YOUR COMPLETE
RETIREMENT PLANNING
ROAD MAP

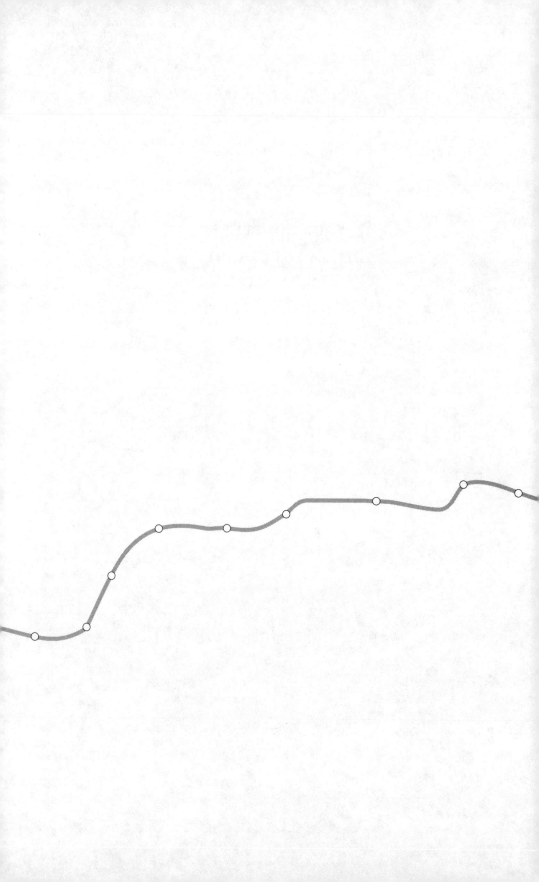

YOUR COMPLETE RETIREMENT PLANNING ROAD MAP

The Leave-Nothing-to-Chance, Worry-Free, All-Systems-Go Guide

ED SLOTT

BALLANTINE BOOKS NEW YORK

Your Complete Retirement Planning Road Map is a commonsense guide to personal finance. In practical advice books, as in life, there are no guarantees, and readers are cautioned to rely on their own judgment about their individual circumstances and to act accordingly. Readers are also reminded that this book is intended for informational purposes only and is not meant to take the place of professional advice. The laws in this area are complex and constantly changing. You should consult with an experienced professional to apply the relevant laws in your state to your unique situation.

Published in the United States by Ballantine Books,
an imprint of The Random House Publishing Group,
a division of Random House, Inc., New York.

BALLANTINE and colophon are registered trademarks of Random House, Inc.

LIBRARY OF CONGRESS CATALOGING-IN-PUBLICATION DATA

Slott, Ed.
Your complete retirement planning road map : the leave-nothing-to-chance, worry-free,
all-systems-go guide / [Ed Slott].—1st ed.
p. cm.
Includes index.
ISBN-13: (invalid) 978-0-345-49455-9
1. Retirement income—United States—Planning. 2. Finance, Personal. I. Title.
HG179.S534 2007
332.024'014—dc22   2006051037

Printed in the United States of America on acid-free paper

www.ballantinebooks.com

2 4 6 8 9 7 5 3 1

First Edition

Book design by Mary A. Wirth

To my wife, Linda, and our children,
Ilana, Rachel, and Jennifer

Author's Note

Legislatively speaking, 2006 turned out to be a banner year for retirement savers. As I write these words, three new tax laws have been enacted by Congress and signed into law by the president. They offer many new, more flexible opportunities for you to sock more of your money away for your retirement and to keep it growing tax deferred for you and your family. I have filtered this latest retirement-planning information throughout this book in the appropriate sections and checklists. And I am alerting you to that important fact here so you will know, as you go through this book creating your road map, that you are working with the most timely, up-to-the-minute data available.

—ED SLOTT

Contents

THE LONG, HAPPY LIFE OF YOUR
RETIREMENT SAVINGS

"Lou was a daredevil. His last words were, 'Watch this!' "

—Obituary featured in *USA Today* (June 22, 2006)

Planning for retirement is no place to be a daredevil, and yet most people are just that, even though they may not think of themselves as one. But anyone who spends a lifetime building up a retirement nest egg and does not take the time to check up on it once in a while to make sure all systems are go is indeed flying without a net and tempting fate.

Imagine getting in your car day after day without ever giving a thought to whether it's got oil in the crankcase or needs a tune-up, without ever having a mechanic take a look under the hood or kick the tires—just to trust that it will always start, always get you where you want to go. You wouldn't think of treating your car that way, and yet if a car breaks down, it can be fixed or replaced. You can call AAA and get it towed, or just leave it by the side of the road and walk away—as I once did years ago when my 1966 Mustang suddenly died on me at the Southern State Parkway tollbooth on Long Island. My dad had to come and pick me up, shaking his head at me in disbelief as my brother gave me his "what a moron" laugh. But, hey, what was the big deal? It was just a car.

The same cannot be said of your life savings. If that breaks down due to lack of proper care and maintenance, it would take another lifetime to replace—and nobody gets a second chance!

So, this book is for all you daredevils out there who seldom if ever look under the hood of your retirement savings, wherever your account (or accounts) may be housed: a 401(k) plan; a 403(b) plan (also known as a Tax Sheltered Annuity Plan) for employees of schools, hospitals, and tax-exempt organizations; a 457 plan (for governmental employees) or any other company-sponsored retirement plan; an Individual Retirement Account (IRA); a Roth IRA; or a self-employed retirement plan like a Keogh, SEP IRA (Simplified Employee Pension) or SIMPLE IRA (Savings Incentive Match Plan for Employees).

What Can Possibly Go Wrong?

Now that I am older and wiser, I do bring my car in for servicing, where the service department manager tells me that he gives it a proper checkup by putting it through a rigorous fifty-eight-point diagnostic using the latest computer technology. If pressed, I probably couldn't come up with more than five things to look at under the hood of my car that might conceivably break down—and he listed fifty-eight!

It suddenly hit me that the same is true for retirement accounts, where many things can go *kaput* without careful monitoring. Most people just open an account, make contributions, maybe make some investment choices, and that's about it until they retire and start collecting. But by then it's too late to fix what may have gone wrong along the way—and believe me, bad, bad things can happen. For example, you could go broke and end up giving most of your retirement funds back to the government. Of course, going broke is not the end of the world. Lots of people go broke. That's why it's important to know how the prospect of having to declare bankruptcy will affect your retirement savings, tax-wise and otherwise. Remember, unless you're in a Roth IRA, where you pay the tax on your contributions up front, your retirement account has yet to be taxed, so not all of the money you have saved all these years is really yours.

A healthy retirement account is always a function of a long period of disciplined saving and investing (unless you inherited it, which is an even better plan and a great shortcut!). You would hate to think that after twenty, thirty, or even forty years or more of diligent saving that you slipped up in the end by passing most of it on to Uncle Sam rather than your family. And that's just one of the things that can go wrong!

So, I decided that a process for giving retirement accounts a regular, thorough look under the hood and kick of the tires, a checkup with the same rigorous precision of an automotive diagnostic, was needed. A system that would ensure no moving parts were overlooked—and thus keep retirement account owners, their beneficiaries and families from being financial daredevils.

Your Complete Retirement Planning Road Map is that system. There are many, many things relating to retirement accounts that demand regular attention and monitoring in order to make sure nothing goes off track. How many can you come up with—without looking at the Contents page, that is? This book looks at more than 250 of them—and,

Ask Ed . . .

Q: **Does your system also tell me how to invest for retirement?**

A: No, this book is not about which stocks or funds to buy. I assume you are already doing that on your own or with professional help, and that you have accumulated some level of retirement savings, large or small, that you will want to protect and preserve, which is where my system steps in. I will say this, however: The best strategy for building retirement savings, one that works all the time, and no one can deny this, is to contribute the maximum you can each year to your retirement account, and to start as early as possible by making saving for retirement a priority from your first day on the job. In other words, pay yourself first, as the saying goes.

most important, shows you how to keep proper tabs on those potential problem areas and tune things up BEFORE they become an issue!

Customized Care for Your Retirement Savings

So, this book is for anyone who is serious about protecting, preserving, and passing the balance (if any) in their retirement account to their heirs *no matter where they are in the planning process.*

For example, you might just be starting to save for retirement in a 401(k) plan at work—in which case, this system of looking under the hood is the perfect way to develop good habits early, from the time you put your first dollar into that 401(k). On the other hand, perhaps you have just retired and moved your retirement savings to an IRA. Or, you might be anywhere in between those two points. Wherever you are in the process of saving for your retirement years, you'll be able to use this system to make sure your money is well protected against *the most common and costly retirement planning mistakes,* and that you won't miss out on any of the many tax breaks you can capitalize on to increase your savings for yourself and your loved ones.

For the first time, you will be assured that you will have done all you can to make the most of your retirement earnings or inherited account, using every possible tax benefit available to leverage exponentially that nest egg into a lifetime of financial peace of mind.

You will then be able to share this information with your family, and boastfully say, "Watch this," with the confidence of knowing that you're not going to go *splat.*

How to Use This Book

My care solution for looking under the hood of your retirement savings consists of five conveniently organized, easy-to-use sections, each made up of a series of checklists relevant to the issues covered in that section. Together, these five sections will address all of the most common retirement savings issues, including many special issues, that most of you will face at some point either as a retirement account owner, account beneficiary, or both. I have purposely excluded, however, some of the more obscure tax issues because this book is intended to be a user-friendly guide for most Americans to keeping their retirement accounts healthy, not an overwhelming and intimidating exploration of the tax code. If you believe you have a complex tax situation it is always a good idea to have a conversation with an experienced tax professional, and I would urge you to do so. The sections are as follows:

- **SECTION I: My Account Inventory**
  As I noted earlier, it is not uncommon these days for people to own and pass on multiple retirement accounts of different types—401(k), 403(b), IRA, and so on—to multiple beneficiaries. So, proper care of a retirement account or accounts begins here with knowing all there is to know about every account you've got and where that information is. Therefore, this section *applies to every one of you using this book.* It shows you how to survey and keep track of each originally owned account or inherited account now owned by you, then summarize that information for fast, easy reference as you move to the subsequent checklists pertinent to you.

- **SECTION II: The Account Owner's Care Solution**
  This section addresses the key ownership issues specifically affecting all holders of an IRA, 401(k) or any other type of retirement account. Failure to address even one of these ownership issues all but guarantees that your account(s) will lose money at some point, either when you start taking distributions or when the money passes to your beneficiaries. Completing this section will give you what you need to avoid these ownership pitfalls. *Keep your beneficiaries in the loop as you plan your decisions in this section. Remember, your beneficiaries will be stuck with those decisions. Inviting their input now will help to ensure a smooth transition down the road and a nest egg that can keep growing instead of losing substantial amounts to taxes.*

- **SECTION III: The Account Beneficiary's Care Solution**
  This section addresses the key issues affecting all inheritors of a retirement account or accounts. It is for any type of beneficiary—spouse,

child, grandchild, other family member, friend, favorite charity, or a family trust. Here you or the inheriting entity will be given the tools to map out what you need to be attending to—and when—in order to take advantage of every available tax opportunity if the person you are inheriting from has not kept you in the loop. *This section will also tip you off to key opportunities and pitfalls to avoid that you should make the account owner aware of (if not too late) in his or her planning because they will affect you. Once you have inherited and transferred title and ownership to inherited account(s), thereafter* **you** *are the account owner and will use Section II in planning opportunities for your own beneficiaries.*

- **SECTION IV: The Special Issues Care Solution**
  This section shows how to address those unique issues that do not apply across the board to every retirement account owner or beneficiary, *but may apply to one and/or the other of you (each checklist will tell you who) at some time.* Here, you will see how to handle these stray issues, such as: accessing retirement funds early without incurring a tax penalty; taking advantage of company stock tax breaks; proper Roth IRA planning; making decisions in the event you or your beneficiary becomes incapacitated. This section is the most complete coverage of these special issues ever compiled for retirement account owners and beneficiaries. If you have a special issue that is *not* covered here, this means yours is a really, *really* special situation that you should address with a professional financial advisor right away.

- **SECTION V: The Follow-Up Care Solution**
  Whether you are the account owner or beneficiary of an inherited account, this section serves as your safety net, providing you with all the reminders each of you will need to check up and follow through on during the year (and by year-end) to keep your respective road maps current and your planning on track. This final section also shows how to make sure either *as an owner or a beneficiary of the account(s)* that your respective financial advisor or fund manager attends to every detail you have covered so that nothing goes

awry on the management end in the implementation and mainte-nance phase of your planning. The checklists here will give you the peace of mind of knowing that your financial advisor has the proper expertise, as well as everything he or she needs from you, to do what you want done correctly—and if not, what to look for in find-ing one who does.

Structured for Practical Use

I have put this book together in a way that allows you to go straight to the section covering the issues specific to you as the original owner or the beneficiary of one or more retirement accounts, and start working on those issues; then move to the section addressing the *special issues* you may face as either an account owner or a beneficiary.

Furthermore, if, for example, you are the beneficiary of an ac-count, whatever you may need to know as an owner-to-be about is-sues facing original owners will be cross-referenced to that section, providing you with an extra check so that no important detail gets overlooked or neglected in customizing your retirement plan care so-lution.

This is the same diagnostic system I use with my own clients and with the financial advisors I train. So, going through it will be like hav-ing me sitting beside you, whispering in your ear, guiding you every step of the way.

An Ongoing Process

Once you have addressed the areas in this book relevant to you, be sure to revisit them as events occur in your life—a birth, a death, a marriage, a divorce, ill health, or new financial responsibilities. This means going beyond your year-end checkup. Anytime there is a change in any of the factors that go into your planning, you can use and reuse this book to make sure your overall plan is always up-to-date and in line with those changes—that your plan will always reflect your *current* situation, including any special circumstances.

How to Use the Checklists

Each checklist is divided into two columns. On the left are all the items you will need to address on the particular issue or subject at hand, and on the right is ample space for including your response to each item. Depending upon the item, your response may just be a simple check mark to indicate that you have attended to the item; writing in a brief "Yes" or "No" to a specific question about the item; or providing more detailed remarks should more information or explanation on your part be required. Unless you can do the *New York Times* crossword in pen without making a mistake (but even then), I urge you to use a pencil since you may want or need to make changes later on.

In fact, the more changes you go through in your life, the more valuable this book becomes as a diagnostic. A 30-year-old person, for example, will experience many more changes in his or her lifetime than a 65-year-old person—i.e., marriage, having kids, financing the purchase of a first home, additional schooling for themselves or college for their kids. Each of these changes can affect how you should set up your retirement account. My system gives you the flexibility to monitor this and make the adjustments necessary to respond to each new life challenge and issue you face.

As a result, you can use this book as a resource for the life of your retirement accounts. That is why I say you should start addressing the issue of retirement distribution planning NOW, and make a lifelong commitment to revisit it.

In the end, the reason you are doing this is for complete financial security, not only for you but also for everyone you care about and have saved for as well. Saving means sacrifice. Somewhere, in order to get something, you had to give something up. *Your Complete Retirement Planning Road Map* ensures that these sacrifices will not have been in vain.

Section I

MY ACCOUNT INVENTORY

for everybody

What It Does

We start here because this section applies to ALL of you who are the proud owner (original holder or inheritor-owner) of an IRA or any other type of retirement account, or multiple accounts (as many people are nowadays). You will use this section to inventory each of your accounts in detail—because you will need to know this information in order to facilitate use of the checklists in the sections of the book that follow.

Your objective here is to gather as much information as possible about your accounts so that nothing escapes your attention. For example, many people who have several retirement accounts sometimes forget about one (don't laugh; it happens!). *This information will be used by your financial advisor, your family lawyer and accountant, your spouse and your kids (if they are your beneficiaries) to determine and carry out your wishes for each account after you are gone.* If your spouse or domestic partner has an IRA and/or other retirement account, he or she will want to complete this part for each of their originally owned and/or inherited accounts as well.

- **General Information—Original Owner Accounts.** This checklist surveys each retirement account you own or have rolled over to your own name from a spouse (it does not include accounts you have inherited from someone else including your spouse if you remain a beneficiary on the account): 401(k), 403(b), Roth IRA, traditional IRA, SEP IRA, and SIMPLE IRA just to name a few of the most common. The rules surrounding these accounts can be vastly different (and complicated); and if you are not in full command of the law, you or your heirs could encounter penalties when the time comes to withdraw funds from them.

- **General Information—Inherited Accounts.** This checklist surveys each account you now own because you inherited it from someone upon his or her death. This is an important distinction because even though the beneficiary of a retirement account does, in effect, become the owner of that account once he or she inherits it, the documentation requirements, planning opportunities, and especially the tax rules can be and often are stricter for inheritors of an account than for the original owners. This checklist will enable you to stay out of trouble.

- **Summary Information—All Accounts.** This checklist summarizes the information you have collected on each of your originally held or inherited accounts for quick referral as you move through the other sections of this book. This summary of basic data from your general information checklists is what you will probably refer to most often while monitoring your retirement savings (and seeing how much it grows!). It gives you a total picture of all your retirement money without having to go back and dig into the details of each account. This summary also will be extremely valuable to your financial advisor (Section V) who will surely have many questions about your

Ask Ed . . .

Q: **How long will it take?**

A: Everyone's portfolio is different. The more accounts you have, the more spadework you will have to do by phone and in person to pull together information on each one. But once this is done, the process of continuously updating your account information should take you no time at all—and you will always have that sense of being well organized and in total control.

account(s), and you can now provide answers quickly in a well-organized, easy-to-read, easy-to-access form.

In order to avoid any confusion, here are explanations of some of the key items you will be covering in this and subsequent sections:

- **Type of Account:** The kind of retirement plan that the funds are in—e.g., IRA, Roth IRA, 401(k).
- **Account _____ of _____:** If you are the original owner or inheritor-owner of several accounts, the one you are describing—e.g., Account 1 of 3.
- **Institution or Company:** The name of the custodian (such as a bank or brokerage firm) or the employer holding the account.
- **Account #:** The identifying number the custodian has assigned to the account.
- **Balance:** The total amount in the account as of your last statement.
- **Basis:** The amount of after-tax funds in the retirement account according to your company plan statement or the Form 8606 filed with your tax return.
- **Primary Beneficiary:** The name of the *key* beneficiary—e.g., a spouse—listed on your beneficiary form for this account (see Section II).
- **Contingent Beneficiary:** The name(s) of your second, third, fourth or however many secondary beneficiaries as listed on your beneficiary form (see Section II) for this account.
- **Date:** When you filled out the information sheet.

What's In It for Me?

Your objective in gathering this information is to find out what you have in retirement holdings, where you have it, and what you need to do to make sure you address all the key planning and distribution issues central to the growth and security of each account. I suggest making photocopies of these and, perhaps, other checklist pages throughout the book should you need more copies. As noted in the introduction, I strongly recommend you fill these pages out in pencil so that you can make changes later on since the process of updating information on your IRA(s) and other accounts is an ongoing one. You might even want to have several copies of the book on hand for that purpose.

What If I Don't?

Overlooking an account in your arsenal of assets could result in that account's not having a named beneficiary, causing it to go through probate—and, perhaps, winding up in the hands of the one person on the planet you *didn't* want to inherit it, ultimately creating a family feud where only the lawyers end up making any money.

This inventory serves as a safety net in the care and feeding of your retirement nest egg. It may even eliminate the possibility of any posthumous family arguments, costly attorney fees, and probate costs occurring as the result of confusion over your holdings and intentions.

Instructions

Fill out a general information sheet for each account you own or have inherited so that you don't forget one later (it happens!). Then summarize the general information on all your accounts in the appropriate spaces of the summary information sheet. If you have multiple owned and/or inherited accounts, photocopy additional inventory sheets and keep them in this section of the book after filling them out. [Your spouse or domestic partner can photocopy the sheets he or she will need too—or, better yet, can buy a copy of their own!]

Use the space marked "Comments" to make any notes to yourself or to record any additional information you fear might fall through the cracks—for example, forgetting to name a contingent beneficiary in the event, however unlikely it may seem to you, that your primary beneficiary dies before you do. If it's all down in black and white for fast, easy reference, there are no cracks or fissures in your care solution. [After each information sheet, I have included an example—for guidance purposes only—of how each sheet may look once you have filled it out.]

Ask Ed . . .

Q: **What should I do with this information once I have pulled it together?**

A: Put it in a safe place that you can locate easily—and that any family member who will need access to it will be able to locate easily, as well. Better yet, make copies and give them to family members or advisors for referral. Do not store it in a safety-deposit box since the box will be hard to access after your death.

EACH OWNED ACCOUNT

Survey each account for which you are the owner not an inheritor.

ACCOUNT OWNER: _____

TYPE OF ACCOUNT: _____
IRA, Roth, SEP, 401(k), 403(b), Keogh, etc.

ACCOUNT_____ OF _____ ACCOUNTS

INSTITUTION OR COMPANY _____

ACCOUNT # _____

BALANCE $ _____ AS OF ___ / ___ / _____

AMOUNT OF BASIS (AFTER-TAX FUNDS) IN ACCOUNT $ _____

PRIMARY BENEFICIARY % should = 100		%
		%
		%
		%
CONTINGENT BENEFICIARY % should = 100		%
		%
		%
		%
		%

COMMENTS: _____

_____

_____

_____

_____

DATE _____

GENERAL INFORMATION

EACH OWNED ACCOUNT

Survey each account for which you are the owner not an inheritor.

ACCOUNT OWNER: _John Smith_

TYPE OF ACCOUNT: _IRA_

IRA, Roth, SEP, 401(k), 403(b), Keogh, etc.

ACCOUNT _1_ OF _5_ ACCOUNTS

INSTITUTION OR COMPANY _The Brokerage Firm_

ACCOUNT # _1234567_

BALANCE $ _552,687_ AS OF _12_ / _31_ / _05_

AMOUNT OF BASIS (AFTER-TAX FUNDS) IN ACCOUNT $ _10,000_

PRIMARY BENEFICIARY % should = 100	Mary Smith	100 %
		%
		%
		%
CONTINGENT BENEFICIARY % should = 100	Ann	25 %
	Bill	25 %
	Carl	25 %
	Donna	25 %

COMMENTS: _Mary is my spouse_

After-tax funds come from IRA nondeductible

contributions made in 1990–1994

DATE _01/15/2006_

EACH INHERITED ACCOUNT

Survey each account you have inherited.

ACCOUNT BENEFICIARY: _____

ORIGINAL ACCOUNT OWNER: _____

TYPE OF ACCOUNT: _____
       IRA, Roth, SEP, 401(k), 403(b), Keogh, etc.

ACCOUNT _____ OF _____ ACCOUNTS

INSTITUTION OR COMPANY_____

ACCOUNT # _____

BALANCE $_____ AS OF _____/_____/_____

AMOUNT OF BASIS (AFTER-TAX FUNDS) IN ACCOUNT $ _____

BENEFICIARY IS: PRIMARY _____   OR   SUCCESSOR _____

YEAR OF ACCOUNT OWNER'S DEATH _____ PRIMARY BENEFICIARY'S DATE OF BIRTH _____

YEAR OF FIRST DISTRIBUTION TO PRIMARY BENEFICIARY _____

PRIMARY BENEFICIARY'S LIFE EXPECTANCY FACTOR BASED ON AGE IN YEAR AFTER
OWNER'S DEATH _____

SUCCESSOR BENEFICIARY % should = 100		%
		%
		%
		%
		%
		%

COMMENTS: _____

_____

_____

DATE _____

GENERAL INFORMATION

EACH INHERITED ACCOUNT

Survey each account you have inherited.

ACCOUNT BENEFICIARY: _John Smith_

ORIGINAL ACCOUNT OWNER: _Ben Jones_

TYPE OF ACCOUNT: _401 (k)_

<small>IRA, Roth, SEP, 401(k), 403(b), Keogh, etc.</small>

ACCOUNT _4_ OF _5_ ACCOUNTS

INSTITUTION OR COMPANY _ABC Widget Co._

ACCOUNT # _123456_

BALANCE $_96,857_ AS OF _12_ / _31_ / _05_

AMOUNT OF BASIS (AFTER-TAX FUNDS) IN ACCOUNT $ _12, 386_

BENEFICIARY IS: PRIMARY _X_ OR SUCCESSOR _____

YEAR OF ACCOUNT OWNER'S DEATH _2005_

PRIMARY BENEFICIARY'S DATE OF BIRTH _01/02/1955_

YEAR OF FIRST DISTRIBUTION TO PRIMARY BENEFICIARY _2006_

PRIMARY BENEFICIARY'S LIFE EXPECTANCY FACTOR BASED ON AGE IN YEAR AFTER OWNER'S DEATH _33.3_

SUCCESSOR BENEFICIARY % should = 100		%
		%
		%
		%
		%
		%

COMMENTS: _Even though the IRS Single Life Table allows a 33.3 year payout, the company says I have to take the full amount out by 12/31/06 and that I will have to pay income tax on everything but the $12,386 after-tax amount. See if company will let me wait until 2007 and transfer balance to inherited IRA._

DATE _11/15/2006_

EXAMPLE 2

GENERAL INFORMATION

EACH INHERITED ACCOUNT

Survey each account you have inherited.

ACCOUNT BENEFICIARY: _John Smith_

ORIGINAL ACCOUNT OWNER: _Sue Brown (Mother-in-law)_

TYPE OF ACCOUNT: _IRA_
    IRA, Roth, SEP, 401(k), 403(b), Keogh, etc.

ACCOUNT _5_ OF _5_ ACCOUNTS

INSTITUTION OR COMPANY _The Credit Union_

ACCOUNT # _11556699_

BALANCE $ _123,682_ AS OF _12_ / _31_ / _05_

AMOUNT OF BASIS (AFTER-TAX FUNDS) IN ACCOUNT $ _0_

BENEFICIARY IS: PRIMARY_____ OR SUCCESSOR _X_

YEAR OF ACCOUNT OWNER'S DEATH _2004_ PRIMARY BENEFICIARY'S DATE OF BIRTH _1952_

YEAR OF FIRST DISTRIBUTION TO PRIMARY BENEFICIARY _2005_

PRIMARY BENEFICIARY'S LIFE EXPECTANCY FACTOR BASED ON AGE IN YEAR AFTER
OWNER'S DEATH _31.4_

SUCCESSOR BENEFICIARY % should = 100	Jennifer	33.3 %
	Victoria	33.3 %
	Kaitlyn	33.3 %
		%
		%
		%

COMMENTS: _Account was my mother-in-law's and inherited by my wife._
I inherited from my wife at her death in 2006.

DATE _11/15/2006_

SUMMARY INFORMATION

ALL ACCOUNTS FOR

MY NAME: _____ DATE: _____

SPECIAL INSTRUCTIONS: Summarize the basic data you have collected on each owned or inherited account. Note in the space marked "Comments" any after-tax funds held in accounts listed in your own or inherited general information sheets.

#	INSTITUTION	BALANCE	AS OF	TYPE	OWNER

COMMENTS: _____

_____

_____

SUMMARY INFORMATION

ALL ACCOUNTS FOR

MY NAME: _John Smith_   DATE: _1/15/2006_

SPECIAL INSTRUCTIONS: Summarize the basic data you have collected on each owned or inherited account. Note in the space marked "Comments" any after-tax funds held in accounts listed in your own or inherited general information sheets.

#	INSTITUTION	BALANCE	AS OF	TYPE	OWNER
1	The Brokerage Firm	552,687	12/31/05	IRA	John
2	The Bank	186,981	12/31/05	Roth	John
3	The Brokerage Firm	72,159	12/31/05	IRA	W. Jones
4	The ABC Widget Co	96,857	12/31/05	401 (k)	B. Jones
5	The Credit Union	123,682	12/31/05	IRA	S. Brown

COMMENTS: _$10,000 basis in IRA #1_
$12,386 basis in 401 (k) & I have to take a full withdrawal
before year-end

THE ACCOUNT OWNER'S CARE SOLUTION

This section addresses planning items that apply if you are the *original owner* (not an inheritor) of any type of retirement account. Most of you reading this book will fall into this category.

As the original owner, you will want to make sure you cover such critical items as updating your beneficiary forms and custodial documents, integrating your retirement account(s) into your estate plan, and knowing how to make the right choices when it comes to decisions involving movement of funds from your company plan into an IRA, and so on.

You'll also want to make sure your beneficiaries can stretch distributions from the IRAs they inherit from you, an option that might require looking at other options such as naming a trust as your IRA beneficiary for postdeath control. All of this and more are covered in the six parts of **"The Account Owner's Care Solution."**

At the end of each part, you will have space to make notes of any important items you may have questions on, want to discuss with family members, your attorney, or financial advisor—or simply items that you may want to revisit later on in the event you want to alter your decision.

Completing this section will also help you to create important "To Do" lists for following up on items you have not yet addressed or have found to be improperly addressed. This will give you an action plan that puts you, the original owner of the account(s), well on your way to completing a thorough retirement plan checkup.

Account Owner Alert!

A HERO Is Not Just a Sandwich. Our government found another way to honor our service men and women who are serving in combat zones when it enacted the Heroes Earned Retirement Opportunities Act (HERO) in May 2006. The act provides a rare opportunity for service personnel to make IRA or Roth IRA contributions (even for their spouses) for tax years that are closed. The HERO Act allows excluded combat zone pay to be included in earned income, for the purpose of making an IRA contribution, for compensation earned from January 1, 2004 through May 28, 2006. You have a three-year period in which to make your contribution. (Example: A 2004 contribution would have to be made by 2007.) The period ends on May 28, 2009. If you don't have the funds, all is not lost. Parents and grandparents and any other interested parties can gift the necessary funds to the serviceperson for the IRA contribution. The maximum contribution for 2004 was $3,000 (plus $500 if you were 50 or older), the contribution limit for 2005 was $4,000 (plus $500 if you were 50 or older), and the contribution limit for 2006 was $4,000 (plus $1,000 if you were 50 or older).

Part 1

MY BENEFICIARY FORM

CHECKLIST

What It Does

Your retirement account beneficiary form is the single most important document in your estate plan because it *guarantees* that the person you name as beneficiary of what may be the single largest asset you own—your retirement savings—will indeed get that asset when you are gone.

Your beneficiary form has a huge impact on the amount and timing of required distributions that your beneficiaries must take and in turn impacts the ultimate value of the account. It also is a key distribution-planning document because the person you name as your beneficiary can affect the required minimum distributions you must take during your lifetime, which, in turn, can impact the potential growth of your savings. So, who to name is one of many important questions that will emerge for you to answer as you complete this form. And completing that task will put you on the path to being able to respond knowledgably to many other planning questions that pop up as you work your way through your complete road map.

So, do I have your attention? THIS FORM IS CRUCIAL! And fill-ing it out—as well as updating it periodically to reflect any changing circumstances in your life, such as a birth, a death, or a divorce that may affect your wishes—is the first thing you should do.

Typically, you will fill out a beneficiary form for each retirement account you open when you open it—and it will remain on file with your account custodian (bank or other financial institution holding the funds). You and your family should also have copies tucked away in a safe place just in case the original is lost. Your work here will guar-antee that won't happen. So, read on.

What's In It for Me?

Actually, nothing—since you will be dead. But seriously, for your own peace of mind until that day comes, if you care at all who will wind up with your hard-earned cash after you die—your family or, heaven help you, the Taxman—and want to know that your family will be able to take advantage of every tax opportunity available to them to keep your hard-earned nest egg growing for decades, *you will want to have an up-to-date beneficiary form on file for every single retirement ac-count you own.* A retirement account beneficiary form is the only way to make absolutely certain that your retirement funds will go to the people you intend—and with the most favorable tax benefits.

What If I Don't?

A recent story in the *New York Post* highlighted the case of Bruce and Anne Friedman from Brooklyn, New York. Anne worked several decades for the New York City school system and accumulated almost one million dollars in her retirement account. When she died, her husband Bruce received not one single penny of it even though she had wanted him to. It turned out that she had never designated him as her beneficiary on her beneficiary form. Whom did she name?

When she first took the job many years ago and opened her retirement account, she was not yet married and so she named her mother, her uncle, and her sister as primary and contingent beneficiaries. Well, her mother and her uncle had long since died, but her sister is still living, and so sis got the whole kit and caboodle. The late Anne's widower husband complained that his sis-in-law "won't give me a cent." Apparently she's either very greedy or she and her brother-in-law never got along too well. Whichever, the fact remains that she doesn't have to give him a red cent, and she has the law to back her up.

If your beneficiary form for each account cannot be found when you die, or does not reflect your current wishes at the time of your death, all bets are off. Your family or other beneficiaries will then have to begin an expensive and time-consuming game of legal hide-and-seek. First, they will have to contact the account custodian to examine the custodial document (see this Section, Part 2) to find out who becomes the beneficiary under the default provision, which kicks in only when there is no beneficiary named. Unfortunately, most default provisions stipulate that the account goes to your estate. This means it passes through your will—if you have one or, if not, through intestacy. Both turn your account or multiple accounts into a probate asset subject to fees and additional legal scrutiny; your will may even be contested by family members who suddenly pop up out of nowhere to claim some of the proceeds as their due even though you barely saw them much and wouldn't recognize them if you tripped over them in a lighted room.

If that isn't enough to give you the cold sweats at night, consider this: If your beneficiary form is not current (as the late Anne Friedman's wasn't) and, for example, lists your spouse—who is now your ex-spouse—as beneficiary, guess what? The beneficiary form trumps all other documents, including a will, in determining where the money goes after you die, no matter how up-to-date your will may be. So, your current spouse or children would be left out in the cold, while your ex-spouse (perhaps for the first time) could think fondly of you because he or she is rolling in your dough.

Ask Ed . . .

Q: **What if I do not want to name my children as beneficiaries? Do I have to?**

A: No. You can name anyone you wish as beneficiary of your retirement nest egg. If you are in a company plan, you generally must name your spouse (though a spouse can waive the benefits in favor of some other beneficiary if he or she desires). But with an IRA you can name a minor, a charity, or a trust if you wish (see Section IV "The Special Issues Care Solution"). But if you want to name a charity, which does not pay taxes on inherited assets, you should still do so through a beneficiary form and not just a will, or the bequest will pass through your estate and thus be subject to probate and to potential contesting by irate family members. Also, if the charitable bequest is not funded properly in your will—as a pecuniary bequest funded with your retirement account, for example—this would subject your estate to income tax on the amount of the retirement assets going to the charity.

Not naming a beneficiary for each account or not keeping beneficiary forms up-to-date also could disqualify your heirs from being able to take advantage of the stretch option [see this Section, Part 3] after you are gone. This option would allow them to keep growing the money you wanted to leave them for decades, building your bequest into a family fortune in tax-deferred funds.

Last but not least, failure to keep your beneficiary form(s) up-to-date can also cause some of your grandchildren to be disinherited. For example, if you name your children as co-beneficiaries of your account and one of your children dies before you, but you don't update the form to name the deceased's child or children as co-beneficiaries of that person's share, the share passes to your other children after you die, disinheriting the deceased's offspring—i.e., some of your own grandchildren.

Bottom line: A properly filled out and up-to-date beneficiary form for each of your accounts that you, your heirs, and your account custodian can always find easily at any time is the way to avoid completely all of these pitfalls.

Ask Ed . . .

Q: **What if I want to name a charity as co-beneficiary with my kids? Can I do that?**

A: Yes, you can leave a portion of your retirement account to your children and a portion to charity by splitting the account, naming the charity as beneficiary of one account and your children as co-beneficiaries of the other (see the Naming a Charity-As-Beneficiary Checklist, Section IV, Part 1). You can do this yourself now to make sure everything goes smoothly so that your kids and grandkids don't lose out on the "stretch" opportunity you may have set up for them in this section, Part 3, or you can leave the split for your children to handle after they inherit—when special rules will apply that may make things a bit more complicated. If you decide to do the latter, be sure to tell your kids ahead of time to go over the Multiple Beneficiaries' Checklist (Section III, Part 3).

Instructions

Fill out the beneficiary checklist in this section—or make multiple copies if needed for multiple accounts, filling out one checklist for each retirement account you own. This will guarantee the following:

1. You have not overlooked or neglected this critical part of the retirement-planning process.
2. You (your beneficiaries and account custodian for whom you will make copies) will be able locate your beneficiary form(s) at a moment's notice.

3. Your beneficiary forms for each account are fully up-to-date and express your most current wishes as to how your retirement nest egg will be distributed after you are gone.

As you complete each item, make notes of issues you may need to fix or address. If there are any items you do not understand, you should go over them with your financial advisor. For example, Item 8 asks if your overall estate plan takes your retirement assets into consideration—meaning, as part of your estate plan—do your 401(k), IRA, and/or other account beneficiaries fit in with your other estate planning document forms and your will? If they do not figure into your overall estate plan, you will want to review that plan to make sure they do.

Be sure to include primary and contingent beneficiaries. And if there are multiple beneficiaries in either category (say, three children) stipulate how much each is to inherit by writing in the word "equally" (if that is your wish) or the fraction or percentage you desire each

Ask Ed . . .

Q: **What should I do if I can't fit the names of all my beneficiaries in the space provided on the beneficiary form?**

A: Write the phrase "See Attached" in the space, and on a separate piece of paper list all your beneficiaries and contingent beneficiaries with the shares each one is entitled to (make sure the shares add up to 100 percent). Then staple that piece of paper to the beneficiary form, not once, but several times across the top or down the side of the pages to make sure it doesn't become detached no matter how many people ultimately handle the form. Never, ever, ever list added beneficiaries on, say, the back of the form. You can't be sure someone will actually turn the form over and see them.

child to get so that it is clear who gets what; "equally" will not automatically be assumed if the word is not on the form and there is no mention of what share each beneficiary is to receive.

Ask Ed . . .

Q: **Once I have completed my beneficiary checklist, how do I keep it updated?**

A: You can either do this through your financial advisor or on your own by contacting the custodian (bank, broker, fund, or insurance company where you have your retirement assets invested) and asking for a new beneficiary form to make the changes. Be sure the advisor or custodian acknowledges that the updated form voids all previous ones, and that he or she, as well as your family, has copies of the new form(s) and has destroyed the old ones. My rule of thumb in making sure account custodians stay current is to contact them a week or two after you've made the changes, and ask them to send you a memo verifying the beneficiaries listed on your form. If they send you a list of the outdated beneficiaries, raise hell. Make sure your estate-planning attorney also has copies of your updated beneficiary form(s) on hand and destroyed all previous ones, as well. You don't want copies of an outdated beneficiary form for any of your retirement accounts popping up later to create potential headaches.

MY BENEFICIARY FORM CHECKLIST

MY NAME: _____ DATE: _____

MY ADVISOR'S NAME: _____ PLAN #: _____

Follow-ups should be added to the To Do lists at the end of this checklist.

1. Where do I keep copies of my beneficiary form?

_____

_____

• Can I produce the copies and are they current? (Do they   _____
match what is on file with the plan? If not, I should request copies from the plan or update the plan forms.)

• Do my beneficiaries or the executor of my estate know   _____
where to find a copy of my beneficiary form?

Comments: _____

_____

_____

_____

2. Is my beneficiary form current?

• Does it consider any recent changes in the IRS rules?   _____
(e.g., the correct life-expectancy table is being used for
required minimum distributions calculations; see Appen-
dices)

• Does it consider state or federal estate and tax law   _____
changes? (e.g., state estate tax decoupling that could
mean estate tax due at my death)

• Does it consider plan limitations? (e.g., no stretch oppor-   _____
tunity; see checklist this section, Part 3)

• Does it consider life events that could change my benefi-   _____
ciary elections?

adoption	_____	beneficiaries to eliminate	_____
births—child or grandchild	_____	deaths	_____
divorces	_____	marriages	_____
special needs beneficiaries	_____	other life events	_____

3. **Have I named a contingent beneficiary on my beneficiary form? What would be the effect of disclaiming?** (See The Disclaimer Planning Checklist in Part 3 of Section IV)

_____

4. **Is my signed beneficiary form on file with the trustee/ custodian/plan provider?**   _____

5. **Do I have an acknowledged copy of my most recent signed beneficiary form?** (In case the plan provider "loses" its copy; may not be able to get a copy from an employer plan)   _____

6. **Does my advisor have a copy of my most recent signed beneficiary form?**   _____

7. **Can my trustee/custodian/plan provider locate and/or produce its copy of my most recent signed beneficiary form?**   _____

Comments: _____

_____

_____

_____

8. **When my estate plan was drafted, did it take into account my retirement assets?** (Retirement assets will pass according to my beneficiary form, not my will; see My Retirement Assets and Estate Plan Checklist this section, Part 4)

_____

9. **My beneficiary form should name a person not an entity as beneficiary unless I am leaving my retirement assets in whole or in part to a charity or a trust.**   _____

10. **Does my beneficiary form allow my beneficiaries to stretch payouts?** (See checklist this section, Part 3)   _____

11. **Does my beneficiary form allow "per stirpes" language?**   _____

Comments: _____

_____

_____

_____

12. Who are my primary beneficiaries and what % do they inherit?
(Should = 100%)

_____

_____

_____

13. Who are my contingent beneficiaries and what % does each inherit?
(Should = 100%)

_____

_____

_____

14. If there are multiple beneficiaries, make sure I have _____
**clearly stated each beneficiary's share on the benefi-
ciary form.**

15. If I have multiple beneficiaries, is there a need for me _____
to create separate accounts for them now?

Comments: _____

_____

_____

Follow-Up

My To Do List	Date Completed
1 _____	_____
2 _____	_____
3 _____	_____
4 _____	_____
5 _____	_____
6 _____	_____
7 _____	_____
8 _____	_____
9 _____	_____
10 _____	_____

My Signature _____   Date _____

MY CUSTODIAL AGREEMENT
CHECKLIST

What It Does

If you have an IRA, then the IRA custodial agreement at the bank or other financial institution where your funds are kept is the *rulebook* for it. By that I mean the agreement lays out all the investment, distribution, and estate-planning options available to you and those who will be inheriting your IRA. Every IRA owner agrees in writing to the provisions of the IRA custodial agreement upon opening the account (though most IRA owners probably have no memory of ever even signing this key document).

Similarly, company plans such as a 401(k) come with their own custodial rulebook called the "Summary Plan Description," or more commonly the "Plan Agreement." All employees receive this when they begin participating in a company retirement plan. Few company plan agreements offer participants any flexibility—they are pretty much stuck with the investment, distribution, and estate-planning options dictated by their company's plan agreement since they can't go shopping for another 401(k) unless they change jobs. But IRA participants are not stuck—even after they sign on the dotted line—because they do have the option of shopping around for the allowed options they want. That's why it is important to know going in what options your IRA custodian will and will not allow, which is where your custodial agreement checklist comes in.

This checklist addresses the key provisions you want to make sure are in your IRA custodial agreement—and should be asking about when opening an IRA or contemplating a change to another custodian.

Ask Ed . . .

Q: **What if my IRA custodian cannot tell me whether my agreement includes all the items you advise?**

A: This is quite possible. You may even be looked at as if you had sprouted another head because it is unlikely anyone there has ever asked about this before and so whoever you're talking to will probably not know the answer. But don't give up the ship. This is an important document with a set of rules you will be stuck with. So, persist until you find someone at the custodial institution who can answer your questions. If you start to lose confidence there is such a someone, just put a bug in the institution's ear that you may move your funds elsewhere. That's usually enough to track down the person who knows what's going on. But if even this does not do the trick, get your IRA money out of there fast and into the hands of another IRA custodian who can tell you at all times the allowed provisions in its agreement.

What's In It for Me?

You will know right away how the funds in your IRA will be distributed both during your lifetime and after your death. This way, you will know in advance whether the custodian offers all the investment, distribution, and estate-planning options that you want—or would want—and will be able to choose wisely. If the agreement contains all the provisions you want, you are all set. If not, you've got a heads-up to move your IRA to another, more enlightened or cooperative custodian. By checking all of this out now, you won't saddle yourself or your beneficiaries with restrictive distribution provisions later on.

Ask Ed . . .

Q: **Is my IRA custodial agreement something I can actually read and understand (like this book), or is it all inscrutable legalese?**

A: Pretty much all legalese, but many times the agreement comes with subject headings that help you locate what you need without having to plow through and decipher the entire document. For example, if you want to look over the agreement's default provision should you die without naming a beneficiary (of course, that won't happen because you've taken care of your beneficiary form, right?) you may see a heading that reads, "Provisions that apply when there is no beneficiary," and will find your answer there—albeit in legalese. Helpful headings or not, if you find the legalese just too much mumbo jumbo to comprehend, run your questions by your financial advisor, who should not only have a copy of your custodial agreement but the answers as well (see Section V).

What If I Don't?

Interestingly, the IRS rules governing IRA distributions are more liberal than what many IRA custodians themselves will permit. But even if the IRS allows it, if the provisions of your custodial agreement don't, the document rules, and you and your beneficiaries pay up.

For example, does your IRA document allow your beneficiaries to stretch distributions from your IRA when they inherit? Most custodians now offer this option, but if you happen to have your IRA funds with a bank, broker, or other fund company that doesn't, your beneficiaries will be stuck taking distributions over a shorter time period, thereby forking over more of their inheritance (your remaining nest egg) to the government, faster.

Your IRA beneficiaries have nowhere near the leverage you have now once they inherit. Let's say that your children (nonspouse beneficiaries) would prefer certain provisions once they inherit, but those provisions aren't in the agreement. Unlike you, they cannot just pull money out and transfer it to another IRA custodian (unless the agreement permits this) or they will trigger a tax on the entire amount of the withdrawal. Bingo, a big chunk of their inherited IRA goes right into the coffers of Uncle Sam.

Ask Ed . . .

Q: **What if I cannot find my original IRA custodial agreement?**

A: Just call your IRA custodian and ask for a copy or to see a typical agreement form. This way, you will be able to ascertain what's typically allowed and what isn't in that custodian's agreement. In fact, some IRA custodians actually post their custodial agreement forms on their websites. Others will simply mail one to you or you can pick one up the next time you stop in at the bank or wherever your IRA is held. Your financial advisor should have copies of your agreement as well.

Here's another example: Let's say you go through the time and expense of working with an attorney to name a trust as beneficiary of your IRA. But if the custodian does not accept a trust as beneficiary, the devil knows what will happen to your money once you are gone—it may become available to people like your children's spouses or to creditors you specifically wanted to avoid by naming a trust in the first place. The whole point of naming a trust as beneficiary (see Section IV,

Part 2) is to retain some degree of control over what happens to your money after you die, so your planning will not be out the window.

Your IRA custodial agreement is not like your beneficiary form, which allows you to make changes. Only the custodian can make changes in your agreement and probably won't do that just for you. So, all you are left with as an alternative is to complain or to move your IRA funds elsewhere. But by finding the potential problem spots in the agreement ahead of time (by which I mean before you die, or as attorneys put it, "before your will *matures*") you can move your money to a custodian offering the options you want.

Ask Ed . . .

Q: **One of the provisions you say to look for is whether the agreement permits a beneficiary to name a beneficiary? Why do I care about that now?**

A: Here's why. Let's say your beneficiary George has a thirty-six-year life expectancy and dies five years into the payout of the inherited IRA. That means there are thirty-one years left on the life-expectancy payout (the stretch IRA option, see Part 3). If George had named his son Bill as his successor beneficiary, Bill can complete the thirty-one years remaining on what would have been George's life expectancy, thus preserving the stretch option. In addition, by allowing the beneficiary to name a beneficiary, if your first beneficiary dies with funds still remaining in the inherited IRA, then the account will pass directly to the successor beneficiary and not through the estate, thereby avoiding costly complications like probate.

Instructions

Review each item in the checklist to see if your IRA custodian allows it. If all the important provisions I've noted here are permitted, then you and your beneficiaries are in fine shape for the future. If just a few are allowed, consider carefully whether and how much each disallowed one may affect you and your beneficiaries. For instance, if your IRA custodian doesn't allow a trust as your IRA beneficiary, and you have no intention of naming a trust, then there is no problem. (Of course if you subsequently decide that you do need to name a trust, then your only alternative would be to move your IRA funds to another custodian offering that option.)

Apply this checklist to the custodial agreement for each IRA you own or are considering.

A Word to the Wise

Participants in a company plan such as a 401(k) should go through this checklist too as way of comparing how well the provisions allowed in your plan agreement stack up against the checklist—even though you won't be able to do anything about it unless or until the time comes when you decide to roll your company plan funds over into an IRA.

MY CUSTODIAL AGREEMENT CHECKLIST

MY NAME: _____ DATE: _____

MY ADVISOR'S NAME: _____ PLAN # _____

Follow-ups should be added to the To Do lists at the end of this checklist.

1. Are stretch distributions permitted? _____

2. What are the default provisions when there is no bene- _____
   ficiary named?

3. Will my custodial agreement accept a trust as my ben- _____
   eficiary?

4. Will my power of attorney form be accepted?

Comments: _____

_____

_____

_____

_____

5. Can my beneficiary name a successor beneficiary? _____

6. Can my nonspouse beneficiary move investments via a _____
   trustee-to-trustee transfer?

Comments: _____

_____

_____

_____

Follow-Up

My To Do List	Date Completed
1	
2	
3	
4	
5	
6	

7 _____

8 _____

9 _____

10 _____

_____   _____
My Signature   Date

Part 3

MY STRETCH OPPORTUNITY

CHECKLIST

What It Does

You won't find the words "Stretch IRA" or "Stretch Retirement Plan" in the tax code because it is a made-up term, one that describes over how long a period of time your beneficiaries can withdraw funds from the account you are passing on to them and pay tax on the withdrawals—in other words, how long they can extend (stretch) payouts of those funds, enabling the balance to grow.

Some financial institutions use made-up terms of their own to describe this extended tax deferral, such as the "Extended IRA," the "Multigenerational IRA," and the "Legacy IRA" to name a few. But don't get caught up in names. It's the option to "stretch" that counts—an option that offers a big tax break that's part of the IRC (Internal Revenue Code) and thus completely legal!

I always say that the only surefire way to build wealth is to eliminate the government as a partner. The more you have to fork over in taxes, the less money you will have. And the longer you can keep the Taxman waiting for his money, the more time it can grow for you and your family and build into a fortune. That's what the stretch option does, and this checklist makes sure you don't blow the opportunity. It sees to it that you set your account up properly so your beneficiaries will be able to seize the stretch option.

Ask Ed . . .

Q: **I have a 401(k) with my company. Is there a stretch 401(k)? I never see any mention of this.**

A: Yes, there is such a thing as a stretch 401(k), but it is more rare than a rookie Mickey Mantle baseball card. The tax rules specifically allow the stretch option to beneficiaries of all retirement plans, including company plans like the 401(k), as well as 403(b) and 457 plans. But company plans are not required to offer it, and most don't because they really do not want to be bothered with the administrative work involved in paying out distributions to your beneficiaries for decades. The priority with most companies is to get you off their books as soon as you die. To find out if your company plan offers the stretch to beneficiaries, check the plan's "Summary Plan Description" referred to in Part 2 of this section on custodial agreements. If it is not allowed, you should consider rolling your company plan funds into an IRA as soon as you are able. That way, you can *guarantee* the stretch option for your beneficiaries, since non-spouse beneficiaries will not be able to do a rollover after you die. In 2007, for the first time, a non-spouse beneficiary, including a qualified trust, will be able to do a direct transfer to a properly titled inherited IRA, but the plan still has to allow this.

What's In It for Me?

Nothing—except the peace of mind of knowing that whatever funds are left in your account(s) after all that skydiving, bungee jumping, and world traveling you've done in your retirement years will go to your beneficiaries (rather than to the government) in a way that allows those funds to continue to grow and flourish.

To set up the stretch, you simply name a person (as opposed to a "thing" such as an estate or charity) as beneficiary on your beneficiary form. This will allow the named person to spread required distributions on the inherited account over his/her remaining life expectancy, according to the actuarial numbers in the IRS's Single Life Expectancy Table (Appendix I).

The younger the person named, the longer his or her life expectancy, thus the greater the financial value of the stretch option. This is because while your IRA and other plan beneficiaries will be subject to Required Minimum Distributions (aka RMDs, see this section, Part 5) just as you are, their RMDs will be based on their ages and life expectancies, not yours. The result, especially with a younger beneficiary, is that very little must actually be withdrawn each year, allowing the bulk of the inherited account to keep growing tax-deferred. It will take decades before all of that money will be forced out through distributions and by then, your children or grandchildren will have had the benefit of a tax-deferred fortune that dwarfs the actual amount you left them.

Ask Ed . . .

Q: Does the stretch concept apply also to Roth IRAs, which are tax-free at withdrawal?

A: Yes, and a Roth Stretch IRA is as good as it gets because although you are taxed up front on contributions, the money you put in grows exponentially and is never again subject to taxes. So not only do you pay no tax on distributions, your children or grandchildren don't either; they can benefit over time from growth in the inherited Roth IRA, all of it tax-free. Uncle Sam gets cut out completely, which is the way to build real wealth (see The Roth IRA Conversion Checklist, Section IV, Part 11).

The numbers are exponential. For example, a $100,000 IRA left to your eleven-year-old granddaughter—whose life expectancy is 71.8 years according to the IRS's Single Life Expectancy Table—could be parlayed into as much as a $4,500,000 fortune (yes that's 4.5 *million*), which is one nice legacy, if you ask me.

Of course, many people leave their retirement plan money to their spouse (The Spouse Beneficiary's Checklist, Section III, Part 2). That works with the stretch option too, and will yield other tax benefits as well.

The bottom line is that you set up the stretch mostly to make life better for your children, your grandchildren, or whomever you love for the rest of their lives—so that the money you earned during your lifetime (unless you spend it all, which is fun too, and means you can skip this checklist) has the opportunity to grow exponentially and benefit them, rather than Uncle Sam—and with Uncle Sam's blessing to boot!

What If I Don't?

Your beneficiaries will hate you. But seriously (I hope), the world won't end if you don't; it's just that very soon after your passing, the tax shelter your retirement account provides will disappear as funds are distributed, and the IRS gets its mitts on your money faster, leaving your beneficiaries no opportunity to continue to grow the account tax-deferred (even tax-free if it's a Roth IRA) for many more decades.

For your beneficiaries to get the stretch option, you must see if your custodial agreement allows stretch distributions—and then make sure you have designated your beneficiary (or beneficiaries) on your beneficiary form. If you designate no beneficiary, and your account passes through your will, then your inheritors are stuck with the distribution rules under that scenario. Those rules depend on whether you pass away before or after your Required Beginning Date (RBD), which is the date you are required to begin taking minimum distributions from your retirement account; with an IRA and most other plans, the RBD is April 1 of the year following the year you turn 70½.

If you die before your RBD, your beneficiaries must withdraw all the funds in your account by the end of the fifth year following the year of your death (the so-called 5-year rule), and the tax deferral is gone forever. If you die on or after your RBD, then the payout to your heirs will be your remaining life expectancy based on the IRS Single Life Expectancy Table. Since the inherited funds will be forced out much earlier than if they were stretched, the taxes your heirs will pay will be higher, and they will be paid sooner, building a savings account for Uncle Sam rather than your family.

Ask Ed . . .

Q: **As great as all this sounds, I cannot see my kids taking distributions over 50 years. They will probably want all the money at once and not care about all these fantastic tax benefits. Can I make sure they stretch?**

A: Yes—by naming a trust as your beneficiary for your kids' benefit (see The Naming a Trust-As-Beneficiary Checklist, Section IV, Part 2).

Instructions

Having named your beneficiaries on your beneficiary form in Part 1 and reviewed your custodial agreement in Part 2 to determine if your plan allows the stretch option (if not, this checklist is moot and you can move to Section IV), use the checklist to set up your IRA, Roth IRA, or company plan properly and to make sure *you* make no mistakes in the stretch setup that may haunt your heirs later on. Conversely, you can use this checklist as a reminder to go over your stretch plans with your designated beneficiaries and refer them to Section III so they can go over what *they* must do once they inherit to ensure they will not blow the stretch opportunity you've created for them.

MY STRETCH OPPORTUNITY CHECKLIST

MY NAME: _____ DATE: _____

MY ADVISOR'S NAME: _____ PLAN #: _____

Follow-ups should be added to the To Do lists at the end of this checklist.

A stretch retirement plan will allow payouts to stretch over my beneficiary's own life expectancy, if done correctly.

1. Have I checked my custodial agreement (see previous checklist) to see if it permits stretch distributions? (Most company plans will not permit stretch distributions to nonspouse beneficiaries.)   _____

2. Have I checked my beneficiary form (see checklist this section, Part 1) to see if it allows a stretch payout?   _____

3. Have I named a person—spouse, children, grandchildren, life partner, etc. (as opposed to a trust or charity) as my designated beneficiary, or beneficiaries, to take advantage of the stretch option?   _____

4. Does my nonspouse beneficiary (if applicable) know how to properly retitle my account when he/she inherits—i.e., John Jones (deceased, date of death) IRA fbo Sam Jones   _____

5. Does my spouse beneficiary know that when she inherits my account and rolls it over to her own account, there is no stretch until she dies and the account goes to her designated beneficiaries (the Nonspouse Beneficiary's Checklist, Section III, Part 1)? (It is always a possibility that the spouse will spend down the account and leave nothing for beneficiaries to stretch.)   _____

6. If I have multiple beneficiaries and each one wants to use their own life expectancy to stretch, do they know the separate account rules (The Multiple Beneficiaries' Checklist, Section III, Part 3)? (I can separate the account now to make sure nothing goes wrong.)   _____

7. Will all my beneficiaries want to stretch my account?   _____

8. Will I need to force my beneficiaries through a trust to stretch the account so I can maintain some form of control even after my death?   _____

9. Have I made sure my beneficiaries know what they _____
must do, how to do it, and when, in order to implement
the stretch opportunity I have set up? (Refer them to
Section III.)

Comments: _____

_____

_____

_____

_____

Follow-Up

My To Do List   Date Completed

1 _____

2 _____

3 _____

4 _____

5 _____

6 _____

7 _____

8 _____

9 _____

10 _____

_____   _____

My Signature   Date

Part 4

MY RETIREMENT ASSETS AND
ESTATE PLAN CHECKLIST

What It Does

Up to this point, you have been focusing exclusively on your retirement assets because they typically make up the largest chunk of your estate. But if you are like most people, you will have accumulated other assets too, such as a home and other property. So, here is where you inventory what you have in other assets in order to coordinate them with your retirement funds as part of your overall estate plan.

Given the state of current estate tax law, which seems to have no certainty to it at all these days, the federal estate tax exemption is already high enough to eliminate most estates from taxation (for 2007 $2 million for singles, $4 million for married couples). If your IRA or other retirement assets combined with your home and other property will add up to an estate valued higher than those figures and thus subject to federal estate taxes (as of this writing), then you need to get serious here and make sure that you title your assets and bequeath them in a manner that will permit most or all of those assets to pass to your heirs estate tax–free.

Even if estate tax is not an issue, however, you still will want your property to go to the people you wish and not to the people you don't wish. That means leaving nothing open to interpretation after you are gone. This inventory and planning assessment checklist will start you off on the right path and keep you there.

Ask Ed . . .

Q: **What if I want to leave my retirement account(s) to certain beneficiaries and my other assets to others? Can I do that?**

A: Sure you can, and it is advisable in many cases, which is why you want to coordinate your retirement account with your overall estate plan. For example, you may have a younger brother you want to inherit the family business and a child you want to inherit your IRA and get to stretch it over his or her lifetime. Or you might want to leave your IRAs to your grandchildren to gain the biggest hit on the stretch option and leave other assets to your spouse (assuming your spouse will have all he or she needs—you never want to leave a spouse with too little in the name of tax planning). Or your kids might be so successful that they don't want you to add to their own estates, so they would rather have you pass certain assets directly on to their children (your grandkids) instead. These are all issues that come up in the estate-planning process.

What's In It for Me?

Estate planning is not just about saving on or eliminating estate taxes; it is also about finding ways to leverage what you have accumulated in overall assets into even greater wealth by using the tax code to keep more of that wealth in the hands of your family. In other words, even if there is no estate tax to worry about, why not seize the opportunity to leave behind an estate that can be of much greater value than it is now?

Life insurance, for example, is a method that can be used to accomplish this, which is why a life insurance assessment is part of this checklist. You may not have thought of it, but life insurance is THE biggest tax break ever created by Congress—bigger even than the stretch option—because properly owned *life insurance in an estate passes entirely **tax-free**,* no matter what the overall value of the estate. Thus, life insurance proceeds can be used by your heirs to pay any estate taxes (should they kick in) without their having to dip into your account and depleting it prematurely.

So, here again, what's in it for you is the knowledge that by going through this checklist, you will once more be doing all you can to make your estate, large or small, as valuable as it can be for your children and grandchildren.

Ask Ed . . .

Q: **You stress life insurance as such a big deal. Do you get a kick-back from the insurance industry?**

A: Let me be very clear about this. I am not now nor have I ever been a shill for the insurance industry. But I strongly believe in life insurance as a surefire way of seeing to it that your family receives tons of tax-free cash after you die—cash that, among other things, they can use to offset estate tax or other financial difficulties without having to sell the family home, business, or other assets to raise cash. Even people who say they can make more profitable investments than life insurance should consider this: The policy generally pays off as soon as you die. No other investment can beat that kind of return as quickly. The amount of life insurance you will need is the amount of wealth you want to create for your family. You pay a relatively small amount of money now for a tax-free windfall forever. That to me is what estate planning is all about and why life insurance is the centerpiece of my own estate plan, and a key part of this checklist.

What If I Don't?

If you are like most people, you have probably put off estate planning for as long as possible. After all, who likes contemplating death, except maybe Woody Allen? But the fact is, YOU are the architect of your estate plan, and if you don't get involved or you don't do it right, you will potentially leave your family one hell of a financial mess at a very emotional and vulnerable time. On the other hand, your government will love you because you will be putting money in its coffers that your family might not have had to pay out so quickly, if at all. So, put yourself in your family's shoes and ask yourself this, "How would I like that to happen to me?"

Furthermore, having no estate plan—or setting one up too willy-nilly—means not only that your family will have to deal with the fallout later on, but also that they will be sorting things out according to their terms, not yours. This could result in the tearing apart of your family over disagreements that YOU could have avoided had you provided them with some guidance in the form of an estate plan.

A Word to the Wise

If your IRA or other retirement account is the bulk of your estate and you do not have other funds from which to buy life insurance, it may pay to withdraw the funds from your retirement account, pay the tax (and, in some cases, even the penalty if you withdraw prematurely), and put those funds into a life insurance policy that can be set up by your insurance professional to be estate- and income-tax-free. Simply by leveraging your taxable retirement assets into buying tax-free life insurance, you have the ability to turn a highly taxed asset like your retirement account into many times its current value, totally tax-free.

Instructions

If you can't remember all the nonretirement account assets you have, or you and/or your estate-planning attorney have overlooked or not considered certain assets as even being part of your estate, this checklist will tip you off to them ("Don't forget to include . . ."). It's impossible for me to suggest every conceivable possibility, however, because each of you has a unique lifestyle and thus will have a wide variety of different types of assets in addition to those I'm suggesting here.

Ask Ed . . .

Q: **Should I ever consider leaving my retirement account(s) to my estate?**

A: As I've written elsewhere in this section, you should always do *everything* you can to *prevent* your retirement funds from passing through your estate—well, *almost* always. There are situations where you might want to do this—for example if you have no children or grandchildren or anyone other than relatives who are so distant you can't remember their names let alone their faces. I had a client like that. His only potential heirs were fourteen distant nephews and nieces. His plan was to spend most of his funds anyway, and then, rather than naming fourteen distant relatives individually to get whatever might be left, he named his estate and left everything to the fourteen equally. That was the easiest route for him to take. But as a general rule, leaving your money to your estate is a BIG no-no.

Use this checklist also to help you locate all your current estate-planning documents—such as your will, powers of attorney and health care proxies, and so on—for informational purposes, and to make any changes.

If you do not have these documents, it is time to pay a visit to an estate-planning attorney and have them drawn up. And when you make the appointment, be sure to bring your retirement plan beneficiary forms and custodial documents with you—and to clearly express your desire to enable your plan beneficiaries to stretch (if allowable)—so that the attorney can help you put together an overall estate plan that takes *everything* into consideration.

A Word to the Wise

Estate planning is about communicating with your family. It can be a wonderful experience you'll wish you had sooner. The dilemma is that someone has to bring the topic up. Your children may be uneasy about doing so, and you may be just as uneasy about addressing your own mortality. The result is a Mexican standoff, and the planning goes undone because important family conversations never take place. Don't let this happen in your family. Use this checklist to start the ball rolling, and that conversation will quickly fall into place.

MY RETIREMENT ASSETS AND
ESTATE PLAN CHECKLIST

MY NAME: _____ DATE: _____

MY ADVISOR'S NAME: _____ PLAN #: _____

Follow-ups should be added to the To Do Lists at the end of this checklist.

Use the first section to determine if your estate will be subject to estate tax; if yes, complete the remainder of the checklist.

1. I have inventoried ALL my assets. _____

Don't forget to include:

- Annuities (that have postdeath value) _____
- Other real estate (list location, deeds, and insurance information) _____
- Rental real estate (list tenants and leases) _____
- Investment real estate _____
- Vacation homes _____
- Boat/recreational vehicle/motor home _____
- Club memberships _____
- Ownership interests in a business (a valuation/appraisal will be needed) _____
- Inheritances or gifts _____
- Valuables (hidden or stored) _____

2. Group property by ownership. (Mine, my spouse's, joint, in a trust, etc.)

- Are there rollover possibilities? (Employer plans) _____
- Have I looked at the titling of my assets to determine how they will pass at my death—e.g., which assets will pass through probate, and so on? (Assets with beneficiary forms, such as retirement plans, do not pass through my will and are not subject to probate as long as I do not name my estate as beneficiary on the forms.) _____

3. I have collected all my planning documents. _____

- Tax returns _____
- Wills, trusts, powers of attorney, health care proxies, living wills _____
- Beneficiary forms (retirement plans, insurance policies, annuities) _____

4. I have completed my Custodial Agreement checklist. _____

5. I have completed a liquidity analysis (a listing of all my _____
assets in order of their liquidity) to assess life insur-
ance needs for paying estate taxes and other expenses
postdeath.

Comments: _____

_____

_____

_____

_____

6. I have gathered all my personal information. _____

Family tree:

• Parents, children, grandchildren _____

• Prior marriages _____

• Children of prior marriages _____

• Distant relatives _____

• Ages, health, birthdays, residency, and future residency _____

• Will my surviving spouse need the money? _____

• Liability issues _____

• Medicaid issues _____

• Family dynamics—who gets along with whom, and who _____
does not

7. What do I want to accomplish?

• The stretch opportunity _____

• Secure the estate tax exemption (a.k.a. the credit shelter _____
amount)

• Postdeath control (beneficiaries are minors, disabled, in- _____
competent, unsophisticated, trust may be needed. (See
the Naming a Trust-As-Beneficiary, Section IV, Part 2.)

• Creditor protection (The Bankruptcy Reform Act passed _____
by Congress in 2005 gives IRAs widespread protections
in Bankruptcy Court.)

• Benefit charity _____

• Build estate for my beneficiaries _____

• Reduce taxes my beneficiaries will pay (including _____
generation-skipping tax)

• Other _____

8. When will my lifetime distributions begin? ⎯⎯⎯⎯

• I am still working. (See checklist this section, Part 5.) ⎯⎯⎯⎯

• Will I need my required minimum distributions to live on? ⎯⎯⎯⎯
(If not, consider converting to a Roth IRA—see checklist
Section IV, Part 11.)

Comments: ⎯⎯⎯⎯⎯⎯⎯⎯⎯⎯⎯⎯⎯⎯⎯⎯⎯⎯⎯⎯⎯⎯⎯⎯⎯⎯

⎯⎯⎯⎯⎯⎯⎯⎯⎯⎯⎯⎯⎯⎯⎯⎯⎯⎯⎯⎯⎯⎯⎯⎯⎯⎯⎯⎯⎯⎯⎯⎯⎯⎯⎯

⎯⎯⎯⎯⎯⎯⎯⎯⎯⎯⎯⎯⎯⎯⎯⎯⎯⎯⎯⎯⎯⎯⎯⎯⎯⎯⎯⎯⎯⎯⎯⎯⎯⎯⎯

⎯⎯⎯⎯⎯⎯⎯⎯⎯⎯⎯⎯⎯⎯⎯⎯⎯⎯⎯⎯⎯⎯⎯⎯⎯⎯⎯⎯⎯⎯⎯⎯⎯⎯⎯

9. Have I assessed the tax and estate planning ramifica- ⎯⎯⎯⎯
tions of my choice of beneficiary?

• Beneficiary vs. designated beneficiary ⎯⎯⎯⎯

• Primary and contingent beneficiaries ⎯⎯⎯⎯

• Successor beneficiaries ⎯⎯⎯⎯

10. Have I assessed estate tax issues? ⎯⎯⎯⎯

• Would there be estate tax (federal or state) if I died now? ⎯⎯⎯⎯

• Would there be a projected estate tax (federal or state) ⎯⎯⎯⎯
based on the asset value and my projected life expectancy as of now?

• Who will pay the estate tax? ⎯⎯⎯⎯

• What funds will be available to pay the estate tax? ⎯⎯⎯⎯

11. Have I assessed all income tax issues? ⎯⎯⎯⎯

• Who will pay the income tax on postdeath distributions ⎯⎯⎯⎯
(exceptions—Roth IRAs, nondeductible contributions,
after-tax funds in company plans)? Will it be an individual beneficiary or trust beneficiary? (Evaluate trust tax
rates vs. individual income tax rates.) (State income tax
rules will vary.) (Consider a Roth trust solution.)

• What funds will be available to pay the income tax? ⎯⎯⎯⎯

• Do I qualify for any special tax breaks? (Section IV, Part 7) ⎯⎯⎯⎯

Comments: ⎯⎯⎯⎯⎯⎯⎯⎯⎯⎯⎯⎯⎯⎯⎯⎯⎯⎯⎯⎯⎯⎯⎯⎯⎯⎯

⎯⎯⎯⎯⎯⎯⎯⎯⎯⎯⎯⎯⎯⎯⎯⎯⎯⎯⎯⎯⎯⎯⎯⎯⎯⎯⎯⎯⎯⎯⎯⎯⎯⎯⎯

⎯⎯⎯⎯⎯⎯⎯⎯⎯⎯⎯⎯⎯⎯⎯⎯⎯⎯⎯⎯⎯⎯⎯⎯⎯⎯⎯⎯⎯⎯⎯⎯⎯⎯⎯

⎯⎯⎯⎯⎯⎯⎯⎯⎯⎯⎯⎯⎯⎯⎯⎯⎯⎯⎯⎯⎯⎯⎯⎯⎯⎯⎯⎯⎯⎯⎯⎯⎯⎯⎯

⎯⎯⎯⎯⎯⎯⎯⎯⎯⎯⎯⎯⎯⎯⎯⎯⎯⎯⎯⎯⎯⎯⎯⎯⎯⎯⎯⎯⎯⎯⎯⎯⎯⎯⎯

12. I have developed my beneficiary plan based on the _____
information I have obtained from evaluating all the
options.

• I have named my primary and contingent beneficiaries _____
on my beneficiary form and shared this information with
them.

• I have considered the effect of a possible disclaimer (see _____
The Disclaimer Planning Checklist in Section IV, Part 3).

• I have updated my beneficiary form for each retirement _____
plan, naming both primary and contingent beneficiaries.

• I have obtained acknowledged copies of my updated _____
beneficiary forms from each retirement plan provider
and given copies to my financial advisor.

Comments: _____

_____

_____

_____

Follow-Up

My To Do List   Date Completed

1 _____

2 _____

3 _____

4 _____

5 _____

6 _____

7 _____

8 _____

9 _____

10 _____

_____   _____
My Signature   Date

Part 5

MY RMD CALCULATIONS

CHECKLIST

What It Does

This checklist takes you through all the steps needed to make sure you calculate your Required Minimum Distributions (RMDs) correctly and take them at the right time, especially if you have funds in several different types of retirement plans, as many people do.

Ask Ed . . .

Q: **You say I must take my RMD even if I do not need the money. OK, so let's say I don't need the money, but I take the distribution anyway like I am supposed to and I pay the tax. Now that I did everything I am required to, can I just roll the distributed funds back into my account to keep them growing tax-deferred?**

A: No. The tax law specifically prohibits you from rolling RMDs back into a retirement account.

You must begin taking your RMD by what is called your Required Beginning Date (RBD), which is generally April 1 of the year following the year you turn age 70½. There are some exceptions to that rule for distributions from company plans, and these exceptions are covered in this checklist, as well.

Even if you don't need the money, you still must take the distribution. This is not voluntary. The RMD is required under the law.

Roth IRA owners are not subject to RMDs, but beneficiaries of Roth IRAs are, and those details will be covered in Section III.

What's In It for Me?

By using this handy checklist, you will be assured of not messing up this crucial component of retirement account distribution planning. And, believe me, you don't want to mess up or the you-know-what will really hit the fan. But I'll get to that in a moment.

Furthermore, this checklist will show you when you can add all your plans together (if you have more than one) and take RMDs from any one or a combination of the accounts to make calculating easier. You cannot satisfy an RMD from an IRA by withdrawing from your 401(k) plan, however. Nor can you can satisfy an RMD from a Keogh plan with a distribution from an IRA. But for RMD calculations, SEP and SIMPLE IRAs are included with IRAs.

Ask Ed . . .

Q: **What is my "first distribution year"?**

A: Not what you think. It sounds like it's the year you take your first distribution, which would make sense if the tax code were in English, but it isn't. Your "first distribution year" is not always the year you actually take your RMD, but the first year that an RMD *is required.* Here's an example: Say you turn 70 on April 23,

2007. That means you will turn 70½ on October 23, 2007 (six months later). Since you turn 70½ in 2007, then that is your "first distribution year," but you do not have to take your first distribution until your Required Beginning Date, which is not until April 1, 2008. So in this case, your "first distribution year" is 2007, but the year you take your first RMD can be 2008. Even if you wait until April 1, 2008 to take your first RMD, the year-end balance you will use to calculate your RMD is December 31, 2006 (the year prior to your "first distribution year" of 2007). It is only the first year's RMD that has these twists and turns. Afterward each RMD must be taken by December 31 of that year, which, following on this example, means your second RMD must be taken by December 31, 2008, based on the balance in your IRA or other plan on December 31, 2007. You use the age you turn on your birthday in each distribution year to calculate RMDs. Here, having turned 70 on your birthday (April 23, 2007), you will look up the life expectancy for a 70-year-old in 2007 on the Uniform Lifetime Table (Appendix II) and divide your December 31, 2006 account balance by that number (27.4 years) to determine your RMD. Now, if you turn 70 on, say, November 12, 2007, this means you will not turn 70½ until 2008, and your Required Beginning Date would be April 1, 2009—so your first RMD will be based on your account balance as of December 31, 2007. If you are unsure of any of this, don't go it alone. Any trained financial advisor (see Section V) should be able to help you with your RMD calculations. Your IRA custodian can help you as well.

What If I Don't?

You will lose your money pretty quickly because the government levies a 50 percent penalty for any RMDs not taken. That's one of the stiffest fines in the whole tax code. And believe me, Big Brother is watching and will know if you missed an RMD because your plan custodian is required by law to rat you out by notifying the IRS of your RMDs. With all this watching and ratting out, it is now extremely difficult to plead ignorance of an RMD as many people did in the past when they missed one. It remains to be seen just how lenient the IRS may be now since it will know that your own plan custodian has given you a timely heads-up.

A Word to the Wise

Don't risk the 50 percent penalty by waiting until the last minute to take your RMD. The banks and other financial institutions are flooded with these year-end requests and as a result your RMD might not get distributed in time. Since RMDs are based on the December 31 balance in your account as of the prior year, you can actually compute your RMD early in the year to avoid the year-end rush—and you should do that if only for the peace of mind in knowing that the calculation is done. Then you can take your RMD a bit later in the year (around November for example, though not later). Keep your inventory of owned accounts [Section I, Part 1] up to date so that you will have the most current information on your balances when you begin making calculations and taking RMDs.

Instructions

Refer to the list you made of all owned (not inherited) accounts (Section I, Part 1) to make sure you include all of them here. You also will need your IRA and/or other plan statements handy showing the balance in each plan as of the end of the prior year. For example, you will need your December 31, 2006 balance to calculate a 2007 RMD. Then follow the checklist right through the calculations of each RMD for each account you own, and you won't go wrong.

Ask Ed . . .

Q: **If I qualify for the still-working exception referenced in the checklist, does this mean I do not have to take any RMDs from any of my retirement accounts until I actually retire?**

A: No! The still-working exception applies only to distributions from your company plan if you are still working for that company—in which case you do not have to begin talking RMDs (from *that* plan), until April 1 of the year following the year you retire. You still must take your RMDs from all other plans and IRAs you have. The still-working exception never applies to IRAs, nor does it apply to a company plan if you own more than 5 percent of the company or are self-employed.

Lifetime RMDs for most IRA and other plan owners are based on the Uniform Lifetime Table (Appendix II) unless the "Spousal Exception" applies. This exception allows IRA and other plan owners to use the Joint Life Expectancy Table to calculate RMDs if the sole beneficiary of the plan for the entire RMD year is a spouse more than ten years younger than you. The Joint Life Expectancy Tables (Appendix III) will give you a lower RMD.

A Word to the Wise

Your trickiest RMD may be the first one because you can take it either in the year you turn 70½ or up to April 1 of the following year. For example, if you turned 70½ in 2006, then your Required Beginning Date (RBD) is April 1, 2007—and you can take your RMD either in 2006 or up to April 1, 2007. In many cases, it might be better to take your first RMD in 2006 rather than waiting to take it in 2007, however. In this way, you will not have to take your first two RMDs in one tax year (2007 in this example) as your 2007 RMD would also be due in 2007. If you take your first RMD in 2006, you can separate the income from both of your first two RMDs into two separate tax years and probably pay a lower tax in each year.

MY RMD CALCULATIONS CHECKLIST

MY NAME: _____ DATE: _____

MY ADVISOR'S NAME: _____ PLAN #: _____

Follow-ups should be added to the To Do lists at the end of this checklist.

1. I am subject to required distributions because I am or _____
will be age 70½ or older by 12/31 of this year.

2. Does an exception apply to my required distributions? _____

• Roth IRAs have no required distributions _____

• My first-year distribution can be delayed until 4/1 of the _____
following year (second distribution must be taken by
12/31 of that year also).

• I am still working (company plans only); if I am less than _____
a 5 percent owner of the company, distributions are not
required until 4/1 of the year after my retirement.

• 403(b) plan balances prior to 1987 are not subject to re- _____
quired distributions until I am age 75.

Comments: _____

_____

_____

_____

_____

3. Determine my distribution year (if turning 73 this year, _____
the distribution year is the current year. If prior year's
age 70½ distribution was deferred to current year 4/1,
distribution year is prior year).

4. What is the balance in each of my retirement plans? _____

• Balance as of 12/31 of the year prior to the distribution year _____

Comments: _____

_____

_____

_____

_____

5. I have looked up my life-expectancy factor (my age on the last day of the distribution year) in the Uniform Lifetime Table (Appendix II) and it is: _____

- EXCEPTION: If my spouse is my sole beneficiary for the entire year and is more than ten years younger than me, I will use Joint Life Expectancy Table (Appendix III) to look up my life-expectancy factor, which is: _____

6. Divide the account balance by my life expectancy factor to calculate RMDs. _____

Comments: _____

_____

_____

_____

7. Take my RMD by 12/31 of the distribution year (unless it is the first-year distribution delayed until 4/1). _____

8. I know there is a 50 percent penalty on any required distribution not taken. _____

9. I know that if I have multiple accounts, distributions can sometimes be taken from any one or a combination of those accounts. _____

- Owned IRAs (including SEP and SIMPLE IRAs but not including Roth IRAs) or IRAs inherited from the same person can be added together. _____

- 403(b) plans can be added together. _____

- All other company or employer plans can*not* be added together. _____

10. I know that if I have pre-tax (deductible) and after-tax (nondeductible) amounts in my IRA that the pro-rata rule will apply. _____

- I must file Form 8606 with my tax return. This form will track my after-tax basis amount and give me the calculation for the taxable and non-taxable amounts of my distribution. _____

- I cannot take after-tax-only amounts out of my IRA(s), even if they are in a separate account. _____

Follow-Up

My To Do List	Date Completed
1	
2	
3	
4	
5	
6	
7	
8	
9	
10	

My Signature   Date

Part 6

MY ROLLOVER/LUMP-SUM
DECISION CHECKLIST

What It Does

My daughter Ilana began driving last year, and as any parent knows, that's when the worrying really begins. Whenever she takes the car, I usually say to her, "Call me when you get there" so that I know she arrived safely.

You should do the same thing whenever your retirement funds leave the nest—and that's the short answer to what this checklist does.

The longer answer is this: When you retire or leave the company you work for to take another job (or for any other reason), you will be asked by your current employer what to do with the retirement benefits you have accrued in your 401(k), 403(b), 457, or other company plan. There are four options: (1) Roll the funds over into an IRA; (2) Take them as a lump sum; (3) Keep them in the current plan for the time being, then transfer them into your new employer's plan when you get settled; (4) Leave them in the employer plan. Each option comes with many considerations that must be weighed carefully to make the right decision for you. As these funds represent every penny you have saved from working over the past however many years—the largest check you will ever get—you will want to make sure nothing bad happens to them due to your making the wrong decision here. Because you may only get one chance.

Ask Ed . . .

Q: What if I do an IRA rollover, but then decide I would like to roll those funds back to my company's plan. Can I do that?

A: The IRS says yes, but it is up to your company plan whether to accept your money back or not. In any case, only taxable IRA funds can be rolled back to a company plan. You cannot roll after-tax funds (funds you have already paid tax on) from an IRA to a company plan. But I would think twice before considering a reverse rollover because once your funds are in the IRA most of your company plan benefits (like NUA or 10-year averaging, see Section IV, Part 7, for example) are no longer available on those funds. So that tilts the scales toward leaving the funds in the IRA where you control them. As you go through the checklist, you will find plenty of benefits from having funds in your company plan, such as federal creditor protection, the ability to delay RMDs if you are still working, the age 55 exception from the 10 percent penalty for early withdrawals to name just the big ones. But the distribution options in an IRA are far better than in a company plan—especially for a nonspouse beneficiary who will be able to stretch IRA funds over his or her lifetime, an option that probably won't be available in the company plan and if your beneficiaries inherit from that plan (as opposed to an IRA), they will probably be hit with the full distribution, which will all be taxable. Presto, no more retirement account. This is not the way to leverage your wealth and keep it building for and by your heirs. However, under the Pension Protection

Act, as of 2007 nonspouse beneficiaries can transfer inherited company plan funds to properly titled inherited IRAs maintaining the tax deferral over their lifetime. As far as federal creditor protection is concerned, virtually all IRAs are protected from bankruptcy (not all judgments, only bankruptcy) under the recent Bankruptcy Act, and many states now protect IRAs too— another reason to stay with the IRA. To find out if your state is one of them, ask your estate-planning attorney or expert financial advisor.

What's In It for Me?

You will have all the facts at hand to make the best—and safest— decision possible regarding the rollover or lump-sum distribution of your company plan retirement funds. You won't have to worry about missing any possible tax breaks or wonder whether your funds will indeed get where they're supposed to go (and I don't just mean to your named beneficiaries) when they leave the nest, but to their actual transfer destination. This last concern may strike you as a bit far-fetched—after all, in our age of computerization how could a check as sizable as a rollover or lump sum distribution NOT safely arrive where it's to be transferred? Well, read on, MacDuff.

Ask Ed . . .

Q: **Part of my plan balance is after-tax funds. Can these funds be rolled over to an IRA? And, after that, be converted to a Roth IRA tax-free?**

A: Yes to the first part of your question—the Economic Growth and Tax Relief Reconciliation Act of 2001 (known as "EGTRRA") does allow that. But no to the second part, at least until 2008, when that will change. But as of this writing, you cannot just convert the tax-free funds and pay no tax at all, unless you have no IRA funds even in other accounts. If you do, then you will have to factor those funds in. This will result in some of the converted funds being taxable—the so-called pro-rata rule. You see, when an IRA contains both after-tax and taxable funds, then each dollar withdrawn from the IRA will contain a tax-free and taxable percentage. That percentage is based on the percentage of after-tax funds to the entire balance in all your IRAs. Let's say you rolled over $50,000 of after-tax funds from your 401(k) to your IRA. There was $450,000 in your IRA and now with this additional $50,000 of after-tax funds, your total IRA balance is $500,000. If you now want to withdraw $50,000 and convert those funds to a Roth IRA, you will still pay tax on $45,000, and the other 10 percent, the $5,000, will be tax-free. The $50,000 of after-tax funds now in your IRA is 10 percent of the total $500,000 IRA balance, so each dollar withdrawn from your IRA will be 10 percent tax-free and 90 percent taxable. If you withdraw the entire $500,000, then all of the $50,000 will be tax-free (since that is 10 percent of the total IRA balance) and the other $450,000 will be taxable. Can you roll that $50,000 of after-tax money into a separate IRA (with no other money in it) and then withdraw tax-free? The answer is still no. Once after-tax funds are rolled into an IRA, they can only be withdrawn under the pro-rata rule where each dollar withdrawn is part taxable and part tax-free based on the percentage of after-tax money in the account. However, beginning in 2008, things will change, and you will be able to roll funds directly from a company plan to a Roth IRA. If your company issues a separate check for your after-tax funds, you can roll the after-tax funds only into a Roth IRA and pay no tax on the conversion.

What If I Don't?

Whenever distributed funds come out of your retirement account, you should follow the money (as the message of Watergate goes) to make sure it arrives at its destination intact. This may sound simple, but many of these transactions end up in the wrong place. And when the error is discovered (typically at tax time), it is often too late to do anything to correct it. You might just as well have signed those funds over to the IRS. All your accountant may be able to say to you at this point is, "Well, at least I do have *some* good news. I saved a fortune on my car insurance by switching to GEICO."

One situation was brought to my attention where the bank rolled more than $200,000 from an account owner's IRA into someone else's account, and the error was not discovered until five years later. The challenge became how to get those funds back into the right account, which might not even be possible at that point. By the way, in case you are wondering how rich a person must be not to miss a sudden drop of $200,000 in his IRA, the answer is—not rich at all. It turns out that for some still-unknown explanation—either a 1099-R form on the erroneous distribution was not sent to the IRA owner, or, like the funds themselves, it went to the wrong account—no red flag went up. Also, you will recall that 2000, the year this mistake occurred, was a year when most people invested in the market saw their portfolios plunge (the so-called "dot.com collapse"). When the owner of the account saw the sudden drop in the value of his holdings on his statement, he simply assumed he'd gotten killed on paper like everyone else in the market and didn't say anything about it to his accountant or custodian until he wanted to start taking distributions and wondered where most of his nest egg went!

Botched rollovers are so prevalent that more than 300 Private Letter Rulings (PLRs)—requests to the IRS from plan owners requesting relief from a botched distribution—have been issued by the IRS in recent years. In the majority of such cases, the cause of the problem was financial advisor error or a mistake made by the financial institution either in providing proper guidance or by moving the money to a taxable account instead of an IRA. In these cases, the IRS granted the victims relief. But a PLR is an expensive process and it can take nine months or more to get an answer—with no guarantee the answer will be a favorable one. Do you want to take that chance? This is YOUR life savings we're talking about.

What else could happen if you ignore this checklist? You will never know until it's too late if you made the right distribution decisions. You will never know until it's too late if you left any big tax breaks on the table simply because you did not know you were entitled to them. You will never know until it's too late that you are paying a lot more tax on the distribution of your tax-deferred funds than you probably should be. Are all of these not reasons enough?

Ask Ed . . .

Q: **How best can I avoid a rollover horror story like those mentioned?**

A: Easy. When moving money, don't do a *literal* rollover (where the money is issued to you and thus temporarily in your possession until you put it in an IRA or other plan). Do a trustee-to-trustee transfer where the funds move *directly* from your 401(k) or other plan into an IRA or other plan without touching your sticky little fingers, and thus becoming vulnerable to the Taxman. The rollover process has three problems. The first is the 60-day rule, which gives you just 60 days from the date you receive the distribution to roll it into another plan. That deadline comes very quickly and people often miss it. The second problem is the once-a-year rollover limitation rule, which prohibits you from doing more than one rollover every twelve months. Why should you care about this? Let's say you have $500,000 in your IRA at Mutual Fund A and you roll $1,000 of that to another IRA at Bank B. You must then wait at least a year before you can roll over any of the remaining $499,000 from your IRA at Mutual Fund A. And you also must wait a year before you can roll the $1,000 in Bank B over to another IRA. And the final problem with a rollover distribution is that it may be subject to a mandatory 20 percent withholding tax if it comes from a company plan. A trustee-to-trustee transfer avoids all these issues. The 60-day rule does not kick in since the money transfers directly. There is no limit on the number of trustee-to-trustee transfers you can do in a year. And there is no 20 percent mandatory withholding tax.

Instructions

Even if you have made a decision about how you want your money distributed, go through each item in this checklist, ticking off those that apply to you; then prioritize them 1, 2, 3 and so forth according to which applicable item is most important to you (1 being most important and 3 being of lesser importance). By going through the entire checklist and rating your priorities, you will expose any conflicts or potential conflicts in your decision-making, and be able to resolve the problem now.

For example, let's say you know you want to get those 401(k) funds into a Roth IRA so they can begin to grow tax-free. You also know that to do this you must first roll those funds into an IRA because you cannot convert from a 401(k) directly to a Roth IRA until the law changes in 2008. So, you mark the line after "ability to convert to a Roth IRA" under the "My reasons to do an IRA rollover" section with a 1, since that is important to you. But you might find other items offering other choices that may also rate a 1 to you now that you think about them, such as "qualifying for tax breaks on the distribution—10-year averaging and NUA" under "My reasons to do a lump-sum distribution." Thus, you find yourself torn because that's important to you, too. Now you have a conflict. By going over every applicable item and rating it, you will know what you will have to resolve ahead of time with your financial advisor, spouse, even your beneficiaries in order to make the right decision for you and your family.

After you make your decision, you will fill out the required paperwork at your employer to actually get the distribution. Here again, you should work closely with an expert financial advisor to avoid any slip-ups. Although many companies have people on staff in the Benefits Department to work on distributions, these people are usually not financial professionals and thus can easily make mistakes. Furthermore, while they may be nice people and very helpful, the bottom line is they work for your employer, not for you. That's why you want an expert financial advisor for guidance here. You want someone who works for *you* and is thus 100 percent accountable to you.

In the end, an IRA rollover will probably be your best choice, but there are so many factors to look at first, and you will find them all here. So, if your advisor—or any of those financial experts you encounter down at the local gym—tells you just to do an IRA rollover without considering anything else, you are getting the wrong advice.

A Word to the Wise

If you are going to roll over your 401(k) or other plan balance to an IRA and request a trustee-to-trustee transfer, but your Benefits Department does not do this and says it must issue you a check instead—with the check made out to *you*—then the IRS will consider you to be in receipt of the money, thereby triggering the three rollover problems I've mentioned. Insist that the check be made out instead to "**ABC Bank as trustee of Individual Retirement Account of (Your Name)**." This way, the check can only be cashed by ABC Bank to go into your IRA, thus qualifying as a direct transfer [IRS Regulation § 1.401(a)(31)-1].

MY ROLLOVER/LUMP-SUM DECISION CHECKLIST

MY NAME: _____ DATE: _____

MY ADVISOR'S NAME: _____ PLAN #: _____

Follow-ups should be added to the To Do Lists at the end of this checklist.

My distribution options available from a company plan are:

    1. Rollover to an IRA

    2. Lump-sum distribution

    3. Move it to my new employer's plan

    4. Leave it in my current plan.

1. My reasons to do a rollover to an IRA are:

- I don't need the money now   _____

- Ability to create a stretch IRA for my beneficiaries. As of   _____
  2007 my beneficiaries will be able to directly transfer
  company plan funds to an inherited IRA, if the company
  plan allows

- Estate planning with an IRA is easier   _____

- Wider choice of investment options   _____

- Ability to convert to a Roth IRA. As of 2008, I will be able   _____
  to convert plan funds directly to a Roth IRA

- Ability to invest in an annuity   _____

- No withdrawal restrictions (after age 59½)   _____

- Ability to consolidate accounts   _____

- No withholding taxes on a trustee-to-trustee transfer   _____

- Access to professional advice (IRA funds can be placed   _____
  with a manager accountable to me)

Comments: _____

_____

_____

How to do a Rollover

2. Trustee-to-trustee transfer

- Unlimited number of transfers per year   _____

- Exempt from 20 percent withholding (applies to trans-   _____
  fers from employer plans only)

- No opportunity for me to use tax-deferred funds   _____

3. 60-day rule

- I will have 60 days from the receipt of my funds to contribute them to an IRA or company plan without penalty _____

- When distributed from company plan, funds are subject to 20 percent withholding (the withheld amount can be rolled over but I must pay out of pocket) _____

- Funds not deposited within 60 days are considered income and subject to tax _____

- IRS now has the power to grant relief and allow completion of the rollover after the 60 days under "special circumstances" _____

- For IRAs only—one rollover per year per account _____

- Roth conversions—60-day rule applies, one per year rule does not apply _____

- 60-day IRA loans—funds are removed from the IRA for personal use and returned within 60 days. (IRS is reluctant to grant relief if the funds are not returned on time) _____

Comments: _____

_____

_____

_____

4. Funds eligible for rollover: _____

- RMDs *No*
- Distributions that are part of a substantially equal payment plan *No*
- Hardship distributions *No*
- Distributions to nonspouse beneficiaries *No*
- After-tax funds:
  To an IRA *Yes*
  Between the same types of plans if the plan agreements allow (Must be a trustee-to-trustee transfer) *Yes*
  Between different types of plans if the plan agreements allow (Must be a trustee-to-trustee transfer) *Yes*
- The same property received—i.e. if I receive cash, I must roll over cash; if I receive ABC stock, I must roll over ABC stock—except for a distribution from a company plan, where I can sell the asset received and roll over the cash from the sale *Yes*

- Funds from plans of other countries—e.g. assets in a Canadian plan cannot be rolled over to a US plan   _____No_____

Comments: _____

_____

_____

_____

_____

_____

The lump-sum distribution

5. My reasons to do a lump-sum distribution are:

- I need the money now.   _____

- I will qualify for tax breaks on the distribution (i.e., NUA and 10-year averaging, see The Tax Breaks for Lump-Sum Distributions Checklist—Section IV, part 7).   _____

- My tax bracket is lower now than it will be in retirement when I start taking withdrawals and paying tax on them.   _____

- No future taxes will be due (they are paid at the time of distribution).   _____

- Source of liquidity for estate planning   _____

Comments: _____

_____

_____

_____

6. Qualifying as a lump-sum distribution:

- Entire balance(s) credited for all like plans of the employer must be distributed in the same tax year   _____Yes_____

- The distribution must take place after a triggering event: separation from service (except for self-employed individuals), attainment of age 59½, death, or disability (Disability is only for self-employed individuals)   _____Yes_____

- I have taken no other distributions from the plan between the triggering event and the lump-sum distribution unless they are in the same tax year as the lump-sum distribution   *Yes (I took no other distributions)*

7. Distribution can be split between funds I keep and _____
funds rolled over to an IRA or another company plan.

Comments: _____

_____

_____

_____

Leave in my company plan or move to my new employer's plan.

8. My reasons to leave my funds in my company plan are:

• I will be working again _____

• No taxes are due _____

• Federal creditor protection _____

• Loan provisions (may not apply to terminated or retired _____
employees)

• Plan holds life insurance that cannot be transferred or re- _____
placed

• I can defer required distributions if still working and not a _____
5 percent owner of the business (see checklist this section, Part 5)

• I am exempt from 10 percent early-distribution penalty if _____
I was at least age 55 when I separated from service

Comments: _____

_____

_____

_____

Follow-Up

My To Do List	Date Completed
1	
2	
3	
4	
5	

6 _____

7 _____

8 _____

9 _____

10 _____

_____   _____
My Signature   Date

Section III

THE ACCOUNT
BENEFICIARY'S
CARE SOLUTION

> "A son can bear with composure the death of his father,
> but the loss of his inheritance might drive him to despair."
>
> —Niccolo Machiavelli (1469–1527)

Even if the person you have inherited or will be inheriting from does everything correctly to enable you to inherit with all stretch and other tax opportunities intact, it can all be for nothing if you make a mistake on your end by not knowing what to do *when* you inherit. So, this section tackles all the critical items all types of beneficiaries must take care of and do (or not do) in order to inherit the maximum amount possible and keep their inheritance growing tax-deferred (or even tax-free) for as long as the law allows. In other words, for beneficiaries, this section can spell the difference between Uncle Sam's beating you out as the biggest beneficiary of all.

When it comes to company retirement plans and IRAs, beneficiaries are divided into two distinct camps. No, it's not good beneficiaries and evil beneficiaries (that's the theme of an earlier work about two well-known beneficiaries named Cain and Abel). The types I am referring to are beneficiaries who are spouses and beneficiaries who are nonspouses. There are distinct tax law differences in the ways these two beneficiaries can inherit retirement plans.

I thought the difference between a nonspouse beneficiary and a spouse beneficiary was obvious until I received the following question from a client a few years ago: "Dear Ed," she wrote, "I am the benefi-

A Word to the Wise

If your benefactor has not kept you in the loop, and it's not too late to alert him to some of the things he can and should do for your benefit when you inherit, this section will tip you off to those key opportunities to grab and pitfalls to avoid—because when you inherit it may be too late to do anything about them. Once you have inherited and assumed legal ownership as a beneficiary of the account(s), thereafter **you** are treated as the owner (with some exceptions) and you will use Section II (for account owners) to plan opportunities for your own beneficiaries.

ciary of my dad's IRA, but I am also married. Am I a spouse beneficiary or a nonspouse beneficiary?" Signed Susan Confused.

"Dear Susan," I wrote back. "You are a nonspouse beneficiary, even though, yes indeed, you are someone's spouse."

The type of beneficiary you are is based on your relationship with the *deceased owner* of the account you have inherited. If you were married to him or her, then you are a spouse beneficiary (even though you are now a widow or widower and no longer married). If you are not the widow or widower of the deceased owner and you inherit, then you are a nonspouse beneficiary (even though you may be someone else's spouse). Got it?

In addition, nonspouse beneficiaries don't always have to be people. An estate, a charity, or a trust that inherits is also a nonspouse beneficiary.

So, this section offers different checklists of what to do when you inherit, depending upon which type of beneficiary you are. It also provides a third checklist for multiple beneficiaries that covers a very common inheritance situation—where an IRA, for example, is left to two children, or to three grandchildren, or to a child and a spouse, or any other combination of multiple (or multiple types) of beneficiaries.

Part 1

THE NONSPOUSE BENEFICIARY'S

(AN INDIVIDUAL) CHECKLIST

For a child, grandchild, relative, family friend,
or other individual who inherits

What It Does

If you are a living, breathing (unlike a charity or trust) nonspouse beneficiary of an IRA or company plan (or will be), this checklist is for
you. It shows you everything you must do to inherit an IRA or company plan correctly. By *correctly*, I mean in order to maximize the tax
deferral of the inherited account for as long as legally possible and to
be aware and able to take advantage of every possible tax benefit available to you that has been set up for you in the bequest.

This checklist covers IRAs, Roth IRAs, 401(k)s, 403(b)s, 457
plans, and all other types of "inherited accounts," a term that in tax
lingo means an account that is inherited by someone (or something)
other than a spouse. What's the distinction? When a spouse inherits,
he or she can do a rollover or a trustee-to-trustee transfer, and from
that point the account is treated as his or her own, not as an inherited
one. To add to the confusion, if a spouse is one of several beneficiaries
and the account is not split by 12/31 of the year after the account

owner's death (the spouse is still one of several beneficiaries) then he or she is considered to be a nonspouse beneficiary. In such a circumstance, this Nonspouse Beneficiary's Checklist is what to use.

In addition, it is common for nonspouse beneficiaries to inherit several different types of retirement plans from one person—for example, your dad could leave you a 401(k) and an IRA—so you'll need to know your distribution options for each plan. They are probably very different. This checklist provides an easy-to-use chart that lays out in one page ALL of the distribution options available to you as a nonspouse beneficiary of the human type. (Charities or trusts get their own separate checklists in this section.)

Everything covered here applies equally to nonspouse beneficiaries of Roth IRAs, as well. The only difference is that distributions from inherited Roth IRAs will generally be income tax-free.

Ask Ed . . .

Q: I just inherited an IRA from my mom, but I am under 59½ years old. Will I pay a penalty on any distributions I take now?

A: No. The 10 percent penalty on early withdrawals before age 59½ *NEVER* applies to a beneficiary.

What's In It for Me?

Using this checklist to make all the right moves with your newly inherited account(s) will ensure that you maximize your inherited dollars for the rest of your life by not missing out on any tax benefits to which you are entitled. This is your inheritance, but because it is a retirement account—unlike, say, an antique automobile—it can provide a lifetime legacy of *income* to you and your own heirs. What you make of this incredible opportunity is up to you, but everything you will need to seize that opportunity is here for you.

Ask Ed . . .

Q: **I inherited retirement accounts from two different people. Can I combine them into one inherited IRA?**

A: No. Each inherited account must be kept separate and in the name of the deceased original owner but with your social security number on it. This does not mean it is not your money. It means that the account must always be recognized as an inherited one—but you still control the distributions and investments the same as on any accounts you possess in your own name. However, you can combine two or more inherited accounts that you inherited from the *same* person into one IRA. For example, if you inherited two accounts from your brother, you can combine those into one inherited IRA that is maintained in his name but under your social security number.

What If I Don't?

You'll blow your inheritance. The money will go quickly to Uncle Sam, leaving you with little more than a memory of what could have been. This is a common occurrence because most beneficiaries do not realize the long-term potential of an inherited account such as an IRA. It is the goose that keeps laying the golden egg, and this is your one chance to have it.

You will see many items in this checklist that may strike you as seeming unimportant or even ridiculous. But I assure you they are not. Missing any one of them could cause your golden goose to break its neck.

For example, something as simple as titling the inherited account in your own name is considered a complete distribution subject to tax. What happens then? The entire IRA balance becomes taxable to you, and the stretch opportunity is over. You'll have to withdraw the funds and pay the tax all in one year, giving you a large amount of added income that not only may bump you into a higher tax bracket that year, but also prompt other tax increases that may result in your giving more money to the IRS than you would have had to. You see, when you pile on a lot of income in a year, you start to exceed certain income limitations that cause you to lose exemptions for your family and deductions based on a percentage of your income. A loss of tax deductions is the same as a tax increase.

Ask Ed...

Q: **How do I find out how long (for how many years) I can stretch the IRA I inherited and calculate my Required Minimum Distributions?**

A: You would look up your age as of your birthday in the year *after* your benefactor's death in the IRS Single Life Expectancy Table (Appendix I) and note the life-expectancy factor that corresponds to your age. That is your stretch period. For example, if you turned age 50 in 2006 when the person you inherited the account from died, you will be 51 in 2007 (the year after the account owner died) with a life expectancy—stretch period—of 33.3 years. Your first RMD is due for 2007. To determine the amount, divide the account balance at the end of 2006 by 33.3. The 2007 RMD must be taken by the end of 2007. For each succeeding year you cannot go back to the Table to calculate your RMD for that year—just reduce the life expectancy factor by one each time—so that in 2008, you'll use 32.3, then in 2009 you'll use 31.3 and so on. The RMD is what it says—the *minimum* you must take. You can always withdraw more than that if you wish, but you will owe tax on whatever you withdraw. Each year's RMD is due by the end of that year.

A financial advisor shared this story with me. A client of his died naming a son the beneficiary of a $560,000 IRA. The son did not like the conservative investments that this advisor and his late father had in the IRA, and basically said, "I am taking the money and moving it to an account where I can do my own trading and investments." The son withdrew the $560,000 and went to move it to a discount broker, but as soon as he took the check to the broker's company, he was told that they could not open an inherited IRA for him. When he asked why, the company told him the bad news. The minute he took the distribution from the inherited IRA, the entire $560,000 became taxable, and the error could not be corrected. The son did not know that a nonspouse beneficiary cannot do a rollover.

His dad might have spent a lifetime conservatively investing this money to grow it to $560,000, but his son wiped it out in seconds—and furthermore had to add the $560,000 distribution to his own income for the year, putting him in the highest tax bracket and causing all of his other income for that year to be taxed at higher rates, not to mention losing many deductions and exemptions because his income was now too high.

So, here's the message: Messing up a single step in the inheriting of a retirement account can result in very bad news all around. But

Ask Ed . . .

Q: **My mom died late in the year and did not take her RMD for the year when she died. What happens now? Who takes her year of death distribution or is she exempt since she died?**

A: Death gets you out of pretty much everything under the tax code, but not RMDs. You, as the beneficiary, must take her year of death RMD, and you also must pay tax on the distribution on your own tax return. The following year, you will start taking RMDs based on your own life expectancy.

you can avoid that bad news by putting this checklist to good use and not missing a beat.

Instructions

This checklist takes you through every critical step in the inheriting-an-account process, beginning with the most important step of all, "Touch Nothing!" Do not move or touch a red cent of that money until you have carefully reviewed all the points in this checklist relevant to your situation, and discussed them with your *expert* financial advisor (Section V). This is an area where just any advisor won't do. Even the advisor your parent or whomever you inherited from used may not be up to the task—because most financial advisors are not trained in what to do with a client's retirement account *after* the client dies. A mistake made by the untrained can end your inherited account; it happens all the time.

It is critical that the inherited account be set up and titled correctly. It is also important that you immediately name your own beneficiary so that if you die while there are still funds remaining in the inherited account—an IRA, for example—your children will be able

Ask Ed . . .

Q: **Can I disclaim an inherited account so that it will go to my children?**

A: Once you disclaim (refuse) an inherited account, you have no say where it goes. It will go to the contingent beneficiary named by the deceased original owner of the account. Of course, if the deceased owner named your children as contingent beneficiaries, then they will inherit the account you have disclaimed—but not on your say-so. (See The Disclaimer Planning Checklist, Section IV, Part 3.)

to continue the stretch you would have been entitled to had you lived (assuming, of course, the IRA custodial agreement [Section II, Part 2] allows that, which hopefully it will because your benefactor has made sure it's there).

If you need funds—to pay estate taxes, for example—after the death of the person you inherited from, and you have not yet had a chance to go through this checklist, then see if it is at all possible to take the money you need from some other asset you may have inherited. The minute you use any inherited retirement account funds, even if it is to pay estate taxes, you will first have to pay income tax on the amount you withdraw and you'll be quickly eroding your inherited funds. Use these funds last. They are too valuable.

THE NONSPOUSE BENEFICIARY'S (AN INDIVIDUAL) CHECKLIST

MY NAME: _____ DATE: _____

MY ADVISOR'S NAME: _____ PLAN #: _____

Follow-ups should be added to the To Do lists at the end of this checklist.

1. I will touch nothing! _____

- I have obtained or will obtain copies of the death certifi-   _____
cate (the plan custodian will probably ask for a copy).

- I have copies of the beneficiary form.   _____

- I have determined the type of retirement account—   _____
traditional IRA (including SEP and SIMPLE IRAs), Roth   Type of plan(s)
IRA, or company plan (401(k), 403(b), 457 plan), etc.—
I am or will be inheriting.

- I know that I can make no contributions to the account   _____
(nonspouse beneficiaries are prohibited from making
contributions to inherited accounts).

2. The plan custodian's copy of the beneficiary form names as beneficiary:

- Primary (if spouse is primary beneficiary and elects to   _____
roll over account to her own, he/she should go to checklist in Part 2 of this section)

  - Designated or nondesignated (a designated benefi-   _____
  ciary is an *individual;* a non-designated beneficiary is an
  entity, such as a charity)

- Contingent   _____

  - Designated or nondesignated   _____

3. The distribution options allowed by the plan custodian are:

- Did the account owner die before or after the Required   _____
Beginning Date (RBD) for his or her required distributions? (For definition of RBD, see Section II, Part 5.)

- The stretch is/is not allowed?   _____

- 5-year rule only?   _____

- Other?   _____

4. I have determined whether to disclaim the account   _____
(Checklist Section IV, Part 3).

**5. If the primary beneficiary is a nondesignated benefi-
ciary, the two payout options are:**

• Death before the RBD, 5-year payout option only. Account must be emptied by the end of the fifth year after
the account owner's death; there are no required annual
distributions.

_____

• Death after the RBD, distributions can be stretched over
the remaining life expectancy of the account owner. (See
chart after item 13)

_____

**6. As primary beneficiary I should do the following if not
disclaiming:**

• Change the social security number on the account to my
own social security number.

_____

• Change the account title to include my name as well as
the name of the deceased owner, which must remain in
the account title—i.e., John Smith, (deceased, date of
death) IRA fbo Charles Smith.

_____

• I have named a successor beneficiary (if the account
document allows).
   —Owner: uses his own age
   —He names a beneficiary: uses her own age
   —She names a successor beneficiary: uses beneficiary's
   age

_____

**7. If the account owner died after his/her RBD, was the
RMD satisfied for the year of death? (Does not apply
for a Roth IRA.)**

_____

• If no, have the balance of the account owner's required
distribution distributed to me as beneficiary by 12/31 of
the year of the account owner's death (distribution is calculated as though the owner were alive for the entire
year). I can still disclaim even after I take the year-of-
death RMD.

_____

**8. Pay estate taxes from other assets, not from the inher-
ited account if possible.**

_____

**9. When changing plan providers, I know to move funds
via direct transfer only (trustee-to-trustee transfer) because as a nonspouse beneficiary I _cannot_ do a
rollover, only a direct transfer.**

_____

Comments: _____

_____

_____

_____

_____

10. **For multiple beneficiaries—see The Multiple Benefi-** _____
    ciaries' Checklist in Part 3 of this section.

11. **For a trust beneficiary—see The Naming a Trust-as-** _____
    Beneficiary Checklist in Part 2 of Section IV.

12. **For tax breaks—see The Tax Breaks for Beneficiaries** _____
    Checklist in Part 5 of this section.

Comments: _____

_____

_____

_____

_____

13. **I must take my first RMD by 12/31 of the year after the** _____
    original owner's death. (10 percent early-distribution
    penalty does not apply to distributions to beneficia-
    ries.)

- Determine age to use for stretch payouts (see chart fol- _____
  lowing this item):

- Look up life expectancy factor from Single Life Ex- _____
  pectancy Table (Appendix I). It is:

- Use the balance in the decedent's account as of 12/31 of _____
  the year of death. If the account was split after that, use
  only the proportionate share of the balance applicable to
  each beneficiary.

- Divide the balance determined above by my life- _____
  expectancy factor to determine my RMDs.

- If I die after the original owner's death but before 9/30 of _____
  year after the owner's death, my age is used for calculating of RMDs going to my successor beneficiary (See The
  Successor Beneficiary's Checklist in this section, Part 4).

The following is a synopsis of options allowed by the IRS final-distribution regulations. All distribution options are subject to the terms of the custodian's agreement in effect at the time of the distribution. The 10 percent early-distribution penalty never applies to beneficiaries taking distributions. All beneficiaries generally have the option of taking a lump-sum distribution and paying income tax on the distribution or choosing to use the 5-year rule. Roth IRA beneficiaries use the Owner Dies Before RBD rules.

	Account Owner Dies Before RBD	Account Owner Dies After RBD
Nonspouse, Designated Beneficiary	Distributions based on the life expectancy of the beneficiary	Distributions based on life expectancy of the **younger of** the account owner or the beneficiary
	Use **Single Life Expectancy Table,** look up attained age in the year after account owner's death to get factor, factor is **reduced by one in each subsequent year**	Use **Single Life Expectancy Table,** look up attained age in the year after account owner's death to get factor, factor is **reduced by one in each subsequent year**
Nondesignated Beneficiary (Charity, Estate or Non-Qualifying Trust)	**5-year rule**	Distributions based on the life expectancy of the **deceased account owner**
	No annual required distributions but account must be emptied by the end of the fifth year after the year of the account owner's death	Use **Single Life Expectancy Table,** look up attained age account owner would have been in the year of death to get factor, factor is **reduced by one in each subsequent year**

14. I know there is a 50 percent penalty on any required distribution that is not taken. _____

15. My required distributions *cannot* be made from any other inherited retirement account unless it is inherited from the same person and is the same type of account (i.e., 2 IRAs inherited from Great-aunt Matilda). _____

16. If I am the nonspouse beneficiary of a Roth IRA inherited in the 5-year period after the account owner established the account, I may be subject to income tax. _____

Comments: _____

_____

_____

Follow-Up

My To Do List   Date Completed

1 _____

2 _____

3 _____

4 _____

5 _____

6 _____

7 _____

8 _____

9 _____

10 _____

_____   _____

My Signature   Date

Part 2

THE SPOUSE BENEFICIARY'S
CHECKLIST

For an inheriting spouse who is
the sole beneficiary

What It Does

Although I am not a chess player, I do know that in chess, the queen can do anything and go anywhere she pleases. She's downright intimidating. She can move, up, down, across, and even diagonally. She *owns* the chessboard.

When it comes to moving inherited retirement money around, a spouse beneficiary, whether male or female, is very much like that queen. A spouse beneficiary has more flexibility than a nonspouse beneficiary because she (or he) can do almost no wrong—and is usually bailed out by some provision in the tax rules if she (or he) does make some tactical blunder. To paraphrase Mel Brooks, "It's good to be the queen." This checklist shows why.

As most people do name their spouse as sole beneficiary of their assets, including retirement account funds, this checklist will apply to most beneficiaries. To avoid staying gender neutral and having to keep repeating the qualifiers she or he and her or him, I'll go with statistics, where the surviving spouse is typically female, and refer to the female gender.

Generally, when a spouse inherits she does a "spousal rollover" and elects to become the new owner of the inherited account rather than remaining a beneficiary. From that point, the IRS treats her as if she were the original owner of the account, and she follows the same RMD and penalty rules as any other original owner of an IRA or other plan. So, the spousal rollover is typically the best option for her.

Under some circumstances, though, she may want to remain a beneficiary for a time rather than do a spousal rollover right away. This might occur if she were younger than 59½ when she inherits the account and needs some of the funds in it to pay off debts or estate taxes. If she were to do a spousal rollover, then took distributions from the IRA before reaching age 59½, she would be subject to the 10 percent early withdrawal penalty, the same as any account owner. By remaining a beneficiary, however, she avoids the penalty because IRA and other plan beneficiaries are never subject to the 10 percent early withdrawal penalty (she will, of course, have to pay tax on any withdrawals). Then, when she reaches 59½, and the penalty is no longer an issue, she can still do the spousal rollover to her own IRA as there is no deadline for a spousal rollover and choosing to remain a beneficiary does not stop her from changing her mind later because she is the queen and can do as she pleases.

Ask Ed . . .

Q: **If I do the spousal rollover and become the IRA owner, can I later change my mind and go back to being a beneficiary?**

A: No. That is one of the few moves the queen cannot make on this particular chessboard. Once you take ownership of the account, it is, in all respects, yours, so you cannot go back and make it a beneficiary account again.

Well, almost as she pleases. Even the queen has to address some issues in making her spousal rollover vs. remain a beneficiary decision—and this checklist takes her through them.

What's In It for Me?

By designating a spouse as beneficiary of his retirement funds, the original owner (see Section I) has set the account up to provide the best opportunities for growth and longevity. He has also made sure that his grieving (one assumes) spouse—YOU—is not suddenly overwhelmed with having to make a slew of choices involving the inheritance at a very emotional and vulnerable time. Therefore, much advance planning and spadework has already been done for you. However, if your deceased husband did not take advantage of Section I to do much advance planning on your behalf, you can still seize the advantage with this checklist of your own.

Ask Ed . . .

Q: **Can I contribute to an IRA for my deceased spouse? He would have qualified had he lived (he was still working).**

A: No. The IRS ruled many years ago that you couldn't make an IRA or any other plan contribution for a deceased person even if that person would have qualified to make a contribution had he or she lived. You can argue with the IRS's logic on many things, but not here. It reasoned in its ruling that it saw no point in funding a retirement account for a dead person since that person is clearly retired . . . for good.

What If I Don't?

For the most part, all you have to do as a spouse beneficiary to take ownership of an inherited account is a spousal rollover—and even if you forget or miss out on doing that right away, you can always do it later on. So, it's hard for you as a spouse beneficiary to get hit with a monkey wrench even if you do mess up. But your own beneficiaries will get hit with a monkey wrench if you don't follow this checklist— so if you care about *their* future, that's why this checklist is here.

For example, let's say you mess up by not naming a beneficiary of your own as soon as you inherit, which the checklist urges. If you never get around to this step or die prematurely, the likelihood is the fund will go to your estate, and your children and grandchildren may lose out on the stretch option, or even be disinherited. Furthermore, if you remarry, the fund might go to your new spouse instead of your children and grandchildren as I'm sure your late first husband and you would have preferred. Even worse, the fund might wind up going to your new spouse's kids and grandkids, shutting out yours and your first husband's altogether.

So, if not for yourself, use this checklist for the benefit of your heirs.

Ask Ed . . .

Q: **My spouse died with all his money in a 401(k). Can I roll that over to my IRA, even though he did not have his funds in an IRA when he died?**

A: Yes. As a spouse, you can roll over 401(k) or other plan balances to your own IRA. The IRS has even ruled that a spouse beneficiary can roll a deceased spouse's 401(k) plan into an inherited IRA in the name of the deceased so that the surviving spouse can choose to remain a beneficiary instead of doing a rollover.

Instructions

Use this checklist to decide the best way for you, as a spouse beneficiary, to inherit—do a spousal rollover or elect to remain a beneficiary, and make other important choices. You have all the options for making your decisions here, but remember, because you are the spouse, you can change your decisions later on. Once you make a decision, be sure to follow the distribution rules that apply to the option you have chosen.

For example, the IRS likes the spouse beneficiary so much that it doesn't want her to have to share her inheritance. That is why there are different rules for when the spouse is the sole beneficiary (no sharing) and when the spouse is one of several beneficiaries (sharing the inherited account with co-beneficiaries—see checklist this section, Part 3). The spouse who is the sole beneficiary has the most flexibility and can take advantage of the distribution benefits available to her. But when a spouse is not the sole beneficiary, she lowers her status to that of a pawn, and is relegated to following the distribution rules that apply to other lowly nonspouse beneficiaries. The difference, though, is that she is usually able to remove her share and go back to being the sole beneficiary of her separate share and thus resume her royal status, regaining all the benefits of being a sole beneficiary (see The Multiple Beneficiaries' Checklist in this section, Part 3).

Ask Ed . . .

Q: **If I were 45 in the year my husband died and left me his account, what RMDs must I take if I choose to remain a beneficiary because I am under age 59½ and do not want to get hit with a 10 percent penalty on any withdrawals?**

A: This depends on how old your spouse was when he died. Let's say he was the same age as you, 45. If you choose to remain a beneficiary you do not have to withdraw anything from the inherited account until twenty-five years from now when he would have turned 70½ (the age when he would have to start taking his RMDs). So, any withdrawals you make during those twenty-five years are voluntary on your part, not required. But let's assume he was 75 when he died and you are 45. In this case, since he had already reached age 70½ when he died, you must begin taking RMDs in the first required distribution year (the year after his death). You will look up the life-expectancy factor in the Single Life Table [see Appendix I) for a 46-year-old (37.9 years), and then divide the account balance as of December 31 of the prior year by 37.9 to calculate your first-year RMD as spouse beneficiary. This distribution is subject to income tax, but no penalty because you have chosen to remain a beneficiary as opposed to taking ownership of the account with a spousal rollover. To calculate the next year's RMD as a beneficiary, see the chart following item 11 in the checklist.

THE SPOUSE BENEFICIARY'S CHECKLIST

MY NAME: _____ DATE: _____

MY ADVISOR'S NAME: _____ PLAN #: _____

Follow-ups should be added to the To Do lists at the end of this checklist.

1. I will touch nothing!   _____

- I have obtained or will obtain copies of the death certifi-   _____
  cate (the plan custodian will probably ask me for a copy).

- I have found copies of the beneficiary form.   _____

- I have, or will, inherit through a trust or a will.   _____

  - If I am the sole beneficiary of the trust or will and enti- _____
    tled to the entire account, I may be able to do a rollover
    based on numerous Private Letter Rulings and be
    treated as a spouse.

  - If I am not the sole beneficiary and I choose to remain a   _____
    beneficiary, I will be treated as a nonspouse beneficiary
    if I am one of multiple beneficiaries and the account is
    not timely split (see The Nonspouse Beneficiary's
    Checklist in Part 1 of this section).

- I have determined the type of retirement account(s) I   _____
  have inherited or will be inheriting—traditional IRA (in-   Type of plan(s)
  cluding SEP and SIMPLE IRAs), Roth IRA, or company
  plan (401(k), 403(b), 457 plan), etc.

- Did the deceased (original owner spouse) die before or   _____
  after his Required Beginning Date for taking Required
  Minimum Distributions (for definitions of these terms, see
  The RMD Calculations Checklist in Part 5 of Section II).

- I will make no contributions to the account (if I do, I will _____
  be deemed to be treating the account as my own).

2. The distribution options available to me as a spouse beneficiary are:

- Spousal rollover   _____

- Treat as my own account   _____

- Elect to "remain a beneficiary"   _____

- 5-year rule only   _____

- Lump-sum distribution   _____

Comments: _____

_____

_____

_____

_____

3. Determine if I should disclaim. (If yes, see The Dis-   _____
   claimer Planning Checklist in Section IV, Part 3.)

4. If not disclaiming, I must change the social security   _____
   number on the account to my own social security number and name successor beneficiaries as soon as possible, even if I am planning on doing a spousal rollover.

5. If the original owner spouse died after his RBD, was the   _____
   distribution satisfied for the year of death? (Does not
   apply for a Roth IRA.)

• If not, take the balance of the deceased owner's required   _____
   distribution (if any) by 12/31 of the year of death (distribution is calculated as though the deceased were alive
   for the entire year, see Section II, Part 5).

6. Pay estate taxes from other assets, not from the inher-   _____
   ited account if possible.

Comments: _____

_____

_____

_____

_____

_____

7. If I am not the only beneficiary, see The Multiple Bene-   _____
   ficiaries' Checklist in this section, Part 3.

8. Am I entitled to any tax breaks? (See The Tax Breaks   _____
   for Beneficiaries Checklist in this section, Part 5.) If so,
   they are:

Comments: _____

_____

_____

_____

_____

_____

9. If I treat the account as my own or if I do a spousal rollover, I become the new owner and I can:

• Make contributions to the account.   _____

• Have Required Minimum Distributions made to me as the   _____
account owner. (See the chart following item 11 and the
My RMD Calculations Checklist, Section II, Part 5.)

10. If I do *not* do a spousal rollover but elect to remain a beneficiary (see chart following item 11 for distribution options if I die with a balance remaining in the account), I can:

• Take distributions before age 59½ with no 10 percent   _____
early distribution penalty (penalty does not apply to beneficiaries). (I should do a spousal rollover after attaining
age 59½.)

• Do a spousal rollover at any time after inheriting the ac-   _____
count.

11. As spouse beneficiary I must take an RMD in the year the deceased owner would have been 70½. (See chart following this item.)

• Determine the age I must use for calculating my RMDs: _____

• Use that age to look up my life expectancy factor from   _____
appropriate table (See chart following this Item and refer
to appropriate appendix).

• Find the balance in the account as of 12/31 of the prior   _____
year and divide that by my life-expectancy factor. (For all
subsequent years I will use the same method.)

**12. I know there is a 50 percent penalty on any required   _____
distribution not taken.**

13. I know that required distributions from an account inherited from my spouse *cannot* be satisfied by distributions made to me from any other inherited account
unless it came from my spouse and is the same type of
inherited account (e.g., 2 IRAs or 2 Roth IRAs.)

_____

The following is a synopsis of options allowed by the IRS's final distribution regulations. All distribution options are subject to the terms of the plan agreement in effect at the time of the distribution. The 10 percent early distribution penalty never applies to beneficiaries taking distributions. All beneficiaries generally have the option of taking a lump-sum distribution and paying income tax on the distribution or choosing to use the 5-year rule. Roth IRA beneficiaries use the Owner Dies Before RBD rules. A spouse is considered the sole beneficiary of the plan when he or she is the sole designated primary beneficiary on the account as of 12/31 of the year after the original account owner's death.

Spouse as Sole Beneficiary

	ACCOUNT OWNER DIES BEFORE RBD	ACCOUNT OWNER DIES AFTER RBD
Remain as Beneficiary	I use the **Single Life Expectancy Table** (Appendix I) and look up my attained age **each year** a distribution is required (recalculation) to get the life expectancy factor	
	I can delay taking my distributions until account owner would have been 70½	I must take my first distribution by 12/31 of the year after the account owner's death
	I am not subject to the 10 percent early distribution penalty	I am not subject to the 10 percent early distribution penalty
Spousal Rollover	I take my first distribution at my RBD I use the **Uniform Lifetime Table** (Appendix II) and look up my attained age **each year** to get the life-expectancy factor	
Take Account as Own	I take my first distribution at my RBD I use the **Uniform Lifetime Table** (Appendix II) and look up my attained age **each year** to get the life-expectancy factor	

Spouse Is Not Sole Beneficiary

	ACCOUNT OWNER DIES BEFORE RBD	ACCOUNT OWNER DIES AFTER RBD
Remain as Beneficiary	I use the **Single Life Expectancy Table** (Appendix I) to look up attained age in the year after account owner's death to get factor; factor is **reduced by one in each subsequent year**	
	I MUST take my first distribution by 12/31 of the year after the account owner's death	
	I am not subject to the 10 percent early distribution penalty	

14. If I inherited a Roth IRA, I realize that distributions of earnings made to me within 5 years of the establishment of the account by my deceased spouse (original owner) may be subject to income tax. _____

Comments: _____

_____

_____

Follow-Up

My To Do List   Date Completed

1 _____

2 _____

3 _____

4 _____

5 _____

6 _____

7 _____

8 _____

9 _____

10 _____

_____   _____
My Signature   Date

Part 3

THE MULTIPLE BENEFICIARIES'

CHECKLIST

For spouse and nonspouse co-beneficiaries

What It Does

United we stand, divided . . . we are better off—as beneficiaries that is. If you are one of several co-beneficiaries of an inherited account, this checklist is for you.

When there are multiple beneficiaries of an inherited account, all

A Word to the Wise

Make sure your co-beneficiaries go through this checklist with you so that you will all understand what to do and how to do it (and when) if you mutually agree that you want to separate the shared inherited account. Then create the separate accounts as soon as possible after the inheritance with the help of an expert financial advisor (Section V) to ensure that everything goes smoothly.

must use the age of the *eldest* beneficiary for calculating their own RMDs. So what? Here's what: Let's say you are one of three people named as co-beneficiary of an IRA or other plan. If you are all very close in age, using the age of the eldest in taking RMDs may not be such a big deal. But what if you are 35 years old, and your co-beneficiaries are your 9-year-old niece and your 90-year-old aunt? According to the IRS's Single Life Expectancy Table (Appendix I), your life expectancy is 48.5 years, your niece's is 73.8 years, and your aunt's is 5.5 years. That means you are stuck with using the life expectancy of the eldest to calculate RMDs for all three of you, and the account's stretch and growth potential for the younger of you goes out the window because all the money in the account has to be withdrawn in 5.5 years.

The situation gets even worse if one of your co-beneficiaries is not a person but a charity or a trust, for example. Since neither is a living being, it has no life expectancy; thus, there is no stretch option at all for any of you.

These are situations you want to avoid as a co-beneficiary, and it can be done by creating what the tax rules call "separate accounts" so that each beneficiary can take RMDs based on his or her own age. This

Ask Ed . . .

Q: I inherited my dad's IRA with my mom. We are each named as 50–50 beneficiaries. Do I still get the stretch?

A: Yes, if you split the inherited account no later than the end of the year following the year of your dad's death. If your dad died in 2007, then you must split the account into separate inherited IRAs by December 31, 2008. But I would not wait that long. You should split up your shares as soon as possible after you inherit. Then both of you should each name successor beneficiaries immediately.

checklist is about how to do that so that each beneficiary can be treated as the *sole beneficiary* of his or her own share and thus maximize the stretch potential individually.

What's In It for Me?

If you are one of several co-beneficiaries of an inherited retirement account and don't want to be stuck with another co-beneficiary's life expectancy in taking your own RMDs, you can be rid of that obstacle for good by using the steps in this checklist to create your own separate account and increase your own payout period, thereby adding greater longevity to your account and maximizing its growth possibilities. Here's why: By extending the term of your lifetime payout, you can take lower RMDs each year, pay less tax each year on those lower RMDs, and build more money tax-deferred for you over your longer-term payout period term—all because the calculations you use will be based on your age alone, not the eldest among your co-beneficiaries.

Ask Ed . . .

Q: **What if three children inherit a parent's 401(k)? Do the separate account rules apply here?**

A: Yes, they apply the same as with an inherited IRA, but the difference is that the co-beneficiaries will probably not get the chance to use them because most 401(k) plans will just send the co-beneficiaries a lump-sum check subject to tax, thereby killing the need to create separate accounts because there won't be enough money left to stretch even if the option were offered, which is unlikely since few 401(k)s will allow one beneficiary to stretch, let alone two, three, or more.

What If I Don't?

You'll likely be stuck with someone else's life expectancy in determining your RMDs and end up giving more of your inheritance to Uncle Sam faster than you had to. Or, you may not even be able to seize the stretch opportunity in the first place if one of your co-beneficiaries lacks a pulse—is a trust, for example. In either case, you will wind up paying more tax, more quickly. This happens to many people because they are unaware that they can create their own separate inherited IRAs from the big one they've inherited mutually.

Ask Ed . . .

Q: **If the original owner of the account dies before taking a RMD for the year and there are several co-beneficiaries, who takes the RMD for the deceased?**

A: Each co-beneficiary takes a proportionate share. For example, if three children inherit a third each, then each would take one-third of the RMD the deceased owner would have had to take had he or she lived—and each beneficiary will pay the income tax on their one-third RMD on their own tax return. But the IRS doesn't care who takes the RMD as long as someone takes it. If one of the beneficiaries wants to cash out their share and the IRA has not been split yet, the distribution to the beneficiary that is cashing out can be used to satisfy the RMD and the other beneficiaries can wait until the following year before they have to take any distributions.

Instructions

The first thing you will want to do in this checklist is to identify your fellow co-beneficiaries and enlist their cooperation in separating ac-

A Word to the Wise

As I pointed out in Part 1 of this section, a nonspouse beneficiary cannot do a rollover, so if you are one of three nonspouse co-beneficiaries, separate accounts can only be set up by doing a trustee-to-trustee transfer, where you do not touch or withdraw the funds. Imagine, for example, that you and your two siblings inherited a $300,000 IRA from your mother and withdrew the $300,000 to deposit in your separate inherited accounts of $100,000 each. The result would be a tax on all $300,000 in one shot—and you would no longer need separate accounts because none of you will have an inherited account.

counts for your mutual benefit. Even most surviving spouses who squabble with their children or children who squabble with each other about everything will see the value in agreeing with each other here.

Make sure the account custodian (financial institution holding the fund) knows that you wish to create separate accounts from the one inherited—otherwise, the custodian might just cash all of you out. Although you have until the end of the year following the year of the original owner's death to create separate accounts, this is one reason why you shouldn't wait that long. Bad things can happen. And that's one of them.

If part of your planning involves a disclaimer (where you, or your co-beneficiaries, wish to refuse your respective share so that it can pass to the contingent beneficiaries), *do not set up the separate accounts until the disclaimers are completed* (see The Disclaimer Planning Checklist in Section IV, Part 3). Once you take possession, you can generally not disclaim anymore, and creating separate accounts could be deemed as taking possession.

The biggest issue presented in separating accounts is when there are any nondesignated beneficiaries—those nonhuman beneficiaries I've mentioned called charities, trusts or estates—that are co-beneficiaries with you. So as not to turn you into a nondesig-

Ask Ed . . .

Q: **If I plan to disclaim my share (so it can pass to my children) but there are other co-beneficiaries on the account with me, how do I make sure that my share goes to my children and not to my siblings?**

A: The original owner of the account will have to have planned to pass the account to his or her named beneficiaries "per stirpes" so that when you as one of those beneficiaries disclaim, your share goes to your children, not your siblings. You cannot put your children in as contingent beneficiaries after you inherit. So, if you intend to disclaim but don't know whether the account is set up for you to do that once you inherit, alert the account owner now because this is an item he or she must set up for you.

Q: **What happens if the inherited account is not split by the deadline? Can it be split later?**

A: There is no time limit for splitting up an inherited account, but if it is not split by the deadline (the end of the year following the year of the original owner's death), then the separate account treatment option will expire. This means that while you can still physically separate accounts after the deadline, the chief advantage of doing so is lost because you will forever be stuck with having to use the age of the eldest co-beneficiary for calculating your RMDs.

nated beneficiary on paper as well, they must be removed from the inherited account by September 30 of the year following the year of the original owner's death. By removed I don't mean having them "whacked." This is not *The Sopranos* (and besides, how do you *whack* a trust?). I mean having them removed as a co-beneficiary by splitting the account or cashing them out (paying out their share in full) BEFORE the September 30 deadline.

THE MULTIPLE BENEFICIARIES' CHECKLIST

MY NAME: _____ DATE: _____

MY ADVISOR'S NAME: _____ PLAN #: _____

Follow-ups should be added to the To Do lists at the end of this checklist.

1. Who are my named co-beneficiaries as listed on the beneficiary form?

_____

- Are all my listed co-beneficiaries designated? (A desig-   _____
  nated beneficiary is an *individual* named on the beneficiary form not an entity, such as a charity.)
- If not, these are the nondesignated co-beneficiaries: _____

Comments: _____

_____

_____

_____

_____

_____

The period between the plan owner's death and 9/30 of the following year is called the "gap period." Designated beneficiaries, for RMD calculation purposes, are those named as of the date of death and who remain beneficiaries as of that 9/30 milestone.

2. I have evaluated my tax and income situation—and   _____
those of my designated co-beneficiaries—to determine
if I should disclaim. (See the Disclaimer Planning
Checklist in Section IV, Part 3.)

3. I know that all nondesignated beneficiaries' shares   _____
must be distributed before 9/30 of the year after the
account owner's death.

4. As co-beneficiaries, we understand that if one of us   _____
dies during the gap period, our respective life expectancy will be used to calculate distributions to our
successor beneficiary.

Comments: _____

_____

_____

_____

_____

_____

5. As co-beneficiaries of an inherited account that has _____
   not been split into separate accounts, if I/we wish to
   split them and use our respective individual life ex-
   pectancies in calculating RMDs, this must be done by
   12/31 of the year after the original owner's death. (And
   preferably earlier to simplify bookkeeping when mak-
   ing withdrawals and investment decisions.)

- Properly title the separate accounts to include the origi- _____
  nal owner's name with my/our own to avoid making the
  entire inherited account balance subject to income tax—
  i.e., "John Smith (deceased, date of death) IRA fbo Jane
  Smith"

- Assets can be moved into the new, properly titled inher- _____
  ited accounts by a trustee-to-trustee transfer only. A
  nonspouse beneficiary can NEVER do a rollover.

- Change the original owner's social security number on _____
  my separate account to my social security number.

- Name my successor beneficiaries (if the plan allows). _____

- See checklists in Parts 1 or 2 of this section for instruc- _____
  tions on calculating my RMDs.

Comments: _____

_____

_____

_____

_____

_____

6. I understand that if there are multiple beneficiaries of _____
   a trust that is the beneficiary of an inherited account,
   there can be no separate accounts and all distributions
   will be calculated using the life expectancy of the el-
   dest of the trust beneficiaries.

7. I understand that if there are multiple beneficiaries, _____
I/we can split accounts after the 12/31 deadline, but will
be forced to continue using the life expectancy of the
eldest for calculating required distributions even after
the account is split.

Comments: _____

_____

_____

_____

Follow-Up

My To Do List   Date Completed

1 _____

2 _____

3 _____

4 _____

5 _____

6 _____

7 _____

8 _____

9 _____

10 _____

_____   _____
My Signature   Date

Part 4

THE SUCCESSOR BENEFICIARY'S

CHECKLIST

What It Does

You may be asking, "What the heck is a successor beneficiary anyway, and why should *I* care? This better be good because it looks like a chapter I could skip."

The short answer is this: For retirement planning purposes, a successor beneficiary is simply the beneficiary's beneficiary. And you should care for the same reason the original owner of the account you have inherited or will be inheriting cared about naming a beneficiary—YOU—in the first place: to keep whatever funds may be left in the account growing and out of the Taxman's pocket for as long as possible after death. Especially if your death were premature, in which case there could be quite a sizable chunk of change left in the account—and quite a long stretch period remaining in which those funds could continue to grow that will be lost.

The premature death of a beneficiary need not be—and should not be—the death of the inherited account itself. But generally that is what happens because most people and many financial institutions do not know what to do when a beneficiary dies, and the account is just cashed out and taxed. The point of planning is to prevent that from happening and to keep the original owner's wealth in the family and building for as long as possible. This checklist takes you through the steps that you as the beneficiary of an inherited account need to follow to ensure that happens, and what the beneficiary's beneficiary needs to be aware of when inheriting so that the best-laid plans of your benefactors do not go awry.

Ask Ed . . .

Q: **Should the successor beneficiary also name a beneficiary as soon as he or she inherits?**

A: Yes. Though it may be unlikely that two beneficiaries—the original and the successor—will die prematurely, it's always better to be safe than sorry. Then the account will go to the "successor, successor beneficiary," who can then complete the remaining term on the stretch that was available to the first successor beneficiary.

What's In It for Me?

If you are the beneficiary of an account that the original owner beneficently set up for you to stretch, isn't it equally beneficent for you to extend the same opportunity to your own heirs? Here, you will learn how to do that and keep what's left in your inherited account growing and away from taxes even after your death. Think of this as creating both a memorial to the original owner's intentions and a satisfying way to fulfill those intentions while making them your own.

And if you are (or may be in the future) a successor beneficiary (the beneficiary's beneficiary), what's in this checklist for you is that which you must know when you inherit in order to keep the balance in your inherited account alive and working for you and your family as long as you can.

Ask Ed . . .

Q: **What if there are two or more successor beneficiaries—for instance, two children inherit their father's inherited IRA? What happens then?**

A: They share the remaining payout on the inherited IRA based on how many years were remaining on their father's stretch period. It makes no difference how many successor beneficiaries there are or whether they split the inherited IRA into separate accounts because whatever they do, they cannot use their own life expectancy. They can only use their father's remaining term of years had he lived. But they also do not have to cash it out and end the inherited IRA, unless they have a very uncooperative IRA custodian.

What If I Don't?

The account will likely be cashed out on your death as the original beneficiary, providing a potential windfall for Uncle Sam, especially, as I've written, if your death is premature and there is a substantial sum left in the account and a long stretch period (your remaining life expectancy had you lived) to go.

For example, let's say you are the sole beneficiary of an IRA inherited from the original owner, and you have a thirty-seven-year life-expectancy payout term on the stretch. But you die prematurely five years into the payout period. If you have named a successor beneficiary on your beneficiary form, your account will not go to your estate, wind up in probate, and be subjected to all the costly bad things that go with probating retirement plans as discussed earlier in this section and in Section II. Instead the balance in the account will go *directly to your successor beneficiary* who can take distributions over the thirty-two years left on the payout schedule based on your life expectancy had you lived. If your estate inherits, yes it could keep the stretch going (if the custodian agreement allows) for the same length of time to the beneficiary of your estate named in your will (who might even be the same person), but the beneficiary will wind up having much less in the account to stretch due to losses incurred by paying taxes and other expenses. So, to prevent the remaining stretch period from being lost, it is always wise for a beneficiary to name a successor beneficiary as soon as possible after inheriting.

Instructions

As a beneficiary, use this checklist for two purposes: (1) to make sure your own beneficiaries know that even your premature death does not have to mean the end of the inherited account, and (2) to show them why it is so important for them to name a beneficiary of their own as soon as they inherit from you. This way, you will both be covered in preserving the inherited account for as long as legally possible even if one or both of you dies prematurely.

What follows are the two most common successor beneficiary situations—and *darn,* wouldn't you just know it, there's a different set of distribution rules for each of them to make things complicated? Apply the checklist to find out if you are using the right set of rules.

1. The IRA owner names his child as beneficiary. The child inherits. As soon as the child inherits, she names her child (his grandchild) as her successor beneficiary just in case there are still funds left in the inherited IRA to be distributed when she dies.
2. The IRA owner names his spouse as IRA beneficiary. When she inherits, she chooses to remain a beneficiary, rather than becoming an owner. She immediately names her child as successor beneficiary just in case there are still funds left in the account to be distributed when she dies. When she passes on, her child can become either a

beneficiary or a successor beneficiary; depending on whether or not she was taking required distributions when she died. If she died after her required distributions began, the child becomes a successor beneficiary.

In each of these cases, the IRA can pass from the first beneficiary to the beneficiary's beneficiary (the successor beneficiary). But what happens then?

Let's say Mike has a $500,000 IRA and dies at age 45. He named his wife Mary as his beneficiary. Mary is 41 years old and decides to remain a beneficiary (not do a spousal rollover) because she may need to withdraw funds and does not want to get hit with a 10 percent penalty for early withdrawal (under age 59½).

Mary immediately names her 1-year-old daughter Rachel as her successor beneficiary, but Mary dies prematurely just nine years later at age 50, and her daughter Rachel, who is 10 at the time, inherits then. What are Rachel's distribution options? Does the entire $500,000 account have to be cashed out in one year? No. The key here is that her mom, Mary, immediately named a beneficiary (Rachel) of her own upon inheriting the account from her husband Mike. That changes everything for the good.

Because Mary's husband Mike died at 45 and she dies at 50 (before Mike would have reached age 70½ if he had lived) then she is treated as if she were the IRA owner (even though she is a beneficiary). Because Mary named her daughter Rachel as her successor beneficiary, when Rachel inherits she is treated not as the successor beneficiary under this special rule, but as if she were the original beneficiary, and can thus stretch distributions over her own life expectancy of 71.8 years (the life expectancy for an 11-year-old—Rachel's age the year after her mother's death—according to the Single Life Table in Appendix I).

If Rachel were not named as Mary's successor beneficiary here, then the IRA would have had to be distributed under the 5-year rule (assuming the IRA went to Mary's estate). But much more happily, a $500,000 inherited IRA that could have been wiped out from being taxed in one year (if it were cashed out because no one knew what to do) can now be stretched over 71.8 years, potentially providing millions of dollars to Rachel over her lifetime, because Mary had known to name her own beneficiary early on.

Ask Ed . . .

Q: **What would happen if Mike had died *after* reaching his Required Beginning Date?**

A: Rachel would be considered the successor beneficiary and would have to withdraw over Mary's remaining single life expectancy had Mary not died—which is 33.2 years,* according to the Single Life Table (Appendix I) and still a decent stretch period. A successor beneficiary can never use his or her *own life expectancy* to extend distributions on an inherited account. The successor beneficiary can only complete the remaining term based on the age of the original beneficiary—in this case Mary—at death.

* Because Mary is a beneficiary, you look up her attained age (50) in the year of her death. The factor is 34.2 which is then reduced by one for each subsequent year.

THE SUCCESSOR BENEFICIARY'S CHECKLIST

MY NAME: _____ DATE: _____

MY ADVISOR'S NAME: _____ PLAN #: _____

Follow-ups should be added to the To Do lists at the end of this checklist.

A successor beneficiary inherits the remaining retirement plan assets, including Roth IRA assets, at the death of the retirement plan beneficiary—and is thus defined as the "beneficiary's beneficiary."

1. I have named a successor beneficiary (or beneficiaries) to inherit my retirement assets at my death. He, she or they are:

_____

_____

- **Note:** If I have not named a successor beneficiary or the plan custodian does not allow me to name one, then at my death any remaining retirement plan assets will pass to the default beneficiary named in the plan document. That is generally the estate, which would make the retirement plan subject to probate. It may get cashed out and be subject to income tax, it could be contested, and may end up not going to the beneficiary of my choice.   _____

- My successor beneficiary can continue to stretch the remaining required distributions over my life expectancy.   _____

- My successor beneficiary can accelerate distributions or liquidate the account. But if there are multiple successor beneficiaries, this could create an accounting problem for the financial advisor trying to keep track of each beneficiary's share.   _____

2. If my successor beneficiary does not disclaim the inherited account or cash out, he or she (or they) must:

- Change the social security number on the account to his or her social security number.   _____

- Change the account title (the name of the original deceased account owner must remain in the account title)   _____

- e.g. John Smith (deceased, date of death) IRA fbo Charles Smith   _____

- Name a successor beneficiary of their own (if the custodian allows).   _____

3. If there is more than one successor beneficiary named,   _____
   and the account is not split, all beneficiaries share the
   required distribution each year.

4. Successor beneficiaries can move the assets from one   _____
   custodian to another but ONLY by using a trustee-to-
   trustee transfer.

5. Guidelines for a successor beneficiary of a nonspouse:

• Name a successor beneficiary of your own as soon as you   _____
  inherit (if the plan custodian allows).

• Take the remaining required distributions of the de-   _____
  ceased beneficiary by continuing to use the deceased's
  life expectancy factor (Appendix I) and reducing that
  factor by one each subsequent year in calculating RMDs.

• **Note:** As a successor beneficiary, you cannot use your own age or life expectancy to replace the deceased beneficiary's payout period. The payout
  period will continue to be based on the age of the original beneficiary. The
  age of the successor beneficiary has no effect on the remaining payout
  term.

• **Example:** Chris is the beneficiary of an IRA. Her first RMD is taken using a
  life expectancy factor of 37. She names her son James as the successor
  beneficiary. Chris dies 5 years later when her factor would have been 32.
  James can continue taking distributions using Chris's factor of 32 and reducing it by one in each subsequent year in calculating his subsequent
  RMDs.

6. Guidelines for a successor beneficiary of a spouse beneficiary:

• Name a successor beneficiary of your own as soon as you inherit (if the plan custodian allows). _____

• If the spouse dies before the original owner of the plan would have been 70½, the successor beneficiary inherits as a beneficiary and can use his/her own life expectancy in calculating the remaining RMDs. _____

• **Note:** This is the only time that the successor beneficiary's age is used in calculating the remaining RMDs.

• If the spouse dies after the original owner of the plan would have been 70½, the successor beneficiary continues to use the spouse's life expectancy factor in calculating RMDs, reducing the factor by one each year. (See example above.) _____

Comments: _____

_____

_____

_____

_____

Follow-Up

My To Do List	Date Completed
1	
2	
3	
4	
5	
6	
7	
8	
9	
10	

My Signature	Date

Part 5

THE TAX BREAKS FOR BENEFICIARIES CHECKLIST

What It Does

As an IRA or company plan beneficiary, you may be in line for big tax benefits, but you cannot rely on the average financial advisor or tax professional to point them out to you or even ask you if you might qualify. So, you will use this checklist to uncover those tax breaks, then go to your tax preparer or financial advisor and make sure they know to take advantage of them for you.

This checklist covers all the tax-saving opportunities that apply to you as the beneficiary of an IRA or company plan. Although one can find all kinds of tax breaks for account owners listed on the Internet and covered in tax books and magazine articles, one almost never sees any listed for beneficiaries of an IRA or company plan. As a result, beneficiaries tend to miss out.

Under old tax law, since a nonspouse beneficiary could not do a rollover, once that check was in hand, the ball game was over. The tax deferral ended as the entire distribution became taxable. But as of the year this book comes out (2007), nonspouse beneficiaries can do a direct rollover (a trustee-to-trustee transfer) of employer plan balances to a properly titled inherited IRA account, if the plan allows. This will allow nonspouse beneficiaries to stretch distributions over their own life expectancies. This checklist highlights some of the biggest, but largely unknown, tax breaks available to beneficiaries of an inherited IRA or company plan. But they do not come automatically. These must be asked for, or they're not given. And to ask for them, you need to know they exist.

You may not even be able to rely on your tax planner or financial advisor to be aware of them. In fact, when I cover them in my training programs for advisors here is where I really see my trainees taking notes at a frenzied pace, all the while mouthing the words, "Wow, I didn't know any of this!" For example, has your tax preparer or financial advisor ever asked you, "Did any of that stock you inherited from your dad in his 401(k) contain any Net Unrealized Appreciation?" Hardly likely. But the answer to that question can yield a huge tax break for beneficiaries, which I will get to later in this chapter. This checklist DOES ask that question, and others, so that you will know enough to seek out the answers.

Ask Ed . . .

Q: **I inherited an IRA from my brother. How would I know if he had ever made nondeductible IRA contributions?**

A: You would have to look at his tax return to see if there is Form 8606 ("Nondeductible IRAs"). Or you can check his IRA statements to see if he made IRA contributions and then cross-check that with his tax return to see if he took a deduction for those contributions. If he did not, then you know he made nondeductible IRA contributions and a portion of each distribution you take from your inherited IRA will be tax-free. You will then have to file Form 8606 yourself to calculate the portion of each IRA distribution that will be tax-free to you.

What's In It for Me?

Even after your tax preparer may have told you there was nothing else you could do to keep more of your inherited IRA or company plan out of the hands of the government, it is likely you will find some goody-goody tax break in here for you. And even if just one of these goodies applies to your situation, this may be enough to cut down seriously on your inherited account tax bill.

For example, let's say you receive a lump-sum distribution from your late dad's 401(k). The plan balance is in company stock and other assets and you put them in your own brokerage account. Now, assume the entire plan balance is $500,000 and $400,000 of that is in company stock with a Net Unrealized Appreciation (NUA) of $300,000. For the tax year of the lump-sum distribution, the plan will send you a 1099-R form for the full $500,000. When you have your taxes prepared, your accountant will tell you that you owe tax on the full $500,000 at ordinary income tax rates. That's what

Ask Ed . . .

Q: How would I know if there was NUA in a 401(k) plan I inherited?

A: It would show that on the 1099-R form you received when the plan assets were distributed to you. Look in Box 6 (titled "Net Unrealized Appreciation in Employer's Securities") of the form. The number in that box is the NUA, and that amount is not taxed at the time of distribution if it is a qualifying lump-sum distribution to you as a plan beneficiary. You do not pay tax on the NUA until you sell the stock. When you sell it, you pay only capital gains taxes on the NUA amount regardless of how long you held the stock. This box is often overlooked by tax preparers, so be sure to look yourself and to alert your tax preparer.

the form says, so why would your accountant, let alone you, question it? So, you will pay the tax and walk away grumbling about what a huge tax hit you had to take. But you would really have something to grumble about if you found out later that you didn't have to take such a big hit—because you did not have to pay tax on the $300,000 of NUA since you had not sold the stock yet. Even when you do get around to selling the stock, which you can sell at any pace you wish, you will automatically qualify for long-term capital gains rates that will probably be less than half of ordinary income tax rates.

What If I Don't?

The items in this checklist are aimed exclusively at cutting your tax bill. And so not taking advantage of them will cost you. You will pay the highest tax possible on the IRA or company plan you have inherited. It's as simple as that.

Instructions

Review each of the items in this checklist to see which tax savers apply to you. It is likely that you may qualify for more than one of them. Very often you will find that what is good for the goose (the original owner) is good for you too. For example, if you inherit a Roth IRA, you may not know that the distributions you take are not taxable either.

Ask Ed . . .

Q: How would I know if the IRA I inherited is a Roth IRA?

A: Roth IRAs have only been available since 1998 and so they are relatively young, just like most of their owners. But it is not impossible for a Roth IRA to get passed on, and if you do inherit one it should be clearly titled as such—though I have seen cases where an inherited Roth IRA was titled as a traditional IRA because the financial institution did not have the proper titling in its system yet for an inherited Roth IRA. What happens then? You'll most likely pay tax on the distributions of the inherited Roth that should be tax-free. So, don't just trust what the title says (or doesn't say). If you are unsure, check the account statements sent to the account owner during his lifetime. They should clearly state that an account is a Roth IRA. If you are still unsure, you can also check tax returns (you only have to go back to 1998, which was the first year you could have a Roth) of the person you inherited from. If he or she converted a traditional IRA to a Roth IRA you will see the conversion income on the deceased's tax returns. If the deceased had made Roth IRA contributions that information would not show up on the tax return, but the financial institution would have records of them. The financial advisor and/or tax preparer for the deceased owner should also know if your inherited account is a Roth or traditional IRA. So, ask them as well.

In a different instance, you may be entitled to tax breaks on the state level that you didn't know about. For example, some states do not allow deductions for plan contributions, even if the deduction is allowed federally. So, if you inherit an IRA, for example, from your dad, who did not receive a state tax deduction for his IRA contributions, then you do not have to pay state income tax on the distributions you take from that inherited IRA. How will you know to ask about this? This and many other reminders are on the checklist.

A Word to the Wise

The biggest and most complex tax break available to plan beneficiaries is the Income in Respect of a Decedent (IRD) deduction. There is so much to be aware of with the IRD deduction alone that I am only reminding you here to check whether you may qualify for it or not, but have created a separate checklist (see this section, Part 6) that goes into the details. Likewise, among the biggest—and most involved—tax breaks available to plan owners AND to beneficiaries (if the owner qualified) are NUA and 10-year averaging on lump-sum distributions. Again, I am only alerting you here to check if you qualify for these breaks. Look for the details in The Tax Breaks for Lump-Sum Distribution Checklist, Section IV, Part 7.

THE TAX BREAKS FOR BENEFICIARIES CHECKLIST

MY NAME: _____ DATE: _____

MY ADVISOR'S NAME: _____ PLAN #: _____

Follow-ups should be added to the To Do lists at the end of this checklist.

1. Are all inherited accounts titled properly and identified _____
   correctly (i.e., a Roth as an inherited Roth)?

2. Am I eligible to claim the IRD deduction? To be eligi- _____
   ble, the inherited IRA or plan must have been subject
   to federal estate taxes in the estate I inherited from.
   (See checklist this section, Part 6.)

3. Does my state allow any tax breaks for distributions _____
   from inherited IRAs or employer plans? (Some states
   exempt all or a portion of retirement plan distributions
   from state taxes even when those distributions are
   made to beneficiaries.)

Comments: _____

_____

_____

_____

_____

4. Does my inherited IRA hold after-tax contributions _____
   (basis)? Distributions of basis will reduce the income
   tax I owe on the distribution. Note: Basis can include
   nondeductible IRA contributions made by the deceased IRA owner (after 1986) and after-tax contributions made to an employer plan that were rolled into
   an IRA (after 2001).

• Look for Form 8606 (Nondeductible IRAs) attached to _____
  the decedent's tax returns.

• If there is no Form 8606 and I think there are after-tax _____
  contributions, I can look for Form 5498 (IRA Contribution Information) or IRA statements to see when contributions were made and check the corresponding tax
  returns to see if a deduction was taken.

• Figure the tax-free portion of the distribution using the _____
  calculation on Form 8606, which must be filed with my
  tax return.

Comments: _____

_____

_____

_____

_____

5. Does my inherited IRA have a different basis for state   _____
   taxes than it has for federal taxes?

• Did the deceased IRA owner live in a state that does not   _____
  allow deductions for contributions to IRAs?

• If yes, for state tax purposes, are distributions partially   _____
  tax-free?

Comments: _____

_____

_____

_____

_____

6. Did I inherit a Roth IRA?   _____

• If the account has been established for more than 5 years   _____
  (counting the time the Roth IRA was held by the deceased owner) then all distributions from the Roth are
  income-tax-free.

• If the account has been established for less than 5 years   _____
  then distributions of contributions and conversions are
  income-tax-free. Distributions of earnings will be subject
  to income tax (but never a 10 percent penalty since that
  does not apply to beneficiaries).

Comments: _____

_____

_____

_____

7. Did I inherit an employer plan?   _____

• Do I have to take a lump-sum distribution?   _____

  • If there is company stock in the plan, I am eligible to use   _____
    the NUA tax break (See The Tax Breaks for Lump Sum
    Distribution Checklist in Section IV, Part 7)

- If the deceased owner was born before 1936, I am eligible to use the 10-year averaging tax break (see The Tax Breaks for Lump-Sum Distribution Checklist in Section IV, Part 7). _____

- If any of the lump-sum distribution is from plan participation before 1974, I am eligible for the capital gain election (see The Tax Breaks for Lump-Sum Distribution Checklist in Section IV, Part 7). _____

- 10-year averaging and the distribution of pre-74 balances are reported on Form 4972. _____

- Lump-sum distributions from an employer plan using either 10-year averaging or NUA can qualify for the full IRD deduction. (See The IRD Checklist in this section, Part 6.) _____

- As of 2007, funds in an employer plan can be transferred directly to a properly titled inherited IRA. If a check is made payable to me, I cannot put the funds in an inherited IRA. _____

Comments: _____

_____

_____

_____

_____

Follow-Up

My To Do List	Date Completed
1	
2	
3	
4	
5	
6	
7	
8	
9	
10	

My Signature	Date

Part 6

THE IRD CHECKLIST

What It Does

The IRD deduction is number one on my list of the most overlooked tax breaks available to beneficiaries of inherited retirement accounts and other property. In fact, it is one of the oldest provisions in the tax code, dating back to the early 1940s. With so many baby boomers inheriting larger retirement plans and other assets than ever these days as their WWII-generation parents pass on, more people are in a position to qualify for this deduction than ever before. But they may not receive it due to their ignorance of its existence, which is why this checklist is here.

IRD stands for Income in Respect of a Decedent, an IRS term (who else could string such words together like this?) that describes inherited income subject to federal tax. An IRA or company plan is probably the most common example. The income in the plan was earned by the decedent during his or her lifetime, but the tax was not yet paid on the funds remaining in the account at death. The beneficiary must pay the income tax as he withdraws from the inherited account.

Ask Ed . . .

Q: **How do I know if the IRA or company plan I inherited was subject to federal estate taxes?**

A: Easy. You look at the federal estate tax return (Form 706) for the person you inherited from to see if the estate paid federal estate tax. If federal estate tax was paid, and the item you inherited is included in the estate, you qualify for the IRD deduction and can claim it on your personal tax return as you withdraw the assets.

Death does not remove the tax obligation; the plan beneficiary (you) must pay income tax when he or she starts taking withdrawals from the inherited account. But the IRD deduction can whittle down this tax obligation big-time. It is much more valuable than most other itemized deductions because it is not eroded by the 2 percent of adjusted gross income (AGI) limitation nor is it even subject to the dreaded alternative minimum tax (AMT). Not checking to see if you qualify for the IRD deduction could be criminal—you may end up having as much as 80 percent of your inheritance confiscated by Uncle Sam.

Ask Ed . . .

Q: **What if the inherited plan is not subject to federal estate tax, but the estate did pay state estate or inheritance taxes? Do I still get the IRD deduction?**

A: No. The IRD deduction is only available when the item gets hit with federal estate tax. State estate taxes do not qualify for the IRD deduction, so on a state level the double taxation still exists. This is getting to be a more common situation as more revenue-hungry states institute estate taxes of their own on estates of lower value where there might not otherwise be federal estate tax due.

What's In It for Me?

The IRD deduction is a way for beneficiaries to *offset* the effect of the double taxation that comes with inheriting assets such as tax-deferred retirement accounts that are subject to federal income tax. But most beneficiaries and their financial advisors are woefully unaware of the existence of the IRD deduction to offset this blow. You'll save a fortune in taxes if you spot even one item in this checklist, such as an inherited account, that may qualify you as a beneficiary for the IRD deduction. And many of you may find more than one.

Ask Ed . . .

Q: **What if I am one of several beneficiaries who inherit an IRA that qualifies for the IRD deduction? Who gets the deduction?**

A: You each take your share of the total IRD deduction in accordance with your share of the inheritance. For example, if the total IRD deduction is $60,000 and there are 3 equal beneficiaries, you are each entitled to a $20,000 IRD deduction as you withdraw the assets. If there are 2 unequal beneficiaries—one inherited 75 percent of the IRA and the other received 25 percent—then the 75 percent beneficiary is entitled to 75 percent of the IRD deduction or $45,000 ($60,000 IRD deduction × 75 percent) and the 25 percent beneficiary is entitled to 25 percent of the IRD deduction or $15,000 ($60,000 IRD deduction × 25 percent).

The IRD tax deduction is large. It often runs as high as 45 percent, meaning that if you inherit an IRA subject to federal estate tax and withdraw $100,000 (on which you must pay tax), your withdrawal also amounts to an approximately $45,000 IRD tax deduction. That can be used to offset your overall tax bill. Imagine someone missing a $45,000 tax deduction because he or she didn't know better! But it happens—all the time.

Ask Ed . . .

Q: **Can I take the entire IRD deduction in one year?**

A: Only if you withdraw the entire balance of the inherited IRA or plan in one year. The IRD deduction is taken in proportion to how much of the IRD income you have withdrawn during the year. For example, if you and your advisor calculate the IRD deduction to be $100,000 and you only withdraw 6 percent because that is your required minimum distribution for the year, then you can claim 6 percent ($6,000), and you will still have $94,000 of IRD deductions to use for future years. You never run out of time to claim the rest of the IRD deduction until the account is used up.

Q: **Is there a dollar limit on the amount of IRD deduction that can be claimed?**

A: No. But you can only take the deduction against IRD income that you report. You cannot just make up a number. So, as long as you have IRD income to take (say from inherited IRA distributions) and you qualify for an IRD deduction, you can claim an amount up to the amount allowed. You can never claim more than the IRD deduction, but there is no limit on the actual dollar amount of the IRD deduction itself.

What If I Don't?

You won't have to worry about your successor beneficiaries killing you; you'll do it yourself. Seriously (I hope), if you do nothing, you may (and probably will) lose out substantially by missing this important tax break.

Ask Ed . . .

Q: **If I missed taking the IRD deduction in past years can I go back and correct my mistake?**

A: Yes, you can go back three years and amend your tax returns to claim the IRD deductions you missed. You'll receive a tax refund plus interest (IRS has to pay you interest even if the mistake was yours). If your state allows the IRD deduction, and you missed taking it in past years, you can go back three years as well to amend your state tax returns and receive even more refund checks. You cannot go back beyond three years (the statute of limitations), but if there are still funds in the IRA or plan balance you inherited, you can keep taking the IRD deduction against your future withdrawals as long as those funds last.

Instructions

Review the checklist to see if you qualify for the IRD deduction. First up, you will find a listing of every conceivable inherited item subject to federal estate tax that will put you in line for this deduction. Many of these items represent income owed to the decedent (your benefactor, the account owner) at death that do not receive a step up in basis. Of course, you'll see IRAs and company plans in the eligible list too, but keep your eye open for receivables, insurance renewal commissions, lottery winnings, legal claims, alimony, and a host of other things you may inherit that can qualify you for the IRD deduction when you withdraw the income.

If you don't qualify, then you can move on to the next section in this book. If you do qualify, use the checklist that follows to find out how to claim the IRD deduction on your tax return. There are different ways to claim the IRD deduction. For example, most beneficiaries will claim it as a miscellaneous itemized deduction, but those who receive a lump-sum distribution may be able to take the deduction on

Form 4972 to directly offset the income if the deceased qualified for 10-year averaging (see The Tax Breaks for Lump-Sum Distribution Checklist in Section IV, Part 7).

Ask Ed . . .

Q: **Why should I care about the IRD elimination strategies on this checklist?**

A: To eliminate the income tax burden on your own heirs by withdrawing more during your lifetime when you become the plan owner. Due to the high combined tax on IRAs, even after the IRD deduction, it can often pay to reduce your IRA and plan balances during your lifetime and leverage those funds into more-tax-efficient vehicles such as life insurance, for example, or for charitable planning, or by converting to a tax-free Roth IRA. This is something you should alert your benefactor to now, if it's not too late.

A Word to the Wise

After you complete the checklist and run your IRD calculations, you should run them by your tax or financial advisor. There may be some items, such as basis, that you may even need your advisor to help you with, so you may wish to consult with him or her beforehand. Then you will be assured you are doing everything right.

Qualifying IRD Items

Use this list to identify Income in Respect of a Decedent (IRD) in an estate that you have inherited or may be inheriting. IRD is income earned by the decedent during his or her lifetime, but unpaid (owed to the decedent) at death. IRD items do NOT receive a step up in basis, but if the estate was subject to federal estate tax, then beneficiaries who inherit any of these items will be able to claim an IRD deduction as they collect the income.

1. Investment Income
   - Interest income—accrued to date of death
   - US savings bonds interest (unrecognized)
   - Dividend income
   - Rental income
   - Royalty income
2. Employee Compensation (Postdeath payments from employers)
   - Regular wages
   - Vacation pay
   - Sick pay
   - Deferred Compensation
   - Employee death benefit
   - Voluntary payments from employer
   - Stock options
   - Postdeath bonus
3. Independent Contractor Income (sole proprietors, professionals, contractors, consultants, etc.)
   - Receivables for services (professional fees, commissions, etc.)
   - Partnership income
   - Insurance renewal commissions
   - Fiduciary fees (due to Fiduciary)
   - Director fees
4. Retirement and Pension Income
   - All tax-deferred retirement plans (qualified pension & profit-sharing plans and IRAs [but generally not Roth IRAs]; including 401(k)s, 403(b)s, Keoghs, etc.)
   - Joint and survivor annuities
   - Deferred compensation
   - Net Unrealized Appreciation (NUA) in employer stock

5. Sales Area
- Sale of a partnership interest—IRC Sec.736(a) payments
- Installment sales—Income portion of installment payments received by beneficiary is IRD
- Executory Contracts—if seller dies between contract and closing, there may be IRD depending on how much of the sale was completed at death.
- Proceeds of property sales owed to the decedent at death are IRD. Examples:
  - Stocks, bonds, funds
  - Land, buildings, equipment
  - Home
  - Business interests

6. Other Income Owed to the Decedent at Death
- Income owed to deceased beneficiary from trust or estate
- Legal claims, lawsuits, damages
- Medical insurance reimbursements
- Alimony
- Tax refunds
- Lottery winnings
- Other refunds or amounts due decedent at death

THE IRD CHECKLIST

MY NAME: _____ DATE: _____

MY ADVISOR'S NAME: _____ PLAN #: _____

Follow-ups should be added to the To Do lists at the end of this checklist.

IRD is income earned by a decedent during his or her lifetime but not received or taxed until after death.

For Beneficiaries

1. Am I eligible to claim the IRD deduction? _____

• Did I inherit assets from an estate that was subject to   _____
  federal estate tax?

• If no, there is no IRD deduction.   _____

2. If yes, go through estate assets on US Estate Tax Return and identify IRD items.   _____

• NO IRD deduction is allowed for state estate taxes paid.   _____

• Lump-sum distributions from an employer plan using 10-   _____
  year averaging (found on Form 4972) can qualify for the
  full IRD deduction and the deduction is not reduced by
  the 3 percent overall itemized deduction limitation.

• IRD items subject to generation-skipping transfer taxes   _____
  can still qualify for the IRD deduction.

Comments: _____

_____

_____

_____

_____

3. Has a distribution been made from the IRA or any   _____
  other IRD item? (There is NO IRD deduction unless
  there is a distribution.)

Look for distributions: _____

• on Form 1099-R, box 7, code 4   _____

• of interest or dividends   _____

• of receivables   _____

• on W-2 forms (e.g. deferred comp)   _____

- of lump sums from employer plans including Net Unrealized Appreciation (NUA) _____
- from inherited Roth IRAs where earnings might be taxable _____

4. The IRD deduction is taken on my tax return (even if I did not pay the estate tax):
- As a miscellaneous itemized deduction, NOT subject to the 2 percent AGI limits and NOT subject to AMT _____
- On Form 4972, Tax on Lump-Sum Distributions (if I took a lump-sum distribution from an employer plan and am using 10-year-averaging) _____

5. Was there any basis in my inherited account? Distributions of these funds do not qualify for the IRD deduction. _____
- Check prior year tax returns for Form 8606, Nondeductible IRAs and Coverdell ESAs. IRA amounts withdrawn tax-free do not qualify for the IRD deduction. _____
- Do any of the balances include after-tax funds rolled over from a company plan? _____

Comments: _____

_____

_____

_____

_____

6. Calculate the IRD deduction: _____
1. Take the federal estate tax amount from page one of Form 706. _____
2. Calculate the estate tax again without including any of the IRD items in the estate. _____
3. Subtract the estate tax in Step 2 from the estate tax in Step 1. The result is the total amount of the IRD deduction. _____
4. Divide the amount from Step 3 by the amount of the IRA included in the estate. This will give me the percentage of the deduction I will be able to claim. _____
5. Multiply the amount of the IRA distribution (if any) I have taken during the year by the percentage from Step 4 to get the deduction amount for the year. _____

7. Calculate how much of the IRD deduction is unused   _____
   and available for future years.

Comments: _____

_____

_____

_____

_____

8. Did I miss the IRD deduction in past years?   _____

- If yes, amend tax returns (federal statute of limitations is   _____
  3 years) or take from future distributions.

- Check state tax returns if my state allows the IRD deduc-   _____
  tion for federal estate taxes (ask advisor) and also allows
  the deduction even if the income is exempt from state income tax.

9. Did I inherit assets that were IRD assets in a prior estate?   _____

- Were the assets subject to federal estate tax in both prior   _____
  estates?

- If yes, I can take a double IRD deduction, one for each es-   _____
  tate in which the asset was subject to federal estate
  taxes. **Note:** §2013, the double IRD deduction, could be
  reduced by credits for estate taxes paid on prior transfers. The credit is on a sliding scale.

Comments: _____

_____

_____

_____

_____

**For Beneficiaries-To-Be (Alert My Potential Benefactors to These IRD Pre-
planning Measures on My Behalf)**

10. What types of assets are included in the estate that   _____
    could become IRD?

- Notify beneficiary, family, and tax advisors of potential   _____
  double taxation of IRD items after death

11. Explore IRD elimination strategies:

• Leverage IRAs/life insurance _____

• Charitable planning/leave IRD asset to charity _____

• Income acceleration strategies _____

  IRA distributions _____

  Roth IRA conversions _____

  Executory contracts _____

  Tax elections _____

    S corp income §1377(a) _____

    US savings bond interest §454(a) _____

    Installment sale income §453(d) _____

Comments: _____

_____

_____

_____

_____

Follow-Up

My To Do List   Date Completed

1 _____

2 _____

3 _____

4 _____

5 _____

6 _____

7 _____

8 _____

9 _____

10 _____

_____   _____

My Signature   Date

Section IV

THE SPECIAL ISSUES
CARE SOLUTION

The entire purpose behind this book is to make sure everything goes according to plan with your retirement savings bequest—whether you are on the giving or the receiving end of that bequest. To further that goal, this section addresses those out-of-the-box issues and concerns that affect those of you who do not fit the exact account owner or beneficiary mold. Thus, the section is not for everyone—which is to say, it is not for ALL account owners or ALL account beneficiaries. But I will bet my own life savings that one or more of these special situations will apply to either or, perhaps, even both of you at some point. That's why I have included this section. It is for those situations specific to YOU.

For example, as an account owner with company stock in a 401(k) you will need to be aware of the tax breaks known as Net Unrealized Appreciation in setting up your account to best advantage for passing on to your beneficiaries. Or you may need to tap your retirement funds early and want to avoid the 10 percent penalty for early withdrawals, have financial or bankruptcy issues, are divorced, or perhaps want to leave some of your funds to charity. Conversely, if you are or will be the beneficiary of an inherited account, and thus on the receiving end of the issues sparked by these special care situations, you will need and want to know what to do, as well.

Part 1

THE NAMING A CHARITY-AS-BENEFICIARY CHECKLIST

For account owners only

What It Does

Every once in a while in my line of work, I run across an individual or a couple who have no beneficiaries—at least none they care about leaving anything to, especially something as important as a retirement account. I would offer myself as beneficiary just for them to have one, but I doubt this would work because there are much better causes than mine to leave retirement money to, and charity is a big one.

If your heirs don't need the money, bequeathing your IRA or company plan to them could push them into a higher tax bracket and may even trigger estate tax. Under those circumstances, some account owners decide that donating this asset to charity is the better route. A charity does not have to pay income tax when it cashes out the inherited IRA. There is no loser here because our tax laws encourage charitable giving so that the government does not have to provide as much to those in need as it would otherwise.

In addition to sparing your well-to-do heirs some potential grief with the Taxman, you may just want to make a difference in the

Ask Ed . . .

Q: I know that in leaving a retirement account to charity, the charity pays no tax when it cashes out, but do I receive a tax deduction for the gift?

A: No. But your estate does—for the amount in the account that passes to the charity, provided it is an IRS-qualified charity, which generally includes religious, charitable, educational, scientific, or literary groups or those organizations that work to prevent cruelty to children or animals. Not sure if the charity you are considering qualifies? You can either call the IRS at 1-877-829-5500 for the answer, or find it in IRS Publication 78 (available online at www.irs.gov or in your local library.

world, one that will endure after you are gone. There's nothing wrong with that. And in such a case, this is the checklist for you. It will take you through the most tax-efficient and family-friendly ways to leave all or part of your IRA or company plan to a charity hassle-free.

It will show you the various ways to structure your plan ahead of time and tip you off to the most common errors that are made in that process. It will also cover family issues relating to your charity planning here that you should *make sure your loved ones are aware of (assuming you want them to know) in advance so they can put in their 2 cents.*

What's In It for Me?

You'll be able to leave all or part of your retirement account balance to charity and reap the best tax benefits while also doing a good deed. Or, you will be able to cut taxes for your heirs by leaving the entire account to charity and your other property (nonretirement account assets) to family members. This way, the nonretirement account property that goes to your family receives a step up in basis, and there is no income tax on the appreciation. This is not the case with an IRA or

Ask Ed . . .

Q: **Would it be wise to do a conversion to a Roth IRA if I will be leaving those funds to a charity?**

A: No. As much as I like Roth IRAs, this makes no sense because unlike a traditional retirement account you pay tax on a Roth when you contribute not when you withdraw. And since a charity pays no tax on withdrawals even from a traditional account, there is no advantage to your funding a Roth that you simply plan to give away—unless, of course, you like paying taxes.

other plan asset. There is no step up in basis for those assets, and family members receiving them will owe income tax when they start withdrawing—unlike a charitable beneficiary, which pays no tax.

So you get a win-win; you will have seen to it that your family pays no tax on the appreciation of its bequest, and the charity has to pay no tax on the retirement account proceeds you have donated.

What If I Don't?

This checklist does not tell you whether to leave your IRA or other plan to charity or not. That's for you to decide with the help of your financial advisor and with (or without) input from your family. But if you do decide to go ahead and leave all or some of your account to charity, be aware that a single mistake you make in this process could wind up making the IRS your BIGGEST charitable beneficiary.

For example, one common mistake is naming the charity in your will rather than on your beneficiary form (see checklist Section II, Part 1) in which case you will have turned a nonprobate asset (your retirement account) into a probate asset, potentially triggering an income tax on the bequest where none existed before. Furthermore, the bequest could be challenged by some remote moneygrubbing family member showing up out of nowhere to contest your will and scuttle your charitable plans. This is just one of the costly errors that might occur if a charitable bequest of your retirement assets is your goal but you don't follow this checklist.

Instructions

Most other types of property can be given to charity during your lifetime, but not IRAs or company retirement plans—unless you cash out and pay the tax on your withdrawal, hoping to qualify for at least a partially offsetting tax deduction on the balance (if any) you give to charity. This is why the only way to give retirement funds in whole or in part to charity in the most advantageous way for all concerned is to bequeath the account at death. So, this checklist takes you through that process.

Under a new tax law, however, you have the ability to make charitable contributions directly from your IRA to a qualified charity for tax years 2006 and 2007. You must be at least age 70½ at the time you make the contribution. The contribution must go directly from your IRA account to the charity, it cannot be paid to you, then you write out a check to the charity. The contribution can be made from taxable funds only, not from any after-tax amounts you have in your IRA accounts. It cannot come from an employer plan or from SEP or SIMPLE IRAs. That sounds like a lot of rules already, but there are more—and all for a provision of the law that exists for less than eighteen months! That's another reason to use this checklist.

If you want to leave your whole IRA or 401(k) to charity, no problem—just spell that out on your beneficiary form (Section II, Part 1). If you want to make sure the charity receives at least some portion of your IRA or 401(k), you will also spell that out on your beneficiary form and can set things up in any of the following ways: (1) Split the account while you are alive, naming the charity as beneficiary of one account and your children as co-beneficiaries of the other account; (2) Leave part of the account to charity and part to your children for them to separate after your death (see The Multiple Beneficiaries Checklist in Section III, Part 3); (3) Leave the account to a charitable remainder trust (see The Naming a Trust-As-Beneficiary Checklist in Part 2 of this Section) where you can dictate the terms so that family members will receive a certain amount of income for a term of years after you're gone and the rest goes to charity.

On the other hand, you might want to name your spouse as your primary beneficiary to make sure she has enough to live on, and then name the charity as a contingent beneficiary. After you die, your spouse can decide how much she can pass to the charity and how much she would like to keep by disclaiming the amount she will not need (see The Disclaimer Planning Checklist in Part 3 of this section) based on her needs at the time.

You should not only involve your financial advisor in your decision-making here, but family members and the charity too so they can all contribute to your vision and your wishes.

Ask Ed . . .

Q: **Instead of naming a charity (or charities) on my beneficiary form and separating accounts so my family doesn't have to do it, wouldn't it be much easier for me just to leave my account to my estate and make all my charitable bequests in my will?**

A: It might be easier, but it will be much more costly because a tax could be triggered in the estate. That's because the bequest of a specific dollar amount in your will—like a $10,000 bequest to a charity—is known in tax terms as a "pecuniary bequest," and if you satisfy a pecuniary bequest with, for example, an IRA, you trigger immediate taxation on the IRA in the estate under Section 691 (a)(2) of the Internal Revenue Code. It's as if you took the retirement plan money out, paid a tax on it, then made the bequest. That defeats the tax benefit of leaving the account to charity.

THE NAMING A CHARITY-AS-BENEFICIARY CHECKLIST

MY NAME: _____ DATE: _____

MY ADVISOR'S NAME: _____ PLAN #: _____

Follow-ups should be added to the To Do lists at the end of this checklist.

1. I have a desire to leave funds to charity.   _____

2. Make sure the charity I am considering is a qualified charity so there will be a tax deduction for my bequest. Contact IRS at 877-829-5500, check IRS Publication 78 (available in many public libraries), or check on the IRS website at www.irs.gov.   _____

3. Should I leave my retirement assets to the charity? Or should I leave other assets to charity?   _____

• At my death retirement assets do not get a step up in basis and are subject to both income tax and estate tax.   _____

• Other assets do get a step up in basis and are only subject to estate tax at my death.   _____

• It is more tax-efficient to leave retirement assets to charity and leave appreciated (nonretirement) assets to individual beneficiaries.   _____

4. If I am planning to leave my retirement plan to charity, don't do a Roth conversion as I will have to pay income tax on the conversion when there would be no income tax due at my death.   _____

5. As an alternative, use life insurance to fund my charitable bequest. Take funds from my retirement plan to buy insurance. The distributions reduce my taxable estate, and there is more to leave to charity.   _____

Comments: _____

_____

_____

_____

6. Should I name both individuals and a charity as beneficiaries of the same retirement plan or split the plan?

- A charity is a nondesignated beneficiary with no life expectancy, which can kill the stretch option if accounts are not split.

- Segregating the portion to go to charity eliminates any postdeath problems for designated beneficiaries with regard to stretch distributions.

- It is more cumbersome to have separate accounts, more paperwork, more fees, and maintaining the balance I want in each account.

7. If I leave my account to be split by my named beneficiaries after my death:

- Beneficiaries must split into separate accounts by no later than 12/31 of the year following my death.

- Charity should be paid out no later than 9/30 of the year following the year of my death.

- If charity is not removed or accounts are not timely split, then there is no designated beneficiary and distributions to beneficiaries will be accelerated.

Comments: _____

_____

_____

_____

8. Consider creating a charitable trust as beneficiary. The most common type of trust used is a Charitable Remainder Unitrust.

- At the death of the plan owner, a distribution is made from the IRA to the trust.

- The plan distribution to the trust is not subject to income tax because of the charitable beneficiary.

- The estate gets a partial charitable tax deduction based on the expected trust payouts to the beneficiary.

- Beneficiaries of the trust receive a stream of income (based on a percentage of the trust balance) in accordance with the trust terms but do not have access to principal.

- Distributions to the beneficiaries are included in their income and are taxable to them. _____
- At the death of the last beneficiary or at the end of the trust term, the remaining assets are paid to charity. _____

Comments: _____

_____

_____

_____

_____

10. **Keep family and beneficiaries informed of charitable intentions and beneficiary designations so there are no postdeath surprises.** _____

11. **Name a contingent beneficiary to allow more flexibility in postmortem estate planning by the use of a disclaimer. (See The Disclaimer Planning Checklist in Part 3 of this section.)** _____

Comments: _____

_____

_____

_____

_____

The following section applies to tax law changes enacted in 2006 that are effective from August 17, 2006 through December 31, 2007 only.

Qualified Charitable Distributions

12. **Consider funding charitable contributions directly from my IRA if:**

- I ordinarily cannot take a deduction for the contribution on my income tax return because I use the standard deduction and don't itemize deductions. _____
- I may not receive a full tax deduction for my gift because it exceeds 50 percent of my adjusted gross income. _____
- I live in a state with no income tax. _____
- A distribution would increase my AGI and put me at more risk of losing deductions, exemptions, and tax credits. _____

13. A qualified charitable distribution could satisfy my _____ Required Minimum Distribution (RMD). In effect, my RMD becomes income-tax-free for the year to the extent of my charitable distribution (but limited to $100,000 for the year).

14. The distribution does not have to be reported as in- _____ come in the year of the distribution, and I do not get a charitable deduction.

Comments: _____

_____

_____

_____

_____

15. I have an opportunity through the end of 2007 to make distributions of any amount up to $100,000 per year directly from a traditional IRA to a charity if:

• I am the account owner (not a beneficiary). _____

• I will be age 70½ (or older) at the time of the distribution. _____

• I do a direct transfer from the IRA to the charity. (I cannot _____ receive the payment, then give it to charity—unless the check I receive is payable to the charity).

• The transfer comes from a traditional or a Roth IRA, not _____ from a SEP or SIMPLE IRA.

The charity is qualified, which means it: _____

• Cannot be a donor-advised fund. _____

• Cannot be a private foundation. _____

• Cannot be a charitable gift annuity. _____

Only taxable amounts are transferred, in which case: _____

• For the purposes of charitable distributions, all my IRAs _____ are considered one IRA (excluding SEP and SIMPLE IRAs).

• Taxable amounts are considered to be distributed first. _____

• A distribution is considered taxable as long as it does not _____ exceed the total taxable amount in all my IRAs.

• I must keep track of my basis. _____

- I would have been able to claim a charitable deduction for the qualified charitable distribution. There can be no benefit received (raffle tickets, meals, etc.) and I must have substantiation (a receipt from the charity for the contribution). _____

16. **I will need either an IRA custodian or a self-directed IRA custodian willing to make direct transfers from my IRA to the charity, or an IRA checkbook to write the checks directly to the charity.** _____

Comments: _____
_____
_____
_____
_____

17. **A qualified charitable distribution cannot be made from employer plans.** _____

18. **If the qualified charitable distribution fails, then the regular charitable deduction rules apply. The distribution is included in my income for the year, and I get a charitable deduction if I itemize deductions.** _____

Comments: _____
_____
_____
_____
_____

Follow-Up

My To Do List	Date Completed
1	
2	
3	
4	
5	
6	
7	
8	
9	
10	

My Signature   Date

Part 2

THE NAMING A TRUST-AS-BENEFICIARY CHECKLIST

For account owners only

What It Does

Most account owners do not need to name a trust as beneficiary. But you won't know if you are one of them until you go through this checklist, where you will determine if you need a trust because you may need some postdeath control over your retirement assets to prevent your beneficiaries from squandering them or because you wish to leave your assets to a minor child (your grandchild, for instance).

If after reading through the reasons to name a trust as your beneficiary you have found no reasons to do so and decide that a trust is not for you and your family (which is by the way what the majority of folks decide), then you stop and move on to the next checklist appropriate to you.

A Word to the Wise

I know that this checklist can be intimidating at first glance—it is even to many professionals. This is because it covers so many arcane areas in the law, such as the Uniform Principal and Income Act, pecuniary bequests, see-through trusts, conduit or discretionary trusts to name just a few. This is why you will need an expert estate-planning lawyer to help you actually set up the trust once you have determined whether you need one or not. And when I say "expert," I mean just that. If the trust is not set up correctly, it may not be properly implemented according to your wishes, and by then it may be too late to do anything about the problems that arise. So, any old lawyer and financial advisor won't do here. You will really need to grill your advisors to make sure they are up to the task, which is why I've included an expert advisor (including estate-planning attorneys) locator tool (Section V, Part 2) for you in this book.

Ask Ed . . .

Q: **What if I find that I need to name a trust for one of my three children but not for the other two?**

A: You can split your account into three: two for the beneficiaries who do not need the trust and the other for the beneficiary who does. Then on the beneficiary form for the children who don't need the trust, you just name them directly. For the beneficiary who needs the trust, you name the trust on your beneficiary form. Or, if you want to have only one retirement account, on the beneficiary form you can name your two children and the trust for the third child to split the IRA equally (or in any percentage you choose).

What's In It for Me?

This checklist will reveal to you whether you have something to worry about with regard to your retirement plan bequest. In other words, you will learn here whether it is in your interest as well as that of your beneficiaries to name a trust beneficiary as a protective measure. And whichever way you go, you will feel comfortable and secure in the knowledge that you have covered this base in your estate planning as well.

Ask Ed . . .

Q: **If I want to leave my IRA to a trust for my children, when can they actually receive the money and who decides that?**

A: You decide this when you express your wishes to the attorney who drafts the trust. If it is a discretionary trust, this means you give to the trustee—a corporate trustee, a spouse, sibling, or other person you charge with carrying out your instructions after you're gone—the power to determine how much of the IRA your beneficiaries should be allowed access to and when, in accordance with your wishes.

Q: **If I need a trust to inherit my account for the sake of some of my beneficiaries, how long should their shares remain in trust? Does the trust ever end?**

A: That is up to you. The trust can go on for their lifetime or end when they reach a certain age. You will decide the term and put that in the trust. For example, if you name a trust as beneficiary of the account because your grandchild is a minor at the time, you might want to put in a provision ending the trust when he or she reaches 21 or whatever age you decide. You can also end the trust in stages; for example, make half of the funds available at age 21 and then have the trust end and all the funds dispersed when the grandchild reaches age 30 or 35 or 40. (Some parents tell me their 50-year-old children are not yet able to handle large sums of money!) Postdeath control is what you wanted, so you have total flexibility to write the rules of your own trust.

Q: If I name a trust as the beneficiary for my IRA, will my children (the trust beneficiaries) still be able to take advantage of the stretch opportunity?

A: Yes, if the trust is a "see-through trust." This means that it treats your kids (your trust beneficiaries) as if they inherited directly. If you wish all your trust beneficiaries to be able to use their individual life expectancy (rather than that of the eldest) for the stretch period, then you would have to leave their shares in separate named trusts. In many estate-planning trusts, the owner lists a spouse as the income beneficiary in order to provide funds for the spouse after their death. If that is the case, the remainder trust beneficiaries (children and grandchildren) will be stuck using the surviving spouse's life expectancy and will not get the full advantage of the stretch. But this may be a trade-off you as the original owner will want to go with depending upon how much postdeath control you seek. (For all the ins and outs of the stretch option, see Section II, Part 3.)

What If I Don't?

Whether you are a control freak or not, if you have accumulated a sizable retirement account (or accounts) that you know you can't possibly go through in your remaining years no matter how many trips you take and other activities you participate in, you will experience a lot of sleepless nights before you're done wondering what will happen to the balance when your spendthrift offspring get their hands on it, or the government does.

Ask Ed . . .

Q: **If I name a trust as beneficiary, is the inherited account still subject to Required Minimum Distributions?**

A: Yes. The inherited account must pay the RMDs to the trust. Once that happens, it is up to the terms of the trust whether the RMDs paid to the trust are subsequently paid out to your beneficiaries. If not, the trust itself will pay the income tax (at trust tax rates, which are almost always higher than the tax bracket your kids or grandkids are in) on the RMDs it has taken. To avoid the trust tax issue, you might opt for a conduit trust, which pays the RMDs taken by the trust to your individual beneficiaries, who will then be taxed on this income at their (typically) lower rate. Or, you can name the trust as beneficiary of a Roth IRA, which will make income-tax-free distributions to the trust.

Q: **What if I want to protect my IRA funds by keeping them in a trust for my kids, but I still want them to have access to the money for emergencies or education or some other prudent reason?**

A: You can do that with a trust by inserting what are called "invasion provisions" (i.e., access to the funds in an emergency) into the trust, or you could give the person you name as your trustee the discretion to decide when and for what reason your kids should be permitted early access.

On the other hand, the good news is that you won't actually know, so, in effect, all those sleepless nights will have been for nothing.

Instructions

Unless you have true expertise in this area, most of the items on this checklist will need to be reviewed with a qualified financial advisor

Ask Ed . . .

Q: **What if I name a trust and after I die my children or spouse see no need for it and want to end it? Can they do that?**

A: Yes, if you give them the authority to do so in the trust itself. But even if you don't, ending the trust may still be possible if all, not just some, of your trust beneficiaries mutually agree. But it will be costly and time-consuming. They'll need a Private Letter Ruling (PLR) from the IRS allowing them to end the trust and have all funds in the inherited IRA transferred directly into their individual inherited IRAs (trustee-to-trustee in order to avoid triggering a tax). A spouse beneficiary who had complete control of the trust could roll the inherited funds from the trust over to her own IRA, but would still likely need an IRS ruling for that as well. The best solution is to name your spouse or children directly as your contingent beneficiaries. This way if they all feel the trust is not necessary, they can easily eliminate the trust after your death by having the trustee disclaim the interest in the trust. The IRA will then pass to them directly without the complications of the trust.

and estate-planning attorney. So, the way to proceed here is to make notes right on the checklist itself of anything you don't understand or will need help with from them. Create your list of questions, then make an appointment with the advisor and/or attorney. Having your questions prepared and ready to go over with them will not only save on time and possibly expense, but will expose very quickly whether they have the "right stuff" or not and if you need to look for advice elsewhere.

A Word to the Wise

If you have named a trust as your IRA beneficiary, do all you can during your lifetime to make that IRA a Roth IRA. Why? Naming a trust as a beneficiary of a Roth IRA removes the trust tax problem. If the trust is an accumulation trust (also known as a discretionary trust) where some or all of the IRA distributions are accumulated instead of paid out to the trust income beneficiary, the distributions will be trapped in the trust and taxed at high trust tax rates. But if a Roth IRA has a trust beneficiary, distributions to the trust have no income tax. Most people who name trusts as IRA beneficiaries do so because there are significant sums at stake and people with that much in an IRA are likely to have incomes in excess of the $100,000 Roth conversion eligibility limit and cannot convert. But under a new tax law provision, they will be eligible to convert their IRAs to Roth IRAs in 2010. Then they can leave Roth IRAs to their trusts and not have to worry about high trust tax rates, because inherited Roth IRA distributions will almost always be income-tax-free.

THE NAMING A TRUST-AS-BENEFICIARY CHECKLIST

MY NAME: _____ DATE: _____

MY ADVISOR'S NAME: _____ PLAN #: _____

Follow-ups should be added to the To Do lists at the end of this checklist.

Should I name a trust as beneficiary of my account(s)?

1. Reasons Yes:

- My beneficiary is a minor, disabled, incompetent, unso-   _____
  phisticated in money matters

- To provide an income stream   _____

- A subsequent marriage—to provide income to spouse,   _____
  remainder to children of prior marriage

- To ensure that my beneficiaries do not withdraw more   _____
  than required distributions

- To avoid estate tax inclusion in my beneficiary's estate   _____

- Generation skipping—not to exceed generation-skipping   _____
  transfer tax exclusion amounts

- Continuation of distributions after death of beneficiary   _____

- Control disposition of large retirement plans   _____

- Creditor protection (The Bankruptcy Reform Act passed   _____
  by Congress in 2005 gives IRAs widespread protections
  in Bankruptcy Court.)

- Divorce protection   _____

- Fund charitable bequests through charitable remainder   _____
  trusts (See The Naming a Charity-As-Beneficiary Checklist in this section, Part 1.)

2. Reasons No:

- To save estate or income tax (There is no tax benefit that   _____
  can be gained with a trust that cannot be gained without
  a trust.)

- You incur trust taxation, payment of trustee fees, and   _____
  other trust expenses

- To preserve the estate tax exemption (required distribu-   _____
  tions may deplete the plan, particularly QTIP trusts)

- The trust may preclude use of the stretch option   _____

- Trust must be maintained for its entire term (could be _____ decades): annual trust tax returns must be filed, trustee has fiduciary obligation to invest trust funds, account to beneficiaries, decide invasion requests, interpret terms of trust, and wind up the trust.

3. Factors to consider before naming a trust as my beneficiary:

- Coordination of retirement plan and trust with overall es- _____ tate plan

- Will my spouse be the income beneficiary of the trust? _____

- Will my retirement plan be consumed by my spouse _____ (leaving my children with little or no plan to inherit and a wasted estate exemption)?

- Will life insurance proceeds be available to my spouse? _____

- Separate trusts must be established before my death if I _____ want my beneficiaries to be able to stretch distributions over their individual life expectancies—or subtrusts must be named on the beneficiary form.

- Who will pay the income tax on the postdeath retirement _____ plan distributions—the trust or trust beneficiary? (Evaluate trust tax rates vs. income tax rates.)

- What funds will be available to pay the income taxes? _____

- Who will be the trustee (bank or trust company, family _____ member(s), professional advisor, friend)?

- Trust provisions to include (e.g., invasion for health, edu- _____ cation, emergency reasons; business investments; pay debts or bills; buy a home, etc.)

- Coordination with required distribution rules (See The _____ RMD Calculations Checklist in of Section II, Part 5.)

- When does the trust terminate? (A trust that terminates _____ as soon as the estate is settled should not be named a beneficiary of retirement funds.)

- Consider using a Roth IRA with the trust (no income tax _____ on required distributions)

Comments: _____

_____

_____

_____

If I have determined a trust is *not* necessary, STOP HERE. Otherwise, CONTINUE:

4. I must name the trust as beneficiary on my account beneficiary form. DO NOT have retirement assets transferred to the trust. That is a taxable distribution and ends the tax-deferred status of the assets. _____

5. Will the custodial document provider accept a trust as my beneficiary and make distributions according to the trust terms? _____

6. Does the trust qualify as a "see-through" trust? _____

• It must be valid under state law. _____

• Trust is irrevocable or becomes irrevocable upon my death. _____

• Those beneficiaries (my trust beneficiaries) with respect to the trust's interest in my retirement plan are identifiable. _____

• The required trust documentation must be provided by the trustee of the trust to the plan trustee, custodian, or administrator no later than October 31 of the year following the year of my death. _____

7. Are all my trust beneficiaries individuals (persons)? (A nonindividual beneficiary may mean an accelerated payout of the account balance—no stretch.) _____

8. Will my estate be considered a trust beneficiary because the trust has language allowing the payment of estate debts and expenses? _____

9. Is the right *type* of trust named? _____

• Conduit or discretionary trust? _____

• Does the trust fit my estate plan? _____

10. Evaluate all beneficiaries of the trust to determine which ones will be considered beneficiaries of my retirement plan according to the retirement plan distribution rules. The age of the oldest of those beneficiaries is the one that will be used in calculating required distributions. _____

11. Will the trust have to comply with Uniform Principal and Income Act, Unitrust, or Power of Adjustment provisions? (Has my state adopted any of these acts?) _____

12. Is the trust intended to qualify for the marital deduction? _____

13. Does the trust refer to a specific company plan or IRA rather than "retirement accounts" or "retirement benefits"? _____

14. Is my chosen trustee aware of the trust terms and familiar with the regulations regarding distributions from a retirement plan to a trust? _____

• How will my trust beneficiaries be paid? _____

• Who will determine the form and timing of the payouts to my trust beneficiaries? Is it the beneficiary? The trustee? _____

• When does the trust end? (Trust beneficiaries should be informed) _____

• Will my trustee need guidance? (Refer him/her to The Nonspouse Beneficiary's Checklist in Part 1 of Section III) _____

• How much of the required distribution will be subject to trust tax rates? _____

15. Is the trust assignable? _____

16. Does the trust contain any pecuniary bequests? (This will accelerate recognition of IRD) _____

Comments: _____

_____

_____

_____

To ensure the proper implementation of the trust after my death, do the following:

17. Do NOT liquidate the retirement plan and put the resulting funds in the trust. That is a taxable distribution and ends the tax-deferred status of the assets. _____

18. Title the retirement account properly. _____

19. File for a federal identification number for the trust. _____

20. If I do not satisfy any required distribution for the year of my death, any remaining distribution must be made to the trust by 12/31 of that year. _____

21. Determine if trust should disclaim any or all of the retirement benefits within 9 months of my death. The trust can still disclaim the balance in the IRA after taking any required year-of-death distributions per Revenue Ruling 2005-36. (See The Disclaimer Planning Checklist in Part 3 of this section.) _____

22. Determine if the trust or the trust beneficiaries qualify for tax benefits. (IRD, 10-year averaging, NUA; see The IRD Checklist in Section III and The Tax Breaks for Lump-Sum Distribution Checklist in Section IV for 10-year-averaging and NUA.) _____

23. My trustee must provide trust documentation (either a copy of the trust or a list of the beneficiaries and their entitlement) to the retirement plan custodian by 10/31 of the year after my death. _____

24. Evaluate my trust beneficiaries to determine beneficiary with shortest life expectancy. (Required distributions will be based on this life expectancy.) _____

25. Required distributions will begin in the year following my death. Distributions should be made to the trust using the trust tax ID number, then be distributed to my trust beneficiaries in accordance with the trust language. (There is a 50 percent penalty on any required distribution not taken.) _____

Comments: _____

_____

_____

_____

_____

Follow-Up

My To Do List   Date Completed

1 _____

2 _____

3 _____

4 _____

5 _____

6 _____

7 _____

8 _____

9 _____

10 _____

_____   _____

My Signature   Date

Part 3

THE DISCLAIMER PLANNING

CHECKLIST

For account owners and beneficiaries

What It Does

A disclaimer is a written refusal by the beneficiary to receive assets, such as a retirement account, that would otherwise pass to him or her. In effect, it treats the inheritance as if the named beneficiary had died before the account owner so that the assets will go to whoever is named next in line, allowing the assets to be removed from one estate and pass to another without triggering income tax.

Ask Ed . . .

Q: **What is a "renunciation"?**
A: It is the legal term for a disclaimer. It means the same thing—the beneficiary is electing to refuse a gift or inheritance.

Changing beneficiaries on an IRA or company plan is different from changing beneficiaries on most other types of property because it is the age and type of beneficiary that determines the postdeath payout term and the Required Minimum Distributions that must be taken. A change, therefore, can have a huge impact on the eventual value of the inherited account. So, proper planning is important.

Disclaimer planning is one of the best estate-planning strategies available because it enables an account owner to create a contingency scenario that permits his or her beneficiaries to alter the deceased's estate plan on an as-needed basis, allowing them to put Plan B into effect if Plan A is no longer viable.

Of course, disclaiming begs the question: "What sane person would ever refuse an inheritance?" Actually, many people disclaim, and few of them are insane (in this area anyway). For example, if a spouse inherits a large estate and on top of that also inherits an IRA, she can disclaim the IRA, and if the children are named as contingent beneficiaries, the IRA will pass to them, and they can stretch it over their lifetimes. The disclaimer provides the spouse with much-needed flexibility.

Now you might ask, "Well, if the spouse didn't want the IRA herself but wished it to go to her children why didn't her husband (the late IRA owner) just name the children instead of her in the first place?" Good question. And here's the answer: Perhaps when the original planning was done, neither she nor the husband was sure if she would need the money or not to live on when he died. So, he

Ask Ed . . .

Q: **How much can I disclaim? Is there a limit?**

A: No, there is no limit. You can disclaim a billion-dollar inheritance if you wish and remove that from your estate with no estate or gift tax being assessed.

Q: **How do I actually do a disclaimer or renunciation?**

A: After inheriting, you should have an estate attorney prepare a disclaimer statement for you, which you will sign and then serve on the plan custodian (the IRA institution holding the funds). I would also file it and have it recorded with the probate court like a property deed simply as further proof that the disclaimer was done within the appropriate 9-month deadline just in case the IRS or anyone else questions you. The stamp of the court on the document is the best proof you can have—especially if the IRA custodian loses your signed statement, which is not uncommon. The executor of the estate should have a copy as well. I would also attach a copy of the disclaimer to the estate tax return if one has to be filed. You should also keep a stamped and dated copy with your permanent tax records—as should the person who receives the property as a result of your disclaimer.

planned for each contingency by giving her the flexibility to disclaim.

In another example, let's say you're an account owner who wants to leave part of your retirement account to charity, but you still want to make sure your spouse has all the money she needs. So, you name your spouse as your primary beneficiary and the charity as contingent beneficiary. After your death, if your spouse finds that she does not need all the funds you left her and wishes to pursue the charitable bequest you had in mind, she can disclaim the share that she wants to go to the charity, and that is where it will go.

So, for account owners, this checklist covers all the points you need to know in order to properly lay out a disclaimer path for your beneficiaries. And for beneficiaries, it alerts you to the fact that a disclaimer plan is in place (assuming the owner hasn't told you already) and points out what you must do on your end if and when you want to disclaim.

Ask Ed . . .

Q: **Can I disclaim for a dead person?**

A: Yes, and in fact this happens frequently. For example if a husband dies and leaves an IRA to his wife and she dies right after that without taking possession, then the executor of her estate (probably the couple's child), can disclaim the inheritance on behalf of the estate so that it passes to the next-in-line beneficiary, allowing distributions to be taken over the child's longer life expectancy.

Q: **My mom has named the three of us as beneficiaries of her IRA. My sister and I have children of our own, my brother does not. I don't need the funds from the IRA. If I disclaim, will my two children get my share, or will it go to my sister and brother?**

A: You can make sure your children get your share of the IRA in two ways. (1) Asking your mom to split her IRA into three separate shares, naming you as her primary beneficiary and your children as her contingent beneficiaries on the share going to you. Or (2) asking your mom to include the phrase "per stirpes" (meaning "per branch" or "by the stem") on her beneficiary form so that if you disclaim, your share follows your branch of the family tree and would go to your children, not to your sister and brother. But you have to be careful; not all IRA custodians allow the use of per stirpes.

What's In It for Me?

As a retirement account owner, you will be at ease knowing that the estate plan you have created for your account has the maneuverability to roll with the punches should your beneficiaries need or want to alter who gets the account and when due to circumstances you could not have foreseen while putting your plan in place. And for a beneficiary, this maneuverability could possibly add years of life and considerably more value to your inheritance. Disclaimer planning can accomplish these goals by laying out a ready-made road map that covers all the bases and contingencies.

Ask Ed . . .

Q: **Can I disclaim if there is no contingent beneficiary?**

A: Yes, you can always disclaim your inheritance, but if no contingent beneficiary is named, why would you want to? The funds could wind up as a probate asset and never reach the person you would like them to.

What If I Don't?

You may stick your beneficiaries with an inheritance path that may not work out best for them—or for your account—because family and financial issues may change between the time you laid out that path and your death. This roadblock to postdeath flexibility could trigger taxes that might severely diminish the account balance if not wipe it out altogether.

The stretch IRA opportunity for a younger secondary beneficiary could be lost as well if there is a need but no disclaimer plan in place for the primary beneficiary to transfer the account. And a hefty gift tax could be levied on the primary and secondary beneficiaries if they tried to effect this transfer without a proper disclaimer plan in place.

Ask Ed . . .

Q: If the deceased owner has not taken his year-of-death RMD, and I as beneficiary want to disclaim the inherited account, which must come first, taking the year-of-death RMD or the disclaimer?

A: In the past, beneficiaries were advised to disclaim before taking the year-of-death RMD. The reason for this was to make it clear that they have accepted no part of the account. But the disclaiming process sometimes caused them to miss the December 31 deadline for taking the year-of-death RMD, leading to a 50 percent penalty. A recent IRS Revenue Ruling (2005-36) now allows beneficiaries to take the year of death RMD and still be able to disclaim the balance afterward—they just can't disclaim the RMD once it is taken.

Q: My dad died at 78 and had not yet taken his Required Minimum Distribution for the year, so I know that as his primary beneficiary, I must take that distribution. What happens if I want to withdraw more than the RMD, can I still disclaim the balance?

A: Since this was not specifically covered in the IRS Revenue Ruling 2005-36, the unofficial answer is yes, you as the beneficiary can still disclaim the balance of the IRA.

Q: Can a beneficiary always disclaim after taking the year-of-death RMD?

A: Not always. For example, Bill dies in January and Mary is the primary beneficiary. Mary has until October (9 months) to disclaim so her daughter Sarah (the contingent beneficiary) will inherit, but the year-of-death distribution does not have to be taken until December 31. If Mary waits until November to take the year-of-death RMD, she cannot disclaim after that since the nine-month disclaimer deadline has passed. Now, you may ask, "Does the year-of-death distribution have to be taken before making the disclaimer?" And the answer again is, not always. Using the same example, if the disclaimer is made in October, the year of death RMD still does not have to be taken until December. There is no guidance as to which beneficiary (Mary or Sarah) should take the year-of-death distribution, so there is an opportunity here to do some postmortem planning and choose which beneficiary receives that distribution. However, if the primary beneficiary does a complete disclaimer prior to the distribution of the year-of-death RMD, then the contingent beneficiary is required to take that distribution.

Instructions

For a disclaimer to be effective in allowing the change of a previously designated beneficiary to another after the owner's death, the disclaimer must qualify. As with everything else, certain requirements determine whether it qualifies or not:

1. It (the refusal) must be made in writing.
2. The property must be disclaimed within nine months of the date of death. This is a strict rule, but there is an exception for minors, who have nine months from the time they turn age 21 to disclaim.
3. The property cannot already have been taken into possession by the primary beneficiary.
4. Whoever disclaims cannot direct who gets the property. It must pass to the next-in-line beneficiary (the contingent beneficiary, if there is one) named by the deceased owner without any interference or direction by the person disclaiming. Furthermore, the property must pass to someone other than the disclaimant (unless the disclaimant is the spouse of the deceased). In other words, except for a spouse beneficiary, you cannot disclaim an inherited account knowing that you will get it back (through the estate, for example) as a result of the disclaimer.

If you are the account owner, use this checklist to formulate your disclaimer plan for each of your retirement accounts, remembering to name a primary and, most important, a contingent beneficiary on each so that the path will be clear as crystal as to who inherits should the primary beneficiary disclaim. Then share this information with your primary and contingent beneficiaries so they will know that this path is available to them.

If you are a beneficiary-to-be and are concerned about whether your potential benefactor's silence on this issue indicates no disclaimer planning on your behalf, bring the issue up now and thrust this checklist under his or her nose.

Ask Ed . . .

Q: **Will changing the title on the account mean that the beneficiary can't disclaim?**

A: Although this issue is not directly addressed in Ruling 2005-36, it would appear that changing the account title would not mean the beneficiary has accepted an interest in the account. This is because many custodial institutions are going to automatically change the title on the account when they change the social security number to the beneficiary's social security number in order to pay out the year-of-death RMD.

THE DISCLAIMER PLANNING CHECKLIST

MY NAME: _____ DATE: _____

MY ADVISOR'S NAME: _____ PLAN #: _____

Follow-ups should be added to the To Do lists at the end of this checklist.

A disclaimer is used when an IRA or plan beneficiary wishes to refuse (disclaim) all or part of the inherited asset so it can pass to the next-in-line beneficiary (usually the named contingent beneficiary). The account owner or plan participant chooses the disclaimer path. The choice to disclaim is that of the beneficiary. A disclaimer is a legal document and as such it should only be drawn up by an attorney.

1. Reasons to plan for a disclaimer (why my primary beneficiary might disclaim):

• My primary beneficiary may not want or need the inher-   _____
ited property (it may be better to keep it out of his/her
estate).

• It may be better for the asset to go to a younger benefi-   _____
ciary to take advantage of a longer stretch period.

• I want the flexibility to maximize my estate-planning   _____
strategies (to fund a credit shelter trust, for example, or
make a charitable bequest, etc.).

• There may be a need to adjust my estate plan after my   _____
death (for example if I have named a trust as my beneficiary and that no longer may be the best choice).

Comments: _____

_____

_____

_____

_____

2. Plan ahead for the right outcome of a disclaimer by:

• Naming a contingent beneficiary so I will know where the   _____
property will go.

• Including a "per stirpes" provision in my beneficiary form.   _____

• Considering how the disclaimer will affect stretch distrib-   _____
utions.

3. Will the disclaimer cause estate tax? If so:

- Who will pay estate taxes on the disclaimed asset (check the tax apportionment clause in my will or trust)? _____

- Is there life insurance or some other source of money available to pay the tax? _____

- Will the disclaimer set up a conflict with estate tax provisions in the will or trust, creating an inadvertent result (a larger share of the estate tax being paid by an unintended beneficiary)? _____

4. Will the disclaimer result in generation-skipping transfer taxes if the asset goes to a grandchild? (The exemption is $2 million for 2006–2008)

5. I have no guarantee that my beneficiary will disclaim. _____

Comments: _____

_____

_____

_____

_____

6. A qualified disclaimer must meet ALL the following tests:

- It must be an irrevocable and unqualified refusal. _____

- It must be submitted in writing. _____

- The disclaimer must be received by the transferor of the interest, his/her legal representative, or the holder of the legal title to the property to which the interest relates no later than 9 months after the later of: _____

  —The day on which the transfer is made _____

  —Or, the day on which the transferor attains age 21 _____

- The person disclaiming must not have accepted the interest or any of its benefits. _____

- As a result of the disclaimer, the interest passes without any direction on the part of the person making the disclaimer. _____

- The interest passes to the spouse of the decedent or to a person other than the person making the disclaimer. _____

7. If the account title is changed after the death of the plan owner, the account can still be disclaimed as long as it remains an "inherited account" (see definition, Section III, Part 1). _____

8. A spousal rollover is considered acceptance of the account, which cannot thereafter be disclaimed. _____

9. Making investment decisions (exercising investment control) is considered acceptance of the account, which thereafter cannot be disclaimed. _____

10. Property cannot be disclaimed in exchange for something else. That is considered acceptance. _____

11. In addition to complying with all the federal laws previously listed, the disclaimer must comply with any other requirements imposed by state law. _____

Comments: _____

_____

_____

_____

_____

12. A beneficiary can do a partial disclaimer of a retirement account. _____

13. A beneficiary can disclaim before or after taking any Required Minimum Distribution (RMD) due upon the death of the plan owner. _____

14. A beneficiary can take more than the RMD and still disclaim. _____

15. When the disclaimed amount is a stated dollar figure (e.g. $100,000), earnings accrued on that amount from the date of the plan owner's death are also considered to be disclaimed. _____

16. An executor or personal representative can disclaim for a deceased person. _____

17. A trustee can disclaim on behalf of a trust that inherits the retirement plan, provided the trustee is not the beneficiary next in line to receive the disclaimed bequest unless the next-in-line beneficiary is the spouse. _____

Comments: _____

_____

_____

_____

_____

_____

18. Steps for doing a disclaimer:

• Provide a list of the account custodian(s) and contact in-   _____
  formation to the attorney preparing the disclaimer.

• Include account number(s).   _____

• Provide name and contact information of administrator   _____
  of employer plan.

• Include the date of death of the asset owner.   _____

• Determine who will handle the delivery of the dis-   _____
  claimer—beneficiary, attorney, trustee, etc.

• File with the court as a precaution to establish the date   _____
  of the disclaimer.

• Make note of when the disclaimer is delivered. If the dead-   _____
  line for making the disclaimer falls on a Saturday, Sunday,
  or holiday, the deadline is extended to the next business
  day. Timely mailing is considered timely delivery.

Comments: _____

_____

_____

_____

_____

_____

_____

_____

_____

Follow-Up

My To Do List	Date Completed
1	
2	
3	
4	
5	
6	
7	
8	
9	
10	

My Signature   Date

Part 4

THE DIVORCE CHECKLIST

For account owners

What It Does

There is no such thing as a joint retirement account. And because a couple's individual retirement savings—whether his is in a 401(k) and hers is in an IRA or vice versa—is likely to be the single largest asset each owns, it is more likely in a divorce situation to be the asset they will have to split up. How it is split up will determine whether the divorce action turns into a ménage à trois, with the Taxman as trois.

Retirement money is tax-sheltered until the shelter becomes a broken home. That's just what happens in a divorce situation. You cannot just give part (or all) of your retirement account to your ex-spouse as part of a property settlement without properly planning each step of the transaction—otherwise, you could expose your entire plan balance to taxes, which may result in your account being liquidated to pay the IRS.

To add to the problem, many divorce lawyers, accountants, and financial advisors are not as familiar with the steps involved in this type of divorce transaction as they are with how to split ownership of a

Ask Ed . . .

Q: **Under the terms of my divorce decree I have agreed that my former spouse will receive my entire IRA in exchange for my receiving a larger share of other assets. How should I transfer the funds in this case?**

A: This is probably the easiest transfer to execute since you don't have to actually move the money in your IRA. You simply retitle the IRA with the name and social security number of your former spouse, since he or she is receiving the entire balance in accordance with your divorce decree. But you can also do a trustee-to-trustee (direct) transfer of your entire account into an account of your former spouse's. With either method, the transfer will be tax-free.

house, say, or other kinds of property that don't come with the complex tax baggage retirement accounts do.

This checklist will guide you and your attorney/advisor through the delicate process of splitting either an IRA or a company plan balance in the event that your marriage bond goes the way of Ken and Barbie's or Jen and Brad's. It covers all those critical circumstances you might never even think of, let alone resolve, at such an emotional time.

What's In It for Me?

Splitting up property in a divorce settlement is traumatic enough to go through without having the Taxman also coming in with an outstretched hand. In most cases, it's also a complicated enough task to work out without having to worry about whether you may make a mistake in the language of the settlement that could send your entire account into the welcoming arms of your ex, or the IRS. If you adhere to this checklist, however, your divorce may not be amicable, but it should at least be tax-free to you insofar as the split of your retirement funds is concerned.

Ask Ed . . .

Q: I am getting divorced, but a few years back I needed to tap some of my funds early (before age 59½), so under the tax rules I began taking periodic withdrawals of substantially equal payments* to avoid the 10 percent penalty for early withdrawal. The problem is that under the divorce decree I have agreed that my ex-wife will receive 40 percent of my IRA. How do I do this without breaking my substantially equal payment schedule (which still has several years left) and getting hit retroactively for all the years I withdrew penalty-free?

A: In several private letter rulings (PLRs) the IRS has said that if a soon-to-be-former-spouse—is to receive a certain percentage (in your case 40 percent) of her soon-to-be-ex-husband's IRA as part of the divorce agreement, and hubby is currently taking payments under the substantially equal payment early withdrawal exception, then the 40 percent can be transferred to the ex-wife's account. Furthermore, hubby's remaining payments can be reduced by 40 percent (the percentage of the account transferred to her) and the payment schedule will not be broken by this action. Hubby will not be subject to back penalties as long as he continues taking 60 percent of his original payment amount from the remaining 60 percent in his IRA according to the terms of his payout schedule.

*Also known as 72(t) payments; see The Early Distribution Exceptions—72(t) Payments Checklist in this section, Part 5.

What If I Don't?

You will probably get the shaft. If you are the one with the IRA or plan, you may also have to pay tax and a 10 percent penalty (if you are under age 59½) on the amount you transfer, just at the time when you will probably have little or no money available to pay that tax and penalty because of all the other divorce expenses that have hit you. Of course, if you are the owner's ex-spouse, you may not care if your former wife or husband has to pay taxes and penalties—just as long as you don't. But if you are that former wife or husband who is reading this, you will want to make sure you do everything right so you keep your fair share of the mine and don't end up with the shaft.

Even a seemingly straightforward agreement to split an IRA or company plan in a divorce settlement can become a minefield of potential headaches and gross inequities if the agreement is not properly worded. Here are two very different examples:

In the first, the divorcing couple mutually agreed that the ex-wife would receive $800,000 (or half) of her ex-husband's $1,600,000 IRA. But when the account was finally split in accordance with the divorce agreement, the stock market had tanked and the value of the IRA was now only $1,200,000. Since the wording of the agreement stipulated that the ex-wife was to receive a specified dollar amount ($800,000) rather than a specified percentage (in this case 50 percent) or fraction (½), the ex-wife wound up getting two-thirds ($800,000) of the account, and her ex-husband (the account owner) got the remainder, which was now down to $400,000, or half what he would otherwise have received, just because of the wording of the agreement. If the agreement had simply stated a fraction or percentage rather than a specific dollar amount, this inequity could have been avoided.

Going with a split percentage or fraction settlement doesn't necessarily ensure an equitable outcome though if, as in this second example, the divorcing couple doesn't get its percentages straight. Their agreement said the soon-to-be-ex-husband's 401(k) would be split by the same percentage as all the other assets to be divided between the two. Unfortunately, there was no consistent percentage in the agreement for all assets. So, instead of an easy, straightforward, and relatively amicable split, things got ugly, a court battle ensued, and a team of expensive lawyers went on the dueling duo's payroll to fight it out over who got what. This could all have been avoided with a more carefully considered and more carefully thought-out agreement, or

Ask Ed . . .

Q: **If I am under 59½ and in a 401(k) that my former wife is to re-ceive a portion of in accordance with the QDRO, can she roll those funds over to an IRA and would I have to pay a 10 percent early withdrawal penalty on the rollover?**

A: The portion of your 401(k) plan that will go to your former wife under the QDRO can be rolled over to her IRA so long as you would have been eligible to roll it to your own IRA if the distribution was made to you. (She can also roll those funds into her own employer plan.) No, there is no penalty; a distribution subject to a QDRO is exempt from the 10 percent early withdrawal tax.

Qualified Domestic Relations Order (QDRO, pronounced "Kwad-row"). This is the order or judgment issued under the domestic relations laws of a state to determine the split of a qualified company plan such as a 401(k) in a divorce settlement. (IRAs are split in accordance with the divorce or separate maintenance decree or a written document related to the decree, not with a QDRO.)

Instructions

If you are going through a divorce, do not—I repeat NOT—move one cent of your IRA or company plan funds without first going through this checklist. Even after you review the checklist, still touch noth-ing—until you have gone over it again with your financial advisor, ac-countant, and attorney to make sure that your retirement funds are split according to the QDRO (if you have a qualified company plan) or according to the divorce decree (if you are splitting an IRA). The funds that are split should be moved only by trustee-to-trustee transfer (a rollover to your ex's account must be done within 60 days or there will be tax consequences, a mistake that kills many an IRA for spouses at-tempting to transfer these assets in a divorce).

Under a QDRO, the account owner's ex-spouse becomes what is known as an "alternate payee" entitled to receive a percentage of the owner's 401(k). But the QDRO cannot force the plan to make a distribution that is against the plan rules, so the ex-spouse may not be able to access these funds immediately. So, all you former spouses out there on the receiving end of a QDRO whose ex is in this position, beware. What good is receiving half your spouse's 401(k) if you cannot get your hands on it because the plan may not allow for withdrawals until many years later? In that case you should negotiate to receive other assets that you can get your hands on *now* in lieu of the 401(k).

Ask Ed . . .

Q: **If as a result of my divorce and in accordance with a QDRO I am to receive a portion of my ex-husband's 401(k) plan, can I qualify for the lump-sum distribution NUA (Net Unrealized Appreciation) tax break on company stock in his plan?**

A: Yes, but only if he is eligible for a lump-sum distribution due to separation from service, reaching age 59½, death or disability (if self-employed) or similar event. Then you can take the NUA tax break on your portion of the lump-sum distribution the same as he can. (See The Tax Breaks for Lump-Sum Distributions Checklist in Part 7 of this section)

THE DIVORCE CHECKLIST

MY NAME: _____ DATE: _____

MY ADVISOR'S NAME: _____ PLAN #: _____

Follow-ups should be added to the To Do lists at the end of this checklist.

1. Insert Contact Information _____

_____   _____
My attorney—Name   Phone Number

_____   _____
My spouse's attorney—Name   Phone Number

_____   _____
My company plan contact—Name   Phone Number

_____   _____
My IRA contact—Name   Phone Number

Comments: _____

_____

_____

_____

_____

2. I understand that any voluntary payments made to my _____
   ex-spouse without a QDRO (for an employer plan) or
   divorce or separation agreement (for an IRA), will be
   taxable to me (plus a 10 percent early distribution
   penalty, if applicable) and my ex will not have a tax-
   deferred account.

3. I understand that a prenuptial agreement does not _____
   waive spousal benefits available in an employer plan.
   Benefits can only be waived by a spouse who signs a
   consent form provided by the employer.

4. Is my advisor familiar with the specifics of how a retire- _____
   ment account is split in a divorce?

5. Is this an employer plan or an IRA? _____

- I understand that a QDRO cannot force distributions that _____ are not allowed under the terms of the employer plan.

- Specify in the agreement or QDRO who will pay fees or _____ penalties related to the splitting of the accounts, if any.

- State the specifics clearly: _____

  —If I want my ex-spouse to receive a specific amount, _____ specify a dollar amount or a percentage of a specific account value as of a specified date.

  —If I want to limit what my ex receives in the event of a _____ potential change in my account balance (such as a market collapse), specify a percentage or a fraction with no as of date to be received. (**Example:** "My spouse gets 50 percent" would mean he or she gets _no more than 50 percent_ no matter what the account balance is on the date of the split.)

6. All movement of funds should be done as direct (trustee- _____ **to-trustee) transfers rather than rollovers.**

Comments: _____

_____

_____

_____

_____

7. With a QDRO: _____

- After the QDRO is delivered to the company, my ex- _____ spouse's share of the assets are segregated and the company has an obligation to preserve them.

- The company has up to 18 months to review and approve _____ the QDRO.

Comments: _____

_____

_____

_____

8. With a divorce or separation agreement for splitting an IRA: _____

• The IRA custodian should get a copy of the divorce decree or separation agreement before I move any funds to my ex-spouse's account. _____

• I should do a trustee-to-trustee transfer to my ex-spouse's account. _____

9. If I have a 72(t) payment plan on the account I have to split, I can split it without breaking the 72(t) schedule and incurring penalties. _____

Note: The IRS has had a major policy shift on this; it is now recommended that you get a PLR if you want to do this.

• I should use a trustee-to-trustee transfer. _____

• My ex-spouse does not have to continue my 72(t) payments on the portion received from my account. _____

• I can reduce my payments proportionally (if my spouse gets half of my account, I can reduce my payments by half). _____

Comments: _____

_____

_____

_____

10. As soon as my ex and I have split my account, update my beneficiary form to make sure my ex does not wind up with the remaining balance at my death. _____

11. If I have an RMD for the year of the split, the transfer of assets to my spouse does not reduce the RMD amount for the year. I must take the full RMD from the remaining assets in my account. _____

12. For tax filing purposes, marital status is determined as of 12/31 of the year (if married on 1/1, for retirement plan purposes I am considered to be married for the entire year). _____

Comments: _____

_____

_____

_____

_____

Follow-Up

My To Do List	Date Completed
1 _____	
2 _____	
3 _____	
4 _____	
5 _____	
6 _____	
7 _____	
8 _____	
9 _____	
10 _____	

_____   _____

My Signature   Date

Part 5

THE EARLY-DISTRIBUTION EXCEPTIONS— 72(t) PAYMENTS CHECKLIST

A Word to the Wise

You should never withdraw funds from your retirement account early for some arbitrary reason like buying a big-screen TV. Withdrawing early is rarely a good idea and should be avoided at all costs—or used as an absolute last resort because you have no other resources you can tap for must-have cash. Remember, you have spent many years of disciplined saving to build the account into what it is, and withdrawing from it early could defeat the very purpose for which you have been saving—a comfortable retirement. It is the hardest money to replace because whether you get hit with the 10 percent early withdrawal penalty or not, you still must pay tax on the withdrawal, and that will eat into the money you can actually spend. So, just because there may be some exceptions to the early distribution penalty rules, don't just jump at them.

What It Does

An early withdrawal under our tax laws is any distribution taken from a company retirement plan or IRA before you reach age 59½. Generally, an early withdrawal not only triggers income tax on the tax-deferred funds that are withdrawn but also a 10 percent penalty on those funds. This checklist is for those of you who may need to tap into your account early and seek to avoid the 10 percent penalty, if possible.

There are several exceptions to the early withdrawal penalty rule. This checklist covers the exception known as "annuitizing" (taking what tax law calls "a series of substantially equal periodic payments") or simply abbreviated as "72(t)" (after the section of the tax law that allows this exception). I'll use the latter reference because it is shorter.

The 72(t) payment exception is a way to take penalty-free early distributions based on an IRS approved payment schedule. This checklist tells you what to consider before deciding whether to take the early withdrawal plunge, guides you through the ins and outs of the basic 72(t) payment rules so that you will execute the plunge safely, and shows you how to create the most-tax-efficient 72(t) payment schedule, one that will eat up the smallest amount of your IRA or plan assets.

What this checklist does *not* do is calculate your 72(t) payments for you. For that you will need a financial advisor with experience in

Ask Ed . . .

Q: **Can I take 72(t) payments from my 401(k) plan?**

A: Yes, but only if you are separated from service and the plan allows the 72(t) exception, which it does not have to. So, check with the plan custodian.

Q: **Do I have to use my entire IRA for making the 72(t) payment calculation?**

A: No. You can split your IRA into several IRAs and use only one to calculate your 72(t) payments, leaving your other IRA funds free of any 72(t) current commitment—and therefore able to be used in the future for other 72(t) payment plans if the need arises.

this area. He or she will use a computer program—such as "Pension & Roth IRA Analyzer" (Brentmark Software—www.brentmark.com)— for calculating the 72(t) payment schedule for you under applicable interest rates. Your advisor should provide printouts of your payment schedule for documentation purposes in the event the IRS ever questions you about how you came up with your payment amounts. So, be sure to ask for them before you leave.

What's In It for Me?

Although not advisable, there are some valid reasons for tapping into your account early. For example, let's say you are already retired but are not yet 59½, and you need funds to pay your everyday ex-

Ask Ed . . .

Q: **If I am taking 72(t) payments and I die, do my beneficiaries have to keep the payments going?**

A: No. Death gets you out of your 72(t) commitment—and with no penalty either. Ain't that great!

Q: What if the plan custodian issues a 1099-R form indicating that the 10 percent penalty applies even though I am taking 72(t) payments correctly? How will I explain this to the IRS and avoid the penalty?

A: This happens all the time. You can set things straight on your tax return by attaching Form 5329 and enter code 2 (distributions made as a part of a series of substantially equal periodic payments) showing that this exception applies to you. Better yet, make the IRA custodian aware you are taking 72(t) payments so that your 1099-R is issued correctly. But at least you have a backup plan if the custodian still messes up.

penses. Or you are doing some estate planning and need to fund some trusts. These reasons are exactly what this exception was created for.

What If I Don't?

Well, if you don't tap your funds early, there's no harm, no foul. A problem arises only if you tap them early and incorrectly. You'll probably get hit with the 10 percent penalty, and that would be a real waste of money, especially at a time that you need it most. Here's why:

The 72(t) payment exception is a way to take penalty-free early distributions based on an IRS-approved payment schedule. But you must *stick* like glue to that schedule, or else you won't qualify for the exception and will have to pay the piper. As if that isn't bad enough, here's the even worse part—the penalty is assessed *retroactively*, which means that you will owe the IRS the 10 percent penalty for all the back years since you began the 72(t) schedule, *plus interest*!

The bottom line is that this can get ugly, so if I still haven't talked you out of it by now, you must really need early access to your money, and should read on.

Ask Ed . . .

Q: **If I am taking 72(t) distributions from an IRA, can I move that IRA to a different IRA custodian without breaking the 72(t) payment schedule?**

A: Yes, as long as you continue the scheduled 72(t) payments from that account. Also, you cannot move the funds to an IRA that has existing funds in it; otherwise, you will have changed the balance and broken the 72(t) payment schedule. If you are going to transfer the funds to another IRA, it must be a new IRA with no other money in it.

Q: **If I have four separate accounts—all of them IRAs, for example—can I use all four in one calculation for a 72(t) payment schedule and then take just one check from one of the accounts? Or, would there need to be four calculations, then a distribution from each of the four accounts separately?**

A: You can add the four balances in the four IRAs, make one calculation based on the total, and take the 72(t) payments from any one or combination of those accounts. But if you use all four in making the one 72(t) calculation, you cannot contribute to those 72(t) accounts nor roll over funds from, say, a fifth IRA not used in the calculation into any of those four accounts. You can only transfer funds among the four 72(t) accounts.

Instructions

Use this checklist to determine (a) if you qualify for the 72(t) payment exception, (b) if it is right for you, and (c) how to go about it correctly. As mentioned earlier, there are other penalty-free exceptions (see this section Part 6) that you might consider as an alternative.

To qualify for the 72(t) payment exception, you must use one of the IRS-approved payment schedules and adhere to this schedule for five years or until you reach 59½, whichever is longer. You may find that you are too young or do not have enough in your IRA or company plan to generate a large enough payment. The IRS-approved 72(t) payments do not let you just empty your retirement savings. You can only take a portion, and it is based on your age. The younger you are, the longer your life expectancy and the lower your payments will be.

So first off, see if taking the 72(t) payments will be enough since they will be taken over time. Many people, especially younger people, find that even the best 72(t) payment method still does not produce the amount of income that they need, especially if they need a big lump sum. For example, if you need $50,000 and, based on your age, your 72(t) payments under the best method come out to only $1,000 a month (or $12,000 a year), that won't help you. If that is the case, the monthly or annual payments simply won't cut it for your cash needs. But if you need the payments on an ongoing basis—for retirement or living expenses as an example—then taking 72(t) payments may work out better for you.

Ask Ed . . .

Q: **What if I begin taking 72(t) payments because I lost my job and needed the money, but later get a new job and no longer need the 72(t) payments? I know I cannot break the schedule without getting hit with the retroactive 10 percent penalty. But since I no longer need the money, can I stick to the schedule but roll the payments back into my account?**

A: No. You cannot do that. Under the law, 72(t) payments are not eligible rollover distributions.

THE EARLY-DISTRIBUTION EXCEPTIONS—72(t) PAYMENTS CHECKLIST

MY NAME: _____ DATE: _____

MY ADVISOR'S NAME: _____ PLAN #: _____

Follow-ups should be added to the To Do Lists at the end of this checklist.

Once a 72(t) payment plan is established, it CANNOT be modified or changed except in the case of your death or disability.

1. Reasons why I might need to set up a 72(t) payment plan:

- Early retirement—my retirement funds are my only source   _____
  of income

- For estate planning—I need to fund a trust, make gifts,   _____
  buy life insurance, equalize assets in my estate

- Financial hardship   _____

Comments: _____

_____

_____

_____

_____

_____

2. Factors to consider before setting up a payment plan:

- What other sources of nonretirement funds are available   _____
  to me?

- Can I afford to deplete my retirement savings now?   _____

- How much do I have in my retirement account?   _____

- Am I too young or too old to qualify?   _____

- Have I really retired?   _____

- Do I have a company plan? (If I separated from service in   _____
  the year I was age 55 or later, my distributions are not
  subject to the 10 percent penalty.)

- Am I ready to make the commitment?   _____

3. The Basic Rules

- I can start at any age. _____

  EXCEPTION: for a company plan I must be separated _____
  from service (if I separated from service at age 55 or
  later the 10 percent penalty does not apply to distributions from the plan).

- Distributions must continue for 5 full years (until the last _____
  day of the fifth year) or until age 59½ (the date I turn
  59½, not the year), whichever is **later.**

- Payments cannot be modified by changing the amount _____
  of the payment, the balance in the plan account, or the
  calculation method.

  EXCEPTION: My death _____

  EXCEPTION: I become disabled _____

  EXCEPTION: My account balance is exhausted _____

  EXCEPTION: An allowed onetime only change from ei- _____
  ther the annuitized or amortized payment method to
  the minimum distribution method. (The IRS has approved three methods for calculating the 72(t) distributions: annuitization; amortization; minimum distribution.)

  Will I qualify for a onetime switch to the minimum distri- _____
  bution method?

  EXCEPTION: Divorce (if all or a part of your account is _____
  awarded to your ex-spouse). If only part is awarded, the
  72(t) distributions can be adjusted proportionally (it is
  recommended that you get a Private Letter Ruling to do
  this).

- I can take no other distributions from the account, even if _____
  they qualify for a different penalty exception.

- No other contributions, rollovers, or deposits can be _____
  made to the account.

- The interest rate used cannot be more than 120 percent _____
  of the federal midterm rate for either of the 2 months
  preceding the month of the first distribution.

- Failure to satisfy any of the basic rules means disqualifi- _____
  cation of all payments made under the plan since incep-
  tion. The 10 percent early distribution penalty will be
  applied to all taxable payments made to me prior to age
  59½.

Comments: _____

_____

_____

_____

_____

_____

4. **Thoroughly analyze income and expenses—once a pay-**   _____
   ment schedule is set up, it generally *cannot* be changed.

5. **Determine the amount desired from the account.**   _____

Comments: _____

_____

_____

_____

_____

6. **Calculate amount allowable using IRS-approved meth-**   _____
   ods, allowable interest rate, and life-expectancy tables
   (software is a big help here; there are also calculators
   available on the Internet).

- Use the Single Life Table (Appendix I) to produce the   _____
  largest possible 72(t) payment from the smallest amount
  of retirement funds.

- If the amount calculated is too large, split the account   _____
  into two smaller accounts—one that will give me the desired distribution amount and one with the excess.

7. **More than one account can be used in the calculation**
   to produce the amount needed. Distributions can be
   made from any one of the accounts or across all the ac-
   counts as long as the required amount is distributed
   annually. Amounts can be transferred between these
   accounts. (Such transfers will probably result in 1099-R
   coding showing a taxable distribution).

- How many accounts will be used in the 72(t) calculation?   _____

8. **Decide on amount/payment method to use.**   _____

9. Will I need a PLR to set up a customized payment schedule for inflation adjustments, etc.? _____

Comments: _____

_____

_____

_____

_____

10. If I must split the account to allow for a smaller distribution amount, transfer all necessary assets *before* taking the first withdrawal. _____

11. Instruct my plan provider, in writing, to set up the 72(t) schedule. _____

• Distributions can be taken more frequently than annually. _____

• Distributions can be set up on a fiscal year rather than a calendar year. _____

12. Maintain detailed records of all calculations and correspondence, in case of an IRS audit. _____

13. Look for modifications that could jeopardize my penalty exception. _____

14. I can convert my 72(t) payment account to a Roth IRA before the payment schedule is completed, but:

• Distributions required under the 72(t) plan must continue from the Roth IRA until the payment schedule is completed. _____

• Distributions required under the plan cannot be converted. _____

15. Follow up with my plan provider (custodian) to ensure that distributions are coded correctly on its tax-reporting system so that the 1099-R is issued correctly, showing an early distribution exception applies. _____

16. At year-end, double-check to be sure the total distribution has been made for the year (check fiscal-year schedules). _____

Comments: _____

_____

_____

_____

_____

_____

Follow-Up

My To Do List   Date Completed

1 _____

2 _____

3 _____

4 _____

5 _____

6 _____

7 _____

8 _____

9 _____

10 _____

My Signature   Date

Part 6

THE EARLY-DISTRIBUTION—OTHER
EXCEPTIONS CHECKLIST

For account owners

Account Owner Alert!

The Pension Protection Act of 2006 created two new 10-percent penalty exceptions. The first is for reservists called to active duty and it creates an opportunity to file for a tax refund for closed tax years for the amount of the penalty that was paid. The exception applies to those who were on active duty for more than 179 days and took a distribution subject to the 10 percent early distribution penalty while they were on active duty after September 11, 2001. They are also being given an opportunity to repay the distribution they took. The repayment must go to an IRA and the reservist will not be able to take a deduction for the repayment. Funds for repayment could come from parents, grandparents, friends and any other interested party. The second exception to the penalty applies to public safety personnel who have separated from service at age 50 or older. Distributions from their plans will not be subject to the 10 percent early distribution penalty. Employees who qualify are policemen, firefighters, and emergency medical service workers who are covered by a governmental defined benefit pension plan offered by state or local governments.

What It Does

If you tap into your IRA or company plan funds early (before eligibility age 59½), you will have to pay a 10 percent penalty on any withdrawals. It is bad enough that most distributions from IRAs and other plans, even if not taken early, are subject to regular income tax, but adding a 10 percent penalty on top of that is criminal. After all, it is *your* money; why shouldn't you have penalty-free access to it whenever you wish?

Ask Ed . . .

Q: **How does the IRS know that I qualify for an exception?**

A: Every distribution from an IRA or company plan generates a 1099-R form that is sent to you and to the IRS. Your 1099-R will be coded to tell the IRS that the distribution qualifies for an exception to the 10 percent penalty. If it is coded incorrectly by the plan custodian (and that happens frequently), you will give the IRS the correct information by filing Form 5329 with your tax return claiming the exception that applies to you. (You can get Form 5329 and the instructions on the IRS website at www.irs.gov under "Forms and Publications.") The IRS usually accepts your word on the tax return, but of course they can audit you just to make sure, so you should keep all documentation (paid bills from schools, hospitals, or home purchases, for example) showing why you qualify for the exception you claimed and how you used the money.

But the government has decided that it is in your best interest to be discouraged from touching these funds until you reach 59½, which is probably good advice. But the enforcement of a 10 percent penalty only adds insult to injury. Still, that's the rule, and you are wise to pay heed to it before prematurely touching one red cent of your retirement account—unless you qualify for an exception to the penalty rule.

One of the more complicated exceptions is to take a series of substantially equal periodic payments—known as 72(t) payments—and because of those complexities, I have given this exception its own separate checklist (see this section, Part 5). All of the other exceptions to the early withdrawal penalty rule are covered here in this checklist, which will guide you through the maze, helping you to identify which exceptions apply to which plans, what you have to do to qualify, and the rules you must follow for each to ensure that you don't make a costly mistake.

What's In It for Me?

If you need to withdraw early, this checklist will help you find an exception that may apply to you and help you to avoid the 10 percent penalty. For example, if you have high medical bills and need to withdraw early from your IRA or company plan to pay for them, you may be able to es-

---

Ask Ed . . .

Q: If I am using the series of substantially equal periodic payments exception—72(t)—can I take extra payments if they qualify for other exceptions? For example can I take penalty-free payments from an IRA that I am taking 72(t) payments from, if they are used for medical or education purposes?

A: No. That will break the 72(t) payment plan even though the medical and education withdrawals are valid exceptions, but they must be used on their own against other (non-72(t) exception)

IRAs. As noted in the previous checklist on 72(t) payments (this section, Part 5), the only exceptions that can be used to modify a 72(t) payment plan without triggering the 10 percent penalty are death and disability.

cape the 10 percent penalty if you meet certain requirements—in this case, that the distribution is used to pay those medical bills in excess of 7.5 percent of your adjusted gross income (AGI).

The checklist also will tip you off to the major tax traps that can befall account owners who qualify for an exception but miss an important detail in the execution, which means that the transaction winds up costing them more money.

What If I Don't?

Again, I am not recommending here that if you qualify for an exception, withdrawing early is, as Martha Stewart might say, a "good thing." I believe quite the opposite. If you are strapped for cash, I'd even recommend taking out a home equity loan before tapping into your retirement account early; at least you will get a tax deduction on the loan interest rather than face a possible tax penalty on the cash withdrawal. But if you must withdraw early, and I guess you feel you must otherwise you wouldn't be reading these words in the first place—then what you risk by not using this checklist to structure your early withdrawal properly is the possibility of paying taxes and penalties (and more of both) that could have been easily avoided. The tax courts are full of such cases. Here's one of them:

A budding attorney attending law school withdrew money from his 401(k) plan to pay his tuition. The IRS assessed him the 10 percent penalty because tax law says that the education exception applies only to distributions from IRAs, not from company plans. So he hired himself as his lawyer and took the IRS to court to show it a thing or two, arguing that he could have rolled the funds from his 401(k) to his

IRA and taken the money from there penalty-free, so what's the difference? The court agreed that had he done this he would have been fine, but pointed out the one big difference: He hadn't. So, he wound up paying the 10 percent penalty (and losing his first case) because he did not know rule number one: If there is an exception available, make sure it applies to the plan you are going to withdraw from. (Rule number two is: Never act as your own lawyer.)

Even if you use the right exception, timing counts too. Funds distributed early must be taken in the same year as the expense to qualify for the exception. So, if you need the cash for education (like our budding attorney) or medical expenses, you must pay the school in the same year as the distribution or pay the medical bills in the same year as the distribution to beat the penalty.

For example, a woman withdrew $17,222.69 from her qualified plan in 2000 to pay for medical treatments that began in 2000. Most of these medical bills though were actually paid in 2001. She and her husband reported the $17,222.69 distribution on their 2000 joint tax return but did not pay the 10 percent early withdrawal penalty (neither of them had hit age 59½ yet). The IRS sent them a deficiency notice stating that they were liable for the 10 percent penalty on the $17,222.69 early withdrawal, or $1,722. They claimed that since they used the funds for medical expenses, they qualified for the medical expense exception, so they did not owe the $1,722. The IRS disagreed, and the next thing you knew, the couple landed in tax court where,

Ask Ed . . .

Q: **Why do you have conversions to Roth IRAs listed as an exception on the checklist?**

A: Because a conversion is really a rollover, and you also will notice on the checklist that rollovers are exempt from the 10 percent penalty.

surprise, surprise, they lost. Why? Because, as the IRS noted (and the court agreed), they had not read the fine print: The exception applies only to those distributions used for expenses (in this case medical) paid *in the same deductible year as the distribution is made.*

Instructions

Now you understand why it is so important to do this right, beginning with using the right exception for the right retirement account. There are exceptions that apply to distributions (a) from both IRAs *and* company plans, (b) from IRAs only; and (c) from company plans only. There have been many instances where early withdrawal taxpayers have lost out by claiming the wrong exception for the wrong plan, the most common of which is when a person withdraws funds early from a 401(k) plan either for education expenses or to purchase a home not realizing that neither of those exceptions applies to distributions from company plans. As you'll see in the checklist, the first-time homebuyer and the education exceptions only apply to distributions from IRAs.

Ask Ed . . .

Q: **Is the $10,000 lifetime cap for the first-time homebuyer exception per person or per couple? In other words, could a couple withdraw $20,000 penalty-free?**

A: The first-time homebuyer exception is per person; however, if each spouse has an individual IRA, they can each withdraw $10,000 from his or her own account penalty-free. One spouse cannot use any part of the other spouse's $10,000 lifetime amount. Both spouses must qualify as first-time homebuyers for this exception though (neither one having owned a house in the past 2 years) for even one spouse to be able to claim the exemption.

So, if you think you may have to withdraw any funds from your IRA or company plan before you hit the milestone age of 59½ (there is even an age 55 exception for company plans), go through this checklist first to find out whether there is an exception to the 10 percent early withdrawal penalty that applies to you. And if an exception does apply, make sure that you will qualify to get it by withdrawing from the right plan under the right rules in the right year.

THE EARLY-DISTRIBUTION—OTHER EXCEPTIONS CHECKLIST

MY NAME: _____ DATE: _____

MY ADVISOR'S NAME: _____ PLAN #: _____

Follow-ups should be added to the To Do Lists at the end of this checklist.

The 10 percent early-distribution penalty applies to all taxable distributions made before the attainment of age 59½ (for IRAs) or age 55 (for employer plans if separated from service at age 55 or older) unless one of the following exceptions applies. The penalty is 10 percent of the taxable amount distributed and is reported on Form 5329.

IRA exceptions, not employer exceptions, apply to SEP and SIMPLE IRAs.

1. Death (applies to all plans and IRAs) _____

2. Disability (applies to all plans and IRAs) _____

- Disability is defined as being unable to engage in any _____
  substantial gainful activity by reason of a medically de-
  terminable physical or mental impairment that can be expected to result in death or to be of long-continued and
  indefinite duration.

- There is no specific form required by IRS to prove disabil- _____
  ity. The retirement plan custodian may require some sort
  of proof.

Comments: _____

_____

_____

_____

3. Medical expenses (applies to all plans and IRAs) _____

- Distribution must be for medical expenses in excess of _____
  7.5 percent of my AGI and the expenses must be paid in
  the year of the distribution.

- The medical expenses must be deductible (even if I don't _____
  itemize) in the same year as the distribution.

- Medical expenses can be for me, for my spouse, or my _____
  dependent(s).

- Medical expenses include dental, prescription drug, and _____
  health insurance premiums.

- I do not have to itemize deductions to qualify for the exemption. _____

4. **Series of substantially equal periodic payments (applies to all plans and IRAs) (see The Early Distributions—72(t) Payments Checklist, this section, Part 5).** _____

5. **IRS tax levy (applies to all plans and IRAs)** _____

6. **Rollover of eligible assets to another tax deferred account (applies to all plans and IRAs)** _____

7. **Active reservists (applies to IRAs, 401(k) and 403(b) plans)** _____

- Must be called to active duty between September 11, 2001 and December 31, 2007 for more than 179 days. _____

- Took a distribution subject to the 10 percent penalty between the date of the call to duty and the end of the active duty period. _____

- Can file an amended tax return for the penalty amount. For closed tax years the amended return must be filed by August 16, 2007. _____

- Can pay back the amount withdrawn during the 2 years beginning on the day after active duty ends. The 2-year period will not end any earlier than August 16, 2008 (2 years after the signing of the legislation). The repayment goes to an IRA and does not affect IRA contribution limits. The reservist does not get a tax deduction for amounts repaid. _____

8. **Health insurance (applies to IRAs only)** _____

- To qualify I must be unemployed and have received unemployment compensation under either a federal or state unemployment compensation law for 12 consecutive weeks in either the current year or previous year. (Self-employed individuals do not qualify.) _____

- Distribution must be made in the year of or the year after unemployment. _____

- The distribution cannot exceed the amount paid (in the year of distribution) for health insurance for me, my spouse, or my dependents. _____

- The exception does not apply to distributions made after I have been reemployed for 60 days. _____

9. First-time homebuyer (applies to IRAs only) _____

- Exception applies if I am purchasing a first-time home for _____
  me or my spouse, or a child, grandchild, parent, or other
  ancestor of me and my spouse. "First-time" is defined as
  having had no ownership interest in a principal residence
  for the past 2 years. If married, my spouse must also
  qualify under the same definition.
- Distribution can be used to purchase, construct, or re- _____
  construct a principal residence.
- Distribution can be used for reasonable financing, settle- _____
  ment, or closing costs of a principal residence.
- The principal residence can be a houseboat, house trailer, _____
  or stock held in a housing co-op.
- Distribution must be used within 120 days beginning the _____
  day it is received.
- Date of acquisition is the date on which a binding con- _____
  tract is entered into or the date on which construction
  commences.
- If distribution will fail to qualify for exception solely due _____
  to delays or cancellation of the acquisition of the primary
  residence, distribution may be rolled over to an IRA by
  the 120th day. (The one-per-year rollover rule does not
  apply.)
- There is a lifetime cap of $10,000 per IRA owner; more _____
  than one IRA owner's distribution can be used in the purchase of one primary residence.

Comments: _____

_____

_____

_____

_____

_____

10. Higher-education expenses (applies to IRAs only) _____

- Exception applies to me and my spouse, our children and _____
  grandchildren.
- Expenses include postsecondary tuition, fees, books, sup- _____
  plies, and equipment.

- Distribution cannot exceed education expenses (less any financial aid) for the year and must be taken in the year of the expense. _____

- Room and board are qualified expenses only if the student is enrolled at an eligible institution on at least a half-time basis. The maximum allowable amount is the amount used in federal financial aid programs or, if greater, the actual amount charged by the institution for the student living in housing owned or operated by the school. _____

11. Conversions to a Roth (currently applies to IRAs only but beginning in 2008 will apply to employer plans also) _____

- IRA distributions that are converted to a Roth IRA are not subject to the early withdrawal penalty at the time of conversion (but may be subject to the penalty if withdrawn too early from the Roth—see this section, Part 11). _____

Comments: _____

_____

_____

_____

_____

12. QDRO—Qualified Domestic Relations Order (applies to employer plans only) (For explanation of QDRO, see the Divorce Checklist in this section, Part 4.) _____

13. Section 457 plans (applies to 457 plans only) _____

- Distributions from 457 plans are exempt from the penalty. Pretax amounts rolled into the 457 plan do not qualify for the exception. _____

14. Early distributions to public safety employees (applies to plans only) _____

- Effective August 17, 2006, for policemen, firefighters, and emergency medical service personnel employed by state or local governments. _____

- Must be separated from service at age 50 or later. _____

- Distribution must be made after separation from service. _____

Follow-Up

My To Do List	Date Completed
1	
2	
3	
4	
5	
6	
7	
8	
9	
10	

My Signature

Date

THE TAX BREAKS FOR LUMP-SUM
DISTRIBUTION CHECKLIST

For account owners

What It Does

Taking a lump-sum distribution means withdrawing all the assets from your retirement plan in one fell swoop—typically at retirement. If you participate in a 401(k), taking a lump-sum distribution could net you a couple of big tax breaks you may not have considered, or, perhaps, never even heard about: NUA (Net Unrealized Appreciation) on company stock in your plan, and 10-year averaging on your distribution. Not everyone with a 401(k) qualifies for these breaks, but if you do, either or both of them can make a big, big dent in your tax bill by helping you get funds out of your plan at bargain-basement tax rates, and maybe even for free.

These breaks do not apply to lump-sum distributions from 403(b) or 457 plans or from IRAs (including SEP and SIMPLE IRAs). And a triggering event must occur for 401(k) owners to qualify for a lump-sum distribution. For the lump-sum distribution NUA tax break, the triggering events are: (1) Separation from service (not for self-employed individuals); (2) Reaching age 59½; (3) Death; (4) Disability (for self-employed individuals only). Triggering events for 10-year averaging qualification are the same, plus these extras: (1) You must have participated in the plan for a minimum of 5 years; (2) You must have been born before 1936; (3) You cannot have elected 10-year averaging anytime since 1986.

Ask Ed . . .

Q: **What if I am separated from service because my employer fires me? Can I still qualify for any of these lump-sum tax breaks?**

A: Yes. Whether you were fired, quit, resigned, or retired, it does not matter. The tax code does not care how or why you left the company; even if you're the CEO and left in handcuffs, you still qualify.

The NUA tax break allows you to withdraw employer stock (stock of the company you work for) from your 401(k) as part of a lump-sum distribution and pay tax only on the original cost of the stock, not its appreciated value over your years of service. So, let's say you have $1,000,000 worth of company stock in your 401(k) and the original cost of that stock when purchased for your plan was $100,000. The NUA amount is $900,000 (the difference between the $1,000,000 value of the company stock at the date of the lump-sum distribution and the $100,000 original cost of the stock). That $900,000 is not taxed until you sell the stock, at which time you pay just long-term capital gains tax, no matter how long you've held the stock. The rule requiring you to hold stock for more than one year to receive long-term capital gains rates does not apply to NUA stock, so you can sell the stock one day after your lump-sum distribution and still pay only long-term capital gains tax (currently at 15 percent).

The 10-year-averaging tax break applies to fewer and fewer people each year because of its additional requirement rules, such as being born before 1936. But if you do qualify, it means you get to pay tax on

Ask Ed . . .

Q: **Can I use the NUA break if I leave the company when I am only 45 years old?**

A: Yes, if you take a lump-sum distribution (withdraw all the funds in your 401(k) in 1 calendar year) after separating from service. There is one hitch here though. Because you separated from service before reaching age 55, you are subject to the 10 percent early withdrawal penalty. That's the bad news. The good news is that the penalty only applies to the amount that is taxable, which is the cost of the stock in the plan. You can still withdraw all of the NUA tax- and penalty-free.

your lump-sum distribution as if you were taking the entire withdrawal over a ten-year period rather than all at once, thereby lowering the overall tax you must pay.

Furthermore, if you were born before 1936 and part of your lump-sum distribution is from pre-1974 plan participation, you can elect (on IRS Form 4972) to pay a flat 20 percent capital gains rate on that portion. You may also choose *not* to elect capital gain treatment where averaging produces a lower tax.

Ask Ed . . .

Q: **Can I use 10-year averaging if I leave the company when I am only 45 years old?**

A: No. To qualify for 10-year averaging on your 401(k) distribution, you must have been born before 1936. If you are 45 years old now, then you cannot have been born before 1936, at least not without backdating your birth certificate.

As with everything else in the tax code, the devil is in the details, so this checklist takes you through all the things you must know in order to secure these potentially huge lump-sum distribution tax breaks.

You also will require the cooperation of the people in the Benefits or Human Resources Department of the company where you work to provide you with the key contact and tax-reporting information on your 401(k) that you will need to keep track of now and to retrace your steps later.

A Word to the Wise

Another little-known fact is that both the NUA and 10-year-averaging tax breaks carry over to your beneficiaries. This means that if you are in a 401(k) and qualify for either or both of these tax breaks, then so do your beneficiaries if they inherit your 401(k) plan and take a qualifying lump-sum distribution. So, be sure to point this out to them, and refer them (if you haven't already) to the Tax Breaks for Beneficiaries' Checklist, Section III, Part 5.

What's In It for Me?

You won't know until you run the numbers, but there is the potential for huge tax savings here depending on the amount of company stock in your 401(k). For example, if you have company stock in your plan, the longer you worked for your company, the more likely it is that your stock has appreciated in value. The greater the appreciation in the value of your company stock, the greater your NUA tax break.

Once you get the numbers for NUA and/or 10-year averaging, contact your tax advisor to determine what the tax benefit for you will be and whether either strategy is right for you in terms of your overall tax-planning goals. Remember that with either break, you will have to pay some tax up front (whereas with an IRA rollover you will have to pay no tax but irrevocably lose both tax breaks). The idea is to see how much less that tax can be.

Ask Ed . . .

Q: **If I separate from service, do I have to take the lump-sum distribution in the year I left the company or in the year after to qualify for the tax breaks?**

A: Once you are separated from service, you can take your lump-sum distribution then or in any subsequent year—as long as you take no partial distributions after your separation from service. Whenever you take it, you must take it all in one calendar year. For example, let's say you separate from service in 2007. You take a lump-sum distribution of your entire 401(k) plan balance in 2011. As long as you take no distributions in 2007 through 2010, then your 2011 lump-sum distribution qualifies for the NUA and 10-year-averaging tax breaks.

What If I Don't?

If you would have qualified for these tax breaks but didn't know about them, or, in taking them, make a misstep along the way, you will probably wind up paying more tax on your lump-sum distribution than you would have had to. Or, you might sell shares of company stock in your 401(k) while your funds are still in there and negate the possibility of NUA tax savings on that portion.

In some cases, these tax breaks cannot be recouped if a mistake is made. For example, if your 401(k) plan balance contains company stock with substantial appreciation, and you roll all or part of that balance into an IRA, that is an irrevocable election and will cost you *and* your beneficiaries the NUA tax break forever.

Ask Ed . . .

Q: How does the IRS know that I am taking advantage of these tax breaks?

A: You report 10-year averaging by filling out and attaching Form 4972 (Tax on Lump-Sum Distributions) to your tax return. If you use the NUA tax break, your employer reports the NUA amount in Box 6 on the 1099-R issued for your distribution. You simply report the cost of the shares withdrawn as income from a pension distribution on your Form 1040 tax return, just as you would any other pension distribution. When you sell the NUA shares, you report that gain as a long-term capital gain on Schedule D with your other stock and property sales. Your beneficiaries will do the same if they take a qualifying lump-sum distribution or inherit the NUA on the stock you withdrew, so be sure to tell them.

Instructions

Knowing about NUA and 10-year averaging is not enough. You must take the distribution *exactly* according to the tax laws. The reason the government is giving a tax break here is because you have agreed to withdraw *all* of your funds from the 401(k) plan instead of keeping them there, tax-deferred.

With 10-year averaging, you must withdraw everything and pay the tax now, so you get a tax break by paying the tax up front. None of the funds withdrawn from the plan can be rolled over, so the tax shelter ends. You need to project the tax before you choose 10-year averaging because in some cases, especially as the lump-sum distribution increases, it may not benefit you to pay the tax up front. You need to know that ahead of time so that you do not go into shock at tax time wondering what the heck happened to your retirement savings.

Using the NUA break is a bit different. You still have to withdraw everything from your 401(k) plan, but you have the option of rolling all or any part of the distribution over to an IRA to retain the tax shelter. Of course if you roll *everything* over to an IRA, there will be no NUA break. But you can roll some of the company stock over to an IRA if you wish and transfer the rest to a taxable account and use the amount of the NUA tax break that is right for you. As with 10-year averaging, you need to project your tax bill in order to make that decision and avoid any nasty surprises at tax time.

THE TAX BREAKS FOR LUMP-SUM DISTRIBUTION CHECKLIST

MY NAME: _____ DATE: _____

MY ADVISOR'S NAME: _____ PLAN #: _____

Follow-ups should be added to the To Do lists at the end of this checklist.

1. Reasons to do a lump-sum distribution (LSD):

- I need to spend some or all of this money right away or   _____
soon after the distribution.

- I qualify for tax breaks on the distribution (10-year aver-   _____
aging, Net Unrealized Appreciation [NUA], or pre-1974
capital gains break at 20 percent).

- My tax bracket is lower now than it will be in retirement.   _____

- I need liquid funds for estate planning (equalizing estates   _____
or to buy insurance).

Comments: _____

_____

_____

_____

_____

2. To qualify as a lump-sum distribution:

- My entire account balance must be distributed to me all   _____
in the same tax year.

- The distribution must occur after a triggering event,   _____
such as:

  —Separation from service (does not apply to a self-   _____
  employed individual)

  —Attainment of age 59½   _____

  —Death   _____

  —Disability (only if I am self-employed)   _____

Comments: _____

_____

_____

_____

3. **When was the last triggering event and when will the**   _____
   next triggering event be? If you have taken distribu-
   tions from the plan after your last triggering event, in-
   cluding RMDs, you cannot do an LSD until you have a
   new triggering event.

4. **What is my age in the year of the LSD?**   _____

   • If I separate from service in the year I am 55 or older, the   _____
   10 percent penalty does not apply to the LSD.

   • Otherwise, if I am under 59½, there will be a 10 percent   _____
   penalty on the taxable amount of the LSD.

5. **Do I have more than one employer-sponsored company**   _____
   plan? If so, all may have to be considered one plan for
   LSD purposes.

6. **What are the assets in the plan(s)?**   _____

   • Company stock. If so, what is the *total* amount?   _____

   • What is the basis amount (the cost to the plan) of the   _____
   company stock?

7. **Where will the cash come from to pay the tax on my**   _____
   LSD?

   Comments: _____

   _____

   _____

   _____

   _____

8. **I must start the distribution process early in the year to**   _____
   ensure that the distribution is completed in one tax-
   able year.

9. **Keeping track of the process:**

   • Contact person and phone number   _____

   • Date contacted   _____

   • Result of contact   _____

10. **I must advise my CPA or tax preparer of the LSD and**   _____
    seek his/her advice on the tax benefits.

Comments: _____

_____

_____

_____

_____

11. I can elect to pay ordinary income tax on the entire   _____
   LSD (but this is not generally recommended).

12. Tell beneficiaries who will be inheriting my employer   _____
   plan(s) that all my LSD options are passed on to them.

13. NUA can be combined with 10-year averaging if none   _____
   of the LSD is going to be rolled over.

• This option works best with distributions under $125,000   _____
  (produces a lower tax).

• I must elect to include NUA amount in income.   _____

• I must use 10-year averaging to calculate taxes.   _____

Comments: _____

_____

_____

_____

_____

Net Unrealized Appreciation (NUA)

14. NUA eligibility requirements, rules and regulations:

• I can only use NUA if I have a qualified plan—(401(k),   _____
  ESOP plans, etc.—that holds stock or bonds of the company for which I work. (I should only consider NUA when
  the company stock in the plan has low basis. In order to
  determine the basis, find out from the company, which
  must keep track of it.)

• Employer stock must be distributed in kind (actual   _____
  shares of stock) to qualify. Stock sold in the plan or rolled
  over is not eligible.

• NUA on stock distributed in LSD is not taxed at the time   _____
  of the distribution. It is taxed when the stock is sold.

• Only the cost of the stock to the plan is subject to in-   _____
  come tax.

- The tax is paid at ordinary income tax rates. _____

- The stock must be transferred to a taxable account. (I do _____
not have to take all of the company stock; I can take just
part of it, transferring the balance to a tax-deferred account where it will not qualify for the NUA tax break.)

- The tax on the NUA is paid at long-term capital gains _____
rates.

- I can roll my other plan assets to an IRA or another plan _____
if I want to and still be eligible for NUA on my company
stock.

Comments: _____

_____

_____

_____

_____

15. How to calculate NUA and its cost (be sure to include the value of the employer-contributed shares and after-tax shares)

- Determine the market value for the company stock. _____
(it should be on the plan statement).

- Determine the cost to the plan of the company stock. _____
(It should be on the plan statement.)

If the company tracks basis share by share, I may have _____
to calculate the cost to the plan by adding up the cost
of the shares I want to use the NUA election on (I can
elect to use specific shares if I want).

- Subtract the cost from the market value to determine the _____
NUA amount.

- Calculate the tax cost of the LSD on the basis amount. _____

- If applicable, calculate the amount of the 10 percent early _____
distribution penalty on the basis amount.

Comments: _____

_____

_____

_____

_____

16. The process:

- Do a direct rollover of noncompany stock assets (or non-NUA assets if I am not using NUA on all of the company stock) to another tax-deferred account first. _____

- Then have the company stock distributed to a taxable, non-IRA account. (20 percent withholding will not apply to this transfer.) _____

- I must withdraw all plan assets, leaving a zero balance as of 12/31 of the year of withdrawal. _____

- If there is a balance left in the plan account as of year-end, I cannot elect to use NUA. _____

- Stock dividends deposited in my plan account after year-end are not an issue. _____

Comments: _____

_____

_____

_____

_____

17. If I have inherited the company stock from someone who took an LSD, the following NUA issues apply:

- There is no step up in basis on NUA; I will owe long-term capital gains tax on the remaining NUA amount. _____

- Growth after the date of distribution will receive a step up. _____

- Make sure the correct basis amount was used in the taxable account (from the 1099-R issued for the year of the distribution, the total distribution amount minus the NUA amount in Box 6). _____

18. The Income in Respect of a Decedent (IRD) tax deduction is also available, in addition to NUA, if the estate was subject to federal estate tax. (See The IRD Checklist in Section III, Part 6.) _____

Comments: _____

_____

_____

_____

10-Year Averaging

19. 10-year averaging eligibility requirements, rules, and regulations:

• I must withdraw my entire plan balance in a lump sum. _____

• I must have been born before 1936 or become the account owner as the result of inheriting it from someone born before 1936. _____

• I must have been in the plan for at least 5 years (does not apply if beneficiary is taking an LSD). _____

• I cannot have previously elected 10-year averaging after 1986 (it is a onetime election). _____

• I cannot roll over any of the plan balance. _____

Comments: _____

_____

_____

_____

_____

20. 10-year-averaging distributions are reported on Form 4972, and they bypass AMT. _____

21. The tax on lump-sum distributions under $70,000 is reduced by the Minimum Distribution Allowance calculated on Form 4972. _____

Comments: _____

_____

_____

_____

Capital Gains Treatment

22. 20 percent capital gains treatment requirements, rules, and regulations:

• I must have been born before 1936. _____

• Part of the lump-sum distribution must be from pre-1974 plan participation. _____

23. I can elect to pay a flat 20 percent capital gains rate   _____
on the pre-1974 portion. (The rate stays at 20 percent
based on rates in effect in 1986 and does not change.)
I should not elect capital gains treatment if 10-year
averaging produces a lower tax.

Comments: _____

_____

_____

_____

_____

24. To recap, I must make sure that:

- I have taken no distributions in the years since my LSD   _____
  triggering event, or I will not qualify for an LSD.

- My entire plan balance is distributed to me by 12/31 of the   _____
  year of withdrawal.

- I do not transfer the company stock I want to qualify for   _____
  NUA to another tax-deferred account.

- I transfer my non-NUA assets to an IRA or other tax-   _____
  deferred account if I do not cash them out.

- I do not sell the company stock in the plan if I want to use   _____
  it for NUA.

- The 1099-R issued by the plan is correct (NUA should be   _____
  shown in Box 6).

- I keep copies of all documentation, company plan state-   _____
  ments, correspondence, calculations, etc.

- I keep track of the NUA basis.   _____

- The correct basis amount (the amount I paid tax on) is   _____
  used in the after-tax account holding the shares of company stock.

- I do not roll over any assets to another tax-deferred ac-   _____
  count if I want to use 10-year averaging or receive capital
  gains treatment.

- I file Form 4972 with my tax return if using 10-year aver-   _____
  aging or want capital gains treatment.

- I advise my beneficiaries that there is NUA in my estate.   _____

Comments: _____

_____

_____

_____

_____

_____

Follow-Up

My To Do List   Date Completed

1 _____

2 _____

3 _____

4 _____

5 _____

6 _____

7 _____

8 _____

9 _____

10 _____

My Signature   Date

Part 8

THE INCAPACITY CHECKLIST

What It Does

This checklist is for those of you who are or may become unable for a number of reasons to make legal and financial decisions on your own behalf or that of your family. It is also for you if you are considering naming a beneficiary for your retirement assets who is incapacitated.

Incapacity is a topic that is not much discussed in the financial-planning media, but I receive questions on it regularly, such as "How do I leave my IRA to a disabled child?" or "What if I become disabled? Who will look after the retirement funds I need to live on and take my required distributions for me?" These are the type of items on the minds of account owners like yourself that this special issue checklist will address.

For our purposes, the term "incapacity" means not just physically or mentally incapacitated but also legally incapacitated—for example, a minor child (a grandchild, for instance). The minor child may be physically and mentally okay, but at 2 years old is hardly in a position to make legal decisions and tax elections now or for a good many years. You don't want to leave your planning decisions in limbo for that long, and to make plans now you need to know all your planning choices—for example, (1) should you leave the account to a special needs trust for the child's benefit or (2) leave it to a Uniform Gifts to Minors Account (UGMA) or Uniform Transfers to Minors Account (UTMA)? These are all viable options covered by this checklist.

It also will address many other need-to-plan-in-advance items such as creating a power of attorney that contains specific provisions that grant the person you appoint (and only that person) the power to make the financial and legal decisions you want. For example, will you want your attorney-in-fact (the person to whom you grant this power) to be able to change the beneficiary on your account? Probably not, but that might happen if you do not address such specifics ahead of time. Of course, to actually set up your power of attorney, trust for a minor child, and so on, you will need the professional services of an experienced lawyer or advisor in these fields. This checklist will not make you one.

Ask Ed . . .

Q: **How will I know if my bank will accept my power of attorney with its specific provisions?**

A: You'll have to show it to the bank and get the bank's acceptance in writing, or punt accordingly if the bank insists you use its own power of attorney form. That's why it is so important to take care of this while you are still healthy and able to, as you may have to decide to move your account to a bank that is more flexible and reasonable in terms of your desired provisions (see the "My Custodial Agreement Checklist," Section II, Part 2).

What's In It For Me?

Here again, peace of mind is the key benefit. If you become incapacitated or have named a beneficiary who is, you will know that the funds you are relying on to take care of you (or that your beneficiary is relying on) will be looked after properly under your terms and conditions by the people you have appointed to do so. You will be assured that your IRA or plan custodian allows the power of attorney or the trust you have set up because you have addressed that point ahead of time so there will be no surprises later on. As with postdeath planning, planning ahead here also means not leaving it to chance that your family will be able to fix things up after the fact if you do nothing now. There is no guarantee they will be able to do so, let alone in accordance with your known wishes.

You want to address the incapacity issue now and set things right the first time to save yourself and your family thousands of dollars in legal expenses from not having to go to court to determine what you should or would have wanted done.

Ask Ed . . .

Q: **I have a disabled child and want to set up a special needs trust to inherit my IRA for him. What will be the effect of the annual Required Minimum Distributions the trust must take?**

A: If your child is getting any type of government benefits due to disability, the amounts the trust distributes to your child are not only taxable but will have to go right back to the government program your child is benefiting from. Usually, the special needs trust will pay only for extra items like amenities that the government program does not provide. The rest of the RMDs should remain in the trust. This accumulation could quickly cause a loss of assets to taxes in excess of 40 percent if there are state trust taxes to pay in addition to the 35 percent the IRS receives. Therefore, an IRA or other plan is not the best asset to leave to a special needs trust. I would look to leave other assets to the trust for your disabled child and leave the IRA or plan asset to other beneficiaries.

What If I Don't?

You will not only be leaving your fate but the fate of your retirement money—and your family—up to chance. There are laws governing what must happen if the owner of a retirement account becomes incapable of making decisions about that account and there is no plan in place or documents available clarifying his or her specific intentions on these matters.

Even if you have a spouse or other family member who can take care of you, remember that your IRA or other plan is an *individual* account, not a *joint* account. That means even your spouse will have no say over what decisions to make about your money or what distributions to take for your benefit should you become incapacitated and have not specified those arrangements. It will be up to the courts to decide. And not only will the courts be less sensitive to your desires or concerned about them in making its decision, they also will be more costly.

Instructions

Intent is all-important not only in postdeath planning but with incapacity planning, too. You will use this checklist to make sure your intent is always clear so that no questions will arise later about choices that you may no longer be able to clarify. This can help to keep the biggest asset you own and will need—your retirement account—out of court, or at least dramatically smooth the proceedings if court involvement does come up for some reason.

For example, let's say that in the event you become incapacitated and must have care, you want other resources (long-term-care insurance, perhaps) to cover those costs so that the balance in your retirement account can go entirely to your grandchild. But a minor cannot legally hold assets (including an IRA or other plan) in his or her name. So, if you leave your IRA to a minor, your plan custodian will not let the minor act for him or herself. And a parent might not automatically be allowed to act for the minor either. Instead, the custodian might require a "guardianship of the property" for the minor, and a parent may have to go to court and ask to be named the "guardian of the property," which normally is not an extensive process. But if your overall intent is for your grandchild to get your retirement funds free and clear, it would be better if you named a custodian for your grandchild *now* under your state's Uniform Gift/Transfers to Minors Act (UGMA/UTMA) so that your intent is explicit and bulletproof.

This checklist will take you through the various items you need to consider in deciding upon and clarifying your intent, but for the specifics on naming a beneficiary, the ins and outs of custodial agreements, and setting up trusts, please refer to their respective checklists (The Naming a Trust-As-Beneficiary Checklist in Part 2 of this section and The Account Owner's Care Solution in Section II).

Ask Ed . . .

Q: **I want my grandchild, a minor, to inherit my IRA and the guardian I name to be approved by the court or the plan custodian. How do I set up the IRA to accomplish this?**

A: You should contact the plan custodian to determine its specific requirements. Generally, the plan custodian will ask to see evidence of the guardian's legal authority before opening the inherited IRA account. If the guardian is a parent (your son or daughter, for example), a birth certificate probably will be sufficient. A parent is usually considered to be the natural guardian, unless there is some objection. For an individual other than a parent, a record of a court-ordered guardianship is generally required. Alternatively, a written opinion of counsel, attesting to the legality of the guardianship in a last will and testament, should suffice.

THE INCAPACITY CHECKLIST

MY NAME: _____ DATE: _____

MY ADVISOR'S NAME: _____ PLAN #: _____

Follow-ups should be added to the To Do Lists at the end of this checklist.

1. What is incapacity?

• Mental incapacity—where I or my beneficiary is unable to   _____
make financial decisions.

• Physical incapacity—where my or my beneficiary's phys-   _____
ical limitations render us unable to make financial decisions.

• Legal incapacity—where my beneficiary is a minor and   _____
not able to make financial decisions.

• Fiscal incapacity—where my beneficiary is not able to   _____
make sound financial decisions or is in financial difficulties.

Comments: _____

_____

_____

_____

_____

_____

2. Planning for incapacity:

• In the event that I or my beneficiary should become inca-   _____
pacitated, I will seek the assistance of a qualified attorney
for Medicaid assistance. The rules are complicated and
differ from state to state. (A Roth IRA may be treated
very differently than a traditional IRA under Medicaid
rules.)

• IRS has granted a Private Letter Ruling (PLR 200620025)   _____
allowing the transfer of retirement assets after my death
to a special needs trust (set up as a grantor trust) for the
benefit of a disabled beneficiary. This strategy may provide some protection in very limited situations.

3. **Types of powers of attorney (POA): (A legal document that gives another person the authority to handle my financial affairs; I should consult an attorney before executing one.)**

- General POA—ceases to be effective when I become incapacitated. _____

- Springing POA—the power is granted today but does not become effective until a specific event "springs" it. _____

- Durable POA—I grant the power when I sign it and that power does not end until my death or until I revoke it. _____

4. **Power of attorney issues:**

- Who should have my POA? _____

- Who are my current beneficiaries? _____

- Could there be any sources of conflict between my POA holder and my beneficiaries? _____

- Will my plan custodian accept a POA? _____

- Can I use my own POA or must I use one provided by the plan custodian? _____

5. **Consider whether or not the following powers should be granted to my attorney-in-fact and included in my POA for my retirement plans:**

- The power to make contributions. _____

- The power to request that required distributions be made. _____

- The power to take distributions other than required distributions. _____

- The ability to do rollover transactions. _____

- The power to change my beneficiary, or a limited power to change beneficiaries. _____

- The power to manage my retirement plan investments. _____

- The power to sign all necessary paperwork with respect to retirement plan transactions. (There may be a delay in processing transactions initiated by the person holding a POA for another person while the plan custodian verifies the power and the identity of the holder.) _____

6. **Review my POA periodically to be sure that it is up-to-date:**

- Is the person holding the power still alive and able to act for me? _____

- Have state laws changed?   _____
- Does my plan custodian still accept my POA?   _____

7. **I might want to set up a trusteed IRA** (a trust set up   _____
   during my lifetime that names a trustee to handle retirement account transactions if I become incapacitated)
   **instead of using a POA: A trusteed IRA is effective both
   while I'm alive and after my death.**

- Check with my plan custodian to be sure it will accept a   _____
  trusteed IRA.

Comments: _____

_____

_____

_____

_____

8. **Things to consider before naming a plan beneficiary
   who is incapacitated:**

- Does he or she have a guardian to act for him or her?   _____
  - —If yes, the guardian is (name and contact information):   _____
  - —If no, court proceedings may be necessary to establish   _____
    a guardian.
  - —Have I named a successor guardian?   _____
- Will I need to set up a trust for my plan beneficiary? (Set-   _____
  ting up a trust requires the services of an attorney spe-
  cializing in that type of trust and who is also familiar with
  IRA trust and distribution rules.)
- If so, which type of trust?   _____
  - —Special needs trust—for disabled beneficiaries.   _____
  - —Spendthrift trust—for beneficiaries who have financial   _____
    difficulties.
  - —Trust for minor beneficiaries—to force the stretch op-   _____
    tion by extending distributions over a minor's life.
  - —A trust can also provide a level of creditor protection   _____
    for my plan beneficiary, depending on state law.

—I should set up a trust for my disabled beneficiary so that he or she will not inherit my retirement plan assets directly if eligible for government assistance programs in order to avoid tax and program repayment issues.

_____

9. If I wish, I can arrange to have two different people be the trustee of the trust and the guardian for my minor or disabled beneficiary: The former can take care of the assets; the latter can take care of my beneficiary.

_____

10. If I name a minor as my plan beneficiary, at what age do I want him or her to have access to my retirement funds?

_____

• Leaving the plan directly to the minor or through an UGMA (Uniform Gifts to Minors Act) or UTMA (Uniform Transfers to Minors Act) means the minor has access to my retirement funds at the age of majority (18 or 21 depending on state law).

_____

• Leaving the plan to a trust means I can control the minor's access to funds through the terms of the trust.

_____

11. Life insurance is a much better asset than my retirement plan for a beneficiary who is receiving government assistance: (1) When it is properly purchased and owned it comes into the special needs trust estate- and income-tax-free and any remaining funds at the death of the special needs beneficiary can go to my contingent or successor beneficiaries. (2) Plan distributions can be used to purchase the life insurance.

_____

Comments: _____

_____

_____

_____

_____

Follow-Up

My To Do List	Date Completed
1 _____	_____
2 _____	_____
3 _____	_____

4 _____

5 _____

6 _____

7 _____

8 _____

9 _____

10 _____

_____   _____

My Signature   Date

Part 9

THE SAME SEX AND UNMARRIED COUPLE CHECKLIST

For account owners and beneficiaries

What It Does

Regardless of whether you have lived together for years without tying the knot in a common law situation or a same sex partnership, as far as the tax laws are concerned, you're *single*. With that in mind there are serious issues you need to be aware of and serious decisions for you to make when it comes to retirement account planning for you and your significant other.

Our tax laws offer numerous built-in legal protections for spouses, but none of them apply to you as an unmarried partner. For example, spouses can leave each other unlimited amounts of IRA or plan money estate-tax-free, but you cannot. If you leave your partner an IRA or plan money that, combined with your other assets, exceeds the current federal estate tax exemption, then your estate will be subject to federal estate tax. Also, married couples can make unlimited gifts to each other, but unmarried partners cannot; they are stuck with the annual and lifetime gift tax limits—but at least they are not shut out of these, which means all is not lost for unmarried couples. In fact, there are some advantages to being unmarried (no, I'm *not* trying to be funny) but not single.

For example, there is no marriage penalty. I don't mean there is no penalty for being married (that's a personal issue). I mean the *tax penalty* married couples face when they file a joint tax return. Often, married couples would pay less tax if they could file as two single people. They don't have that option, but as an unmarried couple, *you do.* Roth conversions have a huge marriage penalty built in because you cannot convert to a Roth IRA if your income exceeds $100,000—a limit that is the same for singles as well as married couples who file a joint tax return. This means 2 single people (as in an unmarried couple situation) can each earn $100,000, effectively raising the limit to $200,000 ($100,000 on each tax return). Unmarried couples will continue to enjoy this advantage until 2010, when the law removes the limitation, thus taking even that advantage away from you.

So, here's the bottom line: Our tax laws do not favor unmarried couples the way they do married couples. This makes careful and considered retirement account planning arguably even more critical for unmarried couples who want to be able to provide for each other. This checklist will take you through the essential points you will need to understand in order to accomplish that.

Ask Ed . . .

Q: **If I name my partner to inherit my IRA, how will the payout period be determined for her as my beneficiary?**

A: The payout will be based on the same rules as for any nonspouse beneficiary. There is no spousal rollover because your partner is not legally a spouse, so distributions will have to begin in the year after your death and be taken over your partner's life expectancy based on his or her age the year after your death (see Section III and Appendix I—The Single Life Expectancy Table).

What's In It for Me?

If your intentions are to leave property (such as your retirement assets) to each other, and to name each other as decision-makers during times of incapacity, disability, or as your beneficiary after your death, this checklist will save you from lots of legal misery that would otherwise probably come your way. It will help to protect you and your partner legally where little or no legal protection would otherwise exist.

Ask Ed . . .

Q: **My partner and I are unmarried but live together. If I withdraw from my IRA before reaching age 59½, but I use the funds to pay medical bills for my partner, am I exempt from the 10 percent early withdrawal penalty?**

A: Not unless your partner is also your dependent. If your partner is not your dependent, you will have to pay the 10 percent penalty. The same rule applies to early withdrawals for other exceptions, such as education expenses and buying a first home.

What If I Don't?

Unmarried couples who leave assets to each other inherit under the same rules that apply to any nonspouse beneficiary (see The Nonspouse Beneficiary's Checklist in Part 1 of Section III). But unlike a nonspouse beneficiary who is a family member and might just inherit anyway under intestacy, if there was no beneficiary form or will, an unmarried partner would not gain any benefit in intestacy and would probably lose out even to a distant blood relative of the deceased. That alone is why planning for unmarried couples who want to provide for each other is so much more critical than for married couples. Your retirement funds might not go to your partner, and you might not inherit your partner's retirement assets. You might not even be involved in the distribution of your partner's property after death or involved in any decisions if you are not the named executor or trustee.

For example, when a spouse has funds in a 401(k) plan and that spouse dies, the beneficiary is automatically the surviving spouse—unless he or she waives that right. But if a partner in an unmarried couple situation has funds in a 401(k), these funds will go to whoever is named as the plan beneficiary. So, if you have failed to specifically name your partner, who knows who will inherit your retirement savings? If it goes to your estate, even that is no guarantee your partner will get it, if your will does not clearly name a beneficiary. There is a good chance that either the government or your relatives, however remote, will have a better claim on your property than your partner. Estate planning, which includes retirement beneficiary planning, is *essential* for unmarried couples, as the law is not with you on any of this.

Ask Ed . . .

Q: **If my longtime companion and I split up, how much of my company plan is he entitled to?**

A: None of it, since he is not your spouse. He has no legal right to any of your property if you are not legally married. If you feel your ex-partner is entitled to some of your retirement plan funds, you can keep him as your primary or contingent beneficiary on your beneficiary form. Of course, you will have to die before he can collect, so I hope the split was amicable.

Instructions

Make sure you and your partner take action to ensure protection of your retirement assets by following the essential points of this checklist. Among them: Be sure to make out an IRA or other plan beneficiary form, specifically naming who you want as your primary and contingent beneficiary (see Section II for details), and then keeping your beneficiary form current.

You will also need to be sure that any children you may have are well protected by naming each other as their legal guardian in your respective wills (if that is what you wish) and including your children's names in all documents. If you do not name each other as their legal guardian, the court may not necessarily appoint you, although even in unmarried couple situations, any parent has a better standing to be appointed legal guardian than someone else. But it is still much easier to avoid the courts in the first place by having this spelled out.

Ask Ed . . .

Q: **Is a same sex couple married in a state that allows gay marriage treated by the IRS as a married couple?**

A: Not under current federal tax rules, where even a same sex married couple that is legally married is not considered married insofar as the IRS is concerned. This may change over time, but not as of this writing.

THE SAME SEX AND UNMARRIED COUPLE CHECKLIST

MY NAME: _____ DATE: _____

MY ADVISOR'S NAME: _____ PLAN #: _____

Follow-ups should be added to the To Do lists at the end of this checklist.

1. As an unmarried partner, I cannot do the following:

• Be accepted as legally married under federal law (currently) even if my union is recognized by the laws of my state. _____

• Claim the unlimited marital deduction at my partner's death. _____

• Make unlimited financial gifts to my partner for tax purposes. _____

• File a joint tax return. _____

• Claim a right of election (the legal right to inherit a portion of a spouse's property) _____

Comments: _____

_____

_____

_____

_____

2. As an unmarried partner, I am able to do the following:

• Avoid the marriage penalty by having to file a separate tax return. _____

• Receive a better deal on Roth conversion eligibility since the $100,000 income cap applies to each unmarried partner individually (this limitation is eliminated in 2010). _____

Comments: _____

_____

_____

_____

3. Retirement account planning for unmarried couples:

- If I want my partner to receive my plan benefits, I must _____ complete a beneficiary form for each account I own (see My Beneficiary Form Checklist in Section II, Part 1 for details).

- When inheriting, my partner and I will be treated as each _____ other's nonspouse beneficiaries (see the Nonspouse Beneficiary's Checklist in Section III, Part 1 for details).

- As an account owner, I must use the Uniform Lifetime _____ Table (see Appendix II) in determining RMDs, even if my partner is more than 10 years younger than I am (see the RMD Calculations Checklist in Section II, Part 5 for explanation and details).

Comments: _____

_____

_____

_____

_____

4. As an unmarried partner, I should make sure the following are part of my estate plan and review them on a regular basis:

- Contingent beneficiaries for all my accounts, keeping in _____ mind the effect a disclaimer (see the Disclaimer Planning Checklist in this section, Part 3) would have.

- Clearly stated custody issues for my children (especially _____ guardianship for a minor child) who inherit my retirement plan or these issues may be contested (see the Incapacity Checklist in this section, Part 8).

- My children are named in all documents and thus well _____ protected.

- A simultaneous death clause in my will, in case my part- _____ ner and I die together.

- Choose a trustee (if I set up a trust), an executor of my _____ estate, name a power of attorney, and so on.

Comments: _____

_____

_____

_____

_____

5. Problems I want to avoid:

• The possibility of any of my bequests being contested by   _____
  family members after my death.

• Dying intestate—blood relatives will have better standing   _____
  if I do not clearly name my choices for beneficiaries,
  guardians, or personal representatives.

**6. Share my wishes with family members by making a   _____
  video record of me stating them.**

Comments: _____

_____

_____

_____

Follow-Up

My To Do List	Date Completed
1	
2	
3	
4	
5	
6	
7	
8	
9	
10	

_____   _____
My Signature   Date

Part 10

THE ALTERNATIVE INVESTMENTS AND PROHIBITED TRANSACTIONS CHECKLIST

For account owners

A Word to the Wise

Terry: *"You was my brother, Charlie, you shoulda looked out for me a little bit. You shoulda taken care of me just a little bit so I wouldn't have to take them dives for the short-end money."*

Charlie: *"Oh I had some bets down for you. You saw some money."*

Terry: *"You don't understand. I coulda had class. I coulda been a contender. I coulda been somebody, instead of a bum, which is what I am, let's face it."*

Your retirement account "coulda been a contender" too, or at least the investments in your plan could have, and that is the big issue here. Remember, like Charlie in that memorable exchange from the movie *On the Waterfront,* you have an obligation to watch over your retirement savings and to make prudent decisions so that you don't lose your money and turn your account into a "bum."

What It Does

"I don't need no stinkin' stocks and bonds in my IRA. Gimme the good stuff!" Yes, the grass is always greener (and so is the cash) in someone else's retirement account. At least that is what many account owners seem to think. They see others making a fortune in real estate and other business investments and they want a piece of that sweet action. But the only money they have to invest in these "sure things" is their retirement savings—so those are the funds they want to use to make their killing. Then, when they strike it rich, they tell themselves, all of the profits will be tax-free from being in a retirement account! Sounds like a plan that's too good to be true! And it just may be. But if you do decide to go the alternative investment route, such as real estate, with your retirement account choices, this checklist will keep you safe and straight on course.

You can put your retirement plan contributions in pretty much any investment you want, except for life insurance and collectibles. But most people stick with what the typical plan custodian (bank, broker, mutual fund, or insurance company) offers, which may be a wide

Ask Ed . . .

Q: If I use a self-directed IRA custodian, will that guarantee that I won't make any mistakes?

A: A self-directed IRA custodian will inform you of the rules and not let you invest your IRA funds in property that is not appropriate for your IRA, but they are not the police and cannot monitor your every move. If you use the property improperly for your own purposes or some other family member does, the custodian is not likely to know or be able to help you out of the bind.

range of investment options but are usually limited to the major investment categories of stocks, bonds, funds, and Certificates of Deposit (CDs). If you want anything with more pizzazz—real estate, a small business, a start-up company, mortgages, equipment-leasing, or other nontraditional retirement plan investment choices—you will have to do it yourself with a self-directed IRA (SDIRA) offered by a bank, broker, fund, insurance, or other company (such as PENSCO Trust Company in San Francisco) that specializes in SDIRAs.

Ask Ed . . .

Q: **If I am contemplating a nontraditional IRA investment, would the opinion of an attorney be helpful in determining if it's a prohibited transaction?**

A: Not really. The only opinion that counts is the opinion of the US Department of Labor, which issues the Prohibited Transaction Exemption rulings (PTEs). You can ask them for a ruling in advance to see if they bless your IRA or plan transaction, but this process can take a year or more and be very expensive. By the time you receive an opinion, your investment deal will probably be long gone.

If you are thinking about unconventional or even exotic investments for your plan funds, you have to be careful because the tax rules are rigid and designed mostly to ensure that you don't cheat the government out of its cut of your tax-deferred funds.

But secondarily, the rules are there to make sure you don't do anything foolish by mistake that might cause you to cheat *yourself* out of your retirement savings. This checklist will help you to structure the alternative investment in your account properly so that you do not miss an essential detail that might derail things before they get started and do damage to your account.

Ask Ed . . .

Q: What if I lend my IRA funds to a family member but receive a fair market interest rate, or even charge a higher interest rate to make sure I am dealing the same as I would with a stranger?

A: Dealing with family members when it comes to your IRA is a prohibited transaction because you are considered to be self-dealing.

What's In It for Me?

The bottom line is that making alternative investments in your IRA is usually not the problem. It is what the IRS says you can and cannot do in making them that is the problem. The prohibitions mainly involve what is called "self-dealing," which can be defined as using the funds in your account for your benefit not that of the account. I know this sounds like splitting hairs, but the IRS looks at your retirement ac-

Ask Ed . . .

Q: You say that if an IRA transaction is prohibited, the entire IRA balance becomes subject to tax and penalty. What if I used only *part* of my IRA funds for the investment and the transaction turned out to be a prohibited transaction? Is my entire IRA still subject to tax or just the part I invested?

A: Your entire IRA is subject to tax and penalty even if you only used a small percentage of it. But a way to avoid this potential nightmare is to first split your IRA into two IRAs. The tax and penalty would then apply only to the IRA making the investment. Your other one is spared.

count (and insists that you look at it too) as a *separate entity* from you. This means that even though it is your savings account, you cannot just treat it as another pocket to dip into for cash you may need to make any old investment. If you do, your entire account may become taxable due to a prohibited transaction penalty, and you could end up taking such a hit that your nest egg is depleted.

The crux of the matter is this: Prohibited transactions are there to monitor alternative IRA investing—and that is why this checklist is so important to review before investing in a choice piece of real estate you've seen that tickles your fancy more than traditional mutual fund investing. Of course, even if you are able to steer clear of all the potential traps involved in alternative investing and prohibited transactions, you should still follow the main precept of wise investing, which is to put money only into what you *know and understand;* otherwise, there is a real chance that you could still lose out big-time.

Ask Ed...

Q: **If I am allowed to invest in the stock of businesses like Microsoft, General Electric or other big, listed companies, can I invest my IRA funds in the stock of my own business too?**

A: The answer is no precisely because it is your business and, therefore, you exercise control over all business decisions. That is considered "self-dealing," whereas even though you may own Microsoft stock, Bill Gates does not have to call YOU whenever he wants to make a decision about Microsoft operations. The fact that your business may be a better investment for your IRA is meaningless as far as the self-dealing rules are concerned—unless you brought in someone else (unrelated to you) to run your business for you. Then you might qualify to invest your IRA in your own business.

What If I Don't?

The big benefit of using plan funds for an alternative investment is that the gain (or income) is not taxed until you take a distribution from the SDIRA. But wait . . . there's a catch (surprise! surprise!); some income inside the SDIRA *is* taxed if you invest in certain businesses. Not only is the income taxed, but since your SDIRA is technically speaking a trust, the tax you pay will be at *trust tax rates,* which are the highest rates in the land. This can easily erode profits inside your plan and is just one trap you could fall into if you blast ahead without going over this checklist.

Ask Ed . . .

Q: **If I have real estate in my IRA and I sell it at a huge profit, is there any way to get any of those profits out of the IRA at capital gains rates?**

A: No. All distributions from IRAs are taxable at ordinary income tax rates. The only way you can beat the tax on real estate or any business profits in an IRA is if the IRA is a Roth IRA (see this section, Part 11). Roth IRA funds are already taxed money so that is the best type of IRA money to use for alternative IRA investments like real estate and businesses. The distributions from a Roth IRA will generally be tax-free, which is much better than any capital gains rates, since you cannot beat zero percent!

Another potential trap is debt financing. You cannot loan money to your account to make investments, but your account can borrow from the accounts of others. If your IRA does borrow, you cannot personally guarantee the loan since that is the same as loaning money to your IRA, which is a prohibited transaction. Who would make a loan to your IRA without a guarantee that you will pay them back, you may be asking. Believe it or not, many individuals and banks will. It is becoming a booming business to target the growing balances in IRAs and the number of people looking at nontraditional investments such as real estate for loan opportunities. These lenders are called "nonrecourse lenders," which means they will loan your IRA money to buy property with just the property as their collateral and no personal guarantee from you. They generally will only lend you an amount up to a certain percentage of the property's value so that if your IRA cannot repay the loan, they can just take the property in foreclosure. If you are able to arrange the nonrecourse financing for property you buy in your IRA, you could still lose the property and your life savings at the same time if you do not know what you are doing. And if you

Ask Ed . . .

Q: **Why do you focus on the rules for making nontraditional investments in IRAs? Don't they apply to 401(k)s or other company plans?**

A: Yes, most of these rules apply to company plans as well. In fact, qualified plans like a 401(k) allow a broader range of options than an IRA, at least as far as prohibited investments are concerned. For example, you can invest in life insurance in a company plan, even though that is prohibited in an IRA. And with a 401(k) certain debt-financed real-estate-related income taxes that you could end up paying in your SDIRA do not apply. But the reason I reference IRAs mostly is that most 401(k)s will never let you do self-directed investing within the plan. They just don't want the liability or the administrative headaches of allowing thousands of employees to start putting their 401(k) funds into real estate and all kinds of other nontraditional investments. They feel it could easily get out of control, in addition to which many employees may not be sophisticated enough as investors to steer clear of the many tax traps with these investments.

make money, some of that money will be subject to income tax now because it comes from a debt-financed asset.

Instructions

Before you even consider making any type of IRA or plan investment other than stocks, bonds, mutual funds, or CDs, consult this checklist to see if there is a chance it could be deemed a prohibited transaction. If you are still unsure, this tells you something too, and you should perhaps not engage in the transaction.

The penalty for engaging in a prohibited transaction with your IRA funds is so severe that you should always err on the side of caution. Measure your nontraditional investment selection against each point in this checklist to see if it will stand up to the Ed Slott test: (1) Is the investment for you, and (2) Can you make the investment without violating the self-dealing rules?

Ask Ed . . .

Q: **What if my IRA owns an interest in an apartment building and I pay some of the maintenance bills personally, but am reimbursed by my IRA? Is that a prohibited transaction?**

A: Yes. Paying bills for an investment owned by your IRA is the same as loaning money to your IRA, and loaning money to your IRA is a prohibited transaction.

Also, as you reflect on this checklist, consider the long-term impact on your beneficiaries of having the types of nontraditional investments you are thinking about. If you die holding these types of nontraditional investments, you will want to make sure your beneficiaries know what to do about taking RMDs after they inherit. Which then begs the question, Will they understand these types of investments as well as you do—e.g., what should be sold and for what price? Think this through as you go over the checklist, then have a conversation with your family.

After that, go over everything again with your accountant or financial advisor, or plan custodian, as one final precaution that everything you are doing is okay—before you take the big step and actually do it.

A Word to the Wise

The Right Way to Reduce Risk Investing IRAs in Nontraditional Assets

- Establish separate IRAs for each nonstandard asset.
- Assemble a team of professional experts and use them.
- Only buy assets from unrelated third parties.
- Don't use the asset for personal use, and that includes allowing family members use of the asset.
- Check the scenario with your IRA custodian.
- If you are unsure if it is a prohibited transaction, ask the Department of Labor (DOL) for approval before doing the transaction.
- Don't try to use your professional expertise to benefit your IRA asset (buy a piece of land and use your architectural firm to draw up the plans for the building to go on the land).
- Don't rely on the "expertise" of family members.

THE ALTERNATIVE INVESTMENTS AND PROHIBITED TRANSACTIONS CHECKLIST

MY NAME: _____ DATE: _____

MY ADVISOR'S NAME: _____ PLAN #: _____

Follow-ups should be added to the To Do lists at the end of this checklist

WARNING: Are you aware of the risks of making nontraditional IRA investments? Violation of the rules could result in the disqualification of your IRA, leaving your entire account balance subject to income tax (and a 10 percent penalty if you are under age 59½). Generally you will need a self-directed IRA custodian to hold your IRA.

1. What types of transactions are prohibited?

- Borrowing from or lending money to my account. _____

- Pledging my account as security. _____

- Buying, selling, or leasing any property to or from my account. _____

- Buying property for personal use with funds from my account. _____

- Investing in my own business or in a business wherein I or any other prohibited participant have a majority interest. _____

- Receiving compensation for managing my account. _____

- Disguised transactions—doing business with an LLC or multiple entities in which I, or other prohibited participants, have a majority interest (this includes the purchase of insurance through other entities). _____

2. What types of investments are prohibited?

- Collectibles (art, rugs, antiques, gems, stamps, alcoholic beverages, etc.). (Exceptions are made for some coins and metals.) _____

- Owning life insurance in my account. _____

- Funds used to purchase prohibited investments are considered to be distributed and taxable to me in the year the investment was purchased. The 10 percent early-distribution penalty will apply if I am under the age of 59½.

3. Who is considered a prohibited participant?

- Myself. _____

- A beneficiary of my account. _____

- My fiduciary (anyone who exercises or has discretionary authority, control, or responsibility in managing or administering my account or in disposing of its assets; or who provides investment advice to me on the account for a fee or has any authority or responsibility to do so.

- Members of my family (spouse, parents, lineal descendant, and any spouse of a lineal descendant).

4. My IRA assets must be kept separate from my personal assets, and:

- No prohibited participants can work for my IRA investment.

- No prohibited participants can do maintenance, repairs, or remodeling on property owned by my IRA.

- No prohibited participants can use their personal funds to pay bills due on investments in my IRA, even if my IRA reimburses them.

- No prohibited participants can use any property in the IRA for any personal use, not even to store unused personal property.

- No prohibited participant can receive any personal benefit from my IRA investments.

5. Tax benefits such as capital gains, step up in basis, depreciation, and losses cannot be taken advantage of for investments inside my IRA.

6. Financing inside my IRA will be more difficult because:

- I must use nonrecourse loans.

- I cannot lend money to my IRA or personally guarantee a loan for it.

- Debt-financed income may be subject to Unrelated Debt Financed Income (UDFI) taxes.

7. I understand that all of the preceding rules and warnings apply to the investment of my IRA funds in any business owned by my IRA, any other prohibited participant (including myself), or any other person or entity if the IRA investment could be construed to be a conflict of interest or provide a benefit to me.

Comments: _____

_____

_____

_____

_____

8. If the proposed nontraditional investment triggers a tax on my IRA's income:

- Unrelated Business Income Tax (UBIT) is assessed on in-   _____
  come earned by a business owned by the IRA, e.g. a pizza
  parlor.

- UBIT is calculated at trust tax rates.   _____

- Exceptions to UBIT include investment income, royalties,   _____
  rent from real and personal property (rent from personal
  property cannot exceed 50 percent), gains on the sale of
  property—except for business inventory).

- The first $1,000 of income is exempt from UBIT.   _____

- If my investment is debt-financed, income in the IRA at-   _____
  tributable to the debt-financed portion of the investment
  is subject to Unrelated Debt Financed Income (UDFI) tax.

- Both taxes are reported on Form 990-T, which is signed   _____
  by the self-directed IRA custodian, and the tax is paid
  from IRA funds. (Note: The payment of the tax is an expense of the IRA and is not considered a distribution
  subject to income tax.)

9. To avoid disqualification, I will: _____

- Assemble a team of professional advisors for their exper-   _____
  tise in investment selection.

- Choose a self-directed IRA custodian to hold my IRA and   _____
  check my investment scenario.

- Ask the Department of Labor for approval before going   _____
  ahead with the transaction if I am unsure whether it is
  prohibited.

- Not use my professional expertise or resources (or those   _____
  of other disqualified participants) to benefit my IRA.

- Consider using a Roth IRA for the investment (if the   _____
  transaction is disqualified, there is generally no tax effect;
  if it works, earnings will be income-tax-free).

10. Make sure my named beneficiaries are capable of managing this IRA if they were to inherit it. _____

11. Make sure I fully understand this investment and invest only in what I know. _____

Comments: _____

_____

_____

_____

_____

12. If buying real estate in a self-directed IRA:

• Have I evaluated the benefits of purchasing the real estate outside of the IRA assuming I have the ability to do so? (REMINDER: The following tax benefits are not available when real estate is purchased in the IRA. Capital gains tax rates, step up in basis, depreciation and other related deductions, and losses.) _____

• Do I have enough cash in the IRA to purchase the property and pay all the annual expenses on it for as long as I own it? _____

• Have I found a nonrecourse lender to work with me if I must borrow? _____

• Have all payments to purchase the real estate come from my IRA (including the initial deposit) and do all documents show the title of my IRA account as the property owner? _____

Comments: _____

_____

_____

_____

_____

13. Will I need to establish separate self-directed IRAs for each nontraditional investment? _____

14. I understand that annual fair market valuations will be required for my investment (this may require the help of an expert). _____

15. I should periodically review the prohibited transactions and prohibited participant rules to ensure that I am not violating them with the nontraditional investment in my IRA.   _____

16. I understand that required distributions will begin at age 70½ or upon my death. If there is no liquidity in the IRA or no other IRAs from which to make the distribution, then distributions of shares of the investment will have to be made to me or to my beneficiaries. Thus, a valuation of the asset will have to be established as of the prior year-end to calculate the correct RMD, and a valuation of the distributed share will have to be established as of the distribution date to ensure that I have taken the correct RMD amount.   _____

Comments: _____

_____

_____

_____

_____

Follow-Up

My To Do List	Date Completed
1	
2	
3	
4	
5	
6	
7	
8	
9	
10	

_____   _____
My Signature   Date

Part 11

THE ROTH IRA CONVERSION
CHECKLIST

For account owners

What It Does

Here's a quick Roth IRA conversion fact sheet:

- To "convert" means to roll your traditional IRA to a Roth IRA. (Beginning in 2008 you will be able to roll employer plan funds to a Roth IRA)
- Traditional IRAs include SEP and SIMPLE IRAs and those funds can also be converted to Roth IRAs.
- There is no need to have earned income, or any income to be able to convert.
- There is no limit on the amount of traditional IRA or plan funds that can be converted as long as you qualify to convert to a Roth IRA.
- You cannot convert if your modified adjusted gross income (MAGI) exceeds $100,000, or if you file married separate. The Tax Increase Prevention and Reconciliation Act (TIPRA) eliminates these requirements beginning in 2010.

- You pay ordinary income tax on the amount you convert to a Roth IRA.
- You can undo a Roth conversion for any reason whatsoever, up to October 15 of the year following the year of the Roth conversion. If you convert in 2007, you have until October 15, 2008, to change your mind and undo part or all of the 2007 Roth IRA conversion.
- Contributions and converted amounts can be withdrawn at any time.
- Withdrawals are income-tax-free forever to you and/or your named beneficiaries if the withdrawal is qualified: You have held the account for a minimum of 5 years (the 5-year period begins with the establishment of the Roth IRA), and, in addition, have met any *one* of the following conditions: (1) You are at least 59½ (withdrawals of converted amounts before age 59½ within the 5-year exclusion period for that conversion will be subject to a 10 percent penalty on the amount withdrawn); (2) Death; (3) Disability; (4) You withdraw as a first-time homebuyer (maximum lifetime cap of $10,000 per IRA owner).

These are the facts, and they are all well and good. But here's the question: *Should* you convert your traditional IRA to a Roth IRA or roll over your plan funds to a traditional IRA so that you can convert to a Roth IRA, which the tax laws currently require you to do if you have a 401(k) or other employer-sponsored plan (as of 2008 you will be able to roll your employer funds to a Roth)? The answers to these questions are what you will find as you go through this checklist. And if you can and do convert to a Roth IRA, you should continue making contributions afterward, if you qualify. See the following fact sheet to keep your Roth happy and healthy.

I am a big fan of the Roth IRA. They are great for account owners because earnings and distributions are tax-free, and they are great for named inheritors who will get to receive an income-tax-free inheritance. If the value of your estate could be large enough to be subject to estate tax, your inheritors will reap another benefit from your hav-

A Quick Fact Sheet

Roth IRA Contributions

- You contribute already taxed funds (after-tax funds) to a Roth IRA.
- You receive no tax deduction for your Roth IRA contribution.
- You can continue to contribute to a Roth IRA after age 70½.
- Qualified withdrawals are income-tax free (a withdrawal made after the account has been established for 5 years and the Roth owner is over the age of 59½ or qualifies for the first-time homebuyer exception).
- You can also have and contribute to a spousal Roth IRA, based on your income even if your spouse has no income.
- Withdrawals of your contribution or converted amounts are always income-tax free.
- Withdrawals of converted amounts may be subject to the 10 percent early distribution penalty if the 5-year exclusion period has not been met and the Roth owner is under age 59½ at the time of the withdrawal.
- Withdrawals of earnings may be taxed and subject to the 10 percent early distribution penalty if it is not a qualified withdrawal.
- There are no required minimum distributions for Roth IRA owners.
- Roth IRA designated beneficiaries can stretch (extend distributions) over their lifetimes the same as traditional IRA beneficiaries.

ing converted because the income tax you will have paid on the conversion will reduce the overall size of your estate. All that being said, I would never tell you to go full speed ahead and convert to a Roth IRA without having first examined for yourself the tax costs and benefits, the pros and the cons, of doing so. This checklist will guide you through that process so you can make your own determination and be able to follow through properly if your decision is yes.

Ask Ed . . .

Q: **You mentioned MAGI. What the heck is that?**

A: MAGI (modified adjusted gross income) is a totally made-up term that appears absolutely nowhere on your tax return. It's put in the tax code to drive you insane, and it works. But for current (but ending in 2010) Roth IRA conversion eligibility you must know what your MAGI is. You figure this by starting with your adjusted gross income (AGI), which does appear on your return at the bottom of page one, and involves adding back the following deductions that are applicable to you: IRA contributions; student loan interest payments; tuition and fee payments; foreign-earned income and housing exclusions or deductions; qualified savings bond interest exclusions (from Form 8815); and exclusions of employer-provided adoption benefits (shown on Form 8839). You then subtract required distributions and the amount of the conversion subject to income tax to find your MAGI for Roth IRA conversion eligibility, which currently stands at a $100,000 limit for all taxpayers, except those filing married separate, who are *not permitted* to convert to a Roth IRA. But again, all such roadblocks will disappear for Roth IRA converters in 2010.

What's In It for Me?

A big benefit of converting to a Roth IRA is that a Roth comes with one of the few built-in second chances permitted by the tax code. It's called "recharacterization." And it means this: If the funds you convert grow in the Roth IRA, you can keep them, but if your investments tank, you get to undo the conversion and remove any tax you would have owed on the value that no longer exists. You have until October 15 of the year following the year of the conversion to change your mind (for any reason at all). It's like getting to bet on a horse after the race is over. What a deal!

Also, a Roth conversion is not an all-or-nothing proposition. If you wish, you can convert just a portion of your traditional IRA should you just want to dip your toes in the Roth IRA waters.

Ask Ed . . .

Q: **A change to the tax code in 2005 allows RMDs to be excluded from MAGI for Roth IRA conversion purposes. Does this new RMD provision allow RMDs to be excluded for other tax provisions, like taxation of social security?**

A: No. It only allows you to exclude RMDs for purposes of Roth conversion eligibility, and that's it. Your RMDs still count as income—that is, as part of your adjusted gross income—for all other tax provisions, so no extra break here.

Some will say that converting to a Roth does not pay if you will be in a lower tax bracket when you are ready to withdraw from your traditional IRA. That can be true—sometimes. But even so, you don't know what future tax rates will be when the time comes to have to start paying the piper on your deferred account earnings. At least a Roth IRA takes the uncertainty out of future tax rates since you cannot beat their now-and-forever zero percent tax rate on withdrawals.

With this checklist, you will know once and for all if a Roth IRA conversion is right for you *at this time.* And if not, you will have the checklist available to go back to for future reconsideration should events in your life occur that may change your situation or rationale.

What If I Don't?

As noted earlier, the checklist points out some of the reasons why a Roth IRA conversion may not be right for you at this time. For example it does not pay to convert to a Roth IRA if you will be withdrawing early (before age 59½), as this could subject your converted funds

Ask Ed . . .

Q: Can I convert an RMD from a traditional IRA to a Roth IRA? After all, I've already paid the tax, so this should be okay, right?

A: Wrong! You cannot convert any funds from your traditional IRA to a Roth IRA until you take your RMD even if your MAGI does not exceed the $100,000 income limitation, and you qualify to convert. A Roth conversion is a rollover and an RMD cannot be rolled over (it says so in IRS Regulation § 1.408A-4). Once you satisfy your RMD, then any amount remaining in your IRA can be converted as long as your MAGI (which now does not include your RMD) does not exceed $100,000 and you are not married filing separately.

and earnings to the same 10 percent penalty you would get hit with by withdrawing early from a traditional IRA or other plan. Likewise, it would not be worthwhile to convert if you do not intend to hold on to the Roth long-term (i.e., at least the minimum five-year holding period to avoid paying a penalty, but better yet at least ten years to give your funds in the account a chance to bloom tax-free).

It also does not pay to convert if you don't have the money to pay the tax on the conversion, or you may need to tap into your traditional IRA to pay the tax. After all, you don't want to go broke converting. Furthermore, a Roth IRA conversion may not be for you if you are older; you may not have the years left to recoup the tax you will have to pay now for the conversion.

If you are in need of a tax deduction now, you are better off contributing to your traditional IRA or company plan rather than converting to a Roth. But if that is all that's holding you back from converting, I would rethink this short-term strategy and look long term instead. A deduction might save you in taxes now, but you'll pay for it later when the IRS becomes a partner on your tax-deferred IRA or other distributions for the rest of your life. You'll miss out on what I believe is the

Ask Ed . . .

Q: **I won't know if I will qualify for a Roth IRA conversion until after the end of the year, and by then it will be too late to convert for the past year, so what do I do?**

A: Convert anyway. It pays to do the conversion even if you are not sure if you will qualify. One of the great features of the Roth conversion is that you can always undo (recharacterize) it for any reason and you have up to October 15 of the year following the year you convert to do so. Also, if it is early in the year, you can plan to keep your income under the 100,000-dollar limitation (if that is the problem) by doing things like not taking capital gains or increasing your plan contributions.

greatest opportunity in the tax code to build a tax-free retirement savings account for yourself, then pass it on to your children and grandchildren. So don't be intimidated by the thought of conversion. This checklist is easy to navigate; use it so that you don't miss out.

Ask Ed . . .

Q: **Can my beneficiaries stretch my Roth IRA over their lifetimes the same way they can with an inherited traditional IRA?**

A: Yes, the distributions rules are the same, but even better, those distributions will generally be tax-free. I say "generally" tax-free because they could be taxable to your beneficiaries if you had not held the Roth for the five-year holding period before you died and your beneficiaries started withdrawing. But even in that case, only the earnings withdrawn before the five-year period is up are taxable; after that all distributions taken by your heirs are tax-free forever.

Instructions

If there is any magic at all to building retirement wealth (and building it fast), the magic lies in keeping your money away from the government for the longest possible amount of time, preferably forever, which is what Roth IRAs are all about. So go over each point in the checklist, which addresses all the benefits and the costs of converting to a Roth IRA, as you answer *for yourself* the following question: "Why on earth would I voluntarily pay tax on my retirement funds before I have to?"

Your answer may be, "I wouldn't." If so, then you can move on and, perhaps, come back to revisit that answer another day.

Or, your answer could be, "Sure I'll have to pay tax up front, but in the overall scheme of things it will be a relatively small amount compared to the tax-free windfall I and my family could benefit from long term."

Don't make your decision in a vacuum. Review this checklist of advantages and disadvantages of a Roth IRA conversion with your spouse if you have one, and your children, too, if they are to be your beneficia-

Ask Ed . . .

Q: **What if I do not know my RMD amount yet, but want to convert to a Roth?**

A: You need to calculate your RMD and withdraw it before you can convert any amounts to a Roth IRA. Your RMD amount is based on the prior year's December 31 balance in your account. Your plan custodian (bank, broker, fund company, or other financial institution holding your account) must provide you with the RMD calculation for your account if you request it, so request it, then you'll know. Or calculate it yourself (see "My RMD Calculations Checklist" Section II, Part 5) at the beginning of the year you are thinking about converting.

ries. For that matter, go over this checklist with your own parents; they may still be young enough to gain from a Roth IRA conversion if they qualify, not only for your benefit, but theirs, too. Remember to tell them that the tax laws will change in 2010 to make anyone eligible to convert thereafter, and with special tax payment deals too; so if they will be reaching age 59½ by then, or if you will, converting now (if currently eligible) and getting that 5-year clock rolling for tax-free distributions should factor into everyone's thinking.

Ask Ed . . .

Q: **If I am not eligible to make a Roth IRA conversion now due to the income limit, but would like to convert someday when able, what can I do?**

A: It may seem counterintuitive, but if you haven't already, you start stuffing all you can into your traditional IRA (or SEP or SIMPLE IRA) or company plan right now, as you will be able to convert everything in 2010, regardless of income. So, the more you have in your traditional IRA (deductible or nondeductible) or other plan, the more that can be converted. And for conversions done in 2010, you will be permitted to spread the tax bite over 2 years instead of having to pay taxes on the conversion all at once. The tax-free earnings in the Roth during that time could cover a chunk of the tax bill, or you can start on the way now to accumulating the funds that will be needed to pay the income taxes on the conversion.

THE ROTH IRA CONVERSION CHECKLIST

MY NAME: _____ DATE: _____

MY ADVISOR'S NAME: _____ PLAN #: _____

Follow-ups should be added to the To Do lists at the end of this checklist.

1. Reasons to convert to a Roth IRA:

- Eligible withdrawals from a Roth IRA are tax-free to me _____
  and to my account's named beneficiaries.

- I will have no required minimum distributions (RMDs). _____

- I can continue to make Roth IRA contributions even after _____
  I am age 70½ if I am still working (have earned income).

- I can leave an income-tax-free legacy to my children and _____
  grandchildren who can stretch tax-free distributions over
  their own life expectancies.

- A Roth IRA makes a better trust beneficiary because _____
  qualified distributions are income-tax free.

- If I have a taxable estate, the income tax paid on the _____
  amount converted reduces the value of my total estate
  that will be subject to estate tax.

- Paying the tax now takes the uncertainty out of future _____
  tax rates that go with a tax-deferred account.

- Using Roth funds for an alternative (nontraditional) invest- _____
  ment will lessen the impact if the transaction is prohibited
  since there are no income taxes on Roth distributions.
  (See the Alternative Investments and Prohibited Transactions Checklist in this section, Part 10.)

- I can do a partial conversion in any year that I qualify and _____
  do not have to convert everything at one time.

Comments: _____

_____

_____

_____

2. Disadvantages of converting to a Roth IRA:

- I will have to pay income tax on the amount I convert at _____
  my tax rate for the year (possibly pushing me into a
  higher tax bracket).

- I do not receive a tax deduction for contributions. _____

- I could be subject to a 10 percent early distribution penalty if I withdraw before age 59½. (The same is true of a tax-deferred account.) _____

- I don't have the money to pay the income tax on the conversion unless I tap into my traditional IRA or other plan funds to pay the income tax. _____

- I am older and need my traditional IRA or other plan funds to live on and/or I do not wish to leave my beneficiaries an income-tax-free legacy. _____

- I need the tax deduction now and don't want to pay the income tax. _____

- I know for sure that I will be in a much lower tax bracket when I am eligible to start taking my traditional IRA or other plan distributions. _____

- The increased income can affect the taxability of my social security income, my income tax deductions, exemptions, and the ability to use tax credits. _____

Comments: _____

_____

_____

_____

3. Distributions are income-tax free if I meet the following Roth distribution requirements:

- I have held the account for 5 years (the 5-year period begins on the first day of the first year a Roth account is established). _____

- And, I have reached the age of 59½, or the payment is because of death, disability, or a first-time home purchase ($10,000 lifetime maximum per IRA owner). _____

4. Distributions from Roth IRAs come first from annual contributions, then converted amounts—taxable amounts, then nontaxable, and lastly from earnings. If a distribution is not qualified, taxes and penalties depend on the 5-year exclusion periods that apply to the type of Roth IRA funds distributed (contributions, conversions, earnings). _____

5. Distributions of annual Roth IRA contributions can be withdrawn at any time for any reason tax- and penalty-free. _____

6. If I have an immediate need for cash from the Roth _____
   and have met the 5-year exclusion period for conversions, withdrawals of converted funds will be tax- and
   penalty-free even if taken before I am 59½.

Comments: _____

_____

_____

_____

_____

7. I understand that in order to convert any employer plan _____
   funds to a Roth IRA, I must first roll those funds to a traditional IRA, then convert them to the Roth. (This requirement is eliminated as of 2008.)

8. I must have $100,000 or less in modified adjusted _____
   gross income (MAGI) to do a conversion. (See IRS Publication 590 for the latest version of the MAGI formula.)
   This requirement is eliminated in 2010.

• The amount converted is not counted in the $100,000 _____
  MAGI limit.

9. I cannot do a Roth IRA conversion if I am married, filing _____
   separately. (This requirement is eliminated in 2010).

10. If I am 70½ or older, I must take my RMD from my tra- _____
    ditional IRA for the year before doing a conversion,
    and cannot convert the RMD amount.

11. If I put off (or have to wait to become eligible) convert- _____
    ing to a Roth IRA, for conversions done in 2010 only,
    the tax can be paid ratably in 2011 and 2012.

12. The pro rata rule applies to funds I convert from a tra- _____
    ditional IRA that contains both pretax and after-tax
    amounts. I cannot convert the after-tax amounts only,
    even if they are in a separate IRA. (See the RMD Cal-
    culations Checklist in Section II, Part 5.)

13. I understand there is a 5-year exclusion period for _____
    each conversion (if I do 5 conversions over 5 years, I
    have 5 different exclusion periods), and that:

Converted funds withdrawn before the 5-year exclusion period ends are subject to the 10 percent early distribution penalty if I am under the age of 59½ at the time of the distribution. _____

I must keep track of each 5-year holding period, as follows: _____

_____   _____
Date of Conversion   Amount

_____   _____
Date of Conversion   Amount

Comments: _____

_____

_____

_____

_____

14. **Recharacterization allows me to undo my Roth IRA conversion for any reason, and I have until October 15 of the year after the conversion to do so. To recharacterize I must:**

• Notify both the Roth IRA custodian and the traditional IRA custodian that I am recharacterizing. _____

• Transfer the amount I wish to recharacterize, plus or minus earnings or losses, to the traditional IRA via a trustee-to-trustee (direct) transfer. _____

• Amend my tax return to get a refund of the income taxes paid on the recharacterized amount if I recharacterize after filing. _____

• Conversions that fail because I don't meet the eligibility requirements should be recharacterized by the October 15 deadline. And if I miss the deadline: _____

—The amount converted becomes an excess contribution subject to annual penalties as long as it remains in the Roth IRA. _____

—I will need an IRS Private Letter Ruling allowing an extension of time for doing the recharacterization. _____

15. I can do a partial recharacterization and do not have to recharacterize the entire converted amount, but I cannot choose to recharacterize only assets that have lost value unless they are in a separate Roth IRA account I have established for that purpose. _____

16. I should consider making all current conversions to a new Roth IRA account until the time to recharacterize expires. _____

Comments: _____

_____

_____

_____

17. If I am not eligible to do a Roth IRA conversion now, but will qualify in 2010 when the tax law changes to allow anyone to do a Roth IRA conversion of IRA or other plan funds, I should prepare now by:

• Maximizing contributions to my current retirement plan in order to make the most of the conversion opportunity in 2010. _____

• Consider making nondeductible IRA and employer plan contributions to maximize the amount available for conversion to a Roth IRA in 2010. _____

• Start accumulating the funds that will be necessary to pay the taxes on the conversion. _____

Comments: _____

_____

_____

_____

_____

Follow-Up

My To Do List	Date Completed
1 _____	_____
2 _____	_____
3 _____	_____

4 _____

5 _____

6 _____

7 _____

8 _____

9 _____

10 _____

_____   _____

My Signature   Date

Section V

THE FOLLOW-UP CARE SOLUTION

If you have reached this section, it means you have looked under the hood of your owned or inherited retirement account and checked upward of 250 items to determine how healthy it is and how long and fruitful a life it potentially has. Now you fully understand what I meant in my introduction about most people being financial daredevils when it comes to the care of their retirement accounts. Even the rare few of you who may have looked under the hood from time to time really had no idea just how *many* moving parts should be checked, did you? But now that you have completed my diagnostic, you have a greater appreciation of just how much money you can lose and how much planning can be derailed by just one neglected or mistakenly executed item or transaction. And you are at last almost free of daredevil-itis.

"*Almost?*" you ask. "What *else* could there possibly be left to check?"

Good question, and this section, which in effect serves as the safety net for your safety net, will provide the answer. It is designed to make sure that the route you have mapped for your money will remain free of ruts that might otherwise become huge potholes if not quickly paved along the way. This assurance comes from follow-up, a process involving two more moving parts.

Since many aspects of retirement account care and distribution planning are based on a calendar-year schedule, it is important to take a final look under the hood of your account as the books close each year by doing an annual year-end checkup. That's the first part.

You also will need the specialized help of a tax attorney and/or financial and legal professional to draw up key documents and execute key transactions for you. You want them to do so correctly, the first time. That means being sure the advisors you use are experienced in these matters and well up to the task, which is where the last moving part of my care solution comes in—the Advisor Checkup Tool.

Part 1

MY YEAR-END CHECKLIST

For account owners and beneficiaries

Ask Ed . . .

Q: **You say this year-end checkup is for beneficiaries too? How so?**

A: If you are or will be a plan beneficiary, you will know from going through the various checklists in Section III that there are many timely decisions that have to be made and requirements that have to be met by year-end or even earlier in order to inherit properly (retain the stretch option, for example). Also, beneficiaries of inherited accounts are subject to taking Required Minimum Distributions too and the same 50 percent penalty applies if they miss one or take a wrong amount. This goes equally for Roth IRA beneficiaries. They have to take RMDs from their inherited Roth IRAs by year-end, even though the distributions are tax-free.

What It Does

So how do you follow up on your retirement savings? You can't call your money and ask it how it's doing (though I know many people who do talk to their money all the time. No comment). You follow up by, among other things, making sure that each one of your key retirement account transactions is checked and that you have taken care of all your To Do's.

As you should know by now, whenever you move IRA or other plan money, or take distributions, bad things can happen, and it only takes one mistake, or one bungled keystroke by a data entry person at a financial institution to end a retirement account by causing it to be taxed and stripped of its sheltered status.

There is one sure thing about IRA and plan distribution mistakes; eventually they get found out. Every time money is distributed from a retirement account, a Form 1099-R is generated by your plan custodian, and copies go to you and almost everywhere else, including, of course, to the IRS. So if a mistake is made by you, your plan custodian, your advisor, or anyone else, it will get picked up, often too late for you to do anything about it except pay through the nose.

The most common mistake is missing a Required Minimum Distribution, which will trigger an immediate 50 percent penalty on the

Ask Ed . . .

Q: **I notice you include Roth conversions on your year-end checklist. Can't those be undone even after the end of the year in the event of a mistake or change of mind? So, what's the problem?**

A: Yes, Roth conversions can be reversed (technical term: recharacterized) up to October 15 of the year after the conversion. The reason Roth conversions are on this checklist is to remind you to get them done by year-end if you decide to convert. You don't have until April 15 to do a conversion for the previous year.

amount that should have been withdrawn. But there are others. And this checklist will help you identify all those potential problem areas—the timely maneuvers you must make—and remind you to take one more look before year-end to make sure you have taken care of them.

What's in It for Me?

You'll avoid a potential mess, as well as save your money and lots of time by eliminating years of paperwork, letter writing to the IRS, complaining to your advisors, begging the government for mercy, and beseeching your attorney for a discount, none of which are productive activities. I know this is true because I receive e-mails daily from people all across the country who are in that boat. They have made a costly error (or it was made by their financial advisor, bank, or broker from not following instructions properly or knowing the rules) and they are desperate to find a way out and turn things around when, in most cases, it is already much too late. You will be very glad this isn't you.

What If I Don't?

Maybe you are an eternal optimist, which is great for your health, but not for your retirement savings. You will be flirting with Murphy's Law, which says that anything that can go wrong, will, and usually at the worst possible time.

Imagine deciding to roll your 401(k) balance of, say, $400,000 to your IRA during the year, instructing your plan custodian accordingly, believing it was done, only to find out too late that the funds never made it into an IRA but ended up in a regular taxable account, due to a clerical coding error. That would mean your having to pay tax on $400,000—plus a $40,000 (10 percent) penalty if you were younger than 59½ at the time (or under age 55 depending on which rule applies to you). Could you get this fixed? Possibly—in fact, probably—but not without an IRS Private Letter Ruling, a process that is expensive and offers no guarantees. You have the best chance of correcting a fund transfer or plan distribution mistake, for example, in the year it is made.

That's why this final check up before year-end is so important. Otherwise, you could not only be flirting with Murphy's Law, but also playing Russian roulette.

Ask Ed . . .

Q: **I just inherited my husband's IRA and plan to roll it over to my own IRA. Must I do the rollover before year-end?**

A: No. There is no deadline for a spousal rollover, but you still should do it as soon as possible because your RMD will likely be lower if you take ownership rather than remain a beneficiary (see Section III, Part 2). Also, if you were to die suddenly before doing the rollover, your beneficiaries might not get the stretch option. Remember, procrastination is a thief, and not just of time.

Instructions

When I say year-end follow-up, I don't mean the literal last day of the year. I mean during the year, perhaps even close to the end, but never really *the* end. It is almost impossible to get anything done in the last week of the year, let alone the last day, when everyone is overwhelmed scurrying about trying to get things done at the last minute so they can get out the door for the holidays. It is in the heat of battle when mistakes are sure to occur. And the last week of any year is a battle in almost all businesses, I can assure you.

For example, I once got a call from a broker on the last business day of the year (Friday, December 30, 2005). He told me he had mistakenly taken a $120,000 distribution for his mother from her retirement account for the year rather than her actual RMD amount, which was about a tenth of that figure. When he asked his firm to correct his mistake by undoing the distribution and putting the funds back in, the firm refused because it was New Year's and not only the books but also the doors were closing. I told him he could go for a PLR on his mother's behalf, claiming his own negligence as the reason, and he would probably get it. But in the meantime, what would Mom say about messing up her IRA? How about, "Gimme back those presents and take this lump of coal, sonny."

Here's a recommendation: Plan to do your year-end checkup *before Thanksgiving*. To me, Thanksgiving signals the end of the year. Most people really don't do much from Thanksgiving until New Year's anyway (unless, of course, you are in a holiday-related business, in which case it is even more unlikely that you will have time to address IRA distribution and other retirement-planning issues, so my Thanksgiving rule applies even more so to you). It's November, and so you will still get to see another statement in time to correct any mistakes or even make planning improvements before the year ends. But if you wait until December, you won't see a statement until, well, January, when year-end has already passed, and it may be either too late to fix a problem or require lots of work and cooperation on the part of your plan custodian to reopen last year's books to make a change just for you. You might need the Jaws of Life.

A Word to the Wise

Instead of thinking of this as your year-end planning checklist, think of it as your "year-round planning checklist." Year-round is even better than before-Thanksgiving planning. It is always the best way to follow up on your plan decisions and transactions, required or otherwise. For example, whenever you move IRA or plan money, that distribution should show up on your next month's statement. So, it makes sense to follow up that month to see if the funds actually made it to the right place in the right amount. If you use this checklist as a reminder from month to month, almost any problem can be fixed or strategy improved upon. It is the passage of time that solidifies most errors, turning them into stone.

MY YEAR-END CHECKLIST

MY NAME: _____ DATE: _____

MY ADVISOR'S NAME: _____ PLAN #: _____

Follow-ups should be added to the To Do lists at the end of this checklist.

Before Year-end

1. **Have I (the owner or beneficiary) satisfied all my required**   _____
   distributions for the year?

• RMDs   _____

• RMDs from inherited Roth IRAs   _____

• Year-of-death RMDs from inherited accounts   _____

• 72(t) early distribution payments   _____

        _____

Comments: _____

_____

_____

_____

_____

2. **For Roth IRA conversions in the current year, company**   _____
   plan funds must be rolled over to a traditional IRA and
   all funds must leave my traditional IRA before year-
   end.

3. **Lump-sum distributions from company plans must be**   _____
   completed in order to qualify for 10-year averaging
   and NUA treatment.

4. **Check to see that all employer stock qualifying for**   _____
   NUA treatment has been transferred to a non-tax-
   deferred account.

5. **Check to see that all 60-day rollovers were completed**   _____
   on time.

6. **If I want to split an inherited account, I must do so by**   _____
   year-end (12/31) if the account owner died the previ-
   ous year.

7. **Check plan beneficiary forms and update them if nec-**   _____
   essary.

Comments: _____

_____

_____

_____

_____

After Year-end

8. Check the 1099-R issued by the plan for accuracy. _____

9. Make sure all checks issued by the plan at year-end are _____
   received and deposited in the appropriate accounts.

10. Check year-end statement for accuracy: _____

• Are all deposits/contributions for the year recorded cor- _____
   rectly?

• Are all distributions for the year recorded correctly? _____

Comments: _____

_____

_____

11. IRA deadlines to meet in the upcoming year:

• 9/30—Beneficiary determination date _____

• 10/15—Roth recharacterization deadline _____

• 10/31—Trust documentation deadline _____

• Pending 60-day rollover deadlines _____

Comments: _____

_____

_____

_____

Follow-Up

My To Do List	Date Completed
1 _____	_____
2 _____	_____
3 _____	_____
4 _____	_____

5 _____

6 _____

7 _____

8 _____

9 _____

10 _____

_____   _____

My Signature   Date

Part 2

MY ADVISOR CHECKUP TOOL

A Dirty Little Secret

This last piece of the retirement distribution-planning puzzle is not a checklist, but rather a lengthy word to the wise, and a tool.

The checklists in this book are to educate you so that:

1. You will become keenly aware of all the issues involved in the proper care and maintenance of your retirement account.
2. You will have a written record of all your choices and decisions, deadlines and reminders, which you can quickly put your hands on, update, and share with your family (who will need this information at some point).

But any truly comprehensive care system cannot be a total do-it-yourself kit. Even a car junkie needs a hotshot mechanic from time to time.

So it is with your retirement savings account, which, as I noted in the introduction, is unlike any other type of asset you own because it is loaded with built-in taxes, complex distribution rules and rigid dead-lines that demand specialized attention at some point to ensure proper execution, the first time. This is why I have stressed throughout this book, and am offering as a final word to the wise to you here, that after you have gone through these checklists on your own, you should work with a financial advisor to execute your wishes. Not just any old finan-cial advisor, either. You need—and your savings deserve—a financial advisor trained specifically in the IRA and retirement plan distribution issues you have just reviewed.

But here's a dirty little secret: Most financial advisors are not that experienced in this area. In fact, about 1 percent are specifically trained and equipped for such hazardous duty—and I am likely being generous with that figure. This means that more than 99 per-cent of all the financial advisors in this country are not prepared or lack the expertise to work with you and your family on the care of your retirement accounts. And that sad statistic is not entirely the fault of the advisors either—because here is another dirty little se-cret: The banks, brokerage firms, and other financial companies they work for do not prepare or encourage them to develop this ex-pertise. Why not? Because most of these institutions are stuck in just one mode—the investing mode. This means they are so focused on that single area that they are virtually ignoring the really big ele-phant in the room—the 76 million baby boomers coming up on re-tirement who need to know (and need to know *now*) how to set up their accumulations and tap into them in the most tax-advantaged way possible.

You see, the job of a financial advisor is not just to make you money (which is certainly important) but also to help you *keep* it. This rounding out of expertise is what truly transforms a reasonably fair or good financial advisor into a great one—indeed, into an *expert* financial advisor. And an expert financial advisor is what you should have now that you've got your retirement planning road map in hand.

What to Do

So, how do you know if your financial advisor is an expert, and, if not, how do you find one that is?

Here's a test. Show this book to your current financial advisor after you have gone through the checklists. If the advisor looks as surprised as you did when you first opened this book at the volume of moving parts under the hood that must be checked, you should feel a red flag rising. And if the advisor becomes outraged when you share some of my observations in this chapter, consider that red flag flying high and look for assistance elsewhere.

If word of mouth or the phone book fails you, here's another checkup tool you can use. It's called "Ed Slott's Elite IRA Advisor Group" and you can find it on my website (www.irahelp.com) by clicking the line Looking for an Advisor Who Knows IRAs? It is my mission to create more competent financial advisors for consumers to use and to educate consumers to expect—indeed demand—a higher level of expertise from the financial advisors they work with. In an effort to accomplish both goals, Ed Slott's Elite IRA Advisor Group is a listing of all the financial advisors across the country I have trained personally.

To become members of this elite group of not just competent but *top-notch* financial advisors, they must first attend my intensive two-day workshop (I refer to it as Basic Training) in retirement account distribution planning. I then give each of them more advanced training year-round where I teach them how to apply the same system of checklists used in this book to better serve their clients and keep them up to date in their education and expertise with my books and articles, my workshops, streaming video on my website, my newsletter, and other alerts. When each Elite Group advisor has completed two years of advanced training, he or she becomes a member of my "Master Elite" group, also listed on the site, where you can review each member by state or, using a zip code search feature, narrow the names down to those closest to your home or business.

I created this registry (the only one of its kind) specifically to help people like you connect with a financial advisor who will know where you are coming from and know how to get you where you want your road map to take you because they are schooled in the same system. Is this the only way to find a competent advisor? Probably not. But it will definitely help to narrow your search.

Can you expect to pay more for the services of an expert financial advisor? Yes, just as you would for the services of any other type of professional with specialized skills and training. But it won't cost a fortune, certainly not in the long run, especially when you consider the cost you would otherwise be paying in grief, time, energy, *and* money undoing the damage a less expensive nonexpert financial advisor can cause.

You Need an Estate-planning Attorney with Special Expertise, Too!

In addition to an expert financial advisor, you likely will also need an estate-planning attorney to craft many of the legal documents referred to throughout this book—a will, trust, powers of attorney, living will, health care proxies, and so on. Here again, just any old estate-planning attorney won't do. When a good portion of your assets consists of your retirement account, you need an estate-planning attorney with the know-how to incorporate that account with all its separate rules and regulations into your *overall* estate plan. Many estate-planning attorneys are not familiar with these rules and, for example, may set up a will or create a trust to handle retirement assets the same way they would any other piece of property. In fact, though most estate-planning attorneys won't admit it, deep down they *hope* you will spend every dime of your retirement savings before you die so that they don't have to deal with it in your estate after you're gone.

The financial advisors I train are always asking me for the name of an attorney who can prepare a trust to inherit an IRA (what I call an "IRA trust") because it is so hard to find one. If you want to see whether your estate-planning attorney is up on this, a good way of telling is to review the checklist in Section IV on naming a trust a beneficiary and ask if he or she is familiar with the many—or *any*—of the points that must be addressed in this one area alone. If not, then you'll know you must look elsewhere to find an attorney that has this specialized knowledge.

You can start by again going to my website and this time clicking the line "Looking for an Attorney Who Knows IRAs?" where all the estate-planning attorneys I have personally trained are listed, also by state. (In creating this listing I want to acknowledge The American Academy of Estate Planning Attorneys, the first attorney group to undergo this specialized training from me.)

If you have taken a lifetime to build your retirement savings and taken time out of your life to go through this book, address all the points it covers that apply to you and your beneficiaries, and create a care plan for yourself, you need a financial advisor and estate-planning attorney capable of carrying out that plan correctly and protecting what you have built. This advisor checkup tool will help achieve that goal.

One last point. If you go to my website to seek the name of financial advisors and estate planning attorneys, you will notice the disclaimer and legal warning. You should read and carefully consider the information in that disclaimer before contacting these professionals.

Appendix I

SINGLE LIFE EXPECTANCY TABLE

To be used for calculating postdeath required distributions to beneficiaries **(from the April 2002 Final Regulations)**

AGE OF IRA OR PLAN BENEFICIARY	LIFE EXPECTANCY (IN YEARS)	AGE OF IRA OR PLAN BENEFICIARY	LIFE EXPECTANCY (IN YEARS)	AGE OF IRA OR PLAN BENEFICIARY	LIFE EXPECTANCY (IN YEARS)
0	82.4				
1	81.6	21	62.1	41	42.7
2	80.6	22	61.1	42	41.7
3	79.7	23	60.1	43	40.7
4	78.7	24	59.1	44	39.8
5	77.7	25	58.2	45	38.8
6	76.7	26	57.2	46	37.9
7	75.8	27	56.2	47	37.0
8	74.8	28	55.3	48	36.0
9	73.8	29	54.3	49	35.1
10	72.8	30	53.3	50	34.2
11	71.8	31	52.4	51	33.3
12	70.8	32	51.4	52	32.3
13	69.9	33	50.4	53	31.4
14	68.9	34	49.4	54	30.5
15	67.9	35	48.5	55	29.6
16	66.9	36	47.5	56	28.7
17	66.0	37	46.5	57	27.9
18	65.0	38	45.6	58	27.0
19	64.0	39	44.6	59	26.1
20	63.0	40	43.6	60	25.2

61	24.4	81	9.7	101	2.7
62	23.5	82	9.1	102	2.5
63	22.7	83	8.6	103	2.3
64	21.8	84	8.1	104	2.1
65	21.0	85	7.6	105	1.9
66	20.2	86	7.1	106	1.7
67	19.4	87	6.7	107	1.5
68	18.6	88	6.3	108	1.4
69	17.8	89	5.9	109	1.2
70	17.0	90	5.5	110	1.1
71	16.3	91	5.2	111+	1.0
72	15.5	92	4.9		
73	14.8	93	4.6		
74	14.1	94	4.3		
75	13.4	95	4.1		
76	12.7	96	3.8		
77	12.1	97	3.6		
78	11.4	98	3.4		
79	10.8	99	3.1		
80	10.2	100	2.9		

Appendix II

UNIFORM LIFETIME TABLE

(For use by all IRA owners and plan participants except those whose named beneficiary for the entire year is a spouse more than 10 years younger than the owner)

AGE OF IRA OWNER OR PLAN PARTICIPANT	LIFE EXPECTANCY (IN YEARS)	AGE OF IRA OWNER OR PLAN PARTICIPANT	LIFE EXPECTANCY (IN YEARS)
70	27.4	93	9.6
71	26.5	94	9.1
72	25.6	95	8.6
73	24.7	96	8.1
74	23.8	97	7.6
75	22.9	98	7.1
76	22.0	99	6.7
77	21.2	100	6.3
78	20.3	101	5.9
79	19.5	102	5.5
80	18.7	103	5.2
81	17.9	104	4.9
82	17.1	105	4.5
83	16.3	106	4.2
84	15.5	107	3.9
85	14.8	108	3.7
86	14.1	109	3.4
87	13.4	110	3.1
88	12.7	111	2.9
89	12.0	112	2.6
90	11.4	113	2.4
91	10.8	114	2.1
92	10.2	115+	1.9

Appendix III

JOINT LIFE EXPECTANCY TABLE

(For use by owners whose spouses are more than 10 years younger)

AGES	0	1	2	3	4	5	6	7	8	9
0	90.0	89.5	89.0	88.6	88.2	87.8	87.4	87.1	86.8	86.5
1	89.5	89.0	88.5	88.1	87.6	87.2	86.8	86.5	86.1	85.8
2	89.0	88.5	88.0	87.5	87.1	86.6	86.2	85.8	85.5	85.1
3	88.6	88.1	87.5	87.0	86.5	86.1	85.6	85.2	84.8	84.5
4	88.2	87.6	87.1	86.5	86.0	85.5	85.1	84.6	84.2	83.8
5	87.8	87.2	86.6	86.1	85.5	85.0	84.5	84.1	83.6	83.2
6	87.4	86.8	86.2	85.6	85.1	84.5	84.0	83.5	83.1	82.6
7	87.1	86.5	85.8	85.2	84.6	84.1	83.5	83.0	82.5	82.1
8	86.8	86.1	85.5	84.8	84.2	83.6	83.1	82.5	82.0	81.6
9	86.5	85.8	85.1	84.5	83.8	83.2	82.6	82.1	81.6	81.0
10	86.2	85.5	84.8	84.1	83.5	82.8	82.2	81.6	81.1	80.6
11	85.9	85.2	84.5	83.8	83.1	82.5	81.8	81.2	80.7	80.1
12	85.7	84.9	84.2	83.5	82.8	82.1	81.5	80.8	80.2	79.7
13	85.4	84.7	84.0	83.2	82.5	81.8	81.1	80.5	79.9	79.2
14	85.2	84.5	83.7	83.0	82.2	81.5	80.8	80.1	79.5	78.9
15	85.0	84.3	83.5	82.7	82.0	81.2	80.5	79.8	79.1	78.5
16	84.9	84.1	83.3	82.5	81.7	81.0	80.2	79.5	78.8	78.1
17	84.7	83.9	83.1	82.3	81.5	80.7	80.0	79.2	78.5	77.8
18	84.5	83.7	82.9	82.1	81.3	80.5	79.7	79.0	78.2	77.5
19	84.4	83.6	82.7	81.9	81.1	80.3	79.5	78.7	78.0	77.3
20	84.3	83.4	82.6	81.8	80.9	80.1	79.3	78.5	77.7	77.0
21	84.1	83.3	82.4	81.6	80.8	79.9	79.1	78.3	77.5	76.8
22	84.0	83.2	82.3	81.5	80.6	79.8	78.9	78.1	77.3	76.5
23	83.9	83.1	82.2	81.3	80.5	79.6	78.8	77.9	77.1	76.3
24	83.8	83.0	82.1	81.2	80.3	79.5	78.6	77.8	76.9	76.1
25	83.7	82.9	82.0	81.1	80.2	79.3	78.5	77.6	76.8	75.9
26	83.6	82.8	81.9	81.0	80.1	79.2	78.3	77.5	76.6	75.8

AGES	0	1	2	3	4	5	6	7	8	9
27	83.6	82.7	81.8	80.9	80.0	79.1	78.2	77.4	76.5	75.6
28	83.5	82.6	81.7	80.8	79.9	79.0	78.1	77.2	76.4	75.5
29	83.4	82.6	81.6	80.7	79.8	78.9	78.0	77.1	76.2	75.4
30	83.4	82.5	81.6	80.7	79.7	78.8	77.9	77.0	76.1	75.2
31	83.3	82.4	81.5	80.6	79.7	78.8	77.8	76.9	76.0	75.1
32	83.3	82.4	81.5	80.5	79.6	78.7	77.8	76.8	75.9	75.0
33	83.2	82.3	81.4	80.5	79.5	78.6	77.7	76.8	75.9	74.9
34	83.2	82.3	81.3	80.4	79.5	78.5	77.6	76.7	75.8	74.9
35	83.1	82.2	81.3	80.4	79.4	78.5	77.6	76.6	75.7	74.8
36	83.1	82.2	81.3	80.3	79.4	78.4	77.5	76.6	75.6	74.7
37	83.0	82.2	81.2	80.3	79.3	78.4	77.4	76.5	75.6	74.6
38	83.0	82.1	81.2	80.2	79.3	78.3	77.4	76.4	75.5	74.6
39	83.0	82.1	81.1	80.2	79.2	78.3	77.3	76.4	75.5	74.5
40	82.9	82.1	81.1	80.2	79.2	78.3	77.3	76.4	75.4	74.5
41	82.9	82.0	81.1	80.1	79.2	78.2	77.3	76.3	75.4	74.4
42	82.9	82.0	81.1	80.1	79.1	78.2	77.2	76.3	75.3	74.4
43	82.9	82.0	81.0	80.1	79.1	78.2	77.2	76.2	75.3	74.3
44	82.8	81.9	81.0	80.0	79.1	78.1	77.2	76.2	75.2	74.3
45	82.8	81.9	81.0	80.0	79.1	78.1	77.1	76.2	75.2	74.3
46	82.8	81.9	81.0	80.0	79.0	78.1	77.1	76.1	75.2	74.2
47	82.8	81.9	80.9	80.0	79.0	78.0	77.1	76.1	75.2	74.2
48	82.8	81.9	80.9	80.0	79.0	78.0	77.1	76.1	75.1	74.2
49	82.7	81.8	80.9	79.9	79.0	78.0	77.0	76.1	75.1	74.1
50	82.7	81.8	80.9	79.9	79.0	78.0	77.0	76.0	75.1	74.1
51	82.7	81.8	80.9	79.9	78.9	78.0	77.0	76.0	75.1	74.1
52	82.7	81.8	80.9	79.9	78.9	78.0	77.0	76.0	75.0	74.1
53	82.7	81.8	80.8	79.9	78.9	77.9	77.0	76.0	75.0	74.0
54	82.7	81.8	80.8	79.9	78.9	77.9	76.9	76.0	75.0	74.0
55	82.6	81.8	80.8	79.8	78.9	77.9	76.9	76.0	75.0	74.0
56	82.6	81.7	80.8	79.8	78.9	77.9	76.9	75.9	75.0	74.0
57	82.6	81.7	80.8	79.8	78.9	77.9	76.9	75.9	75.0	74.0
58	82.6	81.7	80.8	79.8	78.8	77.9	76.9	75.9	74.9	74.0
59	82.6	81.7	80.8	79.8	78.8	77.9	76.9	75.9	74.9	74.0
60	82.6	81.7	80.8	79.8	78.8	77.8	76.9	75.9	74.9	73.9
61	82.6	81.7	80.8	79.8	78.8	77.8	76.9	75.9	74.9	73.9
62	82.6	81.7	80.7	79.8	78.8	77.8	76.9	75.9	74.9	73.9
63	82.6	81.7	80.7	79.8	78.8	77.8	76.8	75.9	74.9	73.9
64	82.5	81.7	80.7	79.8	78.8	77.8	76.8	75.9	74.9	73.9
65	82.5	81.7	80.7	79.8	78.8	77.8	76.8	75.8	74.9	73.9
66	82.5	81.7	80.7	79.7	78.8	77.8	76.8	75.8	74.9	73.9
67	82.5	81.7	80.7	79.7	78.8	77.8	76.8	75.8	74.9	73.9
68	82.5	81.6	80.7	79.7	78.8	77.8	76.8	75.8	74.8	73.9

AGES	0	1	2	3	4	5	6	7	8	9
69	82.5	81.6	80.7	79.7	78.8	77.8	76.8	75.8	74.8	73.9
70	82.5	81.6	80.7	79.7	78.8	77.8	76.8	75.8	74.8	73.9
71	82.5	81.6	80.7	79.7	78.7	77.8	76.8	75.8	74.8	73.8
72	82.5	81.6	80.7	79.7	78.7	77.8	76.8	75.8	74.8	73.8
73	82.5	81.6	80.7	79.7	78.7	77.8	76.8	75.8	74.8	73.8
74	82.5	81.6	80.7	79.7	78.7	77.8	76.8	75.8	74.8	73.8
75	82.5	81.6	80.7	79.7	78.7	77.8	76.8	75.8	74.8	73.8
76	82.5	81.6	80.7	79.7	78.7	77.8	76.8	75.8	74.8	73.8
77	82.5	81.6	80.7	79.7	78.7	77.7	76.8	75.8	74.8	73.8
78	82.5	81.6	80.7	79.7	78.7	77.7	76.8	75.8	74.8	73.8
79	82.5	81.6	80.7	79.7	78.7	77.7	76.8	75.8	74.8	73.8
80	82.5	81.6	80.7	79.7	78.7	77.7	76.8	75.8	74.8	73.8
81	82.4	81.6	80.7	79.7	78.7	77.7	76.8	75.8	74.8	73.8
82	82.4	81.6	80.7	79.7	78.7	77.7	76.8	75.8	74.8	73.8
83	82.4	81.6	80.7	79.7	78.7	77.7	76.8	75.8	74.8	73.8
84	82.4	81.6	80.7	79.7	78.7	77.7	76.8	75.8	74.8	73.8
85	82.4	81.6	80.6	79.7	78.7	77.7	76.8	75.8	74.8	73.8
86	82.4	81.6	80.6	79.7	78.7	77.7	76.7	75.8	74.8	73.8
87	82.4	81.6	80.6	79.7	78.7	77.7	76.7	75.8	74.8	73.8
88	82.4	81.6	80.6	79.7	78.7	77.7	76.7	75.8	74.8	73.8
89	82.4	81.6	80.6	79.7	78.7	77.7	76.7	75.8	74.8	73.8
90	82.4	81.6	80.6	79.7	78.7	77.7	76.7	75.8	74.8	73.8
91	82.4	81.6	80.6	79.7	78.7	77.7	76.7	75.8	74.8	73.8
92	82.4	81.6	80.6	79.7	78.7	77.7	76.7	75.8	74.8	73.8
93	82.4	81.6	80.6	79.7	78.7	77.7	76.7	75.8	74.8	73.8
94	82.4	81.6	80.6	79.7	78.7	77.7	76.7	75.8	74.8	73.8
95	82.4	81.6	80.6	79.7	78.7	77.7	76.7	75.8	74.8	73.8
96	82.4	81.6	80.6	79.7	78.7	77.7	76.7	75.8	74.8	73.8
97	82.4	81.6	80.6	79.7	78.7	77.7	76.7	75.8	74.8	73.8
98	82.4	81.6	80.6	79.7	78.7	77.7	76.7	75.8	74.8	73.8
99	82.4	81.6	80.6	79.7	78.7	77.7	76.7	75.8	74.8	73.8
100	82.4	81.6	80.6	79.7	78.7	77.7	76.7	75.8	74.8	73.8
101	82.4	81.6	80.6	79.7	78.7	77.7	76.7	75.8	74.8	73.8
102	82.4	81.6	80.6	79.7	78.7	77.7	76.7	75.8	74.8	73.8
103	82.4	81.6	80.6	79.7	78.7	77.7	76.7	75.8	74.8	73.8
104	82.4	81.6	80.6	79.7	78.7	77.7	76.7	75.8	74.8	73.8
105	82.4	81.6	80.6	79.7	78.7	77.7	76.7	75.8	74.8	73.8
106	82.4	81.6	80.6	79.7	78.7	77.7	76.7	75.8	74.8	73.8
107	82.4	81.6	80.6	79.7	78.7	77.7	76.7	75.8	74.8	73.8
108	82.4	81.6	80.6	79.7	78.7	77.7	76.7	75.8	74.8	73.8
109	82.4	81.6	80.6	79.7	78.7	77.7	76.7	75.8	74.8	73.8
110	82.4	81.6	80.6	79.7	78.7	77.7	76.7	75.8	74.8	73.8

AGES	0	1	2	3	4	5	6	7	8	9
111	82.4	81.6	80.6	79.7	78.7	77.7	76.7	75.8	74.8	73.8
112	82.4	81.6	80.6	79.7	78.7	77.7	76.7	75.8	74.8	73.8
113	82.4	81.6	80.6	79.7	78.7	77.7	76.7	75.8	74.8	73.8
114	82.4	81.6	80.6	79.7	78.7	77.7	76.7	75.8	74.8	73.8
115+	82.4	81.6	80.6	79.7	78.7	77.7	76.7	75.8	74.8	73.8

AGES	10	11	12	13	14	15	16	17	18	19
10	80.0	79.6	79.1	78.7	78.2	77.9	77.5	77.2	76.8	76.5
11	79.6	79.0	78.6	78.1	77.7	77.3	76.9	76.5	76.2	75.8
12	79.1	78.6	78.1	77.6	77.1	76.7	76.3	75.9	75.5	75.2
13	78.7	78.1	77.6	77.1	76.6	76.1	75.7	75.3	74.9	74.5
14	78.2	77.7	77.1	76.6	76.1	75.6	75.1	74.7	74.3	73.9
15	77.9	77.3	76.7	76.1	75.6	75.1	74.6	74.1	73.7	73.3
16	77.5	76.9	76.3	75.7	75.1	74.6	74.1	73.6	73.1	72.7
17	77.2	76.5	75.9	75.3	74.7	74.1	73.6	73.1	72.6	72.1
18	76.8	76.2	75.5	74.9	74.3	73.7	73.1	72.6	72.1	71.6
19	76.5	75.8	75.2	74.5	73.9	73.3	72.7	72.1	71.6	71.1
20	76.3	75.5	74.8	74.2	73.5	72.9	72.3	71.7	71.1	70.6
21	76.0	75.3	74.5	73.8	73.2	72.5	71.9	71.3	70.7	70.1
22	75.8	75.0	74.3	73.5	72.9	72.2	71.5	70.9	70.3	69.7
23	75.5	74.8	74.0	73.3	72.6	71.9	71.2	70.5	69.9	69.3
24	75.3	74.5	73.8	73.0	72.3	71.6	70.9	70.2	69.5	68.9
25	75.1	74.3	73.5	72.8	72.0	71.3	70.6	69.9	69.2	68.5
26	75.0	74.1	73.3	72.5	71.8	71.0	70.3	69.6	68.9	68.2
27	74.8	74.0	73.1	72.3	71.6	70.8	70.0	69.3	68.6	67.9
28	74.6	73.8	73.0	72.2	71.3	70.6	69.8	69.0	68.3	67.6
29	74.5	73.6	72.8	72.0	71.2	70.4	69.6	68.8	68.0	67.3
30	74.4	73.5	72.7	71.8	71.0	70.2	69.4	68.6	67.8	67.1
31	74.3	73.4	72.5	71.7	70.8	70.0	69.2	68.4	67.6	66.8
32	74.1	73.3	72.4	71.5	70.7	69.8	69.0	68.2	67.4	66.6
33	74.0	73.2	72.3	71.4	70.5	69.7	68.8	68.0	67.2	66.4
34	73.9	73.0	72.2	71.3	70.4	69.5	68.7	67.8	67.0	66.2
35	73.9	73.0	72.1	71.2	70.3	69.4	68.5	67.7	66.8	66.0
36	73.8	72.9	72.0	71.1	70.2	69.3	68.4	67.6	66.7	65.9
37	73.7	72.8	71.9	71.0	70.1	69.2	68.3	67.4	66.6	65.7
38	73.6	72.7	71.8	70.9	70.0	69.1	68.2	67.3	66.4	65.6
39	73.6	72.7	71.7	70.8	69.9	69.0	68.1	67.2	66.3	65.4
40	73.5	72.6	71.7	70.7	69.8	68.9	68.0	67.1	66.2	65.3
41	73.5	72.5	71.6	70.7	69.7	68.8	67.9	67.0	66.1	65.2
42	73.4	72.5	71.5	70.6	69.7	68.8	67.8	66.9	66.0	65.1
43	73.4	72.4	71.5	70.6	69.6	68.7	67.8	66.8	65.9	65.0
44	73.3	72.4	71.4	70.5	69.6	68.6	67.7	66.8	65.9	64.9
45	73.3	72.3	71.4	70.5	69.5	68.6	67.6	66.7	65.8	64.9

AGES	10	11	12	13	14	15	16	17	18	19
46	73.3	72.3	71.4	70.4	69.5	68.5	67.6	66.6	65.7	64.8
47	73.2	72.3	71.3	70.4	69.4	68.5	67.5	66.6	65.7	64.7
48	73.2	72.2	71.3	70.3	69.4	68.4	67.5	66.5	65.6	64.7
49	73.2	72.2	71.2	70.3	69.3	68.4	67.4	66.5	65.6	64.6
50	73.1	72.2	71.2	70.3	69.3	68.4	67.4	66.5	65.5	64.6
51	73.1	72.2	71.2	70.2	69.3	68.3	67.4	66.4	65.5	64.5
52	73.1	72.1	71.2	70.2	69.2	68.3	67.3	66.4	65.4	64.5
53	73.1	72.1	71.1	70.2	69.2	68.3	67.3	66.3	65.4	64.4
54	73.1	72.1	71.1	70.2	69.2	68.2	67.3	66.3	65.4	64.4
55	73.0	72.1	71.1	70.1	69.2	68.2	67.2	66.3	65.3	64.4
56	73.0	72.1	71.1	70.1	69.1	68.2	67.2	66.3	65.3	64.3
57	73.0	72.0	71.1	70.1	69.1	68.2	67.2	66.2	65.3	64.3
58	73.0	72.0	71.0	70.1	69.1	68.1	67.2	66.2	65.2	64.3
59	73.0	72.0	71.0	70.1	69.1	68.1	67.2	66.2	65.2	64.3
60	73.0	72.0	71.0	70.0	69.1	68.1	67.1	66.2	65.2	64.2
61	73.0	72.0	71.0	70.0	69.1	68.1	67.1	66.2	65.2	64.2
62	72.9	72.0	71.0	70.0	69.0	68.1	67.1	66.1	65.2	64.2
63	72.9	72.0	71.0	70.0	69.0	68.1	67.1	66.1	65.2	64.2
64	72.9	71.9	71.0	70.0	69.0	68.0	67.1	66.1	65.1	64.2
65	72.9	71.9	71.0	70.0	69.0	68.0	67.1	66.1	65.1	64.2
66	72.9	71.9	70.9	70.0	69.0	68.0	67.1	66.1	65.1	64.1
67	72.9	71.9	70.9	70.0	69.0	68.0	67.0	66.1	65.1	64.1
68	72.9	71.9	70.9	70.0	69.0	68.0	67.0	66.1	65.1	64.1
69	72.9	71.9	70.9	69.9	69.0	68.0	67.0	66.1	65.1	64.1
70	72.9	71.9	70.9	69.9	69.0	68.0	67.0	66.0	65.1	64.1
71	72.9	71.9	70.9	69.9	69.0	68.0	67.0	66.0	65.1	64.1
72	72.9	71.9	70.9	69.9	69.0	68.0	67.0	66.0	65.1	64.1
73	72.9	71.9	70.9	69.9	68.9	68.0	67.0	66.0	65.0	64.1
74	72.9	71.9	70.9	69.9	68.9	68.0	67.0	66.0	65.0	64.1
75	72.8	71.9	70.9	69.9	68.9	68.0	67.0	66.0	65.0	64.1
76	72.8	71.9	70.9	69.9	68.9	68.0	67.0	66.0	65.0	64.1
77	72.8	71.9	70.9	69.9	68.9	68.0	67.0	66.0	65.0	64.1
78	72.8	71.9	70.9	69.9	68.9	67.9	67.0	66.0	65.0	64.0
79	72.8	71.9	70.9	69.9	68.9	67.9	67.0	66.0	65.0	64.0
80	72.8	71.9	70.9	69.9	68.9	67.9	67.0	66.0	65.0	64.0
81	72.8	71.8	70.9	69.9	68.9	67.9	67.0	66.0	65.0	64.0
82	72.8	71.8	70.9	69.9	68.9	67.9	67.0	66.0	65.0	64.0
83	72.8	71.8	70.9	69.9	68.9	67.9	67.0	66.0	65.0	64.0
84	72.8	71.8	70.9	69.9	68.9	67.9	67.0	66.0	65.0	64.0
85	72.8	71.8	70.9	69.9	68.9	67.9	66.9	66.0	65.0	64.0
86	72.8	71.8	70.9	69.9	68.9	67.9	66.9	66.0	65.0	64.0
87	72.8	71.8	70.9	69.9	68.9	67.9	66.9	66.0	65.0	64.0

AGES	10	11	12	13	14	15	16	17	18	19
88	72.8	71.8	70.9	69.9	68.9	67.9	66.9	66.0	65.0	64.0
89	72.8	71.8	70.9	69.9	68.9	67.9	66.9	66.0	65.0	64.0
90	72.8	71.8	70.9	69.9	68.9	67.9	66.9	66.0	65.0	64.0
91	72.8	71.8	70.9	69.9	68.9	67.9	66.9	66.0	65.0	64.0
92	72.8	71.8	70.9	69.9	68.9	67.9	66.9	66.0	65.0	64.0
93	72.8	71.8	70.9	69.9	68.9	67.9	66.9	66.0	65.0	64.0
94	72.8	71.8	70.8	69.9	68.9	67.9	66.9	66.0	65.0	64.0
95	72.8	71.8	70.8	69.9	68.9	67.9	66.9	66.0	65.0	64.0
96	72.8	71.8	70.8	69.9	68.9	67.9	66.9	66.0	65.0	64.0
97	72.8	71.8	70.8	69.9	68.9	67.9	66.9	66.0	65.0	64.0
98	72.8	71.8	70.8	69.9	68.9	67.9	66.9	66.0	65.0	64.0
99	72.8	71.8	70.8	69.9	68.9	67.9	66.9	66.0	65.0	64.0
100	72.8	71.8	70.8	69.9	68.9	67.9	66.9	66.0	65.0	64.0
101	72.8	71.8	70.8	69.9	68.9	67.9	66.9	66.0	65.0	64.0
102	72.8	71.8	70.8	69.9	68.9	67.9	66.9	66.0	65.0	64.0
103	72.8	71.8	70.8	69.9	68.9	67.9	66.9	66.0	65.0	64.0
104	72.8	71.8	70.8	69.9	68.9	67.9	66.9	66.0	65.0	64.0
105	72.8	71.8	70.8	69.9	68.9	67.9	66.9	66.0	65.0	64.0
106	72.8	71.8	70.8	69.9	68.9	67.9	66.9	66.0	65.0	64.0
107	72.8	71.8	70.8	69.9	68.9	67.9	66.9	66.0	65.0	64.0
108	72.8	71.8	70.8	69.9	68.9	67.9	66.9	66.0	65.0	64.0
109	72.8	71.8	70.8	69.9	68.9	67.9	66.9	66.0	65.0	64.0
110	72.8	71.8	70.8	69.9	68.9	67.9	66.9	66.0	65.0	64.0
111	72.8	71.8	70.8	69.9	68.9	67.9	66.9	66.0	65.0	64.0
112	72.8	71.8	70.8	69.9	68.9	67.9	66.9	66.0	65.0	64.0
113	72.8	71.8	70.8	69.9	68.9	67.9	66.9	66.0	65.0	64.0
114	72.8	71.8	70.8	69.9	68.9	67.9	66.9	66.0	65.0	64.0
115+	72.8	71.8	70.8	69.9	68.9	67.9	66.9	66.0	65.0	64.0

AGES	20	21	22	23	24	25	26	27	28	29
20	70.1	69.6	69.1	68.7	68.3	67.9	67.5	67.2	66.9	66.6
21	69.6	69.1	68.6	68.2	67.7	67.3	66.9	66.6	66.2	65.9
22	69.1	68.6	68.1	67.6	67.2	66.7	66.3	65.9	65.6	65.2
23	68.7	68.2	67.6	67.1	66.6	66.2	65.7	65.3	64.9	64.6
24	68.3	67.7	67.2	66.6	66.1	65.6	65.2	64.7	64.3	63.9
25	67.9	67.3	66.7	66.2	65.6	65.1	64.6	64.2	63.7	63.3
26	67.5	66.9	66.3	65.7	65.2	64.6	64.1	63.6	63.2	62.8
27	67.2	66.6	65.9	65.3	64.7	64.2	63.6	63.1	62.7	62.2
28	66.9	66.2	65.6	64.9	64.3	63.7	63.2	62.7	62.1	61.7
29	66.6	65.9	65.2	64.6	63.9	63.3	62.8	62.2	61.7	61.2
30	66.3	65.6	64.9	64.2	63.6	62.9	62.3	61.8	61.2	60.7
31	66.1	65.3	64.6	63.9	63.2	62.6	62.0	61.4	60.8	60.2
32	65.8	65.1	64.3	63.6	62.9	62.2	61.6	61.0	60.4	59.8

AGES	20	21	22	23	24	25	26	27	28	29
33	65.6	64.8	64.1	63.3	62.6	61.9	61.3	60.6	60.0	59.4
34	65.4	64.6	63.8	63.1	62.3	61.6	60.9	60.3	59.6	59.0
35	65.2	64.4	63.6	62.8	62.1	61.4	60.6	59.9	59.3	58.6
36	65.0	64.2	63.4	62.6	61.9	61.1	60.4	59.6	59.0	58.3
37	64.9	64.0	63.2	62.4	61.6	60.9	60.1	59.4	58.7	58.0
38	64.7	63.9	63.0	62.2	61.4	60.6	59.9	59.1	58.4	57.7
39	64.6	63.7	62.9	62.1	61.2	60.4	59.6	58.9	58.1	57.4
40	64.4	63.6	62.7	61.9	61.1	60.2	59.4	58.7	57.9	57.1
41	64.3	63.5	62.6	61.7	60.9	60.1	59.3	58.5	57.7	56.9
42	64.2	63.3	62.5	61.6	60.8	59.9	59.1	58.3	57.5	56.7
43	64.1	63.2	62.4	61.5	60.6	59.8	58.9	58.1	57.3	56.5
44	64.0	63.1	62.2	61.4	60.5	59.6	58.8	57.9	57.1	56.3
45	64.0	63.0	62.2	61.3	60.4	59.5	58.6	57.8	56.9	56.1
46	63.9	63.0	62.1	61.2	60.3	59.4	58.5	57.7	56.8	56.0
47	63.8	62.9	62.0	61.1	60.2	59.3	58.4	57.5	56.7	55.8
48	63.7	62.8	61.9	61.0	60.1	59.2	58.3	57.4	56.5	55.7
49	63.7	62.8	61.8	60.9	60.0	59.1	58.2	57.3	56.4	55.6
50	63.6	62.7	61.8	60.8	59.9	59.0	58.1	57.2	56.3	55.4
51	63.6	62.6	61.7	60.8	59.9	58.9	58.0	57.1	56.2	55.3
52	63.5	62.6	61.7	60.7	59.8	58.9	58.0	57.1	56.1	55.2
53	63.5	62.5	61.6	60.7	59.7	58.8	57.9	57.0	56.1	55.2
54	63.5	62.5	61.6	60.6	59.7	58.8	57.8	56.9	56.0	55.1
55	63.4	62.5	61.5	60.6	59.6	58.7	57.8	56.8	55.9	55.0
56	63.4	62.4	61.5	60.5	59.6	58.7	57.7	56.8	55.9	54.9
57	63.4	62.4	61.5	60.5	59.6	58.6	57.7	56.7	55.8	54.9
58	63.3	62.4	61.4	60.5	59.5	58.6	57.6	56.7	55.8	54.8
59	63.3	62.3	61.4	60.4	59.5	58.5	57.6	56.7	55.7	54.8
60	63.3	62.3	61.4	60.4	59.5	58.5	57.6	56.6	55.7	54.7
61	63.3	62.3	61.3	60.4	59.4	58.5	57.5	56.6	55.6	54.7
62	63.2	62.3	61.3	60.4	59.4	58.4	57.5	56.5	55.6	54.7
63	63.2	62.3	61.3	60.3	59.4	58.4	57.5	56.5	55.6	54.6
64	63.2	62.2	61.3	60.3	59.4	58.4	57.4	56.5	55.5	54.6
65	63.2	62.2	61.3	60.3	59.3	58.4	57.4	56.5	55.5	54.6
66	63.2	62.2	61.2	60.3	59.3	58.4	57.4	56.4	55.5	54.5
67	63.2	62.2	61.2	60.3	59.3	58.3	57.4	56.4	55.5	54.5
68	63.1	62.2	61.2	60.2	59.3	58.3	57.4	56.4	55.4	54.5
69	63.1	62.2	61.2	60.2	59.3	58.3	57.3	56.4	55.4	54.5
70	63.1	62.2	61.2	60.2	59.3	58.3	57.3	56.4	55.4	54.4
71	63.1	62.1	61.2	60.2	59.2	58.3	57.3	56.4	55.4	54.4
72	63.1	62.1	61.2	60.2	59.2	58.3	57.3	56.3	55.4	54.4
73	63.1	62.1	61.2	60.2	59.2	58.3	57.3	56.3	55.4	54.4
74	63.1	62.1	61.2	60.2	59.2	58.2	57.3	56.3	55.4	54.4

AGES	20	21	22	23	24	25	26	27	28	29
75	63.1	62.1	61.1	60.2	59.2	58.2	57.3	56.3	55.3	54.4
76	63.1	62.1	61.1	60.2	59.2	58.2	57.3	56.3	55.3	54.4
77	63.1	62.1	61.1	60.2	59.2	58.2	57.3	56.3	55.3	54.4
78	63.1	62.1	61.1	60.2	59.2	58.2	57.3	56.3	55.3	54.4
79	63.1	62.1	61.1	60.2	59.2	58.2	57.2	56.3	55.3	54.3
80	63.1	62.1	61.1	60.1	59.2	58.2	57.2	56.3	55.3	54.3
81	63.1	62.1	61.1	60.1	59.2	58.2	57.2	56.3	55.3	54.3
82	63.1	62.1	61.1	60.1	59.2	58.2	57.2	56.3	55.3	54.3
83	63.1	62.1	61.1	60.1	59.2	58.2	57.2	56.3	55.3	54.3
84	63.0	62.1	61.1	60.1	59.2	58.2	57.2	56.3	55.3	54.3
85	63.0	62.1	61.1	60.1	59.2	58.2	57.2	56.3	55.3	54.3
86	63.0	62.1	61.1	60.1	59.2	58.2	57.2	56.2	55.3	54.3
87	63.0	62.1	61.1	60.1	59.2	58.2	57.2	56.2	55.3	54.3
88	63.0	62.1	61.1	60.1	59.2	58.2	57.2	56.2	55.3	54.3
89	63.0	62.1	61.1	60.1	59.1	58.2	57.2	56.2	55.3	54.3
90	63.0	62.1	61.1	60.1	59.1	58.2	57.2	56.2	55.3	54.3
91	63.0	62.1	61.1	60.1	59.1	58.2	57.2	56.2	55.3	54.3
92	63.0	62.1	61.1	60.1	59.1	58.2	57.2	56.2	55.3	54.3
93	63.0	62.1	61.1	60.1	59.1	58.2	57.2	56.2	55.3	54.3
94	63.0	62.1	61.1	60.1	59.1	58.2	57.2	56.2	55.3	54.3
95	63.0	62.1	61.1	60.1	59.1	58.2	57.2	56.2	55.3	54.3
96	63.0	62.1	61.1	60.1	59.1	58.2	57.2	56.2	55.3	54.3
97	63.0	62.1	61.1	60.1	59.1	58.2	57.2	56.2	55.3	54.3
98	63.0	62.1	61.1	60.1	59.1	58.2	57.2	56.2	55.3	54.3
99	63.0	62.1	61.1	60.1	59.1	58.2	57.2	56.2	55.3	54.3
100	63.0	62.1	61.1	60.1	59.1	58.2	57.2	56.2	55.3	54.3
101	63.0	62.1	61.1	60.1	59.1	58.2	57.2	56.2	55.3	54.3
102	63.0	62.1	61.1	60.1	59.1	58.2	57.2	56.2	55.3	54.3
103	63.0	62.1	61.1	60.1	59.1	58.2	57.2	56.2	55.3	54.3
104	63.0	62.1	61.1	60.1	59.1	58.2	57.2	56.2	55.3	54.3
105	63.0	62.1	61.1	60.1	59.1	58.2	57.2	56.2	55.3	54.3
106	63.0	62.1	61.1	60.1	59.1	58.2	57.2	56.2	55.3	54.3
107	63.0	62.1	61.1	60.1	59.1	58.2	57.2	56.2	55.3	54.3
108	63.0	62.1	61.1	60.1	59.1	58.2	57.2	56.2	55.3	54.3
109	63.0	62.1	61.1	60.1	59.1	58.2	57.2	56.2	55.3	54.3
110	63.0	62.1	61.1	60.1	59.1	58.2	57.2	56.2	55.3	54.3
111	63.0	62.1	61.1	60.1	59.1	58.2	57.2	56.2	55.3	54.3
112	63.0	62.1	61.1	60.1	59.1	58.2	57.2	56.2	55.3	54.3
113	63.0	62.1	61.1	60.1	59.1	58.2	57.2	56.2	55.3	54.3
114	63.0	62.1	61.1	60.1	59.1	58.2	57.2	56.2	55.3	54.3
115+	63.0	62.1	61.1	60.1	59.1	58.2	57.2	56.2	55.3	54.3

AGES	30	31	32	33	34	35	36	37	38	39
30	60.2	59.7	59.2	58.8	58.4	58.0	57.6	57.3	57.0	56.7
31	59.7	59.2	58.7	58.2	57.8	57.4	57.0	56.6	56.3	56.0
32	59.2	58.7	58.2	57.7	57.2	56.8	56.4	56.0	55.6	55.3
33	58.8	58.2	57.7	57.2	56.7	56.2	55.8	55.4	55.0	54.7
34	58.4	57.8	57.2	56.7	56.2	55.7	55.3	54.8	54.4	54.0
35	58.0	57.4	56.8	56.2	55.7	55.2	54.7	54.3	53.8	53.4
36	57.6	57.0	56.4	55.8	55.3	54.7	54.2	53.7	53.3	52.8
37	57.3	56.6	56.0	55.4	54.8	54.3	53.7	53.2	52.7	52.3
38	57.0	56.3	55.6	55.0	54.4	53.8	53.3	52.7	52.2	51.7
39	56.7	56.0	55.3	54.7	54.0	53.4	52.8	52.3	51.7	51.2
40	56.4	55.7	55.0	54.3	53.7	53.0	52.4	51.8	51.3	50.8
41	56.1	55.4	54.7	54.0	53.3	52.7	52.0	51.4	50.9	50.3
42	55.9	55.2	54.4	53.7	53.0	52.3	51.7	51.1	50.4	49.9
43	55.7	54.9	54.2	53.4	52.7	52.0	51.3	50.7	50.1	49.5
44	55.5	54.7	53.9	53.2	52.4	51.7	51.0	50.4	49.7	49.1
45	55.3	54.5	53.7	52.9	52.2	51.5	50.7	50.0	49.4	48.7
46	55.1	54.3	53.5	52.7	52.0	51.2	50.5	49.8	49.1	48.4
47	55.0	54.1	53.3	52.5	51.7	51.0	50.2	49.5	48.8	48.1
48	54.8	54.0	53.2	52.3	51.5	50.8	50.0	49.2	48.5	47.8
49	54.7	53.8	53.0	52.2	51.4	50.6	49.8	49.0	48.2	47.5
50	54.6	53.7	52.9	52.0	51.2	50.4	49.6	48.8	48.0	47.3
51	54.5	53.6	52.7	51.9	51.0	50.2	49.4	48.6	47.8	47.0
52	54.4	53.5	52.6	51.7	50.9	50.0	49.2	48.4	47.6	46.8
53	54.3	53.4	52.5	51.6	50.8	49.9	49.1	48.2	47.4	46.6
54	54.2	53.3	52.4	51.5	50.6	49.8	48.9	48.1	47.2	46.4
55	54.1	53.2	52.3	51.4	50.5	49.7	48.8	47.9	47.1	46.3
56	54.0	53.1	52.2	51.3	50.4	49.5	48.7	47.8	47.0	46.1
57	54.0	53.0	52.1	51.2	50.3	49.4	48.6	47.7	46.8	46.0
58	53.9	53.0	52.1	51.2	50.3	49.4	48.5	47.6	46.7	45.8
59	53.8	52.9	52.0	51.1	50.2	49.3	48.4	47.5	46.6	45.7
60	53.8	52.9	51.9	51.0	50.1	49.2	48.3	47.4	46.5	45.6
61	53.8	52.8	51.9	51.0	50.0	49.1	48.2	47.3	46.4	45.5
62	53.7	52.8	51.8	50.9	50.0	49.1	48.1	47.2	46.3	45.4
63	53.7	52.7	51.8	50.9	49.9	49.0	48.1	47.2	46.3	45.3
64	53.6	52.7	51.8	50.8	49.9	48.9	48.0	47.1	46.2	45.3
65	53.6	52.7	51.7	50.8	49.8	48.9	48.0	47.0	46.1	45.2
66	53.6	52.6	51.7	50.7	49.8	48.9	47.9	47.0	46.1	45.1
67	53.6	52.6	51.7	50.7	49.8	48.8	47.9	46.9	46.0	45.1
68	53.5	52.6	51.6	50.7	49.7	48.8	47.8	46.9	46.0	45.0
69	53.5	52.6	51.6	50.6	49.7	48.7	47.8	46.9	45.9	45.0
70	53.5	52.5	51.6	50.6	49.7	48.7	47.8	46.8	45.9	44.9

AGES	30	31	32	33	34	35	36	37	38	39
71	53.5	52.5	51.6	50.6	49.6	48.7	47.7	46.8	45.9	44.9
72	53.5	52.5	51.5	50.6	49.6	48.7	47.7	46.8	45.8	44.9
73	53.4	52.5	51.5	50.6	49.6	48.6	47.7	46.7	45.8	44.8
74	53.4	52.5	51.5	50.5	49.6	48.6	47.7	46.7	45.8	44.8
75	53.4	52.5	51.5	50.5	49.6	48.6	47.7	46.7	45.7	44.8
76	53.4	52.4	51.5	50.5	49.6	48.6	47.6	46.7	45.7	44.8
77	53.4	52.4	51.5	50.5	49.5	48.6	47.6	46.7	45.7	44.8
78	53.4	52.4	51.5	50.5	49.5	48.6	47.6	46.6	45.7	44.7
79	53.4	52.4	51.5	50.5	49.5	48.6	47.6	46.6	45.7	44.7
80	53.4	52.4	51.4	50.5	49.5	48.5	47.6	46.6	45.7	44.7
81	53.4	52.4	51.4	50.5	49.5	48.5	47.6	46.6	45.7	44.7
82	53.4	52.4	51.4	50.5	49.5	48.5	47.6	46.6	45.6	44.7
83	53.4	52.4	51.4	50.5	49.5	48.5	47.6	46.6	45.6	44.7
84	53.4	52.4	51.4	50.5	49.5	48.5	47.6	46.6	45.6	44.7
85	53.3	52.4	51.4	50.4	49.5	48.5	47.5	46.6	45.6	44.7
86	53.3	52.4	51.4	50.4	49.5	48.5	47.5	46.6	45.6	44.6
87	53.3	52.4	51.4	50.4	49.5	48.5	47.5	46.6	45.6	44.6
88	53.3	52.4	51.4	50.4	49.5	48.5	47.5	46.6	45.6	44.6
89	53.3	52.4	51.4	50.4	49.5	48.5	47.5	46.6	45.6	44.6
90	53.3	52.4	51.4	50.4	49.5	48.5	47.5	46.6	45.6	44.6
91	53.3	52.4	51.4	50.4	49.5	48.5	47.5	46.6	45.6	44.6
92	53.3	52.4	51.4	50.4	49.5	48.5	47.5	46.6	45.6	44.6
93	53.3	52.4	51.4	50.4	49.5	48.5	47.5	46.6	45.6	44.6
94	53.3	52.4	51.4	50.4	49.5	48.5	47.5	46.6	45.6	44.6
95	53.3	52.4	51.4	50.4	49.5	48.5	47.5	46.5	45.6	44.6
96	53.3	52.4	51.4	50.4	49.5	48.5	47.5	46.5	45.6	44.6
97	53.3	52.4	51.4	50.4	49.5	48.5	47.5	46.5	45.6	44.6
98	53.3	52.4	51.4	50.4	49.5	48.5	47.5	46.5	45.6	44.6
99	53.3	52.4	51.4	50.4	49.5	48.5	47.5	46.5	45.6	44.6
100	53.3	52.4	51.4	50.4	49.5	48.5	47.5	46.5	45.6	44.6
101	53.3	52.4	51.4	50.4	49.5	48.5	47.5	46.5	45.6	44.6
102	53.3	52.4	51.4	50.4	49.5	48.5	47.5	46.5	45.6	44.6
103	53.3	52.4	51.4	50.4	49.5	48.5	47.5	46.5	45.6	44.6
104	53.3	52.4	51.4	50.4	49.5	48.5	47.5	46.5	45.6	44.6
105	53.3	52.4	51.4	50.4	49.4	48.5	47.5	46.5	45.6	44.6
106	53.3	52.4	51.4	50.4	49.4	48.5	47.5	46.5	45.6	44.6
107	53.3	52.4	51.4	50.4	49.4	48.5	47.5	46.5	45.6	44.6
108	53.3	52.4	51.4	50.4	49.4	48.5	47.5	46.5	45.6	44.6
109	53.3	52.4	51.4	50.4	49.4	48.5	47.5	46.5	45.6	44.6
110	53.3	52.4	51.4	50.4	49.4	48.5	47.5	46.5	45.6	44.6
111	53.3	52.4	51.4	50.4	49.4	48.5	47.5	46.5	45.6	44.6
112	53.3	52.4	51.4	50.4	49.4	48.5	47.5	46.5	45.6	44.6

AGES	30	31	32	33	34	35	36	37	38	39
113	53.3	52.4	51.4	50.4	49.4	48.5	47.5	46.5	45.6	44.6
114	53.3	52.4	51.4	50.4	49.4	48.5	47.5	46.5	45.6	44.6
115+	53.3	52.4	51.4	50.4	49.4	48.5	47.5	46.5	45.6	44.6
AGES	40	41	42	43	44	45	46	47	48	49
40	50.2	49.8	49.3	48.9	48.5	48.1	47.7	47.4	47.1	46.8
41	49.8	49.3	48.8	48.3	47.9	47.5	47.1	46.7	46.4	46.1
42	49.3	48.8	48.3	47.8	47.3	46.9	46.5	46.1	45.8	45.4
43	48.9	48.3	47.8	47.3	46.8	46.3	45.9	45.5	45.1	44.8
44	48.5	47.9	47.3	46.8	46.3	45.8	45.4	44.9	44.5	44.2
45	48.1	47.5	46.9	46.3	45.8	45.3	44.8	44.4	44.0	43.6
46	47.7	47.1	46.5	45.9	45.4	44.8	44.3	43.9	43.4	43.0
47	47.4	46.7	46.1	45.5	44.9	44.4	43.9	43.4	42.9	42.4
48	47.1	46.4	45.8	45.1	44.5	44.0	43.4	42.9	42.4	41.9
49	46.8	46.1	45.4	44.8	44.2	43.6	43.0	42.4	41.9	41.4
50	46.5	45.8	45.1	44.4	43.8	43.2	42.6	42.0	41.5	40.9
51	46.3	45.5	44.8	44.1	43.5	42.8	42.2	41.6	41.0	40.5
52	46.0	45.3	44.6	43.8	43.2	42.5	41.8	41.2	40.6	40.1
53	45.8	45.1	44.3	43.6	42.9	42.2	41.5	40.9	40.3	39.7
54	45.6	44.8	44.1	43.3	42.6	41.9	41.2	40.5	39.9	39.3
55	45.5	44.7	43.9	43.1	42.4	41.6	40.9	40.2	39.6	38.9
56	45.3	44.5	43.7	42.9	42.1	41.4	40.7	40.0	39.3	38.6
57	45.1	44.3	43.5	42.7	41.9	41.2	40.4	39.7	39.0	38.3
58	45.0	44.2	43.3	42.5	41.7	40.9	40.2	39.4	38.7	38.0
59	44.9	44.0	43.2	42.4	41.5	40.7	40.0	39.2	38.5	37.8
60	44.7	43.9	43.0	42.2	41.4	40.6	39.8	39.0	38.2	37.5
61	44.6	43.8	42.9	42.1	41.2	40.4	39.6	38.8	38.0	37.3
62	44.5	43.7	42.8	41.9	41.1	40.3	39.4	38.6	37.8	37.1
63	44.5	43.6	42.7	41.8	41.0	40.1	39.3	38.5	37.7	36.9
64	44.4	43.5	42.6	41.7	40.8	40.0	39.2	38.3	37.5	36.7
65	44.3	43.4	42.5	41.6	40.7	39.9	39.0	38.2	37.4	36.6
66	44.2	43.3	42.4	41.5	40.6	39.8	38.9	38.1	37.2	36.4
67	44.2	43.3	42.3	41.4	40.6	39.7	38.8	38.0	37.1	36.3
68	44.1	43.2	42.3	41.4	40.5	39.6	38.7	37.9	37.0	36.2
69	44.1	43.1	42.2	41.3	40.4	39.5	38.6	37.8	36.9	36.0
70	44.0	43.1	42.2	41.3	40.3	39.4	38.6	37.7	36.8	35.9
71	44.0	43.0	42.1	41.2	40.3	39.4	38.5	37.6	36.7	35.9
72	43.9	43.0	42.1	41.1	40.2	39.3	38.4	37.5	36.6	35.8
73	43.9	43.0	42.0	41.1	40.2	39.3	38.4	37.5	36.6	35.7
74	43.9	42.9	42.0	41.1	40.1	39.2	38.3	37.4	36.5	35.6
75	43.8	42.9	42.0	41.0	40.1	39.2	38.3	37.4	36.5	35.6
76	43.8	42.9	41.9	41.0	40.1	39.1	38.2	37.3	36.4	35.5
77	43.8	42.9	41.9	41.0	40.0	39.1	38.2	37.3	36.4	35.5

AGES	40	41	42	43	44	45	46	47	48	49
78	43.8	42.8	41.9	40.9	40.0	39.1	38.2	37.2	36.3	35.4
79	43.8	42.8	41.9	40.9	40.0	39.1	38.1	37.2	36.3	35.4
80	43.7	42.8	41.8	40.9	40.0	39.0	38.1	37.2	36.3	35.4
81	43.7	42.8	41.8	40.9	39.9	39.0	38.1	37.2	36.2	35.3
82	43.7	42.8	41.8	40.9	39.9	39.0	38.1	37.1	36.2	35.3
83	43.7	42.8	41.8	40.9	39.9	39.0	38.0	37.1	36.2	35.3
84	43.7	42.7	41.8	40.8	39.9	39.0	38.0	37.1	36.2	35.3
85	43.7	42.7	41.8	40.8	39.9	38.9	38.0	37.1	36.2	35.2
86	43.7	42.7	41.8	40.8	39.9	38.9	38.0	37.1	36.1	35.2
87	43.7	42.7	41.8	40.8	39.9	38.9	38.0	37.0	36.1	35.2
88	43.7	42.7	41.8	40.8	39.9	38.9	38.0	37.0	36.1	35.2
89	43.7	42.7	41.7	40.8	39.8	38.9	38.0	37.0	36.1	35.2
90	43.7	42.7	41.7	40.8	39.8	38.9	38.0	37.0	36.1	35.2
91	43.7	42.7	41.7	40.8	39.8	38.9	37.9	37.0	36.1	35.2
92	43.7	42.7	41.7	40.8	39.8	38.9	37.9	37.0	36.1	35.1
93	43.7	42.7	41.7	40.8	39.8	38.9	37.9	37.0	36.1	35.1
94	43.7	42.7	41.7	40.8	39.8	38.9	37.9	37.0	36.1	35.1
95	43.6	42.7	41.7	40.8	39.8	38.9	37.9	37.0	36.1	35.1
96	43.6	42.7	41.7	40.8	39.8	38.9	37.9	37.0	36.1	35.1
97	43.6	42.7	41.7	40.8	39.8	38.9	37.9	37.0	36.1	35.1
98	43.6	42.7	41.7	40.8	39.8	38.9	37.9	37.0	36.0	35.1
99	43.6	42.7	41.7	40.8	39.8	38.9	37.9	37.0	36.0	35.1
100	43.6	42.7	41.7	40.8	39.8	38.9	37.9	37.0	36.0	35.1
101	43.6	42.7	41.7	40.8	39.8	38.9	37.9	37.0	36.0	35.1
102	43.6	42.7	41.7	40.8	39.8	38.9	37.9	37.0	36.0	35.1
103	43.6	42.7	41.7	40.8	39.8	38.9	37.9	37.0	36.0	35.1
104	43.6	42.7	41.7	40.8	39.8	38.8	37.9	37.0	36.0	35.1
105	43.6	42.7	41.7	40.8	39.8	38.8	37.9	37.0	36.0	35.1
106	43.6	42.7	41.7	40.8	39.8	38.8	37.9	37.0	36.0	35.1
107	43.6	42.7	41.7	40.8	39.8	38.8	37.9	37.0	36.0	35.1
108	43.6	42.7	41.7	40.8	39.8	38.8	37.9	37.0	36.0	35.1
109	43.6	42.7	41.7	40.7	39.8	38.8	37.9	37.0	36.0	35.1
110	43.6	42.7	41.7	40.7	39.8	38.8	37.9	37.0	36.0	35.1
111	43.6	42.7	41.7	40.7	39.8	38.8	37.9	37.0	36.0	35.1
112	43.6	42.7	41.7	40.7	39.8	38.8	37.9	37.0	36.0	35.1
113	43.6	42.7	41.7	40.7	39.8	38.8	37.9	37.0	36.0	35.1
114	43.6	42.7	41.7	40.7	39.8	38.8	37.9	37.0	36.0	35.1
115+	43.6	42.7	41.7	40.7	39.8	38.8	37.9	37.0	36.0	35.1
AGES	50	51	52	53	54	55	56	57	58	59
50	40.4	40.0	39.5	39.1	38.7	38.3	38.0	37.6	37.3	37.1
51	40.0	39.5	39.0	38.5	38.1	37.7	37.4	37.0	36.7	36.4
52	39.5	39.0	38.5	38.0	37.6	37.2	36.8	36.4	36.0	35.7

AGES	50	51	52	53	54	55	56	57	58	59
53	39.1	38.5	38.0	37.5	37.1	36.6	36.2	35.8	35.4	35.1
54	38.7	38.1	37.6	37.1	36.6	36.1	35.7	35.2	34.8	34.5
55	38.3	37.7	37.2	36.6	36.1	35.6	35.1	34.7	34.3	33.9
56	38.0	37.4	36.8	36.2	35.7	35.1	34.7	34.2	33.7	33.3
57	37.6	37.0	36.4	35.8	35.2	34.7	34.2	33.7	33.2	32.8
58	37.3	36.7	36.0	35.4	34.8	34.3	33.7	33.2	32.8	32.3
59	37.1	36.4	35.7	35.1	34.5	33.9	33.3	32.8	32.3	31.8
60	36.8	36.1	35.4	34.8	34.1	33.5	32.9	32.4	31.9	31.3
61	36.6	35.8	35.1	34.5	33.8	33.2	32.6	32.0	31.4	30.9
62	36.3	35.6	34.9	34.2	33.5	32.9	32.2	31.6	31.1	30.5
63	36.1	35.4	34.6	33.9	33.2	32.6	31.9	31.3	30.7	30.1
64	35.9	35.2	34.4	33.7	33.0	32.3	31.6	31.0	30.4	29.8
65	35.8	35.0	34.2	33.5	32.7	32.0	31.4	30.7	30.0	29.4
66	35.6	34.8	34.0	33.3	32.5	31.8	31.1	30.4	29.8	29.1
67	35.5	34.7	33.9	33.1	32.3	31.6	30.9	30.2	29.5	28.8
68	35.3	34.5	33.7	32.9	32.1	31.4	30.7	29.9	29.2	28.6
69	35.2	34.4	33.6	32.8	32.0	31.2	30.5	29.7	29.0	28.3
70	35.1	34.3	33.4	32.6	31.8	31.1	30.3	29.5	28.8	28.1
71	35.0	34.2	33.3	32.5	31.7	30.9	30.1	29.4	28.6	27.9
72	34.9	34.1	33.2	32.4	31.6	30.8	30.0	29.2	28.4	27.7
73	34.8	34.0	33.1	32.3	31.5	30.6	29.8	29.1	28.3	27.5
74	34.8	33.9	33.0	32.2	31.4	30.5	29.7	28.9	28.1	27.4
75	34.7	33.8	33.0	32.1	31.3	30.4	29.6	28.8	28.0	27.2
76	34.6	33.8	32.9	32.0	31.2	30.3	29.5	28.7	27.9	27.1
77	34.6	33.7	32.8	32.0	31.1	30.3	29.4	28.6	27.8	27.0
78	34.5	33.6	32.8	31.9	31.0	30.2	29.3	28.5	27.7	26.9
79	34.5	33.6	32.7	31.8	31.0	30.1	29.3	28.4	27.6	26.8
80	34.5	33.6	32.7	31.8	30.9	30.1	29.2	28.4	27.5	26.7
81	34.4	33.5	32.6	31.8	30.9	30.0	29.2	28.3	27.5	26.6
82	34.4	33.5	32.6	31.7	30.8	30.0	29.1	28.3	27.4	26.6
83	34.4	33.5	32.6	31.7	30.8	29.9	29.1	28.2	27.4	26.5
84	34.3	33.4	32.5	31.7	30.8	29.9	29.0	28.2	27.3	26.5
85	34.3	33.4	32.5	31.6	30.7	29.9	29.0	28.1	27.3	26.4
86	34.3	33.4	32.5	31.6	30.7	29.8	29.0	28.1	27.2	26.4
87	34.3	33.4	32.5	31.6	30.7	29.8	28.9	28.1	27.2	26.4
88	34.3	33.4	32.5	31.6	30.7	29.8	28.9	28.0	27.2	26.3
89	34.3	33.3	32.4	31.5	30.7	29.8	28.9	28.0	27.2	26.3
90	34.2	33.3	32.4	31.5	30.6	29.8	28.9	28.0	27.1	26.3
91	34.2	33.3	32.4	31.5	30.6	29.7	28.9	28.0	27.1	26.3
92	34.2	33.3	32.4	31.5	30.6	29.7	28.8	28.0	27.1	26.2
93	34.2	33.3	32.4	31.5	30.6	29.7	28.8	28.0	27.1	26.2
94	34.2	33.3	32.4	31.5	30.6	29.7	28.8	27.9	27.1	26.2

AGES	50	51	52	53	54	55	56	57	58	59
95	34.2	33.3	32.4	31.5	30.6	29.7	28.8	27.9	27.1	26.2
96	34.2	33.3	32.4	31.5	30.6	29.7	28.8	27.9	27.0	26.2
97	34.2	33.3	32.4	31.5	30.6	29.7	28.8	27.9	27.0	26.2
98	34.2	33.3	32.4	31.5	30.6	29.7	28.8	27.9	27.0	26.2
99	34.2	33.3	32.4	31.5	30.6	29.7	28.8	27.9	27.0	26.2
100	34.2	33.3	32.4	31.5	30.6	29.7	28.8	27.9	27.0	26.1
101	34.2	33.3	32.4	31.5	30.6	29.7	28.8	27.9	27.0	26.1
102	34.2	33.3	32.4	31.4	30.5	29.7	28.8	27.9	27.0	26.1
103	34.2	33.3	32.4	31.4	30.5	29.7	28.8	27.9	27.0	26.1
104	34.2	33.3	32.4	31.4	30.5	29.6	28.8	27.9	27.0	26.1
105	34.2	33.3	32.3	31.4	30.5	29.6	28.8	27.9	27.0	26.1
106	34.2	33.3	32.3	31.4	30.5	29.6	28.8	27.9	27.0	26.1
107	34.2	33.3	32.3	31.4	30.5	29.6	28.8	27.9	27.0	26.1
108	34.2	33.3	32.3	31.4	30.5	29.6	28.8	27.9	27.0	26.1
109	34.2	33.3	32.3	31.4	30.5	29.6	28.7	27.9	27.0	26.1
110	34.2	33.3	32.3	31.4	30.5	29.6	28.7	27.9	27.0	26.1
111	34.2	33.3	32.3	31.4	30.5	29.6	28.7	27.9	27.0	26.1
112	34.2	33.3	32.3	31.4	30.5	29.6	28.7	27.9	27.0	26.1
113	34.2	33.3	32.3	31.4	30.5	29.6	28.7	27.9	27.0	26.1
114	34.2	33.3	32.3	31.4	30.5	29.6	28.7	27.9	27.0	26.1
115+	34.2	33.3	32.3	31.4	30.5	29.6	28.7	27.9	27.0	26.1

AGES	60	61	62	63	64	65	66	67	68	69
60	30.9	30.4	30.0	29.6	29.2	28.8	28.5	28.2	27.9	27.6
61	30.4	29.9	29.5	29.0	28.6	28.3	27.9	27.6	27.3	27.0
62	30.0	29.5	29.0	28.5	28.1	27.7	27.3	27.0	26.7	26.4
63	29.6	29.0	28.5	28.1	27.6	27.2	26.8	26.4	26.1	25.7
64	29.2	28.6	28.1	27.6	27.1	26.7	26.3	25.9	25.5	25.2
65	28.8	28.3	27.7	27.2	26.7	26.2	25.8	25.4	25.0	24.6
66	28.5	27.9	27.3	26.8	26.3	25.8	25.3	24.9	24.5	24.1
67	28.2	27.6	27.0	26.4	25.9	25.4	24.9	24.4	24.0	23.6
68	27.9	27.3	26.7	26.1	25.5	25.0	24.5	24.0	23.5	23.1
69	27.6	27.0	26.4	25.7	25.2	24.6	24.1	23.6	23.1	22.6
70	27.4	26.7	26.1	25.4	24.8	24.3	23.7	23.2	22.7	22.2
71	27.2	26.5	25.8	25.2	24.5	23.9	23.4	22.8	22.3	21.8
72	27.0	26.3	25.6	24.9	24.3	23.7	23.1	22.5	22.0	21.4
73	26.8	26.1	25.4	24.7	24.0	23.4	22.8	22.2	21.6	21.1
74	26.6	25.9	25.2	24.5	23.8	23.1	22.5	21.9	21.3	20.8
75	26.5	25.7	25.0	24.3	23.6	22.9	22.3	21.6	21.0	20.5
76	26.3	25.6	24.8	24.1	23.4	22.7	22.0	21.4	20.8	20.2
77	26.2	25.4	24.7	23.9	23.2	22.5	21.8	21.2	20.6	19.9
78	26.1	25.3	24.6	23.8	23.1	22.4	21.7	21.0	20.3	19.7
79	26.0	25.2	24.4	23.7	22.9	22.2	21.5	20.8	20.1	19.5

AGES	60	61	62	63	64	65	66	67	68	69
80	25.9	25.1	24.3	23.6	22.8	22.1	21.3	20.6	20.0	19.3
81	25.8	25.0	24.2	23.4	22.7	21.9	21.2	20.5	19.8	19.1
82	25.8	24.9	24.1	23.4	22.6	21.8	21.1	20.4	19.7	19.0
83	25.7	24.9	24.1	23.3	22.5	21.7	21.0	20.2	19.5	18.8
84	25.6	24.8	24.0	23.2	22.4	21.6	20.9	20.1	19.4	18.7
85	25.6	24.8	23.9	23.1	22.3	21.6	20.8	20.1	19.3	18.6
86	25.5	24.7	23.9	23.1	22.3	21.5	20.7	20.0	19.2	18.5
87	25.5	24.7	23.8	23.0	22.2	21.4	20.7	19.9	19.2	18.4
88	25.5	24.6	23.8	23.0	22.2	21.4	20.6	19.8	19.1	18.3
89	25.4	24.6	23.8	22.9	22.1	21.3	20.5	19.8	19.0	18.3
90	25.4	24.6	23.7	22.9	22.1	21.3	20.5	19.7	19.0	18.2
91	25.4	24.5	23.7	22.9	22.1	21.3	20.5	19.7	18.9	18.2
92	25.4	24.5	23.7	22.9	22.0	21.2	20.4	19.6	18.9	18.1
93	25.4	24.5	23.7	22.8	22.0	21.2	20.4	19.6	18.8	18.1
94	25.3	24.5	23.6	22.8	22.0	21.2	20.4	19.6	18.8	18.0
95	25.3	24.5	23.6	22.8	22.0	21.1	20.3	19.6	18.8	18.0
96	25.3	24.5	23.6	22.8	21.9	21.1	20.3	19.5	18.8	18.0
97	25.3	24.5	23.6	22.8	21.9	21.1	20.3	19.5	18.7	18.0
98	25.3	24.4	23.6	22.8	21.9	21.1	20.3	19.5	18.7	17.9
99	25.3	24.4	23.6	22.7	21.9	21.1	20.3	19.5	18.7	17.9
100	25.3	24.4	23.6	22.7	21.9	21.1	20.3	19.5	18.7	17.9
101	25.3	24.4	23.6	22.7	21.9	21.1	20.2	19.4	18.7	17.9
102	25.3	24.4	23.6	22.7	21.9	21.1	20.2	19.4	18.6	17.9
103	25.3	24.4	23.6	22.7	21.9	21.0	20.2	19.4	18.6	17.9
104	25.3	24.4	23.5	22.7	21.9	21.0	20.2	19.4	18.6	17.8
105	25.3	24.4	23.5	22.7	21.9	21.0	20.2	19.4	18.6	17.8
106	25.3	24.4	23.5	22.7	21.9	21.0	20.2	19.4	18.6	17.8
107	25.2	24.4	23.5	22.7	21.8	21.0	20.2	19.4	18.6	17.8
108	25.2	24.4	23.5	22.7	21.8	21.0	20.2	19.4	18.6	17.8
109	25.2	24.4	23.5	22.7	21.8	21.0	20.2	19.4	18.6	17.8
110	25.2	24.4	23.5	22.7	21.8	21.0	20.2	19.4	18.6	17.8
111	25.2	24.4	23.5	22.7	21.8	21.0	20.2	19.4	18.6	17.8
112	25.2	24.4	23.5	22.7	21.8	21.0	20.2	19.4	18.6	17.8
113	25.2	24.4	23.5	22.7	21.8	21.0	20.2	19.4	18.6	17.8
114	25.2	24.4	23.5	22.7	21.8	21.0	20.2	19.4	18.6	17.8
115+	25.2	24.4	23.5	22.7	21.8	21.0	20.2	19.4	18.6	17.8
AGES	70	71	72	73	74	75	76	77	78	79
70	21.8	21.3	20.9	20.6	20.2	19.9	19.6	19.4	19.1	18.9
71	21.3	20.9	20.5	20.1	19.7	19.4	19.1	18.8	18.5	18.3
72	20.9	20.5	20.0	19.6	19.3	18.9	18.6	18.3	18.0	17.7
73	20.6	20.1	19.6	19.2	18.8	18.4	18.1	17.8	17.5	17.2
74	20.2	19.7	19.3	18.8	18.4	18.0	17.6	17.3	17.0	16.7

AGES	70	71	72	73	74	75	76	77	78	79
75	19.9	19.4	18.9	18.4	18.0	17.6	17.2	16.8	16.5	16.2
76	19.6	19.1	18.6	18.1	17.6	17.2	16.8	16.4	16.0	15.7
77	19.4	18.8	18.3	17.8	17.3	16.8	16.4	16.0	15.6	15.3
78	19.1	18.5	18.0	17.5	17.0	16.5	16.0	15.6	15.2	14.9
79	18.9	18.3	17.7	17.2	16.7	16.2	15.7	15.3	14.9	14.5
80	18.7	18.1	17.5	16.9	16.4	15.9	15.4	15.0	14.5	14.1
81	18.5	17.9	17.3	16.7	16.2	15.6	15.1	14.7	14.2	13.8
82	18.3	17.7	17.1	16.5	15.9	15.4	14.9	14.4	13.9	13.5
83	18.2	17.5	16.9	16.3	15.7	15.2	14.7	14.2	13.7	13.2
84	18.0	17.4	16.7	16.1	15.5	15.0	14.4	13.9	13.4	13.0
85	17.9	17.3	16.6	16.0	15.4	14.8	14.3	13.7	13.2	12.8
86	17.8	17.1	16.5	15.8	15.2	14.6	14.1	13.5	13.0	12.5
87	17.7	17.0	16.4	15.7	15.1	14.5	13.9	13.4	12.9	12.4
88	17.6	16.9	16.3	15.6	15.0	14.4	13.8	13.2	12.7	12.2
89	17.6	16.9	16.2	15.5	14.9	14.3	13.7	13.1	12.6	12.0
90	17.5	16.8	16.1	15.4	14.8	14.2	13.6	13.0	12.4	11.9
91	17.4	16.7	16.0	15.4	14.7	14.1	13.5	12.9	12.3	11.8
92	17.4	16.7	16.0	15.3	14.6	14.0	13.4	12.8	12.2	11.7
93	17.3	16.6	15.9	15.2	14.6	13.9	13.3	12.7	12.1	11.6
94	17.3	16.6	15.9	15.2	14.5	13.9	13.2	12.6	12.0	11.5
95	17.3	16.5	15.8	15.1	14.5	13.8	13.2	12.6	12.0	11.4
96	17.2	16.5	15.8	15.1	14.4	13.8	13.1	12.5	11.9	11.3
97	17.2	16.5	15.8	15.1	14.4	13.7	13.1	12.5	11.9	11.3
98	17.2	16.4	15.7	15.0	14.3	13.7	13.0	12.4	11.8	11.2
99	17.2	16.4	15.7	15.0	14.3	13.6	13.0	12.4	11.8	11.2
100	17.1	16.4	15.7	15.0	14.3	13.6	12.9	12.3	11.7	11.1
101	17.1	16.4	15.6	14.9	14.2	13.6	12.9	12.3	11.7	11.1
102	17.1	16.4	15.6	14.9	14.2	13.5	12.9	12.2	11.6	11.0
103	17.1	16.3	15.6	14.9	14.2	13.5	12.9	12.2	11.6	11.0
104	17.1	16.3	15.6	14.9	14.2	13.5	12.8	12.2	11.6	11.0
105	17.1	16.3	15.6	14.9	14.2	13.5	12.8	12.2	11.5	10.9
106	17.1	16.3	15.6	14.8	14.1	13.5	12.8	12.2	11.5	10.9
107	17.0	16.3	15.6	14.8	14.1	13.4	12.8	12.1	11.5	10.9
108	17.0	16.3	15.5	14.8	14.1	13.4	12.8	12.1	11.5	10.9
109	17.0	16.3	15.5	14.8	14.1	13.4	12.8	12.1	11.5	10.9
110	17.0	16.3	15.5	14.8	14.1	13.4	12.7	12.1	11.5	10.9
111	17.0	16.3	15.5	14.8	14.1	13.4	12.7	12.1	11.5	10.8
112	17.0	16.3	15.5	14.8	14.1	13.4	12.7	12.1	11.5	10.8
113	17.0	16.3	15.5	14.8	14.1	13.4	12.7	12.1	11.4	10.8
114	17.0	16.3	15.5	14.8	14.1	13.4	12.7	12.1	11.4	10.8
115+	17.0	16.3	15.5	14.8	14.1	13.4	12.7	12.1	11.4	10.8

AGES	80	81	82	83	84	85	86	87	88	89
80	13.8	13.4	13.1	12.8	12.6	12.3	12.1	11.9	11.7	11.5
81	13.4	13.1	12.7	12.4	12.2	11.9	11.7	11.4	11.3	11.1
82	13.1	12.7	12.4	12.1	11.8	11.5	11.3	11.0	10.8	10.6
83	12.8	12.4	12.1	11.7	11.4	11.1	10.9	10.6	10.4	10.2
84	12.6	12.2	11.8	11.4	11.1	10.8	10.5	10.3	10.1	9.9
85	12.3	11.9	11.5	11.1	10.8	10.5	10.2	9.9	9.7	9.5
86	12.1	11.7	11.3	10.9	10.5	10.2	9.9	9.6	9.4	9.2
87	11.9	11.4	11.0	10.6	10.3	9.9	9.6	9.4	9.1	8.9
88	11.7	11.3	10.8	10.4	10.1	9.7	9.4	9.1	8.8	8.6
89	11.5	11.1	10.6	10.2	9.9	9.5	9.2	8.9	8.6	8.3
90	11.4	10.9	10.5	10.1	9.7	9.3	9.0	8.6	8.3	8.1
91	11.3	10.8	10.3	9.9	9.5	9.1	8.8	8.4	8.1	7.9
92	11.2	10.7	10.2	9.8	9.3	9.0	8.6	8.3	8.0	7.7
93	11.1	10.6	10.1	9.6	9.2	8.8	8.5	8.1	7.8	7.5
94	11.0	10.5	10.0	9.5	9.1	8.7	8.3	8.0	7.6	7.3
95	10.9	10.4	9.9	9.4	9.0	8.6	8.2	7.8	7.5	7.2
96	10.8	10.3	9.8	9.3	8.9	8.5	8.1	7.7	7.4	7.1
97	10.7	10.2	9.7	9.2	8.8	8.4	8.0	7.6	7.3	6.9
98	10.7	10.1	9.6	9.2	8.7	8.3	7.9	7.5	7.1	6.8
99	10.6	10.1	9.6	9.1	8.6	8.2	7.8	7.4	7.0	6.7
100	10.6	10.0	9.5	9.0	8.5	8.1	7.7	7.3	6.9	6.6
101	10.5	10.0	9.4	9.0	8.5	8.0	7.6	7.2	6.9	6.5
102	10.5	9.9	9.4	8.9	8.4	8.0	7.5	7.1	6.8	6.4
103	10.4	9.9	9.4	8.8	8.4	7.9	7.5	7.1	6.7	6.3
104	10.4	9.8	9.3	8.8	8.3	7.9	7.4	7.0	6.6	6.3
105	10.4	9.8	9.3	8.8	8.3	7.8	7.4	7.0	6.6	6.2
106	10.3	9.8	9.2	8.7	8.2	7.8	7.3	6.9	6.5	6.2
107	10.3	9.8	9.2	8.7	8.2	7.7	7.3	6.9	6.5	6.1
108	10.3	9.7	9.2	8.7	8.2	7.7	7.3	6.8	6.4	6.1
109	10.3	9.7	9.2	8.7	8.2	7.7	7.2	6.8	6.4	6.0
110	10.3	9.7	9.2	8.6	8.1	7.7	7.2	6.8	6.4	6.0
111	10.3	9.7	9.1	8.6	8.1	7.6	7.2	6.8	6.3	6.0
112	10.2	9.7	9.1	8.6	8.1	7.6	7.2	6.7	6.3	5.9
113	10.2	9.7	9.1	8.6	8.1	7.6	7.2	6.7	6.3	5.9
114	10.2	9.7	9.1	8.6	8.1	7.6	7.1	6.7	6.3	5.9
115+	10.2	9.7	9.1	8.6	8.1	7.6	7.1	6.7	6.3	5.9
AGES	90	91	92	93	94	95	96	97	98	99
90	7.8	7.6	7.4	7.2	7.1	6.9	6.8	6.6	6.5	6.4
91	7.6	7.4	7.2	7.0	6.8	6.7	6.5	6.4	6.3	6.1
92	7.4	7.2	7.0	6.8	6.6	6.4	6.3	6.1	6.0	5.9
93	7.2	7.0	6.8	6.6	6.4	6.2	6.1	5.9	5.8	5.6

AGES	90	91	92	93	94	95	96	97	98	99
94	7.1	6.8	6.6	6.4	6.2	6.0	5.9	5.7	5.6	5.4
95	6.9	6.7	6.4	6.2	6.0	5.8	5.7	5.5	5.4	5.2
96	6.8	6.5	6.3	6.1	5.9	5.7	5.5	5.3	5.2	5.0
97	6.6	6.4	6.1	5.9	5.7	5.5	5.3	5.2	5.0	4.9
98	6.5	6.3	6.0	5.8	5.6	5.4	5.2	5.0	4.8	4.7
99	6.4	6.1	5.9	5.6	5.4	5.2	5.0	4.9	4.7	4.5
100	6.3	6.0	5.8	5.5	5.3	5.1	4.9	4.7	4.5	4.4
101	6.2	5.9	5.6	5.4	5.2	5.0	4.8	4.6	4.4	4.2
102	6.1	5.8	5.5	5.3	5.1	4.8	4.6	4.4	4.3	4.1
103	6.0	5.7	5.4	5.2	5.0	4.7	4.5	4.3	4.1	4.0
104	5.9	5.6	5.4	5.1	4.9	4.6	4.4	4.2	4.0	3.8
105	5.9	5.6	5.3	5.0	4.8	4.5	4.3	4.1	3.9	3.7
106	5.8	5.5	5.2	4.9	4.7	4.5	4.2	4.0	3.8	3.6
107	5.8	5.4	5.1	4.9	4.6	4.4	4.2	3.9	3.7	3.5
108	5.7	5.4	5.1	4.8	4.6	4.3	4.1	3.9	3.7	3.5
109	5.7	5.3	5.0	4.8	4.5	4.3	4.0	3.8	3.6	3.4
110	5.6	5.3	5.0	4.7	4.5	4.2	4.0	3.8	3.5	3.3
111	5.6	5.3	5.0	4.7	4.4	4.2	3.9	3.7	3.5	3.3
112	5.6	5.3	4.9	4.7	4.4	4.1	3.9	3.7	3.5	3.2
113	5.6	5.2	4.9	4.6	4.4	4.1	3.9	3.6	3.4	3.2
114	5.6	5.2	4.9	4.6	4.3	4.1	3.9	3.6	3.4	3.2
115+	5.5	5.2	4.9	4.6	4.3	4.1	3.8	3.6	3.4	3.1
AGES	100	101	102	103	104	105	106	107	108	109
100	4.2	4.1	3.9	3.8	3.7	3.5	3.4	3.3	3.3	3.2
101	4.1	3.9	3.7	3.6	3.5	3.4	3.2	3.1	3.1	3.0
102	3.9	3.7	3.6	3.4	3.3	3.2	3.1	3.0	2.9	2.8
103	3.8	3.6	3.4	3.3	3.2	3.0	2.9	2.8	2.7	2.6
104	3.7	3.5	3.3	3.2	3.0	2.9	2.7	2.6	2.5	2.4
105	3.5	3.4	3.2	3.0	2.9	2.7	2.6	2.5	2.4	2.3
106	3.4	3.2	3.1	2.9	2.7	2.6	2.4	2.3	2.2	2.1
107	3.3	3.1	3.0	2.8	2.6	2.5	2.3	2.2	2.1	2.0
108	3.3	3.1	2.9	2.7	2.5	2.4	2.2	2.1	1.9	1.8
109	3.2	3.0	2.8	2.6	2.4	2.3	2.1	2.0	1.8	1.7
110	3.1	2.9	2.7	2.5	2.3	2.2	2.0	1.9	1.7	1.6
111	3.1	2.9	2.7	2.5	2.3	2.1	1.9	1.8	1.6	1.5
112	3.0	2.8	2.6	2.4	2.2	2.0	1.9	1.7	1.5	1.4
113	3.0	2.8	2.6	2.4	2.2	2.0	1.8	1.6	1.5	1.3
114	3.0	2.7	2.5	2.3	2.1	1.9	1.8	1.6	1.4	1.3
115+	2.9	2.7	2.5	2.3	2.1	1.9	1.7	1.5	1.4	1.2

AGES	110	111	112	113	114	115+				
110	1.5	1.4	1.3	1.2	1.1	1.1				
111	1.4	1.2	1.1	1.1	1.0	1.0				
112	1.3	1.1	1.0	1.0	1.0	1.0				
113	1.2	1.1	1.0	1.0	1.0	1.0				
114	1.1	1.0	1.0	1.0	1.0	1.0				
115+	1.1	1.0	1.0	1.0	1.0	1.0				

Appendix IV

RETIREMENT PLANNING RESOURCES
FOR CONSUMERS AND FINANCIAL ADVISORS

WEBSITES:

www.irahelp.com

Here you will find a wealth of retirement planning and distribution information and breaking news. You will also be able to get on our mailing list and have the latest retirement and IRA tax law and ruling alerts e-mailed to you when they are released by Congress, the IRS, and other authorities. In addition, you can join our Discussion Forum, a free resource open to anyone with a question about retirement planning, distribution, and estate planning. There are thousands of questions and answers posted here for your reference, so chances are whatever questions you may have about how to handle your retirement savings will be answered here. The website also provides a complete listing of all my seminars, advisor training workshops, and education programs for consumers, company employees, credit unions, and professional advisors throughout the year.

www.leimbergservices.com

For more estate planning information, tax strategies, and almost daily briefings on how to make the most of the new estate planning opportunities, I highly recommend you sign up with Leimberg Information Services Inc. (LISI). You'll gain access to this incredible e-mail/database resource that contains a wealth of up-to-the-minute information and analysis on employee benefit planning, IRA, pension, and estate planning cases, rulings, and legislation. You'll receive fast, frank, incisive commentary by the nation's leading experts in each specific area and a virtual daily newsletter. Amazingly, all of these services are included in the $24.95 monthly fee. Take a free look and then sign up for LISI at www.leimbergservices.com.

www.pensco.com

PENSCO Trust Company is a leading financial institution in the area of self-directed IRAs for those making nontraditional types of investments, such as real estate, mortgages, private placements, and other property, with their IRAs and other retirement funds.

NEWSLETTERS:

Ed Slott's IRA Advisor

My monthly newsletter (twelve issues per year)—$125 a year. Each issue contains clear and accurate explanations of the latest IRA- and retirement-related tax rulings, cases, and tax law changes and also shows you how to use this information to benefit your clients and build your practice, including easy to view summaries of key points and advisor action plans. Order the online version (at www.irahelp.com or call 800-663-1340) at the same $125, and get much more. With the online version you gain access to our complete online research library of back issues, back to 2001 when the IRS overhauled the retirement distribution rules. For financial advisors especially, this can be invaluable if a client, prospect, CPA, or attorney has an issue and you need to look up a ruling, court case, or a tax law change quickly and know you have the right answer. Whatever you are looking for, chances are that it has been covered in a past issue. To make your search easier, you can also use the December issue, which includes a cumulative index of all the items we covered for that year. They will all wonder how you know so much and found the correct answer so quickly!

BOOKS:

Parlay Your IRA Into a Family Fortune (Viking, 2005) by Ed Slott, a three-step strategy for creating a lifetime supply of tax-deferred, even tax-free, wealth for you and your family.

The Retirement Savings Time Bomb . . . and How to Defuse It (Viking, 2003) by Ed Slott, a five-step action plan for protecting your IRAs, 401(k)s, and other retirement plans from near annihilation by the Taxman.

Life and Death Planning for Retirement Benefits by Natalie B. Choate (Ataxplan Publications, 2006, $89.95 plus $7 shipping. Call 800-247-6553, or visit www.ataxplan.com). Now in its sixth edition, this is the industry bible on retirement distribution and estate planning, the essential reference resource for every financial advisor, attorney, CPA, and estate planner who advises their clients on these issues. You cannot seriously be in this business without it.

The Advisor's Guide to the Retirement Distribution Rules by Seymour Goldberg, published by the American Bar Association. Order online at: www.abanet .org/abastore. (Type Product Code 1610053 into "search" box.) Format: Download. ABA Member Price: $79.95 / Non-Member: $89.95. Seymour Goldberg is a senior partner in the law firm of Goldberg & Goldberg, P.C., Jericho, New York. He is Professor Emeritus of Law and Taxation at Long Island University. Goldberg is the recipient of the American Jurisprudence Award in Federal Estate and Gift Taxation from St. John's University School of Law. He is also a member of the IRS Northeast Pension Liaison Group. He can be reached at (516) 222-0422, extension 15.

ESTATE, TAX, AND FINANCIAL PLANNING SOFTWARE:

NumberCruncher. An estate and financial planning program created by Stephan R. Leimberg and Robert T. LeClair that is essential for every financial advisor. I use this program for all the estate, income tax, and compound interest computations in my books, newsletters, and advisor course manuals, but most of all we use it to do planning for our clients and you should too. "NumberCruncher" includes a financial planning module in addition to the estate-planning module. It's the only program professional advisors need to instantly put real numbers on any type of planning situation. It includes every imaginable tax and financial planning calculation. It sells for $395 (plus shipping and handling) and can be ordered at www.leimberg.com.

Pension & Roth IRA Analyzer. This program from Brentmark Software may be used to evaluate various strategies of taking distributions from traditional IRAs, Roth IRAs, and qualified pension plans. Calculates up to four alternatives simultaneously for varying types of distributions; handles issues such as new tax law changes; additional contributions to pension fund; distributions to fund living expenses (subject to minimum distribution rules); insurance premiums and proceeds, and pre-59½ distributions that avoid the 10 percent penalty; and Roth conversion analysis. Estate tax may be handled by the entry of taxable estate values or by having the program calculate the taxable estate if you enter the value of other assets. Income tax rates may be entered on a yearly basis. Growth of other assets may even be modeled as realized or unrealized capital gains, if desired. Multiple beneficiaries (up to five) are handled by the program also. Order online at www.brentmark.com, or by phone at 800-879-6665. It is priced at $395.

Index

Acknowledgments

Beverly DeVeny deserves much of the credit for this book since it could not possibly have been completed without her hard work and input. Beverly is an IRA expert and I am lucky to have her on staff as an IRA technical consultant. She has checked and rechecked every word of this manuscript for accuracy, but as always, I take responsibility for any errors. She did an amazing job here on a very tight schedule that involved working late at night and on weekends, all the while traveling to seminars, preparing course manuals, answering countless e-mails from financial advisors, consulting with advisors and consumers who call our office with their IRA issues, and helping with our newsletter, "Ed Slott's IRA Advisor." Thank you, Beverly, for the fantastic job you do year-round.

Thank you to all of the financial, insurance, and tax advisors who attend my seminars and support my work on behalf of America's retirees and retirees-to-be. If not for you, my message would not get out to the very people who can benefit from it most. I applaud you for investing in your continuing IRA education so you can help your clients make the best moves with their retirement savings.

I also must thank the numerous financial institutions that support my retirement planning training programs, seminars, and workshops. These include insurance companies, broker-dealers, mutual fund companies, banks, brokerage firms, financial planning firms, and other sponsoring organizations who bring me in to train and educate their staff and clients. Without your funding of these educational programs, consumers would not be as well served. Thank you for your vision in helping to improve the financial lives of your advisors and their clients and families. Here is just a partial list of many of these companies I work with: Principal Financial Group, ING, WM Funds, Fidelity Investments, Oppenheimer Funds, MFS, Merrill Lynch, UBS, Smith Barney, RBC Dain Rauscher, A.G. Edwards, AXA Distributors, Jackson National Life, Prudential Financial, Genworth Financial, CUSO Financial Services, John Hancock Funds, New York Life, Met Life, Nationwide Financial, Ameriprise, Wachovia Securities, LPL Financial Advisors, AIG Sun America, Securities America, Asset Protectors, and many others. Again, thank you all.

Thanks also to the people at Random House who helped me bring this book to you, especially Jane von Mehren (Publisher, Random House Publishing Group Trade Paperbacks) who I have worked with before. Jane shares my vision and was a key player in getting this book to market. Thanks also to my editors, Ben Loehnen and Christina Duffy, for guiding me through the process, and to the others at Random House who assisted in making this book possible:

Gina Centrello (Publisher, Random House Publishing Group)

Libby McGuire (Publisher, Ballantine)

Subrights: Rachel Bernstein

Production: Lisa Feuer, Crystal Velasquez, Alexandra Krijgsman, and
  Grant Neumann

Marketing: Kim Hovey, Stacey Witcraft, and Katie O'Callaghan

Sales: Jack Perry and Kelle Ruden

Publicity: Patty Park and Brian McLendon

Art: Derek Walls and Gene Mydlowski

Thanks to Joy Tutela, my literary agent at the David Black Agency Inc. for putting up with me and taking care of everything from contract negotiations to getting my books on the shelves. Thanks for your support day in and day out.

John McCarty collaborated with me on my previous books, *The Retirement Savings Time Bomb . . . and How to Defuse It* and *Parlay Your IRA Into a Family Fortune,* and did so again on this one, the third installment in my retirement distribution planning series and the last piece of the puzzle to protecting your nest egg from the Taxman. John and I share the same sense of humor. He is a workhorse and we function together like a watch, especially on tight schedules. Everything I write reads much better because of John's writing and editing skills. Publishers love his work and ability to meet deadlines too! Thanks, John.

I also must thank the New York State Society of CPAs, The American Institute of Certified Public Accountants (AICPA), The Estate Planning Council of New York City Inc., and the National Conference of CPA Practitioners. These are the professional organizations that gave me an opportunity to hone my professional and technical skills by providing me with a forum at their conferences and meetings. This is where it all began for me, so I encourage anyone in any profession to get involved with your own professional organizations. You will develop lifelong relationships that will help you succeed at your chosen field. This has been especially true for me and I thank all of my colleagues at these groups who have helped me along the way and still provide incredible support.

Tax legend Sidney Kess is an example of the kind of people you meet along the way in life who love to help. He has mentored me and many others. Sid is always helping someone become more successful and everyone has the same wonderful things to say about him. Thank you, Sid, for giving me the chance to speak at your programs and get my feet wet.

Sanford M. Fisch is the Founder and Chief Executive Officer of the American Academy of Estate Planning Attorneys, an exclusive group of highly trained attorneys who have expertise in creating estate plans for clients with retirement assets. I acknowledge Sanford here for his vision and commitment to the continuing education of the Academy members. He saw that more and more consumers had retirement savings plans and needed to find attorneys who were trained in distribution planning as well as estate planning. Sanford made sure that this specialized training was made available to all Academy members. The Academy became the first attorney group in the country to take our specialized retirement distribution training so that the attorneys could competently integrate their clients' retirement plans with their overall estate plans. Many of the Academy members have taken this training and continue to do so. I encourage both consumers and professional advisors to work with them. I have also posted the names of the trained attorneys on our website (www.irahelp.com) so that you can more easily find them. I applaud Sanford Fisch and the American Academy of Estate Planning Attorneys for their efforts to continually enhance their education and for their commitment to their clients.

Million Dollar Round Table is a first-class organization whose members include the world's finest insurance professionals. I am so thankful to Million Dollar Round Table and Top of the Table for their consistent support of my books and programs and for inviting me to speak at their functions. It is always a high honor to be able to present to their members and I deeply appreciate the many opportunities MDRT has provided me to do so. I am always looking forward to the next meeting so I can reconnect with my many MDRT friends. Thank you for including me in your prestigious programs.

Thanks to AALU (Association for Advanced Life Underwriting) for inviting me to present at your exclusive annual meetings. This is a great honor and I love being a part of your program.

Thanks to my friends at *Financial Planning* magazine including Jennifer

Liptow, Dan Goldeman, Marion Asnes, Pamela Black, and Pat Durner, a first-class team if ever there was one. I am proud to be associated with you as a contributor to this fine publication for the past fifteen years.

Thanks to the editors and publishers of the Bottom Line Publications, including *Tax Hotline* and *Bottom Line Personal,* for including me on their editorial boards and featuring me in many articles. The exposure through the Bottom Line networks is really amazing and I thank you for that opportunity. Thanks also for the wonderful job your staff of excellent writers and editors do to make your publications so accurate and informative.

Sandeep Varma is one of the best and most successful financial advisors in the country, but the reason I acknowledge him here is because he is also a great friend, and a generous and honorable person. He has a well-earned reputation for giving of himself to many national charities and organizations where he solves clients' problems with creative solutions that many times benefit the charities as well. Sandeep and his wife, Nisha, run Advanced Trustee Strategies Inc. in San Diego, California. Sandeep, Nisha, and their entire staff are great people to work with. I am glad to know you, Sandeep, and I value our friendship.

Mark Rozell is my own estate-planning attorney and I thank him for helping me implement a plan that protects my family, my employees, and my business.

Alan Kahn is my financial advisor and insurance professional. As you know from my books, even though I do not sell life insurance, I believe in the concept as a means to leverage current assets and protect my family. Since I practice what I preach, I want to thank to Alan for making sure this was taken care of for me and my family.

Seymour "Sy" Goldberg is my friend and the person I must always credit for showing me the light of retirement distribution planning and the impact it has on so many people and advisors. Sy is a true visionary. He saw this market emerging years before anyone else and I was lucky to meet him early on in my career. Thanks for sharing your IRA brilliance with me, Sy.

Thanks also to my IRA colleague, Natalie B. Choate, Esq. for her support of my IRA newsletter and advisor training programs. Natalie is a true IRA guru and we spend much of our time spreading the IRA gospel throughout the country with our numerous seminars. Thanks, Natalie, for all your help. The work you do benefits so many financial advisors and their clients. See you on the road!

Denise Appleby is an all-around retirement expert with her own financial planning firm, Appleby Retirement Consulting, and is a technical advisor to me. In addition to being a distinguished member of Ed Slott's Elite IRA Advisor Group (Master Elite), Denise has every designation you could possibly think of including the Accredited Pension Administrator (APA) from the

National Institute of Pension Administrators; the Certified IRA Services Professional (CISP) designation from the Institute of Certified Bankers; the Chartered Retirement Plans Specialist (CRPS) designation from the College for Financial Planning; Certified Retirement Services Professional (CRSP) designation from the Institute of Certified Bankers; and the Certified Retirement Counselor (CRC) designation from the International Foundation for Retirement Education (InFRE), just to name a few. Thanks, Denise, for all your technical assistance and support.

Retirement planning tax law is not easy stuff and I could not possibly do it all alone. In addition to Sy Goldberg and Natalie Choate, and our own Beverly DeVeny and Denise Appleby, I would also like to thank and recognize several other IRA experts. Bob Keebler, Mike Jones, Stephen Krass, David Foster, Gordon Weis, Steven Lockwood, Martin Shenkman, Guerdon Ely, Jeremiah Doyle, Steven Trytten, Tom Gau, Mary Kay Foss, Sally Mulhern, Joel Bruckenstein, Gary Lesser, John Bledsoe, James Lange, Barry Picker, Bruce Steiner, and Victor Finmann.

Thanks to Stephan R. Leimberg, a great friend and an amazing person, who believes in sharing and giving. Steve, along with his partner, Robert T. LeClair, runs Leimberg Information Services Inc. (LISI), the best estate, tax, and retirement planning information service available. I appreciate your support, Steve, and thank you for the meaningful work you do. I love telling advisors about you.

Thanks to Marvin R. Rotenberg, the Director of Individual Retirement Services, Retirement Solutions Group at Bank of America. Marvin is responsible for creating distribution strategies from qualified plans and IRAs for clients with substantial net worth. Marvin is one of the nicest people I know and so generous with his time and resources, along with Mark LaVangie and Richard B. James, who work with Marvin. They all help with the editing of my newsletters and books and are always there for those tough IRA questions. They have been a valuable resource for me for many years and I appreciate our friendship. Thanks, guys.

A big part of retirement distribution planning involves the software tools that make life easier, and for that I thank Gregory Kolojeski, president of Brentmark Software, for the products he produces that I use in my books and advisor training seminars. Jane Schuck is Brentmark's field representative and brings real value to Brentmark's software products because she is always willing to spend time with advisors, showing them how to make the most of these important tools. Thanks, Greg and Jane.

Bill Nelson of the Nelson Financial Group in Dayton, Ohio, is a super financial advisor and trainer. He is in the stratosphere when it comes to selling and is literally one of the top producers in the world. Bill is also the founder of the Learning Institute for Financial Executives (LIFE School). This is a comprehensive program that helps financial advisors aid their clients in growing, distributing, and leaving their money in a tax-efficient manner. He shows other financial and insurance advisors how to create the success that Bill has had. Bill is making a big difference in the lives of millions, including mine, through his genius and his generosity in sharing that genius with others. If you are an insurance or financial advisor you should look into Bill Nelson's LIFE School to jumpstart your business now and serve your clients better. You can call Bill at (937) 426-7032, and mention my name! Bill is a credit to his profession and I admire his work and his message.

Special thanks to Paul Peterson, president of Emerald Publications, the nation's leading provider of innovative marketing and technology tools that help financial professionals succeed. Also, special thanks to financial-planning wizard Bill Nelson, the mastermind behind *Retirement Unlimited,* a hands-on personal finance workshop that shows individuals how to get the most out of my IRA strategies. To find out more about *Retirement Unlimited* or to order it, call (800) 233-2834.

Donald Jay Korn is one of the truly great tax and financial writers and I am lucky to have him as an interviewer and writer for my newsletter. Don has a long list of other professional credentials including *The New York Times, Investor's Business Daily, Financial Planning* magazine, *Bottom Line* Publications, and many others. Thanks, Don, for your great work taking very technical tax topics and making them easier for us all to read and learn from.

Thanks to Dan Sullivan and Dan Taylor at The Strategic Coach. This is one of the great programs available for helping people reach professional goals that once seemed only distant dreams. They do fantastic work and I encourage others to get to know the "Coach" program. Thanks for a lifetime of success.

Doug Davidoff of Imagine Consulting has helped my company find its way and helped it grow by creating business plans and strategies. We consult with Doug year-round. His ideas make sense and have helped us move the company to the next level. Thanks, Doug.

Publicity is a part of getting our message out and I thank Brian Feinblum at PTA (Planned Television Artists) for the job he has done for me with my national radio tours. I have found him and his staff to be highly professional, honest, and reliable. They do what they say they will do and that, as they say, is saying something these days. Thanks, Brian.

Thanks to my long-time media friends Ken and Daria Dolan. They not only provide reliable financial information to millions of people, but they are really nice folks, and I enjoy being part of their radio and television programs.

This book and my others have all shared the goal of educating readers so they can take the steps necessary to protect and preserve their life savings. But I also make it clear that they need competent advisors to help them properly execute their planning decisions. This goal is now even more attainable for every reader thanks to all the financial advisors who are members of *Ed Slott's Elite IRA Advisor Group*™ and *Master Elite IRA Advisors*. These are some of the best and most qualified and educated advisors in the country. These groups are my pride and joy. I love to see the difference they are making in their clients' lives. Thanks to these advisors for helping get my message out to the public to accept "only the best advice" when it comes to your retirement savings. These Elite IRA Advisors are making people's lives more financially secure.

Laurin Levine is the managing partner of our company and a true friend to me. Laurin runs all aspects of our various businesses and has helped build the company from the minute she came aboard many years ago. Anyone who knows me probably also knows Laurin and knows why I think so highly of her. Thank you, Laurin, for our success, which would not have been possible without you.

Laurin has two secret weapons in our office: Pat Pakus and Glenda Zolezzi. They are the ones who make sure all the details are taken care of, whether it is making and fixing travel plans for me, sending out seminar packages and promotional materials, or taking calls from newsletter subscribers, clients, and financial advisors. They do it all. Thank you too, Pat and Glenda, for being such a big part of our team.

Margot Reilly and Mike Lichter, CPA run our tax practice year-round and have been with me for many years. Thanks to Margot and Mike I can be out on the road doing my seminars knowing that they are taking good care of our clients, which is our number one concern.

Chris Paliani is our director of operations and is a truly good person who cares about others. Chris is one of the most dedicated people I know and he shares our goals and dreams. Chris also has great people helping him, including Ryan Fortese, Pat Hawk, and Janet Flood. They work with Chris extensively on our advisor training programs and our Elite IRA Advisor Groups and do all of our strategic marketing. You are all very much appreciated for the job you do. Thank you very much for your dedication to our vision and helping us grow. The future is brighter with all of you on board.

I thank my family for being supportive of my work and rigorous travel schedule, which keep me away from home and from them too much of the time. But when I am home my wife Linda, and my children Ilana and Rachel are great to be with and I look forward to every minute I get to spend with them. Thank you for your love and understanding of my work.

My dad won't see this but I wish he could have. I still thank him every day for what I am and what I have and the family and business values he instilled in me. Thanks go equally to my mom, the youngest 80-year-old I have ever known, who, with my dad, has always supported my goals and dreams. I credit every accomplishment to my wonderful parents and I hope I can do the same for my children.

About the Author

ED SLOTT is a nationally recognized IRA distribution expert, a professional speaker, and hosts the website www.irahelp.com. He regularly presents continuing professional education seminars on IRA distribution planning and estate planning at major conferences for financial advisor firms, mutual fund companies, brokerage firms, insurance professionals, financial planners, trust companies, banks, CPAs, and attorneys. He has established Ed Slott's Elite IRA Advisor Group™, whose members attend advanced continuing education programs for financial advisors, who, as part of their practice, specialize in retirement distribution planning. In addition, Mr. Slott has created The IRA Leadership Program™ (www.iraleadership.com), developed specifically to help financial institutions, financial advisor firms, and insurance companies become recognized leaders in the IRA marketplace.

Mr. Slott is the author of the top-selling *Parlay Your IRA into a Family Fortune* (Viking, 2005) and *The Retirement Savings Time Bomb . . . and How to Defuse It* (Viking, 2003)—both have hit Amazon.com's "Hot 100" list. He is also the writer and publisher of *Ed Slott's IRA Advisor Newsletter* and a personal finance columnist for numerous financial publications.

Additionally, Mr. Slott is a past chairman of the New York State Society of CPAs Estate Planning Committee and editor of the IRA Planning section of *The CPA Journal*. He is the recipient of the prestigious "Excellence in Estate Planning" and "Outstanding Service" awards presented by the Foundation for Accounting Education.

A frequent contributor to *The CPA Journal, The Practical Accountant,* and *Trusts and Estates,* and a past editor of the estates and trusts section of *The CPA Journal,* Mr. Slott is a member of the National Conference of CPA Practitioners and a former board member of The Estate Planning Council of New York City. He is often quoted in *The New York Times, Newsday,* the *Wall Street Journal,* the *Washington Post,* the *Los Angeles Times,* the *Boston Globe, Time, Newsweek, Fortune Magazine, Forbes Magazine, Money Magazine, Kiplinger's Personal Finance*

Magazine, USA Today, Bloomberg Personal, Medical Economics, Investor's Business Daily, Smart Money, and a host of additional national magazines and financial publications. He has appeared on NBC, ABC, CBS, CNBC, CNN, FOX, PBS, National Public Radio, and Bloomberg TV and radio.

Mr. Slott is also an Internet consultant to numerous financial information websites.

For information on booking Ed Slott as a keynote speaker for your next conference, meeting, or company event, or to learn more about Ed Slott's IRA Leadership Program™, a customized full-day advisor training and marketing program for companies that want to be recognized as leaders in the IRA market and increase their retirement-related business, contact:

Laurin Levine
Ed Slott and Company
telephone: (800) 663-1340
fax: (516) 536-8852
e-mail: *laurin@irahelp.com*
address: 100 Merrick Road
                    Suite 200 East
                    Rockville Centre, NY 11570
website: www.irahelp.com

Singer From The Sea

Singer From The Sea

SHERI S. TEPPER

AVON · EOS

AVON BOOKS, INC.
1350 Avenue of the Americas
New York, New York 10019

Copyright © 1999 by Sheri S. Tepper
Interior design by Kellan Peck
ISBN: 0-380-97480-0
www.avonbooks.com/eos

Library of Congress Cataloging in Publication Data:

Tepper, Sheri S.
Singer from the sea / Sheri S. Tepper.—1st ed.
p.   cm.
I. Title.
PS3570.E673S57   1999   99-10231
813'.54—dc21   CIP

First Avon Eos Printing: April 1999

AVON EOS TRADEMARK REG. U.S. PAT. OFF. AND IN OTHER COUNTRIES, MARCA REGISTRADA,
HECHO EN U.S.A.

Printed in the U.S.A.

FIRST EDITION

QPM   10   9   8   7   6   5   4   3   2   1

The following are Maori words used in the text. Long vowels appear in bold face. Ng and wh are letters peculiar to Maori. Ng as in singing. Wh is usually pronounced F. R is close to L, not rolled.

awhero	hope
haere mai	welcome
he	a, an, some
hohonu	deep
huna	conceal e.g., mea huna, secret thing
kaikaukau	swimmer
kamakama	quick
karanga	call, shout
kuia	old lady
e kui	form of address
mai	hither, to me
mana	charisma, power
marae	meeting place. Also fortress, tribal center
matangi	wind
matawaka	ancestral canoes
mea	thing, article
morehu	saved, survivor
nga	the, plural e.g. nga matangi, the winds
nui	large, great
oranga	safety
parauri	dark skinned
taiao	world
tahunga makutu	wizard
tapairu	honored lady
tapu	sacred, forbidden
te	the, singular e.g. te taiao, the world
Tenopia	Zenobia
Tewhani	Stephanie
tumau	servant
wairua	spirit
wahi	place, site
whakaeke	arriving visitors
whakamomori	wait patiently (malghaste usage, "those who")
whakautu	response
whetu	star

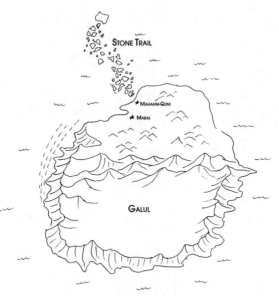

STONE TRAIL

★ MAHAHM-QUM

★ MARAI

GALUL

MAHAHM

UPLANDS

HIGH HAVEN

HAVENOR ★

SCHOOL ★

MIDDLING WELLS ★

DROWNED RANGE

LANGMARSH

MERDUNE

HAVEN POOL

REUSAL ON MERE

MERDUNE LAGOON

ROCKWARD ★

SEALANDS

POOLWICH ★

RIVER REUSAL

DANIA

WEIRMILLS ★

WELLSPORT ★

POTCHER WATER

BARFEZI

BLIGGEN ★

RIVER GIDE

FRANGIA

HAVEN

IN GENEVIEVE'S DREAM, THE OLD WOMAN LUNGED UP THE STAIRS, HANDS clutching like claws from beneath her ragtag robe. "Lady. They're coming to kill you, now!"

She dreamed herself responding, too slowly at first, for she was startled and confused by the old woman's agitation. "Who? Awhero, what are you talking about."

"Your father's taken. The Shah has him. Now his men come for your blood! Yours and the child's. They're coming."

The smell of blood was all around her, choking her. So much blood. Her husband, gone; now her father, taken! Dovidi, only a baby, and never outside these walls!

Genevieve dreamed herself crying, "They're coming after Dovidi? How did the Shah know about the baby?"

"Your father tell him."

Endanger his grandson in that way? Surely not. Oh, surely, surely not. "I'll get him. We'll go . . ."

"If you take baby, you both be killed." The old woman reached forward and shook her by the shoulders, so vehement as to forget the prohibitions of caste. "I take him. I smutch his face and say he one of us. They scared to look and they never doubt . . ."

"Take me, too . . ."

"No. You too tall. Too strange looking. They know you!"

"Where? Where shall I go?"

"I sing you Tenopia. Go like Tenopia. By door, your man's cloak with his sunhelmet, with his needfuls still there, in pockets." She pulled at the rags that hung from her shoulders, shreds tied together to make a tattered wrapping. "Take this! You tall for woman, so you walk past like man. Malghaste man. Go now!"

In her dream, she babbled something about getting word to the ship,

then she went, thrust hard by Awhero's arms, strong for a woman her age. She fled to the courtyard, to the door through the city wall, a door that stood ajar! She could see directly into the guardpost outside—empty. Never empty except now! It smelled of a trap!

Beside the door hung the outer robe with its sunhelmet hood lining, behind the door half a dozen staves stood below a pendant cluster of water bottles, like flaccid grapes. She shut and bolted the inviting door, snatched the cloak, a staff, a waterbottle, and fled back through the house to the kitchen wing, calling to someone as she went past the kitchens to the twisting stairs that only the malghaste used. Awhero had shown her the hatchway below, and she went directly to it, struggling into the robe as she fled, draping the rags around her shoulders to make it look as if she were clad only in tatters. As she slipped through the hatchway she heard voices shouting and fists thundering at the door she had barred.

She came out in a deep stairwell where coiled stairs led up to the narrow alley. The alley led to the street. She went up, and out, head down, a little bent, the staff softly thumping as she moved slowly, like any other passerby. Ahead of her was the narrow malghaste gate through the city wall, never guarded, never even watched, for this was where the untouchables carried out the city's filth. The stained and tattered rags marked her as one of them. Outside that gate a small malghaste boy guarded a flock of juvenile harpya, their fin-wings flattened against the heat, and beyond the flock was a well with a stone coping. The area around it was sodden, and she felt the mud ooze over her toes as she filled the bottle, slung it over her shoulder and walked away on the northern road, still slowly, as any malghaste might go. She did not run until she was out of sight of the town.

In her dream she was being hunted by dogs.

She woke to hear them baying, closer than before.

No. No, not dogs. Arghad's hunters came on wings, not feet, and they had pursued her for two days, now. The Mahahmbi had no dogs, but their birds-of-prey had dogs' loyalty to their masters, dogs' ability to track by scent, and they could scream a signal from the sky when they detected their quarry. She had left her smell behind, on towels, on clothing, on all the baby's things. There had been much of her to give the hunters!

Two nights she had moved over the desert, sometimes running, sometimes staggering; almost three days she had hidden on the desert sleeping when she could. Through last night, the wind had been from the south, and she had fled into it, blinking its grit from her eyes. This morning, the third morning, it had swung around, coming from the west, and she

had lain down on the lee side of a dune, in the shade cast by a line of bone bushes, her head to the north, her feet to the south as Tenopia had done, aware, even through her exhaustion, of the symbolism of the act. Tenopia-songs paid much attention to the interior meanings of simple things. Tenopia: the heroine of women's songs sung by the malghaste in Mahahm-qum.

Lying with her feet away from the city signified that though matters of her mind were in the city behind her, her survival lay in moving away. Dovidi was behind her, and pray heaven he was safe. The menfolk were there, perhaps, if they were not dead. She could do nothing about any of them, but she might save herself. Any hope of doing so lay south, toward the refuge of the malghaste. If her mind struggled with this, her feet did not, for they staggered southward while she was only half awake, into the long shadows east of the stone dike that belted the base of the dune.

Long ago, when this world had been volcanic, the edge of a huge surface block had been thrust upright to make a mighty rampart running north and south. Within the block, layers of igneous rock had been separated by thicker layers of softer, sedimentary stuff, now much worn away to leave paths sheltered from the wind by parallel walls, stone lanes she could use now as Tenopia had used them long ago.

North was the sea, where the shepherds pastured their flocks on the seaweed washed ashore by the sea winds. East or west was desert scattered with hidden oases, already occupied by Mahahmbi. When Tenopia had gone southward, however, toward the pole, she had found refuges along the way. If one went far enough, the malghaste said, one might find Galul, mountainous Galul, with forests, shade, flowers, running water. Perhaps it was true. Or, perhaps it was only a prisoner's myth, the Mahahmbi idea of heaven, achieved as a reward for some unthinkable virtue.

Though the rag-tatters over her sand-colored robe were the best camouflage she could have; though her feet left no lasting tracks in the wind-blown sand; still she stank of fear, of stale sweat, and of the breastmilk down the front of her bodysuit that had soured before drying. Now the stiffened fabric chafed her with every step, and the odor floated on the still air for the winged hunters to sniff out. When Tenopia had come this way, she had sung to nga tahunga makutu matangi, the wizards of the winds, asking their help in confusing her trail. She knew no invocation to bring the tahunga makutu to her aid. She would have to rely on her own two feet.

The dunes rose higher on her left, the sand ascended in the path she followed; eventually it rose to the top of the walls, burying the stone

lanes. She took a sighting south, on a distant outcropping, and held to that direction, swerving only briefly between two thorny mounds, around another, hearing the shrieks from the heavens fade behind her. The hunters were going off at a northeasterly tangent, getting farther away. When the stone dike reemerged it was only a shallow ridge, rooted in the ribbon of shadow along its eastern side. She slipped into the shade, her feet plopping into it as fish into water, feeling the coolness rise to her knees, hips, to her waist as the wall loomed higher, topping her head at last and continuing to rise in erose scallops and notches. A few yards to her left a parallel wall emerged from the sand, and before long she moved in a blessed corridor of shade and calm air, away from the forge of the sun, the huffing bellows of the wind.

Both the shadowed lane and the hunters' misdirection were blessings. Perhaps the wind wizards had decided to help her without being asked. Or perhaps Awhero had sent someone into the desert with a sack of the baby's diapers, to draw the hunters away. Several times Genevieve had heard either men or birds frighteningly close, but they had always turned aside. She caught her breath at the memory of panic, yesterday's fear adding to this moment's weariness. She bent to ease a sudden pain in her side, aware of an overwhelming thirst. She reached for her waterbottle . . .

Gone. Left where she'd been sleeping!

She collapsed against the stone, head falling onto her knees, arms wrapped around her head, holding herself together, denying the terror that threatened to erupt in hysterical screaming or laughter or shouts of nonsense. Think, Genevieve, she told herself. Think. The bottle had only a swallow or two left in it, not worth going back for. Besides, if the men gave up on their current line of search and backtracked into the wind, they could still come across her trail before dark. Also, when Tenopia had escaped from the Shah of Mahahm-qum, she had reached a sanctuary on the third evening. This was Genevieve's third evening, and she might already be within sight of the place the old woman called te marae, he wahi oranga. Water or no, better go on than back.

She stood up again, putting one foot in front of the other, fighting the urge to lick her lips. They were already split and bleeding. Licking them only made them worse. The Mahahmbi wore veils across their faces when in the desert, and they carried unguents for their lips and eyelids. That is, the men did. Women had no need of such stuff, for women did not go into the desert. Except for Tenopia. And, come to think of it, she didn't know what time of day Tenopia had run from Mahahm-qum. Gene-

vieve herself had fled at noon, or thereabout. She might have another half day to go.

She climbed drifting sand as the walls on either side of her were covered once more. Beyond the dune was an area of gravelly hills, spotted with thorn. She stopped to take her husband's locator from the pocket of his robe and check her direction, following the line into the distance to find a landmark on the horizon. She had come this far from landmark to landmark, south on south, and thank God for the locator, though now, with the sun almost on the horizon, she could almost set a track at right angles to the shadows of the thorn, streaming away to her left, shadows that went down the dune and all the way to the top of another . . .

Color! At the shadow's end, a flicker of green, seen out of the corner of her right eye. There, and again. She veered to the left, across the buried walls, and followed her own attenuated silhouette up the dune, gray granules flowing as she slipped, plunged, wallowed the last few meters, struggling to the top on hands and knees.

Below was the valley described in Tenopia's song, skullstones and dry bones, a dry streambed littered with round white rocks. On the south and east, black-streaked cliffs made a barricade against the sands, underlining bald and wrinkled mountains. Across the dried streambed the walled refuge squatted ugly as a toad, built of the same stone as the cliffs and topped by one stubby tower that flew the long triangle of the banner: a licking flame of green bearing a single gold leaf.

"In desert, hope is small," Awhero had said. "Leaf is sign of hope, small, almost unnoticed. Yet it holds infinite promise, does it not?" There were no leaves in Mahahm-qum. The banners of Mahahm were black, with a blazing yellow sun, and there was sun enough in Mahahm-qum to make ashes of anything living.

Light flashed in her eyes, reflected from the highest window of the tower, only a glint. Lenses. Someone knew she was here. She paused, wondering if the gate would open to emit an attacking horde. Or perhaps just one strong man. Either way, she could do nothing about it. Almost three days of walking in the sand had taken her strength. Too little sleep and water had taken her resolve. Fear had taken her will. She floundered downward in another scrambled avalanche and staggered onto the flinty soil of the riverbed. From there it was only a short distance up the equally hard packed slope to the walls.

The gate was of heavy, sun-grayed planks, rough hewn from huge trees, fastened with spikes of iron. The wood had come from somewhere else. Somewhere behind the far black line of cliffs? From some chasm

among those dun-colored mountains? Or maybe from Galul itself, where water ran and things grew green? Not from hereabout, certainly, for nothing grew in this desolation except black thorn, bonebush, and blood lichen.

She leaned against the door for a moment, staring at the wall, built of the same ashy stone as the cliffs, equally cheerless and forbidding. A protruding beam high above her head ended in a carved skull between whose wooden teeth a bell rope emerged like a tongue, an oily strand with a loop in the end, slightly above the level of her eyes. Almost too late she saw the stem of thorn woven through the loop. Unwary or desperate visitors would pay with agony for interrupting the labors of those within.

Genevieve thrust the crook of her staff through the loop and hauled it down, hard. After a long pause, she heard a sonorous clang so remote in both space and time as to seem unconnected to any action she had taken. She tugged again, and again. Two more long delayed and measured tolls of the distant bell. She said to herself, "We will wait to see what happens. We will not lick our lips. We will not have hysterics. We will simply wait to see what happens . . ."

Not much. A cessation of some background murmur that had been unnoticeable until it ended. A unison of treading feet, which would have been worrisome had they been approaching rather than retreating. Since the place was not eager to welcome her, she turned her back on it and stood facing outward, searching the sky and the horizons for her pursuers. She couldn't see them, which didn't mean they weren't there. What she could see was the everlasting monotone of the desert: gray sand, gray earth, creeping dikes of gray stone among hard gray dunes dotted with the ash white of bonebush, the bleeding scarlet of lichen, the angular thickets of thorn made impenetrable by hundreds of needle-sharp daggers that seeped glistening beads of toxin. The thorn meant more than mere pain. A puncture could fester for weeks before healing. Delganor had told them that, or one of the trade representatives. Everything anyone could find out about Mahahm had been dissected and discussed, and she had listened to all of it, to everything any of them knew about Mahahm. It had not been enough.

The skeletal lines of bonebushes were less forbidding than the thorn, but more eerie, each branch an arm or thigh bone, each twig a finger bone, always growing four or five together in a patch of blood lichen. The thorn grew only where there were many bonebushes, and the bonebushes grew only where lichen had established a hold. Now, in the slant-

ing sun, the lichen glowed crimson, as though it were freshly bled onto the soil. She did not want to think of blood. Had Delganor bled? Was the Marshal dead or dying? Cut down by a hundred seabone daggers. Left lying in all that red for someone to find, or not. If she went back to the house, would any of their party be there, lying in their blood?

She turned back to the gate and rang again. Clang, then again clang, and clang. Three, as before. Temperate, she told herself in a mood of weary fatalism. Not hasty. Not importunate. Merely a measured reminder that someone waited, whenever they got around to seeing who it was, or wasn't.

"Who are you?" a voice asked, near her ear.

She swung around, eyes darting, finally locating the tiny sliding hatch in the door. It had opened without a whisper and the person within was invisible in the shadow. The voice was as anonymous as wind; man, woman, child, devil or angel, it could be any.

She cleared her throat, but the words rasped nonetheless: "My name is Genevieve." She bowed her head and took a deep breath. "In Mahahm-qum, an old woman named Awhero told me to seek Tenopia's haven beneath the green banner."

"Who are you running from?"

"Those who were coming to kill me and my baby, men who have already probably killed my husband and father . . ."

"Et al," she whispered hysterically to herself. "Et al . . ."

She raised her head to find the hatch closed once more. She waited. After a time she thrust the staff through the loop and clanged again, another measured three.

This time she saw the hatch slide open. "Don't be impatient. You may enter. The small opening to your left."

It was a considerable distance to her left, a narrow slot around and behind a great wallowing buttress, like the buttocks of some huge animal that had stood forever, pushing up the wall. The passage did not extend through the wall but only into the buttress itself, a slot that only a slender person might traverse, a child, a woman, a young man without arms or armor. She took two steps and a metal grille moved behind her, closing the entrance and leaving her standing in a iron caged space so tight she could not spread her arms. Stone circled her except for the grille at her back and another at her left where a lantern was held by an invisible hand. A woman's voice, perhaps the same voice, said, "Take off your clothing. All of it."

"This is not hospitable," she said, suddenly furious. "This is what *they* no doubt wanted of me, that I be naked and helpless."

A laugh, without humor. "Woman, you do not know them if you believe that, and as for us, we have no designs on your body. We do need to assure that you carry nothing to our hurt, but you may choose. If you like, we will open the grille and you may go out the way you came."

Fighting tears, she leaned her staff against the stone and took off the hooded robe with its porous, insulated helmet that kept the sun from frying the brain, then the under-robe Awhero had given her. Finally, with some struggle, she removed the silken bodysuit that covered her from throat to below her elbows and knees, laminated to her belly and thighs by the dried breast milk.

"How old is your child?" someone asked. A softer voice. Not so crisp.

"Almost a month," she said, gulping tears. "His name is Dovidi."

"Sandals, too," said the first voice. "And stockings. Put everything through that hole by your foot."

The lantern wagged, showing her the gap in the grille, large enough to put shoes or wadded clothing through.

"Turn around, slowly."

She turned, holding her hands out, away from her body. She heard whispers.

". . . one of the intended . . ."

". . . all nonsense, look at that unmistakable nose . . ."

". . . rather as we had been told?"

After a long pause, her outer robe came back, and she wrapped it around herself.

"Where did you get these sandals?" someone asked.

Where had she got them? "I was told they were a gift," she said. "From the wives of the Shah. So that I could walk with them in their garden. My own shoes were . . . what do they say?" For a moment she couldn't remember the caste word and substituted another. "Befouled?"

"Arghaste. That is the Mahahmbi word. It means 'soiled by being foreign,' that is, from originating elsewhere than Mahahm. You yourself are arghaste, while the untouchables are malghaste, soiled by birth. In addition, you are evighaste, soiled by being a woman. Even wearing Mahahmbi shoes, you would not have been allowed to walk in their garden. It was a ruse, a ploy. Something, perhaps, to gain time."

"But I had walked in their garden," she cried. "I'd been there before!"

Silence. Ominous. Gathering.

Then another voice. "Describe the occasion. Where? Who did you meet?"

"I don't know where. A walled place, not too far from the house we rented. There were three of them, the Shah's wives they said. They were all new mothers, and one of them said . . . they'd earned the right to go . . . to paradise. To Galul."

A long silence, then very softly: "What did they look like?"

"They wore veils, heavy ones. I saw one face, only for a moment. They said . . . no! She said, the only one who made sense, she said they had earned this . . . candidacy, whatever it was."

A long pause, then a weary sigh. "Perhaps, under those circumstances you would have been allowed to walk with them."

"Except that we didn't walk," said Genevieve. "We sat. I said something, and they would say nonsense. At least one of them could talk as well as I, but all but one spoke only nonsense aloud. They gave me some tea. I didn't drink it. I didn't like the smell."

Another silence, less ominous. "Perceptive of you. What did you do with it if you did not drink it?"

"Dripped it into my robe, under my veil. You can see, the stain is still there. I had no time to wash it before I left."

"Did the wives sound young? Or old?"

"The one who spoke said she was thirty-three years old. She said she was old for the trip, but her husband hadn't wanted her to go until now. I assumed the others were younger."

A pause. Then, "Why did you pick these clothes for this journey?"

Despite herself, the tears came. "I didn't pick anything. Awhero gave me the robe and told me to wear it when I went out. I had the under-robe and the sandals on because I was summoned to visit the women again. And Father had gone to find out the details from the Shah's people. Then Awhero came running in to tell me assassins had taken him and were coming for me and Dovidi. I didn't doubt her. Others of our party were away, my father was missing, there was fighting where my husband had gone! My husband's spare sunhelmet and cloak were still hanging by the side door. Awhero said take them, so I threw them on and ran."

"Where is your son?"

"Awhero said if I took him, he was as good as dead. She said she could hide him, pretend he was one of them. I trust her, but I honestly don't know if he's . . . if he's still alive."

"She's malghaste?"

"Yes."

"You took no food or water?"

"My husband had left a little sack of way-food in the pocket. I took a water bottle and this staff from the door nearest the guard post. I filled the bottle at the untouchables well, then I started north." She rubbed her head, trying to make the pain go away. "The guards weren't at their post, and it made me uneasy, so I went out the malghaste door."

"Guards wouldn't have been there," said the softer voice. "Not if men were coming to abduct you. The guards would have been invited to be elsewhere, so they could later say they had seen nothing, that perhaps you had been stolen. Women are stolen. It's always believable. Where is the bottle you carried?"

"Wherever I stopped to sleep this morning. I heard the birds screaming, so I rolled away from under a bonebush, and then I ran. When I found it was gone, I didn't dare go back and look for it. It can't be far from here, for I only walked an hour or so before seeing the banner."

"What is this device in the pocket?"

"A locator. It's just . . . it focuses on the navigational beacon in orbit above Haven and it can tell you where you are. It's more useful in Haven than here . . ."

"An off-world device!" The pitch went up, the sharpness slashed. "You're from Havenor? From the Lord Paramount?"

"I'm not, no, though the leader of our party is. I suppose he is. We did come in an airship. I'm sorry. I thought you knew. Though, why would you know? We've been here for some time. I guess I thought everyone knew . . ."

"Was this device brought with you?" The words were sharp, demanding. "Did anyone in Mahahm-qum see it?"

Why did they care? Then, wearily, she understood. "No, the people in Mahahm-qum don't know I have this device. They probably have no idea I can keep to a direction in the desert, which would explain why they kept finding my trail and losing it. They don't know that I had talked to Awhero or that I knew anything about Tenopia or this place. Awhero called it *wahi oranga*, or *marae morehu*. That is what the name means, isn't it? Place of refuge?"

A long silence. Evidently they had closed a door across the grille, for she heard nothing. The lantern had gone with the voices. She pulled the cloak around her and slumped against the grille, head on bent knees, simply waiting. At least nothing from outside could get at her here. When the voice came again, it actually wakened her from a doze.

"We'll open the door. There's a small room here, where you can be

comfortable for a while. You'll stay here while we check what you've told us."

"What about my other clothes?"

"We'd like to know what they gave you in that tea, so we'll keep that robe for a time. Here's your bodysuit, and we'll find you some other clothing. We're keeping the sandals. Someone will carry them away from here, a good distance away from here. The soles have tracking devices in them."

"Tracking devices?"

"Scent emitters. Sometimes women escape, but their shoes are made to lead hunters directly to them. You're lucky. The devices were blocked with mud . . ."

"The well," she cried. "When I filled my bottle at the well. It was muddy."

"Was your ship here, on Mahahm?"

"Outside the city. As I went out, I yelled at the communications man to tell them what was happening." Or had she? She remembered doing it. But then, she might have imagined doing it.

"The people of Mahahm-qum would expect you to go toward your ship. They would not expect you to have listened to a malghaste woman's tales. So, because they are creatures of their preconceptions, it is unlikely they have any idea where you are. If we are lucky, they will assume you are dead. One of us may backtrack to the place you left the bottle, however, as we would prefer that it and the sandals be found somewhere else, a long way from here. On the way to some oasis."

A breath of air came from her left as the grille slipped into a wall pocket and a door opened upon a white plastered room where the day's last light pooled around the high, barred window and seeped a melancholy dimness onto the narrow bed and stone floor below. Beside the bed a small table held a glass carafe of water topped with an inverted cup. She almost fell over herself in her scramble toward it.

"Slowly," said the voice from somewhere across the room. "Take it slowly. A few sips, then a few more. Otherwise you may vomit it up, and that would be a waste. Don't eat anything until you've bathed and settled down and are no longer thirsty. Bring your staff, and also the lantern. It will soon be dark."

The lantern stood in its own circle of light on the floor by the grille. She fetched it and set it upon the table where a bowl covered a plate of fruit, sliced meat and a loaf of brown, crusty bread. Though she ached with hunger, she obeyed the voice. She sat on the bed with the cup in

her hand, drinking little by little, refilling the cup twice. The dryness of her throat and nose slowly eased. For the first time she noticed the little jars near the plate, one of them half-filled with something waxy, herbal, perhaps an unguent.

"Can I use this on my lips?" she asked the walls, turning the jar in her hands, seeing the label too late to forestall the question. "For desert-burned skin."

"Never mind," she said, swallowing hysterical laughter that caught in her throat when she read the label on the other jar. "To dry your milk. Take one with each meal."

To dry her milk. She choked on tears, swallowed them. Well then. Whatever help they might offer, it wouldn't run to getting Dovidi back, not soon. She had best plan on staying here for some time and be thankful for what it offered: drink, food, and a place to wash herself. Someone had definitely mentioned bathing.

She picked up the lantern and walked the perimeter of the room, three meters by five, the entry door now closed off by a sliding panel. Through a pointed arch opposite the entry she found a boxlike hall with three more of the sliding panel doors: left, right, and straight ahead. Two of the panels were immovable, but the one to her right slid easily, opening on a stone-floored alcove furnished with a large, shallow copper pan, an ewer of tepid water, cloths, a low stool, and in the corner, a privy hole like those in the house they had used in Mahahm-qum.

Shutting the panel behind her, she set the lantern on the floor, threw off the dusty robe and ladled water into the pan. Sitting on the stool she washed her feet and legs before standing in the pan to wash the rest of her. The water had a sharp, resinous smell, some cleansing agent that rinsed away without residue and took the grime with it. Even the sweaty stiffness of her hair dissolved when she poured water through it. When she had finished washing herself she fetched her bodysuit and sloshed it about in the pan until the dried milk was gone. She wrung it out and spread it across the stool. The dirty water went down the privy hole and the folded cloths went over the edge of the pan. One dry cloth was long enough to wrap around her body, covering her aching, swollen breasts. She wasn't expecting company, and it covered her almost decently. Certainly it would do to eat in.

When she returned to the table she found a comb lying atop a folded shift, a perfectly simple white garment woven of the same fiber as the robe Awhero had given her. Plant fiber of some kind. Less harsh than wool. Well then. Someone was watching her, someone who could come

in and out without her hearing. Not precisely a comforting thought, though the items spoke of concern for her welfare. Give them, her, whoever, credit for trying. The shift covered her from neck to elbows and ankles. The comb pulled the snarls from her hair. She left the wet strands loose down her back while she rubbed unguent onto her hands and feet and face. Later, when she had rested, she would braid her hair out of the way.

Then the food. The bread was chewy and full of crunchy inclusions, nuts and seeds and shreds of the same rich, peppery pod Awhero had once given her in the rooms below the kitchen. The meat and slices of melon were delicious, the one partially dried and salty, the other juicy and sweet. After a brief spasm of rejection which was almost anger, she took one of the pills from the jar and swallowed it. Emotionally, she hated the idea, but she would need all her strength. If Dovidi couldn't use her milk, it would be stupid to stress her body to produce it.

When she had eaten less than half the food, she caught herself drowsing, head on chest, breathing deeply, lips half opened around a partly chewed mouthful, a bit of bread still in hand. She roused enough to cover the food remnants and drink a last half cup of water before setting the cup over the neck of the carafe. If she was being observed, let them give her a good rating for neatness and parsimony. Who knew how long this ration was intended to last?

Her last thought before sleep was of Awhero. She wished the old woman knew she had come this far safely . . . well, seemingly safely. At least there were no hunters, no voices from the sky. At least she was away from the thorn and the sun. She did not think of the Marshal or Delganor or Dovidi. She did not think of anything but this moment, well fed, comfortably warm, and without thirst. As Tenopia had said, she could afford neither grief nor anger. She could not afford anything but the day, each day from waking to sleep, each such day to be set down after all other such days, a long journey which one must not think of as even having a direction. If one went on, steadily, perhaps at the end there would be explanations, even justification.

The end was the only possible destination. One could not, ever, go back to the beginning.

GENEVIEVE'S TOWER WAS SLENDER AND TALL, AN ARCHITECTURAL CONCEIT added at the last moment to the otherwise undistinguished structure of Blessingham School. Gaining access to this afterthought could not be accomplished on the way to or from anywhere in particular. Climbing the hundred steps to the single room at the top was both inconvenient and arduous. Despite the nuisance, Genevieve had chosen the tower room. For the quiet, she said. For the view. For the brightness of the stars at night.

Though these were at best only half reasons, they satisfied Mrs. Blessingham better than the real reason would have done—a reason which had to do with the billowing foliage of the surrounding forest, the isolation of the star-splashed night, the silence of the sky. On stormy nights the boughs surged and heaved darkly as a midnight sea, and on such nights Genevieve would throw the casements wide and lean into the wind, the white curtains blowing like flung spray as she imagined herself carried jubilantly through enormous silken waves toward an unknown shore.

The imagined sea, the waves, the inexorable movement of the waters were implicit in the instructions her mother had given her. The jubilance, an emotion she had touched rarely, and only at the edges, was an interpolation of her own which, she feared, might be shaming if anyone knew of it but herself.

As Mrs. Blessingham would have observed: the tower was nowhere near the sea; Genevieve had never seen the sea since she had been no farther from Langmarsh House than a single trip to Evermire; Genevieve, like other noble daughters, would not have been allowed to swim. As Genevieve did not wish to explain: *her* sea was not a planetary wetness, exactly. It was inside her as much as it was out there in the night, and though she wasn't quite sure what her instructions amounted to vis-à-vis swimming or sailing or floating, they meant more than simply disporting herself in the water.

Every evening Genevieve submitted patiently as her hair was braided by the lady's maid trainee—who took twice the time Genevieve would have taken to do it herself. Each evening she was courteous as she was helped into her nightgown, though she was perfectly capable of getting into a nightgown without assistance. She waited calmly, without fidgeting, as the bed was turned down, and she smiled her thanks when the trainee departed with a curtsey, shutting the door behind her. The moment the latch clicked, however, Genevieve slipped from her chair and put her ear to the door, hearing the retreating clatter of hard soled shoes down steep stone stairs. Only when that sound had faded did she open the window and lean out into the night to evoke the ocean feeling, the inner quiet that dissolved daytime stiffness and propriety in a fluidity of water and wind, a thrust and swell of restless power.

Though by now, her twentieth year, she did this habitually, even earnestly, it had begun as a requirement. The ritual was among those her mother had taught her, and every night, whether in storm or calm, Genevieve did as she had been taught to do. Standing in the window with closed eyes, she focused outward, cataloging and shutting out all ordinary sounds: rustle of the trees, shut out; murmur of voices from the kitchen wing, shut out; clack of the watchman's heels on the paving of the cloisters, out; whisper of song from the siren-lizards on the roof-tiles, out; bleat of goat in the dairy, out; each day-to-day distraction removed to leave the inner silence that allowed her to listen.

The listening could not be merely passive. Practitioners, so Genevieve's mother had emphasized, must visualize themselves as spiders spinning lines of sticky hearkening outward in the night, past time, past distance or direction, toward something that floated in the far, waiting to be heard. Sometimes she spun and spun, remaining in the window for an hour or more, and nothing happened. Sometimes she heard a murmur, as though some immense far-off thing had swiveled an ear and asked, "Where?" or "Who?" or even, once or twice, frighteningly, "Genevieve?"

And once in a great while the web trembled as though the roots of the mountains and the chasms of the sea were resounding with song. At such times, her body reverberated to the harmonics as she retreated to her bed, and sometimes the singing continued during the night, or so she assumed, for her body still ached with it when she woke in the morning.

Senior girls had their pick of rooms in order of their achievement scores in DDR: discipline, dedication, and religion. Genevieve, ranking first, had chosen the tower room.

"Rapunzel, Rapunzel," her friend Glorieta teased, quoting from a yore-lore fairy tale.

"Let down your hair," whooped her twin, Carlotta.

"Better let down her nose," said snide Barbara, a resentful and distant runner-up. "It's longer."

Silence, then a spate of talk to cover embarrassment.

"Your nose is your misfortune," Mrs. Blessingham had said on more than one occasion. "But your talents make up for it."

It was a hawkish nose, one that ran, so said the wags, in Genevieve's family. As for the talents, no one knew of them but Genevieve—and Mrs. Blessingham, who was one too many.

"The nose would look better on the Marshal than it does on you," Glorieta had admitted, referring to Genevieve's father. "Pity it had to be on the female side, though even on you it has distinction."

Genevieve often daydreamed herself away from Haven, to a place where her nose was quite normal, even beautiful. In her dream world, the singing she listened for with such effort was simply part of the environment, a song she herself could produce without anyone telling her to hush. The fantasy was pervasive. On occasion Genevieve would come to herself in the middle of a meal, unable for a moment to remember where she was because she had been in a place more vivid than reality. Even when awake and alert, she often longed for that other world, though hopelessly, for even if it were real, she couldn't go there. No one emigrated from Haven. Haven had cut the umbilicus that had tied it to the rest of humanity.

Shortly after settlement the Lord Paramount of Haven had announced to the settled worlds that he and his people were resolved to keep to themselves, eschewing all outsiders or outside things—except, that is, for the Lord Paramount's short list of essential imports. If something was wanted that wasn't on the Lord Paramount's list, if the people of Haven couldn't produce it by traditional methods, approved by God as stated in the covenants, then they had to do without. Thus, even if Genevieve's nose might be normal elsewhere, elsewhere was eliminated as an option. Her nose was her nose, this world was this world, and for noblewomen to sing was counter-covenantal. Genevieve, Marchioness of Wantresse and future Duchess of Langmarsh, would simply have to live with her nose and her silence.

"If mother were alive, she'd let me get it fixed," Genevieve whispered to Glorieta, during afternoon recreation, walking through the gardens on their way to the badminton court, their skirts swishing around their ankles,

the long sleeves of their high-necked blouses daringly turned up to expose delicate wrists.

"She would not!" said Glorieta. "Surgery is very dangerous, and that same nose is in your mother's family portraits. I've seen them."

And she had, of course, when she and Carlotta had visited Genevieve over the seasonal holidays. There they hung in the great hall of Langmarsh House: Genevieve's mother, Marnia, Duchess nose of Langmarsh; Genevieve's grandmother, Lydia, Countess nose of Wantresse; Genevieve's great-grandmother, Mercia, Duchess nose of Sealand, and so on and so on. And, in the place of high honor, many times great-great-grandmother; dark skinned, dark haired and mysterious, Stephanie, who had become Queen of Haven by virtue of marrying the Lord Paramount.

"Besides," Glorieta continued, "if the nose was good enough for a queen, it's good enough for you. And since there's no male heir, you'll be Countess Genevieve of Evermire and Wantresse, Duchess of Langmarsh, Mistress of the Marches, so any nose you have will be quite all right."

Which rather summed it up. Genevieve's father, the Marshal—i.e. Arthur Lord Dustin, Duke of Langmarsh, Earl of Evermire etcetera, Councilor to the Lord Paramount and Marshal of the Royal Armies—had desired a male heir. The Duchess Marnia had become pregnant four times after Genevieve's birth, each pregnancy ending in miscarriage or stillbirth, as had the pregnancies of other wives married into the Dustin clan. The subject of genetic defect (whispered by the physicians) could not, of course, be mentioned to the Marshal and as was her covenantal duty, Marnia tried for a fifth time. Her physicians had strongly advised otherwise, and as they had feared, the baby had been stillborn and Marnia herself had died soon after.

The Marshal should have had sons. He was at his best as a leader of men. At the first sound of an alarm trumpet, his cold intelligence would turn from its mundane aggravations, ubiquitous as the itch, to focus his smoldering angers upon the matter at hand. Even when outnumbered, the Marshal won battles, and facing equal forces, he swept the field. Though malcontents were rare on Haven, though battles were few, the Lord Paramount felt any battle was one too many. Therefore the Lord Paramount—though not fond of many men—was very fond of the Marshal.

A dozen sons might have diverted his attention from Genevieve, giving her some peace. As it was, she fell often beneath his reptilian eye, her dreamy insufficiencies and languishments tabulated and filed away for future reference. Though she was attentive to her duty, she seemed to him insufficiently blithe. Men liked women who were untroubled, and Gene-

vieve too often seemed to be thinking about something. He had, therefore, simplified his life by packing Genevieve (then eleven) off to Mrs. Blessingham's school, which was conveniently located in Avanto, the county seat of alpine Wantresse, only one long day's ride from Langmarsh House.

Subsequently the Marshal, to the surprise of most everyone, had remained a widower, though he had sporadically shopped about for a son-in-law to be the future Duke of Langmarsh. During the summer festivals or when Genevieve was home during the Northerlies, the Marshal made a habit of introducing her to likely sons of the nobility, always without consequence. After one such holiday, the Marshal wrote to Mrs. Blessingham suggesting that his daughter was "too like her mother to be satisfactory," "couldn't something be done to her face?" and she should be "livened up a bit," a message which was received with something very like despair.

"Did you meet any new men? What did you think of them?" Glorieta asked after each interlude, eager for sensation.

Genevieve refused to titillate. "That's what father always asks me. I always say each one is very nice, but mostly they aren't. They always look at my nose."

"How did you like *them?* I'm not your father, you can tell me the truth!"

"My loins did not twitch," Genevieve replied. It was quite true, though she wasn't at all sure she would know if her loins did twitch. Barbara said twitching was unmistakable, one couldn't miss it, but if one had never experienced any such thing, how would one know? Genevieve had invented a dozen persons that she could imagine being; she had invented a hundred scenarios in which those characters might act; she had never imagined one with twitching loins.

"Lust is not something we wish to dwell on at our stage of life," said Miss Eugenie, the instructress in spiritual health. "The less said or thought about one's loins at this stage of life, the less trouble one will have later on. It is Mrs. Blessingham's view that for covenantal and Godly Noblewomen, sexual feelings and attractions should be avoided as long as possible. The practical applications of sexuality are best dealt with when the necessity presents itself. Now we are more concerned with acquiring resignation and dedication, for the sake of our souls."

The state of one's soul was considered important both for noblewomen and those aspiring to that state: i.e., daughters of the wealthy bourgeoisie whose papas coveted a title in their families. All such women were expected to be pious, to have imperturbable poise, rocklike dedication to the covenants, and a broad background of conversational information cov-

ering all the fields of general interest in Haven. Since all aristocratic women were presumed to be future mistresses of establishments, they had also to master the skills of personnel management and training, the economics of a large household and the basics of court etiquette and dress. These were studies enough, all told, to fill all the years before the question of twitching loins would become urgent (one dared hope) at the imminence of marriage.

Though many lower-class women would be married before twenty, covenantal women were "allowed the gift of youth," as it was phrased in the covenants, as compensation for the oath every noblewoman took at marriage: "I vow a covenantal life spent in my husband's service." Thirty was the accepted age of marriage for noblewomen; most bore no more than two or three children; and any extra risk they might encounter by delaying childbearing was supposedly compensated through the services of off-planet physicians—though some of them perished in childbirth nonetheless. Off-planet physicians and medical supplies—along with grav-sleds, various weapons and "a few other oddments"—had always been on the Lord Paramount's "short list" of essentials.

Late marriage was a comforting thought, Genevieve admitted to herself, though red-haired, green-eyed Barbara thought otherwise.

"I am sick unto death of Mrs. Blessingham's. I don't know why they are so determined here to delay us, delay us, delay us. No marriage until late twenties. No babies until one is thirty, at least. And no sensible reason for any of it except that the older we are, the better prepared we will be. It's ridiculous! Pray heaven some impecunious but stalwart lord will show up so Papa may impress him with my dowry and I may go elsewhere!"

"Before you could marry a lord, you'd have to be accepted by the Covenant Tribunal," retorted Carlotta. "Probably the Tribunal won't even accept a commoner your age!"

"Oh, pooh! Covenant, covenant, that's all I hear. You nobles certainly like to make life difficult and boring for yourselves."

To which Genevieve silently but wholeheartedly assented. The covenants were like a strict nanny, always saying no or don't or can't. "No singing, Jenny. Singing girls are like crowing hens. Both of them come to the same bad ends." "No running, Jenny. Covenantal girls conduct themselves with decorum." "No dreaming of Prince Charming, Jenny. Don't forget:

" 'Covenantal daughters marry who . . .
ever their papas tell them to!' "

Daughters of the covenants were required to bear their children at

home and nurse them for at least a year, thus joining noble nurture to noble nature. Daughters of the covenant were required to rear their daughters as they themselves had been reared, through an untroubled and godly girlhood to a dutiful maturity of gracious submission.

Long ago, when she was much younger and had not learned to display resignation, Genevieve had rebelled against that duty. "Why?" she had cried to her mother. "Why do I have to when I don't want to!"

Her mother had replied, softly as always, "Because our great-great-great-grandmothers assented to it, Jenny. When our forefathers bought Haven, they recruited strong, healthy young women to be the royal and noble mothers of all future generations, and the young women were allowed to choose to come to Haven or not, as they pleased, but if they opted to come to Haven, they agreed to obey the covenants."

"I didn't agree! What right did some woman a thousand years ago have to agree for me?"

"Because that's how it works, love. We all do what our ancestors found to be best. Why learn hard lessons over and over?"

"Nursing babies for a year!" young Genevieve had said scornfully. "Della's sister's baby is only six months, and she's weaning him already!"

"Year-long nursing is in the covenants," Mother had said, little lines of worry between her eyes.

"It wasn't in the original covenants. I read them my very own self!"

"Jenny, I've asked you to stay out of the library. Your father will . . ."

"I read them," she had insisted, pouting. She had also read the history of the settlement, and could understand very well why young women might have promised almost anything to get away from the planets they had lived upon. Besides, the covenants back then were not at all like they were now!

Mother sighed, running a pale hand across her brow, as though to sort out the thoughts that lived inside. "The Tribunal has made some amendments from time to time. I'm sure there are good reasons for all the covenants, and we have been taught that women are happiest in gracious submission to the covenants."

If that had been the case, Mother should have been very happy, but she had never seemed so to Genevieve. Of course, what Mother said upstairs in her public voice for the Marshal or the servants to hear, and what mother said down in the cellars when she and Genevieve were alone there, were totally different things. Upstairs was covenant, covenant, covenant, all over everything, like moss, with the visiting scrutator scraping away at it to uncover any hidden notions of disobedience or independence.

Despite her private reservations, Genevieve earned a passing grade during each spiritual audit, however, and that was the public side of things.

The secret side of things happened in the lonely hours of the night, when Mother and she went tip-toeing down the stony stairs into the earth-smelling dark, lit only by their candles. It happened when they pushed open the heavy, dusty doors to go beyond the wine cellar, past the coal store, into the deep, moist world of otherness, when they left the covenants behind. Once hidden away they became, so Mother said, separate minds who taught and learned things not of that world. Those teachings would be realized in Genevieve's time, or if not, passed on to Genevieve's daughters to be realized in some later time. Whichever it might be, they could *never* be practiced or spoken of anywhere else! Never until the time was right. Promise.

Genevieve promised, though she had no idea why she would ever speak of them? Nine-tenths of them, she did not understand at all.

"Mama, what are harbingers?"

"Those who sing the song."

"Mama, what is the song?"

"You'll know it when you hear it."

"Mama, if the scrutator says I have a soul, and the covenants say I have a soul, why . . . ?"

Though Mother always answered the questions, Genevieve did not always understand the answer, for Mother often seemed to live in a different world. At breakfast times, her eyes sometimes were focused on something far, far away rather than being cast down in holy resignation as they should have been, even while the Marshal ranted over the latest letters and promotion lists, bloody bedamn this, bloody bedamn that.

Though perhaps Mother had chosen to take no notice of the Marshal's ways, for he cultivated angers like garden vegetables until each was well ripened and firmly rooted. These habits served him so well on the battlefield that he had never thought to leave them there, neither the hot fury that led him off on daily rants nor the cold wrath that stirred in him seldom but was more fearsome for its rarity.

Genevieve had felt it first on the night of her eighth birthday. There had been guests invited to dinner, and when the guests departed, one neighbor had stayed behind to play a game of chess with the Marshal. He was an elderly and kindly gentleman, familiar enough that Genevieve did not feel shy around him. That day she had been much indulged by mother and the servants, and when the men sat down in the shadowy room with the firelight glinting from the shelves of leather-bound volumes

that stood forever at attention, even the Marshal had not sent her out of the room as he customarily did.

Genevieve was curled on the settle with a new book, though when the two men started playing, she looked at the game board instead of the pages. At first it was only a drowsy watching, but gradually she began to see the why of the moves and her gaze became intent.

The pieces were interesting. She had seen them before, but without really paying attention. Now she had a chance to watch them in action on the board. The little ones, she decided, were like the housemaids. They could not do much or go very far, and they were always in danger of being snatched up, as she had seen the Marshal snatch one up, a pretty one that Genevieve much liked but did not see again after that time. So did the little pieces disappear when they were snatched up, back into the box.

The horsemen were more powerful, able to jump fences this way and that way. Along with the horses, each side had two pieces much like the Marshal, she decided, for they could go all the way across the board on the slant, while the fortresses, which were like her father's battle wagons, had to stick to the roads.

The last two pieces were the Lord Paramount and his Queen. Even if father hadn't said their names, that is all they could be, sitting there quietly, depending upon the marshals and battlewagons and horsemen to protect them while their little serving maids ran this way and that way, screaming, with their aprons over their faces.

In the end, if it was necessary, the Queen would sacrifice herself for the Lord Paramount. Genevieve saw exactly how it happened. The Queen did not show what she could do. She moved only when she had to, never bustling about, but if the Lord Paramount was threatened, she moved to save him. If necessary, she died for the Lord Paramount. As this was in accord with covenantal behavior, Genevieve was not surprised. Lives of service to their lords and masters was the lot of womankind.

The particular night was blustery, but as it was cosy before the fire the two men played for a long time. When father's old friend went home at last, Genevieve climbed down from the settle and eagerly asked her father if he would play the game with her. He, softened by wine and an indolent evening, felt momentarily indulgent. It was her birthday, after all.

"Well, my child, that shouldn't take long, now should it. Shall I help you set up the pieces?"

She shook her head, all eagerness, and set them up herself. He let her move first, and she sent one of her maids out into the world. The Marshal

moved, and then she again, letting her horsemen jump where it was right to go, and her marshals move to stop an advance, and so on, until suddenly her father was staring at her with a kind of fire in his eyes. She looked back at the board, not to miss anything. He moved again, slowly, watching her. She moved. "Check," she said, as she had heard him say. "And mate."

And then she really looked up, excited and proud, only to see that fire burning in his eyes. And she knew it for what it was. Cold wrath. She had done something wrong, terribly wrong.

"Who taught you?" he said in his gravest voice, the one that could not be disobeyed.

She thought frantically. Who had taught her but he, himself. "I watched you, Father." And then without thinking she said words that were not quite true, that were not really at all true but would nonetheless save her from those eyes. "It is one of the games you played with your friend, father. I just remembered your moves."

It was true she had remembered the moves, every move either player had made all evening, and though her game had not been the same game as any her father and his friend had played, the claim was the only thing that would help her. The fire in his eyes damped down to a dull glow.

"This game is not for children," he said. "In future when I play it with my friends, you stay with your mother."

Previously, Genevieve had believed she loved her father, for loving and honoring one's father was a Godly duty, something the visiting scrutator covered in detail.

"You would do anything for your father, wouldn't you?"

"Oh, yes, scrutator."

"Your father is the wisest of men, isn't he?"

"Oh, yes, scrutator."

After her birthday, however, she knew she did not love him, and she was careful to cross her fingers whenever the scrutator used the word *love*. Years later, she came to wonder if her mother had ever loved him, whether her loins had ever twitched for the Marshal.

Barbara said her loins had been twitching since she was eleven. Barbara sometimes leaned from her window and flirted with the commoner boys beyond the wall. Genevieve thought this unseemly behavior might have something to do with Barbara's being a bourgeoise; rich, but a bourgeoise. Barbara sang naughty songs in the showers, even when she was punished for it, and though Genevieve fought against the temptation, she adored Barbara. She envied Barbara's daring attitudes and her highly individual style. She loved Barbara's sense of humor and quick wit and flashes of

intimate perception, though she was careful not to let her admiration show. Any hint that a girl might be too fond of one of her friends provoked the scrutator, and the Marshal would be much offended to think she could possibly prefer any other role to the frugal, complex, and thankless one that he, God, and the covenants had bestowed upon her.

Like Genevieve, Viscountess Glorieta and Lady Carlotta were provincial nobility, sister-twins and only children of Lord Ahmenaj, Earl of Bliggen, a county in the province of Barfezi. Glorieta was a bit the taller. Carlotta was a lot curvier. They both had the light brown hair, the hazel eyes, and the creamy skin and curly, laughing mouths shared by all the Ahmenaj family. The twins were destined for the elder sons of the Count's neighbor, Lord Blufeld, Earl of Halfmore. Their weddings would consolidate the two holdings into an enormous estate, which both the Amenaj and the Blufeld families very much desired.

"Though it is troublesome being a dynastic game piece," Carlotta had once said. "Move here, move there, take that piece, jump, jump, take that piece. And at the end, I suppose I get a Viscountess's tiara as a booby prize, and so what!"

"At least you have a foreseeable future," Genevieve remarked. "You've said yourself you rather like Tomas. And Glorieta really likes Willum. And you love your father's estate, and this way you'll remain attached to it."

Carlotta made a face. "The trouble is that we *both* really like Willum, but Glorieta, being two minutes elder, picked him and left me Tomas, who *definitely* suffers by comparison, and besides, attached is not a word I would have chosen. It makes me sound like part of the livestock."

Which she was, of course, though everyone forbore saying so. All the students were like livestock, even Barbara, for twitch though she would, her father and the Tribunal would have the last word. Unless she eloped, of course. Eloping was scandalous, but it did happen and, knowing Barbara, she might well do it, no matter how uncovenantly it was.

Until that time came, however, they would continue as they had done since they were children: subduing predispositions toward unseemly behavior; dancing and exercising to acquire posture and grace; practicing manners and conversation, which, since women weren't supposed to have opinions, was mostly how to get other people to talk about themselves while expressing admiration that sounded sincere. Lessons were interspersed with short trips to orchestral concerts or village festivals, to couturiers for new clothes in spring and fall, and by increasingly frequent visits from the scrutators and doctors.

Genevieve could never decide which visits were more embarrassing,

the ones devoted to her soul or the ones devoted to her body. Though both the scrutator—a man, of course—and the off-worlder doctor—a woman, of course—tried to be gentle, all that intimate probing was humiliating. Still, one had to be both pure of soul and a certifiably fertile lactator if one was to make a good marriage. Only children born and nursed at home could inherit. With such a well-recognized goal, nothing could be left to chance.

"I think I'll sneak out and get pregnant," said Barbara, angrily. "That'll prove I'm fertile all right."

"That'll prove you right back home." Glorieta grinned. "Locked up in an attic by your papa."

"Spending all your days eating moldy bread and brackish water," said Carlotta reprovingly.

Though Barbara had Genevieve's total sympathy, Genevieve stayed at the fringe of this badinage. Whenever other girls engaged in joking give and take, Genevieve felt herself backing away, pulling a kind of membrane around herself that separated herself from them. Though the other girls never seemed to notice, sometimes Genevieve felt the curtain between her and others was thick as a quilt. They were different somehow. Or she was. Not that she blamed them or herself for being different. Differences were part of existence. Everyone was different in some way, but Genevieve was different in several. She had had a mother who seemed quite unlike other people's mothers. She had a nose which was certainly unlike other people's noses. And, unlike her friends, who were actually quite involved with what they were doing and feeling, Genevieve experienced life as a kind of drama, a play, something staged and unreal, a continuing fantasy.

The usual daily play she called "Mrs. Blessingham's School." The school itself was the setting, and the teachers and other students were the cast. They all knew their lines without any discernable prompting, including silly and playful talk that Genevieve could never think up on her own. Though she was occasionally required to say a few words or perform a brief scene, she was always red with embarrassment, during and after. Even the assignment of a tiny part, a walk-on as it were, made her anxious that her performance would be stilted and unbelievable, or that she would do something that seemed perfectly all right at the moment, which would then turn out to be the wrong thing: like knowing something one wasn't supposed to know; or solving a puzzle too quickly; or saying the absolutely wrong thing! Only as an onlooker did she feel truly easy.

In addition to the "Blessingham's School" play, there were others she watched regularly: "The Ahmenaj Dynasty," which was about Glorieta and

Carlotta; the "Chronicles of Barbara," which was naughty; and of course "Langmarsh House, or The Life of Dustin, Lord Marshal." Occasionally episodes of the other plays were played concurrently with "Blessingham's," intermixing confusingly with one another and greatly adding to the cast of characters, the scenery, and the complexity of the plot.

Through it all, Genevieve remained determined not to have a noticeable role, not even when she herself was dragged onto the stage. "Mrs. Blessingham's School" was a play written by others. "Lord Marshal" was no doubt written by himself. She had had no hand in either of them. Nothing she might do could influence the plots in the least. She refused to be responsible for them.

Over the years she had developed a technique for dealing with those occasions when reality threatened to encroach: she would find a corner where she could sit quietly and visualize herself as a siren-lizard, many of which swarmed through the trees around the school. Trees burgeoned, sap flowed from some deep and mysterious source below, life trickled out into every twig, enlivening the entire organism, but the sirens did not know or care. They merely fluttered from branch to branch, flashing their scaled wings in the sun like rainbow mirrors, dependent upon the tree but unconnected to it. Whenever the scrutator came to talk about her soul, Genevieve visualized her soul as a small, invisible siren-lizard, without any dangerous thoughts or emotions, flitting through the tree of life while it waited to be taken away into paradise. She was, so to speak, required to flash her wings, but she was determined to stay unconnected for several reasons, not least of which involved what Mrs. Blessingham called her "talent."

Genevieve could accept her talent as she did her nose: an annoyance, at best, a grief at worst. Sometimes when it did not manifest itself for some time, she hoped desperately that she had lost it or it had left her, though hope was in vain, for the talent always returned. As it did shortly after her conversation with Carlotta and Glorieta, when Mrs. Blessingham invited Genevieve into her office.

"Genevieve, I hate to trouble you, but I am concerned about the marriage plans being made for Carlotta and Glorieta."

Genevieve felt a deep pang, as though a large bell had rung inside her. She stared at the wall, everything else becoming misty and indistinct. She thought of Willum as she had seen him last at an evening soirée, sitting with Glorieta on the terrace. His eyes—which she had scarcely noticed at the time but now remembered fully—had been full of desire and pain, fear and resolution. She saw shadows shifting, like the library

machines on fast forward, shadows of Glorieta, of Willum, of an older man or men, Willum's father or family perhaps, a shadow of another woman, a young woman whose face she could not see.

Her eyes gradually cleared, focused, and she saw Mrs. Blessingham sitting at her desk, calmly waiting. "Mrs. Blessingham," she murmured, "There will be tragedy connected to Willum. He dreads something that will happen, as if he is determined to do some terrible and irrevocable act. I fear ruin will come . . . to someone close to him."

"I've had bad feelings about the whole thing. You're sure?"

Genevieve gave her a reproachful look. "Oh, ma'am, I can't say that. I can only tell what comes to me in these . . ."

"These certainties."

"This one is not clear enough to be a certainty. Most times whatever this is," she touched her head, flipping her fingers away to show how ephemeral it all was, "this thing in my brain doesn't explain what it is showing me. Most of the time I think it is off somewhere else, letting me see only scraps."

This had been one of the times when she saw bits of scenery, heard bits of conversations, recollected things she had read or overheard or seen that had made no impression at the time. The sound that came with these smatterings was like surf or storm, the undifferentiated noise of hard rain or the crackling of fire, and from this meaningless mosaic an impression emerged, a feeling, a picture, sometimes a voice. Only long practice kept her quiet and passive as this occurred and passed, leaving a sodden exhaustion behind, like a deep drift of autumn leaves wet by rain, icy and clinging, herself buried in them, naked and cold.

"Describe it to me," commanded Mrs. Blessingham, though in a gentler voice.

Genevieve sighed. "I feel that someone dies. I see a body, a young woman. I don't know whether it's Carlotta or Glorieta or someone else, but whatever is happening is connected to them. I know Willum is in it, for I see his face. I hear his voice and a baby crying. I smell blood."

Whenever people came into her certainties, she could only identify those she already knew. Others were indistinct, almost like manikins, stand-ins for real people. She saw someone doing something without being able to see why it was done, or by whom. Sometimes she would see people she did not recognize at all, but this time she knew it was Willum, that same Willum she had recently seen with Glorieta on the terrace, his face full of fear and longing.

"You think he will murder her?" asked Mrs. Blessingham.

"Her, who?" asked Genevieve. "I don't know who dies. A woman, yes. But I don't know who. Of course, Glorieta does prefer Willum."

"That may be the trouble," said Mrs. Blessingham. "They both do. In this case, it seems there's nothing I can do about it. Thank you, Genevieve. We needn't mention this to the scrutators."

"Of course," she murmured. Of course. Even mother had been quite clear that there were certain things one did not mention to the scrutators. About this particular thing, Mrs. Blessingham was the only one who knew, the only one who asked, the only one who used whatever it was Genevieve could do. How Mrs. Blessingham had known about her talent, Genevieve couldn't say. She had never inquired, and Mrs. Blessingham had never told her. This was another of the things Genevieve didn't really want to know. Knowing would mean she had to think about it, plan for it, acknowledge it. She refused to accept it, any of it at all.

During the medical examination, the doctor had taken note of Genevieve's dreamy detachment and had asked many probing questions that Genevieve had tried to answer truthfully while not betraying herself.

"Can you remember being a child? What is your earliest memory?" the doctor asked, head cocked, hands busy taking notes.

"I try not to think about when I was little. It makes me sad."

"You were how old when your mother died? Eleven? You should remember your mother very well."

"I don't think about her," whispered Genevieve. "Really, really, I don't."

This was a lie. She remembered her mother often, but the remembered mother was the cellar mother she couldn't talk about, the mother it was dangerous even to think about! Everything she remembered of the covenantly upstairs mother was implicit in the final scene: the shadowed room, the smell of sickness, though even then it was the cellar mother who had whispered, her voice full of desperate urgency:

"Remember what I have told you, darling girl. It will be hard and perhaps loathsome to you. I am sure the hard road is the one you must take. Yours may be the last generation, the one for whom all the practices were meant. Oh, I hope so. Remember our times together. Follow your talent. And, my love, listen for word from the sea!"

Those were her last words to Genevieve. No one else had ever called her darling. She tried to explain to the doctor without explaining. "I'd rather not care about things too much, doctor. When I do, it becomes . . . troublesome."

On hearing this, the doctor frowned. The life expectancy among noblewomen was unaccountably short, and the doctor felt many of them

died from this lack of involvement, this separation from life. She was sufficiently concerned that she spoke to Mrs. Blessingham about Genevieve's detachment.

"Well, that dreaminess is so typical of dear Genevieve," said Mrs. Blessingham disarmingly. "Her mother was much the same. Thank you, Doctor."

Later she spoke to Genevieve herself. "Is it true you cannot remember your mother?"

Genevieve started to say yes, remembering in time that this was Mrs. Blessingham, who knew almost everything.

"No, ma'am. I remember her perfectly well. I just don't want to talk about her."

"Why is that?"

"Because of what she said when she was dying. She said I was to walk a hard road. She said it might be loathsome."

"I see." Mrs. Blessingham puzzled a moment. "So, since it will be hard and loathsome, you choose to take as little notice of it as possible?"

Genevieve flushed. Perhaps that was true.

Mrs. Blessingham, who almost never showed emotion, actually grimaced, as though with pain. "Genevieve, your mother was here. She was schooled here. I was an assistant here in those days, no older than she, and we were friends. It was her dying request of your father that you be sent here, to me. It was she who told me about your talent, for she had it, also."

Genevieve gaped, hearing this with a shock of realization. "Oh, Mrs. Blessingham, if she saw my future laid out for me, she must have had it, mustn't she?"

Mrs. Blessingham patted Genevieve on the shoulder. "Don't worry about the doctor, my dear. She simply thinks you should be more involved in life. Well, perhaps the upcoming soirées will amuse you. Your father will be attending some of them, surely."

Genevieve's heart sank. Though marriage was deferred until later, girls became betrothable at twenty, and all students over twenty attended the soirées. Elegant suppers were served; there was dancing or entertainment; and the students were paraded before their parents and potential suitors. Oh, no doubt the Marshal would attend, and Genevieve's sagging shoulders betrayed her thoughts as she walked away while Mrs. Blessingham silently berated herself for having mentioned him.

Whether Genevieve loved her father or not, she desperately wanted to please him, as life was infinitely easier when the Marshal was pleased.

In this effort she sought Glorieta's help in deciding what she should wear to the first soirée, which her father was sure to attend.

"Wear the blue. It makes you look about thirteen. The younger you look, the more indulgent the papa."

"I don't want him to be indulgent, Glory! I just want him to be . . . satisfied. If he's satisfied with me he doesn't . . . pick at me, and when he picks at me, it's just . . . horrible."

Glorieta put down her book, revealing an unhappy face and eyes that looked swollen from crying. "Is he bringing anyone?"

"The dinner list says he is," Genevieve said, pretending not to notice Glorieta's face, which set off alarms in her mind.

"Well, now that you're twenty, it's probably better if you don't look thirteen. Here he's spent all this money, sending you here for years and years, and if you don't even look grown-up he'll wonder why he bothered. Better wear something very grown-up, show your tits and be Duchessy." Tits, shoulders, and arms which were carefully covered at every other time were shown off at soirées.

"Like?"

"Like the brown satin with the blush ivory roses that just barely cover your nipples. The one that matches your mahogany hair and your nut-brown skin and shows off how nice and round your front is. Tits are important to gentlemen, you can gild them, just a little, and the dress is very regal."

"I do rather like that one."

"Fine. Then you'll be comfortable in it, and life is so much easier when one is comfortable." She said this with a twist of her lips, as though the word meant more to her than she was saying.

The day of a soirée was spent in readying oneself. Bathing. Grooming. Having one's hair done. No liquids after noon—one simply couldn't run off and pee while wearing an evening gown—but a little snack late in the afternoon, just a bit, so that one wouldn't collapse from hunger during the presentations. Then, dressing. Makeup. Genevieve's satin brown skin, inherited from that long ago Dark Queen, needed very little makeup; just a gloss on the lips, a touch of blush on the cheekbones and a bit of gilding on the curve of the breast to draw attention to the nipples, barely hidden by her gown. Her complexion, brows and lashes were perfect on their own, and nothing could be done to disguise the Nose.

Gowns and girls (in that order of importance, said Barbara) were assembled in the reception rooms by sunset, and the guests began to arrive shortly thereafter. The girls moved into the reception line when their own

families or guests were announced. After joining Mrs. Blessingham in greeting their guests, they moved away so that other girls could take their places. Genevieve saw her father's carriage from the terrace, and she was standing at Mrs. Blessingham's left by the time the butler announced the Marshal, Lord Dustin, and his equerry, Colonel Aufors Leys. She looked up, suddenly aware that virtually every girl in the room had also looked up and was not looking away.

They were not looking at the Marshal, who was his usual impeccably dress-uniformed self, the black of his bemedaled and gold-braided jacket serving as proper setting for his long, vertically grooved face, each set of grooves delineating one small fold beneath his chin. The man everyone was staring at was beside him, and Genevieve was staring too.

"Oh, my," she said to herself. "Oh, my." She almost started to applaud the casting before realizing he was not an actor but a real person. Hair like a sunset and a lot of it, springing up from his forehead in a curly red thicket. Darker brows. Lean, but oh, such shoulders, and what straight, athletic-looking legs! He was obviously the lead character in this scene, and he was coming toward her.

"Mrs. Blessingham," her father intoned, bending over her hand. "Genevieve. May I present my equerry, Colonel Aufors Leys."

Genevieve dropped a curtsey, murmured an acknowledgment, felt her hand drawn into her father's, and was led away with the paradigm close behind, their feet raising little dust puffs of whispers. They sat at a table near the orchestra. They sipped wine and were served hors d'oeuvres. The Marshal excused himself and went to speak to an acquaintance at another table.

"So," said the Colonel without preamble, "How do you think we should handle the Frangian situation, Marchioness?"

If her father had been there, she would have smiled and murmured something about knowing very little about the Frangian situation. If the Colonel had been older, if he had said it in a teasing voice, she could not have replied at all. Colonel Aufors Leys, however, asked the question in a matter-of-fact sort of classroom voice, and she answered without thinking, for in this particular play, which seemed to be a new one, she knew the line.

"I think we ought to leave them completely alone."

The Colonel choked on his wine. "I see," he murmured, around his handkerchief. "The Lord Paramount is related to the displaced Duke of Frangia. He wishes his kinsman to be returned to the ducal palace. I don't think he would care for that advice."

"What the Lord Paramount says may have little to do with reality," she responded, still without thinking. "If he and the Duke were patient and kept any new converts out, the Frangians' very strange religion would wipe them all out before long. Since the Frangians' deity, the *Great Whatever*, is worshipped by refusing to toil, since the Frangians do not have children because children require toil, their population must be getting elderly. Also, they're not at all militant. They'd be easy to control if the Lord Paramount really wanted to do so."

"If?" murmured Aufors, his brows lifting in wonder.

"Yes. If. I have never heard it alleged that the Lord Paramount is a patient man. So, it must be that he has some good reason for talking about controlling the Frangians while not doing it. Though he fulminates against Frangia a good bit, probably to show support for the duke, he lets the people come and go as they like. He lets them make converts and keep their society alive, so he must have a secret reason for doing so. If he has a secret reason, then the last thing he would want is advice from someone who doesn't know his reasons."

"What would you tell him?"

"I'd tell the Lord Paramount he has a much better grasp of the situation than anyone else, and he must do what his royal wisdom dictates."

The Colonel stared at her, mouth slightly open. Then, "What reason might he have for letting them alone?"

"I've never thought about it," she said honestly, proceeding to think about it for a long, slow moment. Then she nodded, saying, "It is probable the Frangians do something or provide something that the Lord Paramount considers useful."

The Colonel blinked gravely at her as he considered this.

Genevieve returned his look, unaware that they were staring at one another. She enjoyed looking at him, and she was pleased to have been able to answer his questions. She was quite sure what she had told him was correct. It was not one of those visions that arrived suddenly in a hissing radiance, but it was the only answer that took into account everything she knew. It was really only a little more complicated than foreseeing the moves in chess.

The orchestra began playing a waltz.

The Colonel had a very thoughtful expression on his face as he rose, bowed, and asked, "Would you care to dance?"

She didn't care to, really, because she had to fight her tendency to hum along with the music, but seeing daughters dancing was one of the things parents paid for at Blessingham's, and no doubt her father would

approve her dancing. She nodded and accompanied him onto the floor, where he held her firmly, never stepped on her feet, and was blessedly silent, which she preferred. Dancing and carrying on conversation at the same time was very trying.

Since the Colonel didn't try to make conversation, whenever he reversed or turned Genevieve could look at the other dancers. Carlotta was dancing with Tomas, the two of them seeming rather bored. Glorieta was with Willum, the same expression on their faces that Genevieve had noticed before. It was a wounded look, with an admixture of fear, revulsion, and pain. It wasn't an expression that belonged in a ballroom, and Genevieve spun away on Aufors's arm, telling herself she had not seen it. During the next dance, Glorieta was with Tomas and Willum was with Carlotta . . . no! Willum was with Barbara!

She made a sound, for the Colonel drew her closer and asked, "What did you say?"

"Nothing," she murmured. "I was just surprised to see . . . one of my friends dancing with the betrothed of . . . another of my friends."

He looked across her shoulder. "The young lady in green?"

She nodded, ever so slightly.

"The girl's a flirt," he said, softly. "She'll get herself into trouble."

Genevieve surprised herself by saying, "I think Barbara would welcome trouble. She is not of the nobility and she gets awfully bored trying to be covenantly." Then she bit her lip, confused by the strange look he gave her.

Two waltzes and a country dance later, Colonel Leys attention was drawn across the room, where the Marshal was preparing to leave. The Colonel bowed his thanks, then, turning so that his face was hidden from the Marshal, who awaited him in obvious impatience, he said:

"I have an apology to make, Most Honorable Marchioness."

"Not at all," she murmured, her eyes on her father, who was beginning to fume.

"Please. I teased you in asking those questions. I expected only the usual, a gush of uninspired coquetry with no thought behind it and no sense in it. I was mistaken. I ask your forgiveness for you are . . . a very intelligent . . . ah, person, Most Honorable Marchioness. I hope we will meet soon again." He bowed, kissed her hand, turned on his heels and went, leaving her standing quite still against the blue velvet draperies of the terrace arch, her mouth slightly open, and his lips still burning on her hand as though he had somehow left them behind.

Carlotta came over, full of questions, to which Genevieve gave mono-

syllabic answers. She noticed a sotto voce spat going on between Glorieta and Barbara, so instead of joining her friends for supper, she said her good-nights while the soirée was still going on.

She was curled up in bed with a book when, much later, Carlotta and Glorieta burst in upon her.

"Oooh," cried Glorieta. "Wasn't he something! Wherever did your father find that one, Jenny?"

"He's Father's equerry," said Genevieve.

"What did he say to you? What did you talk about?"

She hesitated a moment before replying. "All he did was stare at me and ask strange questions."

"What strange questions?" demanded Carlotta, scenting something juicy.

"Not flirty sorts of questions, silly. No, he wanted to know what I thought about the Frangian situation. So, I told him what I thought."

"Which was?"

"Something about just leaving Frangia alone."

"His Majesty, Marwell, Lord Paramount will love hearing that. My father says he's very set on bringing Frangia to heel. He wants no breakaway provinces."

"He didn't ask me what I would say to the Lord Paramount, he asked me what I thought."

"He danced with you!" said Glorieta soberly. "I was watching, and he wasn't asking questions then!"

"He didn't say a word the whole time. With him, words seem to be either a flood or a drought."

"Well, if you didn't like him, you might have introduced him to Barbara." She turned away to the window to hide her face, letting herself out onto the balcony.

"Why did he come?" Carlotta said loudly and hastily. "Just a fill in? Someone for you to dance with?"

Genevieve had not thought about that. On occasion her father did send someone in his place, with or without a possible suitor in tow, but it was usually someone she knew, a family friend from Evermire, or one of the older cousins, always someone solid and respectable and no longer young. "I really don't know," she said.

"For heaven's sake, Genevieve! Don't you care?"

She shook her head, which so infuriated Carlotta that she called Genevieve a long-nosed ice maiden. When Genevieve did not respond, Carlotta leaned close.

"Did you hear Glorieta and Barbara fighting? Willum asked Barbara to dance, and she said yes!"

"Isn't that allowed?" Genevieve asked. "I've seen you dancing with him."

"I'm family," she said. "Barbara definitely isn't! And there's something more to it than just dancing. Glorieta has been crying a lot lately."

Carlotta, it seemed, didn't know the reasons for any of it, for Glorieta refused to talk about it, and though Carlotta and Genevieve whispered about it for some time, Genevieve could not think of anything comforting to say. Finally, Carlotta yawned, collected her sister from the balcony, and they went off to their own beds below.

Genevieve turned out her light and pulled the blankets around her shoulders, but then surprised herself by lying there, worrying about Glorieta. Or Barbara. Or even Carlotta. She couldn't help it, even though she had long ago realized that the characters in her plays were not exempt from tragedy. Characters were sometimes written out. Her own mother, for example, had been written out. Someday Genevieve herself would be written out so her soul could go flitting off into paradise where it would flutter from blossom to blossom, sipping nectar, no longer needing resignation. As for this unexpected plot twist in the Amenaj play, she would watch it, of course, but there was nothing she could do about it. All plays would come to an end eventually.

Nonetheless, she had a difficult time dismissing the quarrel between Glorieta and Barbara. She was also unable to stop thinking about the Colonel. Tonight those three characters had stepped off the stage and engaged her attention at a level that was completely new to her. They had seemed real to her, especially the Colonel, for he had made her want to touch him, even before they had danced, the way she sometimes wanted to hug Barbara, though she never did, for it would be an unpermitted sensuality. The Colonel's arms had felt strong and safe, and his questions had not, truthfully, been all that strange, though he had seemed too casual about the first one and too oddly intense about the others. But then, he was quite young. Thirtyish. And very good looking.

Outside, in the garden, Barbara, still in her ball gown, leaned against the stones of the wall while Willum watched her from four inches away, his hands on the wall on either side of her head, his eyes boring purposefully into hers.

"Glorieta is my friend," she said weakly. "This wouldn't be right."

"If you'd really cared about that, you wouldn't have sneaked out to meet me," said Willum in his slow, slightly arrogant voice.

"Your father won't allow you to marry me, Willum. You're already betrothed."

"Father will allow whatever I want. He thinks two brothers marrying two sisters sounds very nice but may lead to unpleasant complications. He was here tonight; he saw you. He's quite impressed. Besides, Father's getting elderly. He's sixty-four. He doesn't want me to wait ten years to give him a grandson, and Glorieta is set on having her full youth before getting married."

"Well," Barbara said in a teasing voice. "If you're sure . . ."

He pulled her to him and put his lips over her own, holding her tightly. Slowly, her arms went around him. When he released her, she was panting, her eyes were softened and glazed looking, as though she had gone blind in the instant.

She murmured drunkenly. "You'll have to break your betrothal to Glorieta first. I won't have her saying that I broke up her betrothal . . ."

"Oh, you didn't," he murmured, his lips at her ear. "Believe me, you didn't."

"Do you think I was too forward?" Genevieve asked a day or two after the soirée, when her friends had questioned her again and she had given them an abbreviated version of her conversation with the Colonel. "Was I too . . . unfeminine?" At Mrs. Blessingham's school, girls were taught to be concerned about such things.

"You did rather spout," Carlotta agreed. "And you know what Mrs. Blessingham says about spouting."

Mrs. Blessingham went to some pains to teach her girls that when a man of the aristocracy asked a woman "What do you think?" it was almost certainly a rhetorical question. The covenants that governed the nobility, the covenants on which the world was founded, specified with absolute clarity that there should be no conflicts among noblemen and no stridency among noblewomen. Stridency among slaves, inferiors, and women had been tolerated during the human rights struggles of predispersion times, but on Haven, stridency was eschewed, as it made people uncomfortable.

Therefore, said Mrs. Blessingham, young ladies would behave like young ladies, not like political agitators. It was uncovenantly to question men's business or one's own status. If one's husband or father struck a horse or servant or child, or even oneself, the proper response was to retire, to see that injuries were attended to, and to assure that the occasion of anger was not repeated. Men were actually happier if they believed that women did not think of anything except babies and baubles and other such harmless, female kind of things. Happy men were tranquil men; tranquil men made a tranquil society. A tranquil society was the goal of women; sacrificing one's own immediate gratifications for one's family and society was Godly and laudatory; and doing it graciously, with unreserved resignation, displayed perfect purity of soul.

"Do you think we really have souls?" Genevieve had asked Barbara on

one occasion when they were alone and no one could possibly overhear them and report them to the scrutator.

Barbara had frowned, something she rarely did. "Oh, Jenny, I had an older brother, Bertold. Sometimes I hated him. He'd hurt me. He'd twist my arm to make me cry, and then he'd laugh. But sometimes, just once in a while, he was happy, and when he was happy he was so funny and sweet. It never lasted long. He was killed because he was mean and hateful one time too many. He was Papa's only son, and that's why Papa is so set on . . . well, you know.

"After Bertold was killed, I just knew all the mean parts got washed away, and the funny, sweet parts of him were kept, like gold, panned out of gravel, and put in the treasury. Not all of him was worth keeping, but part of him . . . I don't think it was lost."

Barbara sometimes amazed Genevieve. She had such wonderful thoughts, though they, like the gold in Bertold's nature, were sparse among the gravel of Barbara's daily self. One had to go panning for them. And ideas weren't universally admired, either!

"Women should not complicate any matter under consideration by offering opinions," said Mrs. Blessingham. "To be a handsome, poised, amusing, seemingly passive but managerially brilliant woman is your goal."

"I did spout at the soirée," Genevieve admitted shamefacedly to Carlotta. "Father will no doubt be furious."

Though Genevieve heard nothing directly from her father on the subject of "spouting," it was the first thing that came to her mind when she was summoned to Mrs. Blessingham's sitting room a few days later. On the way there, she wondered if Colonel Leys had told her father, or if someone else had, and if now he was angry with her. If he had heard she had misbehaved, his anger could be taken for granted. She was quite pale when she arrived at Mrs. Blessingham's office.

"Heaven, child, you're pale as milk!"

"I thought, perhaps . . . Father . . . something . . ."

"It's nothing that warrants worry! Your father merely sent a note to say he is bringing an important guest to the next soirée." The older woman fixed the girl with a doubtful expression. "I would be concerned, of course, if your father intends to betroth you to someone. By the terms of the covenants, you should have another ten years before accepting that responsibility. I have told him as much, but he does not seem to listen."

"Father does not really listen to women, Mrs. Blessingham."

Mrs. Blessingham, a commoner who had chosen her lifestyle, her work,

and her friends, had grown unaccustomed to including herself in the category "women," and this label made her blink.

"Well, still we must keep Papa happy, since that is what we do. I asked to see you so we can arrange with Dorothea to do your hair and with Gertrude to select your gown and be sure it is fitted properly. You have grown since last year. Most girls do not grow in height at your age, so we must be sure your stockings and small-linens still fit you well."

"Yes, ma'am," she said, as she always said. Then, however, she went on, betraying her own confusion. "Father has not said anything at all about a betrothal."

"I was merely guessing, my dear. He did not say who he was bringing with him, merely that he wished you to make a good appearance. And Genevieve, please. It might be better if you did not spout. You were seen talking at a great rate at the last soirée, and it is never a good idea to go on so volubly. If it was only chatter, it can be excused as mere nervousness or even playfulness, but do avoid speaking about politics. Few women find comments on political matters well received, and those who do tend to be elderly, with years of exposure to the talk of a husband and his colleagues. At the age of fifty or sixty, if a woman is not contentious, she can sometimes offer an opinion without being silenced."

"That seems foolish," Genevieve said, surprising herself. "It seems self-defeating not to let us use our minds."

Mrs. Blessingham smiled rather ruefully. "Genevieve, it would be self-defeating among the commons. The poor are like foxes: they need intelligence in order to survive. The rich, however, have power; they don't need good sense. Also remember that traditional things are sacred, and here on Haven, vapid noblewomen are traditional."

Genevieve dropped a curtsey and left, her face flaming.

"It was Barbara, that cat. She told," said Carlotta.

"No," Genevieve said, trying to be fair. "I think it was one of the guests who heard me talking to the Colonel, and his questions were political, sort of."

"I can't understand why you're so interested in politics. Where do you even learn about it?"

"I'm not all that interested," murmured Genevieve, by now quite aware that any such interests should not be shared with her schoolmates, for they would tell their families, and their families would tell others. Besides, it was true that she wasn't interested in politics exactly. She just wanted to know how things worked and what roles people played, and what the

rules of the game were. The only real way to find such things out was to watch them or read about them.

To this end, she had haunted the library since soon after coming to Blessingham's. It reminded her of the library at Langmarsh House: it was quiet, and if she daydreamed over an open book, no one thought she was strange. The librarian was a crickety little man with a funny beard who never bothered to learn their names and called each one of them "young lady." He had a small office where he sat for hours at a time, reading periodicals, some from off-world, some from the provinces, most of them printed on paper particularly for nontechnological markets. Nothing of the kind was included in the reading material available to students, and Genevieve's curiosity was piqued, particularly when she saw that the librarian stacked the older periodicals outside his door for the maids to take away.

After several days of anticipatory guilt, she filched one from the pile and carried it off to her room. There, for the first time, she read of other worlds as described by the people on them. She read of planets that had been settled with high hopes, only to fail, while others, settled in like fashion, succeeded. Here was Dephesia, fertile and flourishing; there was Chamis, no less fertile, but perishing nonetheless. Here was Barlet's World, healthy amid its forests and seas. There was Ares, on which a mysterious thing had happened, on which a mysterious plague was even now infecting the population. Genevieve found this information totally fascinating.

Thereafter, Genevieve "borrowed" periodicals whenever she could do so unobserved, reading and rereading them in the privacy of her own room before returning them to the discard pile, thankful for the private room that let her read without being questioned. All the girls twelve or older had private rooms, for being alone was something girls had to adjust to. When one became mistress of an estate, one would need to occupy long stretches of solitude without being lonely. Otherwise, one might actually engage in improper behavior, start fraternizing with the maids, chatting with the butler, or flirting with good-looking stable boys, which was not the thing. Not at all.

"No matter how lonely you get, do not get into the habit of chit-chat with the servants." So said Mrs. Blessingham.

And whom might one chit-chat with? One's friends from school, who could be invited to come visit for a fortnight or a season. One's parents or siblings, if any. One's children if one had any and if they and oneself lived to a conversational age. Everyone seemed agreed that women should talk as little as possible, in order not to offend.

Or, Genevieve thought as she stood in her open window staring out at moonlit trees, one might simply have a tower room, above it all, where talking was unnecessary. When she imagined her future, Genevieve equipped it with a tower room, one even higher than this, above the clouds, where the night music would sound clearly and she could sing at the top of her lungs without being heard. This dream was slightly confusing, for if she wanted to be separated from humanity's troubles, why did she read the librarian's periodicals? It was puzzling.

During the human dispersion from Old Earth, a surprising number of habitable worlds were discovered more or less by accident. Haven was a typical example. Te Matawaka Whetu, the largest ship in the Ark Fleet from Old Earth, blew a modulator while transitting a worm hole and was expelled through an unexpected nexus. The ship emerged too near Haven to avoid discovering the planet rather more violently than the crew would have preferred. Te Matawaka Whetu, which had been headed toward another planet in quite another direction, was pulled into a rapidly decaying planetary orbit that ended with the ship crashing into the worldwide ocean where it soon broke up and eventually sank, though not before the crew escape pod was launched along with the Mayday beacon array.

The site of impact was between two landmasses—the only two landmasses—near an arc-shaped isthmus where the escape pod came to rest with all its emergency supplies intact. Some of the wreckage washed up on the smaller continent to the south, as well as upon a number of islands.

Even under the press of disaster, the experienced captain had included in the Mayday signal the fact that the planet was habitable but uninhabited. This guaranteed the rescue of the survivors, for any habitable world was worth at least one rescue mission. When the rescuers arrived they found the crew safe and well, through they could find no significant remnant of the ship, which was listed as having sunk together with all cargo and the cargo handlers. The planet was subsequently registered for settlement—along with several others that the rescue ship located in the immediate area—and when it was officially surveyed by the Office of Planetary Settlement it was listed as having two continents connected by the mountainous isthmus, plus some thousands of islands.

The land area was too small to tempt most investors, though nearby planets discovered by the rescue mission were settled rather soon: Dephesia by a farming society; Chamis by a group of terraformers; Barlet's World

by a group of militant greens; forested Ares by veterans of the final lebens-raum wars among Earth, Luna, Mars, and the Jovian moons that had left all of them uninhabited and uninhabitable. Eventually the exorbitant claim fee for Haven was paid by a small consortium of wealthy men who wished to retire from Urbana-eight, a planetoid which they had much profited from gutting, to something more natural and charming. The group did not care that Haven's land area was small. They preferred it that way, as it would be more exclusive. Easier, so they said, to keep out the riff-raff.

As many wealthy world-buyers did, they recruited craftsmen, farmers, and skilled workers of all kinds who were willing to immigrate in return for employment and land. Young, healthy candidates for wifehood were also recruited, and the world, named Haven, was thus furnished with useful citizens and several social classes even prior to occupation.

Haven, the world, was profoundly wet. Haven, the larger continent, was a great basalt pillar jutting above the worldwide ocean like a titanic tub, its walls feathered with sea birds whose ancestors had escaped from the sinking Ark ship, its rim raised above the reach of the wildest storms. The western half of the continent cupped to hold a huge freshwater puddle filling what was left of the ancient caldera. This lake, soon named Ha-venpool, was deep and fertile and full of fish, the extensive swamps and mires along its eastern edge serving as a nursery for all kinds of water creatures, native and introduced.

Havenpool was ringed about with mountain ranges. A man on the northwesternmost of the Seawall Mountains could stare northeastward across the Great Fall, where Havenpool fell into the sea, to the heights of the Northern Knot and, if he turned clockwise, he would see mountains on every horizon, all of them formed by that ancient mother-of-all-volcanoes that had become the continent itself.

Haven's provinces were Upland, northernmost, atop the high cliffs; south of that was High Haven, the Royal holding that included the seat of the Lord Paramount at Havenor; Dania like a fat "J" hung below High Haven, with Langmarsh to the west along the shore of Havenpool, and Merdune to the east. Sealand stretched along the west shore of Havenpool to the cliffs above the world-ocean; Barfezi ran along the south of the continent, with the province of Frangia sticking out below like a rude tongue. Merdune was on the eastern side of Haven, where the land sloped downward from the Eastrange Mountains to the very edge of the sea, as though an enormous tooth-grooved bite had been taken out of the conti-nent. Merdune boasted the only real seashore on Haven, one that

stretched the length of shimmering Merdune Lagoon, a saltwater bay almost as large as Havenpool.

Very early after settlement, a dispute had arisen between a particular nobleman and the Covenant Tribunal, the ultimate religious authority of Haven. Though many considered this a minor matter, a question of interpretation, the nobleman had subsequently marched with all his followers down the land bridge to the smaller landmass, which he named Mahahm. As the polar ice continued melting, a process that had been going on at least since the planet was discovered, the isthmus became a widely separated string of rocky islands, the Stone Trail, and regular contact between the two landmasses was lost. Though the Lord Paramount at Havenor was still titled "Ruler of Mahahm," the Mahahmbi were known to refer to him less cordially.

The thousands of islands scattered singly and in clusters all around the globe were entirely unexplored by the Havenites. The seas were dangerous and there was little reason to go seeking out relatively small specks of dry land, many of which had been covered by the sea since colonization. According to the surveyors, the Inundation should have finished long ago, but seemingly there was still ice to melt, as the rising shorelines of the Stone Trail and the Merdune Lagoon well certified.

All native animals were amphibious. There were no native birds, though the so-called siren-lizard soared and sang, filling a bird's ecological niche. The only purely land-dwelling creatures—as well as real birds—were exotics brought in by the settlers, everything from cattle to lap dogs to butterflies and peacocks.

The men who purchased Haven desired a world of privilege, culture, and peace. Technology had facilitated the total urbanization of Old Earth, an event which had only briefly preceded its strange demise as a viable world, and technology, the settlers felt, should be eschewed in the interest of tranquility. In tranquil societies, nothing changes very much or moves very fast, if at all, and the buyers yearned for this leisurely pace. They deified tradition. They forbade invention. They adopted an hereditary monarchy and, for the nobility, a state religion: pseudo-Judaeo-Muslim-Christian-monotheism with accretions. The wealthiest man among the settlers became the first Lord Paramount, his colleagues became the lesser lords, the dukes of the seven provinces. Their children became the earls and viscounts of the counties within those provinces, and their children became the barons of the estates within those counties. Each county—some forty of them—was allowed an assembly of citizens, variously constituted, who elected or selected a minister to the provincial council, and

the provincial councils elected representatives to the Lord Paramount's Council of Ministers, a group charged with oversight of interprovincial matters such as the maintenance of roads and bridges or the location and support of schools and medical services for the million or so citizens of Haven.

Preservation of the belief system which supported the tranquil, unchanging culture of Haven was the particular duty of the scrutators, who reported to the Invigilator, an officer of the Tribunal, the body that assured the continuation of the traditions of Haven. Thus, as Haven had started, it continued: a peaceful, changeless, easy kind of a place, where sound basic education, excellent sanitation, advanced medical care, and adequate diets contributed to long life spans for most of a populace ruled by, so everyone among the ruling class agreed, a conservative but well-intentioned aristocracy.

SOUTH OF HAVEN, ON THE MINOR CONTINENT OF MAHAHM, SHAH ARGHAD rose early on the third morning of the Time-of-Renewal, a thrice-yearly holy time during which aspirants for elevation were examined for their faith. The first two days of the examination had been conducted by trusted associates in the annex. Though the Shah seldom left the comfort of the palace, his presence at the second stage of the examination was obligatory. No candidate brought by an aspirant might go to the place of reward without being individually selected and blessed by the Shah. No sacred substance might be dispensed to the aspirants except from the Shah's own hand, making the sole source of all such rewards abundantly clear.

Ybon Saelan, the Shah's most trusted minister, was waiting in the anteroom, already clad in the robe of blessings.

"May your life be extended beneath the everlasting sun," murmured the minister, presenting the sacred goblet.

Upon the clear water floated a slight haze of fragrant dust, and the Shah drank the ritual draught quickly.

"May we all be so livened," murmured the Shah, as he returned the goblet.

His serving men helped him into the royal cloak trimmed with the feathers of hunting birds. They pulled the insulated hood over his head. His horse was waiting in the portico, heat dissipating straps of harptahide dangling from its belly-band, its skull protected by a foam helmet much like the one beneath the Shah's hood. Though it was cool now, in a few hours the desert would be a furnace.

"Are the aspirants assembled?" the Shah asked.

"They await Your Effulgence," murmured the minister.

The Shah mounted his horse, one of only half a dozen on Mahahm, a symbol of royal authority no less than the golden dome of the palace, the prostrations of his servitors, the length of his reign, all by the will of

the Great Sun whose son was the Shah himself. The gates were swung open and he rode at a slow walk into the outer courtyard where the two files of black-robed aspirants were mustered.

Their faces were stern and still, as befitted aspirants. Each pair bowed low as Ybon Saelan pronounced their names and the Shah passed between them. There were fifteen men in each file, and as he reached each pair the Shah inclined his head, intoning, "As the Fire of Heaven wills."

The outer gate swung open as he led the aspirants into the street, where the procession was arranging itself around seven giant harpta lizards, the last one bearing basket panniers, the other six walking between lines of white-veiled candidates. Each candidate was to be accompanied by one of the aspirants from the courtyard or, if the aspirant was infirm, that aspirant's delegate. In the half dozen cases where this applied, the aspirants were already placing the hands of their delegates—often a son or younger brother—upon the head of the candidates while reciting the ritual transfer of responsibility to the younger men. When all was orderly, the minister led the black-clad participants in reciting the oath of the ritual masters, the solemn words confirming that each understood his duties.

"How many stops?" the Shah murmured to his minister.

"Fifteen, Effulgent One. The runners have set the flags accordingly."

"How many candidates?"

"Sixty, Your Effulgence."

"Not enough."

"All there are, Great One. We have examined the rolls carefully."

"And none from elsewhere?"

"None this time, Great One. We anticipate there being several at the next Renewal."

The Shah settled into his saddle. He knew what was anticipated. He knew what was here and now, as well. From somewhere nearby, a baby cried. He stiffened. The sound was quickly muffled. Very well. He took his place at the head of the procession, raised a hand, and ordered the assembly forward, riding slowly as the minister walked beside him.

Though he was impatient to get through the day's ritual, it would do no good to spur the horse. At this hour, still chilled by the night, the harpta could move only slowly, their dual dorsal fins folded together, the intaglio tracery of blood vessels sunken within the fin-flesh. When the sun was a bit higher, the fins would separate slightly, allowing the sun to touch both sides, the veins would fill with blood to be warmed by the sun and to carry that warmth deep into the huge bodies of the beasts. Later, when it grew hot, the blood would be diverted from the fins into

the moist belly-fringes of the beast, and the fins themselves would be lowered on either side to provide shade for the huge bodies beneath— and for the persons who walked there—while the long rows of evaporating belly-fringe conducted heat away from the bodies, keeping the creatures from overheating.

The first red flag was set just outside the city gate of Mahahm-qum; the next one gleamed along the edge of a dune. As they reached these, others would be seen, marking the way.

An hour's slow ride from flag to flag brought them to the first patch of holy growth. The Shah raised his hand for a halt, turned and rode silently back along the line. The masters had arranged themselves between couples of candidates, and the Shah pointed randomly at two of the heavily veiled candidate-master trios. Each candidate couple knelt to receive a silent blessing from the Shah before each ritual master guided his candidates to the vegetation and demonstrated how the holy growth was to be sheared off close to the ground, how every scrap of it was to be placed in the baskets.

With four candidates working, it did not take long. When all had been cut, the ritual masters took the curved knives from the candidates, emptied the baskets in the panniers carried by the last harpta in line, and returned to the candidates for the completion of the ritual. The procession did not wait for the ritual to end, which would take some time. Those involved would return to the city on their own when they had finished. As soon as the last basket was emptied, therefore, the Shah commanded the procession to move forward.

The trek went on all day. In early evening, having made a wide, circular loop through the desert, the Shah led the caravan back toward Mahahm-qum. Most of the harpta had already returned to their half-shore, half-sea pen on the coast; those remaining held their fins erect to gather the last of the sun. Outside the city, the herdsmen removed the harnesses and let the harpta go, all but the one who carried the panniers. This one was guided toward a long, low mud-brick building that emerged from the sands on the outskirts of the city. Seeing the beast approach, guards unlocked and swung wide the doors before removing the panniers and harness from the lizard. It went scuttling off after its fellows, sand splaying from beneath its feet.

The Shah and Ybon Saelan stood for a moment outside, scrutinizing the building with great care. At either side of the front wall, hinged wooden extensions held back the sand. At the front roof-line was another, propped high, the props held by a single mechanism. If the side flanges

were pulled in and the upper one was dropped, the wind-piled sand behind all three of them would flow down in an instant, covering the building. It had been designed so, in the event of . . . anything untoward occurring.

"When was it tested last?" asked the Shah.

"Last Holy Days," replied Ybon Saelan. "It worked perfectly. It took two days to dig it out. The men inside were running out of air."

They went inside, shutting the doors behind them. The panniers had been emptied onto a smooth table, the originally voluminous cargo dried by the day's heat and dry air into a modest pile of dark scraps. A stone roller plied by the guards was reducing the scraps to a fine, reddish powder which was sifted and crushed again, then scooped and brushed with meticulous care into small glazed jars that were sealed tightly before stacking them against the wall amid others.

While this went on, the Shah went to the rear of the room where only one bolted door broke the expanse of wall. He took a key from his pocket, unlocked a panel that allowed him to move the bolt, then pulled the door open to disclose another one with a round of thick glass set into it. The Shah peered in, his lips working as he craned, trying to see right and left and down through the small pane. At last he breathed deeply, closed the doors and locked them once more.

His minister approached, taking no notice of the Shah's preoccupation. "Twelve jars of P'naki, Magnanimous One," murmured the Ybon Saelan.

"Only twelve?"

"The usual amount, sire, within half a jar or so."

"Was all gathered?"

"All we had candidates for."

The Shah grimaced. "One is tempted to increase the raids."

"Serving today at the expense of tomorrow, Great One. The P'naki will not be increased by using up our resources. How many jars for the aspirants?"

The Shah thought long. He had taken particular notice of this year's aspirants for elevation. Too many of those in this morning's muster had been elderly, subject to disease and frailty, and those who had selected proxies would have been there all day still bowed forward, silent, unmoving, waiting for the Shah to postpone or elevate them. As he must! He had postponed too many elevations recently. It would be a mistake to postpone more.

"Bring enough to protect all of them," he said, gritting his teeth.

"Enough for all of them?" wondered the minister.

"All. There is no one among them who had not been there twice

before and not one among them is without friends. They have earned their protection."

The Shah mounted his horse and rode back to the palace, the minister running behind, carrying the small jar and panting a little.

So, let him pant. The crop was so limited and so much in demand. Haven wanted desperately to buy more of it. There should be some way to improve this system. Though perhaps one should merely accede to the will of the Divine Sun. Scarcity brought its own rewards.

He had these thoughts before, but nothing had changed. Too much depended upon it. It had brought him much and would bring him as much again. No. It would not change.

``F~OR THE SOIRÉE, I THINK THE MAHOGANY SATIN," SAID GERTRUDE, THE Wardrobe Mistress. "You look marvelous in it."

Genevieve demurred. "It's what I wore last time. I really look like a Nose in it."

"You know," said Gertrude, head cocked to one side, "you're growing into your nose. Last year, it seemed large, true, but this year, no. This year, it seems a proper part of your face. The art instructor, Master Vorbold, said you would be striking. He was positive it would happen, and I believe it has!"

The mirror agreed, but only if Genevieve stood tall, head carried imperially poised on her long neck, shoulders relaxed, face quiet. Then the face was fine, nose and all, just as it was in the family portraits. Her dark skin was unusual in Haven, but acceptable since it was inherited from Queen Stephanie.

"I'll bet your father's bringing the colonel back," whispered Carlotta, as they were having their hair done. "I'll bet the colonel has asked for your hand."

"No," said Genevieve, with a pang of regret. "Father wouldn't consider the colonel for me." Not in this play or any other.

"Why not?" demanded Barbara. "He's young, he's handsome, he looks healthy!"

Genevieve worked it out. "In the first place, he's a commoner, which means he's uncovenantal. And then, Father is looking for a son. He did not get one by birth, so he will try to get one by marriage. It is much more important that Father get on with the person than that I do, and the Colonel is not the kind of person Father would ever be comfortable with." She said it calmly, but heard it with a pang. What she had said was absolutely true. Now why was that? Why wasn't Father perfectly comfortable with his own equerry?

What was it about Aufors Leys that Father was *not* comfortable with? Not merely his being a commoner, for Father was quite comfortable with some commoners. It wasn't his appearance, which was heavenly, or his manners, which were impeccable. It had to be something, but she couldn't think what. Just something about him. His attitude perhaps. Yes. That was likely it, his attitude of being *real*. Aufors was more *real* than Father was. This idea was difficult to think out, but once having thought it, Genevieve could not unthink it. Aufors Leys was real, but like her father, Genevieve was probably not.

Everyone was ready for the soirée early. Father arrived early, also. He bowed, took her hand, and led her out through the open doors of the ballroom onto the terrace.

"Genevieve, Prince Yugh Delganor will be attending the soiree tonight, as my guest."

Yugh Delganor. She cast out a net of memory, seining for Delganor. A guest at Langmarsh House, not long before school started this year. A tall, thin man with dead eyes, hollow cheeks, and no conversation. As she had been taught, she had given him opportunities for conversation, but each had been a stone dropped into a bottomless well: no splash, no echo. He had been very well dressed. Middle aged. Perhaps older. Not bad looking, but vaguely repellant and utterly without animation. Genevieve had assigned him a walk-on role and had been glad when he had departed.

"I remember the name . . ." she murmured.

His lips thinned. "You should remember more than the name, girl! Yugh Delganor is the Lord Paramount's nephew, son of his younger brother."

"Ah," she murmured. "Prince Thumsort, is it?"

"No, no. Thumsort is the youngest of the three. Delganor's father and His Majesty, Marwell, Lord Paramount were twins. Since the untimely death of the Lord Paramount's son, Delganor is the heir presumptive. Thumsort comes third, since Delganor's sons have also perished."

"Couldn't the Lord Paramount have another son?"

"The Queen is past it, girl! She hasn't had the good sense to die and let him find another wife, and a son out of any other woman would not qualify. Why don't you know all this?"

She murmured, "I don't think you have ever told me of it, Father."

He sniffed. "I keep forgetting this school does not always teach you what may be most important to you. I hope at least you have guessed something of what this evening portends."

Something tore. A bit of that membrane that made a comforting trans-

lucency between herself and the outside world ripped away, leaving a hole. Reality showed through, only a glimpse—ominously dark—and her inner parts cramped in panic. She found voice to say, "Since you had not mentioned this matter before, no, I have no idea."

He frowned, displeased.

She sought to mend the veil that protected her, pulling it together between herself and the reality of his words. "Are you perhaps engaging in some enterprise with Prince Delganor?"

He glared, not at her but at the horizon, barely visible between the trees. "I have been summoned to Havenor, to attend upon the court. It could be a lengthy term of service. When I mentioned other responsibilities, the Lord Paramount kindly thought of your needs. The Lord Paramount does not invite all and everyone to reside in Havenor. He has waited to receive others' opinion of you, of your poise, your behavior, your appearance, the purity of your soul. Prince Delganor gave him an opinion. Aufors Leys has also done so. Delganor is coming tonight to extend the Lord Paramount's invitation for you to reside at court during my posting there."

"I don't understand . . ."

His face contorted in anger. "Of course you do! Do not be willfully stupid, Genevieve! You have been well reared, well educated. Your soul has been kept pure. You are suitable! And because you are suitable, the Prince has condescended to come here tonight in order to deliver the Lord Paramount's invitation. He may ask if you have any objection to leaving school. You will say no. He may ask if you have any matrimonial interest, since that might distract you from the duties of the court, and if he does, you will say you do not."

Stillness, and herself saying in a stranger's voice from a place of clarity. "I did not particularly like him, Father."

He barked, a single *ha*, unamused. "That is of no matter. There will be a good many at court you will not like, any more than I do. Nonetheless, we accommodate ourselves. Who knows? You may find a husband there."

"I am entitled to a decade more of my youth, Father. And I do not think I would like marrying a courtier."

"That, too, is of no matter. Your mother was young when we were wed, she did not much like marrying me, nor I her. It worked out well enough."

She closed her eyes against those words, remembering a face, hearing sounds of agony, smelling the metallic reek of blood. A woman's voice whispering, "Jenny, Jenny, oh, my darling girl . . ." Had it worked well

enough, their marriage? Not for Mother, she did not say. Mother died, she did not say. You killed her, she did not say, feeling the first fluttering of something other than panic, something foreign to her, a loose thread of fury, hanging there, tempting her to grasp it, let what would unravel!

She ignored the thread, saying softly, "My education is unfinished, and I will miss my friends here at school."

"That also is of no matter. The honor you are offered outshines any such concerns, and Mrs. Blessingham can no doubt recommend tutors at High Haven if you wish to continue your education." He turned on her, face hard. "Keep this in mind! This whole matter may be in the nature of a test, to see whether we, you and I, are the kind of people who will make difficulties! Believe me, Genevieve, if you think of doing such a thing, think again. Rejecting an invitation from the Lord Paramount, brought to you by no less personage than the Prince, would not be good for me, and if you are not thoughtful of my reputation, as you have a duty to be, it will not be good for you, either. Whatever the Prince proposes comes directly from the Lord Paramount, and I am sworn to serve the Lord Paramount."

"His invitation is actually your command, then." She was surprised at the calm in her voice. "You are saying that I have no choice."

"No honorable choice, no. Later on, well . . ." He barked laughter, as though at something he had just discovered. "Yugh Delganor may well marry again. It is not impossible he might find you attractive enough to consider you for . . . some very exalted position."

And there she was suddenly, at center stage. The lights were on her, the attention of whoever it was, out there in the darkness, the watchers, among whom she had hoped to stay, always, always. Now the action centered upon her and the plot lines knotted and wove and all other characters faded into shadow. She drew away from him, hearing the rustle of her gown on the tiles loud in the silence, feeling the evening air clammy on her bare shoulders while a greater coldness froze the pit of her stomach.

She whispered, "Does he have family?"

"He has family, yes. He's been married two or three times, but his wives died." He said it offhandedly, as though it didn't matter. "As I recall, his first wife died in childbirth and one of the others died of batfly fever the year it swept the lowlands. Such things happen. I must say, your attitude surprises me."

"Forgive me, Father," she said from that brightly lighted place where she stood, that cell in time where all seemed to converge. "It is only that

I, too, am much surprised. You have never mentioned any of this to me. This invitation comes out of the blue in the hands of a man who was not even polite to me when he visited Langmarsh House. Perhaps he is above politeness."

This time her father laughed with genuine amusement. "Well said, daughter. Perhaps he is, indeed. Whether he is above it or not, I know you will be sensible enough not to insult him. He has received good report from Colonel Leys, who has confirmed Mrs. Blessingham's opinion of you. She has said you are poised and quiet and your purity of soul has been approved by the scrutator. The Colonel has seconded this judgment."

"The Colonel . . ." She shook her head, confused. She had not been quiet with the Colonel. He had not asked about her soul. Not at all!

"The Colonel will be going with us to Havenor," the Marshal said, misunderstanding. "When the Lord Paramount suggested the Colonel give an opinion it was for good reason. Leys is my equerry, and he would be responsible for your safety and comfort at court. His making an assessment of your manner is appropriate." He turned away, as though finished with words.

She tried, unsuccessfully, to think of something that might delay this matter, or forestall it altogether, but before she could think of anything, he exclaimed:

"Ah, there he is!"

She turned her head toward the distant door where Nemesis stood, tall and dark and dressed all in black, his eyes staring in her direction like flawed marbles, blindly.

"Remember to whom you are speaking," her father concluded, tucking her arm firmly under his own and moving off to greet his guest.

Somehow she greeted, bowed, responded to words. Somehow she got out onto the terrace with the tall man, without noticing that her father ushered them there, shutting the doors behind them. She did not come to herself until Delganor had taken her hand in his and was saying, ". . . the Lord Paramount wishes me to convey his pleasure at the prospect of your attendance at the court, in Havenor."

The words reached her ears, but beyond her ears she felt her brain shudder and cramp at his voice. Beneath her glove, the skin of her hand crawled. She could not bear for him to press her hand again or say anything more. To put an end to it, she assented, withdrew her hand in order to make the full, dramatic courtesy, after which she remained bent, watching his heels as he retreated from her. He exchanged a few words with

her father inside the door. She barely breathed, wishing she had dreamed what just happened. This had not been a play. She had not merely watched. She had been present, hideously present, and she would have given anything she owned or ever thought of attaining if she had been elsewhere throughout it all.

Genevieve's invitation to court had come about thusly:

The Marshal, who had been at Havenor on business, was bidden to an immediate audience with the Lord Paramount. Not stopping to put on court attire, he went upon the notice and was admitted into the small hearing chamber where the Lord Paramount spent part of each morning attending to the business of Haven. His Majesty sat on a low dais, in a gilded and padded chair beneath a baldachin hung behind and on either side with weighty purple velvet to shut out the draughts. The carpet around him was strewn with booklets, both talking book and view-cube, and a tottery stack of other such booklets occupied a small gilded table at his side. His crown was slightly tilted, for he habitually leaned his chin on his left hand, turning the pages with right, listening with his eyes half shut, like a dreaming tortoise. He was in this position when he received the Marshal, alone except for two members of the recently imported off-world security force—Aresians sworn to the Lord Paramount's service and protection—who stood on either side of the door, weapons at the ready and eyes scanning the room in ceaseless watchfulness.

The Marshal saw all this as he came through the door, particularly the guards—bulky men, and strong looking, as all Aresians were. The two of them traded him look for look, silently, without a hint of feeling: no animosity, no acceptance, just alertness. The taller one was dark haired with a beard so black that his smoothly shaven skin looked blue. The other resembled him, though he was lighter, a bit thinner. They were good men, both. He wouldn't mind commanding men like these.

"Your Majesty," murmured the Marshal, bending a knee.

"Marshal," said the Lord Paramount, without moving, the pages slowly turning. "You know that new minister, the one from Barfezi? Name of Gormus."

"Efiscapel Gormus, yes, your Majesty, I've met him."

"Don't like him."

"I'm sorry to hear that, sir."

"I don't know what it is about County Potcher in Barfezi! The place breeds these free thinkers like lice, and here's another of 'em, all full of schemes to connect to off-world, join the community of man, open our

arms and our hearts. And our pockets, he doesn't say. And our private business, which is none of off-worlds' affair! Well, I don't like him. Don't like the influence he has on some of the other ministers. Decided I need a balancing weight." He looked up, his eyes fully open, piercing the Marshal with his stare. "I'm inviting you to come to court."

The Marshal paused before answering, for the words had been peculiarly freighted with meaning, and that meaning suddenly penetrated. "You mean, live here, sir?"

"Can't be here without living here, can you?"

"No, sir." He thought, furiously. What was he supposed to say now? He'd never thought of such a possibility. He was no courtier! But he could scarcely say so, at the moment.

"Ah . . . I am deeply honored, Your Majesty, and I will comply as soon as I can arrange the few . . . responsibilities I'll have to see to first. . . ."

The Lord Paramount's eyes had not left the Marshal's face, but now they slid aside, like a snake from a rock. "Of course, of course, for the moment I'd forgotten. You have a family—what is it, a daughter? Delganor mentioned her to me just recently. He met her at your place in Langmarsh. As I recall, he spoke well of her." He breathed for a moment through his teeth, a little whistle, *whee-oo, whee-oo,* in and out. "If possible—though it may not be—she should be with you, of course. All the young women at court have assigned duties, and we'd need to be sure she could acquit herself in a covenantly manner. Let's have someone take a look at her again, just to confirm Delganor's impressions. By the way, what's her name?"

"Genevieve, sir."

The Lord Paramount's eyes were on the turning pages. "Of course. Genevieve. Well, I'm sure she's quiet and respectful, a dutiful daughter, covenantly, pure of soul, a proper candidate." The Lord Paramount looked up, piercingly.

The Marshal found himself feeling slightly queasy, almost sick, like a man hard pressed, unable to catch his breath. It was known that the Prince was seeking a wife, but it would be presumptuous to imagine Genevieve as a candidate for . . . well, what the Lord Paramount was obviously referring to.

He chose to evade the question. "That would be hard for a father to judge, sir."

The Lord Paramount gave him a sharp look. "Ah . . . you think so? Well, I have an idea. Since that equerry of yours would be looking after her here in Havenor, let him take a look at her. We old fellows, we can't

judge women, and it's not our place, anyhow. Though Delganor does very well. Proper judge of livestock, Delganor. Gave me a marvelous stallion, just recently."

"As Your Majesty wishes," murmured the Marshal, backing away from the presence while trying not to show his discomfort. Why had he mentioned having responsibilities? Still . . . if the Lord Paramount had meant what he might have meant . . .

Behind him, in the small council chamber, silence fell. A servant crept through a side door and circled the throne, putting the scattered booklets into a basket and rearranging the pile at the Lord Paramount's side before creeping out once more. The Lord Paramount dropped the booklet from his lap onto the carpet and took the top one from the pile, leafing through it, marking the pages here and there. The Aresian mercenaries by the door continued their restless watch upon the room, raising their weapons briefly as the curtain behind the baldachin opened and Yugh Delganor slipped through to lean familiarly across the Lord Paramount's shoulder.

"So, do I invite the girl to join us all here at Havenor?"

The Lord Paramount smiled. "Give it a little time, Yugh. It isn't as though we're in a hurry, eh? Look at this animal, here. Like a sheep, only tiny. It's a kind of lapdog. I want one. Or several."

"As Your Majesty wishes."

"Ten of them, I think. That way I'll have replacements. They don't last long, pets. Such short lives. Better bring them in stasis. And look here, this admirable new type of rug weaving looms. I must have some of these."

Yugh Delganor scanned the booklet, bowing. "Your Majesty is no doubt correct."

"I'll have Krivel look at it. We may be non-technological, Yugh, but we have to keep up with things, ah?"

"Your Majesty can say nothing less than truth."

The Lord Paramount nodded, the pages flickering in his hands. "Let that young colonel look her over, the Marshal's daughter—look at this dinnerware! Quite marvelous—if you think she's all right and he's a suitable one to . . ."

"Oh, definitely. Very . . . puissant."

"Then he'll no doubt find her charming, despite the nose."

"She may have grown into it by now," the Prince interrupted.

"Despite the nose," repeated the Lord Paramount, an edge to his voice. This time Delganor did not interrupt him. "Then you can go down to her school or academy or whatever it is and invite her. If all goes well, we'll have you wed shortly. Your third wife, won't it be?"

"Fourth, Your Majesty."

"Pity. I remember your first wife. Charming girl. Look at this boiler arrangement, Delganor. Now that's innovative . . ."

The Prince did not reply. He merely bowed and departed, taking no notice of the Aresians who had measured his every movement and recorded his every word. The Prince was a source of much information to the intelligence people on Ares. They drew sustenance from every casual word uttered by the Prince. More than from the Lord Paramount, who spoke unequivocal nonsense most of the time.

After a time the lips of the guards curved in not-quite smiles at the slither of booklets spilling from the lap of the man on the throne, followed by a gentle but unmistakable snore.

"So, likely we'll be getting a new woman to flit about here for a while," said one, Ogberd by name, speaking barely above a whisper without moving his lips. "Destined for the Prince. Brother, it's interesting that they never stay long, do they?"

His brother, Lokdren, assented with an almost invisible nod. "Lady Marissa was the last young one, and none since she married Lord Tranquish. Lately I've felt like an attendant at a home for the aged, and by the Great Sportsman, it's a waste of time!"

"Shhh," hissed the other, with a quick glance at the throne, where the Lord Paramount had stirred slightly. "Aged or not, we are sworn to him, and as the universe knows, we Aresians never waver from our oath of service." His lips firmed as he said sententiously, "Faithful service is our pride. It says so in the Aresian security services prospectus."

The other actually did smile at this, a quick twitch of the lips, his eyes roving the room as they always did, taking note of every gentle movement of curtain, every shift of light, every sound that might presage a visitor. He stiffened slightly at a sound in the hallway outside the door, then relaxed at the familiar tramping of feet. Behind the two, the doors slid soundlessly open to admit the change of guard who eased into the places Ogberd and Lokdren silently vacated.

Outside in the corridor, Lokdren removed his helmet, wiped his brow, and continued the interrupted conversation, though softly. "I'm less concerned with what's in the prospectus than I am what's in our orders. We may be fulfilling the prospectus, but we're damned well not finding out what we came to find out!"

Ogberd's lips twitched. "We've learned a lot about rug-weaving looms and chandeliers and wine-making equipment and miniature sheep, though, haven't we?"

Lokdren shook his head. "More than I care to know, frankly. Time is running out. Father's getting impatient. He sent another indignant message this morning. If we don't come up with something soon, he'll do something irrevocable."

"Do you care?" Ogberd shrugged.

His brother nodded back. "Haven's a nice enough little place. Some of the people are pleasant. I'd hate to see them in father's hands, the mood he's in, put it that way. He won't stop at anything. I'm sure of it."

"Nonsense. Father's an honorable sportsman."

"Is he now? Are any of us? *Given the consequences if we don't find out?*"

"Given the consequences . . ." Ogberd sighed. "Damn. Well, I don't know. Given the consequences . . . I suppose even Father . . . well, I suppose even he could . . . do the unthinkable."

Lokdren thinned his lips and snarled. "Better start thinking about it, brother. Just so it won't be unthinkable, when it happens."

GENEVIEVE, AS HER FATHER DIRECTED, WAS TO TAKE LEAVE OF HER FRIENDS at school, return with her belongings to Langmarsh House, and there oversee the packing of such furnishings and garments as would be needed in Havenor. Meantime, the Marshal himself would go to Havenor and obtain lodgings, which might or might not be to either of their liking. Havenor was always crowded with members of the court and others who came to seek favors from the Lord Paramount, and there was often little to be had in the way of houses or apartments.

"I am sorry to lose you, my dear," said Mrs. Blessingham, with a pang she herself thought unwarranted. Girls were always going away; why should she anguish over this one? Nonetheless, she did anguish.

"I don't want to go," whispered Genevieve, admitting it for the first time to someone other than herself. "Oh, I do not want to go, Mrs. Blessingham. I would so much rather stay here."

"Do you think this journey is possibly what your mother meant?"

Genevieve looked up, spilling tears. "I've thought . . . perhaps it is. Though . . . I'm not sure."

"Think on it, dear." Mrs. Blessingham actually wrung her hands. "Please, Genevieve, it will be wise for you to take a great deal of notice of what's going on around you. You must be alert in Havenor."

So Genevieve went home, all at doubts and dithers, with no idea what Havenor had to offer or what she should take with her. Soon, however, the post packet that plied the River Reusel stopped at Sabique, a Wantresse County village in the valley below Langmarsh House, and from there a fast rider brought up a letter from the Marshal saying he had acquired a large and partially furnished house with a garden and stable, one left tenantless by the recent death of its owner.

The day before they left, Genevieve slipped away from the busy company of packers and folders to sneak down through the cellars of Havenor

to that same remote, deep-pooled cavern where her mother had taken her. She shut the doors behind her, as her mother had always done, and then she memorialized her mother by doing the things her mother had taught her to do. Though the exercise was itself uncomfortable—she had become unpracticed—she was comforted that she still remembered how.

The journey to Havenor was made by carriage, with wagons behind bringing Genevieve's clothing, books, and other belongings. Their route took them down the hill road to Sabique, and thence northward along the Reusel road, which climbed easily but steadily toward the pass leading into the cupped valley of High Haven. Five outriders accompanied them, to help with the wagon in the likely event of snow or the less likely one of brigands. Though brigands were endemic in Dania—stealing women seemed to be their main occupation—they rarely crossed the Reusel into Wantresse.

Genevieve had chosen to bring her own maid, the Langmarshian woman who had tended her since she was a child: ruddy, red-haired Della whose strong arms had comforted Genevieve as they had her own children, long since grown and scattered. Genevieve, behaving most unlike herself, had insisted to the Marshal that she would have Della, not a maid hired in Havenor, since Della's husband was one of the horsemen accompanying the Marshal. Della cared more about joining her John than going for any other reason, and Genevieve was well aware of this. Since Genevieve preferred a known quantity to an unknown one, however, the arrangement satisfied them both.

The journey was accomplished before the first snows, just before, the last miles of it beset by freezing squalls that blew scattered needles of ice into their faces. From the top of the pass above Sabique, High Haven lay before them: a wide dun grassland with ivory Havenor set distantly upon it, like a fancy cake upon a platter. For a moment the sun broke through, and Havenor became an ephemeral toy, a play city full of sugary towers and icing plazas, all glittering in the cold light, and for that moment Genevieve regarded it with something like hope.

They spent the night uncomfortably at the only available inn. On the morrow, as they came closer to the city, Genevieve found the view less auspicious than she had hoped. The chill wind had driven everyone indoors, leaving the streets untenanted, dim and dreamlike behind shifting veils of snow. As they went through the residential area, Genevieve regarded the stern lines of city houses on either side of them with dismay. Their faces were shut up tight, the windows lidded with heavy curtains, the iron-bound doors locked-lip and stern. These forbidding visages be-

came even more dour when they turned onto a broader boulevard where the houses were farther separated and set deeply behind walled and gated gardens beneath bare, black-branched trees. Dusk had come by this time, and though the wind had ceased, the snow was falling hard.

"The houses go on forever," Genevieve murmured in dejection. "Miles of them. It'll be dark soon."

"The end of a trip is always the longest part," soothed Della. "I'm sure we're almost there."

She spoke the truth, for they soon turned between great granite pilasters and heard the tall iron gates shriek open on corroded hinges. From there was only a short way to the house, where they pulled up as the last light left the sky. Della and Genevieve alit to be greeted by Halpern, the butler, while the wagon continued around to the stable yard and the protection of the carriage house.

The interior of the house was scarcely less cold than the courtyard, each cavernous room as gloomy and lightless as a tomb. Not even Genevieve's apartment, on an upper story toward the back, had any feeling of welcome. The dirty windows overlooked a weed-filled wilderness of garden, the drapes were stiff with dust, and the tiled stove was cold.

Della had better luck in the rooms she would share with her husband on the ground floor, for they were kept cheerfully warm by the stoves in the adjacent kitchen. It was there that Della brought Genevieve, to seat her in a chair before the fire and help her rub feeling back into her hands and feet while Halpern set people to fueling the tiled stove in her room, dusting out, sweeping up, warming the linens, and making up the bed.

"My Lady Marchioness," he said, his brow beaded with cold sweat. "No one told me you were coming. Your father did not mention it."

"Let it go," murmured Genevieve. "Don't apologize. I'm here now, so we'll start from where we are."

"Your Ladyship is very gracious."

"My Ladyship is very tired," she said, smiling at him. "Let's not waste time on things not said or done, Halpern. Let's do what we can to make ourselves comfortable."

"And where's the Marshal?" Della demanded angrily of her John. "Here's Jenny, frozen half solid, and not even a fire in her room."

"Gone hunting, so he said," muttered John. "And he didn't tell us you'd be coming today. Or at all! He depends on others to do his day-to-day thinking for him, he does, and the one who does it lately, his equerry, that Colonel, he's not taken up residency here, not yet."

When the Marshal returned a day or so later, having been invited to

hunt stag with a party from the court, he was surprised to find the new arrivals still in confusion as they tried to settle in.

"Ha," he said to Genevieve, when she confessed that things were not yet in order. "I've set up a camp for a thousand men with less fuss than this." He then proceeded to unsettle the entire menage even further by announcing their schedule for the near future: several formal dinners, including one only ten days hence; innumerable courtesy calls with Genevieve over the next several days; attending a command performance of the Royal Orchestra; and an ambitious program of familiarization with the city. Since the cook was newly hired and did not have the kitchen yet to her liking and since the place itself needed a good deal of work before welcoming guests, Genevieve, as putative mistress of this establishment, was more than merely set back.

"I've never done any such thing," she cried to Della. "At home, Father never entertained! Oh, a few old friends, but that was different. I've learned how at school, I'm quite competent to handle it, given time and a certain local knowledge he has given me no time to learn! Where does one hire temporary help? This house, Della. It's filthy! Some of the draperies are in rags!"

Della stood with her hands on her hips and her lower lip thrust out, as she did when in deep thought. "There's nothing for it, my lady, but do it somehow. Have you friends here from among the ladies you knew at school? Any at all?"

There probably were acquaintances in Havenor, though she did not know for sure. At the moment Genevieve could think of only one person she knew to be in the town and was inclined to trust, though she hesitated to call him her friend. "I have met Father's equerry, Colonel Aufors Leys. He struck me as the kind of person who would do everything he could to be helpful. Though he is expected to move into this house at some point, he is now in rooms at an inn, though I've no idea . . . No, wait. I saw Father writing it down."

"Write the Colonel a note," Della suggested. "I'll get John to take it, and we'll see what we can do."

Aufors came at once, let himself in by the side entrance, as requested, and in the small dining room he, Della, and Genevieve held a council of war.

"I am so thankful you have come, Colonel."

She looked so uncomfortable that he decided at once on a soothing informality. "If we are to work together, my Lady Marchioness, you may call me Aufors. I grant you it's an odd name, but I came by it legitimately,

through a rogue of a great grandfather." He turned a radiant smile on her that blocked her throat as though she had been eating feathers.

"Well, Colonel," said Della, with an assessing glance at Genevieve that told her the girl was for the moment speechless. "The Lady Marchioness finds the place to be dirty, and a bit shabby to boot. The carpets are worn, more than even I'd allow. The furniture needs cleaning of a kind no new household can manage. Professionals, I'd say."

"Footmen," murmured Genevieve. "If we're to entertain, we'll need footmen, and I have no idea where to get temporary help, or even to get the flowers we'll need. And Father has recently hired the cook, I don't know her at all well, but I have heard she's dissatisfied with the kitchen. I have this terrible image in my mind of burned roasts and fallen cakes. I know the butler, Halpern, no better than the cook and the other locally hired staff, though it is my understanding Halpern came with the house. If Father had given me a little time, I daresay I could have managed nicely, but all this being dropped out of the sky on my head just baffles me."

Aufors noted it all down. He went to meet with Halpern and the cook, sent a few written inquiries to friends via several hastily obtained messengers, and went over the house before returning to Genevieve. "Here is the name of a man who does professional cleaning and has enough help to do it quickly, and here the name of a decorator who also works quickly and without chatter. Halpern, the butler, approves both choices but thinks they may respond more quickly for you than they would for him, as the Baron who inherited this house has allowed the place to fall into disrepute both as to its maintenance and as to its prompt payment of accounts.

"The flowers will have to come from the greenhouses at court. It would normally take several weeks to get an allocation, but they have a plethora, and I have a friend who's made a friend of the gardeners.

"Your cook does not like the kitchen—and one can quite see why—but minor changes will do for now and she will rise to the challenge. I told her she is probably the only one in the city who could do so under such circumstances. I've explained to Halpern what's toward, and he's so grateful someone is doing something about the house—I gave you all the credit for that, Genevieve—that he'll turn cartwheels if you suggest it. It would be appropriate for you to give him carte blanche in hiring whatever additional help he needs for this first dinner, starting with two or three men to clean up the gardens. I've talked with the man who used to be head gardener here—he's taken a position at a large establishment nearby. He says it's too late in the season to do anything at all decorative, but he suggests trimming the topiary, raking out the paths and the flower beds

and mulching them evenly so they're less an eye-sore. He's committed to his current employer, but for a small commission he'll find a trustworthy crew to take care of this immediate matter for us. Meantime, call on me for any needs whatsoever, such as escorting you this morning to these various tradesmen."

"They should come to her," sniffed Della.

"No, Della, Aufors is quite right," she replied. "My going to them will give them dignity and increase their desire to be helpful."

Della went along with them, for propriety's sake, and the three of them spent the morning going here and there, before returning to the house to await return visitations from those whose help they had just solicited. By evening, all was developing nicely: contract workers would arrive on the morrow, the cook was making shopping lists, and the butler was doing a hasty inventory of the cellars and the plate.

Aufors departed toward evening, after looking over the Marshal's invitation list and shaking his head.

"My Lady, . . ."

"If I am to call you Aufors, you must call me Genevieve."

"Genevieve, I respect your father deeply for he is a great soldier. He has, however, no idea what is involved in keeping an establishment or even what is involved in keeping him comfortable in the field. When he is not immediately engaged with a problem, he seems to go inside his head somewhere, thinking of . . . oh, old battles, perhaps. He simply doesn't notice what's going on! I think he assumes it happens spontaneously: food on his table, water in his basin, clean clothing for him to put on. At Langmarsh he has people who have cared for him since he was a boy, but I doubt he has any idea of what they do.

"If he is to succeed here in Havenor, he must be brought out of himself and made aware. We do not know how long he is to be here, at court, or what his role will be. However long, whatever role, the rules must be observed. I've learned only a few of them. One of them is that enemies are not invited to the same affairs, and your father has already done this." He pointed out the offending entries on the invitation list.

"I know some of the rules are silly, and I know they have to be learned the hard way, for people do not spontaneously tell you what they are. You must find someone to guide you rightly, and you'll need the Marshal's help, or, failing that, his forbearance. Plead with him to be a little less hasty!"

Though she doubted pleading with her father would do any good whatsoever, she nodded her thanks, too full of them to put in words.

When the Marshal arrived, late in the evening, after a day of meetings and irritations, he found the place still buzzing like a disturbed hive.

"What's all this?"

"You have invited thirty people to dinner eight days from now," Genevieve answered in the calm voice she had been practicing for the past hour. "We are preparing for that event, and for whatever other events will follow."

"You don't need all this fuss, surely. I thought Colonel Leys might help you with introductions and so forth, the day of the first dinner."

She forced herself to smile rather than snap at him, which to her own surprise, she very much wanted to do. "If we had waited until the day, Father, you would have had nothing to feed your guests. The house would have been dirty and unwelcoming. Nothing could have been well done. Some of the things the cook needs will take seven or eight days to obtain, and certainly we could not clean the house in less than that."

"Really?" he appeared astonished. "It seems clean enough."

"To one accustomed to camping in the open, it may well do. The dirt and wear and cobwebs are glaringly obvious in a good light, however, and when one has guests, one lights up the house. This is a rule in Havenor, one of many, I am told. If we do not yet know the rules in Havenor, then we must find them out in advance of your issuing future invitations. I fear we have already made several faux pas."

"Nonsense!"

"Father, if you were a junior officer, would you invite to your table two superior officers who were sworn enemies?"

"Of course not."

"Well, here in Havenor we are very much junior residents, yet we have invited two noble ladies who are sworn enemies. If that were not enough, we have invited two other persons who are opposing litigants before the Tribunal. We want everything to do you credit, but we can't manage it if we are not well prepared, so please, Father, allow us a little time to learn the way."

He turned slightly red. "I had guests at Langmarsh House with no more notice than a word to the butler in the morning! In the field, I have had my fellow officers join me for meals on no notice at all!"

Her face grew hot. Without stopping to think she said, "In Langmarsh you had old servants who knew the place intimately, and you entertained old friends, who would take Langmarsh as it was with no more light than a few candles and the fire. In the field, soldiers are accustomed to soldier's fare. This dinner you plan, however, is for people who will arrive with

their ears pricked, their eyes sharpened, and their noses twitching to judge us by everything they hear and see and smell. They will rate the service, the food, the look of the place, and our manners, yours and mine. None of the guests know us well, some may be maliciously inclined to dislike us, and none of the guests, I'll wager, have ever been on a field of battle, nor would they like the setting, the food, or the manners they would find there."

She had been carried away, had heard herself "spouting" and stopped, too late, for she looked up to find his eyes fixed on her, really looking at her, with an expression that she could not read. It was not angry, but neither was it appreciative. Weighing, perhaps. Deciding.

"Where have you picked up all this?" he growled.

She faltered. If he was offended, she couldn't blame Aufors, and apology would only convince him he was right to be annoyed. Well, now was the time to press a momentary advantage.

"As your hostess, I am responsible for the success or failure of social events, Father, and I have been asking questions, as I was taught to do. You sent me to school to learn how to do this! I was a dedicated, faithful student and I have learned. Now you really must let me do it. The house will be in a frenzy over the next several days. I need to be here. If you will make the courtesy calls by yourself, it would help enormously."

He grunted at her, still with a very equivocal expression, and went to his rooms, demanding Terson, his servant, to bring something light by way of supper. Genevieve breathed deeply.

"Good for you, my lady," whispered Della from behind a portiere.

"Good for Aufors," breathed Genevieve. "Now if I can only hang on and Father will just . . . settle down."

The days that followed were too full of work for any enjoyment. The Marshal made his calls alone. Workmen came in and workmen went out. Carpets were taken up (leaving great continents of dust on the floor) to be cleaned and turned; furniture was sent to be repaired; draperies were removed, shaken free of several years' worth of detritus, brushed carefully to reveal unexpected colors and patterns, and those that were whole were rehung while worn ones were shifted about to hide the wear, there being no time to have new ones made.

Foodstuffs were delivered and preparations begun. Wines were fetched from the cellars—thankfully, rather good ones—and set ready in the cooling room. Plate was polished. The dining room was given a complete going over, walls and ceiling as well as floors, evicting generations of spiders from behind the cornices while the huge table was brought to a

silken polish by two newly hired young footmen who flung themselves back and forth along it on lambskins, much to the amusement of the equally new housemaids.

Responses to the invitations arrived, virtually all of them acceptances. Those who refused were replaced by others nominated by Aufors. "These people I'm suggesting are not important," he said, "but they are amusing. Just as every dinner needs a little spice, every dinner party needs a few people to be diplomatic and pleasant, to keep things moving."

On the day of the dinner, Della insisted that Genevieve do nothing but lie about.

"Is everything done, Della?"

Della put out her lower lip, hands on her hips, and nodded firmly. "Everything is as close to done as it's going to get, Jenny. Everything's delivered, put up, put down, plucked, stuffed, cooled, warmed, hung or unhung, as may be. Everything that'll take a polish has been polished at least twice and what won't polish has been hidden behind something that will. The cook's in a temper, which Halpern tells me is a good thing. Her dinners are always delicious, he says, when she's in a temper. The table looks lovely. The flowers just came, sneaked in the back way by somebody who knows or works for the Duchess Bellser-Bar, so he told us. She's a friend of the Colonel, it seems. I think it'll all go fine."

Aufors thought so, too. He swept a bow, saying with a smile, "You've done well, my Lady Marchioness."

"Please don't call me Lady Marchioness. I hate it."

"Well, Genevieve, I must, you know. On formal occasions."

"Well then, when we are alone, could you call me Jenny?"

"Very well." He smiled. "When we are alone."

"Who's the Duchess Bellser-Bar?" she asked in a worried tone, picturing a large and overbearing dowager whom she would at once owe numerous favors.

"Someone I did a very small favor for, once, and she's repaid me by getting your flowers for you. It's no problem, Genevieve, really. Please, erase that frightened look from your face. It's all going to go well!"

"Aren't you ever frightened of anything?" she demanded, very slightly angry.

He considered the question seriously. "The usual things," he confessed. "Death, wounds . . ."

"No, no, I mean just . . . things."

"I am quite frightened of water-babies," he said, the words popping out without any thought at all.

"Water-babies?" She frowned, suspecting he was teasing her. "I've heard of them, but . . ."

"It was nothing, really. When my mother died, she left me a small legacy. Even though my older brother knew he would inherit the farm, he resented the fact she'd left the legacy to me. In his view, eldest took all, regardless. He got even by telling me horrific tales about how my mother had gone to pick cress for salad and had been abducted by water-babies, and because I was her favorite, they would come for me next. He was constantly knocking me down, sitting on me, then peering at my fingers and toes, claiming he saw webs growing between them. He even locked me in the well house once, where it was damp and cold and dark, and hung about outside making frog noises. I was frightened for days afterward."

Actually, Aufors still had occasional night terrors in which he dreamed himself turning into something green, clammy, and cold, but he was not tempted to confess this frailty to Genevieve.

"That's dreadful," she said, indignant on his behalf.

"It seemed so at the time, and I have never been really friendly with my brother since." Which, he thought, was a charitable way of putting it. "Now, let's go down this list of people, and then we'll look at your seating diagram."

They drilled on the names while Aufors changed the seating diagram about, saying, "Lady Alicia, Duchess Bellser-Bar of Merdune, the donor of your flowers, is cousin to Inelda, Countess Farmoor of Dania, who has not spoken to the Lady Alicia since a falling out over a matter of inheritance. The grandmother of both ladies favored the Duchess as more true to the family lineage, and Inelda has never forgiven her. Put them at opposite ends of the table. As a matter of fact, put the Duchess to your left, across from Prince Thumsort. She's done you a favor already, she's an interesting woman and her rank allows you to favor her, though Inelda will dislike you for it. And remember that the Invigilator of the Covenants, chief of all scrutators and a high-ranking member of the Tribunal, is at odds with Count Farmoor over a question of interpretation."

"What does that mean?"

"I have no idea. Nobles do not explain covenant matters to commoners. Tribunal matters are sacred and secret. Commoners are not even allowed to go near the Tribunal Building, for any reason. Nonetheless, I feel sure, seating them together would not be a good idea."

"I'll never learn the names of all the nobles!"

"Not if you had to learn them all, but you don't. Only the other six

provincial Dukes and Duchesses are regularly here in court, together with a handful of the lesser nobility. Your father's military role has kept him free of attendance until now, and if a battle broke out anywhere, he'd probably be excused again. Just remember each Province's Duke is known by the name of the Province, as for example: Duke of Sealand or Duke of Merdune. Each county has an Earl or sometimes a Count, depending upon the original title, who is known by the name of the county, and within counties large estates are held by barons or viscounts. If you forget, flutter your eyelashes and smile."

He started to leave, then turned back. "Oh, I forgot to mention. Since the Prince is coming, there will be at least a couple of Aresian guards with him. The proper protocol is to take no notice of them, not even if they search behind curtains for weapons or run their detecting devices over your body."

"Really!" she breathed. "Take no notice!"

"No notice," he said. "Just . . . pretend they aren't there."

The Marshal came home, looked about himself in amazement, and came up to stick his head in Genevieve's door. "Didn't realize that dining room was so big."

"Well, we've never eaten in there, but it is a banqueting hall. Aufors says . . ."

"Who?"

"Colonel Leys, Father. He says the table is forty feet long."

"You called him Aufors," he said accusingly. "That's rather familiar, an't it?"

She took a deep breath. "He's been very helpful, Father. If it hadn't been for Colonel Leys, we wouldn't have managed nearly so well. We have become friendly over this matter, and he is entitled to a little informality as a member of our household."

He grunted, glaring at her briefly. "Well, I don't like informality, not among my staff. I prefer them punctilious. Who're all the stiff-necked men just wandering around down there?"

She frowned. "The footmen hired for the night. If they're wandering around, it's because they have to be familiar enough with the house not to direct one of the gentlemen into the ladies' cloakroom or vice versa. We'll need them from time to time if you're going to do a lot of entertaining. And when our men from Langmarsh return home—as they must; their families are there—we'll need a couple of local men to do the heavier work." After a pause, she went on to tell him about the Prince's guards.

"That's an unfunny joke, Genevieve."

"It's not a joke, Father. Please, if you choose to disbelieve me, speak to the Colonel."

He grunted, gave her another of those slightly surprised, slightly offended looks, and went out.

She leaned against the wall, whispering to herself, "Give me strength to get through this evening."

As Della was dressing her hair, Genevieve rehearsed the names of the guests. ". . . and Thumsort of Tansay, brother to the Lord Paramount, and his companion, the Lady Charmante, who, Aufors tells me, is actually a man who dresses as a woman, though I mustn't let on for a moment and daren't tell Father. Della, have you ever heard of such a thing?"

"Heard of it, yes, lady. There was one in our village when my mother was a girl. Couldn't abide men's clothes. Said he was a woman's brain trapped in a man's body."

"Strange. I, myself . . ."

"What, my lady?"

She had been going to say that she, Genevieve, had sometimes felt she was a foreign, strange, alien brain caught in a girl's body, but this was not something for Della to hear. "Gardagger, Duke Bellser-Bar of Merdune," she went on with her roll call, "and Alicia, the Duchess, who has provided our flowers for the evening . . . and Rongor, appointed by the Tribune as Invigilator of the Covenants, commander of the scrutators, who would be mightily offended if he knew about the Lady Charmante, as the covenants are strict on matters of gender."

She took a deep breath. "And of course, the heir, Prince of Havenor, Yugh Delganor, who may bring his guards whom we are to take no notice of . . ."

She wore again the mahogany gown with the rose decolletage. It fit her better than any other of her evening dresses, though she realized as she put it on that she would have to have something new for the next dinner, for everyone would have seen this one. According to Aufors, there were rules about that. If any of the guests were repeaters, one wore a gown only once in one's own house, though one could wear it again when invited to other peoples'. Where was she to find a dressmaker?

Her father was at her side and Aufors was at her elbow as the guests arrived.

"The Baron and Baroness Crawhouze," Halpern intoned, in a voice Genevieve had never heard him use before. An echoing, resonant, larger-than-life voice which leant dignity to every word. Oh, my, how could

one live up to a voice like that. One might squeak. One might stutter. Of course, one was not allowed to do so!

"Baroness." She nodded, offering her hand. "Baron, delighted, so pleased that you could come."

"Chahming gull," said the Baron to her father, with a sidelong leer down her decolletage. "Chahming."

"Old goat," whispered Aufors, behind her.

"Don't," she whispered behind her hand. "If I giggle, I'm lost."

The Prince arrived, with his guards, who showed considerable interest in areas behind draperies and shadowed corners but mercifully did not search any of the guests. When dinner was served, they stood straight as lances in the corners, their eyes on Yugh Delganor, who was seated at the Marshal's right. Prince Thumsort of Tansay was at Genevieve's right. The Prince was a talkative, elderly man with strong opinions about fish, which was his business, though, as he was quick to say, his business was kept at arm's length. "Don't handle them. Can't abide handling them. Slimy things. Know all about them, though. From the golden talking fish of Merdune Lagoon to the slippery silver elvers of the Randor Isles, I know every blessed thing from egg to fin. Tansay's fortune is in fish!"

The Duchess of Bellser-Bar was on Genevieve's other side, a tall, voluptuous women with smooth black hair twisted into a complicated bun at the nape of her neck and creamy skin like thick matte velvet on which her separate features stood out as though painted: dark feathered eyes, dark swooping brows, scarlet recurved lips. Before Genevieve could ask about the talking fish, she spoke in a throaty, amused voice, saying:

"Don't listen to Tansy, my dear. His province knows only Havenpool and its fresh-water fish, but for salt-water fish, you must ask someone from my province of Merdune. We call all those Sealand people puddle jumpers, don't you know?"

"Oh, now, Alicia," said Prince Thumsort.

"Oh, now, Tansy," she retorted with a laugh. "Don't bore the girl to death with fish. Tell her about your son Edoard. That's what girls like hearing about. Young men." And she leered at Genevieve, a look of enormous and totally spurious complicity.

"That's him," the Prince retorted, pointing vaguely with his elbow. "Halfway down on your left. The one in the wine-colored coat, with the puffy front to his shirt. I can't see why the young ones like those puffy fronts. Always dropping food on them." And the Prince subsided into his soup.

"Duke Edoard is perfectly charming," murmured the Duchess. "He is third in line of succession, after Yugh Delganor and his father."

"What is he Duke of?" asked Genevieve.

"Not much so long as Thumsort is alive, though he dances beautifully, and he sings in a supercilious way that all the young ladies find absorbing. Shall you be absorbed?"

Genevieve smiled. "I doubt it, Your Grace, though if it is customary, I shall try."

"So do I doubt it, looking at you. Not the usual thing at all, are you?"

"What is the usual thing, Your Grace?"

"Please, don't Your Grace me. Call me Alicia. And I shall call you Genevieve. No, it's quite all right, don't blush. You are the daughter of a Duke, just as I am, though I rather gave the rank away for a time. The fact I eventually married another Duke, or one married me, is just part of the clutter. I read books, so I know it's clutter. Other worlds have not retained all these titles and castes, and they seem to get along quite well."

She took a mouthful of soup, nodding at Genevieve to do the same. "You must keep eating, dear. Little nibbles, little spoonfuls, so your mouth won't be too full if someone asks a question, but always a tiny bit. Otherwise the whole dinner will be over, and you'll have had nothing. Now, the usual thing with girls is that they are rather silly."

"Mrs. Blessingham tries very hard to keep us from being silly," murmured Genevieve. "She says even though our roles are somewhat restrictive, we must not compensate by dramatizing ourselves, for there is nothing we can experience that generations of women before us have not experienced; nothing is new, not our lusts, not our hopes, not even our despair. She says that with few exceptions, nothing is as tragic as it seems, nor is anything quite as joyous as we dream it will be, and of all disasters, romantic notions are responsible for most."

"Dreadful to have one's little excesses smoothed away so uniformly," murmured the Duchess with a little smile. "Smile, dear. Appear to be enjoying yourself, or your papa will worry. And don't be offended with me. I have raised four girls myself; two of my own, Sybil and Lyndafal, and two that Gardagger had by his first wife. Such a tragedy. Gardagger and his first wife went on a tour, you know, shortly after their son was born, and she fell ill of the batfly fever and died! All three of his children were only babies when he married me. Luckily, they were malleable. I quite liked his girls, though they both died young, as did my Sybil." She took several more spoonfuls of soup and a bit of bread. "Your Mrs. Blessingham sounds formidable."

"I considered her so at first, but she was a good friend," said Genevieve. "I looked forward to several more years in her company."

"But?"

"But . . . Father wanted me to come to court. Particularly inasmuch as I was invited to do so by Yugh Delganor."

A shadow crossed the Duchess's face. "The Prince of Havenor? Now, in what capacity did the heir offer such an invitation?"

Startled, Genevieve looked up to see the scarlet lips twist ever so slightly, as though the Duchess had tasted something sour. She said, "I was told it was the Lord Paramount who decided whether individuals were allowed at court, that the heir merely expressed the Lord Paramount's wishes."

"Interesting," commented the Duchess. "Very interesting. Well, here are the footmen, bringing in our fish. Now we will see if Tansy knows as much as he thinks he does."

At the other end of the table, the Marshal was attempting conversation with the Prince, Yugh Delganor, who sat at his right.

"I hear from many sources that you will shortly be going on a mission for the Lord Paramount."

"From many sources?" The Prince frowned. "The mission is not sufficiently advanced to be talked of at all."

"Forgive me if I have transgressed," murmured the Marshal, falling back on the delicately deferential manner he had perfected many years ago as a junior officer. "I assumed it was a matter of public knowledge."

"Well, Count Farmoor knows of it," cried the Countess Inelda, who sat across from the Prince. "He tells me the Prince is going to Mahahm so we won't all die of batfly fever."

"The Count is correct to say I will go," said the Prince. "Though the detail, much less the outcome, of our visit is far from sure. While I prefer not discussing matters that are still so very undecided, I suppose it does no harm to acknowledge that we intend to approach the Shah of Mahahm-Qum in an effort to increase our imports of P'naki."

"Mahahm has a monopoly on P'naki, does it not?" asked Aufors Leys, who sat beside the Countess Inelda.

"One we hope to find some way around. Mahahm's sole export is P'naki, and the revenue from the sale supplies them with virtually all their necessities. Little food is grown there. Almost no fiber, except wool from the sheep that graze on seaweed washed up by the tides. The Mahahmbi have religious proscriptions against many things we would consider essen-

tial, such as wine and good food and various comforts. They have, perhaps, made a virtue of necessity since they have no way to pay for luxuries."

"The entire population of the desert would simply starve and go naked if it couldn't trade in P'naki," said the Countess. "Or so says my husband."

The Prince nodded judiciously. "We need the P'naki, of course, to control the batfly fevers, and while we import all of it we can get, that amount is just enough for the current population of our riparian areas where the flies breed. Though our total population remains level, in accordance with the covenants, people are always moving about. At one time they left the rivers to go up the mountains, now they are coming down from the mountains to settle along the rivers. If we are to keep the fevers at bay, we need more P'naki."

"I should think Mahahm would be glad to increase exports," said Aufors Leys.

"On the contrary." The Prince shook his head with an expression of judicious concern. "The Mahahmbi tell us they can't produce more than they do now, that we'll just have to get along with what they give us."

"Can't the stuff be synthesized?" asked the Marshal.

The Countess shook her head, making her long cylindrical curls swing to and fro, like chimes. "Count Farmoor says perhaps it could be, on any technological world, but not here. Or, I should say, not economically. Only at astronomical cost, in fact. So he says."

The Prince nodded agreement. "Since we're the only planet affected by batfly fevers, the market offers little financial incentives to off-world manufacturers."

The Marshal asked, "The stuff is herbal, isn't it? What growth is it made from?"

The Prince frowned. "We have no way of knowing whether it is herbal or some animal by-product or some combination of both. It comes, so I've been informed, from the desert, but the Mahahmbi consider the desert to be sacred and foreigners aren't allowed into it. They would be furious if we attempted to find out the details."

"From what Daviger says, they're always furious," commented the Countess. "But I'm sure you'll calm them down, Your Royal Highness." She gave him a smile of guileful sweetness.

The Prince ignored the smile, responding with a ponderous nod. "I shall make that effort. At any rate, the Lord Paramount hopes it does come from vegetation of some kind and that we can study the way the thing grows and obtain seeds or scions which we can grow here on Haven,

though our experts are not sanguine about the possibility. We have no desert, and it may grow only in the desert."

"Also, the Mahahmbi may not want to lose the profit they make by having a monopoly," remarked the Marshal.

"We're prepared to pay a generous royalty for it, and if we can prove they'll make more money letting us do it that way, they should accept—"

"And if we can't," interrupted the Countess, "We can expect the fevers to go right on killing our sweet children . . ." She sighed dramatically.

The rest of the conversation at the Marshal's end of the table, though continuous, was unremarkable, while at Genevieve's end the Duchess focused the talk largely upon the royal greenhouses, which she invited Genevieve to visit with her during the coming week. After dinner, Genevieve spoke with Duke Edoard, who took her hand, refused to release it, and invited her to attend the next concert of the Royal Orchestra.

"I will need to see what plans my father has made, Your Grace. And speaking of fathers, I much enjoyed my dinner table conversation with yours."

He smiled. "Your expression of pleasure is polite but unlikely to be fully sincere," he said. "Father usually talks either about the batfly problem or about fish."

"I know little about the batfly problem, but fish can be interesting," she said with a smile.

"Ocean fish, perhaps," he commented, looking across her shoulder at someone else, and thereby missing the fact that his words had sent her somewhere else.

She saw a heaving deck, tilted toward a troubled sea, people actually in the sea, all trying desperately to do something with a portal in the deck, to open it or close it, and all around in the sea was a sound . . . a sound she thought she had heard before . . .

Then she was back, bowing herself away into a corner where she could catch her breath. Aufors was beside her at once, whispering, "What's the matter, Jenny? Did that idiot say something to upset you? You're pale. You look frightened."

"It's nothing." She laughed. "Sometimes I get a little breathless in crowds, that's all." Though of course it wasn't all. Until now, whenever this happened, she had had Mrs. Blessingham to run to, thereby removing—or perhaps only sharing—the curse of foreknowledge. Now she had no one. Certainly not the Marshal, who would be offended and insist upon having her looked over by doctors. Nor Della who, though loyal, would tell her husband everything, and he, in turn, would tell everyone else he met.

Aufors? No. She didn't want him to think her . . . odd. And this "talent" of hers was odd, very, very odd.

In a moment, she was herself again. In a moment she decided it was not foreknowledge she had had, but a vision of something that had already happened, maybe something she had read about, a memory that had been elicited by something Edoard had said.

Aufors sat down beside her. She blinked several times and tried to come up with a neutral topic of conversation. "What did you all talk about at your end of the table?" was the best she could do.

He recounted the conversation concerning P'naki, meantime keeping a close watch on her, seeing the color gradually come back into her cheeks, and with the color, awareness of where she was and what she was supposed to be doing.

She murmured, "I'd like to hear the rest of it later, Aufors, for father is giving me a very strange look."

Aufors had the good sense not to look in the direction Genevieve had. He rose, bowed, and took himself away to be replaced almost immediately by the Duchess.

"What happened to you?" she asked without preamble. "You turned white as milk. Did that brat of Tansy's say something rude?"

"No." Genevieve shook her head, smiling. "No, he invited me to go to the concert as his guest, and then . . . I had this moment's breathlessness. All this is too much excitement for one who was a schoolgirl up until a few days ago."

"My mother had them, those breathless moments." The Duchess took Genevieve's elbow in her hand and turned her toward the corner where they stood, thus hiding her face from the room at large. "She would turn pale, as you are now, and stare off into the distance, saying she had seen a vision of a time or place not present. Her sister, my aunt, claimed it was all pretense, but my grandmother believed her as she, too, was said to have such spells. My daughter Lyndafal, has inherited the trait, though not I. Seemingly it skipped a generation. We are kinfolk, you know, Genevieve. My mother was related to your mother through a common ancestress back a few generations, Lady Stephanie, foster daughter of Duke Fitful of Merdune, who made her Marchioness of Wallachy." The Duchess cocked her head, as though expecting a reply.

Genevieve faltered, "You mean Queen Stephanie? The Dark Queen? I know nothing about her except that her daughters and their daughters have shared her dark skin and eyes and nose. Their portraits hang in the great hall at Langmarsh House."

"I know little about her myself. There was something most mysterious about her; she was a complete unknown, no family at all, but as a child she came to the attention of the Duke, he adopted her, and she became the wife of the Lord Paramount. Among the many children she bore him—almost all girls—were twin daughters, one of whom was Bricia, my great-grand-mother, and the other was Mercia, your many times great-great-grand-mother. Stephanie wrote a strange little book, a collection of tales that she called a history. I have a copy at home. I tried to read it once, but it was terribly dull. There's probably a copy in the library here, for the owner of the house was also Wallachian and quite a collector, so I've heard . . ."

A voice at their side interrupted her: the Marshal. "Your Grace, I'm afraid Genevieve is monopolizing your attention."

"Rather the other way round, Marshal," fluted the Duchess. "I've been monopolizing hers. And do call me Alicia." She took his arm, patted Genevieve on the shoulder saying she would call, soon, then drew him away, leaving Genevieve behind to catch her breath.

Genevieve felt for the moment overfed on information, everything from a P'naki scarcity to the fact that she and the Duchess were related through the legendary Dark Queen. Most fascinating was the news that there were others like herself. Another, at least. Lady Alicia's daughter.

The rest of the evening went, if not swimmingly, at least not badly. The hired musicians played well, and a popular young songstress sang several delightfully mischievous songs in a polished and coquettish manner that much delighted the gentlemen. Yugh Delganor bowed himself away as early as politeness allowed—thoughtfully, as it happened, for none could depart until he had done so—and was shortly followed by the second and third in line for the throne, Prince Thumsort, and his son Edoard, at which point the party broke up in mutual pleasantries. Aside from Yugh Delganor's chilly manner, the palpable frost between the Ladies Farmoor and Bellser-Bar, and the sullenly dyspeptic attitude of the Invigila-tor, everyone had seemed pleased, not least the Marshal.

"Well," he said to Genevieve, when they had departed. "You did very well."

"Colonel Leys was of great help, Father. I could not have managed without his help."

"Good fellow, Leys. Pity he's of such common stock. He could go far, otherwise."

Which burst her bubble completely and set her sniveling to bed, or so said Della.

"I am not sniveling!" Genevieve retorted from her dampened pillow. "I am merely very upset! Aufors was wonderful, he helped us immensely, and all Father said was pity he was common. Besides, getting through this dinner has been enough to cry over, if I like."

"Why, Jenny?" Della took the girl's chin in her hand and looked into her eyes. "Are you falling in love with him?"

"Nonsense," she said, jerking her head away. "I just think it's a pity he can't . . . be respected for what he does. He's a very good, solid person."

"I wouldn't advise your falling in love with him. I think your father has set his eyes higher."

Now Genevieve wept indeed. "If he's thinking about my marrying the heir, I'll die."

Della paled, then nodded slowly. "He watched you tonight. Delganor. I was up in the minstrels gallery, peeking. Whenever you weren't looking, he was watching you."

"I'd *rather* die."

"The look on his face wasn't a lover's look. Forgive my saying so, Jenny, but it was more the look a dog gives to his dinner. He's nothing to set your heart thumping. Like a mourner at a feast."

"It's worse than that. There's something . . . something creepy about him. Something aged and malignant and . . . I don't know. Like the air down in the cellars at Langmarsh House, when we've been away for a while, that kind of musty deadness that takes you by the throat."

"How old is he?"

"At first I thought middle-aged, then I thought really old, but if he's thinking of getting an heir on a new wife, he can't be . . . that old, can he?"

Della stroked her charge's hair, thinking of her own strong, virile John and wondering what it would be like to be so fairy-rose pretty and have all that youth and dewiness given to some nasty old fart who couldn't even smile.

AUFORS LEYS WAS INDEED OF COMMON STOCK, AND HE CLAIMED THAT HERI-
tage proudly, even in a place like Havenor, where those barely tinged by
aristocratic blood spent their lives trading on the stain. Aufors aspired to
no such notice. He was a Langmarshian through and through, a younger
son who had learned to outwit and eventually outfight a bullying older
brother who resented everything about Aufors: his looks, his mind, his
sturdy independence. This latter led Aufors to a soldier's life, both as a
way to escape a hateful sibling and as an honorable career for a man of
small fortune. He acquitted himself well during small scuffles with the
bandit tribes of Dania—in suppressions of intertribal frays in Uplands
and in rounding up fanatical Frangians—rising to the rank of captain in
the process.

Then had come the P'PoP rebellion, an uprising by the followers of a
self-styled "People's Prince of Potcher," a charismatic agitator who claimed
the present Lord Paramount and the lesser lords were far too old to relate
to the present day, that they had outlived their usefulness to their people.
The claim resonated well in the ears of the young, who were given to
inflammatory rhetoric, which so infuriated the Duke he was impelled into
military retaliation. Thereafter matters degenerated into random and sporadic acts of violence followed by increasingly cruel reprisals which spread
beyond Potcher to involve the eastern counties of Barfezi.

The uprising might well have spread across the borders into neighboring provinces had not Captain Aufors Leys moved swiftly among towns
and villages to negotiate firmly but gently any grievances, fancied or real,
against Lorne, Earl Vestik-Vanserdel, the legitimate Duke of Barfezi. Each
hamlet had been promised a bit of this or a bite of that in return for
renewing its oaths of loyalty to the Duke and Duchess, and this diplomatic
coup had not escaped the notice of the Marshal, who promoted Aufors
Leys to the rank of major.

Once the loyalty of the villages had been established, the last stages of the conflict had been absurdly one sided. With no audiences for his bravado, the self-styled Prince of Potcher was soon left with only a few score giddy boys and girls with longbows and a dozen suicidal bomb-throwers whose numbers were reduced each time they acted. The pretender could only flee to a point of no return, where Aufors promptly bottled him. It was this salutary end to the matter which gained Aufors Leys both a colonelcy and appointment to an unspecified term as the Marshal's equerry.

The rank was high for one of his age. It was much too high for one serving as an equerry or, conversely, an equerry's duties were demeaning for one so distinguished in battle. Despite Aufors's gratitude to the Marshal, the disparity did not escape his notice. The Marshal, though harsh, was reputed to be a fair man, however, and Aufors believed his benefactor would be little agitated by Aufors's voluntary departure—which the unspecified term allowed him—so long as it occasioned no inconvenience to the Marshal himself.

With that in mind, Aufors recruited a junior officer of noble blood, impeccable manners, and limited ambition whom he began training for the job. While this went forward, Aufors wooed persons of influence in order to finagle a post where he might gain rank high enough to guarantee an honorable, even luxurious retirement.

Before Aufors's finagle fruited, however, the Marshal invited him to a school soirée. The Lord Paramount's suggestion—the reason for the invitation—was quoted to Aufors by the Marshal himself: "See what a youngster like Aufors thinks; he'll know if she's an acceptable, attractive, quiet, biddable girl who'll fit in."

His military exploits had made Aufors better known to the court than the court was known to him. He was unaware—as was the Marshal himself—of the danger carried in innocent-seeming and transparent words that floated along the corridors of power like jellyfish in the tide, death hidden in every tentacle. Aufors took the assignment at face value. If he assumed anything, it was what any outsider might assume: that the Lord Paramount and the Marshal were thinking of betrothing the Most Honorable Marchioness of Wantresse to some noble scion who was perhaps refusing to get involved until he knew whether Genevieve was "acceptable," or was a lady-too-long-in-waiting being foisted upon the credulous.

Attending an evening party was a small favor to ask of a man who considered himself a good judge of women, and Aufors agreed. He would go with the Marshal to have a look at the girl, have some good food and

wine, and write out his impressions for the Lord Paramount. Seeing that the girl in question was the Marshal's daughter, it might make the wording a bit ticklish, but Aufors felt his diplomatic skills were equal to the task.

By the time he left the soirée, however, the towers of his ambitions had been toppled flat as the Plains of Bliggen. All his careful career maneuvers had been driven from his mind, and he found himself unable to concentrate on anything except a young woman whom he had no reason to think he would even meet again. Her eyes seemed permanently fixed before his own. Her lips curved around his every waking moment. The feel of her bosom, swelling so softly against him in the dance . . . Ah, who would have thought he was so vulnerable?

On the morning after the soirée, Aufors regarded himself soberly in his mirror and told himself he was an idiot. Which idiocy was compounded when the Marshal announced the move to Havenor. At that point Aufors did not resign as equerry and go marching off toward glory, as he had intended. Instead, he not only retained his lowly position as the Marshal's aide but also became a panting dogsbody much involved in the family's relocation. Burning with desire to be helpful to Genevieve, he did it all eagerly and without a second thought.

All this could possibly be explained as one of those infatuations to which even the most sensible men fall prey, or, equally, by the fact that Aufors had a particular mental picture of his mother. She had died when he was very small, abducted and presumably killed by Danian brigands, a presumption that his brother amplified in order to terrorize Aufors. Aufors himself remembered a certain delicacy and grace and how flowery she smelled and how he had loved her laughing manner and diligent care and, above all, how clever she had been at figuring things out and solving problems. Aufors had built upon these impressions a description that differed greatly from the stick-stiff, flat-as-paint person some itinerant artist had supplied for the family hall. Though he carried a copy of that portrait with him, he never looked at it, for it confuted his memories.

Setting likeness aside, Aufors felt Genevieve shared all the other qualities of womanhood he had assigned to that lost and sainted mother, plus those attractions that youth often stirs in youth, particularly when one is pretty and the other is virile. Aufors did not stop to think that he could never be considered a suitable match. He wasn't thinking about matches at all, but about Genevieve, her comfort, her health, her pleasure, and—when he learned of the Marshal's association with Yugh Delganor—her safety. During his soldierly life, Aufors had heard disquieting things about Delganor.

The first of these had been at the end of the Potcher War where he and his officers passed the last evening around the campfire, telling stories, tongues well oiled by a providential cask of wine that someone had "found" along the way. Late in the evening, one grizzled captain made a sotto voce remark at which another officer took umbrage, and voices rose.

"Hold it," said Aufors, his steely tone cutting through the disputation. "What's this about?"

"He . . . sulted th'Lord P . . . p . . . prmount," said one disputant.

"I did not," countered the graying captain, who had been more abstemious than his colleague. "I said he was fortunate to have lived so long. That's no insult."

". . . like maybe he shoulda died, huh?"

"Not at all."

"Enough," said Aufors. "We have a victory to claim on the morrow. It is unfitting for us to indulge in trifling quarrels at such a time. Off to your bedding, gentlemen. Except for you, Enkors." This was the captain, who stayed behind at Aufors's gestured command.

They seated themselves by the fire again, and Aufors—who liked Enkors—remarked, "It's odd you should mention the Lord Paramount's long life after our battle against that renegade up the cliff. That rebel rallied followers around the matter of the Lord Paramount's age, as though living long were a sin! Why should you or anyone remark at the Lord Paramount being old? Men grow old, and so what?"

"There was no disrespect meant, sir, and you know how it is. Things get broadened in the telling."

"No, I don't know, Enkors. What gets broadened? This whole business puzzles me. When this war started, I asked the Duke of Barfezi and a couple of the Earls what all the fuss was about—I mean, if they'd let the man alone, his popularity wouldn't have lasted beyond the next harvest season—and they turned bland as milk and soft as curd, murmuring nonsensically without ever answering me. Such treatment makes a man curious. You needn't fear I'll take offense or repeat anything you tell me. I merely want to know."

One thing Aufors's men knew about him was that he kept his word. Enkors nodded thoughtfully. "Well, Colonel, if you truly want to know. How old are you now?"

"Thirty."

"And who was Lord Paramount when you were born?"

"Marwell, just as he is now."

"Well now, I'm forty-some odd, and when I was born Marwell was

Lord Paramount. And my father, when he was born Marwell was Lord Paramount. And when his father was born, likewise."

Aufors considered this, poking the fire with a stick to make the coals flare. "Well, so the Lord Paramount has a long life. He has off-world doctors, you know. They are no doubt well paid to see to it he lives long."

"Long." Enkors smiled into the flames. "Yes. But my father was fifty when I was born, and his father was sixty when he was born—we Enkors tend to marry late—and any way you add that up, it comes to a hundred fifty years."

"Still," mused Aufors after a lengthy pause, "we have commoner centenarians on Haven, more than a few, and they don't even have off-world doctors."

"True," said the Captain, picking up a stick of his own to join in the fire poking. "But y'see, I thought it peculiar, so I went to the Staneburgh registry—that's the name of my village, Staneburgh—where all the births are entered, and I looked up the birth of my pa to count the years, and then his pa, and then, for no particular reason, two more generations back. Every one of them was born as it says right there in black and white, in the reign of His Majesty, Marwell."

"And how far does that take it back?" murmured Aufors, his eyebrows raised in wonder.

"That takes it back well over two hundred years. And I couldn't look further, for the books before that have been sent to the archives at Havenor, and the book I was looking in was supposed to have been sent, too, according to the clerk, sent long ago, only Staneburgh's a noplace town in County Southleas—a noplace county, itself—and nobody thought to see to it. Now, o'course, nobody will do it for fear of being blamed for not doing it sooner!"

"Two hundred years is long," Aufors agreed, though grudgingly. "Very long."

The Captain nodded, a slow teetering of his head upon his neck, as though to test whether it was still attached. "You're right that it's long. And the Lord Paramount isn't the only one, as I hear tell it."

"Who else?"

"Well, there's most all the Dukes of the provinces—which explains why the Duke of Barfezi wiffle-waffled to you—and there's certain ones at court, mostly the ones living around Havenor, all men, and there's this heir, Yugh Delganor, son of the Lord Paramount's brother, and he goes way back, longer than even the Dukes. He's had two or three wives already, and the Lord Paramount's had more than that. Whatever this is,

this lengthening, seeming it doesn't work on women, or the Lord Paramount won't share it with his wives, not one.

"So, there's sayings and stories and a few jokes of a dirty nature—told in whispers as you'd imagine—but the one thing everyone says is that the ones that live long, they're all men, they're all nobles, and they all go through the women, one after another."

This last remark of Enkors had stuck in Aufors's gizzard, and subsequent to this conversation he had noticed passing allusions and sidelong references he would have missed before. Many people seemed to agree that the Lord Paramount was very, very old. There were quiet comments made at village markets, such as, "You call this chicken young? Why, it's old as the Lord Paramount!" and "If this mutton is lamb, the Lord Paramount is only a hunnert." No one who mentioned the Lord Paramount's long life seemed to have any idea how long it actually was. "Oh, he's nigh a hunnert an some," was as close as Aufors came to getting an estimate when he asked, casually, "How old is he, anyhow?" It seemed that only Enkors had taken the trouble to count up the years, and he had succeeded only because the books of record had not been sent to the archives from Staneburgh. Aufors had subsequently looked up the place. It amounted to one valley and several adjacent ridges enclosing half a dozen farms, one provisioner's shop, and a grist mill.

Since Aufors began his association with Genevieve with the idea she was to be betrothed, and since Yugh Delganor was somehow involved, Aufors jumped to a reasonable but abhorrent conclusion. Being audacious, which so far had not served him ill, he decided to learn whether an equerry to a duke could gain access to the Havenor archives, as this is where not only the Staneburgh registers but also all other registers had supposedly ended up.

He went to the palace offices and was directed down several flights of stairs to a maze of tunnels which, so he was told, housed the archives. There, he accosted one of the clerical staff, a dusty and bustling creature with a halo of elf locks, a pale, lined face, and a wild expression.

"Why, why, what's here for you, Colonel? What's here in the dust, the rust, the musty fust?"

Aufors chose to ignore this oddity and put on his most boyish and sincere expression. "I'm currently serving as equerry to Lord Dustin, Duke of Langmarsh, and though I do well enough with Langmarshian matters, being a native born and bred, I find I'm not well educated in the history and nobility of the other provinces."

"You're no more ignorant than most, dumb as a post," said the madman.

Aufors smiled beneficently. "Maybe so, but I'm a man who likes to know all he can about the job he's doing, so I thought there might be something in the archives that would let me sound less of an idiot. These people at court, they're quick to find you out, I notice, when you don't know what or who you're talking about, and they don't let you forget it if you step wrong!"

The clerk gave him a sympathetic look, raised his eyebrows almost into his hairline, fluttered his eyelashes and his hands, all preparatory to glancing over his shoulder and skulking into the shadows between two stacks of books. From this refuge he summoned Aufors with a beckoning finger.

"My supervisor's another one like that! Don't do this and don't do that! He keeps his brains inside his hat, behind the brim, the hell with him, the sprat!"

"You don't like him?" asked Aufors, wondering whether the man had gone mad on the job or been hired because he was mad enough for the job. There were jobs where madness was an asset. The military was full of them.

"I ask for my vacation, oh, first he says go then he says no. No leave, go grieve. I hate him." He took a deep breath, closed his eyes, and counted audibly from one to twenty-five. Then he opened his eyes and said in a quiet voice, "If you promise not to spill the beans, I'll let you look at the machines."

"Machines?" said Aufors, blankly. He had expected machines no more than madmen.

The functionary smiled bleakly. "Off-world archive machines, Colonel."

"I didn't know we had off-world things . . ."

"When Lord Paramount says not, the things in storage, he's forgot! But no forbidden off-world thing is forbidden to a king!"

"Do you make those rhymes up as you go along, or have you got them all memorized?" asked Aufors.

"A game," said the functionary, flushing. "Sometimes we . . . we archivists play it together. Because we're bored."

"For the moment, could we not play? You mentioned machines?"

"All kinds," said the man sullenly. "Not only medical stuff, but weapons and heavy-duty lifters. Can't say I disagree with having archive machines. Notes one takes and words one jots, but vellum breaks and paper rots. In machines we save the past for that's the only place they last!"

"You can't stop doing it, can you? What's your name?"

The strange one glanced over his shoulder, making a face, obviously

thinking of the superior aforementioned. "Jeorfy. Jeorfy Bottoms. As for the versifying, well, it gets to be a habit. It's hard to talk like a human being when one hasn't been treated like one for years! Come along. Since everyone on Haven is supposed to be half-witted, the machines have been simplified. No offense, Colonel, but I could teach a pig how to use them in five minutes."

The clerk led Aufors down a twisty aisle into a half-hidden cubby equipped with chair, desk, and the same kind of keyboard most literate Havenites were taught in school to use for things like bills of sale, deeds to land, contracts or marriage agreements, that is, all matters needing clarity and permanent storage. Aufors's family used such a device for breeding records, and after the clerk had explained the common usages of the mechanisms and led Aufors through the process, Aufors had no trouble imitating a man deeply interested in three-hundred-year-old squabbles between Langmarsh and Dania.

As soon as the doggerel-body was out of sight and hearing, however, Aufors left the screen busy with its noisy reenactment of the battle for Wellsport while he cleared the screen and entered the words "Yugh Delganor."

"Heir presumptive to the Lord Paramount, son of the Lord Paramount's slightly younger twin brother, Elwin," the screen informed him, going on with a lengthy list of diplomatic and fact-finding missions which the heir had handled for Marwell. The earliest date given was only forty years in the past. Aufors tapped his front teeth with a fingernail, musing, and then keyed in the names of some of the events Delganor was said to have been involved in. A diplomatic mission to Frangia, another to Mahahm. A survey of the Drowned Range off Merdune. Accounts of these missions were complete with dates; the oldest of them dated back a hundred sixty years and gave the Prince's age as thirty. So, he was almost two hundred years old.

Aufors, humming under his breath, entered "Marwell," and received, "current Lord Paramount of Haven . . ." and it went on with a voluminous account of life and accomplishments, without dates. Again, Aufors tried keying in the names of the events themselves. The old Captain had been right. Some of the events were dated well over two hundred years in the past. So. One could not find dates listed under biographies, possibly because someone had purged them, but no one had purged the accounts of historic events.

He tried the names of the Dukes: Gardagger of Merdune, Tranquish of Dania, Wayheight-Winson of Upland, Vestik-Vanserdel of Barfezi. With a

little digging he found events that measured their lives at well over a century. Each of them had traveled for the Lord Paramount, had worked for him and had fought for him. So, he thought, tapping his teeth again, *clickety click*, the Lord Paramount rewarded his faithful servants with a long life. He tried the Marshal. The Marshal was relatively young: he had only recently turned sixty.

The versifying clerk came into view at the end of the corridor, moving angrily, as though propelled, arms loaded with books. As he approached, Aufors blanked the screen, called up the genealogy of the Bellser-Bars of Merdune, and by the time the clerk peered over his shoulder, he seemed totally immersed in the Gardagger family tree.

"Dreadful deadly dull," sneered the clerk, obviously smarting from some very recent encounter. "Almost a total null. . . ."

"Stop," said Aufors, forbiddingly. "I'm too tired to make sense out of you."

The clerk heaved a sigh and spoke, venom dripping from every word. "I don't know why we put up with it. Royalty, I mean. It's unfair, the attention we pay them, neglecting worthier men."

"From what I've read," Aufors replied, somewhat startled by this display of ill feeling, "every society has some way of allocating power. Some places do it by age, some by money, some by war, some by class, like us. All systems have their faults, but everyone has roughly as much life as everyone else, and that's as fair as can be, so far as I know."

"Well!" The clerk turned pale as ash. "If that were true it would all be very nice, but when power means two or three hundred years of life while others get cut off short . . . I'd call that unfair."

Aufors swung around, staring. "Now that's interesting," he commented, as though it were news.

The clerk paled, shuddered. "My sense of preservation's broken," he muttered, wiping his forehead. "Believe me, I should not have spoken."

Aufors grinned at him. "Don't worry. I shan't repeat it. You may depend upon my word . . . if you'll set aside both your sense of self-preservation and your versifying for a moment more."

The clerk barked a laugh, brief and cut off sharply, his eyes focusing on Aufors for the first time, sharp, vital, full of intelligence. "I can't tell you any more. I don't know anything real. Some of the Lord Paramount's colleagues are very old, and the Lord Paramount himself ages slow as a tree. He evidently decides who's to get the gift of long life, whatever that gift may be."

"You don't know what it is?"

"It's a well-kept secret, Colonel. We all assume—we being the dusty grovelers here in the bowels, we burrowers in the racks, we delvers in the stacks—we assume it's from off-world, like the rest of the things forbidden to the rest of us. And we assume it's expensive, for the ones who get it are favorite and few."

"It seems unthinkably criminal to me, to buy such a thing for oneself and keep it from one's people," said Aufors.

The archivist bit his lip and whispered, "You've heard that old proverb, Colonel. 'Thirst makes any wine drinkable . . .'"

" 'And greed makes any crime thinkable,' " Aufors concluded the couplet. He himself could not, at the moment, think of any reward high enough for such dishonorable behavior, but he set that aside for the moment. "I wonder what determines who the favorites are?"

The clerk patted the console Aufors was seated at. "Well, you want to ask, let this do the task. It's very strange that I know how, but never thought of it till now."

"How, then?"

"Give the machine some names or common factors, it'll come up with a list for you. And, Colonel! Delete what you're doing before you leave. I'm not supposed to let anyone in here."

He drifted away, and Aufors entered, *List all persons currently alive in Haven who are more than one hundred twenty years old.*

The list came spitting at him, longer than he had thought it would be. All the names were male. He stared at it for a moment, then asked, *Who was the first person to gain this age on Haven?*

"Marwell, Lord Paramount, reached his one hundred-twentieth birthday in the year 1070 After Settlement."

Which meant he'd been born in 950 A.S. Which, since the current date was 1190, meant he was now almost a quarter of a millennium old, sixty years older than the Prince.

Were there any persons, now dead, who lived longer than one hundred twenty years?

"There were such persons, most recently Lord Wayheight-Winson, Duke of Highlands, who died at age two hundred three."

He should have been able to figure that one out. The Duke's funeral processions had filled Havenor's streets just a short time ago. *How did he die?*

"Senile paralysis," said the machine. "Listed as natural causes in the record."

What was the cause of death of the others?

"Also senile paralysis."

Aufors stared at his fingers on the keyboard. What did all of this have

to do with the covenants? He started to key in the question, but was stopped by voices shouting among the stacks: Jeorfy and someone else. Instead, he keyed quickly:

Print all this information. Then clear all reference to this transaction.

"Printing," said the machine, "Clearing." When it had finished, it switched itself off. Aufors, keeping one eye on the aisle, ran his eyes down the list, noting the men he knew or had heard of. The list and the other information had been printed on fold-tight. When Aufors let go of it, it snapped itself into a flat bundle that would fit easily in a pocket.

He left quietly, taking care not to be seen by whomever the shouter had been.

"What did you find? What's on your mind?" whispered the clerk from the near end of a side aisle as Aufors passed down the corridor toward the door.

"Nothing much," he replied softly, taking care to sound bored. "Mostly the Lord Paramount's relatives."

"What we'd expect," said the clerk. "If you come again, be sure you talk to me, Jeorfy. Jeorfy Bottoms. Nobody else. And please, don't tell anyone where you got the information or I'll end up . . . well, worse off."

Aufors made a solemn promise, expressed his thanks, and went out into the air.

The palace walls at Havenor ran around the edge of a leveled hill, but at one point outside the walls an original stone outcropping had been left untouched to continue upward in a narrow pillar. Some former architect had topped it with an observation deck and furnished it with a stair for those inclined to look at the view or the stars or simply to be alone with their thoughts. Aufors had climbed to this aerie several times in the past and did so again today, finding himself the only sightseer. He leaned across the railing into the brisk wind that was blowing from the southeast.

Dark clouds massed low on the horizon. If he were farther south, he would see the limitless range of the ocean, wandered by billowy petticoats of cloud, brushed by blue brooms of storm, as though the Mother of Worlds swept the seas. Whenever Aufors felt overcome by beauty or joy, he thought of the Mother of Worlds, Queen of the Skies, a deity peculiar to the rural areas of Wantresse.

There were a number of religions on Haven, the largest one being that of the nobility, the One True Church of the Divine Author of the Covenant. The Divine Author was invoked during weddings, dedications, jubilees, and the covenanting of noble girls at puberty. The Divine Author was anthropomorphic, inexpressibly regal, and He dwelt in heaven, which

He had created and maintained as an ecstatic home to which all covenantly men were welcomed after death. There they would be served by angels, allowing their wives, daughters, and other female relatives a well-deserved rest in a separate heaven of their own (as the commentaries on the covenants made clear) where they could flutter on bright wings among the celestial flowers.

The creation and maintenance of heaven were the Divine Author's only duties, so far as Aufors could tell. Seemingly, the nobility didn't want a god who interferred in their lives. They needed no other scripture than the covenants and the commentaries. If they worshipped anything, they worshipped the covenants their own ancestors had written, though, so it was taught, the writing was done by divine inspiration. The members of the Tribunal, the Covenanters, served as clergy; and the Invigilator enforced compliance on those the scrutators found nonconforming. It was a very neat, contained system.

The Frangians, on the other hand, worshipped the Whatever, by eschewing toil of any kind. Toil was seen as an offense against the generosity of Whatever, though there were a few Frangians, the Mariners' Guild, who did toil on ships. They were tolerated by their brethren for it was assumed the ships would be needed to transport all purified Frangians to heaven, which they called Galul and identified as being near the south planetary pole. Since all Frangians were sterilized at puberty—to avoid the toil of parenthood—they would have died out long ago were it not for the converts from elsewhere, who flowed constantly into the province in defiance of the Lord Paramount's edicts.

Though the Covenanters and the Whatevers had the largest numbers of adherents, nothing in the covenants required commoners to give up the religions of their forebears, and there were dozens of beliefs current among them. Aufors had never been particularly interested in religion, certainly not enough to seek spiritual help from it, not even from the Mother of Worlds. Whatever was done for Genevieve, he told himself, it would have to be done without divine intervention, which meant he must do it himself, though he judged himself to be barely capable of it.

Less than a month before he had prided himself on his self-control, now he found himself becoming frantic at the idea of Genevieve being betrothed. It didn't matter whether it was to Yugh Delganor or to any other of the old men whose names he had just learned. Despite his concern, he was not so out of control as to forget that a frantic man is a careless man, a lesson every soldier learns soon or dies wishing he had learned sooner.

All these concerns were simmering in his mind, like so much con-
somme, as yet unjelled, when he returned to his quarters to find a message
from the lady in question: Could he help her find a dressmaker?

Aufors sat upon his bed and laughed until tears ran from his eyes. He
had planned on rank and privilege and an honorable retirement; he had
struggled with the idea of seeking divine intercession; he had determined
to assure Genevieve's salvation; what he would actually do, for the love
of heaven, was find a dressmaker!

An hour or so later he was at her door, ready to provide whatever
help he could. She did not disappoint him in her response to his service.

"Aufors, this is beneath your notice, and I would not ask except that
I have no confidante here in Havenor. While I got on well with the
Duchess Alicia, it's not the sort of thing I want to ask a completely new
acquaintance. You're the one I know best—"

He stopped her apologies with an upheld hand. "Genevieve, say no
more about it. On my way here, I stopped at the home of one of my
colleagues who has a pretty and well-dressed wife. Both of them are gre-
garious people who go about socially, so she knows what is needed. She
gave me three names." He handed her a card on which he had noted
them down in a firm hand. "She says the first woman is totally trustworthy,
though without much imagination. The last one is inclined to imagine
rather more than she might wish, and she counsels a firm hand. She says
in general the first woman does less with more, while the other two do
more with less. The second name on that list dresses the Lady Charmante,
consort of Prince Thumsort."

Genevieve surprised herself by giggling. "The . . . lady was very strik-
ingly dressed at our dinner. If you had not told me what you told me, I'd
never have known. Oh, Aufors, thank you. Father feels our first effort was
so well received he must do another as soon as may be, and after that,
who knows? A whole string of dinners, probably." She sighed, looking
down at her hands in her lap. "If Prince Thumsort comes again, I must
learn more about fish and batfly fever! And, oh, I almost forgot, I have been
invited to a concert by Duke Edoard. What does one wear to concerts here
in Havenor?"

"I'll find out," he murmured, examining her lowered face closely, though
it gave very little away. She did not seem cheered at the thought of
concerts or new dresses, which won his sympathies as he himself preferred
less frippery in both men's and women's clothing. Her hands were tightly
clenched, as though they fought for control. He decided to pry, just
a little.

"I heard your father say that the Lord Paramount envisions some duty for you at court. Have you any idea what that might be?"

Her hands twisted and she shook her head. "No, I don't. And when he mentioned querying what the Lord Paramount might have in mind, I begged him to let the matter alone until we know better what we're doing here. Della thought it wisest, also. You know, I sometimes think Della knows more that's going on than I do."

He chuckled. "She probably does. Certain subjects seem to be taboo among the courtiers, either that or they're talking in a code I don't understand, but the servants speak as they like, especially when they are in their own quarters where no one bothers them, or even notices them. In the army, it's the same with the enlisted men. Most officers don't listen to their talk. I do, because I was one of them, and knowledge picked up in the lat—ah, parade ground is better than ignorance fostered in the drawing room. If Della trusts you, perhaps she will tell you what she hears."

They fell silent for a moment, each much occupied in looking at the other. In the space between them, the air wavered before Genevieve's eyes, like rippled water, then cleared to display a city, squat and earth-colored against a bloody sky. A huge voice sang in the silence, but she could not understand the words. She looked down at her hands, and they were red with blood. Blackness swept around her.

He reached out to her, too late, for she had slumped to the floor all at once, limply and without a sound.

"All right, Jenny, what is this?" he growled, falling to his knees beside her, putting one arm beneath her shoulders to lift her.

She opened her eyes and stared wonderingly into his face as he held her close, her head lying against his shoulder.

"Tell me," he urged, his voice shaking. "You've done this twice. Once at the dinner, then again today. Are you not well? What is this?" He shook her, as he might shake a child, gently, almost pleadingly.

"I saw . . ." she murmured, only half aware of his presence. "I saw a city made of earth, with earthen walls. I heard a voice sing loudly, like a great trumpet blowing. My hands had blood on them . . ."

He picked her up and placed her in a large chair away from the window, keeping his arm around her, thrilling to the touch of her as he had when they had danced together, having the same trouble hiding it now as then. "And the other night?"

She shook her head wonderingly. "I was watching a shipwreck. There were people struggling in the water . . ."

He breathed deeply and stepped away. "And are these the first such visions? No, I can see it in your face. They are not. There have been others?"

"Yes, Aufors." She lowered her face, as though shamed.

"Why didn't you tell me?" he cried. "You should have told me. You might have needed . . . needed someone."

"I had someone. Mrs. Blessingham, at school. She always . . . tended to things. Once she found out my visions really . . ."

"Really what?"

". . . really happened."

"You're a seeress?" He doubted seeresses, but he did not doubt this woman. So. She was a seeress?

"Shhh, Aufors. Father will hear you."

"He doesn't know?"

"Of course not. He'd be furious. He doesn't even like to talk about such things. Mother . . . Mother knew. She was like me. According to the Duchess, Alicia, so was her mother and her daughter. We're related, she says. Several generations back."

"Tell me what you've seen that came true?" he demanded, sounding impatient, even to himself, but so eager to help her that he needed to know immediately, without delay!

She sighed. "Oh, Aufors, many different things. Little things, mostly. A cat hiding her kittens in the hen house. A neighbor losing a chicken coop in a spring flood. Once I saw the roof blowing off the kitchen at school, and that same winter it did. Mostly they're just feelings of things that will go awry, choices that are mistaken . . ."

"And your own future?"

"I don't know. I've never seen anything about my own future, at least, nothing that I know of."

"Except you will be on the deck of a ship . . ."

"No. I think that already happened. Long ago. And the one just now, if I'm in it. I guess I am in it, for I saw my own hands. That's the only one that includes myself."

He sat down, pulling his chair close to hers. "It would be dangerous for you to get yourself involved in the court, Jenny. Somehow we've got to keep you out of that!"

"We can't." She smiled, rather wearily. "I thought there might be some way I could stay away, but there isn't. Father needs me here—this first dinner party made that very obvious, Aufors. He'd have been in a dreadful mess without me. Besides, the Lord Paramount asked me to be here."

"You need someone, surely." He rose, striding to and fro, agitatedly. "The Duchess of Merdune, perhaps she could be . . ."

"You're thinking she might help me? Well, perhaps. She said she would call on me, and since we really are kinswomen, she may actually do so."

"Your father asked me to take an apartment here, in the house. So far, for various reasons, I've delayed, but I could be here tomorrow if it would help you . . ."

"If it would help me?" she asked. "Of course it would help me, but you shouldn't do it for that reason."

"Genevieve . . ." he cried, the word breaking from him uncontrollably, all his feelings in his face. "For what other reason would I?"

He reached for her hand, ready to go on, but she gasped, as though breathing hurt her. Her eyes filled as she held up her hand, palm out, forbidding him.

"It would help me, provided you understand . . . we must stop this familiarity of ours. I know I asked you to call me Genevieve or even Jenny, but I'm afraid it's likely to be . . . misunderstood. Father has already . . . misunderstood it. From now on, you must be Colonel Leys to me, and I must be My Lady to you, and you must not say whatever you just started to say. It is not fair to you, I know, and it is no more fair to me."

"You have a right to be happy!"

She shook her head, her lips trembling. "I am a daughter of the covenant, Colonel Leys. The covenant allows us our youth, but that is about all it allows us. I was happy, at school. I didn't realize until I came here how happy I was there. I knew my way, there, and who my friends were. I had my niche and was comfortable in it. I didn't ask to be brought here, and the people here are strangers . . . no, not merely strangers but strange! As though . . . as though they are not made of the same stuff that you are. As though all their words are paint. Do you understand?"

"Paint?" He frowned. "You mean, painting over, covering up, hiding something."

"Yes. Covering up something. Exactly. As though they all know a secret. Or some of them do, and the others pretend to. I don't know what it is, but it distresses me. Della says I'm merely tired out, and perhaps she's right, but I cannot . . . cannot deal with anything complicated just now. Not until I've watched this play, and caught onto it, and learned what the plot is, you see? If I don't know how it's going, I might get dragged into it. If I were once to be caught in it . . . oh, maybe I could never go back to being what I am."

"What you are?" he whispered, amazed. "You're as real as the earth itself. What do you think you are?"

She was shaking, horrified at herself for what she had already said. Well, she had said it. No point in going back. "I told you! I'm a mouse, a watcher from corners. I don't have anything to do with the plot. I'm happier if I can just stay to myself, watching. Which I must do, until I come to obeying my mother's dying words. No, don't ask. Please . . . please, Colonel . . ."

He frowned in concentration, telling himself not to argue with her, not to accuse her of silliness or stupidity, to take her words seriously though everything in him denied what she was saying. He promised that he would move into the house by morning, after which she sent him away before going upstairs to lie on her bed and cry for all the things she was feeling with no way at all to be rid of them or do anything about them.

When she had cried herself out, she got up, washed her face, returned to her bed, and took up the book that lay open upon the table, determined to lose herself in thinking about something else. After Alicia had mentioned the book, the strange account of their mutual ancestress, the Lord Paramount's wife, Queen Stephanie, Genevieve had found it in the library. She read:

This is a story our people tell:

Long, long ago on another world, our grandmother te kui nui, mother of us all, heard the voice of all worlds singing.

"E, kui," the spirit called. "I have a task for you."

"Oh, Io," cried our grandmother. "Am I not burdened down with tasks? Here are children at my knees, here are sons running wild, here are daughters begging knowledge, here are gardens to be cared for, am I not well laden with burdens?"

And the voice said, "This is a greater task than all of those, and on this task the lives of your children and gardens will depend, for I set upon you the task of sailing among the stars in the long time to come."

And our grandmother did not know what to say for a time, but then she replied, "Oh, great filler of worlds, surely only those who have passed beyond the world may sail between the stars. Are my children not to have the gift of life?"

And Tangaroa said, "The time will come when te wairua hohonu needs a service of you, and against that time, I would prepare you.

"You must go to your sons and grandsons and tell them to build great canoes, and you must take all your children and all your belongings, and you must set sail as I shall guide you, to a new land."

So our grandmother came to her sons and grandsons, who were many, and told

them of the command she had received. And after a time of talk, not all of which was
sensible or respectful, so that our grandmother was forced to shout loudly, our people
set about building the great canoes. And when the first canoe was built, the people came
to grandmother and asked what name it should have.

And grandmother said, "It shall be named nga Tumau Hohonu, the servants of the
deep, and when it comes to land, the people of that canoe shall take that name forever."

So it sailed away. And when the second canoe was finished, grandmother said, "It
shall be named nga Kaikaukau Whetu, the star swimmers, and when it comes to land,
the people of that canoe shall take that name forever."

This is the story my people tell. Others say this did not happen, that it was not
until the great ship left the world that our people were visited by the spirit. And others
say that the spirit never spoke, it was all accidental, that we just happened to be there,
for we and the spirit left the world together. I, Stephanie, sometimes believe one and
sometimes another, but I like to think of the ancestral canoes setting out upon the great
and trackless sea, nga matawaka hollowed from the trees of the forest, sailing on and
on, into the emptiness at the edge of the sky.

However it happened, I came to be he Kaikaukau Whetu, a star swimmer, and I
am still he tumau hohonu, a servant of the deep . . .

Genevieve came to herself with a start at the sound of the first dinner
bell, reverberating in the great hall below. She laid the book on the bed
beside her and sat up, the thoughts and images of the book evoking and
blending with stories her mother had told. Stephanie's story was not unfamiliar, though her mother had used different words to tell it no less enig-
matically than Stephanie herself.

Her thoughts were interrupted by Della, coming with an armful of
newly laundered petticoats. "Come, Jenny," she said in an admonitory tone.
"No time for daydreams. It's time you were dressed for dinner."

And when Genevieve went down to dinner, Della neatened the bed,
putting the book away on the shelf, where it stayed for some time,
forgotten.

Genevieve made appointments with the first and second dressmakers
on the list, saving the third for later. From the first, a colorless little
woman with a pinched mouth that spat pins and wiry fingers that extruded
tape measures, she ordered two gowns, simple ones of classic cut and
exemplary fabric. The whole transaction took less than an hour, once the
measurements were taken.

Karom Veswees, a sinewy and pliant male with beautiful bones and
hands, was a different breed of lizard. "I'd like to do you all in beads," he

said, observing her from several angles, including crouching on the floor to look up at her. "Or maybe feathers! What a marvelous face. You're quite divine, Lady Genevieve."

She was more amused than annoyed. "Sit down," she said, pointing to a chair. "Do not flitter about. This is serious business."

Simpering only slightly, he sat in the chair, hands folded, being the good child. Despite herself, she smiled.

"You see," he crowed, "what a face!"

Genevieve summoned her most businesslike voice, "I am told you dress the Lady Charmante. She was wearing something filmy the other evening, red, with lines of amber and gold in it?"

The simpering look vanished and was replaced with a grimness about the lips.

"Silk batik, from the aboriginal commune on Strayne V, off-planet needless to say, obtained by the Prince for his 'consort.' I'm sorry, Your Ladyship, but if you want something like that, you're out of luck. Unless your father is far wealthier and more dishonest than he is reputed to be."

She frowned at him, then rang for a footman and ordered tea before coming to sit beside him. "You'll stay to tea, won't you, Mr. Veswees? I think you have knowledge I need, and I will buy many dresses from you if you will tell it to me."

He cocked his head. "You're just in from the country, aren't you? You're not up on things."

"Completely at sea." She smiled, deciding suddenly to allow this most improper person into her confidence. "I don't understand this off-planet business. I know our ancestors, in their wisdom, decided that a nonindustrialized life which made small demands on power and raw materials would be more sustainable over the ages. I know the Lord Paramount and his counselors, in their wisdom, have decided that we must make what we need, except for things like medical personnel and a few other essentials. Until a moment ago, I did not know that the list of such things included luxuries like imported silk."

"Well, that particular import wouldn't be publicized, would it?" he said, giving her a searching look.

"There's something that's been bothering me for a number of years, Mr. Veswees . . ."

"Karom. Call me Karom. Everyone does."

"All the more reason I should call you Mr. Veswees." She smiled sweetly. "We learned in school that Haven is what might be called a poor planet, partly in fact, partly by choice. We learned in school that interstel-

lar transport is hideously expensive. We learned in school that the Lord Paramount has a list of things we must obtain from elsewhere—" She interrupted this catalogue when the footman entered. He bore a tea service that must have been poised nearby, ready if she should ask.

Veswees nodded, looking up with a smile at the footman who placed the tea service on the table between them. "Everything you say you have been taught about Haven is quite true," he said.

She went on, "What no one has ever told me, however, is what coin, what medium of exchange we here on Haven use to purchase these off-planet things."

The footman knocked over an empty cup, making a clatter. "Your pardon, lady," he said, righting it with a slightly trembling hand.

The noise had drawn Genevieve's attention away from Veswees's face, and she missed the glance he shared with the footman, rapt attention mixed at once with apprehension and elation. When she looked up, he was as he had been, pleasantly interested, nothing more.

He said in an innocent tone, "I have wondered about it, too. Perhaps we have artists or singers or people with other talents whose services can be sold," he murmured.

"Wouldn't we have heard of this? If someone were that talented, wouldn't that person have a local reputation? Wouldn't we have known of him, or her?"

The footman bowed himself away. Veswees waited until the door had closed behind him. "Perhaps the talents are . . . private ones, Your Ladyship."

She considered him over the rim of her cup. The sexual innuendo had been explicit. She could neither have missed it nor misinterpreted it. "Do you think so?" she asked, as casually as she could.

He sipped, turned the cup on the saucer, played with the spoon. "Don't you think our medium of trade must be something like that? This world of ours is poor, as you say. There were no prehistoric forests to store oil and coal for our use, but we have large rivers to provide hydroelectric power. We have a few mines to supply metal, a few forests that give us wood for burning in our stoves. Our population is kept at a level that can be sustained by these rivers, these mines, and these forests. Nonetheless, we must import certain needed minerals for food additives and for our agriculture. We have no gems of note. We have no rare foods or seasonings or wines. We have no rare ores or biologicals that are in demand— or at least none that are mentioned in the marketplace." He sipped again.

"And then, too, you must have noticed how few . . . pretty young women we have at court."

She thought back to the recent dinner party. There had been no young woman but herself. The others had all been well past middle age, though they would not have thanked her for so judging them. "I do not consider Havenor to be the most healthful environment, Mr. Veswees. It is chilly here, I am told, even in summer. Young women are of an age to have babies, and perhaps they prefer to stay in the provinces with their children."

"Perhaps. Certainly motherhood proves difficult for many of our noblewomen."

She frowned. "Why so?"

He shrugged. "It seems to be a pattern among some of my favorite clients, young women who came here for a time, who returned home to have their children and who never returned. All too often I have heard that they succumbed, usually to batfly fever . . ."

"But the court has off-planet doctors," she said.

"Who can do nothing for batfly fever, or so I've heard."

"Well then," she said. "Tell me about batfly fever, for it is one of the subjects I must learn about."

"Where did you live, before you came here?"

"At school in Wantresse. Or at Langmarsh House, also in Wantresse."

"Wantresse is hill country, and you were fortunate to live high up," he said. "I am told the batfly flourishes at lower altitudes, especially in the moist herbage along the rivers and the lakeshores. The flies are said to carry the fever virus in their blood, which would do us no harm if it stayed there. The flies, however, are said to be infested with mites that suck up the virus, and when the batflies are flying, they are also shedding mites onto everything below, trees, people, animals. The mites are tiny, transparent, almost invisible, and when they burrow into a person seeking blood, the person gets the virus."

"But not in the hills?"

"Evidently not, nor along the shore of salt seas. The batflies, I am told, prefer rainy woods along freshwater rivers and ponds and lakes and during wet years there are millions of batflies dropping zillions of mites onto people, though in drier years, one hardly hears of a case."

"Dreadful! Really dreadful!"

"It would be, we are told, without P'naki."

"And what does P'naki do for us? It's horrid tasting!"

"If you know how it tastes, you must have known what it was for!"

"Well, I knew it was medicine, without at all comprehending the reality. Della gave it to me when I was a tiny child and we were visiting Lord Fenrider, Earl of Evermire. What does it do?"

"A dose every ten or twelve days is supposed to make people poisonous to the mites. Before it even nibbles, the mite simply shrivels up and dies."

She made a face. "I can understand why Prince Thumsort would be worried," she said. "According to his son, Edoard, his father talks only about batflies and fish."

He smiled at her. "Life has many pitfalls, my lady, and few of them make pleasant conversation. I would rather discuss something much more amusing than either flies or fish, such as how we are going to dress you to advantage!"

So derailed, she did not return to the subject until late that evening when, prepared for bed, she sat before her mirror while Della brushed her hair. "What do we have on Haven," she murmured aloud, "to trade for off-planet goods?"

"Pearls," said Della, without missing a stroke.

"Pearls? On Haven? Pearls are an Old Earth thing. You know the ones that Mother gave me. They came from some ancestress, but I assume they were brought from Earth. I've never heard of Haven pearls."

Della smiled at her in the mirror, rather grimly. "They don't talk of it in the marketplace, my lady."

"Well then, why do you say it's pearls?"

"It stands to reason it has to be something! And we've explored all the land on Haven, so it's nothing on land or we'd know about it. So, it has to be something from the sea, and whatever it is, it goes off Haven in ships."

"If no one knows what it is, how do they know what goes off Haven?"

"Nobody knows, but everybody guesses. And we do know some things. We know sometimes a starship comes to Haven. It sends down a little boat, like a sailing ship sends a dory, and it lands down at a place at the edge of the Plains of Bliggen in Barfezi, where it's flat and rocky and out of the way. There's always someone waiting for that ship, someone dressed in the royal livery, all sparkles and gold, and that person marches out to the boat and he hands over a box, not a big box, a small one, the size of a glove box, maybe, and the little boat goes up and away. Then, some later, a bigger ship comes down with people or things for the Lord Paramount, like doctors, or machines. And there's always men on the hills nearby, watching their sheep, and others in the copses up the valleys, burning charcoal, and they watch the ships and they say it's pearls in the

little box, because they can't think of anything else it might be. And one of them's my cousin, and I've heard him tell all about it."

"Something small. Well, it could be pearls, I suppose," mused Genevieve. "Though one would think one would have heard of it, if that had been the case." She yawned. "I am tired out."

"No wonder. All that toing and froing of dressmakers. Did you like that crazy one? Veswees?"

"I did, rather," she said drowsily, sliding between the cool sheets. "He told me what to wear to the concert, which helps. That is, if Father wants me to go. He hasn't said, yet." She mused a moment, eyes closed. "Veswees knows something he'd like to tell me, but he can't, or won't, or shouldn't. And he drew some exciting dresses. He'll be back in a day or two, with muslin patterns, for a fitting . . ."

But Della had already gone.

In the night Genevieve dreamed of Aufors. The two of them were sailing away somewhere, having a conversation with fish. She didn't know where they were going or what they were talking about, but things grew more interesting the longer the dream went on.

A MESSENGER CAME ON THE MORNING WITH A NOTE FROM ALICIA, DUCHESS Bellser-Bar, inviting Genevieve to accompany her on a tour of the royal greenhouses. Genevieve gave the messenger her acceptance, with thanks, and the ducal carriage arrived in an hour. The Duchess was well muffled up, her face half-hidden in furs, for though the skies were clear, the weather continued cold. They rode through a city wild with wind, the trees on the boulevards twisting in a frenzy, the banners atop the pinnacles lashing, everything in motion, even the gemmed and broken light that jigged and glittered from the long, jewel-faceted conservatories.

A footman helped them from the carriage, another opened the doors, and inside a cultivation of gardeners stood slowly from their work, tools still in their hands. The Duchess was obviously a well-known and well-liked visitor, for they greeted her with smiles and moved eagerly to help both her and Genevieve with the furs and scarves that were now unneeded, for the women had come from chill chaos into an eden of blooms, elegance, and moist, calm air.

The Duchess, retaining the scarf around her throat and face, thanked each of them by name, then took Genevieve's hand and walked with her slowly down the graveled pathways among flowering trees laden with epiphytes, urns burgeoning with trailing blossoms, and beds of succulents and rare Old Earth species. As they went she kept her face turned away, drawing Genevieve's attention to this bloom and that leaf until they were out of earshot of the gardeners, at which point she led Genevieve behind a large pillar draped with fuschias and ivy, removed the scarf, and said in a shaking voice, "My dear, I need to presume on short acquaintance. I need your help greatly, very greatly indeed."

Now, with the Duchess facing her, Genevieve could see what the scarf had hidden on the way: an unusual pallor, pinched lines around the lips,

eyes pooling with unshed tears. She reached out a hand, all sympathy for the older woman's obvious distress. "Of course, Alicia. What is it?"

The Duchess took her arm again and drew her farther along the aisles, away from the busy men, her voice barely above a whisper:

"My daughter. My daughter Lyndafal. Genevieve, she's about to have her second child." She buried her face in her handkerchief, blotting her eyes.

Genevieve waited a moment, then said in a puzzled voice, "Is that . . . a troubling thing?"

"She's married to Lord Solven, Earl Ruckward of the Sealand. He's somewhat older than she. She's his second wife. He already has heirs . . ."

"He didn't want another child?"

Alicia looked heavenward, hopelessly, making a frustrated gesture. "Genevieve, could you . . . will you do something for me without my having to explain? I really don't think I can explain. Will you allow that I have good reasons, though they might seem silly? Will you help me without knowing what they are? I must somehow help my daughter get away from Ruckward. I believe with all my heart that her life depends upon it."

Genevieve stared in incomprehension, her mind tumbling with all the questions she was being forbidden to ask. "You can't invite her to visit you?"

"She's due to deliver any day, and Solven won't let her leave the place now. It's within his rights, in accordance with the covenants, so I can't . . . I . . . Genevieve, please!"

Genevieve bit her lip in indecision, finally shaking her head and saying, "You ask me in friendship, which demands I do what I can, but I must ask you, why do you want her to defy the covenants?"

The Duchess took a deep breath. "Knowing would only endanger you, Genevieve. Sometimes we can do in ignorance what we could not do in knowledge. I can only swear to you that it is a matter of her life."

"Why do you ask me? I know almost no one, I have very little freedom of action."

The Duchess grasped her arm. "It's your being from Langmarsh that makes me think you can help. My daughter is a good sailor. Since she grew up in Merdune, she could scarcely be anything else. The baby is due soon. Lyndafal has sent me word by a trusted messenger that on the tenth of Early-winter, whether the child is born or not, she plans to leave the estate in Nether Ruckton and sail out onto Havenpool as she does,

often, in all weathers, sometimes taking her little daughter. This time she will keep going, eastward, along the Randor Islands to Ramspize Point.

"Have you any acquaintances in Evermire who could meet her and hide her? I will pay, of course, and she is a sturdy girl. She can braid up her hair and work as a farmer or fisherman . . ." Her eyes went into her handkerchief again and she breathed deeply. "Oh, I have no right to ask . . ."

Genevieve patted her arm. "I'll talk with Della, my maid. She's related to half the people in Evermire."

"Don't tell her it's my daughter. Make up a story. She will use the name Bessany Blodden. Perhaps she could be a servant girl fleeing from an irate father."

"Something like that," Genevieve mused. "The immediate problem is that I may need to hire a messenger, and while Father provides adequately for the household, he gives me almost no pocket money of my own."

"Oh, child, don't worry on that." She reached into the pocket of her cloak and brought out a clinking bag. "Coin. Not at all traceable, as royal notes would be. Take what you will and keep what's left over as my gift of thanks. How soon, do you think?"

"I don't know. We'll need to meet again." She thought furiously, erupting with, "Are you sure, Alicia? Are you sure you want to do this and that I'm the best person to ask? I know so little of what's going on . . ." Her voice trailed into troubled silence.

"That's why, girl. No one will think of you or ask you questions. You're an infant. You have the experience of an egg. Anything that goes on with you goes on inside you. You don't gossip, you don't twitter. I'm presuming on our kinship, ancient though that is. And on our friendship, young though that is." She burst into silent tears once more, letting them flow without hindrance.

"Shhh. I'll do what I can. You must think of some other jaunt we can take two days hence, and I'll tell you then what's arranged. Now. Dry your eyes. You don't want them seeing you've been crying. It'll make people wonder."

Making people wonder, according to Mrs. Blessingham, was the first step on the slippery slope of perdition. Covenanters disliked wondering. They preferred certainty.

They wandered a while longer while the Duchess calmed herself and fixed her face with the aid of a pocket mirror. When they had stayed long enough for appearance's sake, they smiled and murmured their way back to the carriage and went directly to the Marshal's house, where the

Duchess insisted upon alighting from her carriage and walking away from it with Genevieve.

"I'll see you day after tomorrow," said the Duchess, giving Genevieve a hug. "Tell whoever it is to light a signal fire at the end of the Ramspize. She will guide by that."

"A signal fire," she agreed.

She went looking for Della, finding her out by the stables, which Genevieve considered a more private place to talk than the house.

"Della, I need to ask a great favor of you and maybe of John. I'll pay you well for it, but you mustn't ever speak of it to Father, for he'd be most annoyed."

Della sat down on a convenient keg and looked interested while Genevieve described the plight of a servant girl of whom the Duchess was quite fond, who now worked for the Duchess's daughter, and of this poor girl's husband, who was inclined to be violent and vindictive, so the girl herself needed a place to bide with her child until it was weaned, at least. A secret place.

"I'll wager the Earl got her pregnant," grunted Della. "That's who the Duchess's daughter is married to, Lord Solven, Earl of Ruckward, and that would explain all this secrecy and anger. Well, the Earl has a reputation for being a son of thunder, and it's not the first time he's bred a servant girl, so I can understand how the Duchess and her daughter feel. There's no covenants ruling what us common folk can do, so I can arrange for one of my cousins to meet this girl and her babe. I've family who lives down Southmarsh way, right near the Ramspize, including one old lady who could use some company."

"She'll arrive on Ramspize Point about the fifteenth, Della. Someone needs to light a signal fire on the shore, to guide her where they're waiting. You'll need to go to Evermire . . ."

"I won't need to go anywhere. The Langmarsh men are returning home today, and my John's going with them, to pick up some things the Marshal wants brought from Langmarsh House. He'll find someone trusty who'll go to Evermire and fix it with my cousins. When he gets back, he'll tell me how he's managed it."

"Are you sure John won't mention it to anyone? It would be so dangerous for me, and for the girl . . ."

Della snorted. "And me as well, Jenny. John might not care that much about the girl, or even about you, forgive me for speaking freely, but if I let him know it would endanger me, he'll not say a word. I promise you that."

"Thank you! Oh, thank you!"

Della's mouth twisted ironically. "No thanks needed if, as I believe, the Duchess intends to pay for it. It would have to be her, for I know your father keeps you in short shrift."

Genevieve flushed. "It is her money, yes. A hundred royals for you and John, and another hundred for expenses, and still another to help keep the girl until it's safe for her to return home or she can care for herself. Do you think that will be enough?" She had considered this business of money during the drive home, deciding on this figure at least as a starting point.

"Fifty will do for expenses, including a bit for whoever goes to Evermire and sets it up, but it could take more than a hundred for keeping the girl, so the total is fair. What's her name?"

"Bessany Blodden." She passed over the six fifty-royal pieces she had taken from the bag. Della took the coins, looked them over carefully, nodded her satisfaction, and pocketed them. "My lady," she said, flushing.

"Yes?"

"For you, I would have done it for nothing except expenses, but John and me, we're looking to buy a bit of land in Wantresse. A place to keep us when we're old, and any little money extra goes to that. I thought, since it was someone else's business . . ."

Genevieve laid her hands on Della's shoulder and leaned forward to put their cheeks together. "That's all right, Della. If ever I can, I'll put by a bit for your land. I've done you little enough good so far for all your years caring for me."

Della flushed again, started to speak, then shook her head and turned away.

Genevieve went back to her own room and lay down on the bed to think first about Della's land, for land was a matter of constant concern to the commons. Too much of it was owned by the nobles, far more than they could use. When she'd exhausted what she knew or felt about that subject, she considered what Alicia had asked her to do. The story she and Della had made up between them seemed so plausible she could almost accept it as reality except for one oddness. Why did Lord Solven, Earl of Ruckward, mind if his young wife had a child? And, why was Alicia ready to risk her daughter's soul in this way, for certainly her daughter had taken an oath when she married the Lord Solven! A life in his service. Which didn't include running off!

But then, Veswees's remark about young mothers having a difficult time came to mind. And her noticing how few young mothers there were.

And many of the students at school had been motherless, as Genevieve herself was, the result of noble husbands insisting upon having an heir, or two, or three, with mothers dying in childbirth, because they were older. One would think the off-world doctors so much touted by the court would be able to do something about that. Why did so many noblewomen die? In the villages of Wantresse there were many young mothers. Most of the women servants at school had children that they chattered about and showed pictures of.

Was it because noble heirs had to be born at home, as the covenants required? Perhaps that was what Alicia was afraid of for her daughter. That she would perish bearing a child at home. But that would be safer than in a boat at sea! Surely that was more dangerous yet. . . .

Someone rapped at her door, then opened it. The Marshal, her father, poking his head in, saying impatiently, "Genevieve? Aren't you well?"

"Quite well, Father. Just resting a bit before luncheon."

"Well, get up and put your court dress on. We've received a summons, you and I. The Lord Paramount wishes to meet you."

Della helped her get into the wide-skirted, rigidly boned, high-necked casing that served as daytime court dress. As soon as they were full grown, all students at Blessingham's had court dresses made for their eventual presentations, and managing the voluminous skirts had been part of the curriculum taught by the dancing instructor. Being introduced to the Lord Paramount was a formality, and on formal occasions everyone wore court dress, each of the color assigned to his own rank, from the purple of royalty down to the brown of gentlemen. Only commoners of the lower sort wore red, for it was considered so improper a color that it was never used in clothing or decoration, at least not by those with any pretensions of class.

Once dressed Genevieve and the Marshal went uncomfortably by carriage to the palace at the appointed time, midafternoon, whereupon they were shown into an easeless anteroom where they waited on hard benches for several hours. Genevieve had had the foresight to bring a book, a practice Mrs. Blessingham had recommended for any appointment made by a member of a higher class who might keep people waiting to display his superior rank, and she spent the time patiently turning the pages.

Heretofore, however, the Marshal had only been summoned to court when needed to quell some crisis; he had never before been kept waiting; and he now reacted to this delay by growing angrier with every passing moment. By the time the footman summoned them into the throne room

where the Marshal had been interviewed before, the Marshal was steaming.

The Lord Paramount was in no such agitation. He might not even have moved since the Marshal had last seen him, for he sat as he had then, robed in purple velvet, crown tipped slightly to one side, head leaning on his right hand, eyes half shut, an untidy scatter of booklets around him on the carpet and piled to either side.

"Marshal," he said, slowly sitting upright and opening his eyes. "And his lovely daughter."

"Your Majesty," murmured Genevieve, sweeping a proper courtesy, head bent, hair arranged high, long neck exposed. It was this exposure of the neck that conveyed subservience. One was helpless in such a position. Which the Marshal perhaps thought of, for he bowed not nearly low enough. Her stomach clenched. He might well say something irretrievable!

"How are you settling in?" asked the monarch. "Yugh Delganor says you seem to have found appropriate lodging."

The Marshal, tight-lipped, said, "We were fortunate enough to do so, Your Majesty."

"Over on Belregard. Baron what'sits place. Good. Good. Happened to think that it was about time to decide how we're going to occupy the young lady's time. Have you grown bored yet, Marchioness? Being home instead of at school?"

Genevieve assumed the question was addressed to her, though the Lord Paramount was looking over her shoulder into the air. "No, Your Majesty. Things are still rather unsettled," she murmured.

"Well then, we'll give you a bit more time. Prince Delganor has asked that you be attached to his office when you're ready to take up your duties."

Genevieve managed a charming smile over gritted teeth as she asked, "May one ask what that would entail, Your Majesty?"

The Lord Paramount stared at the ceiling, as though trying to recall what exactly the Prince's duties were. "Ah, the Prince oversees the maintenance of the palace and the welfare of its people. As you might imagine, we get visitors from all the provinces, and the Prince usually relies on a few charming young people to show the little barons and baronesses around the place, escort them through the public parts of the palace, you know. The greenhouses, the galleries, the gardens—only in summer, of course—and the royal stables. That's a favorite, the stables. Children always like horses. So, when you're ready, he'll call upon you to do that."

She said, "I imagine I'll need to familiarize myself with that duty, sir."

"Of course, of course you will, my dear, though it seems you already are, ah? Someone said you and the Lady Alicia were together in the greenhouses just this morning? Good. Good. Ask the Duchess. She'll show you around. She used to help the Prince, when she was younger."

He smiled, half drowsily, and leaned his head back on his hand. "That's all, Marshal. Glad you've settled in so well."

The Marshal bowed; Genevieve made the full court courtesy, remaining with her head bent for a long moment. There, on the carpet, lay one of the monarch's booklets, brightly colored, full of pictures of . . . things. Furniture. Golden dishes. Extravagant carpets. And there were a hundred such booklets scattered near the throne. Export catalogues. Some of them from planets whose names she knew from her reading in the school library.

Her father touched her elbow, she rose, they backed away from the presence and the tall doors were shut behind them. The Marshal took a deep breath, his face purple, as though about to explode.

"Any servant," he growled, as they went out into the hallway. "Any footman can escort visitors about!"

"It's all right, Father," she said hastily. "I don't mind."

His voice rose as he said, "To keep us waiting all that time! He could have had someone apologize for the delay!"

"Shhh," she said, aware that the approaching footman had his eyes fixed intently on them. "As you once pointed out to me, Father, this may be in the nature of a test. To see whether we are the type of people to cause difficulties."

His eyes widened. Slowly the blood drained from his face, leaving his usually ruddy skin quite pale, almost ashen as he mumbled, "So I did."

The footman preceded them on their way out, bowing and gesturing like a mime, obviously well pleased with himself, ears all but quivering. Genevieve remarked casually, "I'm delighted with the duty His Majesty has proposed. It will give me something interesting to do, and allow me quite a bit of exercise. I was amazed at the size of the greenhouses, and the galleries must be equally large. I didn't even know there were galleries."

"Nor I," he mumbled, allowing a waiting servant to place his cloak upon his shoulders. "I'm sure the duty will be very rewarding."

They descended the flight of marble stairs to find their carriage waiting. Inside, as they relaxed onto the cushions, the Marshal's face began to redden again.

The air solidified. Genevieve saw a dim room, stone walls, a cone of light, a dwarfish man crouched over a mechanism of some kind. She heard

her father's voice coming from the mechanism: "Any footman can escort visitors about . . ." The dwarfish man looked up with a gleeful, vulpine expression.

And she was back in the carriage with her father just opening his mouth.

"Oh, Father," she cried, laying her fingers upon his lips. "It's so exciting! And wasn't the Lord Paramount wonderful! Imagine seeing him in person. Quite an honor. Really, quite an honor!"

He started to say something, but she leaned forward and put her hand sideways across his lips, gagging him, her eyes fixed pleadingly upon his own. He was at first angry, then puzzled, but at length he pinched his nostrils together, as though he smelled something unpleasant and turned away from her. She turned away also, but to search the carriage with her eyes, the corners of the joinery, the places the cushions met the frame, the buttons tufting the cushions, seeing nothing, turning back toward her father to see the angry question in his face.

She said, with a wide, false smile. "Aren't you excited, Father? I know you *must* be! Anyone who admires the Lord Paramount as you do would be."

After a long pause he said, "Very excited," in a solemn, rather aggrieved voice. "Oh, very excited indeed."

They said nothing more on the way home, though the Marshal stared at Genevieve in a way that made her quite uncomfortable. When they arrived at the house, they drove directly to the stable yard, from which her father fairly dragged her into the desolate garden. "What possible excuse can you offer for all that?"

"I . . . I just had the feeling, sir, that His Majesty might find it necessary to . . . listen to people he had invited to court. To hear what they said, whether they were loyal to him. I just had the feeling that . . . it would be a mistake to say anything at all negative."

"You had this feeling in our own carriage! And just how would he manage that?"

She thought of the scattered booklets by the throne, wondering if she should mention them. No. She didn't know what they portended, her father had paid no attention, but even he knew about doctors. Let her speak then of doctors.

"The Lord Paramount . . . the Lord Paramount and some of the nobles hire off-world people and buy off-world products, Father. Medical personnel and supplies, for example. We all know that. And when you fight on the Lord Paramount's behalf, I'm sure he gives you off-world weapons if

you need them. People near to His Majesty, those charged with his security, are no doubt also given special tools to keep track of people. You would not necessarily be told of these things, just as they would not be told of the weapons you use."

"Which has nothing to do with spying on people!"

"I am sure such technology exists, Father."

"In our carriage?" he said mockingly.

His eyebrows were lifted, his lips twisted in the lofty manner that she dreaded. Still, it was important that she warn him . . . without telling him how she knew.

Keeping her voice as level as possible, she said, "Our carriage was there, at the palace, for several hours. And not only our carriage would be vulnerable. We had a lot of work done on this house, before our dinner party. And . . ."

"Ridiculous," he snorted angrily. "You're like your mother! Imagining things! Making up ridiculous stories!"

"Perhaps," she said submissively. "But, wouldn't it be a good idea to be careful?"

Now that he had a target for his wrath, he exploded. "Genevieve, you've never given me any real trouble, as your mother did all too often, and if you are wise you will not start now. I'm sure the Lord Paramount does whatever he needs to do to keep order, but you're ignoring who I am! I have always been one of his most faithful supporters! I have fought in his behalf, borne wounds in his behalf. Though his underlings may be thoughtless enough to waste half a day of our time on a mere triviality, His Majesty would never feel it necessary to spy on me!"

His face forbade her saying anything more. She clenched her hands into fists and kept quiet. He went on in a more moderate tone, "You have pleased me with all you've done since we've been here, particularly since it is new to you and there is a good deal more to this business of being a courtier than I had been informed. I cannot allow you to go on in this spirit, however, seeing threats under every bush and around every corner! From now on, my dear, you *will not concern yourself with your safety, or mine;* you will not invent conspiracies to make me aware. I am always aware! Our covenants make the care of women the duty of their husbands and fathers. You can rely on my care and protection as you always have, and you are to set all such concerns aside. Do you understand me?"

"Yes, Father," she said meekly, biting her tongue. He wasn't aware, he was blind to the dangers here in Havenor, but there was no way she could make him see. She knew he collected intelligence on the battlefield for

she had heard him speak of its importance, but he ignored it here, where the battles were no less deadly. He thought the only enemies worth worrying about were the ones with weapons pointed at him, weapons he could see! How much more deadly the ones that were invisible!

He took a deep, simmering breath. "Good. Now go change that costly, ridiculous gown while I change my equally ridiculous garb, and we'll say no more about it."

Certainly she said no more about it. The next day passed simply, and on the day following, Alicia came to call. Almost defiantly, Genevieve took her into the garden, though it was probable that her father was watching. "My house has ears," she explained. "I do not know the servants well. I cannot swear they would not repeat anything they heard in my house."

The Duchess stared at her. "You look . . . different. Why, Genevieve, you look angry!"

Genevieve laughed without humor, shrugging helplessly as she did so. "I am somewhat peeved at Father. He considers my advice impertinent. Or perhaps he thinks I have none to give, that I know . . . nothing of value. As is his right. According to the covenants, I am brainless on such matters."

"Oh, yes, as we are all. Nonetheless, what do you know, Genevieve?"

Genevieve bit her lip, wavering, then answered honestly, "Father and I were summoned to the Lord Paramount day before yesterday. I know that His Majesty keeps close watch on all of us here in Havenor."

"Ah. How does he do that?"

"I think he probably has listening devices that he gets off-world. I think he has them planted in places where he wants to know what people are saying. So, when we go inside, I'm not going to say anything about your daughter. The matter is being arranged, and I have every confidence that someone will be on Ramspize point to meet your daughter on the fifteenth of this month."

"I can't thank you enough. . . ."

"Oh, yes." She made a wry face. "You can thank me enough. You'll probably think your thanks are onerous before they're done. I am to be assigned to Prince Delganor, as a kind of tour guide, showing visiting dignitaries around the greenhouses, the galleries, the stables. Father was furious, though he's settled a bit by now. He feels the duties are beneath a marchioness. I don't know what he thinks I am able to do that would be worthy of my rank! Except, perhaps, to marry someone who would be

helpful to his career. That seems to be the end toward which all the female nobility is driven! Can't they understand it's . . . it's criminal!"

Alicia tittered, a slight, trembling sound. "Criminality has its devotees, when the rewards are high enough. Still, you mustn't say so, dear. Not to anyone but me. When did you arrive at all this?"

Genevieve smiled, though without much amusement. "Truth to tell, Alicia, it came upon me, all at once . . . like a vision."

Alicia peered at her closely. "Ah. Like a vision."

"Yes. Perhaps my cynicism comes in good time. Better I have it early than too late. At any rate, His Majesty said you should acquaint me with my new duties as you had once performed similar ones, and then he remarked on our visit to the greenhouses that morning. I only hope for your sake that he did not overhear our conversation."

"The place I picked was all right," said the Duchess. "One of the gardeners works for me as a kind of . . . gossip. He tells me bits and pieces, what the butler or cook says, what the footmen overhear from dinner table conversation, you know. The palace servants know there are listening devices for they are the ones who install them." She laughed again, this time genuinely. "Though there are bought-men who actually do the listening, Aresians, I've heard, for the Lord Paramount does not trust anyone else. Despite that, the placement of the devices is left to the palace servants, for it is the custom that anything to do with the house is done by the servants of that house. Royals never think of their servants as being people! Lords Paramount don't consider commoners capable of independent thought or motivation, but I've come to know that the palace servants are capable of a great deal. They live upon graft and influence, my dear. A little oil here, to grease the wheels, a little push there, to mitigate a decision. The servants who trade in such matters are careful to leave dead spots between the spy-ears so they and their donors can negotiate privately."

Genevieve shuddered with agonized relief, an emotion too painful to be enjoyed but too reassuring to resent. "Then I'm right. I'm not imagining it. Someone is listening."

"Oh, yes, my dear. Somehow, His Majesty finds out almost everything we say and do, no matter where we are, in our houses, our carriages, our bedrooms, including, I sometimes think, our private closets, and no doubt there are specialists who listen to our most indelicate noises in the hope of decoding a conspiracy. They are listening everywhere but out-of-doors, and, I think, sometimes even there."

"Father wouldn't believe me. No, he chooses not to believe me."

The Duchess nodded understandingly. "I wondered about it to Gardagger only once, sounding properly foolish in case it was a taboo subject, as it turned out to be, for I was told to keep my mouth shut. Either Gardagger doesn't believe it or, more likely, he doesn't care. The older men don't seem to worry about it. As though they are immune to whatever the Lord Paramount is doing."

"Alicia, where do the young mothers go?"

The Duchess turned ashen. Her lips writhed back from her teeth, and she threw back her head, the long tendons of her neck stretching as though she wanted them to break, wanted her head to fly off, fly away. She trembled, a wracking convulsion, as though every muscle was drawn taut.

"They die," she whispered. "While they're nursing, they die. While their breasts are swollen with milk, they die."

"Why do they die?"

The Duchess turned away, hiding her face from the house, tears flowing down her face. "It's the fevers! So they say, all the physicians from Chamis, and the people here at court, but . . . I can't believe it, Genevieve. It doesn't happen to the servants! Not often, at least. It doesn't happen in the little villages. It only happens in Havenor, or in the noble houses."

"So, if I married, if I had a child . . ."

"You'd want to go to a village, Genevieve. Maybe the air is cleaner in the villages, maybe it's in the diet they eat there, or some herb they use for seasoning, but you're almost sure to be safe in a village. You'd want to get there before the child was born if you could, or as soon after as possible, to nurse it and wean it, quick as could be."

"You were a young mother. Twice."

"Yes. But my babies were born in County Benderly in Dania, in a tiny village where no one even knew who I was. When I was twenty, I ran off and married a commoner, Genevieve, and I didn't tell my family where I was, not for years. Such a scandal. I am the youngest daughter of Tranquish, Earl of Rivernigh, Duke of Dania, and he and I were invited to court, like you and your father. The Lord Paramount proposed I should marry this old . . . boarpig of a man, father to the current Duke of Barfezi. My half-sister had been married off to an old man, and she'd had a daughter and had died while she was nursing the baby, and I'd felt a kind of warning, maybe only a suspicion, but I wasn't of a mind to emulate her.

"There was a young guardsman from Dania among His Majesty's guards. I met him when I was leading my little tours at the palace, and we fell in love. He had a small holding in Dania, a good little farm. So,

I ran off alone, first, so no one would suspect him. He met me later, and we hid in plain sight in Dania. It's truth, the searchers couldn't see past the mud on my face and the tangles in my hair! Oh, Genevieve! We sang at our work! The whole village sang! It was wonderful. We had three children, two daughters and a son, all of whom lived! Then, fifteen years after we ran away, my husband disappeared. He went hunting, up into the mountains. He never returned, no one ever found him.

"By that time the man Papa had wanted me to marry was dead, and his son, Earl Vestik-Vanserdel, had a wife, Petrilla, and their children were half-grown. The threat was over, so the girls and I went home to Papa." She looked sorrowfully into the distance, her face saddened by memory, her body slumped with dejection.

After a long silence, Genevieve prompted her. "What happened then?"

"Oh, Papa had remarried again, a woman younger than I. She and I got to be good friends, and he rather ignored us both. Maybe he'd mellowed with age, he was eighty-some-odd by then. And then when I was fortyish, I met Gardagger. He's much older than I, of course, and he had children of his own, by his first wife. She had died shortly after the boy was born. Papa told me I'd be wise to marry him, with strong hints that if I didn't, I might be thrown into the street with my children. Marrying Gardagger made my girls covenantable—my son had chosen to stay in common life—but they were young enough to make the change. So, we married and I came to live here, at court, to raise Gardagger's children and mine. I might have preferred a bit more romance, and a great deal more ardor, but Gardagger is pleasant in his way, and if he's decided he's too old for intimacy, I shan't make a fuss over that.

"Father's new wife, my friend, died of the fever shortly after I left. He married again recently, a very young woman, Marissa. I hardly know her. My daughter Sybil married and moved to Tansay, in the Sealands. She too died of the fevers, while Gardagger and I were traveling. It wasn't until we returned home I learned she was gone. Well, the fever is the fever, after all. One cannot grieve forever. Until I heard from Lyndafal, I honestly thought she would be safe in Sealand."

"How does she know she isn't?" Genevieve asked in a puzzled voice.

"Her message says she's *seen* it. Well, you know, my dear, the way you *see* things. Once she told me that, I remembered my last visit to her when I noticed the way Solven spoke of his future, as though all his plans were only his plans, without her in them. I thought the doctors might have told him something ill about her, but she said no, she was well. But then, since I've been here, at court, I've talked to this one and that, countesses,

duchesses, marchionesses, baronesses, even a princess or two, too many of them with stories of how their daughters married older men and then died in the milk-months, even in places where the fevers aren't much known! Well, that made me think! Perhaps it's something to do with older men! Something in the sperm? Or something that men are exposed to in Tribunal rituals? Something they're well aware of, which would explain the way Solven spoke!" She wiped her eyes.

"And the women all die of the fever?"

"That's usually the cause that's cited. Batfly fever."

"But I thought we used P'naki to prevent batfly fever."

"But pregnant and nursing mothers can't take P'naki, because it deforms the child, or it gets in their milk and makes idiots out of the babies." She made a wild, agonized gesture.

"We should go in," murmured Genevieve. "I see the servants peering at us, standing out here in the cold. Father will be angry, for he thinks I'm deluded and silly, and it would be better not to annoy him."

"Pretend I've been advising you about the garden," said Alicia, pulling herself erect, head high. "Talk of roses as we go in."

They returned to the house discussing the merits of ancient shrub roses versus some of the more exotic varietals available through the greenhouses, and hearing this, the Marshal, who had been hovering by the stairs, red in the face and breathing angrily, decided to make himself scarce. A servant approached to say that Veswees was waiting. Alicia volunteered to stay during the fitting, and they continued to talk of gardens, Veswees chiming in from time to time, though with a very percipient look that said he was aware the conversation was all a mask.

"And how is your friend, the brave Colonel?" he asked around a mouthful of pins.

"Colonel Leys?" asked Genevieve, distressed to find her voice breaking on the name. She cleared her throat. "Colonel Leys is quite well, though I've seen little of him recently. Father seems to be keeping him very busy."

"Ah," the man murmured, "what a pity. Tell me, is it customary for one of the Colonel's rank to serve as equerry?"

"It is not," said the Duchess, looking up from the embroidery she had brought with her. "The Marshal should let the boy go. His career will stifle here in Havenor."

At the thought of Aufors being let go, some toothed thing grabbed at Genevieve's insides and bit her, a sudden pang that came from nowhere and went as swiftly, making her gasp.

"What?" demanded Veswees. "Did I stick you?"

"Only a little," said Genevieve wonderingly. "It's nothing."

The Duchess knotted her thread. "What gossip have you, Veswees? What naughtiness is about in the provinces?"

He laughed. "Ah, well, you've heard that Prince Thumsort has quarreled with his lady?"

"That's no new thing. They quarrel about once a season."

"True. There's a scandal in Bliggen. Or, one should say in Halfmore."

Genevieve looked up, suddenly alert, and the Duchess cocked her head, smiling. "You know the place, Genevieve?"

"Of it," she murmured.

"Well, it seems Viscount Willum has taken himself a wife, though he's been long betrothed to someone else. Not only that, but she's a commoner!"

"Barbara," said Genevieve with absolute certainty. "He married her!"

"Got her pregnant first, I hear," said the Duchess. "You know *her,* Genevieve?"

"She was at school with us," she cried. "I should be happy for her, but, oh, what will Glorieta do? She loved him."

"Perhaps," said the Duchess, "it will turn out better for her, in the end."

The Marshal decided that Genevieve should go to the concert with Duke Edoard. Not alone, however. Colonel Leys and Della would accompany her, awaiting her outside the private box. So chaperoned, Genevieve went.

Afterward, she had no idea whether she had been charming to Edoard or whether she had even known he was there. All she could remember was the music, which had made her think of Stephanie's book. Where was the bit about music? She sought the book eagerly, finding it at last upon the shelf and leafing through it until she came to the lines she had remembered:

Our teachers tell us that each world has a song that is begun with the first life on a world, a song that sounds within the world to foster life and variation. All living creatures are a part of the song which shall be sung forever, until the last star goes out.

Our teachers tell us that sometimes living creatures do not wish to be part of the song; they do not hear it; they rise up against it; they cry that they are larger than the song and more important than the music, and when their words drown out the song, then the world begins to die. Within the song, we are an immortal resonance. Outside it, we are like the tinkle of a tiny bell, gone quickly into nothing.

For many ages our people, the kaikaukau whetu, sang with the spirit of earth.

Then came a time when those who could not hear the song became many, and their voices drowned out the song, and the singers knew they must depart if the song was to go on living . . .

And when that time came, all happened as Io had said. The ships were prepared and the song entered into them, and we went with the song into the depths. And when we were gone, lo, the Old Earth died for there was no music left within the world.

Della's husband returned a few days later, and soon afterward, Della whispered into Genevieve's ear what arrangements had been made and where the Blodden girl would be kept in safety. During her tour of the royal art gallery, Genevieve passed this on to Alicia.

"The place she will go sounds very common indeed," she confessed. "I hope Lyndafal will not mind it."

"Lyndafal loves life," said her mother softly. "She will mind nothing so long as she is alive."

Aufors remained busy, and Genevieve caught only glimpses of him coming or going. Some days passed in relative quiet, except for the Marshal, who blustered about, here and there, interfering with the servants and bothering Genevieve with suggestions about the outside workers, several of whom were still laboring at long-deferred and much-needed repairs to the house. The Marshal had not yet recovered from his annoyance at the way the Lord Paramount had treated them, or at Genevieve's "misinterpretation," so he defined it, of that occurrence. He was therefore inclined to carp at everything, though he remained blessedly nonverbal about the specifics of what annoyed him. Almost, Genevieve thought with a wry smile, as though he thought someone might be listening.

Genevieve herself made occasional clearly annunciated excuses for his bad temper: his gout was acting up, his bed was not comfortable, he was worried about his favorite horse. On one occasion when Della, in Genevieve's bedroom, started to say something about their private arrangement, Genevieve laid her fingers across Della's mouth and shook her head. If any servant from Langmarsh had been asked to install a listening device, Della would have known of it, but Della could not know what some stranger workman might have done. Thereafter, she and Della spoke of any private matter out in the stableyard.

Veswees delivered the first dress about the time the house began preparing for the second dinner party. The gown was a marvel of cut and line, made of a fabric woven in Sealand, a soft blue with barely discernable green and darker blue stripes, cut so the stripes spiraled around her body from the high collar to the hem. Even Genevieve had to admit she looked

quite wonderful in it, nose and all, though the collar required that her hair be dramatically "up," as Veswees said. "Very high, Marchioness. Very high indeed."

"Veswees," she murmured, so quietly as to be almost whispering. "Do you know why they won't let us sing?"

He stared into her eyes, as though searching for something there, some keyhole into which he might put a key, perhaps. Some door he might open. "I know two reasons," he said.

"Tell me."

"The first reason is a simple one. Back some hundreds of years, in the time of some Lord Paramount or other, an oracle spoke to him saying that when a noble young woman sang to the seas, the reign of the nobles on Haven should end."

"How strange."

"That's the story, at least. The other reason is merely something I've thought from time to time. Voices, you know, are very individual. Harp music is harp music, well or badly played, but anonymous. The same could be said for piano, or violika, or cortuba. One string quartet, assuming competence on the part of the performers, is rather like any other string quartet. But if someone sings really well, the voice becomes totally recognizable, does it not?"

She puzzled over this. "And so?"

"And so, if a noblewoman were very talented in music, if she sang in public, if she became very much *followed* one might say, her loss would be greatly felt. Being known, and followed, and grieved over would be quite inappropriate for a noblewoman."

He turned away and busied himself, saying nothing more, his very posture telling her he had said all he would say. Though she had been wondering about this ever since she began reading Stephanie's book, which referred repeatedly to singing, she let the matter drop. If Veswees was uncomfortable speaking of it, probably she herself should be equally wary.

On the afternoon of the next dinner, a pale and weary-looking Aufors Leys came to visit her, bearing formality before him like an offering.

"You have done well, my lady," he said tonelessly, with a sorry attempt at a smile. "This time there are no mortal enemies on the guest list, and your seating plan has been quite thoughtfully worked out."

"Lady Alicia helped me," she said, fighting her desire to reach out and touch him. He looked so sad, and his arms were so close. She could move one hand, only a little, and it would rest on his. She clasped both hands

firmly in her lap, cleared her throat, and looked up at the ceiling. "She's been very kind."

"Your dressmakers worked out well?" he asked, making an attempt at conversation.

"Two of them made gowns for me. The woman did two very pleasant ones, beyond reproach as to taste and fabric, though rather dull. They are no doubt superbly covenantly."

A smile barely flickered at the corners of his mouth.

"Craftsman Veswees finished a very dramatic gown for me to wear tonight, and he's working on two more. Father is quite annoyed at the cost, of course. I don't think he understood quite what he was getting into, coming here to Havenor. Things were much less expensive in Langmarsh."

"The provinces are much less expensive, yes. And preferable not only for that reason."

Long silence, while Aufors shifted from foot to foot and stared at the wall and Genevieve remained a statue graven in stone: Woman, looking at her clenched hands.

"Is there anything else I can do for you, my lady?"

"Oh, Aufors," she cried, unable to contain herself. "Even though I said we must be proper, I hoped you would go on being my friend."

He reached for her hands, squeezed them painfully in his own, and said in a husky voice, "Never doubt it for a moment, Jenny. But don't let me show it, for if I do, my words can only lead me directly to your lips."

Stunned by his words, she drew back, jerking her hands from his amid a flood of feeling that was totally foreign to her. It was like a drunkenness, a tottery feeling, as though both her legs and her brain had lost their blood supply, which had suddenly gone heatedly elsewhere in a frightening maelstrom of feeling. It was as though something clutched her there, clutched and squeezed! She was fainting, drowning, and it took all her strength not to fall forward into Aufors's arms. Instead, she grasped the arm of her chair and flapped the fingers of her other hand at him, as though shooing chickens, meaning *go away, oh, go away, what have I done?*

He gave her a look of tragic intensity and went to gasp for breath outside the room, while she, inside the room, did the same.

Some small gibbering thing inside her laughed in hysteria, drawing her attention to what was obviously meant by a "twitch of the loins!" Good heavens! Was this lust? Was this what Carlotta felt for Willum, or Barbara felt for almost anyone? This incapacitating need? This wanting to be near, to be held, to be . . . well, *that,* yes, the act she had been instructed in

then taught to unthink but which she found herself thinking of all too clearly! This wouldn't do! It couldn't do. Not now. Not here!

By evening, several hours' struggle plus a good deal of determination had somewhat restored her poise, which was essential, for at this dinner Yugh Delganor was again a guest, and tonight, he would be seated at Genevieve's right. Despairingly, she had asked Alicia to sit once again at her left.

"My dear, I shall be glad to be there. Are we to have entertainment?"

Genevieve nodded. "A play. A repertory company is traveling up from Merdune, and Father has arranged for them to do a comedy for us."

"No doubt Prince Yugh will want to know when you'll be ready to start your duties here at the palace. We've done the gardens, the greenhouses, the stables, and one gallery, and you've learned it all, leaving us only the other galleries to do."

"I'll try to learn quickly," Genevieve replied, mimicking the Duchess's meaningless public voice and inconsequential words, designed to put any listener to sleep through sheer vacuity. "We wouldn't want the Prince to become impatient with me."

She hurried as she dressed, realizing with a pang that she wanted to get downstairs as quickly as possible, for that was where Aufors was undoubtedly striding about, arranging last minute details. She forced herself to slow down, taking several deep breaths and assuring herself that she was still only a mouse in the wings, a watcher of all the confusions and entanglements that were going on among other people. Soon she would observe Yugh Delganor's play, and she would remember to crouch very small in a corner if she were to avoid being drawn into the story and made a central part of it.

The attempt to drag her onto center stage was not long in coming. The Duchess faced Yugh Delganor across the table. She attempted conversation, only to have each attempt quashed by a chill monosyllable or two. Even her conversation with Genevieve was stifled by the Prince's manner.

Finally, just before dessert, the Prince spoke. "You are looking well."

Though the words were complimentary, he was looking at the Duchess as though he had discovered a fly in his soup.

"I?" said the Duchess, surprised.

"I was speaking of the Most Honorable Marchioness, Lady Genevieve," he replied, turning his face toward her and continuing in a measured and utterly toneless voice, "You are a very good addition to our company here at court, my lady. Everyone speaks your praises. I am so greatly moved

by your beauty and grace and modesty that I shall obtain from your father permission to ask your hand in marriage."

At that moment a small silence fell, one of those that occurs intermittently in even large gatherings. The words, ". . . to ask your hand in marriage . . ." hung in that silence like the last reverberations of a bell. Genevieve did not reply. She sat in gelid paralysis, her wineglass held halfway to her mouth, her eyes fixed on the red shiver of its contents. The only thought she had was of her mother's voice: the hard road. Her whole being rejected it. It could not be this road. Not possibly. This she could not do!

The silence stretched, then broke into chatter, through which the Duchess Alicia could be heard to say with a tinkling laugh, "Your Highness, surely this is neither the time nor the place. If you are jesting, it is unkind, and if you are not, it is inappropriate to make such a statement in the midst of dinner, when the Most Honorable Marchioness cannot so ignore her duties of hospitality as to give your announcement the consideration it deserves."

Genevieve found her tongue and forced herself to laugh in her turn, lightly, dismissively. "I'm afraid the Duchess is right, Your Highness. This would be an extremely awkward time for me to pay attention to any such very surprising flattery."

"You are surprised?" he asked, eyebrows lifted. "I had thought your father might have speculated with you?"

"Oh . . . no, sir, he has not."

"Well then, you're quite right that the matter is untimely." And he turned to the woman on the other side and asked her about her son, while under the table, the Duchess laid a hand on Genevieve's quivering knee as she might lay a hand on a horse's neck to calm it.

"Wait," she whispered, smiling, "just wait. Smile back at me. Don't let them think you're shocked. Just smile, murmur, take a sip of wine, that's it. When everyone leaves, I'll stay behind."

The last course seemed interminable, and when the guests left the table it was only to reassemble in the conservatory where a stage had been set up. The players were brought on with appropriate fanfare, performing their buffoonish play about a group of vampires who were of the nobility and would drink only noble blood, the bluer the better. Genevieve did not think it funny, but then, she scarcely heard a word of it. Seemingly, some others in the room did not think it funny either, for while some of the younger ladies and gentlemen laughed heartily, the older men did not do so. Even in her confusion, Genevieve guessed that she and

her father had once again, through ignorance, transgressed some canon of taste.

The Prince excused himself and departed during the interval. Others of the older nobility left early, also, and it was a lower ranking, much diminished, though more uniformly appreciative audience who saw the final curtain with a spatter of applause and a spate of chatter. As the last guests departed, Genevieve stood beside her father, bidding them farewell. The Marshal was much as usual. He did not seem to be aware of what had happened during dinner, or that the Prince had disapproved of the entertainment. Genevieve did not enlighten him. Instead, she snatched up a shawl and slipped out onto the terrace where Alicia waited for her, wrapped in a great fur cape.

"What can I do?" Genevieve cried. "I can't do this, Alicia. Yugh Delganor is old. He smells old. All during dinner I smelled him, like mouldy soil in old cellars. All during dinner, I felt him, like craylets crawling on my skin, slick and slimy and strange. If I marry him, I will die, Alicia. I know it, the way I sometimes know things. And I'm sure he meant it!"

Someone made a noise beside the house.

"Who's that?" whispered the Duchess, startled.

A shadow detached itself from the house and came swiftly toward them. Aufors.

"Did he say what I think I heard, Jenny? Is that old man wanting you as a wife?"

Her tears were sufficient answer, and he drew her close, wrapping her in his arms.

"Well," said the Duchess, with a breathless laugh. "That answers one little question I've been interested in."

"I don't know what to do," muttered Aufors, over Genevieve's head. "I'm bound to the service of the Marshal, and though this would be . . . a hideous fate for Genevieve, he will no doubt approve it heartily as fostering his own ambitions."

"Hush," said Alicia. "Now is not the time. We must play for time. You must go back inside, both of you. Do whatever you usually do at bedtime. Wait for the house to settle. Then, Aufors, you bring her to the stable gate of my own house. Genevieve, bring whatever you would need for a journey in the wilderness, stout shoes, warm clothing, you know what she should bring, Colonel Leys, for you have fought in evil weather on hard terrain . . ."

"I'll bring my own kit as well," he said grimly.

"No," Alicia interrupted him. "No. She *must not* be thought to have

gone away with you, Colonel, or you with her! That could mean danger and disaster for you both: for her from her father, for you from the Prince. When morning comes, you must be here in the house, as surprised as everyone else. Now, let us get back inside, before the Marshal misses either of you."

"Is this the right thing?" cried Genevieve. "The Prince has not asked Father yet. We don't know what Father will say."

"My dear child, you do know what your father will say." The Duchess fixed her with a steady gaze, at which Genevieve flushed, shivering. "If you are to have time to consider this matter, you must be gone and be known to be gone before the Prince makes a formal request and before your father makes a commitment of any kind." Her voice became ominous, weighty: "For if he makes a commitment to Yugh Delganor, he will be expected to keep it at the cost of his life or yours, or both."

Aufors grimaced. "She's right, Genevieve. If your father says yes, both you and he will be totally bound by that promise. That much of the covenants is well known! Far better move while you and he still have some freedom of action. When the household is asleep, meet me in the stables. Dress warmly and bring only what you must have with you. I'll make up a small pack of travel necessities for you."

He ran along the house and around the corner, to return through another door, while the women returned to the terrace, the Duchess pulling Genevieve along like a little wagon, she trundling obediently, weighed down by so many feelings of mixed horror and anger that she could not form any intention to do anything at all.

"What has my foolish daughter been up to, dragging you out into the night?" bumbled the Marshal, with a frown at Genevieve. "Most thoughtless of her."

"It was I who took her out into the night," said the Duchess, laying a pale hand against her own forehead. "The conservatory was so warm, I was suddenly taken a bit faint, Lord Marshal. Now, if you'll be so kind as to summon my driver."

In moments she was gone, not without sufficient chatter to distract the Marshal from Genevieve, which allowed her to flee to her room, like a rabbit from a blundering hound. There Della helped her with her clothes, distressed by the sweat on her forehead and the way her hands shook.

"What's the trouble, my lady? You're looking peaked. Did something go wrong? Wasn't the food good?"

"The food was wonderful, Della. I'm just tired. These dinners seems to affect me like running for miles or riding all day. When they're over, I

feel wrung out. Pull the pins from my hair. I'll let it down and brush it. You go on to bed, it's late and you rose earlier than I."

Della went away, with only a normal amount of nursemaidish grumble and instructions. Genevieve braided her hair in a long plait, as she usually did at bedtime, but then wrapped it into a tight knot at her neck, pierced it with enough pins to hold it fast under any circumstances, dressed herself warmly, put her nightgown on over the clothing, and finally packed a small bundle that included a change of shoes and clothing, her comb and hairbrush, and a few little bits of jewelry that might be used instead of money. That made her think of the Duchess's coins, and she tucked the small sack into the full sleeve of her cloak, which she hung in the armoire. Then she lay down, the covers drawn to her chin.

After a time, the Marshal's footsteps came down in the hall. He paused at her door, it opened a crack, he peered in, then he shut the door and moved on.

She remained still, in turmoil, her mind chattering like birds in a tree, saying six things at once, none of them helpful. If her mother had meant this particular hard road, then she had a duty to stay where Delganor could do . . . whatever he was going to do. But what if she only thought so, and her mother had meant something else? She had no way to judge. Surely she could take a little time to judge?

When the house had been silent for some time, she took off the nightgown, replaced it with the heavy, hooded cloak, and slipped down the long hallways and out through the kitchen, easing through the heavy outside door that was often left unlocked because it opened only into the walled and gated yard. Just inside the stable she sat on a pile of hay that had been forked down from the loft to be ready for the stable boys in the morning. When Aufors found her, she was slumped in exhausted sleep with her bundle close at her side.

He shook her. She came awake, eyes wide, mouth open, and he put a hand across it at once. "Shhh."

"Where have you been?" she whispered.

"Hiring passage on the packet that goes down the Reusel at dawn."

"That'll take me along Wantresse. I'm well known there."

"If you were going, you'd be known, yes. But you're not going."

"I thought you said . . ."

"I bought passage as I'd already planned to do. I made quite a fuss about the young lady who was going to Reusel-on-mere. No doubt someone will discover her there, but it'll be another woman who's meeting her new husband, an old friend of mine, for a bit of a honeymoon. He's from

Sealand and she from Upland. I'm paying for the trip as a present, they've never heard your name, and making such a project of it is a bit of legerdemain, a red herring."

"And I?" she asked, getting up to brush the hay from her cloak.

"We'll know better after the Duchess tells us what she has in mind."

They rode double on Aufors's horse, Genevieve behind him, holding him tightly, wondering at the feeling this embrace caused within her. She had no time to reflect on it. The Duchess was waiting for them, together with a tall, bulky man, middle-aged and half-bearded, who regarded Genevieve with grave curiosity.

"I'm not sure this is right," Genevieve murmured. "Father told me not to concern myself for my care or safety, that it was his concern. Perhaps if I told him . . ."

"Your telling would have precisely the same effect that it has had heretofore," said the Duchess, in a bleak voice. "Aufors, go into the stable, there's a good boy, my dear. For your own safety, I don't want you to hear what's said here."

When he had gone, Genevieve whispered, "Alicia. Mother told me . . . she told me my way would be hard. She had the gift. The one Lyndafal and I share. Perhaps I am meant to stay here and . . ."

"Do you, yourself, know this is true?"

"No," she cried. "Not surely!"

"Then wait until you know it!" She turned to her companion. "This is Garth Sentith, a friend of mine from Merdune. and you are now Imogene Sentith, his daughter. The two of you are riding east tonight, to slip across the border into the Tail of Merdune, and thence down the canyons to the shore. From there you will sail southward across the Lagoon to the town of Weirmills, beside the Potcherwater, where Garth has a perfumery business I have long patronized.

"Now, Genevieve, here is pen and paper. Write me a brief note telling me that you are running away because Yugh Delganor frightened you half to death at dinner this evening. Write that you must leave before your father makes any compromising promises you might be unable to fulfill. Say you must have time to think on this. No, don't look at me all witless! I must have a reason to speak to your father before he does anything imprudent. I will say I found your note on my door, and this will give me an excuse to let a little reality into his head. I know what I am doing, so write it!"

Genevieve wrote, scribbling, the Duchess prompting. When the Duch-

ess read it over, the penmanship needed no change to appear frantic and panicky.

Alicia went to the stable door and summoned Aufors out once more: "You are to return to the Marshal's house, Aufors, where you will pretend you have been all night, deeply asleep. For the time being, you are not to think about Genevieve. Her safety depends on your not knowing where she is. Also, try not to show that you are worried over where she might be, though I realize you may be unable to do that. She, meantime, will be sitting quiet, being helpful and safe, so we all hope, far from here. Now say your farewells, for Genevieve must be well out of High Haven by morning."

She turned away, the bulky man beside her, and Aufors, with a gasp that had as much pain as ardor in it, drew Genevieve into a close embrace, laid his lips on hers, and held her there while the night spun around them both. Neither of them were conscious of time. The kiss could have lasted either a little moment or forever, and it was only his awareness of her danger that made him thrust her away, holding her tightly by the shoulders.

"Oh, my love," he murmured huskily. "This may be the best thing I've ever done, helping send you out of harm's way, or the worst, letting you go without me. Here I am, presuming. I don't even know if you return my affection—no, don't look at me like that. Say I didn't know, not until just now."

She begged, "Can't you come with me? Oh, Aufors, I'm so . . . at a loss . . ."

He drew himself up and said firmly, "I believe the Duchess knows what she's doing. I have known her for some time. I know that she plans from knowledge, whereas you and I have only intuition. When she says I might endanger you, she's right. I've learned on the battlefield that once the decision is made, for good or ill, it must be done with firm conviction. Now go, and let me put on a surprised face for the Marshal!"

Garth came then to take Genevieve's hand and lead her away. She went reluctantly, looking back over her shoulder as Garth took her through the gate and to the alley's end where two horses waited, their hooves muffled. While Aufors watched from the gate, they rode away, almost silently. By dawn, he knew, they would be well on their way to wherever it was they were going, certainly out of Havenor, across the border of High Haven, and well lost in the lands of somewhere else.

THE PLANET ARES, WHICH WAS NOT FAR FROM HAVEN IN A SPACIOTEMPORAL sense, had been resold several times before finally being settled, a millennium after its discovery, by a group of men who traced their ancestry to the frontiers of space exploration, a time when infinite space called resolute men into the wilderness to build an honorable society in which men were men, women were women, and everyone knew and accepted the difference. Aresians were more hearty than humorous, more intrepid than intuitive, more stalwart than studious. They eschewed the intellectual in favor of action, including sport of all kinds. They found a particular ecstacy in hunting or in doing things at high speed, preferably accompanied by loud noises and strong smells and with much drinking and jollity of a ribald sort to follow.

Their belief system was called Hestonism, a homocentric faith with a god who looked and acted like the best among them, fair minded and honorable and masculine in his approach to problems. If asked, any Aresian would have said that God was an honorable competitor, a good shot, and comfortable on the playing field. Sporting metaphors were customary in explaining the relationship between deity and laity, an intermediary clergy being considered both effete and ineffectual.

The ineffectual was eschewed as un-Aresian. People, no matter of what age or sex, should be *doing something*. If they were not *doing something*, the chances were, they were up to no good. Games had been provided by God to keep young people busy, and there was no juvenile predisposition so nefarious that it would not submit to daily sessions of competitive ball-carrying, rock-climbing, or game-shooting.

Aresians were well aware that others were less honorable than themselves. Had this not been the case, they would not have needed a world of their own in which their native superiority could manifest itself. Aresians felt there was no challenge that could not be met by well-toned muscle

augmented by superior fire power under the approving eye of a deity who kept His omniscient eye upon the target and His omnipresent hand on the trigger.

Upon their arrival on Ares, therefore, the Aresians built sensible armories against whatever enemies might emerge in time, and they manufactured machines for the subduing of the natural world. Subjugation of nature was one of the things strong men did, and they gloried in it, digging deep for the ores they needed and cutting down whole forests to feed their furnaces. Whenever they had a few hours free of toil, they vied with one another in games and sports, in hunting or fishing, at tramping and striving against one another in exploits of physical endurance. They bred doggedly, and proud families with litters of robust and vehement children were the norm.

Relentless sport took an inevitable toll upon the world. Though Ares was largely wooded when it was settled, the animal life was not plentiful, and most of it was extremely specialized and habitat dependent. Human population grew exponentially, though it took a century or two for it to cover all sections of the planet. Once it did, however, the native animal life was soon disposed of, even that preeminent trophy animal, the latigern, a graceful, antlered beast that had once grown to an enormous size that could be dangerous if encountered during mating season by a man without weapons. Since no Aresian was ever without weapons, and since Aresians had arrived at near total destruction of latigern habitat, the animal was driven to the verge of extinction by the turn of the seventh century, Post Settlement. The last few specimens were captured in 702 and put in stasis to be sold to other-world zoos. Such establishments always bid high for the last few specimens of anything. The last latigern were, in fact, purchased by the Lord Paramount of Haven several years later, along with the last few of several other species on the market at the time.

In 708, Post Settlement, something quite inexplicable occurred. One midnight the people of Ares were wakened by a trembling in the earth. Those who had read of such things thought it might be a crustal-quake, though it did not rise to any climax nor did it dwindle away to nothing, but merely went on shaking, a vast shivering as though, some people said, the world had caught a chill. The tremor was the same in the cities as on the farms, neither stronger nor weaker in any location, and it persisted for some hours as glassware rattled, dogs howled, and children cried fretfully.

Along in the small hours of the morning, those citizens who had not been able to get back to sleep (by no means the majority, for Aresians tended toward the phlegmatic) noticed lines of fire rising from the eastern

horizon. The first lines were followed by others, near and far, from all visible parts of the planet, beginning at different times but all rising deliberately until they met at the zenith. Though the people could not see it, monitors later revealed that the fiery lines rose in concentric circles from the entire darkside of the planet. As the planet turned to daylight, the easternmost lines detached from the planet and passed upward even as new lines of fire sprouted along the line of falling night.

When one full revolution had passed, so that the fire had gone upward from all parts of the world, a sharp shock was felt; the ground rebounded as though some enormous personage had tapped it in annoyance. This was followed by a momentary swaying, as though the world were uncertain in its orbit, and then by a deep, sonorous but musical hum from space that for a moment made a strange, haunting melody full of weird harmonics, though this was lost as the sound fell in pitch, lower and lower, becoming also softer and softer until it finally ceased.

There was, of course, much conjecture about the cause of this strange occurrence. Some thought Ares had been visited by aliens who had used the fiery lines as some kind of scanning device. Expeditions were sent to examine the sites of the upwellings, some of which had been accurately triangulated by observers, but nothing was found to explain what had happened. There was no charring of any surface, no appearance of great heat having touched the ground. Shortly after the occurrence, however, the few remaining forests that had been set aside as parks died, almost overnight, and the few native land and sea animals who had survived in hidden places were found lying quite dead out in the open. All life native to the planet simply stopped.

It was a strange and unsettling occurrence which confirmed the settlers opinion that the universe was an inimical place, though they, themselves, had not been injured in any way. Since the occurrence seemed to have nothing at all to do with them, the matter was recorded in the archives and in time was largely forgotten.

Livestock had been imported early on, and vast tracts of fields and pastures had soon replaced the trees. Several sizeable cities had grown up, in the area of most salubrious climate, though the climate had deteriorated greatly after the forests and seas had died. Off-world fish had been imported to restock the seas, and prey animals had been brought in for the hunt, though both failed to flourish, forcing the people to turn to non-blood-sports for their amusements.

If any planetary population could be said to be contented, the Aresians were the most likely candidates. They were well settled in a world struc-

tured much to their liking by their own hard work. Their only problem was that wresting a living from the planet took increasing effort the longer they lived upon it. The planet that had been settled with such dedication was no longer as fruitful as it had been.

In 747 Post Settlement, a new syndrome emerged to trouble the medical professionals on the planet, though it was subsequently determined that the syndrome might have existed undetected for four or five decades previously. All the victims were persons of middle age or older. A typical case might be a man or woman who arose one morning complaining of feeling "odd," though not odd enough to seek medical care. The person went about the daily routine more slowly than usual, slowing still more as the days passed, often commenting to friends and family that something important had been misplaced and could not be found. This might go on for thirty or forty days, after which the patient simply stopped moving entirely.

While under care, the typical patient continued quiet and withdrawn, content to sit and stare into the middle distance without being interested in food or drink or conversation, though some of the afflicted still wondered aloud where they might have put whatever it was that was missing. When urged to communicate, a patient might remark that speech took too much energy away from his or her trying to remember something very urgent, and persistent questioning caused agitation.

Without exception, the afflicted would continue in this vein, whether calm or agitated, until a sudden cry of what seemed to be joy was followed by a fit of laughter and then by an hour or so of unintelligible murmurings which carried a great weight of hopelessness and pain, followed by a lapse into unconsciousness swiftly followed by death.

There were at first only a handful of such patients, but their numbers grew with each year that passed. It was thought by some that a poisonous asteroid or comet or cloud of cosmic material had impinged upon the planet to cause these effects as well as the weirdness that had occurred on "the Strange Night," as it came to be called.

Ygdale Furnashson was High Chieftain among the Aresians. He had three sons, and in the manner of the historic quests of his people—and having already sought such advice as was available from scientific and off-planet sources—Ygdale sent his sons out among the settled worlds to question whether any people, anywhere, had any information that would cast light on what had happened to Ares on the fateful night and whether that event had anything to do with the current plague.

The two older boys found nothing helpful except the fact that a similar

disease was decimating the populations on Chamis and had already virtually destroyed Verben's World. Counting Ares, this meant half the settled planets in the area were in trouble. The younger son of the Chieftain found some additional information, though it was not what he had been looking for. He came home to report that he'd heard rumors that on Haven not only was settlement doing very nicely, but men were living to be several hundred years old. Additionally, Haven was rumored to trade the long-life substance, whatever it was, for off-world goods and services. The stuff had been bought and used by a few people on Chamis and Verben's World, all of whom, it was said, were still alive.

This was enough for Ygdale to work with. Though unaccustomed to protracted thinking, he could do it when necessary. He queried further, learning that the Lord Paramount of Haven had a fondness for shopping, that he much enjoyed brightly colored booklets, copiously illustrated, with elaborate and even fanciful claims and descriptions of the merchandise. Ygdale had such a catalog prepared forthwith, touting the advantages of an Aresian security force. He also arranged bribes to several of the Lord Paramount's servants to be sure that the Ares-Force booklet was always on top of the pile. He reminded his sons that taking an advantage of an opponent's weakness was not at all dishonorable.

Only ten Aresian years passed between the discovery of the disease and the dispatch of an Aresian mercenary force into the employ of the Lord Paramount of Haven, who paid for the service with a quantity of the substance the Aresians called "long-life stuff." Ygdale used part of the shipment for himself, and passed the rest on to his most trusted supporters. He assured them that this was only step one in Ares's recovery from whatever ailed it, for the mercenary force that was being sent to Haven, though it was fully as reliable, strong, able, observant, and protective as represented in the prospectus, was also made up entirely of disciplined Aresians under the command of Ygdale's elder sons and assigned the duty of finding out where the life stuff came from, how it was procured and manufactured, and how best large quantities of it could be obtained.

So it was that while the Prince of Haven wined and dined, while Genevieve wept and the Marshal preened himself in Havenor, Ogberd and Lokdren Ygdaleson, elder sons of the Chieftain of Ares, were well established in the palace at Havenor, where they might be found in the mercenaries' quarters, lifting weights, running a treadmill, and engaging in other exercises designed to keep them fit.

Nearby was a device which erupted, from time to time, with angry words and sounds of temper.

"Where's that listener planted?" a junior officer asked, adding a weight to his bar.

"In the office of the Mahahmbi minister of state," Lokdren replied, panting. "Ybon Saelan. He's the one with the best access to the Shah. If you want to know what's being said, ask Ogberd. He understands the dialect better than I do."

Ogberd took over Lokdren's abandoned treadmill, leaned on its control panel and drawled, "The minister's aggravated about some religious rite that's coming up."

"How did you get a listening device planted in the minister's office?" asked one of the newer men.

Lokdren wiped his face, took a long drink from his water bottle, and replied, "Provincial sales agents go to Mahahm to sell them grain or fiber or whatnot in return for some medicine they get from there."

"Long-life stuff?"

"Naw. Something to prevent fevers. The salesmen have to go to the minister's office to get their residency papers, and I bribed one of the salesmen to plant the listener."

"Why there?"

"We've looked everyplace we can look here on Haven for the long-life stuff, so we thought it was time to have a look at Mahahm."

"There's lots of places in the provinces of Haven we haven't been to," offered another junior officer.

"True," Ogberd muttered. "But it's hard to get out into the provinces unless we can get a duke or a count to hire us, and only a couple of them have, so far. We've been in and out of every noble house here in Havenor, though, as escorts to the Prince, and the stuff isn't stored in any of them." He set the dials on the treadmill and positioned himself.

"Meantime," said Lokdren, heading for the showers, "things are gettin' worse at home."

Ogberd grimaced. What Lokdren said was all too true. Life expectancy dropped every year as more and more people were cut down by the stopping-sickness. None of the men who had received the life stuff from Haven had succumbed, however, which kept their concentration intact. Haven had the substance and seemed to be doing all right; Ares didn't have the substance and was failing. Therefore, obtaining the life stuff was the key to survival.

Before turning on his machine, Ogberd reasserted this in a confident voice. "We've told the Chief we can conquer the planet tomorrow if we want to, but he doesn't want to invade until we know where the stuff

comes from! We've been here better than two years and I'm beginning to doubt His Majesty even knows where he gets the stuff."

"So, maybe we should make him tell us who does know."

Ogberd nodded with a grim smile. "You think we haven't considered it? And suppose it isn't even found here? Hmm? Suppose they get it from off-planet? Suppose it's a compound: some stuff from here, some stuff from somewhere else? Then we've blown our cover over nothing!" He started the machine and began to run with great efficiency.

The others looked at one another with upraised brows. Every man present, including the elder sons of the Chieftain, was serving in anticipation of a just reward, but if they couldn't find out where the reward was, then the past two years plus whatever time they spent in the future could turn out to be a waste of futures that were already threatened.

"So?" asked someone from a corner of the room.

"So," Ogberd breathed, "the Chief is going to decide. If we can't find out in a reasonable length of time, he's going to invade."

"The whole planet?"

"Havenor here, and Mahahm-qum in Mahahm. That way we're bound to net at least a few of the people who know."

"And what's a reasonable length of time?" asked the same voice.

"Not long," panted Ogberd, gritting his teeth. "Not long at all."

Very near the beginning of his reign, Marwell, Lord Paramount of Haven, had had a secret elevator built in a hidden shaft that dropped from his bed chamber behind the throne room into the lowest levels beneath the palace. No one but himself knew of this or even suspected it. The Lord Paramount went to his bed chamber openly each evening, summoning his servants there, and so far as anyone knew, the only access was through one of two doors, the one behind the throne room, which was always guarded, and the one from the servants' hall, which was always observed. Over the decades, Marwell's sleeping chamber had been repeatedly planted with listening devices and recorders by palace servants, bribed to do so by Prince Delganor. The chamber had been, as repeatedly, cleared of all such trifles by the same men, paid by Marwell himself.

Though the Prince had bribed the Lord Paramount's servants at least twenty times to search the chambers behind the throne room, nothing useful had been found there. The men who had built the shaft and the elevator several centuries before had known all about it, of course, but they had been sequestered while doing the work and had not lived long enough afterward to tell anyone. By this time, the secret elevator held a comfortable chair along with various weapons and items of clothing and equipment, and its corners were stacked ceiling high with Haven's entire supply of P'naki, which it was the Lord Paramount's practice to dole out at need.

The older the Lord Paramount became, the more lightly he slept, the more often he checked the elevator's contents and mechanical readiness, and the more often he supplied the elevator with small necessities which by now included his second-best crown and an ordinary, anonymous set of clothing and shoes, just in case, he sometimes told himself, he needed to disappear for a while.

"For a while," was always part of the thought. He never, even in his most suspicious moments, supposed that he would have to disappear permanently.

ON THE MORNING FOLLOWING GENEVIEVE'S DEPARTURE, WHILE THE MAR-
shal sat at breakfast, Her Grace the Duchess of Merdune was announced
by Halpern. She sailed in around the butler, rather disconcerting the Marshal, who had not heard them coming.

"Madame," said the Marshal, rising. "You'll be wanting my lazy daughter, who is not yet out of bed."

"Do sit down, Marshal," she said, going to the sideboard, where an
elaborate breakfast was arranged. "Let me join you for a cup of tea, perhaps
one of these scones. Ah! Zybod ham left over from last night. Delicious!
I must have a slice of that! Actually, it's you I've come to see."

"Me? Well, Madame, I'm flattered. What can an old war horse do
for you?"

A footman brought her plate from the sideboard as she sat in the chair
nearest the Marshal, leaning confidentially toward him. "An old war horse
can be understanding, sir. You can be understanding."

"Of what?" he asked, drawing back suspiciously.

"Of why Genevieve has left home."

He snorted. "Left home? Nonsense, woman. She's upstairs in bed."

"I think not. I'm almost sure she's gone away. . . ."

The Marshal's eruption interrupted her. He shouted for a footman,
telling him to find Della, Genevieve's maid, and bring her here, at once.
The Duchess sighed and concentrated on her breakfast while Della arrived,
was sent away, and returned rather ashen in the face to confirm that
Genevieve was indeed gone.

Angrily, the Marshal dismissed her and demanded of Alicia, "All right,
what is this?"

She beckoned him to lean close to her, softly whispering into his ear,
"I found a note at my door this morning, from your daughter. Last night,
during dinner, Yugh Delganor spoke of marriage to Genevieve."

"Did he indeed?" said the Marshal, eyebrows rising, eyes gleaming. "Well, I'd said as much to—"

The Duchess's hand across his mouth silenced him. She shook her head, motioning at the room around him, then whispering again:

"Genevieve went into a panic, sir. I believe she is in love with someone else."

"She what!" He turned an ugly red and rose with such force that his chair went crashing behind him. "She had no business being in love with anyone!" he cried, stalking away from the table, his napkin flapping on his chest.

She got up to take him by the arm, shush him, tug him back into his chair, and pat him on the knee as she murmured, "I don't think it's a business at all, sir. Businesses we control. Love, we cannot. At any rate, she was gravely upset by last night's dinner, so upset that she has run away."

She drew him close again, putting her lips within an inch of his ear. "She thought, quite rightly I believe, that since the Prince had not actually spoken to you or proposed to her, and since she had not given him any encouragement whatsoever, no promises could be considered broken."

"And who is she in love with?" snarled the Marshal.

"She didn't say she was in love with anyone, but I think from my own observation it is probably Colonel Leys."

The Marshal shouted, "I'll have the bastard shot! So he went with her, did he?"

The Duchess gave up any attempt at silence. So long as the Marshal stayed away from the subject of the Prince's possible proposal, he might rave as he liked. "I'd be surprised if he even knew about it, much less went with her."

"So you say!" He summoned a footman and demanded that Colonel Leys be summoned, without delay. Then he turned on the Duchess once more, saying sneeringly:

"So why are you here, Your Grace? Come to beg forgiveness for her?"

"Not at all, sir. I merely read her note, and since I knew you would be upset to find her gone, I came to tell you what had happened."

"*After* it happened," he shouted.

The Duchess said frostily, "I suggest you moderate your battlefield bellow, Marshal. We are equal in rank, and I do not take it kindly. Besides, you do not want this overheard . . ." again she gestured at the room around them, ". . . by every servant in the house. Neither my butler nor I check the door for messages during the night hours, nor have you any right to assume so."

He said through clenched teeth, "Well, I'll let her know what to expect. I'll have her run down by nightfall, I assure you, and all your good offices will not win my forgiveness. She may well have upset some long-considered plan of the Lord Paramount. She may have been brought here for this particular reason. I don't suppose that occurred to you?"

He glared at her, barely noticing how her expression hardened, how her lips thinned into an angry line. She rose, went to the tall windows opening on the terrace and flung one of them wide, sailing out through it. The Marshal followed her into the open air, steam rising from his forehead.

The Duchess turned to confront him. "Tell me, Marshal, does your daughter have a mind?"

"Of course she has a mind. I would have thought until now, a rather good one."

"But she is forbidden to use it, is that it?"

"She is certainly not allowed to use it to disobey me!"

"Oh. Had you forbidden her to fall in love with Aufors Leys? I had thought it was you who introduced them."

Fuming, the Marshal leaned across the stone baluster and spoke into the air. "Madam, you are serpent worded. Your sentences fairly slither. You know full well what I mean, and you know more than that. You know this . . . defection may have set my own life at risk."

"You curse Genevieve where you shouldn't and deny her credit she has earned," she murmured, bringing her lips close to him once more. "Her going has not harmed you, but her staying here might well have! If you value your life, Marshal, you will attend to what I say! *I heard the exchange at dinner last night, every word of it.* So long as you remember that Yugh Delganor had not actually asked you for your daughter's hand, no matter how he may have hinted at or alluded to or implied an interest, so long as you did not certainly know what he intended, so long as you had not agreed to any such intention, so long as you had not told Genevieve of his intentions, *you* are not at fault, nor is *she.*"

He stared at her, chewing on his lower lip, his face only very gradually losing its flush as his icy lizard's mind disengaged from its choleric tantrum to survey the battlefield.

"On the other hand," she went on icily, "if she had stayed here, and if you had promised her to Yugh Delganor, and if she had been physically or mentally unable to fulfil that promise, then your life might well have been at risk."

"She would not have been unable," he snarled.

"Marshal, you may command men into battle. You cannot command them not to die in battle. The same is true here. She might well have died of it."

He frowned. "This is hysteria!"

"Am I to infer you wish to see her dead?"

He made a gesture of disdain. "Bah, they're fragile things, women. Few of them live long. One or two children, they fade like flowers, which is why we give them their youth. We never wish to see them dead, and yet they die. It's their nature."

She drew herself up, like a tower. "Don't talk foolishness, sir. I deny your judgment of women. The village women I meet are often in their eighties or nineties, outliving their husbands by many years. They are not fragile. They do not fade. Why is it not their nature?"

He fumed, chewing at the inside of his cheek as at a cud. "We're inbred, I suppose. We of the nobility."

"If you do not wish to consider Genevieve, consider this," she murmured icily. "Though a royal wife may spread ephemeral favor among her relatives, once she is dead, the favor rots with her."

He stared. "Nonsense."

"I do not argue nonsense," she said. "You may check for yourself. Find out what has happened to previously favored families of royal or noble wives who are now dead! If you are more concerned for yourself than for your daughter, then consider yourself." She lowered her voice once more. "Those close to the Prince do not last long, nor do their kin. Your best future will be found in service to the *Lord Paramount*; your best chance at survival will be to keep the Prince at arm's length."

"He'll ask for her. The Lord Paramount. Or the Prince."

"Until one of them does, you wouldn't think her departure important enough to concern either of them, would you? You certainly wouldn't *lend* it importance by bringing the matter to their attention."

He stared, glared, shook his head. "Suppose not, no. Though His Majesty did ask me to bring her here."

"But you wouldn't trouble His Majesty if she were indisposed, or if she went home to Langmarsh for a few weeks. She hasn't taken up her duties yet, and after all, we don't know where she went or when she may return, so you have no real information to give them. If they ask you about her, why then you tell them what happened. The silly girl was frightened by something that happened at dinner last night, and she ran away, leaving a note with her friend, the Duchess."

"When I brought Delganor to her, back at school, she didn't mention to me she was in love."

"I doubt she was, then."

Behind them, in the dining room, the door opened and Aufors Leys came in. Hearing this, the Marshal and the Duchess reentered the room, closing the tall window behind them.

Aufors's eyes widened when he saw the Duchess. He bowed. "Sir, you sent for me?"

The Marshal's eyebrows went up. "So you're here, eh?"

"Of course, sir. I have several days' leave planned, as you know, but I didn't intend to depart until this evening."

"Never mind, never mind. I had the impression you might have gone away somewhere."

"No, sir," said Aufors, managing to look extremely puzzled. "Though I did oversleep this morning."

"And where are you going for your leave, Colonel?" asked the Duchess.

"An old friend of mine is being married in Reusel-on-Mere, and he's asked me to stand up for him."

"Right," snarled the Marshal. "You told me, weeks ago. Well, well, go shave yourself. You look disorderly. We'll talk later."

"Yes, sir." And Aufors Leys departed, taking note in passing of the Duchess's quietly triumphant expression.

She would have been less pleased if she had heard the Marshal's commands to an aide, given soon after she departed. All roads out of Havenor were to be scoured for a runaway daughter. If found, she was to be brought home to him, at once. An intelligent women herself, the Duchess had overestimated the Marshal's intelligence. Not an ambitious women, she had underestimated his ambition. So are many misread by other's lights. The Marshal did not for one moment believe that a family alliance to Prince Delganor could bring him, the Marshal, anything but good. The Duchess was obviously a woman to whom the covenants meant nothing. Her warnings were ridiculous, the result of pique or jealousy or female connivance. Women were always warning you against this or that. Genevieve's mother had been full of such warnings. No doubt the Duchess would have preferred the Prince for one of her own daughters. Perhaps she still did.

Having assumed this, the Marshal rested on the assumption as on a rock, without bothering to turn it over to see what lived beneath it. He

particularly did not ask whether the Duchess had a marriageable daughter, for he preferred not to know that she did not.

While all this scurry went on in the house of the Marshal, the Lord Paramount of Haven, guarded as always by two Aresians, sat down to a late breakfast, only to be interrupted by the arrival of Yugh Delganor, who seemed in an unusual state of annoyance.

"The girl's run off," the Prince said, with an angry grimace.

With well-feigned innocence, His Majesty looked up from his imported quail, served on a bed of Farsabian rice. "What girl?"

"The one we planned for me. Langmarsh's daughter. My listener heard the Duchess of Merdune telling the Marshal about it earlier this morning. Seemingly, I frightened her rather badly at dinner last night."

The Lord Paramount had known this for hours, but he did not say so. "Ah. Well! Does this upset your plans for her?"

The Prince snarled. "It could well do. Though I doubt she'll be hard to find. Her father's already sent people after her, as have I."

"Who did she elope with? That young man, the equerry, what's his name?"

"Colonel Leys? No." He barked laughter. "I wouldn't have minded if she'd eloped with someone. That would have been easy enough to fix. One of my men tells me that someone bought passage for a young woman on the Reusel packet, the someone much resembling Colonel Leys, so she's probably prevailed upon him to help her run off home to Langmarsh House."

The Lord Paramount mused, "Your business is scheduled for later this year, Delganor."

The Prince shrugged. "There's more than one way to crack a craylet, Your Majesty. So she's run off home. We'll give her a little time to calm down. Either her father will round her up, or you'll discover that she's displeased you by leaving without permission, and my men will find her for you. Under threat of royal displeasure, our subjects are usually biddable enough."

His Majesty nodded and smiled while marking down in memory what Delganor had just said. In the Lord Paramount's pocket was a small, off-world machine on which everything anyone said to him was recorded. In the Lord Paramount's luxurious rooms was another little machine into which, every evening, the Lord Paramount unloaded those parts of his day's record that qualified as "Delganor's presumptions." He did not wish

to forget even one of them, and certainly Delganor's use of the words "our subjects" was a presumption, if not a damned arrogance.

He smiled again, "You're very clever, Delganor. Really, extremely clever."

"Your Majesty is too kind," the Prince demurred, though with little sense of satisfaction. Of course he was clever. He was so clever that the former royal heir had died "accidentally," and this old fool thought it really had been an accident. When this old fool found himself dying earlier than expected, as the Prince planned he should, he'd probably think that an accident as well. Delganor liked making such plans, which he found juicy and savorsome in anticipation. So far, all his advancements had been covert. Covert they would continue to be until he himself was Lord Paramount.

"Will the Marshal confide to you about his daughter running off?" wondered the Lord Paramount in the same innocent tone. "Full of blustering apology?"

"He'd be a fool to put himself in the wrong," murmured the Prince. "Though his naïveté continues to surprise me. Even though he was orphaned at an early age and had no father or uncle to enlighten him, you'd think a man his age would have taken notice by now, would have asked a few questions, would have attended a few Tribunal meetings and started looking about for a candidate of his own. Instead he blunders about like an ape in an apiary, infuriating the inhabitants and missing all the sweetness! Well, if he takes good counsel, he'll not say a word. And later, when we get righteously angry at him, he'll be all surprised innocence, or do his best to act so."

"Ah," said the Lord Paramount, with every show of disappointment. "I had hoped we might have a bit of excitement out of it."

"Not soon." The Prince smiled grimly. "Eventually, yes, if Your Majesty would like to take part in the final act of our drama."

"Thank you, no," murmured the Lord Paramount, leaning his head on his hand and smiling a secretive, bland smile. "Not at my time of life. Thank you. No."

The Prince missed the secretive smile. The Aresian guards, who missed nothing that happened in that room, did not.

THE DUCHESS HAD PLANNED GENEVIEVE'S ESCAPE AS WELL AS SHE WAS ABLE; Garth Sentith was as appropriate an escort as could have been found even with longer notice; but however thoughtful and sensible the plan, it lacked the necessary redundancies to cope with disaster, and disaster struck before they were well gone from High Haven.

When they had come only a few miles outside Havenor, Genevieve's horse slipped on an icy rock and lamed the right front leg. Garth Sentith put Genevieve on his own horse, put the horse's pack and light saddle on his own back, and turned the lame horse back toward the city, letting it find its own way home, which it would in good time, lame or not. He would, he said, hire another horse at the next post.

The post was a considerable distance off. Their night's travel on foot brought them only partway to the border between High Haven and the Tail of Merdune, and they were both weary by the time light oozed up over the eastern hills. As soon as it was light enough to see by, Garth began looking for a place to hide Genevieve during the day-light hours.

"Do you think someone will be coming after me?" Genevieve asked.

"I don't know," he answered. "But if they do, we want to be prepared for it. The horse is the problem. It isn't easy to hide a horse, so I'll look for a place where I can be more or less out in the open with the horse and you can be well hid. That way, the horse is explained innocently enough, and since there's no connection between you and me, they're unlikely to suspect anything."

Genevieve agreed that this sounded sensible, and when they came across a wooded area at the foot of an east-facing cliff with a good many cavelets in it—though most of them were mere bubbles—they set up camp as Garth had suggested. The area was obviously often used by travelers, for there were circles of blackened rock, dried saplings laid across lower

branches to provide framework for shelters, and even a small stack of firewood ready collected under the lee of a large boulder. Genevieve selected a small cave hidden behind some boulders about twenty yards away, where she put her own saddle and pack.

At the back of the cave a fallen stone made a shadowed space, and she lit a lantern to scan for unwelcome inhabitants before unrolling her bedding there. The flame wavered and smoked, as though in a strong current of air. A few moments of poking and prying established that air was indeed coming from the back of the shadowed area where a cylindrical opening extended into the cliff, like the neck of a bottle. The air coming from this duct was surprisingly warm, which made her curious enough to squirm into it, pushing the lantern ahead of her. Two body lengths in, she found further movement blocked by a rusty grille some three feet across. Beyond it, something rustled and stilled, and rustled again.

She squirmed out and went to ask Garth to take a look at this. He cut a sapling and used it to push his own lantern in far enough to see the grille, took off his gloves to feel the air, and nodded thoughtfully a time or two.

"I'd say this could be a vent for the storage vaults below Havenor. Though they've no doubt grown in the telling, according to reliable people, they started out as extensive natural caverns that have been enlarged ever since the first settlers. I never thought much about it before, but it stands to reason they would need to let some air out and pull fresh air in. Or, the grille could have been put here in the long past to prevent someone's falling into a chasm with a hot spring. Either way, I see no reason you shouldn't take advantage of the warmth. You'll sleep better for it, won't you, Imogene?"

"Yes," she said, after a moment, recollecting that she was now Imogene. "But there's a sound. Like something moving."

"It's warm," he said. "And it's moist. No doubt siren-lizards or tivvies appreciate warmth, as you will if you put your bed in this recess. Tivvies are harmless and you'll be well hidden."

"You are welcome to share the warm," she said, smiling wearily at him. "It's long enough for both of us."

He patted her shoulder. "The horse won't fit, and we dare not leave the horse out of our calculations. No, the horse and I will be out there, and you'll be in here, safe, and we'll both get on with our journey as soon as conditions permit."

They shared bowls of soup beside Garth's fire. When he had finished,

Garth set his bowl on a convenient rock, leaned forward and said urgently, "Imogene, this unforeseen happening makes me believe we need an agreement in case of emergency. Your horse going lame has taught us that even good plans can go awry, so it would be best for us to be prepared."

"Of course," she said. "I understand."

"You are Imogene Sentith. You will need to remember your name, and that you are my eldest daughter and that I will be distraught over your absence. You have a brother, Ivan, and a sister, Ivy. Your brother is a stripling of fourteen, your sister a child of twelve."

"Do I look anything like your daughter?"

"No, my dear, you're much prettier, but then, no one here has ever seen Imogene."

"Why are you doing this, Honorable Sentith?"

"Not honorable, child, just plain Sentith, though I think you'd better get into the habit of calling me Papa."

"Papa," she said obediently, feeling the word twist upon her tongue as if it had changed identities. "And do you call me Imogene?"

"No, I call you Imma, and I hug you often, which you must not mind, for while I admire young women a good deal, I am faithful to my good wife, Ivalee, and I shall not bother you with unwanted attentions." He said this in a grave and bumbling voice, nodding his head, thus doubling his assurances.

"I didn't think you would." Genevieve smiled. "I should know about the town where we live, shouldn't I?"

"There is little to tell about Weirmills. It is in a valley protected from both warm southerly winds and cold northers by the surrounding mountains, but it receives a good deal of rain, which makes the meadows burst with bloom, a good thing for the business of a perfumer, which is what I am. Weirmills is a little place, getting its name from the great weir built across the river to provide power to the weaving mills on either side."

"And our house?"

"The shop, a small one, is in the front of the ground floor, with our kitchen and living room behind it. We sell dried herbs and fresh ones, plus all sorts of herbal and floral attars and oils and mixed fragrances. Upstairs are the bedrooms, four of them, one for you, one for Ivy, one for Ivan, and one for your mother and me. We have good plumbing in Weirmills, for our people are wise enough to know it does not take technology but only determination to have clean water and a sensible disposal of waste, so there is a bathhouse and flush latrine at the back."

"And what are we doing out here on the road, Papa?"

"Well, we're on our way back home from Upland, where I've been bargaining with the Glass Masters for several thousand bottles to be sent down the Merdune Lagoon in the spring."

"What sort of bottles?"

"This sort," he said, taking one from his pocket and passing it to her. The tiny thing was as long as her little finger, shaped like a teardrop stopped at the tip with a brilliant gem of colored glass through which the firelight glittered. "That's what they call their sparkle bottle. The stops come in different colors."

"So the Glass Master story is real?"

"Oh, yes, my dear. The story is real. When you must lie, my dear, lie as little as possible. That way you'll have the least to remember."

"And what did I do all day while you were meeting with the glass blowers?"

"You had a very bad cold, and you stayed the whole time in the little house I rented at the Crags—which is a kind of hostelry—nursing your poor stuffed-up head."

She laughed. "That's easy to remember. It was a dull little house with two bedrooms and a common room. I saw no one, did nothing, went nowhere, right?"

"Exactly. A dull little house with a smoky fireplace. You couldn't taste anything, so you weren't even hungry. And we arrived after dark, so no one saw you, and some days later, we left before dawn, so no one saw you then, either. If you wish, you may speak resentfully about all that, coming so far from Weirmills, to see so little."

He nodded, still thoughtful, while Genevieve made sure everything she had used was cleaned and put away. Garth, on the other hand, left his bowl and cup and spoon where they could be seen.

"You need to know the route," he said, as she was about to wish him good night. "The road we are on leads to Upland, with a fork to the right at the north pass road, a long, winding roadway to the coast, and south along the coast road is the little town of Midling Wells. If we are separated, one from the other, we will meet there, in Midling Wells, at Fentwig's house. And, if we are separated, you must think of some innocent way it could have happened."

"I will think of something if needed, and I will meet you in Midling Wells," she agreed, wondering how in heaven's name she was supposed to get there if separated from her only guide. "At Fentwig's House. Well then, good night."

"Good morning," he said, with a glance at the glowing sky. "Rest easy. I will wake you when it is safe to go on."

She went back to her cave, spread her bedding into the warm recess, and crawled into it gratefully. The recess had been smoothed, either by man or nature, and though the surface was hard, she soon fell asleep. Some hours later, she was wakened by voices coming from outside.

"Get up, I say. You! What's your name?"

"Why, sir, I am Garth Sentith."

"What are you doing here?"

"I'm on my way home to Merdune from a business trip to the Glass Masters in Upland."

"This isn't the road to Merdune! You should have taken the north pass road."

"If I'd gone directly, yes sir, but I stopped a day in Havenor, to buy a gift for my wife."

"And where's that?"

"In my pack, sir. And be careful with it, please, for it's breakable."

There was a moment's silence, during which Genevieve climbed out of her bedding to retrieve all of her belongings and bring them into her tunnel. From the light at the cave entrance, which fell high on the south side but not at all on the left, she thought it was probably midmorning.

"Pah, a looking-glass," said one of the voices.

The other said, "Have you seen anyone on the road? Particularly a young woman? On foot or ahorse?"

"No," said Garth, "but then, I've been asleep."

"Well, merchant, get yourself packed up. We're on our way north and we'll escort you to the north pass."

"I don't want to trouble you, sir. And I'd like a bit of breakfast before starting out . . ."

"Pack yourself up, I say, and go hungry until you're at the border. That is, unless you want to interfere with the orders of the Marshal . . ."

"And the Prince," said the other voice. "Both of 'em are set on finding this young person, and to do it ex-pee-dishus-lee, we're to clear the roads and keep them clear, all the way to the borders."

"That's it," said the first man. "Consider yourself part of the clearance."

"Of course, of course," said Garth.

The lighter voice said, "Meantime, we'd best look around. Be sure this one's alone."

"Oh, he's alone, right enough. One horse, one rider, one pack."

"Can't tell from that. He might be cleverer than he looks."

"It's you want to be cleverer. Go, waste your time, I don't care."

Panting with dismay, Genevieve, wriggled back toward the grille, pulling bedding and belongings along with her. It was farther than she had thought, but she kept wriggling feet first, deeper into the recess expecting to encounter the grille with her feet. Suddenly she realized there was nothing beneath her lower legs, nothing her feet could find on any side, and as she started to ease her way back, her ankles were firmly grasped by someone or something, and before she could make up her mind whether screaming would be a good thing or a bad thing, she was pulled down the tunnel and out, like a cork from a bottle, while someone whispered fiercely in her ear, "Shhh. Don't make a sound."

Since the someone was busy gagging her, there was no significant sound she could make. Her bedding was pulled down on top of her, and the saddle and pack on top of that, and she heard the unmistakable sound of metal being latched.

"There," said the voice in her ear, "the grille's locked! Even if they find the cave, they won't find you, not if you hush and quit struggling."

Genevieve reminded herself that she did not wish to be found by either the Marshal or the Prince, and stopped struggling.

Outside in the cave, someone bashed about. "Hey, Garton! Come see this!"

Other shouts, murmurs, finally the sound of someone approaching the grille. "It's shut off back here! There's a grille over it."

"Probably an old mine shaft," said the same voice that had accosted Garth.

"But it's warm, Garton."

"Thunkle, you're an idiot, you know that. Of course it's warm. There's warm springs all over High Haven. The whole valley was a volcano once."

"Oh," said Thunkle. "I forgot."

"Is it old? The grille?"

"It's rusty."

"Well, then. There's nobody there, is there?"

"No."

"Then come on. We've got this fellow to see to the border, and we don't want to waste any more time."

Sound receded. In the stillness, Genevieve felt herself carried, heaved, then dropped carelessly, her head crashing against an unyielding surface.

"Watch it," cried a voice. "She's not a sack of potatoes!"

"I tripped," said someone else, sulkily.

Genevieve didn't care. The blow had been the final insult, and she felt

herself going away, somewhere else, into a buzzing darkness where there was nothing at all to think about.

When she regained any perception at all, it was of movement, her body being slowly jostled as she was moved by wheels. She could not move or speak, but she could see:

Dim light far up and gray. Massive things at either side. Darkness mostly.

She could hear:

At least two wheels on the cart squeaked slightly, dissonantly, like an insect chirp. Slow drip of water into a pool, each plunking drop making its own tiny echo, the ripples spreading, reaching the edges and returning to intersect the new plunk to make an interference of wavelets. Something peeping, a lizard, perhaps, signaling others of its kind.

She was crumpled uncomfortably on the floor of a vehicle that moved among mountains, their edges obscuring then revealing the dismal light, like moons behind mist.

The place smelled of dust. As the vehicle trundled along, it created a little cloud of dust that went with them, enveloping them. The vehicle made a sudden turn, and her head banged against something hard. She whimpered.

"It's all right," said someone. "We won't hurt you."

She hadn't thought they would, until then. The reassurance had the opposite effect from the one intended. She was sure they would hurt her, or that one of them would. The one who had spoken. There was something viscous in that voice, a gelatinous insincerity. And the other one? If the first did something evil to her, would the other concur? Or watch, interested? Passive? She trembled.

"No," said a younger voice. "We really won't hurt you. You don't need to shiver all over like that. The only reason we tied you up was so you wouldn't make any noise."

A rough hand patted her, as one might pat a dog. This touch did what the voice had not, reassured her. It wasn't the touch of a . . . well, that kind of touch. She turned her head a little, letting one eye see higher up. Shadows against that far gray light. A massive carved throne, high in the sky against the light. A curlicued bedstead? A rocking horse? A great swag of bunting from one precipice to another. A man up there, poised to leap. No, it had to be a statue of a man, holding a bow, a man with wings holding a bow, dark against the high gray light.

None of it made any sense. She relaxed, letting it happen. The water sound grew louder, *plunket . . . plunket . . . plunket . . .* and the wheels began

to swish through a shallow pool, a wide, wide pool that reflected light from above, ripples fleeing from their wheels. Obviously, they were underground. In a cavern. Just as those men had said, the ones who'd been looking for her.

Far above her, to one side, a balloon hung limply from the ceiling, its basket dangling, slightly tipped. She had seen a balloon like that at a provincial festival, filled with hot air, round as an apple against the blue. People had paid to go up in it, to see the world from on high. It had to be pulled down by a capstan, but it always floated up again, when the bellows were applied to its little fire basket full of coals. She had much wanted to go up, but her father had said no. Such activities were for commoners, those easily amused by novelty.

The light grew slightly brighter the farther they went. They passed a precipice of doors stacked one on another, some upright, most recumbent, doors paneled, painted, carved; doors of gilt and metal, reaching from the level of her eyes into the far, dim upness of the place. They entered a chasm between escarpments of carpets, rolled, flat, folded, draped down the sides, lengthy runners twisted into rough garlands hung in catenary curves up the sides of the carpet cliffs. Then, abruptly, they left the rug chasm and came into an open space.

The rough hand returned to take her gag away. "There now. Is that better?"

"Who?" she murmured. "Who?"

"Bottoms," he said cheerfully, as he untied her. "Jeorfy Bottoms. My friend here is Zebulon. Zebulon Coffin. Not a cheerful name, is it? Bottoms now, that's cheerful. Always get a laugh out of Bottoms."

He busied himself with much tinkling and rattling. Light happened, a lantern, and in its orange glow she saw she was on a flat platform with a seat at one side and a control lever at one end. From the open side, two men in gray coveralls regarded her intently, the younger one with amusement and interest, the pudgy, older one with an avid stare that made her apprehensive.

She gulped. "I'm Imogene Sentith," she said.

"Oh, right," said the younger one, with a demonic grin. "And I'm the Lord Paramount of Haven."

"And I am his Prime Minister," said the other, with a sneer. "We heard you, you know. Talking out there. You're not his daughter. You're just pretending, and we want to know why."

"Why do you want to know?" she cried. "It isn't your business."

"Is so," said the older of the two. "Anything goes on in this cavern is my business! This is my place! My job! And you came poking into it."

"She didn't, you know," said Jeorfy, in a conversational tone. "Don't get all in an uproar, Zeb. We pulled her in."

"What is this place?" she whispered.

"The Lord Paramount's cavern," said Zeb. "Where he keeps the things he gets from off-world." He sniggered. "Where I keep 'em, for I'm the actual keeper. Him," and he jutted an elbow toward Jeorfy, "he's my assistant, and he's just arrived."

Jeorfy drew himself up, raised one hand, and declaimed:

"After years without a word, I was suddenly transferred. They removed me from the archives, where I'd spent eleven years, and I'll hate them all their damn lives for they took me from my peers."

He stopped, grinning like a maniac. "If it weren't for Zebulon, my dear, I'd have been here totally alone."

"If you don't quit versifying stupidities, Zebulon will transfer you violently," growled the other, over his shoulder. "It's damned annoying, Bottoms!"

Jeorfy grinned at her again, but fell silent as they rumbled among further promontories of goods and furniture, shortly arriving at the door of a small room built of packing cases against the cavern wall. Genevieve pulled herself upright, assisted by Jeorfy, and stood dazedly looking about herself at endless stacks of cartons and boxes and crates towering into vanishing points against the vault and its widespread galaxies of dim lights.

She shook her head at the monstrous accumulation. "I thought there were very few things bought off-world."

Zebulon laughed, a dry, scraping sound. "Oh, woman! That's for public consumption, that little tale. Why, the Lord Paramount buys all sorts of things off-planet. Piles of them. Stacks of them. Look at them! And this is only one cavern! There's others! Bigger!"

Genevieve stepped down from the vehicle, dusting herself off, and Jeorfy led her into the small room. It was warm, dry, and furnished with several well-padded chairs and a neat bed against the wall. It was also well lighted by a sun-bright panel set into its ceiling, and Genevieve sat in the chair beneath it, grateful for the outdoors feeling it gave her. Though the cavern was huge, it had a claustrophobic, tomblike atmosphere.

She slapped at her neck, where something clung, dashing the thing to the floor. Jeorfy grabbed it up, in the moment, tossing it out into the

cavern and closing the door behind it. The door was covered in mesh, not metal or fabric, but something she had not seen before.

"What was it?" she cried, feeling her neck and bringing blood-stained fingers before her eyes. "It bit me!"

"Cave-lizzy," said the older man. "When they're tiny, they'll bite, you give them a chance. Unless you teach 'em not."

"Like this," said Jeorfy, going to the door and whistling. At once there were several tiny forms clinging to the mesh, and Genevieve went to look at them, jeweled little creatures, ruby and sapphire and emerald, with frills around their necks, webs between their legs and sharp little muzzles, siren-lizards in miniature. Jeorfy went to a cupboard and took out a packet, unwrapped the dripping contents, opened the door a crack and held it out. His hand was covered at once with a whistling, squeaking, chomping horde of the little creatures.

"Every so often, the grown-up ones come into the caves to make their stinking nests and lay their eggs," said Jeorfy, conversationally. "They hatch into these little ones, and at this age they're supposed to eat fish. These caves used to be full of rivers, and the rivers were full of fish. But when the Lord Paramount drained the caverns, oh, long ago, the fish were all drained away somewhere else. So, these hatchlings, they'll eat us instead, or we could poison them all, but that'd wipe out the big lizards, and the nobles like lizard skin boots, so, we feed 'em instead."

"What do you feed them?"

"Fish. It comes in from outside somewhere. And it's only every ten or twelve years that the big lizards reproduce. This time next year, all these little ones will be grown up and flown out into the world. The grown ones are aquatic. It's only when they're little they can fly."

She smoothed back her hair, settled her collar, and said firmly, "You know, I have to get back to Papa."

"He's not your papa," said Zebulon. "And you don't need to get back to him just yet. Why, you're the only amusement that's come along in ten or twelve years."

Jeorfy gave Zebulon a puzzled look before turning to Genevieve once more. "So, tell us your real name, pretty girl."

"Henrietta Hazelbine," she said. "Daughter of the Count of Ob." There was a county Ob in Frangia, but so far as she knew, there was no Count of Ob, nor had there been for many years. Still, it was worth a try.

"And who are you running from?" asked Zeb.

"A nobleman who wants to marry me, but I don't like him."

"Aha!" said Jeorfy. "There! It's the Prince, I'll wager. Didn't I say! He's after another wife, isn't he? That's it, isn't it?"

"Why do you assume so?" she asked, astonished.

"Because all the oldies, every so often, they seem to get remarried, or they adopt a niece, or they take on a mistress. He's only had three wives, so maybe he needs another one. He hasn't had one for fifty years or more."

"Fifty years?" she faltered. "How old is he?"

"A hundred eighty, a hundred ninety, somewhere in there," said Jeorfy. "You'd be the fourth."

"They all died, I know that," she said, remembering her father's anger when she had asked about Delganor's wives. "I only heard about two of them."

"It was probably the first one you didn't hear about. She was the only one who got away, I have no doubt."

"Jeorfy!" threatened Zebulon. "Talk like a sensible person!"

"Got away?" asked Genevieve.

"Ran away, eluded, absconded, disappeared," said Jeorfy, making a face at his companion. "Felt that she'd be safer in a wig and a false beard!" He nodded slowly. "That's merely a guess. At any rate, he never found her."

"Where did you find out all this?" she asked.

Jeorfy cocked his head impudently, "A man came to the archives, with very charming ways. I learned after he'd left me his name was Aufors Leys. I let him use the archives to look up some history, and what he didn't say about it spurred my curiosity."

"Enough. One more and I'm leaving you here alone!" shouted Zebulon, his face red with fury.

Jeorfy mimed apology, bowing, wringing his hands in pretend-distress, then turned to say cheerfully to Genevieve, "The Colonel was far better at dissimulation than I. When I tried it, they caught me at it. I'm down here as punishment."

Keeping a blank face, she asked, "How did you know I was up there?"

Jeorfy said, "Zebulon was just showing me around and we happened to be there. That grille is the back gate to this cavern, so to speak . . ."

"Among others," muttered Zeb.

Jeorfy paid no attention to the interruption. "Of course, the current powers that be, up there, don't know there's any way out except the locked gate they put me through. They think we're cut off from the world down here, incommunicado. Which is why I'm here. I know too much. Or they think I do."

Zeb mused, as though talking to himself, "I like that particular way out. There's lots of travelers come by there. I can come out at night and listen to them. I hear all kinds of interesting things."

Genevieve rubbed her forehead wearily, trying to decide whether she should insist they let her go or simply go along for a while longer. Jeorfy accurately read her expression.

"Don't worry, girl," said Jeorfy. "Your so-called papa isn't up there anymore. He's been escorted to the border. You agreed to meet in Midling Wells, and that's where we'll take you. We can, can't we, Zeb?"

"Near to there," said the other, reluctantly.

Jeorfy nodded. "Your so-called papa isn't fool enough to wander around in the wilderness just hoping you'll show up, and with the number of men on the roads, he won't have a chance to come back here."

"Is this where you live?" she asked, looking around the small room with something like dismay. She didn't want to stay for a long time, and it would be very crowded with all three of them in it.

"This is just a rest stop," Zebulon said. "I fixed me up a bunch of them, here and there, like plums in a pudding. So I can stop and be comfortable whenever I want."

"How do you live? What do you eat?"

Zebulon sniggered, grasped her by the arm and dragged her back onto the cart. This time she sat on the seat next to Jeorfy while Zebulon drove them down dark chasms between huge, dusty piles of merchandise, other shadowed aisles squirming away on either side like wormtracks. Near the bottom of one stack a crate had been opened, and Jeorfy leapt from the machine long enough to pull a container from the open crate and place it on their wagon.

"Zybod ham," crooned Zebulon. "From the planet Kuflyk. This ham, it's in perpetual preservation. You'd think it'd taste like dust, but it's good, oh, very good. It's why I stay, I think. The food. This ham with goat cheese and fresh bread—well, bread that tastes fresh—is remarkable. Quite remarkable."

The look he gave her was a hungry one, and he licked his lips in a lecherous way. Genevieve kept her face turned resolutely away from his as they went on. They circumnavigated a continent of carved furniture, beneath tottery mountains of marquetry, past veins of veneer, lodes of inlay, eroded towers of tapestry and trapunto over sheer cliffs of stacked cabinetry, bronze fittings, and mirrored surfaces, all scaled and corrupted by time. They slid beneath a leaning tower of paintings, gilt frames jutting like angled crystals, stretched canvases slit and tattered into dust-stiffened

stalactites. They passed cataracts of chandeliers, tumbling gold and prismed glass, shining here and there as a vagrant beam reflected through the gray film. They eased along the bottom of a chasm, crowded on either side by great broken cartons full of crystal and porcelain and lizard nests, the packing material sodden with the excrement of the generations of babies who had hatched there.

Speaking of nesting gave Jeorfy an idea. "We should get this girl a bed," he announced.

"Next left," said Zeb, and they swerved around a corner to stop at a topless pile of mattresses, the bottom ones squashed flat as paper beneath the enormous weight of all those vanishing into the gloom above. Zebulon scrambled high onto a plateau, dust billowing around him as he kicked several mattresses from the dusty layers. The first ones plummeted and burst on impact, but the last few, with surfaces almost clean, landed more or less in one piece.

"What's it all for?" cried Genevieve, when they had loaded the best one aboard the platform. "The Lord Paramount couldn't use all this in a million years."

"Not likely," snarled Zebulon, returning to his lever, "besides which, we've got perfectly good mattress-makers in Haven. And chandelier-makers. And furniture-makers."

"I think I've figured it out," said Jeorfy. "The Lord Paramount has little enough to amuse himself, so he sees something in the off-world catalogs that catches his eye, and he orders it, that's all. All the planets send their catalogs to the Lord Paramount. I've seen 'em, because when he was finished with 'em, they brought 'em to be filed in the archives. Catalogs for food, fabric, machines. Weapons. Gadgets. Even *pets!* Zeb says there's a whole aisle of pets in stasis down here. Animals you've never seen!"

Genevieve heard this with a feeling of certainty. Jeorfy was right. She herself had seen the catalogs stacked around the Lord Paramount's high seat. "What does he trade for all this?" she asked wonderingly. "This is a poor world."

"Now that's what I'd like to know," murmured Zeb, with a leer in her direction. "I suppose Jeorfy'd like to know that, too."

"I've heard it said it's pearls," she offered, pretending not to notice the leer.

"No," said Jeorfy, shaking his head. "I've heard that, but it's not pearls. When I saw all this down here, I wanted to know what we traded, oh, yes, so I looked it up in the archives. Archives was mute, didn't give a toot."

Zeb snarled, "Trade goods is something ordinary folk aren't allowed to know about. Just the nobles know about trade goods."

"How could that be?" Genevieve asked. "I mean, I'm a noble, and I don't know anything about anything. And it's not as if I can do anything that ordinary people don't know about. I mean, my maid knows when I take a deep breath! She knows more about what's going on than I do. Nobles are surrounded all the time by ordinary folk."

"I can tell you one bunch, one place they're not surrounded by commoners," remarked Jeorfy, with a significant nod. "And that's the Tribunal."

"The Covenanters? I didn't know that."

"It's true," remarked Jeorfy. "I was surprised when I read about it, but that's how it is. Whoever installed the inventory system down here connected it to the archive machines upstairs. Zebulon didn't even know that until I came. The nobles, the Lord Paramount, and the Prince and all, even they don't know that! So, I've been digging around, and I came across some Tribunal edicts forbidding common people from going anywhere near the Tribunal."

"What do you mean, the systems are connected?" Genevieve asked.

"It means from down here we can read anything that's in the archive machines except what they've locked up since they caught me looking. They find out I can still get into those machines, they'd disconnect us in a minute, or kill us."

Zebulon made a sharp right turn and headed off in the new direction at top speed. They had come to a section of the cavern where the crates stacked on either side were huge, each one towering three and four men high. Genevieve cocked her head to read the lettering on them as they went past. BIOSTASIS, they read, followed by a code number.

"What's Biostasis?" she asked.

Zeb answered. "That's what we told you. Pets. Animals. I think the Lord Paramount wanted to have a zoo, so he bought all kinds of animals, but never set the zoo up. The animals are in stasis. You open the box, the insides go to work, and out it comes, alive. I'll show you."

He stopped the wagon, and beckoned her to follow him as he wriggled his way into the enormous stack. He stopped before a fogged window and rubbed it clear. "See!"

She looked in, seeing forms, fur, perhaps the edge of a wing? Maybe. Another window showed an unmistakable antler, huge. There were a dozen cases of that particular code number, all from the same shipper. From one case an eye looked at her, unmistakably.

"It's looking at me," she murmured to Jeorfy.

"Can't," he said. "It's asleep."

She felt the look. The thing might be asleep, and in that case it was dreaming her, but it definitely perceived her, one way or the other!

She leaned closer, looking deep. She saw an ear, trembling. Perhaps she did not see it tremble, perhaps she only felt it, the fragile tympanum responding to a sound so deep she could not hear it. "Something's talking to it," she said firmly.

"Nonsense," said Jeorfy, coming to thrust his face in beside hers and peer into the case. "Who could be talking to it?"

"I don't know," she murmured. Still, she was sure the thing in the crate knew she was here, and knew something was talking to it, and was fully aware, though perhaps only in dream, of what was going on. She backed off to estimate the size of the crate. Very, very large. The size of an elephant, perhaps, one of the old, now-departed animals of Old Earth.

"Come on," said Jeorfy, uncomfortably. "It's the same with the war machines. The Lord Paramount has a lot of them down here, too, and they're sort of alive. They take up a lot of space."

"What are war machines for?"

"They've been here since the year one. Inventory has 'em listed as protection against invasion. Like from off-world."

"Does my . . . ah, that is, do the armies know about them?"

"Nobody knows about them. The weapons they know about are simple by comparison, and cheaper. They're all stored up from here, on the first level under Havenor, where they're easier to get to."

She cried, "We're not a rich world! Why would anyone invade us? And who buys such things?"

Jeorfy shrugged. "The Lord Paramount or the Prince would be my guess. Or some oldie duke."

"What do you mean exactly, when you say 'oldie'?" asked Genevieve.

"Someone a hundred fifty, two hundred years old," snarled Zeb. "Like the Prince and the Lord Paramount and all the Dukes, living off the rest of us, like a vampire." He made another swift turn and brought the vehicle to a halt at the end of a long line of vehicles, some large, some small.

She turned, eyes wide. "My . . . ah father's a Count. He's nowhere near that old."

"Maybe he's not old enough yet." Jeorfy made a face. "According to the archives, they turn into oldies later."

"How old do they get?"

"Oh, two or three hundred. Maybe more."

Genevieve stood to one side, lost in wonderment, while the men re-

moved the cargo from the carrier and carried it into a nearby room, one much like the previous chamber except that this one had been profession- ally built with stout masonry walls and a 'pitched, tiled roof. From the large combined office-cum-parlor a short corridor extended past a kitchen, a toilet, a bathroom, two bedrooms, and a number of empty living spaces, all of them brightly lighted and well ceiled against the dust. In one of the empty rooms Jeorfy placed the mattress they had salvaged and put Gene- vieve's belongings upon it.

They returned to the largest chamber. "Our official post," said Jeorfy, gesturing at the wall, which was lined with screens and panels. "Those are the inventory machines."

Zeb said, "Everything the Lord Paramount ever bought's supposed to be listed there." He sniggered, unpleasantly, as seemed to be his habit as a kind of punctuation to his private thoughts.

"What are you supposed to be doing here?" she asked curiously, drop- ping into a chair.

"It's just ordinary maintenance," Jeorfy answered, with a slightly worried sidelong glance at his companion. "Every little while there's something new that comes down on the elevators, and we're supposed to put it in new stacks, and number the stacks and enter the numbers in the machines. And the machines keep track of how long stuff has been here, and lists off the things that have to be destroyed because they're no good anymore . . ."

"Or dangerous," said Zeb.

"Right, so when the machine tells us something has run out of time, we're supposed to take a suitable lifter and load whatever expired and move it through one of the tunnels to a fire chasm, where we push it over."

"And what do you get for all that?" she wondered.

Zeb twisted his mouth into a particularly nasty smile. "Nothing that makes it worthwhile. I tell you, I dream of getting out of here!" He said it angrily, with another of those leering, hungry glances at Genevieve. She looked away.

Jeorfy caught this and said quickly, "Well there is another good thing they don't know about."

"And that is?" sneered Zeb.

"The tunnels. They go everywhere. We could go to Merdune, under- ground. Hell, we could probably go to Sealand, underground, under Ha- venpool, the whole way."

"Except you'd starve," said Zeb. "The vehicles won't go that far without refueling, and the only power source is right here. You'd have to walk, and it'd be a damn long walk."

"So you can take me underground to a place near Midling Wells?" asked Genevieve.

"Somewhere near there," said Zeb, turning away to busy himself at the kitchen cabinets.

"Don't worry, pretty girl," said Jeorfy, with a troubled glance at his companion. "We're not monsters, not sex maniacs, not dreadful anything but dreadful bored, probably."

Zebulon made no comment, merely continued putting together a meal while Jeorfy asked Genevieve questions about everything under the sun. By the time dinner was ready, he had elicited more than she had intended to tell about her schooling, her reading, and her life in general.

Genevieve, she cautioned herself. You're tired and you're spouting. You're chatting. You're doing everything wrong! The self-caution came too late. She had already mentioned her feelings of loathing regarding Prince Delganor, an indiscretion that stopped Zebulon's activities momentarily while he stared at her with his leering smile.

When they were seated around the table, Jeorfy asked. "These off-world publications you read at school? They weren't catalogs?"

"No, no. They were accounts of current happenings."

"Did you notice, were any of them from Ares? Or Verben's World? Or Chamis?"

"There was a story about Chamis," she said, her forehead furrowed. "About the world becoming . . . depopulated. I mean, it's going down-hill. Why?"

Jeorfy shook his head, puzzled. "I've been looking back over the records that were kept, oh, say three or four hundred years ago. Before Marwell was elevated, it was Lord Paramount Gorbagger. He bought little stuff from about a dozen different worlds. And so did Marwell, but he bought a lot. Then as time went on, Marwell kept right on buying more and more, but from fewer and fewer planets. Now he gets most of his stuff from Ares. Including his bodyguards."

"Some settlement worlds don't make it," Genevieve acknowledged. "Actually, Haven is one of the older settled worlds that are still going. Ares is one that's having a hard time, like Chamis. People can't figure why some worlds make it and some don't. It's as though some worlds lack something people need in order to live, but no one knows what it is."

"Now that's interesting." Jeorfy frowned. "I'm going to use the machines to look that up. I'm going to order some of those publications, too."

"You don't have a purchase order," snarled Zeb.

"I can make one up," said Jeorfy. "You think anybody's keeping track?

That's a laugh. I can fake a number and then take the stuff out of the shipment when it arrives."

Genevieve put down her fork. "How does stuff get ordered and come here for storage? Where is it brought? Who handles it?"

Jeorfy said, "Stuff gets ordered from the palace. I used to do it myself. Then it gets paid for somehow, before it comes or at the same time as. The smaller stuff is delivered down at Bliggen and sent up here on barges and wagons. That gets sent down the chutes. But Zeb says huge stuff is always landed right here in High Haven. After dark, by some kind of beam or other that sets it right down on the elevators."

"Hasn't been any huge stuff for decades," mumbled Zeb. "Those big animals was the end of it."

Genevieve put her hand to her mouth, only half-hiding a yawn. "It's very interesting Mr. Coffin, but I'm so . . . I'm so tired. I only had about an hour last night, and all that running and hiding and riding . . ."

"Surely, surely," said Zebulon. "You go ahead. Jeorfy and me, we need some sleep, too. Been a long day."

She nodded her thanks, finished the food on her plate, then excused herself. Within moments, she was lying on top of the bed they had brought for her, her bedding pulled over her, soundly asleep.

Outside, in the other room, Jeorfy asked again, in a worried tone, "We will take her where she's going, won't we?"

"Oh, you can say that, yes," Zeb answered, not meeting his eyes. "We'll definitely take her where she's going."

On that same high vantage point where Aufors Leys had once stood to contemplate his relationship with the Marshal's daughter, Ogberd Ygdaleson, Captain of the Lord Paramount's Aresian mercenaries, Sometime-General of the Aresian army, leaned upon the railing in off-duty laxity, surreptitiously wiping his eyes. He did not see his brother ascending the steep flights behind him; he did not hear him until Lokdren was within a pace of him.

"Brother? Og?" Lokdren murmured, unsure of his ground under these unusual circumstances. Ogberd was not an emotional man. His men had never seen a tear in his eye. "What's happened? Have we had news from home?"

Ogberd took a deep breath, shivered all over like a fly-bit horse, and nodded, wordlessly. He wiped his eyes once more, put his kerchief back into his sleeve, gritted his teeth, and said between them, "Granpa. He's gone into it."

"Aaaah," said the other, with a grimace. "How far gone?"

"He's at the wandering stage. Ma says he keeps looking for something. Granma asks him what it is, and he shakes his head. He doesn't know. Something. Something he's lost. She says he keeps listening for something. She asks what he's listening for. He says he used to hear it, he doesn't hear it anymore. They've done everything they can think of. The Chief hired some off-world quacks to take a look at the situation. They came up with pure vacuum. Not an ion. Gorge and vomit! If we'd just been faster!"

"Come on, Og. We've tried everything anybody's even thought of."

"Then we should have thought of something else," Ogberd mumbled.

Lokdren shook his head. "I've got dust in my ears from the nothing that's come into them, so its hard to know where else we could have done."

Ogberd sniffed, staring at the horizon. "I told them at home nothing was bein' said. Father was raging. He said we just weren't listenin'."

"Ah?"

"So I told him we had been listenin'. I told him the Prince is conspirin' to overthrow the Lord Paramount. I told him the Lord Paramount knows all about it. I told him the Prince murdered the Lord Paramount's son, first in line for the throne. I told him the Lord Paramount did the same to his own brother who was conspirin' to replace him. I told him they treat their women like so many chessmen, move them here, move them there, wed them off to this one or that one. I've listened, I told him, and there's plenty being said, just nothin' about what we need to know."

Lokdren nodded slowly and came to lean beside the other man, the railing protesting gently at his added weight. "And we've got listeners planted all over Havenor and Mahahm and half the provinces by now, but they don't yield anything either!"

Ogberd nodded. "I told Father he could always gamble on finding out after instead of beforehand."

"Last report said the birthrate's down again."

"Gorge and vomit, man," blurted Ogberd. "You think I've somehow missed that?"

"Sorry. Didn't mean you'd missed anything."

"Nobody means. Damn it. Why in hell is Ares going down the drain-hole and this damn world bobbing along like a cork? Any one of our people would make five of these Havenites! And our women! These women don't even start to measure up. I ask you! I've wracked my brain. You think it's only this stuff we're after? Stuff the people don't even seem to

know about? Somehow, after all this time, that's getting to seem less and less likely."

"It's what everybody at home thinks." Lokdren spoke in a soothing tone. "It's what the Chief thinks. When the Chief thinks beefsteak, better we don't go around talking chicken."

Ogberd lowered his voice. "Yes, right, but you know, I've been wondering lately. Here's all these women going missing. What if we've got the wrong end of the stick. Like, what if the stuff doesn't come from this world at all? What if the Lord Paramount is trading women off-world for it?"

Silence. A long brooding silence, until Lokdren said, "Well, then hell, we'll take the women over and find out where they're bein' sold, and we'll do the sellin' ourselves."

The two men leaned together, bearing a weight of woe. When they left, a person moved from a cleft in the rock where he had stood throughout their meeting. Veswees. He stood looking after the two men, pondering, going over in his mind all that they had said.

It meant something to him even now. When he could get some time in the library files, he felt it would mean even more.

Genevieve wakened in the dark, too late to struggle, already gagged, already mostly tied. She struggled against bonds being tightened, and went on struggling against being lifted from her bed, carried and dumped unceremoniously onto a cart. She held her breath in hope as her abductor went away, but he returned to place something beside her. When the platform moved into a better light, she saw that it was her baggage, everything she had brought with her when she arrived. The driver was Zebulon, a strangely elated Zebulon, shifting from foot to foot and humming under his breath. When they had gone some way, he began to sing.

"Take her where she's going, yes, we'll take her to and froing, and I'm the only one who'll know that's not where she planned to go, oh, no, oh, no . . ." He cackled, a high, manic giggle that went on endlessly, trailing away only to repeat itself once, twice, a dozen times more. When it ended at last, Zebulon wiped his face on his sleeve and muttered,

"He's not the only rhymer, is he? Not him. Well, we'll just say she ran off. Fell in a chasm. He'll never know. He'll never know. And we'll get . . . oh, a good price for her. They'll want her. They're looking for her. Hide her away for a while. She's got fat on her. She won't starve in

a week, no, not a week. Even a month, maybe. Water, that'd be the problem. We'll, I'll water her now and again, that's what."

She wrenched her hands, trying to get them apart. They were tied too snugly. Her knees and ankles were flexed and tied. Wherever he was taking her, she had no choice but to go along.

"Water her now and again," hummed Zebulon. "Now and again."

LORD SOLVEN, EARL OF RUCKWARD, WAS IN A FURY. EVEN IN A MAN KNOWN for irritability, his present rage was extraordinary. It had to do, everyone knew, with the Lady Lyndafal, Countess Ruckward, who had put the new baby on her shoulder, walked down from Ruckward House to the shore, and gone out sailing with the child as she had often done in all weathers with her older daughter. This time, however, she had disappeared and had quite possibly drowned.

There were those who had seen her go and thought it foolish of her, just days from childbed as she was. Still, she habitually sailed around the bay, or across to Seapasture, the nearest of the Randor Isles, a lovely parklike place with grassy banks grazed by shaggy, long-horned sweet-breathed cattle. No one wondered at her doing it, for she did it all the time, and since the baby had come, she had taken the baby, too, saying the baby liked it, and it was true the baby stopped crying the moment her basket went in the boat, seeming to rejoice in the rocking motion and the chuckle of the water. So, Lady Lyndafal and the baby went out sailing, and the little white sail went back and forth and back and forth, and then away behind the island, and then out and back behind the island again until nobody watched it anymore and besides, why should they?

Come along dusk, people began to wonder who'd seen her last, and then come dark and they began to worry that nobody had seen her for hours, and then come deep dark and people began to shout and start running about, even before the Earl knew of it and fell to cursing and threatening. Hadn't he put all his men into boats, hunting her? Hadn't he screamed down the heavens, looking for her? Him, who hadn't looked at her twice in the months before the child was born?

Well, indeed he had. He sent a boat out to scour Seapasture Island for her, which was not so easy as one might think, for it was dark with no moon and a veil of wispy cloud hiding even the stars, and at the first

scrape of a hull on the beach, the shaggy cows that pastured there gathered around and demanded to be given something good, their noses pushing wetly and their long horns clacking, immovable as rocks. Cows and dark together brought the endeavor to naught but effort wasted and more screaming threats from the Earl.

On the morrow, they tried again and were able to confirm that she was not on Seapasture Island. So they went on to Little Swamp Island, the next island in the chain, though it was impossible to search the island thoroughly, full of trees as it was, trunks growing out of the water and dropping stems down from their branches to make the whole an impenetrable tangle. After sailing around it and shouting until everyone was hoarse, they decided she wasn't there, either. The third island out was much too far out for her to have sailed before she vanished, so it was obvious she couldn't be there. By evening, the search was given up.

How tragic, cried those who enjoyed conjecture. How tragic there'd been a waterspout, or a wind gust, or the baby had fallen in, or she'd tipped the boat over trying to save the baby, or she'd gone in for a swim (though she'd never been known to do any such thing) and the boat had sailed off without her. How tragic, said the sentimentalists, that it had happened just when the Earl had announced his intention of taking her on a wonderful trip down to that marvelous resort on the Plains of Bliggen.

No matter what the intentions had been, they'd been blown off the parapet and into the moat, and here was Earl Solven in a temper that couldn't be dealt with, not by anybody sane at any rate. It was to the tune and tempo of such turmoil that the people of Ruckward passed the first day and second night after the Countess's disappearance.

By which time the cause of all this annoyance, the woman who would call herself Bessany Blodden, was working her little boat out of a tangle of trees on the east side of the fourth island out from county Ruckward, where she had been since the previous evening.

Lyndafal had been afraid the child might cry in the night when, with sound traveling so far over water, it could lead people in her direction. The baby, however, had been hungry whenever she was not asleep, which kept her busy rooting at the nipple like a little pig, grunting contentedly and otherwise quiet as could be in her mother's arms while Lyndafal waited for first light to take advantage of the wind and get herself beyond finding. She figured she had four more days to make it the rest of the way east to Ramspize Point, where, pray heaven, someone would be waiting for her.

Just now her greatest worry was not herself or the baby in the basket but her other daughter, Evaline, left at Ruckward Manor with Dora. Two

years old, Evaline. Too headstrong and noisy to bring on this trip without risking all their lives, but otherwise sweet and dear and all too vulnerable. Well, Alicia would soon hear of Lyndafal's "disappearance." She would come to Ruckward to beg Evaline's company for a time. The Earl had never paid much attention to Evaline. He wouldn't care where the child went, so, pray heaven, Evaline would be taken back to Merdune where she'd be safe. If she ever could be!

Lyndafal had thought she herself was safe. She had believed it, utterly. She had convinced her mother.

"He loves me," she had said of the Earl, who had come courting at the school she attended in Baiverberg, introduced to her there by the Duke of Merdune, Lyndafal's step-father.

"He may think so," her mother had whispered. "I am sure he wants you."

"No, Mama, he really loves me. He loved his first wife, too, but she died. He's a good man, really he is."

Her mother had not answered, had merely stared at her, as though looking into a crystal ball, trying to find a separate dweller within, someone who might respond independently, differently. "Have you had a . . . vision of your being married to him?" This mentioning of visions was a rare thing. The Duchess did not have the talent, though her mother had had it. Lyndafal never knew whether her mother envied the talent or rued it, so they spoke of it seldom.

"Mama, the only visions I've had about me are sailing in a little boat with my children." Not children, precisely. Child, but it was the same thing. She wanted half a dozen, at least.

The Duchess's eyes were teary as she said, "I wish Gardagger had not introduced you to Earl Solven, for I believe you are too young. Still, you want children, and having them is easier when one is young. Oh, Lyndafal. I wish your grandmother were alive to counsel us both. I'll not stand in your way, but be careful."

"I will be, Mama. And Solven will take good care of me."

He had been ardent, and she had loved their lovemaking. He had been attentive, and she had loved that, too. And when the ardor waned with her first pregnancy, she had said to herself, well, it is appropriate at this time. The newness wears off, but he loves me none the less. And Evaline had been born, and there had been that joy, and then she became pregnant with this little one.

When had she realized that she was no longer safe? When had she understood that she never had been? Was it the cool way that Solven had

spoken to her during this last pregnancy, a kind of terminal detachment in his voice. Was it the way he had stopped looking at her, as though he was trying to forget she was there. Was it his avoidance of those times when they had formerly been alone together, as at breakfast or during late afternoon walks in the garden. Suddenly he had been very busy morning and night with his estate men. Suddenly he had had many trips to take, here or there.

Had she been convinced of her danger that time she heard him speaking with the heir to Ruckward, his son by his first wife, referring to Lyndafal as, "The woman, Lyndafal."

She had heard him use that same tone in speaking of a mangled dog that had had to be put down. "The bitch, Runner." In his mouth it was a knell. It had chilled her. She had told herself she was being foolish. She had told herself she was simply imagining things. Pregnant women did imagine things!

Then, only then, the vision had come, herself lying on dry soil, her cheek pressed into the grit, the sun burning the skin of her back, her head tipped down so she could see the gush of blood soaking into the soil. Near her, a circle of men, passing her little child among them, talking in low voices.

And from somewhere near, her husband's voice, aware but untroubled, in that same tone of detachment.

"So. It is done."

And a strange voice answering. "Congratulations on your ascension, Solven. It has been well done. And here is another who will be candidate for you . . ."

Lyndafal had wakened with the dream fully in her mind. She had taken no time to consider its meaning. She had not been dead in the dream, her child had not been dead, but the tone of it had been enough. If death was not present, it was not far off. She knew an absolute truth with a part of her mind that was not accessible to reason. She either accepted the warning her vision had given her or she ignored it at her peril.

If the dream had not been enough, the following day might have warned her, for on that very morning Solven had begun wooing her anew, hugely pregnant as she was. He had apologized for having been distracted. He had apologized for having neglected her. His hand had patted her cheek, had stroked her arm, his eyes sought hers with pretended love, and she had seen the lie squirming there like a leech, seen it, and known it for what it was.

He had purred at her. "I've arranged for us to have a trip, dear love.

When this baby is born, we're going to the resort in Bliggen. I've heard wonderful things about it!"

Though she was weary with the weight of the unborn child, she tried to sound normally interested and unafraid. "But the baby, Solven. The baby will still be nursing, and you know what the covenants have to say about nursing. A mother must nurse her own child for a whole year."

He could scarcely argue. It was part of the covenants, one of the amendments added by the Tribunal during their years on Haven. A child receiving noble nature and noble nurture was fit to assume the noble title. Breast milk was one of the three female sacraments—resignation, bearing, nurturing—bestowed by the mother upon the female child.

Solven had merely smiled tenderly. "No problem, sweetheart. We'll take the baby with us."

That day she had called Dora to her, whispering into her ear, putting the letter into her hand, together with money and a promise of an equal amount when the letter was delivered. Dora would find a messenger, and even if the letter was intercepted, there was nothing in it to condemn her. It was written in a personal code mother and daughter had used and refined for years, one that conveyed meaning through idle phrases of chit-chat. *Well, Mama, soon I will be out of danger, as I'm due the tenth. Soon after, we're leaving here. It would be fun to go on a sailing boat, across past Ramspize to Poolwich, but we'll probably travel by road, down through Bliggen . . .*

The message concluded with some jotted figures, 9 royals 1, 5 royals 1, 4 royals 2, 9 royals 2, and 3 royals 1, totalling 29 royals 9. *Please, Mama, send me thirty royals to buy special somethings for Evalene for her birthday!*

Hidden in this brief missive was the message:

Danger. Tenth. Leaving here. Sailing boat. Ramspize.

The day before she left she had received her answer: Thirty royals and the coded message, *Meeting you. Watch for a fire.*

While Solven had prepared for their trip to Bliggen, Lyndafal had prepared likewise, awaiting the birth, praying it would be neither late nor hard. It had been harder than the first, but rather earlier than late, and she had forced herself to move, to heal, to go out sailing on Havenpool.

Now she used an oar to push free of the mud. The boat slipped out onto the waters, buoyant as a duck. It took only a moment to step the slender mast and see the light linen sail fill with wind, still blowing season-ally from the northwest as she had hoped. She had gambled it would blow strongly enough to let her escape.

The baby went on sleeping. The island receded behind her. Number four, she reminded herself. There were a dozen, all told, and she needed

to keep track of where she was. She hoped to rest on the seventh tonight and tomorrow. She would go by the eighth island at night, for it was populated by fisherfolk, and the last few islands were close together, mere rocky peaks covered with waterbird nests and deep-piled guano that had been mined by the farmers of Ramspize and Southmarsh before the last fever epidemic.

She glanced at the sleeping child, rocking in her basket. This was what she had dreamed before she married Solven: herself and her child, sailing in a little boat. She had taken it for a vision of happiness. She had never guessed what it really was, had not even recalled its details until now. She threw her head back, staring at the sky, swallowing her tears. The warning had been there, but she hadn't seen it. What good was a talent that was so misleading? And why did she have it at all? Mother didn't. Grandmother had, evidently, and maybe she'd known what it was good for.

As had been her habit since setting out, she turned in her seat every few moments, looking at the water around her, at the horizon to see if any boats were there. She was so accustomed to seeing nothing that she looked all around, turning without really using her eyes, for a moment quite sure that she was indeed seeing nothing.

Then her eyes widened, for she had glanced across what stood upon the glistening horizon: a striped sail that identified a fishing boat from Sealand. As it came closer, she saw that the stripes were yellow and blue, which meant the boat was from Ruckward itself. It was setting directly toward her, and she thought she could make out the tiny figures of men on the foredeck, waving and pointing in her direction.

"Oh, heaven, whatever help there is for women, help me," she cried, the words coming from someplace deep inside her she had never plumbed until this instant. "Oh, help me for the love of all that is dear," as she stared helplessly at her pursuer.

The pursuit continued, though the following ship was obviously confused by something happening off to one side, a foaming, swirling disturbance in the water. At first Lyndafal thought it was a maelstrom, but the activity seemed to be all on the surface, a circle of creamy foam sequined with flashing light. The men on the other boat stopped pointing in her direction and scurried from the foredeck to busy themselves with nets. Even across all the distance between she could hear their eager shouts as the swirling water moved away from their line of travel, to the west.

On that ship, the Captain shouted orders, the sails were tightened to sail nearer the wind, while ahead of them a sparkling curtain of golden

fish leapt upward from the waves as though to escape something beneath them.

On that ship a young sailor turned to his older mate and asked, "So, we're letting the little boat go? What'll Lord Solven say when he hears that?"

"It won't get away, boy! We can sail rings around it. There's no land near enough for her to get to! Those are golden-eyes out there boy, worth their weight in royals. Now's time to put money in our pockets, more money than that bastard Solven will ever pay us! Besides, we don't even know it's her!"

And Lyndafal, on the tiny boat, fell into the bottom of it as it lurched and dipped and began to flee across the water like a bird, the sail actually bellying backward as something carried her faster than the wind away from that other ship. She did not bother to think. She crawled to the rope and dropped the sail, allowing the boat to go even faster. It dashed, throwing a high spume of water on either side.

Island number five spun by. The boat kept on, never diminishing its speed. Another island loomed. And another still, the seventh, where she had planned to rest tonight. The boat swerved around behind it, beaching itself on a sandy beach near a wooded inlet. When a few quiet moments passed with no further happening, she pulled the boat from the sand and waded with it to the inlet where she found cover from the sea. Once the boat was hidden, she took the baby into her arms and stepped onto a mossy bank amid a wooded glade.

As she turned back toward the water, she saw a circle of gold turning in the shallows, a shiny cog wheel like those that turn endlessly in the backs of watches or the workings of music boxes, and beyond the wheel, deeper in the water, a larger wheel, and another deeper yet.

Breathless, she watched as the wheels spun. She thought of all the wheels at work in the universe, those of planets, of stars, of galaxies, round and round and round. When she had observed it long enough to know she was not imagining it, the wheels broke into hundreds of scaled creatures no longer than her fingers that darted away into the depths while she gaped at the place they had been.

Unlike many in Havenor whose highest ambition was to see and be seen, certain agents of the Prince made it their business not to be seen at all. Those who ran afoul of them more than once presumed, quite correctly, that they were immune to the Lord Paramount's law. They were laconic, lean, and lurkish to a man, and chief among them was a man called Wiezal, a name he preferred because it was not his own. Wiezal made it a rule to maintain his private business quite private, though in addition to his own affairs, he was willing to go hither and yon at the Prince's bidding, finding out this, stealing that, and occasionally finding himself in proximity (coincidentally, of course) to someone about to die unexpectedly.

When Genevieve was found to have disappeared, Yugh Delganor summoned Wiezal and set him upon the trail. Wiezal soon found that Aufors Leys had booked passage on the Reusel packet, informed the Prince of this fact, and then went off down the River Reusel with a couple of his pack members, slavering upon the spoor. All of them were tireless and clever hunters who either returned with their prey or, if it was in no condition to be returned, with enough of it to prove its demise.

When Wiezal returned a few days later, however, he was not his usual self. Instead of his customary sidling, head bobbing approach to the Prince, he remained standing by the door, shifting from foot to foot, his appearance more than ordinarily stoatish.

"Well," the Prince inquired in a soft voice, "is she at Langmarsh?"

"No, sir. She is not." Wiezal's voice was petulant, indisputably annoyed.

Delganor raised his head to peer down his nose, keeping his voice soft and unthreatening. "Well then, where did she go?"

"The thing is, Your Highness . . . well, the woman Colonel Leys bought passage for wasn't her."

Delganor frowned. "Then who was it?"

Wiezal breathed deeply and leaked words like a faucet dripping. "The passage was for the daughter of one of . . . well, the Colonel's officers, man he fought with in Potcher." Deep breath. "She was engaged to another officer. This woman went to Reusal-on-mere. She met her man there. His name's Enkors. They got married. Colonel Leys was there. He stood up for the groom. The journey was a wedding present."

"Then where in the deepsea is the Marshal's daughter?"

"Don't know!" snarled Wiezal. "We're looking! There's people out. If she don't turn up in Langmarsh, we'll look elsewhere."

"We don't have forever, Wiezal."

"Shouldn't take forever. Just got misled, that's all."

"Purposefully misled, do you think?"

As he thought seriously on the question, Wiezal lifted a nostril, which lifted one side of his lip, letting a sharp tooth show at the corner. "No. Seems the Colonel promised this wedding long ago. Not something he just thought up. Coincidental, more like."

"I understood the Colonel was in love with the girl."

Wiezal shrugged. "Nobody saw them together. Not without her maid or somebody there. Maybe she loves him. Or visus vercy. It didn't get far, if so. Besides, Marshal wouldn't have it."

So the Marshal wouldn't have it, ah? Which might explain the fact she'd run off without her lover! That was a complication to keep in mind. "Wiezal, find Colonel Aufors Leys. I want him here, before me, soonest. And Wiezal . . ."

"Sir?"

"I don't want him damaged. I need him in good working order."

"Ah. Soon as may be."

"Sooner than that."

Wiezal slipped out and away while Delganor sat in his chair and brooded. No matter how well he planned, there were always these little glitches. The flow of his life was not clear and straight. There were opacities. Eddies. But small, small, nothing in the way of a maelstrom or a tidal wave. Not that Haven needed fear tidal waves. It took long, sloping shores for tidal waves to build their force, and there were no long, sloping shores around Haven. No long sloping shores in Delganor's life, either. His way was straight up, a cliff to scale, a peak to ascend. There was only one height beyond his own, the rule of Haven, including Mahahm, which would belong to him in time.

In fact, Mahahm might belong to him before the rest of Haven did.

They were a poor people in Mahahm, and this mission to offer them royalties for P'naki would whet their appetites. Later he would make another such trip, to offer something else they hungered for. Delganor had seen Mahahm. There was only one thing there to satisfy any hunger at all, and with that one satisfied, they had to hunger for something else. He would find out what it was, just as he would find Genevieve, sooner or later. These were not major matters. They were merely, annoyances.

They were not the only annoyances of that morning. Before noon, another visitor was announced: a messenger from Lord Solven, Earl of Ruckward.

He came in at a march, clicked his heels, bowed, and said: "My master the Earl of Ruckward presents his compliments, Your Highness."

"No doubt," said Delganor. "And does he present else?"

"His apologies, Your Highness. The Right Honorable Earl of Ruckward wishes you to know well in advance that he may be unable to accompany Your Highness on the trade mission scheduled for later this year. Lady Lyndafal, the Countess of Ruckward, has unaccountably disappeared, and the Right Honorable Earl is greatly distraught."

The Prince sat as one petrified, unmoving, seeming scarcely to breathe. At last, barely above a whisper, he murmured, "The child."

"Sir?"

"She had a child? Didn't she?"

"Two children, Your Highness. A toddler daughter, and the infant, also a girl."

"And where are they?"

"The older child is with her father at Ruckton, sir. The baby disappeared with the Countess. Both mother and child are feared drowned."

Delganor's teeth ground together audibly. He took a deep breath and said, "Tell the Earl that I sympathize with his feelings and appreciate his timely information. Tell him, please, that I will be in touch at a later time."

The messenger bowed and left. The Prince sat still as stone, occasionally baring his teeth and drawing back his upper lip, almost as Wiezal had done, though the teeth thus displayed were gray-white, lifeless as dry bone. He sniffed the air, as though he smelled something inimical but could not identify its source. Once, as though barely able to believe what he said, he murmured almost inaudibly, "Another one."

Long before Genevieve's departure, Aufors Leys had obtained leave from the Marshal and scheduled his trip to attend Enkors's wedding in Reusel-on-mere. With Genevieve gone, there was no reason to change his

plans. He anchored Enkors in his determination to wed after forty-some-odd years of single life, and blessed the bride, a no-longer-young but no-less-for-that maiden with more good sense than beauty and a body, Aufors judged, that would come as a happy surprise to his old colleague. During their several long conversations, Aufors enlightened Enkors as to his discoveries in the archives.

"Makes you wonder," said Enkors, slightly tipsy, "if maybe that Prince o' Potcher didn't have it right. About some lords bein' a bit old for the job."

Aufors suggested it wasn't the thing to say where it might be overheard, and Enkors had looked guiltily around himself, saying, "Right, Colonel. Oh, right."

It took Aufors two days and nights to get back using post horses, after which he went about his usual work, quite aware that the Marshal was watching him a good deal of the time. Aufors was not himself and did not pretend to be so. Though he had made a pretence of jollity during Enkors's wedding feast, he was not a happy man. He accomplished his duties commendably, as always, but his downcast eyes and strained expression betrayed his distress. He blamed the Marshal for what had happened, and he was not of a mood to make the old soldier feel less guilty, presuming he felt guilty at all.

The Marshal had found himself itched by an unfamiliar feeling of disquiet, though it had nothing to do with his daughter but rather with Aufors himself. Why had he suspected Aufors Leys, a man who had done him nothing but good? Why had he suspected a man who was obviously just as upset as the Marshal himself? After all, it wasn't Aufors's fault if the stupid girl had fallen in love with him!

In this mood of forgiveness, the Marshal found the Colonel in the stable yard with the farrier, looking over the horses to see which needed shoeing. When the farrier started his work, the Marshal invited the Colonel to join him at luncheon. Surprisingly, the Colonel begged off, saying he wasn't feeling all that well.

"Come now, Colonel. You and I must talk."

"About what, sir?"

"About these recent happenings, Colonel. All this about . . ."

"About Genevieve? What can I say about Genevieve? She is lovely, generous, and intelligent. She has a good deal of kindness about her, and what good will it do us for me to say that?"

"What I want you to say," snapped the Marshal, "is why Yugh Delganor's expression of interest in her sent her over the wall that way."

"She cannot bear him, sir."

"So? So she cannot bear him. She would be Queen, Colonel! Isn't that enough to make up for being unable to bear him?"

Aufors found himself simmering with a rage he could barely conceal. "She may suspect, as do I, that she would not be Queen for long or, indeed, might not survive to be Queen at all. The wives of Haven's royalty do not thrive."

"That's treasonous!" the Marshal shouted, guilt forgotten in a sudden ecstacy of fury.

Aufors said stubbornly, "It's a simple statement of fact. None of Yugh's wives have lasted longer than a year or two, and few members of their families remain alive. The same is true of the Lord Paramount's wives, except for this last woman, whom he married when he was already aged and so was she, a political match, as was said at the time. Heaven knows what the others were."

"What are you alleging?"

Aufors drew himself up to his full, haughty height, confronting the Marshal at eye level. "I do not allege. I describe a condition that exists. If I say that most of the people who walk along the Great Falls Trail in Tansay end up dead at the foot of the cliffs, I am stating a fact. I don't know why they end up there. Rock slides, perhaps. Collapses of terrain. Attacks by beasts. Slippery footing coupled with drunkenness. I don't allege, I simply say the trail is demonstrably dangerous. If I cared about someone, I would have her view the Falls from some other place. Because I care about Genevieve, I would rather see her as a live Marchioness than a dead Queen."

The Marshal huffed, like a bull, working himself up toward another explosion. "You're saying I don't care about her."

"I'm saying nothing of the kind. I have no idea whether you care about her or not. How would I know?"

"You certainly have reason to know!" he shouted. "She has always been well-cared-for, in accordance with the covenants. She has been given her youth. She has enjoyed the house and gardens in Wantresse. She has been well dressed, well kept and fed, well trained—"

Aufors interrupted, as loudly: "Which is also true of your horses, sir. Rather more true, actually. You spend a good deal more time with your horses. Nonetheless, you would sell any one of them for a good price."

The Marshal turned red with fury, his neck swelling.

"Forgive me," said Aufors between his teeth, controlling himself with a good deal of effort. "I have no right to speak so. It is obvious to me I can no longer maintain the neutrality and balance which are necessary for

me to work beneficially for you, Lord Marshal. I have been training some-one to take my place, and I think it would be best, sir, for you to hire him at once as I offer my resignation as your equerry forthwith."

He had said far more than he meant to say; the Marshal had heard a good deal more than he had thought to hear; and they parted in mutual fury. The Marshal started to say that officers were obliged to fulfil their specified terms of service, but then bethought himself that he had not appointed Aufors to a specified term, leaving him quite free to go elsewhere.

Aufors sent a note to the selected replacement with a written introduc-tion to the Marshal. He then went to his quarters and packed his belong-ings, arranging with one of the footmen to store them for later dispatch. Meantime the Marshal sat simmering in his office. When Halpern came in and respectfully requested a word, the Marshal only nodded, not trust-ing himself to speak.

"Sir, I hate to trouble you with such a matter at a time like this, but if Lady Genevieve is to be away for very long, we will need to hire a housekeeper."

"I don't understand you," grunted the Marshal.

"You have several dinners planned, sir, as well as certain other social events. The Marchioness was handling all the arrangements. I could per-haps catch up to it, sir, but then I would have to have someone to fill in for me. Her absence just at this time is most sorely felt. . . ."

"For heaven's sake, man. What has she to do with it? You people do the work, do you not?"

"No sir, that is, not all of it, sir."

"So, how much time did she spend on this? A few moments a day?"

Halpern looked shocked. "She began with the cook at seven in the morning, sir, and she often finished up with the accounts after you had gone to bed, with very little time to herself in between."

The Marshal stared at him. "You're joking."

Halpern bit back a retort, turning rather red himself, saved by the cool intrusion of another voice: Duchess Alicia, who stood in the doorway, accompanied by an embarrassed footman.

"I am sorry, Marshal, I couldn't help but overhear. Lest you grow angry at an irreplaceable part of your establishment, thereby further handicap-ping yourself here in Havenor, let me assure you that Halpern does not overstate the case. Genevieve spent many hours every day seeing that your social affairs and this establishment were well managed. Did you think it happened by magic?"

"My dear lady, I simply don't see what all the fuss is about. Halpern makes it sound like a . . . a profession!"

"Dear Halpern, leave me with the Marshal. Perhaps I can enlighten him." She went so far as to pat the departing butler on one trembling arm before seating herself beside the Marshal.

"Well, sir. Let us try a bit of education. What does it cost to prepare and serve a dinner for thirty people?"

He frowned. "I have no idea."

"Genevieve knew, to the penny. If she had not known, it would have cost you twice what it did. You would have been overcharged by your wine merchant, the confectioners, the butcher, and any number of other persons who live on the fat meat that falls from the tables of the ignorant. Unless you are far wealthier than we all assume, in short order you would have been ruined. Genevieve knew how much to spend heating this house this winter, how to get repairs done economically, how to handle the servants to keep them contented and working well. If Halpern decides to leave your employ—which is entirely possible, considering your manner toward him—who will you get to take his place who knows half what he knows about this place? Genevieve knew the answer to that, and also how to keep him more or less satisfied."

"All right, all right," he growled. "Perhaps there is more to it than I thought. So, I'll let Aufors do it . . ." He stopped, biting his lip. "Damn!"

"So Aufors has resigned," said the Duchess, accurately reading his expression. She was silent and thoughtful a long moment, then she came to herself and said, "It doesn't surprise me. He would have gone long ago except for Genevieve."

He went on fuming wordlessly, while she sat a time, peering intently into his brooding, granite face. At last, she said:

"Well, you seem set in edgy stone, and I have no time to spend smoothing you into something gentler. I came to bid you farewell, for I have received word that my daughter has also disappeared. I'm leaving today for Ruckward, by way of Reusel-on-mere. My granddaughter needs Grandma to comfort her."

"What should I do about Aufors?" he asked, not even having heard her. "What should I do about Genevieve?"

She sighed, shaking her head at him. "Send him after her. Believe me, he'll find her eventually. Tell him you have no objection to their marrying."

"That would be ridiculous! He's a commoner!"

"He's uncommon, Marshal, and you know it! More uncommon than nine-tenths the nobility!"

"But . . . Delganor . . ."

"When and if Delganor says anything, you apologize and say you're dreadfully sorry, but the young ones were so in love it seemed appropriate, sensible, *prudent*, for them to wed."

"He'll be furious."

"I don't know. He may be. On the other hand . . . he may not. Now, I must go. My carriage is waiting." She rose, pulled on her gloves, and sailed out.

The Marshal growled and glowered as he heard her speaking to Halpern in the hall, and by the time he figured out what he intended to do, Aufors Leys was halfway down the alleyway behind the stables. Though a footman was sent after him, the man returned much out of breath, saying he could not catch the Colonel and no one knew where he had gone.

Finally, and only then, did the Marshal realize what the Duchess had said. Her daughter, too, had disappeared.

"Another one," he muttered gloomily.

"Your Highness."

A footman was at the Prince's door. "Your Highness, Colonel Aufors Leys requests an audience."

"That was quick," murmured the Prince. "Did Wiezal bring him?"

"No, sir. He came, just now, of his own accord."

The Prince sat up and blinked twice, slowly, like a lizard, looking over the footman's shoulder into some vast distance. A tiny smile moved across his lips, evanescent as cloud shadow.

"Well, well. Do let him come in."

Aufors entered in military fashion, his cape flowing from his shoulder, his tall bonnet in the crook of his arm, clean-shaven as an egg, his back straight as he bowed. "Your Highness."

The Prince purred, "Colonel Leys. Is there something I can do for you, Colonel?"

Aufors licked dry lips and said, "Your Highness is generous to grant me a hearing. We met, as you may recall, at the home of the Lord Marshal. You may recall his daughter."

"Ah, yes," said the Prince vaguely. "Lovely girl."

"Quite so, Your Highness. I know that it is preferred that young women here at court not be attached, as they are all given duties to perform, but she and I are in love. It was nothing either of us intended; it just happened."

"Ah," said the Prince, with a slight frown. "I see. Well. That is most

interesting, but I fail to see what . . . it has to do with me. . . ." He allowed his voice to trail away.

"Something that happened at dinner apparently frightened her terribly," said Aufors, keeping his eyes down and thereby missing the slight amusement that again crossed the Prince's face. "She has run away; she may be in danger, away from the protection of her family."

"Frightened her?" mused the Prince, frowning slightly. "What could have happened at a dinner party? I knew most everyone there, scarcely a villainous crowd." He peered down his nose, as though expecting a comment on this judgment.

Aufors made none. "I can't say what frightened her, sir. But I feel that I must find her, wherever she has gone. It is apparent to me that she feels unprotected and insecure."

"Then why in heaven's name didn't you go with her?" asked Delganor, without thinking, real irritation in his voice. "I should have thought you would have done so!"

Aufors dropped his jaw, only momentarily. "I . . . I wasn't consulted about her going, sir."

Nor, he thought, about Duchess Alicia's going, either. Since the Duchess was his only connection to Genevieve, he had gone to her house at once, only to find she had departed for Ruckward. After a time weighing the various possibilities and consequences, he had decided to tell the Prince what he intended. In that way, he could not be accused of dishonorable conduct.

"What do you propose?" asked the Prince, in an irritated tone.

"Inasmuch as she was to take up certain duties here at the palace under your aegis, Your Highness, I felt it only proper to tell you that I intend to find out where she has gone, to follow her, and to offer her my protection by marrying her, despite the Marshal's opposition to the match."

Once more in full command of himself, the Prince said, "I am certainly not pleased."

His stern face and unyielding mouth made this quite believable. Aufors gritted his teeth and was humble. He had practiced being humble all the way to the palace, and he was determined to do it well. "No, sir. I am truly desolated by that fact."

The Prince drew a deep, dramatic breath, a very audible sigh with only a touch of petulance in it. "Young people. Oh, young people. So urgent. Well, I too was once young. Though the young lady has behaved foolishly—even ungraciously, one might say—you, yourself, Colonel, have

behaved as honorably as one would expect of the hero of the Potcher War."

He mused, drawing his brows together, frowning, tapping his finger on the arm of his chair, cocking his head, pursing his lips, slightly changing position and then doing it all again, the perfect picture of a man concentrating on an issue. He said at last:

"Well. I will make you an offer, Colonel. Though I am greatly displeased at her impetuous behavior—scarcely what one would expect from one so carefully educated, one whom I myself recommended to the Lord Paramount—I will not make an issue of her departure. I will withhold my displeasure in return for your promise to accompany me on my planned trip to Mahahm. I need trustworthy people, and your honorable actions concerning this matter do you credit. Also, it is at least nominally a military mission, so it's in your line of work."

Aufors felt his tight jaw relax, his rigidly locked knees start to tremble, ever so slightly. He had thought he risked everything. His life, perhaps. He had believed it necessary to risk everything including his life, and he was now not only surprised but dumbfounded. All he could think of to say was, "Your Highness is most generous."

"The terms are agreeable, Colonel? For you and the lady to accompany our mission? Hmmm? In return for my permission for you to marry."

The evanescent little smile had gone. The slight frown of disapproval had gone. There was nothing now in that face or voice to give anything away, but nonetheless, something in that voice brought Aufors's eyes up, to meet the expressionless gaze of the Prince.

He considered. The offer seemed generous. Aufors would have accepted a sentence of death in order to let Genevieve escape from this man, and this bargain was far less than that. If there was a trap in it, it was a trap for himself, not for her.

"If she consents to marry me, Your Highness. You have my word."

The Prince made a gesture, waving this away. "No ifs, Colonel, but you had best go to the Marshal and explain to him that I have consented to your marriage with his daughter—that is, when and if you find her—in return for your accompanying me to Mahahm. I think, once he hears that, he will not oppose, as you put it, the match."

"Thank you, Your Highness, for your generosity."

Aufors bowed and backed away from the presence, not seeing the little smile return, not raising his head until he stopped in the anteroom to wipe his beaded forehead. He stank of fear-sweat. Why, in heaven's name? He hadn't known he was terrified. He had sworn to himself he would face

death without being terrified, but something about the Prince, something . . . well, he could understand Genevieve's aversion, put it that way.

Understand though he did, he couldn't take time to think about it. Instead, he got on his horse and went back to the Marshal's house, where he made a stiff-necked admission of his interest in Genevieve and a more or less accurate account of his meeting with the Prince. The Marshal yelled, ranted, threatened, while Aufors said he understood the Marshal's feelings. The Marshal pronounced himself taken aback, confused, and angry. Aufors apologized again. The matter volleyed several times more, with ebbing impetus, after which the two of them ended up, as the Marshal had suggested the day before, having lunch together.

"So HE SAID *YOU* COULD MARRY HER," SAID THE MARSHAL, OVER HIS SOUP. "If he didn't care who married her, why was he thinking of doing it himself?"

"I can't say, sir."

"Whatever he was thinking, it doesn't change what I think! I do care who marries her!"

Aufors took a deep breath. "The Prince said that in view of his permission, you would probably be kind enough not to object."

The Marshal fumed. They'd gutted him! Usurped his prerogatives! If the Prince permitted it, that meant the Lord Paramount permitted it, and what the Lord Paramount permitted, the Marshal was not accustomed to question.

He snarled, "You'll be going off to find her, then."

"Yes, sir. I'm taking tonight's packet down the Reusel."

"You think she went to Langmarsh?"

Aufors did not intend that the Duchess be brought into the conversation. He equivocated. "Langmarsh is a good place to start looking."

"I suppose. I suppose." The Marshal buttered a bit of bread and chewed it, calming himself. "I don't understand it. I confess that to you, Aufors. It's just . . . like this business of being at court! The Lord Paramount asked me to come to court as a kind of balance to some of the new ministers. They seem to be a bit liberal, commonish, you know what I mean."

"I myself am commonish, sir, so I suppose I do."

"Didn't mean it as a slur, Colonel. Simply meant it to express ideas that go against the covenants. Haven was set up as an aristocracy. Our covenants reflected our culture, either as it had once been or as we wished it to be. You other sorts were invited to come along, and the ones who chose to did come along, no slavery or coercion about it. So, now, a few generations later—"

Aufors interrupted, "Well, sir, it's actually been around twelve hundred years or so. Given as few as three generations a century, that would still amount to thirty-six generations, scarcely a few."

"The number doesn't matter. The fact is the people agreed to live under an aristocracy. They agreed to do without high technology, so our culture could be preserved. Our women agreed to a certain role in that culture. Now some commons are agitating to share rights that belong to the nobility—or even the royals!—and the Lord Paramount doesn't like it."

Aufors accepted a plate of vegetables and rare beef and picked up knife and fork. "So you were invited to court as a counterbalance: a solid weight of aristocratic disapproval from one with a great reputation as a warrior."

The Marshal cut a large bite of beef. "Pah, the kind of opposition these people could make doesn't need a warrior. The least conflict, they'd run screaming. No, these are the kind who talk and talk and talk, scream and scream, march up and down with placards, but they do nothing."

"What is it these 'commonish' people want, Lord Marshal?"

"I asked Prince Thumsort that! He says the men want to marry their daughters to whomever they choose. Well, no one interferes with their doing so now except one time in a hundred! Some particularly pretty girl may fit a baron's idea of a proper upstairs maid, so her wedding gets delayed a few years and she has a child or two more than she'd thought of, but in the end she goes back to her lover, if he's still about, richer than when she began. They want freedom to engage in whatever trade they like. Well, mostly they can and do, unless it removes them from traditional work. They want freedom to innovate, so the traditional work will be easier! Innovation leads to technology, we've told them that, over and over. Man gets tired digging ditches by hand, and he goes and invents a mechanical digger. Does he care that it'll destroy our way of life? Not in the deepsea he doesn't.

"They want higher pay for those who work for the noble houses, they want funds set aside for women who are noticed by nobility! It's impossible. Any woman picked out by a noble should be damned proud of it, and those who work for the noble houses should be honored to be there!"

Aufors smiled.

"What?" the Marshal demanded.

"I've heard it claimed that women themselves should do the choosing of their mates since anything else is tantamount to slavery and rape."

The Marshal scowled. "I won't argue the merits of our customs with you, Colonel. It's not something I'd ordinarily discuss except with my own

class. The thing I started out to say was, why am I here in Havenor? Since I've been here, there hasn't been a single meeting of the ministers! Not one! There hasn't been an occasion when I could be useful as a counterweight to anything! So. Why am I here?"

Aufors took a deep breath and said, probingly: "I have been struck by all the attention paid to Genevieve."

"Well, yes, but I thought that was because of Delganor."

"I think not. If he had been set on her, would he have treated me as he did?"

"He was magnanimous."

"Prince Delganor has no reputation for magnanimity."

"Perhaps he is more generous than he is said to be," the Marshal replied, in a grumpy voice.

Aufors merely nodded. Though he thought it unlikely the Prince was better than said to be, he could not deny the Prince had behaved well. Better than the Marshal, and with less justification. But then, the Prince did not have the habit of rage, as the Marshal did. Whatever he felt was kept hidden. That, in itself, might be a cause for concern.

Though Aufors left Havenor a full day and a half behind the Duchess, his use of the river packet put him in Reusel-on-mere in a day and a half, well before she arrived there. Reusel-on-mere was a small place with several good inns, its existence justified by the confluence of the Reusal with a number of small streams which together formed the mirror smooth blue of the Mere. Below this sizeable lake, the river was wide and slow, running between the farms of Dania and the fens of Southmarsh, a route for both cargo and passenger ships that traveled to and from Poolwich on Havenpool.

Aufors felt the Duchess's arrival would take some time, for her carriage was large, the road was not at its best during this season, and no doubt she would pause for meals and rest. To catch her whenever she arrived, Aufors took a room in the same inn from which Enkors had been married, one with a good view of all roads into or out of the town, and he offered a good tip to the inn servants to keep a lookout should she arrive while he was away.

It did not take him long to find out that someone had been asking a good many questions about himself and Enkors and about the woman who had come down on the packet the day Genevieve disappeared.

"What were they like, these men?" Aufors asked a garrulous tavern keeper.

"Oh, you know the sort, sir. Sneaky men. Eyes never still, always back and forth, like a caged follet. Not there one moment, there the next, gone the one after."

Aufors heard the same said several times, put two and two together and added it up to the men known to be employed by the Prince. In which case Yugh Delganor's ignorance of Genevieve's departure had been bogus. He had pretended not to know, but he had known, and he cared about it enough to put men upon her trail.

Had he thought he loved her then? Or, at least, been attracted enough to care about her welfare? Perhaps the latter. Perhaps he had felt obliged to do something since it was he who had frightened her. It could not have been more than that, or he would not have accepted Aufors's declaration in such good part. But if it had been only that, why tie Aufors to a promise of service? Well, because, Aufors told himself soberly, any such promise from an honorable man is like money in the pocket. A note that can be called at need. The prospect increased his discomfort.

The Duchess turned up about noon the following day. When Aufors greeted her as she dismounted from the carriage, she had all she could do to greet him politely.

"I did not expect to see you, Aufors. I advised you to stay where you were."

"I did expect to see you, Your Grace, but much has happened you do not know of."

She shook her head wearily. "What has happened that I should know? No. don't tell me. I can't hear anything until I've had a bath and a few hours' rest. The inn in Sabique gets worse by the decade. I stayed there last ten years ago, and I believe they have not turned the mattresses since, much less invested in new ones. The dust in the corners dates from before the Inundation, and it would not surprise me to learn that the bread I was served dates from that same era."

"Was the night before no better, Your Grace?"

"Worse, if anything." She turned to her coachman, who was unloading luggage from the boot. "What was the name of the place, Yarnson?"

"Wohsack, Your Grace."

"Wohsack. Indeed. And woe I had there. Well, I know this place, and it is far better. I am too tired to talk to you now, Aufors. Join me for dinner, about sunset, and we will enlighten one another."

As they did, in the Duchess's rooms, at a table laid before the fire, where, said the Duchess, it was most likely safe to talk for she had refused the first room the innkeeper had offered and picked one out for herself.

She heard Aufors's tale while she ate, shaking her head gravely when he had finished.

"And he actually told you to marry the girl."

"I've said so three times, Your Grace."

"Call me Alicia, Aufors. When we are alone, you can do that without offending the gentry."

"As Your Grace wishes, Alicia. Not that I mind offending the gentry. I have mightily offended a couple of them lately."

She leaned forward and began striking her glass with a spoon, making a tinkling sound as she whispered into his ear:

"And now you want me to tell you where she is?"

"Why else would I be here?" he whispered in return.

"Why, to help me, as I have helped Genevieve."

He dropped his fork onto his plate with a clatter. "Help . . . I'm sorry Your—Alicia. I didn't know you needed help."

She wiped her lips delicately, saying in an ironic tone, even as she put a finger before her lips, "Oh, but the Marshal must have told you my daughter has disappeared."

"He did not! Nor did anyone at your house, when I went looking for you four days ago!"

The Duchess smiled bleakly. "Well, she has disappeared. I am on my way to Ruckward County, where my son-in-law lives. To fetch my grand-daughter." Now she shushed him in earnest, leaning to his ear once again.

"But surely . . . surely you will want someone to search for your daughter," he murmured softly.

"Yes," she murmured softly. "And no."

He regarded her closely for a long, silent moment. "You know where she is," he said with his lips alone.

She read his lips, then stared past him, out the window, where the sky above the mountains shone purple with evening. She rose, drew him to his feet. "Let us wander out onto the terrace and watch the stars coming out."

One of the windows opened upon the terrace, and once there, they leaned upon the balustrade as she said softly, "I say to you that I know where a former servant of mine, a girl named Bessany Blodden, is staying. She has a new baby with her, and I would much like Bessany to be escorted from where she is currently to Merdune, far, far east of here."

"She has left her husband?" Aufors murmured. "She is . . . afraid?"

"Oh, one could say that, certainly."

"Your Grace . . . Alicia, I would volunteer for this duty in a moment if it were not for Genevieve. But she . . . she is my first concern."

The Duchess smiled, genuinely amused. "Well, Aufors, my young friend, if you will consent to escort Bessany Blodden where she is going, you will find the one you seek, and I cannot think of any other way you will do so."

Aufors said, "You want this . . . Bessany taken where Genevieve is."

"How perceptive! Yes, I want Bessany and her baby taken where Imogene is."

"And you don't want to do it yourself?"

"I am too much observed. As you are, but you are better equipped to elude the ones following you, Colonel. There are at least three of them. Meantime, I have no objections to my pursuers following me to County Ruckward. They will find nothing of interest there."

Aufors nodded. "Well then, how do we do this thing?"

"You do it," she whispered, leaning toward him, and pushing a tightly folded little paper into his hand. "And do not cavil at the hoops you must leap through, Aufors. They are there for Genevieve's protection. And my own. And yours."

"But Alicia, why did . . ."

"Hush! Ask me no whys. It is better if you remain ignorant of whys. Just go, and do not let this note fall into anyone else's possession."

He read the paper when he returned to his own room. It did not tell him where Genevieve was. It did tell him where Bessany Blodden and her baby were. Also, it gave him the name of an inn along the Potcherwater that he and Bessany should visit, along with the name of the cook at that inn. Presumably, the cook knew something that would assist them.

Gravely, Aufors memorized what was on the paper before he burned it.

SHORTLY AFTER AUFORS'S DEPARTURE, A ROYAL MESSENGER CALLED UPON the Marshal. The man bore a large red envelope heavy with seals and a dangling superfluity of gold ribbons. It contained the notice of a ministerial meeting, the agenda of that meeting, and background information on the issues. Two important matters were to be considered: Firstly, the need to increase P'naki imports from Mahahm; secondly, the question of changing the age at which noble young women would be expected to marry.

Also included in the packet was a letter from the Lord Paramount telling the Marshal what position he was expected to support. The Lord Paramount approved the lowering of the official marriage age for young women, inasmuch as the actual marriage age was much closer to twenty-two than thirty. His Majesty also approved of the attempt to increase the supply of P'Naki.

The Marshal read through the material he had been given and found it lacking in basic data. He went to the archives and dug out many facts which supported the Lord Paramount's position, which made the Marshal feel both proud and useful. He readied himself for the meeting with considerable care, as he might have done for a strategy session with his officers in time of battle, though his naive belief that this preparation was warranted was supported only by his total ignorance concerning the Council of Ministers.

The actual event enlightened him. The brief agenda was barely mentioned before the ministers were off in full cry over something else entirely. Women were disappearing from rural areas of Dania; daughters, some of them, but also a few youngish wives, mostly commoner women, but a few noble women as well. Tranquish, Duke of Dania, charged his colleagues in Merdune and Barfezi with harboring abductors in their respective provinces. Neither Lorne Vestik-Vanserdel, Duke of Barfezi, nor Gardagger Bellser-Bar, Duke of Merdune, were present, but their spokesmen were,

along with allies and interested persons, and when the council of ministers adjourned for lunch some hours later, neither the question of P'Naki nor the matter of marriage age had even been mentioned. Though the Marshal kept a wary eye on Efiscapel Gormus, said Gormus said nothing at all but yawn and scratch himself at intervals.

"What is all this?" growled the Marshal to Prince Thumsort, who served as minister for his own home county of Tansay.

"Tranquish thinks it's either Merdune or Barfezi taking his women. Merdune and Barfezi think it's Tanquish himself. I think the women probably ran off on their own. Women are like sheep, one jumps a fence, all the rest must jump it too."

Though this remark cut very close to the bone, the Marshal chose to ignore it. "Why would anyone want Danian girls?" he asked. "As I recall, the mountain nobility tend to loud voices, hefty bodies, and chapped faces."

"Marshal, don't try to make sense of it. Every time we meet, some of the commoner ministers bring up this business of their womenfolk running off. They usually accuse a neighboring province, either of harboring malefactors or of being in complicity. About once every five years, the ministers set up an investigative committee, and when they look into it, it turns out the women ran off to the city, or they eloped with someone, or they were pregnant by someone Papa didn't approve of."

"When will we get to business?" growled the Marshal, wishing to end this discussion of women running off. "I don't intend to waste another half-day on this nonsense."

"Get to business?" Prince Thumsort asked, eyebrows raised in surprise. "Oh, you mean the agenda? We won't. We never do."

"But we *need* more P'naki!"

"Oh, His Majesty has that well underway. While the ministers argue, he goes right ahead, you know. He says it gives the people a sense of taking part without noticeably slowing down the necessities of government. Eventually, they'll decide it's best, and a day or so later the Lord Paramount will announce it's done. That gives them participation and gives him a reputation for efficiency."

"And lowering the age of marriage?" asked the Marshal, his own eyebrows almost at his hairline.

"The Tribunal has already decided that question. Including it on the agenda was just a way of informing the public. Our young men are so urgent that girls aren't waiting until they're thirty, so why make a fetish of that age, ah?" The Prince winked and smiled, a secretive sort of smile.

"Then what in deepsea does he need the ministers for?"

"Need us?" He bridled, ducking his head into a wealth of chins, grinning widely. "Well of course not, Marshal. He doesn't need us. We're just part of the cover, don't you know?"

The Marshal did not understand all these winks and sidles, and his ignorance was explicit in the volume of his, "I don't know, no!"

And suddenly Prince Thumbsort gave him a different sort of look, one full of surprise and apprehension, as though he had perhaps said something thoughtless, unwise, even dangerous. "Heh, heh, heh," he chuckled. "Just joking, of course. The Lord Paramount needs all of us, Marshal. Of course he does."

"Not a nice joke, not at all," the Marshal rumbled. "Why, he told me himself he needed me here."

"As he does," Prince Thumsort soothed. "As he most certainly does. You especially, Lord Marshal."

Aufors bought a horse in Reusel-on-mere and rode westward along the road that marked the county border between Wantresse and Southmarsh counties. The day was fine, crisp but not overly cold; the reeds in the marshes south of him glittered with frost while the stubble fields of Wantresse were full of birds, scavenging for the odd beakful of grain missed by earlier gleaners. Fifty miles along the road he would find a post house, where he would spend the night, and another fifty miles would bring him to a small village where Wantresse stopped and Evermire began. Bessany Blodden and her child would be found another half-day's ride farther on.

By riding harder and longer, Aufors could have shortened the trip, but men who ride hard and fast are usually on a mission, for themselves or some other, and Aufors had decided it would be safer to appear unhurried, unworried, unconcerned, which would give him time to figure out, first, how to get rid of the rider or riders who stayed just out of view back on the road, and second, how he would transport a woman and infant back toward Merdune. A full day of riding into the wind gave him no idea about the former but a sensible notion about the latter. Sailing up the Potcherwater at this season would be a good deal easier than riding horseback. He had been well funded by the Duchess, so passage would be no problem. The wind was steady from the northwest. The Potcherwater was placid and deep from Wellsport all the way to County Gide; he knew Barfezi well from the Potcher War; and the river would take him to the very town where the inn stood, the one where the cook would, presumably, tell him where to find Genevieve.

Once this had been decided, he turned his mind to the other thing. All in all, he thought he might lose his follower by simple misdirection. Any followers were in search of Genevieve, not Aufors. Therefore, if the rider or riders thought Genevieve was known to be in a particular place, he or they might stop following Aufors and go on to that place. He made a little plan, then let his mind drift onto other things: to the research he had done in the archives, to the unexpected amiability of Prince Delganor, to the things that Duchess Alicia knew but didn't say, to the possible reasons her daughter had had for running away from her husband. He strongly suspected that all these happenings were linked, but he could not find any common factor among them.

About noon, he saw three riders approaching from the west, whipping their horses as they came. When they saw him, they pulled up their lathered mounts, one among them shouting, "Hey, you there, have you seen anybody on this road this morning?"

Aufors eased himself in the saddle. "Yes. Several."

"Who?" cried the first man. "Who've you seen?"

Aufors shook his head, smiling slightly. "I have no idea. I don't know the people hereabout."

"Come," cried the first, rather angrily. "Men, women, what?"

Aufors took a deep breath. "Four men, several miles back, with a flock of sheep. A whole clutch of people and children threshing grain with oxen. That's on the Wantresse side. On the Southmarsh side, I saw several young fellows hunting ducks."

"Did you see a woman with a baby?"

Aufors allowed himself a ponder on this subject, finding it possible to answer with complete truth. "I don't think I've seen a woman since I left the Reusel. There may have been women with babies at the threshing, but I don't remember seeing any."

The three muttered together, then the questioner turned to Aufors. "You'd have noticed this one. Long red hair and a pretty face."

"I'm sorry, I didn't notice anyone like that. Who is it that's missing?"

"The Earl Ruckward's wife. And his infant daughter. They were thought drowned, but someone told the Earl his wife had been seen here, on the Wantresse road."

"Taken, you think?" asked Aufors, his mouth open. "Abducted?"

"Why should you think that?"

"Well, stands to reason a young woman with a child, an infant, wouldn't be traveling alone. And if her husband doesn't know where she

is, then chances are she was abducted. There's a frightful lot of it going on, I've heard."

"Where? Where is it going on?"

"Well," Aufors eased himself and again adopted his pondering expression. "All during this trip I've heard there was a great deal of abducting going on in Nighshore county in Sealand. And in Dania, both." The last of which was certainly true. People at the inns were talking of little else.

The three before him looked at one another in puzzlement. "Nobody said we should look for her there. Just said ask if she'd been seen, along here."

"Not by me, I'm afraid," Aufors responded. "I'll keep my eyes open for her, however."

"If you see her, send word to the Earl. He's staying at Poolwich, at the Elver's Wife." And the three rode on eastward, galloping furiously.

Aufors gave silent thanks for the encounter, which had warned him to stay clear of Poolwich. Also, if the men took all the talk of abductions seriously, it could well deflect the search. Meantime, he would definitely plan to sail up the Potcherwater, preferably on some old tub that no one would look at twice.

Before arriving at the post house, he put a stone in the horse's hoof and then, when he stopped, complained loudly about the horse being lame and the necessity of giving it a day's rest on the morrow. At supper, he was accosted again by searchers, as well as by a single rider who had come in some time after Aufors himself. All claimed to be hunting Earl Solven's wife. Aufors pretended to get quite drunk with them after dinner, saying he didn't care about Earl Solven's wife for he was on his way to a wife of his own, who was waiting for him at Poolwich.

"So why're you on this road?" demanded the single rider. "The Reusel road would have taken you there easier."

"Oh, don't I know that," moaned Aufors. "But I work for the Marshal, and he has me running messages to Fensbridge, near the Ramspize, to do with all these Danian cowherders coming across the border. Well, I'll do that first, then go on down to Poolwich along the coast road." He took another large swallow and muttered, "That is, I will when my horse gets over being lame! If the damned beast ever does!"

On the morning, while Aufors watched from behind his window curtain, the single rider went off the way he had come in company with two others who had been in the post house the night before. Within minutes, Aufors was off as well, though in the opposite direction. At the inn where he stopped that night, he met yet another group, and it was there he

learned that the Earl Ruckward had posted a reward of fifty royals for the return of his wife. No wonder every man with a horse was out galloping the roads. Fifty royals was a year's income for many of them.

Early on the following morning, he left the inn and rode westward again, this time for only a few miles, turning southward on a narrow track that wound among the low hills above the coastal fens of Southmarsh. The road was all but deserted. He saw a swineherd with his beasts mid-morning, and not another person or animal the rest of the day. At midaf-ternoon, he came upon a croft crouched low at the foot of a hill, and behind it a copse of low woods and a stone dolmen like two hooded figures peering seaward, precisely as his directions had specified. An old woman came out to greet him as he came down the lane, stopping him with a hand on the horse's nose and a glare from fierce old eyes.

"And what would you be wanting, young man? There's naught here to interest a young man who's up to any good."

"Well," murmured Aufors, "this young man comes from the mother of a certain one. And that mother wants this certain one and her baby taken safe into Merdune. And it's best we go soon as can be, for there's riders everywhere along the main roads, and it'll be a short time before they're sifting along these little lanes, like ants after sugar."

"Riders?" she asked, wonderingly.

"Someone's offered a large reward, old woman. One that might tempt even you."

"Pah!" she spat. "Can I be tempted with money? Not likely. What would it buy me, at my age? Food? I've plenty. A lover? And what would I do with him? Peace of mind? Hardly, not with what's going on. But I take your point. Enough riders going hither and yon, someone's bound to see something. And that makes me wonder if any such person as you describe would be safe on the road, even with you."

"No." Aufors smiled. "She would not. So it would be up to me or her or you to make her look like something else. Either that, or hide her completely."

"And how would you do that?"

"Well, maybe I'd surround her with a raggedy old mother and a dirty young husband, and I'd dress her in simple clothes, and I'd probably dye her hair. Black, I think, for black tangles nicely. I'd smutch her face and glue down an eyelid to make a squint, and I'd black a tooth or two as well, just to add verisimilitude."

"Verisimilitude, is it?" She cackled. "And the baby? How would you disguise the baby?"

"Boys around here wear rooster-tail-feathers on their cradle boards, do they not? I'd dress the baby's cradle with such."

"Always wanted to travel," she murmured. "Always did."

"You're here alone?" he asked.

"Except for a certain one. And her baby. And a half-dozen old sheep, and a dog."

"Sheep and a dog would be good additions. Do you have a cart?"

"I do. A good one, too. One my youngest son built, just before he went down to Bliggen, seeking adventure. Wanted to have adventure while he was young, he said. Well, happen he did, though I can't say what or where."

"How long ago?" asked Aufors, sympathetically.

"Too long for hope to last," she said, wiping her eyes furtively on her sleeve. "Now, just for the sake of talk, what would the mother's name be, the one whose business you're on?"

"Alicia," he said, smiling.

"Good enough." She turned and stumped away on her gnarled cane, pausing at the door to give him time to tie his horse.

"And how might I address you, ma'am?" he asked, stopping to let her go in first.

"Ma Muddy, that's me. It's a fen name, and only half a joke."

He stepped through the door and stopped, frozen in place. Genevieve sat before the fire! He gasped, she turned, and he knew then she was not his love, did not even greatly resemble her except in silhouette. The skin and hair were different, but the line of the forehead, the chin, yes, and especially the nose were almost the same! Full face, this girl was broader across the cheeks, however, and her mouth was narrower.

"Bessany?" he asked. "And the baby?"

She lifted the baby into the light. "Did my mother send you?"

"Yes. I am to take you to Merdune."

"Has she gone to Ruckward?"

"She should be at Poolwich by now, where Earl Ruckward is staying also. Four days for your mother to cross the sea."

"Are they hunting me?"

Aufors nodded. "All up and down the roads. Earl Ruckward has published a reward. He must love you very much?"

She laughed chokingly. "Oh, he loves me, yes. I am his candidate for something unimaginable."

"For what?"

"Why, to whatever he aspires to. Heaven knows what."

The baby began to fuss, and she put the infant to her breast, head and breast warm glowing globes in the firelight, the one covered with wispy red hair curled into elflocks.

"How do you know?" Aufors asked.

"I saw something. It frightened me."

"What did you see?" the old woman asked, coming forward to stir up the fire. "You didn't tell me of any seeing?"

"I saw myself lying in a great red stain of blood. Nearby I saw my husband surrounded by old men, passing my child from hand to hand among themselves, as though deciding what to do with it."

"Ah," the old woman moaned. "They do that. I've seen that, myself. When the Duchess died, she left a wee girl, and I saw them passing the child around, like a prize."

"How will we go?" asked Bessany, looking into Aufors's eyes.

"We will dirty my horse and comb him backwards, putting burs in his mane. We'll hitch him to Ma Muddy's cart," he said. "We will dye your hair . . . If we can, Ma?"

"Oh, aye. Thalnip hulls make a dye. I've plenty."

"Well then," Aufors went on, "the child will wear a cap with bits of dark horse hair thrust in around the edges and rooster feathers on the cradle board. And we will dirty our faces and halter the sheep to follow, unless the dog will bring them along, and we'll ride south tomorrow, across the marsh, the shortest way we can to the Reusel, and across it, avoiding Poolwich like the plague."

"The fen road," said the old woman, beginning to bustle at the fireside. "Though short don't describe it, for it wanders. Still, it's not a way anybody would look at. Too long. Too soggy. It'll bring us out at Ferrybend, well east of Poolwich, and from there, if we're lucky, we can travel the short road to Wellsport, where my nephew's a barge man."

"He'll help us?"

"We'll count on his family devotion. I'll take the mattress, to pad the cart. And I'll pray for good weather. Nothing worse than winter rain on the fens."

"Come sit," said Bessany to Aufors. "You look weary."

"This is the third day of riding," he admitted. "As a soldier, it was a common thing, but I'm out of practice."

"How's my mother? Is she well?"

"Very well, though saddened by your plight," he said. "Very determined to get your older daughter back to Merdune."

"She didn't want me to marry Solven," she said. "Gardagger encouraged

me, of course, though since he's not my father, he couldn't have forced me to do so. Mother said there was a danger in marrying older men."

"Marrying them, or the sons of them. The wives don't prosper," said Aufors. "Not according to what I find. Few of them live to be old, and they mostly the childless ones."

"Seemingly that is true," she murmured. "I wish I knew what all this was about."

"Has your mother told you nothing about old, old men? And why she feared your marrying?"

She sighed and laid the babe in its box near the fire. "My sister and I were born in a village, daughters of a commoner father. Mother read us stories out of books, and she told us myths and tales of ancient times on Old Earth, but she said nothing of nobility on Haven. After father was dead, we came to live in the city, and then we met our grandmother for the first time. She took us, my sister and me, for a long walk one day, and she asked us if my mother, her daughter, had taught us anything about . . . certain things."

"What certain things?" he demanded, rather angrily. "I've really had enough of this mystification!"

"Well, so had I," she said. "For I knew nothing about anything she was speaking of. Something about the song of the world, and harbingers, and the swimmers in the stars. I remembered star swimmers, for mother had read us a story about it when we were little, and that's all it meant to me, a story. Then Grandma asked us if we ever had what she called waking dreams, and I said I did, and my sister said she did not. And that was the end of that. Grandma said our mother had been unfitted for the learning, and I was too old to be taught. She sighed, and wept and said perhaps it didn't matter. But I went on having waking dreams just the same, though they have misled me as often as not."

She looked down at her child, tears in her eyes, and Aufors shook his head, angry at himself for upsetting her. Perhaps when he next saw Alicia, or Genevieve, they might enlighten him. He suspected very strongly that both of them knew more than they had ever told him.

In the tunnels under High Haven, Jeorfy Bottoms drove one of the smallest freight carts slowly down a lengthy, narrow aisle between two stacks of crates. The dust on the floor before him was deep as velvet, untouched and opulent. As he drove under overhanging surfaces, he could look up at labels where the dust had not settled: medical supplies on his left; machine parts on his right. Neither stack had been disturbed for over

a hundred years, according to the universal dates on the boxes, and the thick gray layers attested to that fact. According to the expiration dates on those same labels, most of these materials should have been dumped into the chasm long ago. Obviously, no one had bothered to do so, up to and including Zeb.

Around the next corner lay a great pile of cartons beneath a lizard rookery, the whole now a petrified heap of guano that must have taken at least a century to accumulate. Most of the stacks in this area were equally fouled or dilapidated, and Jeorfy had seen few if any newer stacks, which could only mean that Zebulon, and possibly the people before him, had been taking the newly arrived stuff directly from the elevators to the fire chasm. There were file entries up to about ten years ago, but none since then. Lately, Zeb hadn't bothered with any of it.

Jeorfy could imagine what Zeb would say to him if he asked. Zeb had already said it, more than once:

"My reward is the same whether I do the work or not. I get the same pay: too little. I live under the same conditions, not good. I ask for a little consideration, and they tell me men are begging for work, men without wives or hope of family, thousands of us, they say. So, why sweat?"

At which point Jeorfy had mentioned that a modicum of sweat could buy them a sweet life. There were bound to be valuables among the stacks. They could take those valuables out through the ducts, sell them outside, and make a fortune.

"They'd find out," Zeb had groused.

"I'll make us new identities," Jeorfy had said. "They wouldn't find out, believe me. Nobody has any idea what's down here."

At first, Zeb had seemed interested in this, but when he had gone looking for the few valuables he'd thought he remembered, he couldn't find them. Jeorfy checked the files and found them to be no help at all. Zeb and his predecessors had kept track of the things they liked or needed, and that was the limit of their performance. The files listed all kinds of treasures, but the stacks weren't there! Where were they?

"All right," Jeorfy had said. "You know where the food is, so we'll start with food. We'll start by taking the packaging off the Zybod hams and we'll claim they come from Barfezi. We'll claim it's a special process, long aging, stuff like that. Edibles are a bit bulky, and the profit on each item will be small, but the volume is huge, so we can build up a clientele and find more expensive stuff as we go along."

Zeb had reacted to that suggestion like a boy told to do the chores. Words like "bulky" and "small profit" sounded too much like work to Zeb.

Zeb was opposed to work. What Zeb wanted was to take his new identity, the one Jeorfy was going to make for him, and leave the caverns just as soon as he could find one nonbulky and high-profit item that would give him enough money to live on. Once he was out, he might hire people to come back down and search, but he wanted out first.

Zeb had made that remark over and over. When the girl came, he'd been funny about her, kind of sneaky. Well, she wasn't the daughter of the Count of Ob in Frangia, Jeorfy knew that much. There had been no nobility in Frangia since religion took over the province. Whoever she was, Jeorfy knew damned well she hadn't packed up all her luggage and sneaked off while they slept. There weren't any vehicles missing. There weren't any footprints, either, so had she flown away?

It would be logical to wonder, right? Logical to go looking for her? Jeorfy thought so, but not Zeb. Zeb said no point in wasting the energy, she'd come back when she was hungry. All too casual, Zeb. All too easy about it all.

All of which made it quite clear to Jeorfy that Zeb thought he'd found his nonbulky, high-profit item, a girl running away from someone who would pay money to get her back! And, knowing Zeb, Jeorfy wasn't sanguine about the item surviving Zeb's attempts at a transaction. Zeb was far gone, a slothful monster, capable of occasional frustrated thrashing about that just got him in deeper. Jeorfy, however, had no intention of letting the girl suffer. He liked her a whole lot better than he liked Zeb.

Which was why he was out here, following Zeb the best he could by sound, aiming for the same general area, but staying out of sight, which wasn't as easy as he'd supposed! It was like following somebody through a maze by listening to his footsteps!

The aisle he was following came to a dead end against another towering stack. Oh, hell, go back and try again, he said to himself, though he'd take a minute first to go pee in a corner.

He turned off the engine and immediately heard another one, not far away, a heavier machine than his own, probably one of the stackers and lifters. Zeb had started out this morning saying he was going to spend the day clearing an old area, so . . . maybe he was and maybe he wasn't.

Leaving his machine where it was, Jeorfy clambered up the side of the nearest stack. When he came to the flat top he was covered with dust and bits of dung, but he persevered, crossing the plateau in slow, easy stages so as not to raise a cloud, not to crash through some carton, not to sneeze or fall. When he came near the edge he hid himself behind a

projecting crate and regarded the scene below with concentrated attention.

Zebulon Coffin was removing crates from a stack back along the way and piling them across the aisle below. Not only was he stacking them to block the aisle, but he was leaving a narrow door at the bottom, half hidden behind one large box. Moving carefully, Jeorfy crept along the trembling edge to look down into the chamber behind Zebulon's barrier. The girl, whatever her name was, was lying there, seemingly unconscious, feet and arms tied, mouth gagged. She didn't move. Jeorfy watched for a long moment and was just making up his mind to go down to her when the stacking machine went silent.

Jeorfy drew back, and a moment later Zeb skulked through the opening, went to the girl and leaned over her.

"Hey!"

She didn't move.

He struck her, not hard, once, twice, three times: *splat, splat splat.*

She opened her eyes.

Zeb said, "I've got water here, you want some?"

She moved restlessly, neither a nod nor a shake, merely a shrug. He leaned forward and took the gag from her mouth. "Like last time, eh? You make a sound, I take the water away. You drink it nice and quiet, you can have it."

"Why are you doing this?" the girl begged. "Why?"

"Somebody wants you," he said. "Somebody'll pay for you."

She laughed, chokingly. "You've got piles of stuff here that somebody would pay for. Mountains of it."

"I'm not interested in moving mountains," he snarled. "You, you're running away from something, somebody wants you, and somebody will pay to get you."

"They won't pay to get me if you let me die down here."

"You won't die. This is just to get you away from Jeorfy. I need him for things. He's going to make us new identities, he is. I need him for the inventory machines. Never learned to run 'em. Never had to run 'em. My assistant did that. But after I killed him, I had to wait ten years for another one."

"Your . . . partner? You killed him?"

"He nagged me. All the time. Store the new stuff. Get rid of the old stuff. Make a new stack here. Make a new stack there. He didn't do it. He didn't want to do it. He just sat there *tappy tappy* all day, nagging at me. I'd go out and make something up and come back and he'd tell me I

couldn't have made a new stack there because there was an old stack there. I got sick of it. I thought I'd get a new helper right away, somebody easier to get along with, but they just let me wait. Ten years I waited."

"For Jeorfy," she murmured.

Zebulon looked up, shaking his head slightly. "Jeorfy's not bad to have around, but he's got no loyalty. I could tell that, right away. He wouldn't cooperate, selling you. So, I had to hide you, first, then I'll figure out what comes next. . . ."

As the conversation progressed, the watcher above became grimmer and grimmer, until at last he shuddered all over, like a startled horse, and began the slow trip back across the plateau. Oh, he'd had his suspicions about Zebulon Coffin. Right from the first, he'd had his suspicions. There were just too many things that didn't add up in either an arithmetical or a psychological sense.

He followed his tracks back to familiar ways, then drove back to the dwelling, where he put his few belongings on the little cart along with a number of other useful items. He fetched tools from the storage compartment on his cart and used them to open the carapaces of conveyances that stood dusty and unused at the far end of the vehicle line. From these he removed several fully charged fuel cells, carefully closing and locking the carapaces afterward. The ones he had lifted were now almost dust free. He frowned, stroked his chin for a time, then went into the dwelling and fetched a piece of mesh, like that used in the doors. Shoveling dust onto a square of the mesh, he used it to sprinkle dust over the vehicles, then blew a few clouds across it, returning them to their unused appearance. After a moment's thought, he decided to take the mesh with him.

Finally, he went back inside and wrote a note to Zebulon saying that he was going to look for valuables in the farther stacks away west—the opposite direction from where the girl was hidden—not to worry if he didn't return that night.

After which he went back the way he had come, stopping at intervals to listen for sound. When he came to less-traveled ways, he followed his own tracks into the same dead end where he had parked earlier. He put the mesh inside his shirt and went up the tottery stack again, and over the top. The new barrier was much higher than it had been, and if he had come upon it from the front, it would have effectively stopped his looking farther. Now, however, Zebulon was gone, along with his machine, so Jeorfy climbed down into the blind alley where the girl lay.

"Come girl," he said roughly, shaking her. "That old dog has you buried like a bone, and he'll eat you for breakfast if we let him."

"Who. Oh, Jeorfy! How did you find me?"

"More or less by accident, Henrietta or Imogene—though I'm sure those aren't your real names—but discover you I did. Here's your hands free; now rub them to life while I untie the rest of you. Damnation. Have to cut it. I won't leave it here, either. Let him wonder, the old mule—stubborn lazy, mule that's what he is. Let him wonder where you are, where the ropes went. Come now, we have to climb over, not to leave tracks. Take what you can carry, I'll bring the rest."

He stopped as they went up the side, shoveling dust from hidden areas into the mesh with his hands, sprinkling it over their tracks, again and again until they reached the top, where he looked down to be sure he had obscured any evidence of their climb. They crossed the pile and went down the other side. At the vehicle, he said, "Did he feed you?"

She shook her head, saying shamefacedly, "And there's no toilet in there. I'm all . . ."

He flushed, saying indignantly, "It's all right, girl. We'll stop a little way along and you can change your clothes. Just now, we need to get well away from here."

He took the cart out of the blind alley, winding among the stacks and coming at last to a much-traveled intersection where one more set of tracks would not betray them. He drove slowly, listening for any sound.

"Where is he?" whispered Genevieve.

"He hasn't worked that hard in years," murmured Jeorfy. "My guess is, he's asleep. Probably back at the dwelling."

They came to one of the way-stations Zeb had built and Jeorfy filled water bottles while Genevieve washed herself and her clothing, wringing it out and bundling it up to dry at some later time. They ate a quick bite, but took no more time than needed. Now Jeorfy headed for the corner of the caverns he had already selected, swerving again and again onto arteries less and less traveled, sometimes circling briefly, though always returning to the direction he had predetermined.

They came upon a key station and stopped once more while Jeorfy tapped away for an hour or more. Genevieve yawned on the cart and tried to stay awake, though she couldn't give herself any good reason for doing so. The dust became thinner and less disturbed the farther they came, the lighting gloomier, the vault lower until at last they reached an aisle leading into darkness that bore no evidence of travel at all. After circling here and there, leaving tracks in all directions, Jeorfy pulled into the way and climbed the nearest pile to tumble an avalanche of cartons behind them,

a barrier that looked accidental. Now theirs were the only tracks left behind them.

"Do you know where we are?" she begged.

"More or less. I brought the map of the caverns with us. I also erased all the other maps, which means Zebulon doesn't have one. He can find his way around the places he's familiar with, but I don't think he's ever explored the rest of it. This tunnel leads out, at least on the map it does. If all goes well, you'll be near the Tail of Merdune in time to catch your friend."

"How did you know Zebulon was holding me like that?" Genevieve asked. "He seemed almost crazy. Did you know he killed the other man that was down here with him?"

"I heard him say so," said Jeorfy.

"You're not talking in rhymes anymore."

"That was when life was uninteresting," he said with a sharp laugh. "When life is really interesting, trifling amusements can be dispensed with. That's Zeb's trouble. He can't get interested in anything, not really. He's gone crazy, I think, from being down here so long. Well, as anyone would! Life here had no purpose! Somebody likes the idea of having this stuff. Somebody cared enough to have made or equipped this place to put it. But nobody cares enough to see that it's done properly! The Lord Paramount sits up there, buying all kinds of things for centuries, piling it up for centuries, and he doesn't even know what he's got, much less use it for anything."

"That's true," murmured Genevieve. She stretched, moaning a little at the stiffness in her back. "When we get out, are you coming back here, Jeorfy?"

"There's a fortune here, for the right man. Those army machines are worth a king's ransom. They can be programmed to fight any foe one has in mind! And the animals! Ah, I'd love to set them loose. More important, there's a way here to find things out. At that last key station, I tried an idea I had about getting through the block they put in the archives, and it worked. I didn't take time to use it much, but now that I know it works, I'll be back to find things out."

"Like what?"

"Like what coin the Lord Paramount uses to buy all this stuff. And why some of the worlds His Majesty used to buy from aren't there anymore. And what's going on, out there, on other worlds. I get tired of Haven, don't you?"

"I haven't had a chance to get tired of it yet," she said. "I've hardly seen any of it."

"It's frozen, Haven. I know it's supposed to be tranquil, but by deepsea, girl, it's more like moribund, soulless!"

She gave him a long, level look, somewhat troubled. "Jeorfy, when you say that word, soulless, what do you mean?"

"I mean this place has no soul to it. No . . . change. No growth. In nature, nothing stays the same, but here in Haven, it's like we're frozen in time."

She frowned. "Are you religious, Jeorfy?"

"Well, as we're nigh on required to be, yes."

"Do you think you have a soul?"

"The churchmen say so, don't they, though I've never figured out quite what it's supposed to be."

"I have a little book, written by Stephanie, you know Stephanie? The Dark Queen."

"I've seen the name in the archives. She was the second wife of the Lord Paramount before Marwell. She bore him so many daughters he threatened to do away with her if she didn't produce a son."

Genevieve shifted on the hard seat, making herself more comfortable. "Stephanie said each living world has a soul that includes all the creatures in it. And if we kill all the other creatures, you know, like they did on Old Earth, then the spirit departs."

"It dies?"

"No, it goes away. Somewhere else. And once that happens, the world has no soul. Do you think that could be true?"

He nodded to himself, thinking. "Well, if everything on a world is tied together, if each thing is part of something else and you can't take it away without changing the other thing, then *if* there are souls, it stands to reason the souls would apply to the whole rather than to the part. Wouldn't it?"

She nodded, slowly. "That's what I thought. Partly because of the way I feel sometimes, looking at a sunset or during a storm of rain when the trees move and sigh, and I get this feeling, this kind of 'wholeness' feeling, as though I was feeling the whole world moving in me. I don't get that feeling in cities, or just from other people. So, it could be, you know, that the world has a soul and we're part of that, and when we're right with it, we can feel part of it, too . . ."

"Besides," said Jeorfy, "all of us humans are pretty much alike, aren't we, so if we all had souls, our souls would be very much alike. You read

old, old books, and the people in them are just like the people now. Same emotions, same hopes and fears. Same sins. Same virtues. But worlds . . . now worlds are unique and they're always changing."

"Right. And then there's what's happening to Chamis . . . and Ares."

"What about Chamis and Ares?"

"Chamis was one of those worlds where the settlers killed off all the native life right away, and it was one of the first worlds that Marwell bought from. But, lately it doesn't have anything to sell and the population is dropping like a stone. And Ares is another one they pretty much stripped when they settled. Within a few centuries, it was mostly bare. And now it's losing so much population that they called in experts from other worlds to try and find out why, but no one knows why. If Stephanie was right, the world spirit probably left both places."

Jeorfy stared at her. "Did you know, *our* population is decreasing?"

Genevieve blinked slowly at him. "Decreasing? I suppose it goes up and down a little, all the time. It's supposed to, isn't it?"

"It's supposed to, yes. But it doesn't. It went up when we first settled. Then it reached the plateau at about a million three, just as everyone expected, and it was more or less flat for a long time. The last several hundred years, though, it's gone down. At first just a little. Lately, more."

"How much down is it?"

"About ten percent."

"Is that a lot?"

"Of course it's a lot, because the rate of decline is increasing. Say it took ten years to lose ten percent, another two years we'll have lost another ten percent."

"Maybe it's just that people are moving around. They're coming down from the mountains to live by the rivers, I know that."

"They're coming down from the mountains because there are too few of them left up there to handle things. Living on the mountains is labor intensive. It takes a lot of hands."

Now Genevieve sat up. "Jeorfy, are you sure?"

"That's what the files say. They keep track of population. The Tribunal's got a system of registering births and deaths that tells them how many people there are. Each little area registers its own births and deaths, and then the books come into the archives and are entered there. It's slow, but it's accurate."

"Ten percent," she mused. "How strange. Is it in one place? Or everywhere? Is it fewer babies? Or fewer old people?"

He shook his head. "I didn't have time to look at the details, my dear. But I shall, when I return."

By this time they had come far beyond the storage areas, and the way was too narrow for anything but the level path on which they rode, a sinuously endless lane that was always the same at the edge of their lights, always the same behind them: pale gray dust and dark gray stone. The dust-fall was much lighter, a veil instead of a carpet. Genevieve drove while Jeorfy rested, and vice versa. Once they stopped so both could sleep, turning off the lights to save the fuel and curling up in their blankets on the cart itself, for fear of losing it in the dark. Several times, Jeorfy changed the fuel cell on the little cart.

"Zeb didn't even know they could be changed," Jeorfy said, shaking his head. "The designer didn't make the job simple, and Zeb's no mechanic. He won't have any idea we could get this far. What I'm hoping is that he thinks I fell in the chasm and you escaped. That'd be best. And I pray there's enough fuel to take us to the end. If the maps are right, there should be, just."

They saw light filtering in among the rocks above them shortly before the fuel ran out. Trudging the last few paces of the tunnel, they made a left turn, and another, to see a bright vertical slit between two rock columns, a narrow eye of light through which they pushed into the outside world after feeding their luggage out piece by piece. Behind them the sun rose over the mountains of Merdune. Below them a narrow trail ran along the edge of the forest.

"We're facing west," said Jeorfy, "looking back at the way we've come. We're right into the edge of the Merdune forest. That trail ahead of us runs north and south along the forest edge, and if the map is right, there should be two trails through the mountains down to the shore of Merdune, one north of us and one south of us, which is your shorter route. I'm afraid your friend will be ahead of you, but I packed plenty of food and water to get you to Midling Wells. If you don't meet up before, you'll meet him where he planned."

He assembled their packs, carefully balancing the one Genevieve was to carry. He patted her shoulder, smiling. "You go south, and I'll go north. I'll know the man by name or voice, and if I find he has delayed, awaiting you, I'll send him after his daughter Imogene. Go with heaven."

"What are you going to do, Jeorfy? I don't like leaving you like this."

"Well, I created myself a new identity at that key station," he said. "And now my new self is going to recruit some helpers. And when I've got a few men and materials together, I'm going back into the caverns!"

"Who is the new man you are?"

"Jeorfy Bliggard, from Bliggen."

"And where will you be recruiting?"

"Somewhere. Haven't decided yet. Somewhere that people aren't totally happy with the way things are. Dania, maybe. I hear there's lots of malcontents in Dania."

"But if I need you, Jeorfy . . ."

"Ah, well, if you need me, lady, just use the archive machine. Leave a message for someone named Jeorfy Bliggard and sign it Imogene. Wherever I am, I won't be far from the machines."

He turned away from her, trudging northward and looking only once over his shoulder. Genevieve put the pack on her back, already arranged with the light saddle on top, and started away down the trail to the south. An hour later, she heard horses approaching from that direction and stumbled into the trees to hide from whoever it might be. Between two mossy boles she saw a disconsolate rider with his chin on his chest and a spare horse trailing behind.

Weary and distracted, she let him go on by, unthinking. Only as he retreated from her did she realize who it was and burst from the trees, crying, "Garth! Papa! It's Imogene."

GARTH SENTITH STOOD IN HIS STIRRUPS TO LOOK OVER THE TOP OF THE last rise that separated him and his weary charge from the sloping meadows leading down to the shore of Merdune Lagoon and the town of Midling Wells. He was so long silent that the quiet penetrated Genevieve's fog of exhaustion.

She looked up and murmured, "Have the wells run dry, the town blown away or been flooded by the lagoon?"

He turned with a little smile. "No, Imogene. The weather is good, the way is clear, and the town looks its usual sleepy self. I'm merely being cautious. Normally, I come here in midsummer during the flower harvest. There are many roses and tuberoses upon these long, sunny slopes, along with lavender and fragrant thyme, and many of my most popular scents derive from them, at least in part."

"So they'll be surprised to see you now."

"A little surprised, but not shocked, for I've occasionally visited here out of season. And they won't be shocked at you, either, for I've often spoken of my children."

"What do we do now?"

"We ride down into the village and stop at Fentwig's house, which is where I usually stay."

The horses stepped to the top of the rise, and for the first time, Genevieve saw the sea. It foamed like lace at the edge of the long meadows, receding into blue haze, endless, eternal. The wind in her nostrils came from it, bringing an odor she had never smelled before: something deep, briny, primal. Her eyes remained fixed on that blue as the horse started down the long slope, and she came to herself with a start and an exclamation only when Garth took her by the shoulder.

"I asked if you were looking forward to a good night's rest?" he said, peering into her face. "Were you asleep already?"

"Daydreaming," admitted Genevieve. "I could use a bed, and a bath."

"Fentwig's House is near the bathhouse, which is clean and well maintained. I suggest you make do with a sponge bath tonight, and tomorrow visit the baths before we set sail."

"We sail tomorrow?"

"Possibly. Or as soon as we find a boat we can hire or rent or borrow. During this cold and windy season, many of Merdune's fishermen neglect their traps and nets in favor of work by the fireside or in the barns."

They rode down the long slope, where flat rosettes of green showed amid the dried stalks of summer flowers. "The green stuff is called Icefern or Evergrow," said Garth. "It has a resinous, sharp smell that goes well with other scents."

"How did you get into the perfumery business?" asked Genevieve.

"It was my grandmother's, then my mother's, then mine," he said. "It provides a good living."

As they neared the village, a few people out on the streets stopped and stared at them. "Few visitors come from this direction," murmured Garth. "But, considering everything, I think it was best to avoid the trails. If that dusty villain in the caverns figured out where you and your friend went, he might have sold the information to someone who would come after you."

"I think Zebulon Coffin would have let me die of hunger or thirst while he was making up his mind what to do with me."

"I've met people like him." Garth nodded sagely. "Men of customary inaction who can be spurred to sporadic excess. Such men often start ill-planned projects that they lack either energy to complete or the wit to abandon."

"That's Zeb," she agreed.

Garth nodded, murmuring, "I'm disturbed by what you tell me about those caverns. Knowing that the Lord Paramount has great stockpiles of extravagant goods, many of them simply rotting away, would bother many citizens of Haven. Is this what the taxes levied by the Council are actually spent for?"

He grimaced and laid a cautionary finger across his own lips. "Still, caution is in order. All we will say to Fentwig is that we lost our way in the dark and missed the trails."

They had come close enough to the town to catch the sound of voices and the honking of geese, near enough to smell wood-smoke and roasting meat. Genevieve was suddenly ravenously hungry, and she clucked to her

tired horse who put his ears forward and hastened his steps, no doubt in equal anticipation of food and rest.

A narrow livestock gate at the upper or western end of town led to a short street that debouched upon a paved square, and on the north side of the square was a sprawling timber-and-wattle building with a thatched roof and a curly sign above the door, "Fentwig's House." When they dismounted, the stocky, white-haired innkeeper came bustling out, breaking into a smile when he saw Garth.

"You must have lost yourself good and proper," cried the host. "What are you doing coming down from the woods that way? You're miles from either of the passes!"

"Went astray in the dark," admitted Garth, with a moue and a shake of his head. He turned to Genevieve, bowing in Fentwig's direction. "Fentwig, my friend, this is my daughter, Imogene. I've told her all about your delectable food and comfortable beds."

"She looks tired out," said the innkeeper's wife, also stout and white haired, who had just emerged onto the stoop. "Come in, both of you. Miss Sentith, it's good to meet you. You'd like a bath, I daresay."

"Gar . . . Papa suggested I visit the baths tomorrow," said Genevieve as she stepped through the open door into a neat little foyer, and from that into a large room with a warm stove in its middle.

"Aha," cried Mrs. Fentwig. "He hasn't been here for months, so he doesn't know! We now have a bath-room, two, in fact, one for ladies and one for gentlemen. We already had water piped in for other things, so Fentwig decided to bring water from the nearest hot spring uphill. We built a room, all nicely tiled, and the cooper made us half a dozen comfortable tubs. It's all clean and toasty warm in there, so you have a bath, dear, you look as though you could use one. Nothing like hot water to soothe away a long day on a horse!"

"Go along, Imma," said Garth, waving her away in Mrs. Fentwig's care. "Take your packet with you. Meantime, I'll see to getting us some rooms."

"Roast leg of lamb for supper tonight," Fentwig cried after Genevieve's departing form. "Boned and rolled around a stuffing of dried mushrooms, mint, basil, thyme, and parsley, with roast garlic and sea-potatoes on the side."

"Oh," said Garth, rubbing his hands together and turning with his back to the fire. "How fortunate I feel."

"Up at the Highlands, were you? Did you buy those bottles you were set on?"

"I did. Lovely little things they are, too. Here's a sample." And again,

he dug out the little bottle and presented it for inspection. "Wouldn't any woman, old or young, like a dear bottle like that, sitting before the mirror on her pretty-shelf?"

"Well, Mrs. Fentwig would, for sure, and our daughters no less. When you come this way next, Sentith, bring one for each of my womenfolk."

So they chatted about nothing very much while Genevieve lay in a curtained cubicle, warm water up to her chin, half floating, the scented steam gathering on her face, for Mrs. Fentwig had come in to whip the bathwater with a bundle of herbs that had lent a soft, clean smell, like rain in a garden. Though Genevieve had been careful not to think of Aufors during all the miles she had ridden for the last two days, the warm water loosened all her constraints and her mind flew to him like iron to a magnet, clinging. Oh, Aufors! The touch of the water was the warmth of his mouth, the embrace of the flannel was the touch of his hands, and there was a tremor inside her, a molten feeling, as though she had become a little fire mountain, flowing with white hot stone, no longer rigid and hard but liquid, shapeless, capable of running over or around everything, anything in its path. Oh, this was a twitch of the loins indeed!

She had not really known she was in love with him until the moment of leaving him. She had wanted to be with him, surely, because he flattered her and she felt wonderful in his company, but she had not known this feeling until he held her. Barbara had been right, quite right, a twitch of the loins was unmistakable! Oh, she would willingly *give up* being part of the nobility if that would let her be with Aufors. She would love to be common, common as he! As Alicia's first husband had been! And safer for it!

She sighed, giving up thought. Thought did no good at all.

So determined, she dozed until the water began to cool, at which point she came out of the water like a pearl from the waves and dove into the folds of the thick towel that had been warming on the pipes from the hot spring, and thence into clean garments while the tub glugged itself empty. She was rosy and warm when she went back through the common room into the kitchen where both the Fentwigs were busy.

"Imma, my dear, but you look rested."

"I am, Papa. The lovely bath was almost enough to make me forget my disappointment in Upland."

"Disappointment, my dear?" asked Mrs. Fentwig. "Who would disappoint such a lovely child?"

Which led to the story of the bad cold and how she had seen abso-

lutely nothing, so the whole trip had been less than amusing. "But, I feel very well, now, and I'm looking forward to the sail home."

"Sail, Sentith? This time of year?" Fentwig opened his eyes wide, miming astonishment.

"Now should be possible," said Garth. "It's windy, I grant you, but—"

"Windy! This season is a good bit more than windy. If you're going to sail south, well, you'll have to wait a few days on the Northerlies, which'll be even breezier! The islands of the Drowned Range don't protect the lagoon as well as once they did, now they're being drowned all over again!"

"Still, it's the quickest way home," said Garth comfortably. "Eight or ten days instead of twice that on a horse! We can sail close to shore and put in if there's a gale, and I'm sure you'll find someone to take us."

"Some lunatic," opined Mrs. Fentwig. "Like Weird Wigham."

"Weird Wigham, exactly," cried Garth. "The very person!"

"Who is Weird Wigham?" begged Genevieve.

Garth said, "Why, Imogene, he's a strange old youngster or young oldster who rejoices in doing the different on weekdays and the ridiculous on holidays. And he has a boat, which is the most relevant thing about him."

"Dinner first," pronounced Mrs. Fentwig, much to Genevieve's approval. "Then a good sleep, and Wigham tomorrow."

Wigham was a long armed and stringy fellow who leapt through life with a jerky lack of conviction, like a marionette handled by an unpracticed puppeteer. His white hair billowed around his head like a fume of smoke. His protruding ears were reddish, as was his skin elsewhere, though little of it showed, for he was habitually dressed in a brightly woven shirt covered by stout canvas overalls stuffed into a pair of enormous red boots. Wigham's boat was called the *Unlikely Duck*, though it was referred to by Wigham himself as *Unlikely*, which leant a strange flavor to the conversation.

"*Unlikely*'ll get there," said Wigham. "*Unlikely*, she's a good old girl."

Old she was, as even Genevieve could see, though she looked well enough kept. She had a small, clean galley below, and beyond it a tiny cabin with two bunks hung high on the bulkheads with slant-backed cupboards below, out of the headroom of the table and benches, plus a tiny cubby forward, with a short bed athwartships and one tiny porthole. "You can have the cubby, girl," said Wigham. "Your pa an' I'll do with the cabin.

Since it's only me taking you and your pa's indifferent as a sailor, we'll anchor near shore at night to get our rest."

"The wind's blowing the wrong way, isn't it?" Genevieve asked, for she hadn't taken time to rebraid her hair, and it streamed northward like a flag.

"Now it is. The Northerlies'll be comin' any day, howsomever, and once they do, they'll be goin' on an' on until we're sick of 'em."

"Will we see the Golden Talking Fish of Merdune Lagoon?" she asked. "Prince Thum—ah, yes, someone I met on this trip said someone named Prince Thumsort talked about them."

She knew she had made a faux pas, but she thought she had covered it until she saw that Garth's face was white, and no less Weird Wigham's. This individual took himself onto the top of his cabin with a leap and a cackle and there began to do a rooster dance, hands tucked into armpits and elbows flapping, crowing as he bowed and pranced, head darting this way and that.

"He's dancing to avert ill luck," murmured Garth.

"I'm sorry," she faltered. "Did I say something wrong?"

"Well, he doesn't know who Thumsort is." Garth smiled. "But he caught on to the 'Prince' part of the title. Weird isn't fond of the nobility."

"Don't know who he is," crowed Wigham from his perch, "but he's no business talking of . . . them."

"The man she spoke of comes from over in Sealand," called Garth. "You know they haven't good sense over there."

"Well, I know *that*. Nowhere near the sea! Not good sense at all. Well, young lady, your papa should have warned you. That's not something we talk of here in Merdune. Don't take them lightly. Nosir."

Genevieve actually started to say that the Duchess of Merdune had been there at the time, but caught herself before the words came out. Instead, she apologized, saying she was very sorry, she hadn't realized.

"Those particular fish," whispered Garth, "are said to be magical by some, and it is considered unlucky to speak of them."

Weird came down from the cabin top and the two men set about their business, Wigham ignoring her ostentatiously, though Garth nodded and smiled behind his back to indicate that Wigham's displeasure would pass.

Soon they agreed that Wigham would lay in ship's supplies and see to the sails, Garth would see to the foodstuffs, and meantime Imogene might buy herself a few books at the Midling Wells shop, for the boat offered no amusement and the weather might be too chilly for spending much time on deck. They would set sail when Weird Wigham, in his sole

opinion (this intention delivered in a declamatory voice, with one or two flaps of the wings) declared that the Northerlies were underway.

So for three days they stayed at Fentwig's House, eating well and catching up on their sleep. Genevieve spent some of the time walking along the shore, well wrapped against the chill, tirelessly investigating the shoreline. There were many shells to be picked up, and in some places stone walls and truncated chimneys protruded from the surf, the remains of farms that had been swallowed by the sea when the waters rose. At two houses just above the waterline, people were busy moving house, barns, fences, and stock to higher ground.

What time she was not exploring, she spent in the lovely bath. In either case, lest she make another mistake in conversation that would give pretense away, she stayed as far as possible from Mrs. Fentwig, who was an avid talker and a keen questioner.

On the fourth day, quite early in the morning, they left their horses to be used by Fentwig until Garth's return, and departed on *Unlikely* as she plowed sturdily away toward the south. After a precautionary lap or two about the deck, wings flapping and voice raised in imprecation against all evils of air, water, or reef, Wigham settled to the wheel. The winds were brisk, and though both Garth and Genevieve were arrant amateurs, their help was needed to set the sails. Genevieve surprised herself by learning first to keep her footing on a surface which tipped in every direction, sometimes in several of them at once, and then by learning what each rope was for and how each of them worked. By afternoon she was able to haul on this one or let go that one at command. So the first day passed swiftly by. Though Genevieve found herself sore from the unaccustomed bracing and bending, reaching, and pulling, by evening she was becoming adjusted to the rocking and pitching of the little boat. By nightfall they were at the southern end of the Tail, ready to run along the Rump on the morning. They anchored in a small bay open to the southeast, and when dark fell, they could see the lights of Eales, where the Covenantor's Tribunal stood, its watch towers blooming in the southern dark like so many stars.

During the night, Genevieve dreamed of swimming. It seemed to her that she swooped and soared, and she woke with the feeling still strong for the ship was indeed swooping as it moved. With momentary panic, she realized that it was no longer anchored but was speedily going somewhere. She crawled from her cubby into the cabin, where Garth and Wigham lay exhaustedly asleep, and when she went between them and struggled her way onto the deck, she had to cling to the railing for dear

life. She could not find the land that had lain close on the evening before. Spray washed over her, wetting her to her skin and the pitching, rolling ship seemed to be determined to go in three or more directions at once!

She opened her mouth to shout for the menfolks and half turned toward the cabin to summon them, but was frozen in place, clinging to the rail, as she stared across a narrow river of water between the ship and something huge and marvelous that paralleled their track. It was golden. It glowed. Though it lay almost entirely within the water, protruding only slightly above the wave-roughened surface, it was many times larger than the ship. It rolled away from her, disclosing amid wrinkled lids one great eye that stared across at her. The eye stared, the boat flew, the night roared with wind, and the long moment slipped by until the golden being rolled away from her and slipped beneath the waves once more, momentarily waving its enormous tail behind it. From below, coming up at her from the planks beneath her feet, Genevieve heard the sound of its singing.

Without any decision at all, from long training in the cellars of Langmarsh House, she leaned over the rail and sang a reply into the night, the sound going out over the water, a higher echo of the sound from below. She stretched across the rail, far, far out, putting out one hand to feel the spray, feeling the call of the depths, wanting to let go, leap out . . .

Then the sail flapped angrily, the boat heeled. Genevieve staggered and shouted in sudden fear. The men, thus wakened, stumbled onto the deck and soon found the broken anchor rope, nibbled along its underwater length and at one point chewed through.

"What did this?" cried Garth.

"Damfino," muttered Wigham, not meeting his eyes "Not anything I've seen, I'll tell you. Rope-eaters we have now! It an't enough they chew the planks, now they're eating the ropes."

"You should've used chain," growled Garth.

"Well, and if it was cheap, I would," growled Wigham in return. "But chain is metal and metal an't cheap, and we've never had rope-eaters before. Now an't this a pickle?" He muttered and gibbered, pulling his hair into witches' locks and turning this way and that in an attempt to get his bearings.

"Where are we?" whispered Genevieve, not daring or even wishing to speak of what had happened to her. She had heard the song of the depths. She had sung it in return. She knew exactly what it was—or what her mother had called it.

"East, a good way," said Wigham, bracing himself at the rail. "Over

the deeps of the Lagoon. Oh, it goes down, here, way down. The sea's come up over the reefs these last few years, and the coral didn't close off all the ways between the isles, in any case. Under the coral, deep down, there's tunnels that go out to the sea." He paused, as though regretting what he had said, adding as amelioration: "Or so they say."

Garth called, "There's the tops of the Mountains of the Tail, away north. They're just lit by morning."

Like a rose satin ruching on the skirt of the sky, the stiff folds of the mountains lay against the northwest horizon, extending in a ruffled arc to eastward, where soft-lit satin became saw-toothed iron against the dawn. Wigham, shouting instructions to the two of them, tried to tack back to coastal waters, all to no avail, for the wind pressed them strongly to the southeast as the northern mountains slowly disappeared over the horizon.

"We can wear ourselves out tacking toward the coast," said Wigham at last, "or we can give in to fate and sail on to the Drowned Range. We're past half there already, and though it'll lengthen the journey slightly, it'll be easier on us and *Unlikely*. There's anchorage all along the Range on the lee sides of the islands."

Garth confessed himself ignorant of the geography of the Drowned Range, and it was with some trepidation that he watched out the rest of the morning while the little boat plowed strongly through the waves, leaving a curled wake full of dancing fishes behind her. Genevieve scarcely noticed. In her mind she was still back in the night, clinging to the rail, singing with immensity. What had it meant? Mother had never told her what it meant! Perhaps she, herself, had not known.

"Why are they following us?" Garth asked, pointing to the fishes in the wake.

"They always do that," called Wigham, from his position at the wheel. "They like looking at us."

This brought Genevieve to the aft rail, where she looked down at the fish in return, small fat golden fishes with large eyes that faced more front than sideways. Beneath them, never appearing above the water, lay an enormous golden shadow.

"Do you eat that kind?" Garth cried.

Wigham shook his head. "Bad luck to eat that kind."

Genevieve noticed he had not actually looked at the fish, to see what kind they were. In fact, ever since the chewed rope had been found, he had kept his eyes resolutely away from the water around the boat. She had been going to mention the golden shadow, but thought better of it.

"What kind do you eat?" she called.

"Mostly skinny silver fish of various kinds. And on the reefs there are squeels and nonopuses and saltwater craylets." His elbow wings flapped several times, telling her she was approaching a forbidden topic.

She asked nothing more. The golden shadow had departed. Except for the small golden fish, there was only water dancing in the wind and throwing sequined light into their eyes, splintered as a shattered mirror. No land showed at all, and only Wigham's compass told them they still kept to the same course. Genevieve helped prepare and eat a scratched-together luncheon. Hours later, when the light began to fail, she and Garth again went to the food stores, but within moments Wigham called them on deck to point out a line of foam eastward and a lone light southward, red in the center, with a white beam either side.

"That's the light at Near Ledge Isle," cried Wigham. "Hold off supper until we come to anchorage. We'll sail a little farther east, then turn south to bring us in on the lee side of Ledge Isle, with Far Ledge Isle seaward. You two hold yourselves ready now, and we'll be at quiet water in the hour."

As they were, though they were covered with gooseflesh and soaked through before they lay to in a cupped bay of still water opening only to the north. Lacking an anchor, they might float gently ashore, said Wigham, but they could not be driven asea.

"Looky there," he called. "Water-babies!"

Genevieve leaned on the rail to see the curious creatures swimming below, much like human babies when seen from the back, mostly buttocks and kicking legs, but when they turned over they were froggy things with wide mouths and hair that floated like waterweed. They seemed harmless enough as they circled the boat, swimming on their backs, peering up at the humans, gargling from their wide mouths as though they laughed.

"Those are Haven creatures, are they Wigham?" asked Garth.

"Some say. Some say they're born to Merdune women who go swimmin' when they shouldn't. And when the women's times come, why then, the midwives deliver these things, and they run them to the shore, fast as may be, to get them in the water."

"Surely not!" cried Genevieve, suddenly remembering why Aufors had been so frightened. Poor boy, who had been teased about becoming part-fish and had nightmares as a result!

"Probably not," corrected Garth. "Though I've heard stranger things."

Wigham flapped his wings and told them to get themselves dried and warm. As for him, he would row ashore with the remnant of the anchor rope and tie *Unlikely* to the rocks, just in case. Then he'd hike himself to

the Ledge Isle light and its attendant hamlet, hoping to buy an anchor and a line. Garth said he would go along, as he had never seen the light, so they went, leaving Genevieve to start a fire in the stove and make tea. She poured a cup, generous with the sugar, and drank it while she put together a stew of lamb and potatoes and onions, following directions Garth had given her, sotto voce, earlier in the day.

"Imogene," he had told her, "would know how to cook, so you must pretend you know."

Actually, she did know, for she had spent many a holiday afternoon in the Langmarsh kitchen helping Della and the cook. While the stew simmered, she changed into dry clothes, warming her feet by the stove before putting on her boots. Then she wrapped herself well and carried her wet clothes and bowl of stew onto the deck, where she spread the clothes to dry before sitting sleepily on a hatch cover to watch the reflections of the light in the water and listen to the chuckle of the wavelets along the hull as the boat rocked soothingly, well out of the wind.

"Genevieve," whispered the wavelets. "Come to the rail, Genevieve."

Obediently, she rose and went to the aft rail, leaning over it to look into the depths. The water-babies were gone. In their place was a shining light, softly golden green, spreading from the area around the boat like a stain that broadened and lengthened until all the little bay was lit with its peridot glow. It came, she thought, from that something huge that lay below and swam in a light of its own, lending that light also to the fat golden fishes that flowed in linked arcs, like threads being woven into patterned lace. Beneath this filigree the gold of the depths came higher yet, making a brighter circle at the stern of the boat. For a moment, she thought she saw something there, as though the golden stain encompassed an enormous face. Two eyes, this time, and a mouth that could swallow the sea.

The fat fishes continued to swim, the golden light below hung in the water. She stared. The boat rocked.

"Why did you have your fishes chew through the anchor rope?" Genevieve asked drowsily, half-hypnotized by the movement of the creatures.

"Because you do not belong here, Genevieve. Your road is not this one. Your road is the one you are running from. You must keep the oath of your lineage, your promise to your mother. You must go back."

She heard it clearly in her mind though she was perfectly aware that her ears did not. The golden light pulsed in time with her heart; her vision spun out into it, seeking shape, form, identity. Her heart broke at the words. What spoke? Who spoke?

"Who speaks?" she said.

A line of silver bubble started among the golden filigree, arrowed up at her, lunged from the water and streaked into the air, snatching the rail of the boat as it flew. A shape. Manlike, maybe. Man-sized, certainly, but with a great frill around its head, like a fringed collar, very bright and beautiful. It gripped the railing firmly and said without moving its mouth, "You have heard the harbinger song, Genevieve. You have sung it in reply. You will go with Delganor."

"No," she cried aloud, the word skipping on the waves like a stone, splashing up echoes. "No!"

The shining being bobbed its head. Still it did not move its mouth, yet it seemed to say, "You will go with Delganor. It has been long planned that one of Stephanie's line would go where he goes, see what he sees. You are the one. We have heard your listening. When you sang, we knew you were the one. Your mother saw it. We see it. Stephanie's line has spread widely, and in you it has come together. You will follow the necessary way. You will go with Delganor."

She leaned upon the rail, sick to her heart, the pain spreading outward, through all her body and mind. "Not Delganor."

The being cocked its head. "Yes. All here hangs in the balance, trembling upon the cusp. You are needed now. Others may be needed later. Return, Genevieve. And call upon us at need upon the sea, Genevieve. Call upon us at need."

"Who are you?" she cried. "Who are you?"

"A messenger of te wairua taiao," whispered the being as it left the railing with a sudden slithering motion. The design of fishes broke apart, random golden sparks that swam away in all directions. The golden-green glow dropped into the deeper darkness, and Genevieve closed her eyes, then opened them once more. She was leaning on the aft rail. The pain that racked her was real. She stumbled back to her hatch cover, telling herself she had dreamed, but no. Her supper was still quite warm; not enough time had passed to fall into dreaming sleep.

So, she had not dreamed, she had had a vision. Or she had not had a vision, she had actually heard a being speak! Or heard something speak through it, which made more sense. She had seen fat golden fish with a light beneath them, a light that spoke in her mind. A light that knew her by name! That spoke of her lineage, her duty!

Her duty to go with Delganor. Her duty to return, then, to Delganor. Perhaps real. But perhaps it was all a trick, a trick by Delganor himself.

Anyone who could listen, as he did, could do other things as well. Create illusions. Create voices!

She tried to convince herself of this as she sat shuddering upon the hatch top, her supper growing cold in her hands. Hours later, chilled through, icy with sorrow, she heard the cheerful voices of Garth and Weird Wigham, joined in a slightly tipsy song that kept time with the splash of the oars.

Supplied with a new anchor and rope, the *Unlikely Duck* made her erratic way down the Drowned Range, from island to island, giving Genevieve and Garth a chance to view a part of Haven neither had seen before. Since the islands were the rugged peaks of volcanic mountains sunk—and still sinking—in the Inundation, they had no gentle beaches. Here and there a wooded valley might plunge into the sea, and everywhere tiny streamlets meandered from the heights through boulder bound pools. Huts clung to the precipices and round water towers loomed over tiny terraced fields that clung to the sides of the mountains, supported by tall walls of dry-laid stone. All these works of man—towers, walls, and terraces—had been built through centuries of incessant labor.

At this season the terrace tops were furred with golden stubble, horizontal lines of brightness against black rock that towered above ice-glittering, echoing fjords. The journey was mesmerizing. Here great waves swept over the reefs between the islands, sometimes a gentle susurrus of ripples, sometimes great shouting geysers of spray that erupted from blow holes on the lagoon side. As nowhere else in Haven, here was the feel of the great sea, the presence of it, the push and sway of it, and, so Garth said, the threat of it as well.

"It's a big ocean," he remarked to no one in particular.

"And gettin' larger," said Wigham. "These islands out here, they get smaller all the time. People moving up the slope and up the slope . . ."

"Well," said Garth, comfortably, "it's said the poles haven't melted entirely yet."

"My pa said they was finished meltin' when he was a boy. Guess there was ice somewheres nobody knew about."

Garth shrugged, a trifle uncomfortably. "Monsters out there," he remarked. "So I'm told."

"Oh, monsters right enough," replied Weird Wigham. "I've seen a man go looking for his craylet traps to find them broken up, squeezed into scraps."

"Does it happen often?" Genevieve asked, wonderingly.

"Not so often they stop setting traps," said Weird. "Often enough to make them talk of killing the creatures, though there's no weapons along the Drowned Range that would do the job. The Lord Paramount might, maybe, if he wanted, but so far, he an't wanted."

"I doubt it would do any good," mused Genevieve. "If one monster were killed, or two, or a dozen, or a dozen dozen, no doubt there are millions more out there."

"Is that true?" asked Weird. "Is the ocean that large?"

"The ocean is very large," said Genevieve in a distant, musing voice. "Its surface is about four hundred times larger than the land area of Haven, and if we were to calculate its depth, its true volume of living space would be thousands of times as great. So for every monster you might find here, at Merdune Lagoon, there are probably thousands more where you will never find them. For every mound of swelling gold, rising like a cloud from the depths, there are no doubt a thousand more that no one sees . . ."

She caught herself, too late. Both Garth and Weird looked at her in astonishment blended, on Weird's part, with more than a touch of hostility.

Weird flapped mightily, crying, "Your daughter talks high and mighty, don't she, Garth? Are all young ladies these days so uppity?"

"Mostly they are," said Garth glumly, with a sharp glance at Genevieve. "Even when they've left school, like Imogene here, they read books. You've heard it said, a little learning's dangerous."

"And less is more so," retorted Genevieve, suddenly angered in her turn. "Why, if people do not know what lives in these seas, how can they live sensible lives in this little space?"

Both men turned away, not letting her see their faces, even Garth making a gesture that she recognized as a common one—to avert ill fortune. She was ashamed of her bad temper at once, but oh, she was weary of this journey. Weary and lonely and confused. Though she had at first been grateful to Alicia for helping her escape Delganor, now it seemed she had not escaped at all, or had gone aside from her future only momentarily, until a great fish reminded her of it!

"Softly, daughter," murmured Garth. "It will only be a day or two more."

"Yes, Papa," she replied in a subdued voice. "I'm sorry I spoke out of turn."

"Have you . . . seen what you speak of?"

"Perhaps," she said. "Or perhaps it was only a dream."

He sighed. "The Duchess told me you . . . see things sometimes. She said to keep it hidden if we could. All in all, you've handled all this better

than I expected. My own daughters would have done no better. But how is it you know all this about how large the ocean is? I thought you girls were limited to pretty chatter and the economics of housekeeping. I didn't know you learned geography."

"We don't," she said, somewhat shamefaced. "But we learned to read, and once one can read, one can learn anything. I know this ocean is a very large ocean, and when the great waves come spouting out of holes at us, or when I look across the reefs at the endlessness of it, it reminds me how tiny this boat is. I believe there are creatures in this sea far larger than this boat and more knowledgeable than we can imagine."

He listened to only part of this. "It is a small boat," he agreed. "And these are cramped quarters to grieve the loss of one's love in."

She laughed, almost gaily. "How could I lose what I didn't even know I had? At school, when we talked of such things, it was never mentioned that one's first kiss could also be the last!"

"Oh, come, come, now. Not the last, certainly."

He patted her shoulder, while she thought privately that he was a good deal more sure of that than she was.

Two days later, early in the morning, they came into port at Headway, a shoreline town at the foot of the cliffs that made up the Head of Merdune. Garth rented a light carriage and a strong horse, and they set out at once for Weirmills, driving all day on the switchback road that took them to the heights overlooking the everlasting sea. At sunset they came up onto the top and looked down a long grassy slope to the Lake of the Eye. From the Eye a little stream ran away westward, scarcely more than a rivulet, but still the start of the Potcherwater, and on its near edge, sprawled untidily among its meadows, was a rural clutter of shabby barns, listing hayricks, and ill-mended fences.

"We will stay in that village tonight," said Garth. "Tomorrow, only a few hours west, down the little Potcherwater, we will home to Weirmills."

"There are people on the road," said Genevieve. "See, coming toward us?"

There were two riders on the road. Genevieve stiffened. They looked . . . one of them looked . . . no, both of them looked familiar. But, who?

From afar, the figures spied them against the sky. One turned to the other, then whipped up his horse and came at a gallop while the other followed, more slowly.

"Who?" said Garth. "Who can that be?"

"Aufors," she cried. "It's Aufors." She put her heels into the horse's sides and he, nothing loath with oats and hay awaiting in the town, plunged recklessly down the road.

When Garth arrived, they were leaning from their horses, making a kind of bridge of embraces, which Garth gently disentangled as the other rider came up, a woman.

"You must be Genevieve," said the newcomer. "My cousin."

"And you," said Genevieve, staring into a face that was only a slightly changed version of her own, a face with the same eyes, the same nose precisely. "You are Duchess Alicia's daughter. Lyndafal."

Night, cool, a small balcony open over the stable yard of a country inn. White curtains streamed into the room, blown by the night wind. The fire in the grate flared up, playing across the rose-brown skin of the woman by the hearth. The figure at the open balcony door closed it once more and resumed his seat by the fire. Aufors, with a worried face.

"So you were held captive by this man for how long?"

"I don't know. There are no nights and days down there. A few days, I suppose."

"Did he . . . hurt you?"

"Of course he hurt me," she muttered, taking a deep breath. More calmly, she said, "And he humiliated me. I was tied up and not allowed to use a toilet. But he did no lasting damage."

He nodded heavily, glancing at her lowered face from the corner of his eyes, wanting to ask a more specific question but deciding against it. "And then on the lagoon, there was a being who said you must go with Delganor?"

"If it was actually speaking, that is what I heard, yes."

"A manlike being." There was much he wanted to know about this being, but she seemed reluctant to speak of it. He had the feeling that if he pushed the matter, her fragile calm might be totally destroyed.

"Something that came from the sea," she said fretfully. "I think it had a head and a torso and four limbs, so it may have been manlike. Oh, Aufors, I really don't know!"

"Or maybe . . ." he swallowed deeply, "it was froglike."

"Frog, toad, monkey, I don't know." She looked so hag-ridden, so weary, that he turned away to the rumpled bed where they had come together like two comets, driven throughout all the ages of the universe to a fiery, impetuous meeting that should have lit up the skies with its heat. There they had lain until a few moments before, delaying any thought of

reality. Now there was too much reality to suit him. He could not bear the thought of her held captive, the thought of her at the bidding of strange forces. He could not bear the thought of the man in the cavern, the manlike thing on the lagoon, both of whom had had her at their mercies. Or lack thereof.

Now he pled, "Marry me, Genevieve."

She shook her head sadly and said no.

"I must go with Delganor," she said, several times.

"Have you *seen* anything to do with Delganor?" He cried, hopelessly.

Genevieve shook her head again. "No. I have seen a city built of mud under a blazing sky. I have seen—or more properly heard—a huge voice crying or singing. I have seen blood on my hands and felt terror. Lyndafal has seen herself lying in the dust while her child is passed from hand to hand." Though Lyndafal possessed the seeing, sometimes, vaguely, she had not learned from Alicia any of the things that Genevieve had learned from her mother. There had been no cellar-singing in Lyndafal's life, nor any of . . . the other things. Somewhere in that lineage, the lore-line had been broken.

Genevieve ran her hands over her face, surprised to find that she still felt like the same person. She had expected to be changed, utterly changed. She gritted her teeth and went on, "The fish, if it was a fish, said our lineage was designed for this."

"*Our* lineage?"

"Well, according to Alicia, Lyndafal and I are both descended from Stephanie. She was Queen of Haven, once, though that title is only a courtesy one. Lords Paramount rule and Queens sit still while they do it. The idea that a lineage can be designed for anything makes me rather angry. Who, here, knows how to design a lineage save in the sense that livestock is selected to be more thrifty or hardy?"

"Wouldn't the . . . trait selected for be dissipated in each generation?"

"Perhaps it is not entirely in the genetic material," Genevieve mused. "Perhaps it is merely a thing, an idea, a belief or a skill that is implanted in every member of that line. There are descents tied to the female line, you know. This nose has afflicted generations of my foremothers."

"Are there only the two of you?"

"I would think not." Genevieve furrowed her brow in thought. "I had a little book, in Havenor, written, supposedly, by Stephanie herself. Someone had drawn a genealogy in the back of it, Stephanie's line. One of Alicia's foremothers, Mercia, had ten daughters, and each of them had three or more. One of them, Lydia, had five daughters, and they all had

daughters. And my mother had sisters who had daughters. So did Lynda-fal's. The family runs to girls. There are probably . . . oh, dozens, maybe even hundreds of us."

"But Alicia doesn't have your . . . 'talent.'"

"That may be a separate thing. All of us might have the pattern, but only some of us might be able to use it. If that's what it is. Like a dress pattern." Genevieve smiled, thinking of Veswees. "We all have the pattern inside us, but only some of us can turn it into a dress." She stood up, bent, stretched, then came into his arms, settling on his lap, nestling there.

"I love you, Aufors. I have no doubt of that at all. But I cannot marry you. I must go back. I have no doubt of that, either."

"But he gave me permission to marry you! I told you."

"I know. But it doesn't work the other way around. He didn't give me permission to marry you. That worries me. It feels like a trap, one my road leads straight to, or through. So I go back, my darling."

He gathered her tightly, his eyes full of tears. "You're sure?"

"I'm sure. I've fought it. I've run from it. I've worried over it, thinking up every excuse I can come up with. None of it's any good. I promised. I'll keep my promise. And then, when I've kept it, if I'm able, I'll marry you."

He tugged her back into the bed and they came together again in a spirit that was part desperation, part ecstacy, part renunciation, part something deeper and older and more profound than either of them could have identified if they had tried.

And even in the heat of it, he wondered why she would not marry him, and if it was for the reason she had given him, or for some other reason she had not told him at all. In the night he dreamed of her in the caverns, at the mercy of that old man, and on the sea, at the mercy of whatever it was who had come up out of the depths, and he awoke from that dream as he had awakened from others, shouting in terror, waking her also into fear. It required some time to settle them both.

"Only a nightmare," he said to her and himself, clammy skinned and sweating. "Only a nightmare."

Aufors and Genevieve returned to Havenor, neither hurrying nor delaying, but with deliberate inevitability. Despite the intensity of the passion that had overmastered them in Weirmills, Genevieve allowed them only that one night, insisting that their love must be held in abeyance. Not now, she said. Not yet. "Not yet" became words bitter on Aufors's tongue, particularly on the twenty-fifth day of their travel when he caught Genevieve in tears.

"What is it?" he asked, reminding himself to be as gentle as possible. Shouting at her would not help, so he had proven to himself early in the journey, and lately she had seemed tired and listless.

"I'm pregnant," she said. "I think."

He staggered, forgetting himself to shout, "Oh, by the deepsea, Genevieve. We must be married. We must!"

"Shh," she said. "No, Aufors. Not yet."

He heard himself pleading, "If not now, it may be never!"

"That will be as it will be. And I don't want you to tell Father when we get to Havenor!"

"It'll become apparent, soon enough."

"Maybe not. I have a kind of idea. Don't ask me. Just let me . . . deal with it."

"At least I'll be there to care for you."

"You mustn't. I can't take that. This trip is hard enough, being so close to you without . . ." She drew a sobbing breath. "You said Father had a new equerry. You must live somewhere else, do something else."

"Genevieve, for the love of heaven, your father expects us to be married."

"Well, I'm not saying no. I'm just saying not now."

"Why?"

"You've asked me before. I can't explain it. I have some other thing to

do, something I was born for. I can't deal with my own life until I've dealt with that!"

"But you don't know what it is!"

"No. Not yet."

Not yet. The bitter words. He was beginning to lose faith in not yet. He was beginning to seek reasons thay lay outside the reasons she gave. Though he would have denied it, a tiny seed of doubt had germinated and sent down a hairlike root to find sustenance in his guilt over not being with her on that journey, in his fury at her father, in all the mystification and double talk that went on around him. Perhaps something had happened to her that should not have happened.

They had come through Barfezi by way of a boat upon the Potcherwater, through County Vanserdel, where Lorn, Duke Barfezi had his seat, where they had hired horses and gone north to the ferry across the Reusel. This brought them into Langmarsh, where they rode upward along the same road where Aufors had begun his journey. Though it would not have hurt Genevieve to travel faster, Aufors was in the grip of an obsession, and he insisted upon a slow, untiring pace as they climbed to the pass above High Haven. Two more days brought them to Havenor, where they went first, at Aufors's suggestion, to the home of the Duchess Alicia. She was, so the servants said, still in Merdune, with her granddaughter, grieving the loss of her daughter. They did not expect her return to Havenor at any proximate time.

"I wanted to see her," Genevieve confessed, when they had remounted. "I thought she might make some things clearer to me."

"Then, I, too, would like to have seen her," Aufors said, bitterly. "I much need things made clear to me."

"Aufors . . ." she said pleadingly.

"Genevieve," he mocked. "My darling, I love you. But I am mightily out of temper with you, all the same."

They rode to the Marshal's house, finding him not at home. "Blessedly," said Genevieve. "Now, dearest, go away. First let the Prince know that I would not marry you, and therefore you have promised him nothing."

"The Prince will not like those words."

"Dress them how you will."

"And you won't relent?"

She shook her head, faced him with a puzzled frown. "Never doubt that I love you, Aufors. Please. Never doubt it. Even when . . . when things seem strange. Everything is strange. I am doing everything wrong,

so it seems to my senses, and yet in my mind, it feels . . . that I am doing the right thing."

"What *are* you doing?"

She laughed, saying with a catch in her voice, "Well, right now I'm going to sit down with Della and let the seams out of my dresses."

After finding himself a place to stay in Havenor—which he had no time to do before leaving—Aufors shortly begged an audience with the Prince.

"I presume you found her," the Prince said in an uninterested voice that covered a fully satisfied mind.

"I did, Your Highness. And asked for her hand, as I said I would. She has, however, refused me."

"Refused you!" Satisfaction vanished. The Prince seemed, for the moment, speechless.

Aufors gritted his teeth. "She is of the opinion, sir, that she should not have acted as she did. That to marry me would somehow make her . . . fall short in your eyes."

After a long silence, the Prince said through gritted teeth, "So you're back with the Marshal?"

"No, sir. I've taken rooms in Havenor. I had already trained a replacement to serve as equerry to the Marshal. I am seeking a command in His Majesty's armies somewhere in Dania."

Something in Aufors's voice drew the Prince's keen attention. Some quality of . . . what was it? Shame, perhaps. Embarrassment? Ah.

"Your ambition will have to be delayed," said the Prince, now with the slightest curve of lip, an knife-edged smile of penetrating chill. "You may as well stay where you are. You promised to assist me on the Mahahm mission, and that mission has already begun. Planning is well along."

"But sir . . . My agreement to do so was conditional upon my marrying the Marshal's daughter. If she would not have me . . ."

Delganor snarled, "That was your condition, Colonel. I did not accede to it. Review what we said, please. You had my permission. She had my permission. In return for that permission, you and she were to accompany me. The fact that she chooses not to take advantage of my condescension makes no difference to our bargain."

Aufors remained immobile and expressionless, though with considerable difficulty. "I am at Your Highness's command. Since Genevieve is not my wife, however, I cannot speak for her."

"The departure date has been scheduled. The Marshal will be accompa-

nying us, at the Lord Paramount's request. He can, no doubt, speak for the girl."

Aufors bowed. "As Your Highness wishes." He began to back away, toward the door.

"You have not been dismissed," said the Prince with vicious deliberation. He watched Aufors closely as he said, "Since she did not marry you, I may, perhaps, prevail upon her to marry me. That is, if she is still the kind of young woman a Prince would find suitable. Would you say that she is? To your certain knowledge?"

The threat was implicit. It was not a subject Aufors could lie about, or Jenny might find herself married to the Prince! Aufors remained bowed until he gained control of himself, thereby missing entirely the expression on the Prince's face: one of avid and unpleasant glee.

Aufors managed to make the only reply possible. "Your Highness, I am afraid she would no longer be . . . suitable. I was guilty of anticipating our marriage. Genevieve is with child."

"You are dismissed," said the Prince in a bored voice that covered the pleasure he was taking in this interview. Life held few moments as delicious.

"But, sir . . ." said Aufors.

"So? She's pregnant," the Prince drawled, eyebrows raised. "You must answer to her father for that, not to me. As for me, I am pleased at the news. It is said to be good luck to have a pregnant woman or new mother along on trips over the sea. Run along, Colonel. I'm sure it will all work out, in the end."

Genevieve received Aufors's report as calmly as she could, allowing herself no expression of distress that would further upset him. He was quite troubled enough, more than enough. It took several hours of talk and soothing before he would settle with any pretence of patience into the waiting game she was determined they should play. He was not left idle long, for he was soon drawn back into the Marshal's employ during every moment he could spare from the duties assigned by the Prince. Though the mission to Mahahm was not to be a large or numerous one, there were many decisions concerning supply and logistics to be made. There were new weapons and devices to be tested and installed on the Lord Paramount's airship. There were men to be recruited and trained in their use.

During the time that followed, Genevieve tried to maintain a discreet distance from him. She tried not to look at him directly, not to speak to

him too lengthily or too personally. She did this out of conviction it was right, without realizing how her coolness enriched his distrust, not necessarily of her, for he loved her unreservedly, but of the situation, of something evil and amorphous that encompassed them both.

As the season wore by, as Genevieve's let-out dresses gave way to more flowing ones that Veswees made for her—becoming her confidant in the process—Genevieve blessed the approaching mission to Mahahm, for it kept her father's attention fully occupied elsewhere. Any notice he had to spare was taken up by a few minor skirmishes in Dania. "Women raiders," he said, with a twist to his lips that forbade questions. "Thieves, stealing daughters!"

By the time of their departure, Genevieve was some 220 days along—according to the midwife she had consulted on Veswees's recommendation—with only fifty or so days to go. She, Aufors, and the Marshal were to join the Prince at the much-touted resort in Bliggen, a place that often served as the staging area for trips to Mahahm. Though the rest of the party would travel horseback, Aufors, concerned for Genevieve's comfort, made arrangements for her to travel by river packet to Reusel-on-mere, by boat from there to Poolwich, and by another boat down to the shores of Bliggen, in Barfezi, where she could be met by a comfortable carriage and brought the rest of the way. It was this detail that finally caught the Marshal's attention and let him, for the first time, focus on Genevieve. What he saw did not please him, and the outburst was notable for both volume and invective.

Ten days of bitterness followed, capped by the Marshal's command that Genevieve and Aufors be married, forthwith.

"Now it's a matter of duty," Aufors told her caustically, when he went to inform her of her father's decision. "He says the Prince assented to our marriage, the Prince insists we both go on this mission, and he, the Marshal, is not going to be gossiped about and have his family name put to scorn. Better marriage to a commoner, he says, than the shame of a totally uncovenantly child."

"You're sure the Prince doesn't want me himself? Not anymore?"

"He wants you on this trip, Jenny! Seemingly that's all he's ever wanted, really."

"I can't understand that," she cried.

"Maybe he's had an omen, I don't know! Maybe he's consulted a seeress. Deepsea, Jenny, I don't know what's in the monster's mind! Stop all this play! Unless you know, for certain, that our marriage is a bad idea, and why it's a bad idea, then let us do it. Now. At once."

Della, who had learned all of what was going on during the process of letting out seams, offered the opinion that Genevieve should do what both her father and Aufors wanted her to do.

"Your ma told you to go with Delganor, so you say. So, you'll be going with Delganor. Your ma never said marry Delganor, did she now?"

Genevieve shook her head. "No, Della. But she said the way would be hard, and if I'm married to Aufors, it won't be hard at all. That's what's kept me from it, all this time."

"Ha," snorted Della. "So that's it! If you think being married isn't hard, no matter to who, you're still a child. Marriage is about the hardest thing in the world, girl. If people knew all about marriage in advance, likely they never would. They do it when they're green in hope, like you, with the sap of passion flowing. So do it while you've got the incentive!"

Aufors had the necessary documents. He had had them with him since first leaving Havenor in search of her. He took them, as soon as they were filled out, to the archives to have them recorded, thus making it official. Under the laws of Haven, this was all that was required for commoners to marry.

Since Genevieve would be traveling through Bliggen, she considered stopping at the Ahmenaj estate, where Glorieta and Carlotta would no doubt be spending the impending holidays. After some thought, she decided against it. There was too much on her mind; her school friends were too perceptive not to see she was distracted and too pertinacious to let it be.

She had not figured on Carlotta, who had her own network of spies and informants. When Genevieve arrived at Poolwich, at the mouth of the Reusal, Carlotta was there, determined to accompany her the rest of the way to Bliggen.

"I had to get away from home," she confided, almost at once. "I couldn't bear it any longer. Glorieta is in mourning . . ."

"What? Who?" Genevieve cried.

"Oh, no one's died, though you'd think the plague had taken half the family the way she goes on. No, it's Willum. He grew tired of allowing Glorieta her youth and eloped with our schoolmate, guess who?"

"I had heard that from my dressmaker," said Genevieve, remembering that last soirée but one, Barbara in Willum's arms on the dance floor. "There was evidently some gossip about it at court."

Carlotta pinched her lips together angrily. "Barbara's pregnant already. Maybe she was pregnant before! She may have even had the child by now. Well, she said she'd elope and she did. She said she'd run off and

get pregnant, and she did. I wish her the joy of it. If Willum could do that to my sister, I have no doubt he'll end doing something worse to Barbara!"

"Did he explain? Did he offer any reason?"

Carlotta snorted. "What reason could he offer? His father, Earl Blufeld, wanted him married; Willum wanted a wife in his bed, and he didn't want to wait ten years for her. All Glorieta does is sniff and say she'd have given up her youth for him, but he wouldn't let her. All he did was tell her he loved her and ask her to have faith in him. Faith. Fah."

Genevieve felt a premonitory stirring, that uncertain tremor that presaged a vision. "I could have sworn he loved her. I saw his face, looking at her. I could have sworn . . ."

"Let's talk about something else, Jenny. I'm so glad to see you, fat though you are! Speaking of elopements, you did get the handsome Colonel after all, father or no father."

The tremor vanished, blown away by this spate, like a candle flame in a gust of wind, and Genevieve was content to talk about Aufors, even allowing herself, when asked, to say that her father was reconciled to the match and the Prince had consented to it. Beyond that she did not say. It was good to have a friend beside her again, but she did not want more talk than was necessary about herself and the Marshal, the Prince, and Aufors.

As they went down the Danian coast aboard the *Tern*, they saw several bargeloads of cargo from Bliggen, destined for the Lord Paramount, so it was said by the bargemen. Both the barges and the *Tern* tied up at a mooring between Poolwich and Wellsport while the provincial taxmen examined the cargoes of both. The process seemed interminable, and Genevieve leaned across the railing to talk to a garrulous oldster below.

"So where did the goods come from?" Genevieve asked.

"Come down in a sky-ship, they did," said the bearded bargeman. "Just like always, on the prairie out there in Bliggen. And from there, they come to the shore on drays, and when we get 'em to Poolwich, they'll go on drays again, up across the Reusal onto the Wellservale road."

"You make this trip often?"

"Oh, aye. Time on time. Up we go with stuff for the Lord Paramount, and back we come with stuff for Mahahm. Grain and the like."

"How does the stuff get to Mahahm?"

"Well, them Frangians, they haven't a speck of sense among 'em, but down to the south, where the Notch is, the land falls off in three or four great shelves, and on the lowest one—which is a good deal lower now

than it used to be, the way the water's rising—there's this port with a wall around it, and the people inside that wall, they an't Frangians, quite. Oh, they speak like, and they dress like, and I suppose they believe like, but they don't act like."

"You say port, so there must be ships?"

"Oh, aye. They sail out along the Stone Trail, carryin' cargo to Mahahm. Grain and fiber and food of all kinds."

"I've never heard about that."

"Well, not many have because not many have ever been there. I was there once, years ago, when my pa took me. My pa was in the ship-rigging trade out of Shaller, in Merdune, afore it got drownded. They sent for some of his folk to come over there and teach 'em better ways to rig their ships, so that's how I know."

"And what do the ships bring back from Mahahm?" Genevieve asked.

"Not a thing. Sand for ballast, and otherwise empty," said the old man.

"No P'naki?"

"I hear that comes in the Lord Paramount's airships, that does. So's to be sure of it gettin' here safe."

"But if the sea's so dangerous, aren't the sailors fearful of the voyage?"

"Not so's you'd know it. Oh, no doubt they lose a ship now and again, but don't we all? Hmm? Even on Havenpool that can happen."

Someone shouted a summons, the excise-men scrambled into their little boats and skimmed off for shore, and both barge and ship continued on their way, leaving Genevieve to wonder.

The trip ended at a small port in Bliggen, where Genevieve parted from Carlotta, was met by her carriage, and spent a day traveling across the boring plains, arriving well after dark at the resort. It was there she first saw the passenger list for the airship that would carry them to Mahahm.

"Aufors, I'm the only woman on it," she cried.

"The list isn't complete," he said. "Is it?"

"I wouldn't know. But if it is, I'm the only woman. I'll need a maid at least, with the baby coming. . . ."

On the morning, Aufors asked for and received an audience with the Prince. The royal suite was all velvet, gilt, and carved surfaces, and the Prince sat at an ornate desk littered with paper. He looked up, when Aufors was announced.

Aufors bowed sweepingly. "I have come to beg that some other woman be included in the party, Your Highness. Otherwise my wife will be very much alone."

The Prince looked back at the papers on the desk before him. "She

was educated at Blessingham, was she not? She has learned how to manage solitude?"

"Not interminable solitude, sir."

"I can assure you, it will not be interminable." The Prince smiled tightly, though with genuine amusement. "I am not fond enough of Mahahm to stay long."

Aufors gritted his teeth and tried again. "May one inquire why there will be no other women in the party?"

Delganor drew himself up and said, coldly, "There would have been had Earl Solven, his wife, and child joined us as was planned. The Countess and her child would have been company for the Marchioness. I am not unmindful of the feelings your wife expresses, but I am unable to assuage them."

"She will need help with the baby, sir."

"Your continuing to press me on the matter is close to presumption. I will consider your concern for her, however, and be lenient."

"Your Highness is too kind." Aufors bowed, to hide his flaming face and the fact that he choked on the words.

"As for assistance with the child, we can hire someone when we reach Mahahm. As for her needing company, you are her best company, as she has made clear. If your duty to me conflicts with your concerns for her, I know I can trust your honor implicitly, Leys, though I cannot speak for hers." The Prince went back to his papers, looking up with a malicious smile at the sound of the door closing.

Delganor could not see through it, fortunately, for Colonel Leys was raging at the insult. Something was going on around him, something he could not see, hear, or smell, could only feel like a foul touch on his skin or a chill draft down his neck. Wrongness. A new kind of wrongness with the Marshal; a very old kind of wrongness with Yugh Delganor; and, even though the reasons for going to Mahahm were indeed urgent and well understood, a sort of wilful wrongness with this journey and even with Genevieve. When one tried to think out what was wrong, however, it all came down to the fact that Genevieve's presence on an arduous, lengthy trip made no sense.

"You are quite red in the face, love," said Genevieve, with a slightly worried frown.

He looked up, startled at her presence. "I am angry," he said, before he thought.

"At Prince Delganor?" She smiled, a tight little smile, very controlled, a new expression she had found on her face a few days before and had

made much use of since. "I get angry at him for half a day at a time, and it is very helpful, for it keeps me from being afraid of him."

This echo of his own fear touched him with panic he refused to let her see. "Oh, no, sweetheart, you mustn't be afraid. You are among friends, family . . ."

She smiled. "Well, family, at least, though Father has seemed more than ordinarily unfamilial and laconic lately. He acts as though I've metamorphosed into something obscene instead of merely being pregnant. He's been spending a lot of time with the Invigilator, though what an Invigilator is doing here, heaven only knows."

She smiled the tight little smile once again. "I asked one of the men who accompany the Prince if it really is usual to have a pregnant woman along, and he said yes. He says it brings good luck. Why does that impress me so little?"

Aufors put his arms around her, holding her tightly. "There might still be some way out of this."

"No," she replied. "I've told you. This is a way laid out, Aufors."

"Oh, by all that's heavenly, I wish you could explain it to me!" he cried in pain and frustration.

She heard the pain and tried to respond to it. "Suppose when you were a small boy, your father took you to the top of a hill and pointed down the road, saying, 'My boy, this is your road. You will walk this road, just as I have walked this road, and your sons will walk this road, and you must promise me you will not turn aside from it.' So you make the promise. Later, perhaps, you become reluctant, but the promise was made. At some point, you have to trust that your father pointed out the road because it was important, and you have to choose to keep your promise or break it. If you are honorable, perhaps you choose not to demand such a promise from your own son, but that's as far as you can go."

"But you don't know where it goes!" he cried furiously.

"I don't. No. I have to trust that my mother knew what she was asking me to do, or that her mother did, before her." She hugged him. "Indulge me, Aufors. There must be a good reason for it."

At dinner that night, Aufors again raised the topic of help for Genevieve, though he did it while speaking with the Marshal and under the guise of talking about something else. "It would be a mistake for us to hire malghaste for any reason. Hiring a member of the caste to perform any intimate function for us would be an admission that we ourselves are unclean. The Mahahmbi could then use that as an excuse for not dealing with us."

The Marshal nodded, ponderously, but Yugh Delganor interrupted his response. "My dear boy, I have been there before, and they have not refused to deal with me."

"Forgive me, Your Highness, but always before you were there merely to say hello and give them gifts and best wishes from the Lord Paramount. You've never before asked them to change something about the P'naki trade. I've been told the Mahahmbi do not like change."

"We can scarcely take all the people we will need with us, can we?" grumbled the Marshal.

"I suggest very seriously that we do exactly that," Aufors replied. "Everyone including service personnel. Not only must we refuse their malghaste servants, we'll also have to pretend the people of Mahahm are unclean to us to precisely the same degree we are unclean to them. That starts us off on an equal footing of mutual disdain."

"You're remarkably well informed," said Delganor, one nostril lifted slightly. "Where did you pick all this up?"

"I sent for various documents from the Lord Paramount's archives, as well as the reports of provincial trade representatives who have lived there from time to time. It seemed best to know something about the habits of the people before we meet them."

"I would have been able to tell you all you needed to know," said Delganor, with unmistakable annoyance.

"I didn't wish to trouble Your Highness." Aufors bowed his head and let the matter drop.

Despite his obvious annoyance, the Prince took Aufors's advice, for the final list of people going on the mission was inclusive: the airship crew and officers, who would not leave the ship; Rongor, the Invigilator of the Tribunal, added to the list at the last minute for some unexplained reason; household help, including a very good cook; a communications man; three guards who would double as stewards for the Prince, the Marshal, and for Aufors and Genevieve, a physician, who would attend to the needs of both the household and the crew, and an assistant, a nursemaid. All of them male.

Aufors reported that he had met the physician and the man who was to look after the baby. "I can't call him a maid, though he comes close. Your friend Veswees told me about him. He's a commoner from Bliggen who just happens to be very womanly and to love babies . . ."

"Veswees gave you the name? Before we left Havenor?"

He stopped, puzzled. "He did, yes."

"How did he know we would need a male helper? Are Mahahmbi customs common knowledge at the court?"

He stared at his boots for a moment. "I don't know, Jenny. "I never thought to ask. Maybe he knows more about this than we do." He threw up his hands. "Which wouldn't have to be much! From the looks of it, there'll be no contact between us and the Mahahmbi except across a conference table, if we're lucky enough to get them to confer. We'll see nothing of the place at all, except the inside of our dwelling."

"We won't get to see Galul? It's supposed to be a paradise, isn't it?"

"We don't even know if there is a Galul. It may be mythical."

On the day scheduled for departure, they went down to the mooring field where the airship had been loading for the past several days. Though the gas bag was as large as Genevieve had expected, the nacelle containing the bridge and the cabins seemed tiny. The individual cabins were mere closets, only big enough for the berth to fold down with a person standing next to it. With the berth up, there was room for one comfortable chair and a kind of desk table, both of which had to be folded away before the berth came down again. Sanitary arrangements were shared. Most belongings had to be packed away in the nacelle of the tethered cargo balloon which would float along behind them.

The small dining room was also the lounge, the recreation room, the gym, the library. The galley was only the galley, but as all the food was prepackaged, it was only a closet in size.

"How long will we be aboard?" Genevieve asked, viewing her quarters with some distaste. "It seems very small."

"It is very small," said the officer who was helping her stow her belongings. "But it's built well. The gas envelope and the engines are very well engineered, as they should be if we are to return when our mission is complete."

"Why does it have cannon?"

"All six of the Lord Paramount's airships have cannon. For our protection, if we should be attacked."

"Are we likely to be attacked?" she asked.

"Hardly," he murmured with a sniff. "For we are on the Lord Paramount's business."

Halfway through the journey Genevieve wished they would be attacked, just to break the boredom. The voyage was supposed to take ten to fifteen days by the calendar—depending upon the wind, which kept trying to push them back to Haven—but it seemed to be lasting a year. Each day she did her exercises and ate the dull food which always tasted

the same though it was called different things on successive days. Each day she read until her eyes were tired, avoided her father, the Prince, and the Invigilator, none of whom would look at her anyhow, talked to the men on board, the ones who would talk, until she knew all their life stories intimately, played cards with the baby-tender or with Aufors, and at night, tried fruitlessly to sleep. Aufors was her almost constant companion, and she queried him endlessly about his childhood and career and demanded to see the pictures that he carried of his mother and his brothers. Unfortunately, the berths were too narrow to allow double occupancy, even by slender people.

She spent hours watching the sea. The captain, who noticed her boredom, gave her a copy of the chart of islands and suggested she amuse herself by modifying the coastlines as required as they flew over.

"They change a little, all the time, as the ocean rises," he said.

"Why does everyone say the Inundation is over?" asked Genevieve. "It's obviously not."

"For the most part it is. There are no more polar icecaps, not above the ocean, but we believe there is some ice left in caverns at the poles. We don't expect it to rise much farther, but it's still useful to modify the charts."

When they flew low, she could see shadows moving in the water, the shapes of great sea creatures, and sometimes she even saw them at the surface, though always from afar. When Genevieve searched the sea's surface through her glasses, she occasionally saw a pool of that same glowing gold she had seen in Merdune Lagoon, and at night she sometimes wakened to the sound of singing, a deep and urgent melody, like the song a mountain might sing. With other persons so close around her, she made no attempt to answer. Aufors, queried, said he didn't hear it. She didn't ask anyone else.

One day Genevieve and Aufors were on the tiny deck while one of the men was fishing, his line tied to a strut. Something huge caught hold of the line and pulled. The ship tilted to one side; Genevieve and Aufors also fell across the railing where they clung, hanging over the side, staring down at an enormous creature below, one with shining hide and a huge maw that held the line in its teeth. The ship heeled violently with each twitch.

Genevieve leaned out over the sea, hearing it call to her. She loosed one hand and reached out, rising on tiptoes, feeling herself diving . . .

The shipman was clinging to a post, yelling. Aufors braced himself against the rail as the deck tipped toward the vertical and slashed at the

line with his dagger. The taut line twanged away; the ship righted itself; Aufors grabbed Genevieve as the Captain came raging onto the deck to find out what had happened.

Genevieve was still bent over the railing, still feeling herself plunging through the air, arms extended over her head, diving . . . diving. There were people in the sea, struggling around the wreckage of a ship, trying to get a huge door open while waves washed around them . . .

"Jenny, get away from that railing," Aufors cried, pulling her away. "What is it?"

She shook her head, her vision dimming. "It's . . . it was a very big fish, wasn't it?"

"All this excitement," said Aufors with a forced smile belied by his extreme pallor. "Come away from there."

She accompanied him, confusedly trying to sort out her feelings. Twice now she had felt that call from the sea. Twice she had seen the people in the waves, struggling. Something that had happened, or would happen. She said nothing to Aufors. He was already upset, and her confusion would only make it worse.

"What did the thing look like?" the Tribunal officer wanted to know, at the dinner table, though he asked Aufors, not Genevieve. He made it a point never to speak to Genevieve.

Aufors did his best to describe it. "Like a fish, I think. But very, very large."

"The seas are full of huge beasts," said Delganor. "The Frangian sailors have cataloged a great many of them."

No further incidents of the kind occurred. They woke one morning to find themselves being circled by sea birds, and shortly thereafter they intersected the line of islands, tiny ones, then one larger and greener— the final one in the chain, said the Captain—and beyond it the low dark line upon the sea that marked the edge of Mahahm. They sailed over a flurry of white lace where the ocean surged upon outlying rocks, and then across a bay that stretched deep and blue and empty except for a two-masted ship anchored beside a jetty leading to a small, high-walled enclave.

"The Frangian enclave," whispered Genevieve to Aufors. "Where the supplies from Haven are delivered."

Aufors examined the coast. Aside from the Frangian boat, there was nothing on the sea or the coast: no swimmers, no fishermen.

"I should think they would fish that bay," the Marshal said in a puzzled voice.

"There is no shallow water and the monsters lie just off shore," Delganor announced. "Not the biggest ones, of course, but even the smaller ones are fearsome."

The shore itself was barren, pierced here and there with tall, slender watchtowers, like nails fastening the land to the sea. A scattering of black tents marked the tide line, where sheep grazed upon piles of dark seaweed. Beyond the shore stretched a narrow line of dun-gray dunes, then the dun-gray city of Mahahm-qum—ghost-painted here and there with shadow tints of blue and rose—and beyond that nothing but angular rocky hills interrupted by flowing dunes to the limit of their vision. They lowered the ship on a rocky plain a kilometer from the sea, less than half a kilometer from the low town whose tallest structure, a tower covered with faded blue tile, was perhaps twenty meters tall.

No one came to help them moor the ship. Evidently this was expected, for shovels and sheets of canvas were dropped onto the ground, men slithered down swaying ropes to shovel sand onto the sheets, running ropes through loops around their edges to form sandbags that weighed them down. Solar-powered pumps compressed the gas into cylinders, and the gas bag dwindled in size and buoyancy. Other men went down, other bags were filled, until at last the ship could be winched down upon them, a flaccid fowl upon her eggs. The cargo balloon was similarly diminished and fastened down. A short gangway was dropped. They could clearly see the town and tower baking under the hot, yellow sun. The town, seemingly, did not see them.

They waited. The communications man flashed his mirrors at the walls and, when this drew no response, ran out a line of flags. Neither attempt drew any reaction from the town. The sun made a furnace of the sand. Those who had gone outside came in again, under the shade of the gas bag.

"The best thing to do," said Delganor, "is simply to wait. Any show of impatience will only gratify them."

Genevieve sat in her chair and stared at the city she had already seen in a vision or a dream. The actuality was, if anything, less attractive than her preconception. Walls and roofs were built of mud. Most buildings were only one story high with barrel-vaulted roofs, some few with groined roofs, fewer yet with wind burnished walls or domes, covered with faded tiles. The taller buildings had projecting beams at the level of the floors. The beams were of Danian cedar, one of the ship's men said in answer to Aufors's query, one of the items purchased by the Mahahmbi from Haven. The towers were laid up in circles of mud brick broken by upward spiraling

arches that revealed the steps twining around the inside. At the tops were peaked pavilions of poles and faded fabric, also sand worn and tattered, though the banners flying above them bore blazing yellow suns on fields of utter black.

Genevieve had fallen asleep by the time a group straggled from the city gate and approached the ship, most of them carrying long, woven mats with handles at the sides. One of them led a huge, wallowing lizard with tall fins on its back. Aufors, masked and gloved, went out to talk with them. When he came back and took off the mask, his expression was grim.

"What?" barked the Marshal.

"Sir, they are laying a mat at the foot of the landing ramp. We are to step down on it. Another will be put in front of that, and as we move forward, the one behind will be picked up and brought front. We are not to soil their country by setting foot on the soil of Mahahm."

The Marshal stared out the port, calculating. "It'll take hours for all of us to get into the city that way."

"We don't go into the city. The house we arranged for is by the city wall; they've cut a door through the wall directly into it. We are not to set foot in the city, not even on mats."

"It will still take hours for all of us."

"I think their idea, sir, is both to make our visit inconvenient and to restrict the number who go. Of course, the fewer we are, the more helpless we are."

"Damn it, Aufors! There are other non-Mahahmbi here. They aren't outside the walls."

Delganor had listened to this interchange with an expression of lofty disinterest. He descended from his height to comment, "The Shah has seemingly chosen to take umbrage at us. They don't like outsiders breaching their conventions."

"Conventions?" barked the Marshal.

"Of which there are many," said the Prince, turning to peer out at the clutter of men and mats.

"This is intolerable," said the Marshal, with an angry glance at the Prince's back. "What do you think Colonel?"

"I think it's all hokum, Sir, done for effect. It's an attempt to set us at a disadvantage, as was their suggestion we hire malghaste servants."

The Marshal hooted. "Then we shan't let them get away with it. I think the Prince, the Invigilator, and I should insist on seeing the house, and when we return, if anyone goes, we'll all go, including the grav-sleds

with our cargo. While we're gone, all of you get into those suits we brought, the cloaks and the gloves and the metal visors. I don't want a square centimeter of skin or hair showing on anyone when we get back." He turned to the Prince with a peremptory expression. "Your Highness, let's attend to this."

The Prince, seeming slightly amused by this usurpation of command, did as was suggested, the Invigilator following along without change of expression. From inside the lock, Genevieve could hear the interchange.

Her father: "Nonsense. Who would bring a woman to a place like this? It is not fit for women. Take us to the house we are to occupy. No, there won't be any others getting off the ship until we've seen the house. If we don't like it, we'll go away."

They went, Prince and Marshal and Rongor looming over the furtive shapes in cloaks and veils, off toward the small gate in the city wall. There was a recently built guardhouse at the gate—the mud bricks darker and rougher than those smoothed by incessant shore winds.

"What's that lizard thing the man is leading?" Genevieve whispered to one of the cargo handlers.

"According to the envoy, that's how people move around during the hottest times of the day. The beast is called a harpta. It will lower those fins at command, and you can walk in the shade."

"That beast is huge! It could easily crush anyone walking beside it," she whispered. "I think it would serve to discourage travel. Which is no doubt the point of the exercise."

After a time the three Havenites came through the distant gate and stalked arrogantly toward the ship, looking over the heads of the mud-colored mob that gathered and roiled like dirty water. Delganor and Rongor stayed on the sands, speechifying to the Mahahmbi delegation while the Marshal came aboard.

"All right. Now we go out in full array, all masks in place, please, everyone gloved. Aufors, keep your wife with you, and come about fifth in line, heads up, please, and lengthen your strides as much as you can." He turned to the others. "Ignore the mats. They've made their attempt at embarrassing us, now we ignore it. The grav-sleds come last. Get the cargo inside the walls—there's a open area there—drop your loads and return to the ship with the empty sleds. Captain, I'm trusting you to keep everything stowed and ready, just in case we have to leave in a hurry."

When the Marshal gave the word, they poured down the ramp, pointedly ignoring the men with the mats as they marched directly across the sands. The lead men brushed the guards out of the way as they went past

the barrier, down a short tunnel cut through the city wall, through a new iron-bound door, and into a scorched courtyard with empty pots around its edges and a dry fountain at its center.

A ground floor and upper story surrounded this vacancy on three sides, the city wall closed it on the fourth. They had been told the place would be furnished. It was not furnished. No matter, said Aufors, there are furnishings among the cargo, all cunningly designed to unfold and expand. Except for being under a roof and among walls, it was just like setting up camp, something most of the men had a long practice at doing.

Aufors spoke to three of the men, and then, so quickly it was almost a miracle, Genevieve had a room of her own upstairs, a bed, a desk, her books, a view through the open door, though only of the seared atrium below. It was done so neatly, with so little fuss, that it made her want to cry. She did cry, with the door shut so no one would hear. This was a terrible place. The only improvement over the airship was that one had more cubic feet of stifling air to oneself.

THEY MADE A DESERT CAMP OF THEIR FIRST EVENING IN MAHAHM, WITH SOME men snatching sandwiches while others huddled over the dry well, talking on the link to the ship. Several of them went out, past the barricade, returning with one of the grav-sleds and something bulky atop it which they maneuvered over the top of the well. A blinding light erupted from below the device, followed by a rushing sound, then steaming muddy water welled up the shaft, overflowing the housing, running away through the door and tunnel, past the guardhouse and under the barricade, toward the sea, while the Mahahmbi guards danced wildly to escape being boiled about the feet.

"How did you do that?" Genevieve asked Aufors, when he brought his mud-stained self to the door to see if she had survived the geyser. "How did you get water in the well?"

"I modified one of the laser cannons from the ship. Made a decent mining drill out of it, didn't I?"

"Where'd you learn that?" she asked, astonished.

"Soldiers have access to cannon, Jenny. Once you've done field repairs on a few, they loose their mystery, off-planet technology or not. I may not know how all of the parts work, but I know which ones go where. Anyhow, my digging about in the archives told me there's an underground river below us. All Mahahmbi towns are on the sites of former oases, and all oases had subsurface water; some of them even had pools at the surface. The subsurface water is still there, and from the long, narrow shape of the town, I'm guessing most buildings are drilled into it."

"Where does the river come from? Where does it go?"

"The presettlement geology report says it starts up in those mountains south of us. The area was probably covered by polar ice at that time. Now the river is completely underground, and it must be completely enclosed or we wouldn't get this flow. Our well was deliberately stopped up before

we arrived, just to be disobliging. Now we're working on a seal for the well so we can get all the water we need without having a river through the door."

"How did they stop it up?"

"With considerable labor and tons of rubble. One of the men took a water sample out to the ship and they ran it through the analyzer. It's perfectly clean."

She considered this. "Aufors, if there's all that water available, why don't they have agriculture? If they put water on this desert, it should bloom, shouldn't it?"

He hugged her. "From what we've seen so far, we'll probably find that it's either forbidden by their religion or beneath their dignity. One or the other."

The doctor knocked, put his head around the door, then came in to apply his little monitor to her swelling belly and another to her head. He read the results and recommended a bath and a good sleep immediately.

The tub had been set up in a stone-floored room below, which Genevieve managed to get to without encountering Rongor, the Prince, or her father. The quiet room reminded her of the bathroom at Fentwig's House, and she lay a long time in the tepid water, luxuriating in the feeling of weightlessness. That night she slept in a real bed, one wide enough to turn over in, one wide enough for Aufors to slip in beside her, and when morning came, she began finding her way about the place.

The building was in the form of an E with the open side jammed against the city wall to make two unequal courtyards joined by a passageway. From the desert, they had entered the larger courtyard where stairs ascended along the inside of the city wall to the surrounding balconies. At the top of the stairs a narrow slit through the city wall gave a view of the airship and the sun-blasted lands around it. No window looked out upon the city street; the only access to the city was a heavy door at the end of a hallway from the small courtyard, through the top of the E.

The house was large. Genevieve counted over twenty rooms on the ground floors alone. From the smaller courtyard, stairs descended into the kitchens, one level underground, where it was discernably cooler. Off the kitchens were several stone-walled cellars that had perforated pipes running along the walls. Sometime during their first night these seepers came alive with water, and morning found the rooms moist and cool. From these rooms, air ducts extended upward through the walls of the house, opening through grilles along the floors of the upper rooms. Opposite the grilles, holes in the ceilings opened into hollow T-shaped pots suspended with a wire from

U-shaped brackets and resting in smooth saucers. Wind-fins rotated the pots, turning them into the constant breeze, and as the wind went through the top of the T, hot air from the house was drawn out as well, allowing cooler air to flow in from below. In a few hours the ground floor was quite comfortable and even the upper floor was more bearable.

Genevieve found two men working in the moist cellars, filling pots with soil into which they set dormant plants that had been brought on the ship.

"Who thought of that?" asked Genevieve, wonderingly.

"Ah . . . your father," said Aufors. "Or, he made me think of it. He remarked to me one evening that you had enjoyed the gardens of Wantresse. The plants will not take long to leaf out. When they begin to do so, we'll move them up into the courtyard."

She put on a smile and thanked her father, at which he showed obvious discomfort. As he recalled his remark to Aufors, one that equated women's weakness with their fondness for flowers, it was not one she would have thanked him for.

Genevieve and Aufors had been given the rooms at the end of the balcony upstairs. "You won't be wakened by people tromping by in the night," said Aufors. "Those of us on night duty will use the other courtyard, to keep the noise down."

"Night duty?" Genevieve faltered. "What night duty?"

"Your father considers this a military operation," he smiled. "The Prince and the Invigilator evidently agree with him. The guards will work three four-hour shifts a day so at least one of them will be alert all the time. I have to agree that it's best in situations like this to keep an eye open always."

The other upper rooms over the larger courtyard were occupied by the Marshal and various of the other personnel, while Delganor's suite occupied most of the space below, along with rooms for general use and several apartments tucked away in cooler, sky-lighted areas behind the better-lit rooms. The smaller courtyard was occupied by the household servants and support staff, including the communications man who maintained the link to the ship and slept next to his equipment.

All the floors were tiled, as were the lower parts of the walls. There were both solid panels and lattices to pull across the openings to provide privacy. The only thing truly disgusting about the place, Genevieve thought, were the toilets cut into the city walls, tight little tiled closets with a hole in the floor over which one squatted. Several times each day, silent, rag-clad malghaste came from somewhere in the bowels of the place

to pour buckets of water down these channels to clear them. The waste ran, so said Aufors, through a cloaca to a subterranean reservoir outside the city which was washed out by a diversion from the subsurface river. The system had been built long ago, when the oasis was still here, when the people may have been quite different in their manners and perceptions.

"If so much is known about all this," Genevieve murmured to him, "if this place was surveyed long before settlers came, then why is it all so mysterious? Galul either existed then, or it didn't. Even if the archives don't mention anything seen by ships, surely they have access to the presettlement reports."

"Presettlement maps," Aufors replied, keeping his voice low, "show only an ice-field at the southern end of Mahahm. Whatever exists there now, it's come there since the Inundation."

The ship and its crew remained where they were for the time being and the first few days were spent in shifting additional supplies, mostly foodstuffs, from the cargo nacelle to the house. Once the ambassadorial group had settled in and considered itself secure, the Captain planned to return across the straits to the nearest island, half a day's flight away, where a camp could be established for the men while they awaited a summons from Delganor or the Marshal.

Two of the guards had been with the Prince on former trips to Mahahm-qum; they spoke the local dialect and were able to slip out anonymously to fetch what foodstuffs were available in the market, some local, some imported, some—milk and cheese and meat—from the sheep that grazed the piles of seaweed along the shores. Everything else they would need, they had brought with them.

They had been in residence only three days when, rather late in the evening, the man on guard heard a knock at the small gate that opened into the city streets. He opened the spy hole, conferred with the person outside, then came to report to the Prince, who was in the large courtyard with the Marshal, Genevieve, and Aufors.

"One of the foreigners who live here in the city, sir," he said. "A Danian. His name is Thusle."

"Upstairs," whispered Aufors to Genevieve. "Don't let him see you."

"Oh, Aufors," she whispered in return, "can't I stay? I haven't seen anyone new . . ."

He shook his head. "The presence of a woman is private information. We can vouch for our staff, but we can't vouch for some garrulous old cuss who blathers on about this female he just met. Besides, the Prince and the Invigilator . . ."

She grimaced. "You're right. I'll just listen from upstairs."

Aufors frowned, casting a quick look around. Delganor had already gone to greet the guest. The Marshal and the Invigilator were in one of the lengthy and private conversations they seemed to be having a good many of lately.

He murmured, "Keep out of sight."

She went to her own quarters and pulled the grilles across the arches that opened into her room. Sitting just inside, she listened avidly while the old man was greeted, given wine and a dish of olives.

"Well, so you arrived safely," he said. "I was afraid you would not. There has been some talk in the marketplace. Some talk of Mahahmbi rebellion against the expectations of the Lord Paramount."

"He is Lord Paramount of Mahahm as well as of the rest of Haven," said the Invigilator in his cold, forbidding voice.

"He is Lord Paramount in absentia," the old man murmured. "Who here has ever seen the Lord Paramount? No, they welcome visitors who come on ordinary business. Your Highness knows, for Your Highness has been here before. Perhaps welcome is too strong a word, but you catch my meaning. It's this effort to increase the P'naki they don't like. If this visit was an ordinary visit, there'd have been no trouble at all. It's this other thing that has them upset."

The Prince spoke, drawling. "This will not disrupt our normal relationship, one hopes."

"It may not, Your Highness. But . . . it will help if the demands regarding the P'naki are moderated. Everything I hear indicates that the Mahahmbi are correct when they say there is no more to be had. Their religion forbids any modification of their rites, the P'naki is a religious matter, and religious matters are impervious to argument."

"Even if some modification could result in a large royalty paid to Mahahm?" asked the Marshal.

"Even so. Religion is religion, Marshal." He turned to the Prince. "Your Highness should understand, having been here before."

Genevieve peeped through the grillework. The old man held out a trembling hand. She did not doubt his sincerity. When offered more wine, the old man rejected it, saying, "I could be whipped for smelling of it, Colonel." He did accept a cup of tea and a spice-scented pastille, and thereafter departed into the darkness.

"Well," said the Invigilator. "It will be more difficult than we thought, Your Highness."

"Difficult, yes," mused the Prince. "I must think on this."

*　　*　　*

What followed next was expected and unexpected, both at once. The baby came, which was expected, and Genevieve experienced childbirth, which she had read of but was still greatly surprised by. The doctor was kindly and skilled, the nursemaid was immediately at hand, all went well, though lengthily, and after a day and a half of effort, Genevieve found herself lying exhaustedly at ease in her bed, a tiny head nestled to her breast.

As soon as they left her alone, she pulled herself erect, placed the child before her and unwrapped him. She had to see. When Aufors came in, she was running her fingers along the baby's head and neck, and she looked up at him almost guiltily.

He smiled. "Are you seeing if he is all there? All fingers and toes?"

After a moment, she returned his smile. "All his fingers and toes are there, yes, Aufors."

He leaned forward to pick up his son, wrapping him warmly in the blanket she had removed and saying doubtfully, "He looks very wrinkled. His little neck is actually corrugated."

She moved, a bit painfully. "I understand that they all look very much like that. Della's sister had a baby when I was quite small, and I recall that it was very wrinkled, too."

"Shall we name him, or wait until he fattens a bit?" He grinned at her. "So we can see what he'll look like. Though, come to think of it, he has your nose."

She didn't want to talk about the nose. Naming the baby was a better topic. "What shall we name him?"

"Dovidi," he said. "It's a family name. If you don't mind?"

"Oh, Aufors, I don't mind. Dovidi he shall be."

That night she woke to a cacophonous howl from half a dozen towers, close and distant. She rose, going to the cradle to see if the baby was asleep, which he was, rosy and warm, thumb in mouth. She turned to find Aufors behind her.

"I heard you get up," he said. "Is something wrong?"

"No. Just . . . I do hate this place."

"Why in particular?"

"It's always either too noisy or too quiet," she murmured. "The sound of those screamers is hideous."

"Prayer leaders," he smiled. "They're a hereditary caste with mutated larynxes and nasal cavities. If they can't be heard for a mile or more, they

aren't accepted into the guild or whatever it is. They're very proud and it's only seven times a day."

Privately, Genevieve thought she could make a better noise that would carry farther with her thumb in her mouth, as Dovidi's was. But then, no one knew that except herself. "Where did you find out about them?"

"We've received visits from some of the other trade representatives. They've told us a few things. I'm afraid it's going to be a long mission."

She confessed, "I know I said it wouldn't bother me, being here, but I was wrong. It does."

Though he held her and patted her gently, it did nothing to ameliorate her feelings of embarrassment. Having declared she could manage perfectly well, she was ashamed to admit she was not managing at all. It wasn't that she was alone, precisely, for the men of the staff were around most of the time, here and there, always willing to chat. It wasn't that she had nothing to do, for she'd brought needlework, a lute, books, and the baby took endless hours. It was simply that she had no woman to talk with, no woman to cozy with, nothing to put her own motherhood in focus with, as though Dovidi in his cradle were a unique event with no parallel in the universe. The lack of comradeship left her vulnerable to any possibility of company.

She awakened late one night, thirsty, and the carafe beside the bed was empty. She slipped out of her room, down the stairs, through the passage to the small courtyard and thence to the kitchen. While there, she heard a woman's voice, and, puzzled, she followed the sound through a panel door that stood ajar, a panel she had not seen before, one that led down another level. She had not realized there was a lower level, but she could not argue with her eyes or her nose that between them perceived a musty-smelling, dimly-lit and stone-floored room at the bottom of the stairs. She took a step and almost fell over a huddled body.

"Oh," she murmured, "sorry."

The body didn't move. She leaned over, tapped it. It shivered.

"For heaven's sake, get up," she said in her labored Mahahmbi. It wasn't enough unlike Haven talk to be a different language, but it was pronounced differently and had a lot of words for local things that had no counterpart on Haven. Though she could understand almost all of it she heard, she had had minimal experience using the language.

"Please," the body whimpered.

Abruptly, she realized what she must have done. "Oh, I am sorry. I'll bet you're malghaste, aren't you? I'm not supposed to be here."

The body moved, squirmed away from her, not looking at her. An old woman.

"I won't tell," said Genevieve. "Honestly, I won't tell. Nobody will ever know. Please, talk to me."

She saw actual amusement in the flash of the woman's eyes. "They'll kill me if you do, if I do, if you do, lady."

This stopped her only for a moment. "They'll kill you if I ask you to talk? That is, if you talk? And if I tell?"

A nod. The figure turned to face her, legs crossed, somber cloth wrappings half hiding her face. "You've had baby, lady. We've heard him crying."

Genevieve rubbed her flat stomach thoughtfully. "No one's supposed to know that I'm even here, much less that my baby is. He's a week old now."

"Week?"

"Ah. Sorry. Let's see. It's an old, old human division of days, seven days. The only time we use it is in figuring the age of infants. Two weeks, six, eight, then we start on months. The only time we say months is when we're talking about babies or pregnancy. It's a survival, I guess. You probably use a seasonal count. Most planets do."

"Twelve days to period. Times six equals season. Times four plus new year holy day equals year. We work here season by season, we malghaste. Season on. Season off."

"Did you know I was here?"

"Oh, yes. We overhear your people talking. You are one handsome one calls Jenny."

"That's short for Genevieve. What's your name?"

"Awhero," she said, *Ah-fhair-oh*. "Old name in ancient earthian language of our people. In our tongue it means Hope."

"Awhero."

"Why did you come here?" the old woman asked.

She thought about this a moment, seeking a simple reason. "My husband was required to come, by the Prince. The Prince also required me to come. Also, this was my first child, and I wanted to be near my husband."

"No, no. Why did you come down here?" The old woman patted the stones at her feet.

"I was wakeful. Thirsty. And lonely. I heard your voice. I didn't think. Who were you talking to? Why are you even here at this time of night?"

"When I am assigned here, it is easiest just to stay. Someone must wash out privies. Someone must scrub floors and walls and burn sulfur

when you are gone, to get rid of your unclean spirits. Or bury some of you, if you die."

Genevieve blinked at this. "And you're it?"

"Me. Yes. Also, I listen for the persons of Shah. I am spy." The old woman grinned, toothily. "All malghaste in houses of arghaste are spies."

"Arghaste?"

"Foreigners, unclean ones. Like you."

Genevieve drew a deep breath. "Have you told anyone I'm here?"

The old woman laughed. "Not yet. I did not even tell one-who-asks-me how you got water. I said I did not see how you did it." Her shoulders shook with laughter. "Always they ask us, and always we lie to them. They think we are impenetrably stupid, but they still ask us. "

She was just Awhero, no other name. She had two daughters and a son. They, too, were malghaste. If parents were malghaste, then the children were also malghaste. But, in a way, Awhero said, it was better for women than being born to the other Mahahmbi castes, the religious, the royal family, the merchants.

"Why is that?" Genevieve asked.

"I like to live. I have almost seventy years. If I had been born woman in another caste, I would not live so long."

Genevieve was curious about that, started to ask about that, but she heard her husband's voice from upstairs and knew the interlude was over.

"I'll come back," she said. "May I?"

"I may die if you do, if I do, if you do," she replied.

Genevieve figured that out on her way upstairs. If Genevieve came back, and if Awhero had stayed, and if then Genevieve said anything about it, Awhero might die. So. She would say nothing about it.

ONCE AWARE OF AWHERO'S CELLAR, GENEVIEVE HAUNTED THE PLACE. Whenever Dovidi woke at night, she slipped from the room she shared with Aufors and took the baby down to the kitchens. Three men were on night duty, one near each outer door and one in the communications room, but all three of them were usually dozing, and when this was the case, she did not even stop in the kitchens. It was only a step through the concealed door and down a short flight into Awhero's cellar. There she sat on a cushion holding the baby, nursing him, playing with him, while Awhero—accompanied by a sister or a few cousins or a clutter of old aunts who, it seemed, never went anywhere without their tambours and flutes—sang ballads and laments or chanted lengthy episodes from the life of Tenopia.

Tenopia was malghaste, so it was claimed by the malghaste themselves, though she had come from the sea. As a young woman she had left Galul and gone into Mahahm, where she had been found by the son of the Shah, sitting beside a well in an oasis. The son of the Shah was so taken with her beauty that he took her into his own household, despite Tenopia's habits of disobedience. Among other derelictions she had sneaked away from her attendants without a veil; she had danced on the desert; she had sung with the great voices . . .

"Voices, Awhero?" Genevieve interrupted startled, looking up from the baby. "What voices?"

"Great voices that sing in night, from sea."

"Here? In Mahahm-qum?"

"Sometimes we can hear them here, in Mahahm-qum. We hear them better when we are in Galul."

Giving Genevieve no chance to ask more about this, Awhero resumed her chant, the drums their tapping, the little flutes their piping, and Genevieve did not choose to interrupt. She was so caught up in sleeplessness

and nursing at all hours, so tuned to the slightest catch in the baby's breathing, the least murmur—all of this interspersed with worry about Aufors and the Marshal—that she was not thinking clearly. The time spent among the malghaste was more dreamlike than real. Their music was dream music, the joy in their singing faces was sublime, like the presumed bliss of angels. Genevieve told herself that once she caught up on her sleep, she would ask sensible questions and understand all of it much better. Meantime, she let herself relax among the women, who became more numerous with every night that passed.

One morning, while most of the staff were at breakfast, there came a thundering from the in-city house door. Aufors gestured for the guard to stand aside, put on his gloves and the mask that hung ready at the door, and opened the hatch to confront Ybon Saelan, minister of the Shah, who asked to see Prince Delganor.

"The Prince is not seeing anyone," Aufors said, in the elegant and stylized Mahahmbi he had been practicing for a season. "In any case, we don't admit anyone by this door. We use the gate outside the walls to avoid defiling ourselves with the uncleanliness of your streets." He then shut the hatch and reported to the Marshal, who was of the opinion that the minister would go away.

Either duty or curiosity prevailed, however, and a short time later the same man showed up outside the city wall at the other door. The household had long been prepared for the eventual arrival of someone, if not this man, another; if not today, on some other day; and the minister was admitted with instructions to remove his boots, a calculated rudeness, since all Mahahmbi removed their shoes indoors. Barefoot, he was ushered into the larger courtyard, now colorfully furnished under bright awnings, with water splashing, plants growing, and a pleasant smell of roasting meats. Here he was told to await the Marshal and was very pointedly not asked to sit down.

"Minister Saelan," said the Marshal when he emerged in his own good time, face and hands hidden. "I am the Lord Paramount's Marshal. My assistant, Aufors."

Aufors nodded, a precisely calculated nod which acknowledged the minister's presence while showing only the least modicum of respect. Genevieve watched all this from a screened window upstairs, somewhat apprehensively. The Prince had long since delegated this first meeting to the Marshal (reserving his own appearance for some later stage of negotiations), and Aufors had choreographed the exchange, but the Marshal was

not always biddable, and he sometimes pushed things farther than necessary.

"Will you be seated," Aufors murmured, as both he and the Marshal sat down under the awning. If the emissary wanted to get into the shade, he would have to sit.

"I prefer not," said Ybon Saelan grimly.

"As you like," said Aufors, as the Marshal kept a lofty silence. "Tell me, is the temperature normal for this season? The climate seems much milder than we had expected."

"It is . . . as usual," said the sweating emissary. "I have come to bring greetings from the Shah, Arghad the Effulgent."

"Ah, well, how nice." The Marshal nodded, took a glass from the table and sipped it. "May I offer you some ice water with lemon?"

"Ice . . . It is forbidden."

"Oh? Too bad. It's very cooling. However, one cannot help but admire your constancy to your culture. Will you convey my greetings to the Shah? Since we do not use the city streets, I have been unable to send a messenger with greetings, but it was very kind of him to send you. Was there anything more?"

Ybon Saelan bowed, slightly lower than before. "Nothing. No."

"Very kind, very kind," said the Marshal vaguely. "Aufors, do see our guest to the gate."

"What in deepsea was that all about?" Genevieve asked when Aufors came upstairs to take off the paraphernalia.

"The man was sent to ascertain our discomfort and to reply evasively to our complaints of having no water, no furnishings, no cooling. He is probably still trying to figure out how we got the water back and where all the furniture and greenery came from."

"Now what?"

"Now the Shah knows we're not uncomfortable, we're not thirsty, we're not dying of the heat. He knows we've plenty of fresh food. He knows their attempt to confuse and bamboozle us over this uncleanliness issue has backfired to make him and his people just as dirty to us as we are to them."

"Which means?"

"That the next play, my love, is up to him."

Ybon Saelan left Prince Delganor's quarters and went at once to the palace, where, in the toilet off the anteroom of the Shah's divan, he secretly put on a pair of kneepads under his robes. The ritual crawling

and prostrations on the rough red pebbles laid into the rammed-earth floor could be ruinous to one's legs. On his now-padded knees he progressed from the totem of the Shah down a line of ever rougher and more uncomfortable stones to the foot of the steps to the dais, a mud platform plastered and painted with designs in black and yellow. There he stopped and made an abasement.

"Hail the Voice of Prophecy, the Tongue of the Lord, the Teeth of the Scripture, the Word of God," intoned the minister, his mouth a finger's width from the floor.

"He who is recognizes you," said the Shah, staring across the Saelan's bent form at the far wall.

"I bask in the light of your gaze, O Divine Master. I prostrate—"

The Shah smiled grimly. "Enough prostration, Saelan. So? Are our guests well? Are they contented?"

The minister took a deep breath and spoke the truth. "Prince Delganor's delegation from Haven is seemingly quite contented, Exalted One."

His Effulgence stopped looking at the wall and stared directly at his minister. "Contented without water?"

"They have water, Exalted One."

"Water! Where did they get water?"

"I do not know, Shining One. Perhaps they brought it with them."

One of the Sworn Ones at the side of the throne shook his head slightly. The Sworn Ones had computed the bulk of the grav-sleds, and they would have known if any appreciable amount of water had been brought onto Mahahm.

"They did not bring it with them," said His Effulgence.

"Then I am at a loss, sire."

"Find out, find out," said Arghad to the two Sworn Ones, who slipped silently away from the throne to be replaced by two others, as alike as sand ripples on a dune. The Sworn Ones were all of one family, a lineage that had served the Shah for generations. Its members resembled one another; they thought alike; they balked at nothing, so long as the Shah commanded it.

The Shah beckoned to Saelan, who crept up the seven steps to the throne and knelt on a thin cushion on the top step, the Shah's indulgence to an aged and loyal servant.

"You're saying the Prince and his entourage are not uncomfortable enough to go away," said the Shah.

"They seem prepared to stay for some time, Effulgent One."

"Do they have women?"

"I saw no women. I saw no signs of women. I did see quite a few men, though no faces. They seem determined to regard us as unclean. I am told they have a religious functionary with them. One Rongor."

The Shah frowned in a puzzled manner. "A heretic, you mean. The Prince didn't bring candidates, then?"

"I cannot say, Exalted One."

"Why did he not take our warning when he arrived? By the devils of the deep, Saelan, we made it clear they were unwelcome. Did he assume we had given him a dry and empty house by accident?"

"It is evident that Prince Delganor did not recognize it as a warning, Exalted One. As an expression of displeasure, no doubt, but not as a warning. So our malghaste spies say."

"Then he is a fool."

"As are all who do not look upon the glory of thy face, Master."

"I know he brought women! He wouldn't have wasted the trip. He had to bring at least one! And he should have followed our custom. Any women should have been given to us the moment they arrived. Such is our agreement with Haven! Why do we provide P'naki otherwise?"

"As Your Mightiness says. Several of those in the Prince's group are strangers to us, however. They are people ignorant of Mahahm, uninformed about our relationship with the Lord Paramount of Haven, unenlightened as to our Divine Purpose on this world. They are people who might take offense at giving us the women, and they may have power back in Haven."

"Then why did the Prince bring such people?"

"Perhaps he had no choice. Perhaps the Lord Paramount ordered it. So, the Prince may have decided not to try both things at once. Perhaps he has decided to talk about increasing P'naki first; then later he will return for the other. We know he values us greatly. As does the Lord Paramount of Haven."

"He would have brought women anyway," said the Shah, loftily. "Just in case. He is that kind. And, barring accident, they are probably still here, with their babies."

"They may be. Though our spies do not say so."

"Very well. We want the women and babies now. The Frangian boat arrived yesterday, bringing several candidates, some provided by traders, to curry our favor. The Time of Renewal is upon us. These arghaste cannot be allowed to interfere with it. If the men will not leave the house because of discomfort, let them leave for something else. An invitation, perhaps.

And we will find out whether there are women by making an invitation to the women themselves!"

The minister's eyes opened wide in shocked surprise. He stuttered as he said, "An invit . . . t . . . tation, Great One? There is only one invitation suitable for foreign women, for evighaste . . ."

"We must think of another that is suitable. We need to learn who has come with the Prince. The Prince's aide, perhaps. He has one?"

"There is an old one called the Marshal. There is a lesser one by name of Aufors."

The Shah leaned back on the cushions of the high throne. "Ah, that gives me a better thought. Suppose you tell them we have had a cleansing ceremony that allows us to meet. Invite the Prince and this Marshal and this Aufors, along with the man of religion, to take a tour of the marketplace. Buy them each a seabone dagger as a gift from me. The Prince knows the meaning that lies in the gift of a knife. He will understand the gift if the others don't. Take your time. Cultivate them. Smile. Chat. Take them to the teahouse. Tell them if they have women with them, the women are invited to walk in the garden with my wives . . ."

"Your Effulgence!" the minister cried in surprise.

"Why not? The arghast evighaste, if there are any, were brought here as candidates. I have Mahahmbi evighaste who are also candidates. The ones from outside can walk with my own, for among candidates there is no true foreign presence. When the women have walked with my wives and returned without harm, invite the religious man and the Prince and the Aufors man to go hunting for argivers, in the desert. Roast argiver is a dish all visitors should taste. Tell them tales of Galul. Lull them."

"As the Great One wishes."

"Take no others, only those three, then see that this lesser assistant, this Aufors, meets a useful death before the eyes of the Prince and the so-called religious. The Prince may misinterpret a dry house, he may ignore the gift of a blade, but he will not misinterpret the blood of his own man when it is shed before his eyes! He will realize then that we know he brought women, that we know they were not given to us as agreed. Then he will pay attention and forget this nonsense about the P'naki. The religious man will also change his thoughts. When they have stopped being foolish, the Prince may take part in the ritual."

"As Your Effulgence wishes, Great One."

The Shah smiled and quoted from scripture: "Some things may not be changed, for they are as they are, as was willed, as is so. Amen."

"Amen," murmured Ybon Saelan.

*   *   *

That night, Genevieve heard Awhero sing of the escape of Tenopia. Tenopia had been disobedient: she had eaten with the malghaste; she had danced with the wizards of the winds; and at last the Shah had imprisoned her for these offenses and sentenced her to "a certain kind of death." Awhero's chant detailed Tenopia's escape from her prison and her flight into the southland, toward Galul. This last journey was fraught with difficulty, for all the Shah's men were hunting her as she fled without food or water, into the heat of the desert.

". . . comes third day," sang Awhero, "she hears sky-hunters screaming. Wind-wizards she calls upon, to eat sand-tracks behind her. Wind-wizards she calls upon, to breathe her scent north to sea. Lo, as evening comes, banner of Marae te Morehu licks green against gray sky. Great door hears her hand, knocking with stones. Great door gives her entry, haeremai, for she is one of them, speaking with voices of deep, nga tumau hohonu."

The other old women raised their voices in chorus:

"Did not Tenopia know day to come, hour to strike, time for deep-friends to stand forth?"

They rocked back and forth, smiling. Awhero leaned forward, taking Genevieve's hands for the first time in her own, commanding: "Now, sing it with me, arghaste woman."

Genevieve, half-hypnotized by the drumming and the swaying of their many bodies did not even think about it. This was a cellar, like that other cellar. Though it was without the deep pools that lay beneath the foundations of Langmarsh House, it smelled the same, it resonated in the same way. She was commanded to sing, as she had been commanded before so she sang with Awhero, clearly where she could, la-laing where she could not remember the words, her voice stronger than all of theirs together, her song making the stones shake. Once through the song, and then again, this time remembering almost all of it. When she finished, tears were streaming down her face and she sobbed into her hands.

"You sang well!" exulted Awhero. "Why are you crying?"

"It reminds me of singing with my mother. And the words, tumao hohonu, I have read them in the stories of Stephanie."

"Ah, you say Stephanie, we say Tewhani. That is how we say her name, daughter of Tenopia, mother of many daughters. You are one. Your voice is beautiful. It is unmistakable that you are of kindred."

"What kindred?"

"The kindred of Galul."

"What do you mean? Kindred of Galul?"

"Where long-nosed women are. The children of sea, sisters of deep-swimmers. Those who knew Tenopia before she went unto Mahahm, those who sent her daughter Stephanie—Tewhani—forth into Haven. Oh, we will teach you that song next time!"

"Now, tonight," Genevieve cried heedlessly, wiping her eyes. "Stephanie was my ancestress. Oh, Awhero, I need to know tonight!"

Awhero shook her head. "No. Not now. We are weary, and so are you. Tomorrow will be soon enough."

Sobered, Genevieve assented. "But I need to know, where . . . where my mother's people came from. I *need* to know." She caught herself, taking a deep, sobbing breath. "Oh, what am I doing! I sang out loud! If Prince Delganor heard me! If Father heard me!"

"They did not hear you." Awhero smiled. "We have all doors shut between here and there. They do not listen, they do not hear, and tomorrow we will sing songs of your people who came from Tenopia's womb."

"I'm not supposed to sing!" Genevieve cried.

"We know," said Awhero. "Haven women have been here before, women with their babies, and they have never sung, not even lullabies to their children. They have come, women and children; children have stayed, some, some have gone, all women have stayed, somewhere . . ." Her voice trailed away, then rallied.

"We are surprised that you sing so well!"

"My mother taught me," said Genevieve. "Deep in the cellars of our house, like here." She flushed, remembering other things she had been taught, as well. Things she could not do here.

"Well, time is coming when women must come up from cellars. Those at marae say it is time, and past time."

"Tomorrow then," said Genevieve.

"Soon," said Awhero.

Genevieve was still sleeping when Ybon Saelan came to the residence, this time to invite the Prince, the Marshal, the Invigilator, and the Colonel to join the Shah's representative on a tour through Mahahm-qum. A cleansing ceremony had been held. They were no longer unclean.

Aufors came to tell Genevieve about this breakthrough, then the four men went forth under sunshades carried by runners. When they returned bearing gifts from the Shah, the Marshal seemed to think the event marked a definite advance, though the Prince only smiled his cold, distant smile, without acknowledging any improvement in affairs. Still, there was a cer-

tain amount of jocularity at dinner as the gifts were passed around: curved knives with hilts of a substance no one among them had recognized.

"Seabone," said Genevieve when it came to her hand, seeing superimposed visions of men chopping bone on the shore, of other men carving it.

The Prince actually looked her, or glared, rather. "How do you know that?"

She flushed, fumbled, "Something I read, Your Highness. The Mahahmbi make dagger hilts from the skeletons of great seabeasts washed up on the shores." She was disturbed by this. Something about the picture was awry. Something about it didn't feel right, even more so when the Marshal sought her out later to give her astonishing news. The Shah had sent word that any women in their party were invited to walk with the Shah's wives in their garden. Special shoes had been provided which would mitigate the uncleanliness associated with non-Mahahmbi footsteps in so sacred a place.

"Did you tell them I was here?" asked Genevieve.

"Oh, yes," said the Marshal, not meeting her eyes. "A harpta will come for you in the morning."

Later, when she and Aufors were alone, she asked, "Who exactly told the Shah I was here?"

"The Prince," he said with a grimace. "What he actually said was that I had brought my wife along. If he hadn't, your father would have. I was more than a little surprised, and I wish they had kept quiet about that."

At bedtime, she examined the sandals they had sent. Thick-soled, to keep the feet from the heat of the sand. Lettered all around the soles with unintelligible phrases, and with a rather rank smell, as though the leather were badly tanned. Aufors walked with her up and down the balcony as she tried them out. The smell was off-putting, but wearing them was bearable.

The baby did not wake her in the night, but he wakened very early in the morning, before it was light. Genevieve carried him down to the kitchen and found Awhero standing in the door to the lower stairs.

"Is it true?" Awhero asked. "You go to walk with Shah's wives?"

"So they tell me," Genevieve answered.

Awhero croaked. "Oh, lady, I do not like it."

Genevieve didn't like it either. She made a face. "What could go wrong with it, Awhero? If I keep my tongue on leash."

"They will not speak so you can understand. Women of Mahahmbi speak woman's language, so as not to soil men's language on their dirty tongues. We Malghaste, we seldom speak where Mahahmbi can hear us,

so what words we say are not relevant. High-caste women, they do speak before men, so they have their own tongue. Now, it is true that they hear men speaking, and they pick up language, so they may understand you. You can try, but oh, keep to simple things. How hot is sun. How green are trees of garden. How bright flowers. How grateful you are to join them there."

"Perhaps I can explain to them why we are here, so they can tell the Shah . . ."

Awhero cackled with laughter, echoed by the dozen or so of the cousins and aunts who straggled down the stairs behind her, listening. "Oh, lady, lady. Women of Mahahmbi do not speak to men at all. They are allowed to say two words in men's language: *abn*, which means *yes*, or *asfa*, which means *at once*. It would be disrespectful to say anything else. Most you can hope for is that they might talk of what you say where men might overhear them, and even then men would pretend not to understand." She shook her head, making a grinding sound with her teeth. "Wait here. I have gift for you."

She went off down the stairs, returning in moments with a soft white robe, holding it up to show that it would cover Genevieve from head to toe.

"Under your outer robe," Awhero said. "Wear this. And do not let any of your skin show on street."

"Why, Awhero? I have clothes."

"Not like this. I tell you, wear it. Remember that she who shows skin on street may be executed for being whore, so do not give them excuse. This is like robe Tenopia wore, when her Shah planned evil, woven from seed bolls of same plant, trimmed around hem with her words to wizards of winds. I think there is evil coming, so wear it."

When Aufors heard what Awhero had to say about the invitation, he scowled. Though she had said nothing about the old woman to anyone else, Genevieve had told Aufors about her conversations in the cellars, and he, after a spasm of concern over the impropriety of it all, had promised he would keep it a secret. Since then he had eagerly sought the malghaste point of view to enlighten his own understanding of the Mahahmbi.

"This mission of ours seems to be to make one miscalculation after another," he muttered. "Wouldn't you think the Prince would have been better informed than to expect the Shah's women to speak for us?"

"I think that was Father's idea," she replied. "I think he came up with that one all by himself, and I haven't a clue as to what the Prince knows or doesn't know."

In the morning, a harpta was led to the door by half a dozen handlers. Aufors stalked on one side of her as the lizard lurched on the other, its stout body bending from side to side as it walked on splayed feet, its fin sometimes shading her and sometimes not. It had an evil, rotten smell. The edges of its scales were like knives. If one were bumped by a harpta, one could be badly cut or scraped. Genevieve was bumped, but Awhero's soft robe saved her from any serious discomfort.

They came to a narrow, blue-painted gate, which one of the escort opened, pointedly looking away from Genevieve as she entered. Inside was a simple courtyard with gravel paths and little patches of greenery set around a pool of fish. Three figures, covered as she was, head to toe, sat on stools in the shade of a shallow portico covered with dusty vines.

Genevieve approached them, bowed, said, "I am happy to see you."

One of the figures replied, a nonsense syllable, which set the pattern for all subsequent interchange.

"Thank you for inviting me to share your garden."

"Walla, bulla, taka taka, bum."

"Your fish are quite remarkable."

"Lilla-lalla zim zam."

And so on, for the better part of an hour. By this time, Genevieve was making a game of it. "How heavy the heat of the sun, sun sun, how delightful the night when it's cool cool cool. Do you ever go out for a run, run run, or do you just act like a fool, fool fool?"

"Lalla ap," said the spokeswife.

A serving person came into the portico with a pot and cups. The spokeswife poured for all of them. The wives raised their veils, momentarily exposing their faces, dreamy, self-contained, placid.

The spokeswife leaned forward to give Genevieve her cup and whispered softly, in a careless voice, "You are laughing at us."

Genevieve sat back, flushed and confused. They had obviously understood everything she had said, and might properly resent it.

"I was laughing at myself," she said. "For being here."

"Are you the only woman in your party?" The words were quite clear, but the question was asked in a dreamy, inconsequential tone, one that gave it no importance whatsoever.

"Does it matter?" she said, determined to give nothing away.

"Have you a new baby?" The same tone, incognizant, almost sleepy.

How answer this question? She did not want them to know about Dovidi. "If I had a child, I am sure my child would enjoy this garden."

"Cralliopop. Guggle," said the wives to one another, unmoved.

The spokeswife rose and came to sit close to Genevieve.

"We are sad for you," she crooned into Genevieve's ear. "We three have new children, each of us. And now, we are candidates for the journey to Galul. Now, with these children, our third children, we have earned the right. Galul is paradise."

"I am happy for you if you desire this. Where is Galul?"

The woman swayed on her seat, as though to music only she could hear. "Far, far south. In the high mountains, where it is cool and green. I am old for the trip. Thirty-three. But my master and lord did not want me to go until now. I begged him. Though it was wrong to speak to him, I did. He punished me for speaking, but the wounds have healed and he has done as I asked. Perhaps, you may earn the journey if you speak to your master. Do not fear the pain of his displeasure. It goes away, in time."

She rose and returned to her chair, nodding slowly at Genevieve, who was holding her cup beneath her veil, slowly dripping its contents onto her soft inner robe, where it wouldn't show. They had raised their veils, but she had not. They had drunk their tea, but she was wary of it. It had a strange smell.

Shortly thereafter, a serving person came to tell Genevieve that the harpta was waiting. So was Aufors.

They returned in silence to the gate of the residence, and then, seeing the lizard proceed through the city gate, they ran as if with one mind to the slit atop the stairs and from there watched the handlers and the giant beast going down to the sea. There the lizard was divested of its harness and allowed to dive into the waves.

"Ah," Genevieve said. "It's aquatic! Of course it is! Just as the lizards on Haven. There'd be nothing for it to eat here, on land. It must eat seaweed!"

"What happened?" demanded the Marshal, as he came up the stairs.

"Nothing," she said. "They talked a kind of gibberish. We didn't walk in the garden at all. We just sat and talked incomprehensible nonsense to one another, except that one of the wives said two intelligible things. She said that they had new babies, their third—did I forget to say there were three wives present?—and this entitled them to be candidates to go to Galul . . ."

The Marshal paled at the mention of Galul. He turned away. Over his shoulder he asked, "Did they give you anything to eat or drink?"

Genevieve had noticed her father's reaction. "Yes. They gave me tea . . ." She let her voice trail away, for some reason not wanting him to know she had not drunk it.

The Marshal nodded as though with satisfaction. Aufors urged her to rest and followed her into their rooms.

"You started to say something about the tea they gave you, then you stopped. Why?"

"It was a strange question for Father to ask, did they give me anything to eat or drink. And then, he reacted strangely when I mentioned Galul. I just . . . suddenly wanted to keep it to myself, that's all. The fact that he and the Prince told the Mahahmbi I was here after making such a thing out of keeping it secret is confusing, and I'm sure today's invitation doesn't mean what they think it means . . . or . . ."

"Or?"

"Or," she said bleakly, "they both know what it means, but they are not telling me. Us."

"How much did you drink of the stuff they gave you?"

"None. I didn't like the smell of it, or the fact that they acted drugged, though I think we should keep that between us. I pretended to drink it while I dribbled it onto my inner robe, hidden by my veil. Most of it dried on the walk back."

"Let me have the stained robe for a while," said Aufors, his eyes narrowed. "Assuming it was a drug, why would they have wanted to drug you?"

She laughed, a very chilly laugh. "And why do I suspect it may be a good idea to let my father think they succeeded?"

He said bleakly, "And the Invigilator. He and your father have grown very close, lately."

"Next time I see Awhero, I'm going to ask some questions."

She did not see Awhero that night, for the warren beneath the house was empty, and though she planned to sneak away early on the following morning, events moved rather too quickly to allow it.

First, into the bedroom where Genevieve lay beside the chortling baby, Aufors entered with an announcement: "Here's your robe, love. It's a little damp around the neck. I soaked some of that tea out of it, I want to know what it is, but the only analyzer is on the ship. We used it to check the well water for purity, remember? So, since I'm going out to the ship, the doctor and the nursemaid want to go along to send messages home to their families. Will you be all right here alone for a while?"

"I'm not alone, Aufors. Father's here." She said it with a wry, ironic smile.

Aufors shook his head very slightly. Her father was here, and so was the Prince, but that did not mitigate her being alone. Still, the com-man

was in the house, together with the three guards and the household servants.

Aufors had not been long gone when a messenger arrived to invite the Prince, the Invigilator, and Colonel Leys, to go hunting with the Shah. The Prince and Invigilator announced themselves pleased to go. While the Prince put on riding clothes, he gave anyone within earshot a short lecture on the hunting birds of the Mahahmbi. Though the escort said repeatedly they could wait for the Colonel to return, the Prince refused to delay. He did not give any weight to Aufors having been invited, as he had always felt that others valued him as he valued himself. If he, the Prince, went, no more could be desired. Gloved and veiled and walking in an important manner, he and Rongor went out into the desert, where they mounted the proferred horses and rode away.

As was usually the case when Delganor and Rongor were elsewhere, the whole household relaxed—too soon, for a representative of the Shah arrived almost immediately to invite "The Colonel's woman" to walk again with the wives of the Shah in their garden. The Marshal agreed all too eagerly, and the man said he would return for the Colonel's wife at once. Since the nursemaid hadn't returned, the Marshal appointed the off-duty guardsman to watch the child and announced to Genevieve that she was to accept the invitation.

Though the sun was already high, moving toward the hottest time of a fiery day, Genevieve nursed Dovidi, put on the proper shoes and the proper robes, including the robe Awhero had given her, regardless of the dampness around the neck. Though she was soon dressed, the messenger did not immediately return, and soon the Marshal grew impatient.

"That man should have been here to fetch the woman some time ago," he remarked to the courtyard at large. "I'm going to find out what is holding him up."

"Do you know where he is, sir?" asked one of the guardsmen.

"No doubt I'll find him at the palace, and you two can come along to be sure we get there unhindered."

Full of impatient mutters, he left with both the remaining guards. Dovidi was asleep, and Genevieve left him under the eyes of the third guardsman while she went out onto the balcony. The house was oppressively silent, as though it were totally vacant, though Genevieve assured herself that Aufors had not been gone long and there were others still present. The staff was there, along with the cook and the communications man, all in the small courtyard. She went to the stair top to look out through

the wall-slit toward the ship and its auxiliary, surprised to see them sur-rounded by antlike movement and the red sparkle that identified the laser cannons. At the distance she could not see what was happening, though a gust of wind brought the sounds of shouting and screams . . .

Before she could react, someone scrambled on the stairs behind her, and she turned to see Awhero scuttling up toward her, robes thrashing and tangling around her skinny frame. She gasped, "Lady, they're coming to kill you, now!"

The words made no sense. "Who? Awhero, what are you talking about?"

"Your father's taken. Shah Arghad has him and other two men at palace. There is fighting by airships. Now Shah's men come for your blood. Yours and child's. They're coming!"

She tottered. The world filled with blood, a sea of blood, and she choked at the smell of it. Whose was it? Where had it come from? And then it was gone, leaving her as her visions always left her, shaking and weak.

She faltered, "Coming for Dovidi? How did Arghan know about the baby?"

"Your father tell him."

Her mind tumbled, refusing to believe. "I'll get Dovidi. We'll go to the ship . . ."

"If you take him, you both be killed. Fighting out there on sand, where ship is. No way you can get there. No. I take babe, my people take him, we dirty his face and say he one of us. . . ."

"Take me, too . . ."

"You too tall, too pale. The Shah's women, they *heard* you, they *know* you."

"Where? Where shall I go?"

"Remember song of Tenopia. They won't think you go that way, in-land, no. Your only chance! Take your man's cloak, there by gate. Take these rags, disguise. I take baby-boy, you go like Tenopia!"

"Tell Aufors . . . tell him where I went," she cried.

Awhero scrambled toward the baby's room as Genevieve stumbled down the stairs. The outside door had been left inexcusably ajar when the Marshal left, and the Mahahmbi who usually manned the sentry booth outside were gone. The booth was empty. She barred the door, grabbed up a staff and waterbottle, and fled through the passage into the back courtyard, where she detoured past the communications room.

"Assassins coming, crewman!" she cried at his blank and unbelieving face. "Bar the city door. Look to your own safety."

"But my lady," he cried. "Marchioness . . ."

"No time," she called to him. "No time. Tell the ship! Tell my husband I'm escaping. Bar the door!"

She pulled on the robe and settled the spongy cap within the hood as she went down into the cellars and out into the world. Then, like Tenopia, she ran for her life.

WHEN AUFORS, THE DOCTOR, AND THE BABY-TENDER ARRIVED AT THE SHIP, each preoccupied with his own concerns, they passed among several men quietly at work among the anchor ropes, whom they passed by with little regard, separating at the ramp top, the two off-worlders toward the com-room and Aufors toward the bridge in search of the so-called "tech," the crewman who had been trained to use and care for the off-world machines.

He found not only the tech but also the Captain, who looked up with a harried face and snapped, "Colonel! What do you think of this?"

Aufors followed his pointing finger across the tech's shoulder to the console before him, an enigmatic box covered with blotchy screens.

"What are they?" Aufors asked, confused both by the equipment and by the shadows he saw moving there.

"The devices are off-world detectors; I'm told the shadows are men," grated the Captain, "and they're all around us. Every pile of sand out there has a clutch of Mahahmbi hiding behind it. Men don't hide unless they've got something truculent in mind!"

Aufors made no argument. It was unlikely the Captain had gained his position by being hysterical.

"We already know they don't like us," Aufors mused. "They've made their displeasure clear as ice. Up until yesterday when we supposed a thaw occurred."

"I would judge it was no thaw," said the Captain. "Only a minor melt, to get us off guard."

"Have your men stand by the ropes," said Aufors. "You may need to get off quickly."

"Oh, that was done the moment I saw them," murmured the Captain. "Quietly, so as not to stir things up. Also the cannon are readied and the gunners are standing by."

"How many cannon?"

"All four. Bow, stern, and midships, both sides. The bastards have us surrounded."

Aufors looked at the bottle he was holding. "I need your analyzer."

"Hardly the time for intellectual inquiry," snapped the captain.

"Exactly the time for this inquiry," Aufors replied. "As it may well confirm evil intent."

"If you need confirmation, you must be a hard man to convince!" the Captain snapped at Aufors's back as he stepped into the cubby where the device was housed.

He had seen the tech use it to test their drinking water, after the well was opened, and he followed the routine he had observed then, pouring his sample into a clean vial, inserting it, pressing a button, and waiting while the mechanism hummed and chuckled to itself for quite some time. Murmurs came from the control room, together with several muffled curses from the captain. At last the results came up on a screen, a meaningless clutter of letters and numbers. "How do I translate the results?" he called.

"Tell it you need lay language," barked the tech, without looking up.

Aufors told it, somewhat self-consciously, and the screen changed its message: *Substance is proprietary to Galaxo-pharm, trademark Unforz. Purpose is euphoric, sedative, relaxant. Effective on most mammalian life forms. Typical uses: by surgeon to allay apprehension in patient; by zookeeper, to handle deadly or delicate creatures during transport or prolonged handling; by wardens transporting dangerous criminals.*

"Out here, Colonel!" snapped the Captain. "Here they come."

Aufors emerged from the cubicle in time to see the screens erupt with dark blotches. Loosing his own light weapon in its holster, he made for the ramp to see what he had been too distracted to see when he came in. Halfway up the ramp stood a crewman, a line leading from his hand to a latch at the base of the nearest anchor rope, a latch which had replaced the knotted tie he had seen there previously. It took only a glance to confirm that all the latches were connected to the single line.

The man at the rope cast a glance in Aufors's direction, then knelt behind the railing, out of sight of the robed men pouring over the dunes, blades glittering, voices raised in wild ululations. Without warning, the cannoneers in the nacelle began shooting: soundless, invisible blasts that exploded into sequin showers, like sparks from a poked campfire, though where these sparks fell they were followed by cries of fury or pain.

From inside, the doctor cried, "Colonel. A message from the town. Your wife, she's fled from assassins. The Shah has her father!"

Aufors ran up the ramp. The doctor stood just inside the door, chewing his lips and combing his hair into disarray with unsteady hands.

Aufors demanded, "Genevieve fled where? Is she coming here?"

The doctor shook his head, eyes widely fixed on the battle outside. "Don't know. That's the message the com-man just got from the residence. He's trying to find out . . ."

A reduction in the sound level made Aufors turn toward the ramp once more. On one side the remaining attackers were floundering up the nearest dunes, in full retreat. Whatever their plan had been, it had gone awry, for they surely hadn't meant to leave all those charred bodies upon the sand. Those attacking from the other side were not yet convinced, and the bow gunner swung his weapon in that direction.

"Didn't they know we had cannon?" the doctor asked in a frantic voice. "Should I go out and see to the wounded?"

"Do nothing of the kind," snapped Aufors, on his way to the control room. "Stay where you are. There's still battle going on out there."

As it did, for some time, though with decreasing violence. Finally, though the tech went on twisting dials and tapping buttons, the Captain, hovering behind him, could see only a few shadows remaining behind dunes, moving little if at all. Wounded, most likely. Or dying.

"Can you spare half a dozen men?" Aufors demanded.

"If it is your aim to bring the Prince safely to the ship, yes."

"By the deepsea!" cried Aufors. "It's my aim to bring whoever's left at the residence!"

"Go! Go!" grated the Captain. "We're here at the Prince's command. We shouldn't leave unless commanded by the Prince, but he cannot command if he cannot reach us!"

"Message those at the residence to come out by the desert door, and have your cannoneers cover their retreat. . . ." Aufors's voice trailed off as he went out again, picking half a dozen men with weapons from those muttering in the way and leading them down the ramp, where he put them into rough formation, well spread out and with the calmest of them guarding the rear.

They trudged toward the city, those at the rear walking mostly backwards. It was both impossible and foolish to run on the shifting surface, but the slow trudge gave them entirely too much time to think. Or, so Aufors felt. Why had they heard nothing from the Prince? From Gene-

vieve's father? Why had no one said anything about Dovidi? Genevieve wouldn't have left him! Therefore . . . what?

It did no good to wonder. He would find them or he would not. The thought was one he often resorted to in battle. This time it did no good. A distant shout brought his eyes up, and he saw a man plunging outward from the guard post outside the residence doorway. He was immediately followed by others, and in a moment Aufors could identify them all: three household servants, one steward-cum-guard, the cook, the cook's helper, and lastly the communications man who had kept them in touch with the ship.

When this man came abreast of Aufors he stopped for a moment, gasping, "The place is empty, Colonel. No point in going any nearer. I've followed the protocol and triggered the devices in the com-room. All the off-world stuff'll go up in a few moments . . ."

Aufors grasped him by the arm. "By the deepsea, man! My son! Where's my son?"

"Be easy, Colonel. He's out of there. The old woman took him, that malghaste. She showed him to me as she went by. She said he'd be safe, no one would look among them so long as you didn't mention who took him, not to anyone."

Aufors turned, and they trotted toward the ship. "To anyone?" He gave the man a piercing look.

"I'm safe, sir. If anyone asks, anyone at all, I'll say your wife took him when she went. I owe her that much and more. We'd have been dead meat if she hadn't warned us as she went out . . ."

"Went where?" Aufors demanded. "Where could she go?"

"Down, sir. She went down into the cellars and away. That's the way the old woman went, as well. I don't know how she knew there was a way out down there, your wife, I mean. . . ."

"I know how she knew. What I don't know is where I'm to find her. Or Dovidi."

"I can't tell you, sir. All the old woman said was, tell the Colonel to be patient, keep his mouth shut—pardon me, sir, but I'm just quoting what she said—for his son is safe with the malghaste." He turned to look over his shoulder. "Hadn't we better get a move on, sir?"

Men were massing at the city gate. Aufors picked up his pace and they slogged toward the ship under the cyclopian gaze of the nearest cannon. Though the crowd at the gate grew larger, no one came after them.

"Why did she run?" asked Aufors.

"Somehow, she knew they were coming. The assassins." He laughed, a little wildly. "I wish she'd given us more notice."

"The place was attacked?"

"Oh, they attacked right enough. If she hadn't warned me, they'd have overrun the place, but as it was, she barred the outer door and I got the city door barred just before they came hammering at it. I put a man on the roof, to watch, and he said they were bringing ladders down the street just when the message came to get out. They'll be in over the roof by now . . ."

His words were lost in a crumping noise that shook the soil beneath them and made them stagger. Over their shoulders they saw the gatehouse disappear behind a cloud of dust and smoke that spewed through the opening in the city wall. The crowd outside the city gate howled.

"The Prince?" cried the Captain from the ramp top.

"He wasn't there, sir," answered the com-man. "He'd gone off with the Invigilator, hunting . . ."

As they came up the ramp, the crowd at the city gate screamed itself into a frenzied attack. The man at the slip line tugged it loose and followed them inside where the Captain had men waiting to pull the ramp aboard. As the ship wallowed sluggishly upward under its slowly inflating balloon, they looked down onto the approaching mob, now a sea of blades waving impotently as the ship ascended to the slow hiss of gas being released into the huge bags. Behind the dunes, no one moved, though a few huddled forms still lay there.

The Captain tallied the men aboard and reported to Aufors. "All here but the Prince, the Invigilator, the Marshal, and two guards."

"And my wife and child," snapped Aufors. "I can't believe this attack. It makes no sense at all!"

"You'll have to make some sense of it, Colonel, for you are now in command," said the Captain through his teeth.

The com-man from the residence had his head out a port, watching the confused mob below. Aufors grasped his shoulder and pushed him into a seat, then sat across from him and demanded, "Tell me everything that happened after I left. Every detail!"

The man rubbed his head and took a deep breath. "I guess the first thing was a messenger came from the Shah to invite you and the Prince and the Invigilator to go hunting with His Effulgence."

"Me?" snarled Aufors. "By name?"

"You, sir. By name. Or rank, rather. The Colonel, that's what the man said. Well, you were out here at the ship. The messenger said they could

wait until you returned, but the Prince said he could do without you quite nicely. He was a bit miffed, sir, them asking for you along with him and the Invigilator. Anyhow, off the two of them went with the Shah's man—"

"Out of which door?" demanded Aufors.

"The desert door, sir. I stood there with the guard, while he mounted and rode out onto the sands. Well, he was no sooner gone than another messenger came to the city door, to invite the lady to walk in the garden again."

"Aha," said Aufors.

"Does this mean something?" the Captain asked.

"It would seem they were picking us off a few at a time, wouldn't it?" Aufors grated. Then, to his informant, "Go on. What next?"

"Let's see, sir. Ah. I guess the next thing was the Marshal agreed your lady would go. Since the baby-tender was out here with you, the Marshal took the man who was off duty and set him down next the baby. Baby went to sleep. Meantime, your lady was getting herself dressed."

"When was this?"

"Not long after you left. Well, she was soon dressed, but the escort didn't come for her. No one came. Well, you know the Marshal, sir. He waits on no man, and he was soon thundering about full of bloody bedamn this and bloody bedamn that, putting on quite a show . . ."

Aufors whispered, "A show? You felt he was acting?"

The com-man paused, mouth open. "Now you mention it, sir. Yes. He was, and in no time at all he said he was going off to the palace to find out the arrangements. He went by the street door, and he took the other two guards with him."

Aufors blinked slowly, not giving voice to his fury. He had always admired the Marshal's skills, but it seemed to him now that off the battlefield, the man was an idiot.

The com-man read his face. "Well, I knew you were wondering, sir, just how it was we didn't have the outer doors covered. Well, the Marshal and the men weren't long gone when your lady was warned, somehow, that they were coming for her."

"But not for a garden walk," Aufors said bleakly.

"No, sir. So, she went by me shouting to bar the door and message the ship. I saw the way she went, then I did what she said, barred the door and sent the message. Then I checked the door through the city wall. That one was barred, no doubt by your lady, sir, for she told me to get the other one. While I was there, the old woman came down the

stairs and went by me with the child, as I've said, and went through toward the kitchen. The man who'd been baby-tending was behind her, and I told him to stay by the door while I followed her as far as the way down and out, then I got back to the com. By that time, everyone was gathered in one place, outside the com-room, and when I got your message to evacuate, I set the charges in the com-room and got everyone out."

"How did the Marchioness know they intended harm?" the Captain asked.

The com-man replied, "It had to be the old woman, Captain, Colonel. Who else? And if the Shah had wanted the two of you to begin with, Colonel, it would explain the two attacks, both out here and on the residence. Stands to reason it was you they were after. They already had Delganor, the Invigilator, and the Marshal."

"They miscalculated," said the Captain.

"They and we," Aufors said. "Because of failed intelligence, Captain. We didn't know they intended to pick us off. They didn't know about the cannon or your off-world detectors. We didn't know they were after me or Genevieve, and they didn't know Genevieve would be warned. Why they wanted her is a mystery to me, unless it has to do with all their nonsense about women, but why did they want me? They already had the Prince."

"My judgment would be that they can't use the Prince for what they have in mind," said the Captain in a dead, cold voice. "I've been here before, Colonel. On one occasion, a few years back, an officer of my crew was cut into pieces and left at the bottom of the ramp, merely, so the Prince said, to make a point. Perhaps they felt they needed to make another point."

"To the Prince?" asked Aufors. "And you think I was to have been the victim?"

The Captain shrugged. "You are not of the nobility, Colonel, so your death would not offend the nobility of Haven. Invigilator Rongor is of the nobility, as is the Prince. Noble or not, you are high enough in rank to leave a noticeable hole, as am I. Either one of us would probably serve as a warning, but if they kill me, the ship might not make it back to Haven, and they wouldn't want that. Their trade depends upon Haven and the nobility. You would serve well to make a point."

"I would, or my wife."

"No, not the lady. Forgive me, sir, but the Mahahmbi don't think women make any point at all. If they took your woman, they'd expect

you to find another. The Mahahmbi consider women disposable; they buy them or steal them, just as they buy or steal equipment, with no more importance than that."

Aufors narrowed his eyes. "So they want to make a point to the Prince. The Prince, and no doubt the Invigilator as well, want them to increase P'naki production, so the point being made must be *let this matter alone!* They do not want to talk about increasing P'naki."

The Captain sighed and pursed his mouth. "Likely it is the matter of P'naki, yes, sir."

Aufors started to put his anger into words, then shut his mouth, for the Captain was speaking to the men who had crowded into the control area, and nothing would be gained by shouting at the Captain in front of his men. Shout he would, however. At someone. Sooner or later.

The Captain was saying, "We haven't enough fuel to hang here against the wind indefinitely. We'll have to moor ourselves on the nearest island while we decide what to do next. Helmsman, steer us across the strait. The rest of you, sort yourselves out. Find rooms to bed in and clear the ways."

The others went, but Aufors stayed.

"So you're still digging," the Captain murmured.

"Shouldn't I be?" he replied angrily.

"Yes, Colonel. Of course you should. You're angry with me because you think I should have told you many things you weren't told. I was under orders not to do so. You and I, sir, we obey orders, do we not?"

"Usually," Aufors grated, thinking to himself that there were a good many he would not obey, including ones that put his fellow men into harm's way.

"Also," the Captain went on, "you are in love with your wife, you delight in your son."

"You may be sure I'm going after them."

"Oh, yes, and you're also curious about what's going on, just as I have been for years, except that I've not had the resolution to do anything about it except listen to whispers. That's all I know: whispers. There is one aboard, however, who might know more than I. Ask the doctor, Colonel."

"Ask him what?"

The Captain grinned mirthlessly, his skull face reflected in the dials before him, fixing Aufors with glittering eyes. "I've always felt the doctor knew more than the rest of us about P'naki."

* * *

In the throne room at Havenor, the Lord Paramount was receiving a report from one of his spies, a man the Prince would have been unhappily surprised to see kneeling subserviently before His Majesty.

"Well, Wiezal! So Prince Delganor is now separated from the ship and from his men!" The Lord Paramount sat up quite straight and settled his crown straight on his head. "How did you find that out?"

"You asked me to arrange to keep tabs on the mission, Your Majesty. Accordingly, we put listening devices on the ship, and we stationed men all along the islands to relay the message along the Stone Trail, to Frangia, and thence to Bliggen, and thence up the road to Havenor. We receive the message only a few hours after it has left the vicinity of Mahahm."

"But the Prince is currently with the Shah? Correct? And the Shah does not want any trifling with . . . P'naki?"

"It's rather confusing, Your Majesty, full of noise and cross talk, and our off-world technicians have to sort it all out when we receive the record here. All we really know is that the Prince, the Marshal, and the Invigilator are with the Shah, that the Marshal's daughter has run away, and that her husband will no doubt go looking for her."

"Always running off, that one, isn't she?" said the Lord Paramount in an interested voice. "Ran off from Delganor, before. Said at the time she had good sense. Well. Events have conspired to give us an opportunity!"

"Indeed, Your Majesty."

"And quite good time, too. Delganor was becoming . . . almost overt. Are my good little Frangians out there, Wiezal?"

"Waiting, Your Majesty."

"Let them come in. And stay to listen."

They came in, three lean, browned men with squinty eyes and callused hands. They bowed. The Lord Paramount nodded.

"Shipment on the way, is it?"

"The supply ships are halfway to Mahahm, Your Majesty," said their spokesman. "Trip shouldn't take much longer, depending on the wind."

"Slight change in plans," said the Lord Paramount. "I presume you can communicate with your ships?"

"Oh, yes, Your Majesty. Indeed."

"One of my airships is moored on an island near Mahahm. When your ship gets there, send someone ashore and give the Captain this message: He and the ship are to return to Bliggen at once, without waiting for the Prince. If he asks for a code phrase that tells him the message is really from me, tell him 'Down with sneaks and lurkers.' "

" 'Down with sneaks and lurkers,' your Majesty?"

"The Captain will know the message is from me. Then, when your ships arrive offshore of Mahahm, they should send a little boat ashore and tell the Shah's man that payment is to be made directly to them, not returned by Prince Delganor in the airship. Understand?"

"Perfectly," said the spokesman.

"Payment is to consist of the usual shipment of P'naki, twenty jars, well sealed, the Marshal and the Invigilator, alive and in good condition, and the dead body of Prince Delganor in any condition at all, so long as one can ascertain it is indeed the Prince. Your people are not to unload the food or other supplies they are carrying until payment is received. Now, pay attention. The substance in the jars is extremely condensed when you receive it. It gets prepared for use here in Havenor. Warn your people not to unseal it on the ship. Damp air destroys the efficacy, and none of us want to see more of our people dying of batfly fever."

"We understand, Your Majesty."

"Once they're sure they have the Prince, they may dump his body overboard," continued the Lord Paramount, "Suitably weighted. And as always, we do not talk about our arrangement." He looked significantly at the Aresians on either side of the door, each with a hand on his weapon. "Do we? My cousin, the Duke of Frangia, would be most upset if he learned I had delayed his return to the provincial throne because of my gratitude to the Mariner's Guild of Frangia."

They replied in unison, "Silence is sworn, Your Majesty."

"Thus Frangia continues in peace in the Whatever." The Lord Paramount smiled. "As it has for some time now."

"Peace and Whatever," they intoned, bowing themselves out backwards.

Wiezal was summoned forward from the corner in which he'd placed himself.

"Have I forgotten anything?" asked the Lord Paramount.

"Not if it works," said Wiezal. "You'll have the Prince done for, you'll have your shipment you want, and you'll have the Marshal and Invigilator back."

"It's true that I've asked for the Marshal back," said the Lord Paramount fretfully. "But I'm not at all sure I want him! The man is as thick as craylet bisque! Asked him once if his daughter was a good candidate for . . ." His voice faded, as though he had forgotten what he was saying. He nodded, then said jerkily, "Well, he didn't follow me at all."

He stared distractedly at Wiezal, who responded by looking puzzled. He was puzzled more and more lately, when it came to things the Lord

Paramount ordered or said or claimed he had said. The man was getting . . . well, *forgetful* was the most tactful word Wiezal could think of.

The Lord Paramount came to himself with a start. "I'm rambling. Just rambling. He'll be wiser now. I'm sure Rongor has put him in the picture. That's an Invigilator's job, right? Thick as craylet bisque. Amazing." He sat back on his throne and reached for the top catalog on the pile.

Wisely, Wiezal went.

Genevieve woke in the marae. For a long time she lay in the tall stone room with her eyes half closed, listening for Dovidi's breathing, only slowly realizing that he wasn't there. Her throat tightened as she tried to remember where she was, when she was: not on the ship, not in Mahahm-qum, not on the desert. Panic ebbed. She was at the marae, and three days had passed since she fled the city.

She opened her eyes to stare upward. Pallid light gathered once more around the high window through which the cool of the night had flowed, as into a well.

"With one frog in it," she murmured.

"What frog?" asked a familiar voice from across the room.

She sat up, pushing her tangled hair away from her face. A woman occupied the chair across the room, hands lying in her lap, sandaled feet together beside a cloth bundle, face quiet. Genevieve had never seen her before.

"I was thinking the room is like a well," confessed Genevieve. "It is full of night cool, and I am the frog in it."

The woman smiled, very slightly, as though smiling were an alien habit, one she had only recently learned of. "Well, there are at least two of us frogs, relishing the cool of the morning. Have you rested?"

"I must have. I didn't wake." Without warning, her eyes filled with tears. "I woke up thinking of Dovidi. I've left him. I've abandoned him. . . ."

"You feel guilty over that?"

"Of course I do. He'll think I've abandoned him."

"No. He won't. Babies recognize things they have seen, smelled, tasted, or felt, but they don't remember them separate from the event until they are older. Don't you believe Awhero will keep him safe?"

Genevieve searched inwardly for the answer to that, finding a complete certainty. "I know she will if she can."

"Then blame your hours of sleep on your confidence in her. Unless you believe it is your duty to be forever guilty of some unspecified sin. Some women do. If you are one of them, you will be little good to us or yourself."

Though the woman had spoken as though she didn't care, she was watching Genevieve with concentrated attention.

Genevieve thought about this, running her fingers into the tangled mass of her hair. "No. That's not my duty, but I grieve over his absence. I miss him. He has been with me a while now, inside or beside."

"Of course you miss him. If you had been less intelligent about his safety, you might have brought him with you as a foolish woman would, putting instinct ahead of good sense. If you had done that, neither of you would have survived. A baby wailing in the sands and those winged hunters would have been on you in moments. You were right to let him go. The old woman was right to take him."

"Do you know her?"

"Certainly I know her. Awhero is what you might call a ham, an eccentric, a woman who has grown to love the part she plays. She has virtually invented the role of malghaste for others to copy, but she is nonetheless reliable. The child will be all right: dirtier than with you, more shared among caretakers than with you, passed about a great deal more from one to another, no doubt, but all right."

Genevieve took up her comb and applied it to the tangle, working the snarls out. "I must get word to my husband . . ."

The woman shook her head, slowly. "There's no way we can do that. Our runners tell us that the ship left the city three days ago. He knows you're alive, and that is enough for now."

"There was fighting!" she cried, suddenly remembering.

The woman made a shushing motion with one hand. "The Colonel was not injured in the fighting. In fact, all the Havenites survived except three. . . ."

"Who?" she cried. "Who was killed?"

"The two guards who were with your father and a man of religion who was killed after the ship left, despite his being, I am told, a member of the nobility. Your father and the Prince are now the guests of the Shah, and they are unharmed. Our messengers tell us that everyone who survived the initial encounter, Havenite or Mahahmbi, is irritated beyond measure, for many died by the guns of the ship, and those deaths, at least, were not supposed to have happened."

Genevieve gritted her teeth at this cool analysis. "What was supposed to have happened?"

The woman grimaced. "Judging by prior and similar events, you and your family were to have been taken for an . . . exemplary use. After which your father was to have seen where his interest lay and the Prince was to have moderated his demands. Since your husband made himself unavailable for sacrifice, however, the religious gentleman took his place. Much, one supposes, to his dismay."

Genevieve could not control her annoyance. "Whoever you are, you seem very cool about all this. Does any of it matter to you?"

A curious expression fled across the woman's face, a mere flicker, leaving it as impassive as before. "My name is Melanie, Marchioness, and you do not yet know me or mine well enough to ask that question, much less to judge us. What you confront here, we have confronted for many lifetimes."

Genevieve gritted her teeth. "I'll try to get to know you better, but I beg you, don't call me Marchioness. I did nothing to earn the title save be born to it. I would as soon never have had it since it brought me to the notice of the Prince. I did everything I could to escape the Prince while remaining true to a vow I made my mother, long ago."

The woman's voice softened. "So it seems."

"Then you know a great deal more than you did last night!"

"Ah, well, we made detailed inquiries during the night. All the bloodshed took place three days ago, but Mahahm-qum returned to peace promptly. The thrice yearly Time-of-Renewal was upon them, four days of ritual and mystery, and when that time comes, calm must prevail. On the third day, today, the Shah himself goes out into the desert, and he could not do so if there were unrest. If he did not go, the hopes and dreams of those close to him would wither, resulting in a loss of support, which would dismay as nothing else does." Her mouth twisted, as though she wanted to spit. "Even as we speak, the Shah is welcoming the aspirants whom he will lead into the desert with the candidates. While he does so, the city holds its breath, waiting."

"I'm missing all the fun?" said Genevieve, watching her informant through narrowed eyes.

"Ha," the woman barked. "Fun of the Shah's sort? Yes. And be everlastingly grateful for that."

"Are you going to tell me what all this is about?"

"You don't know what it's about?"

"How could I?"

"I have no way of knowing what you know or don't know, not yet. In any case, we can do better than tell you. Today, you will see for yourself."

"We're going back to the city?" she asked, dismayed despite herself. Her body still ached from the struggle to gain this refuge.

"Not to the city, no, and you won't have to walk." The woman stood and came to peer into Genevieve's face. "You're still weak; your face is burned, your lips are raw. Walking on deep sand is difficult and exhausting. You probably ache."

"I do, yes."

"Well, take comfort. Today will require little physical strain." She returned to the bundle and took it up, delivering it into Genevieve's hands. "I'm returning your soft robe. The stuff you spilled down your front wouldn't have killed you, but if you'd drunk it, you wouldn't have had the wits to escape. We know that drug; the soporific effect lasts for days. Now, put it on. There's a new pair of sandals inside. We're expected at breakfast."

"My hair." Genevieve tugged at a recalcitrant snarl with fruitless tenacity. "I was too sleepy to braid it."

Suddenly Melanie smiled, like a sunrise. "Sit quiet. I used to do it for my own daughters; let me do it for you."

She was a generation older than Genevieve, as old as Genevieve's mother might have been. Her hands were gentle as she worked out the tangles, humming to herself as she did so. It was this familiar sound that made Genevieve realize why the woman seemed familiar to her.

"You sound like my mother," she cried, aware all at once of what had escaped her until that moment. "You almost have my nose! The family nose, my mother's! And Lyndafal's!"

"When you come to breakfast you will see that many of us have Stephanie's nose, and Tenopia's, though most of ours are not as impressive as yours. We, too, are descended from that line."

"Are there many of Tenopia's descendants here?"

"Some, but most of her descendants are in Haven."

"Queen Stephanie was descended from Tenopia?"

"She was a direct descendant. She and some of the other daughters and granddaughters were appointed by Tenopia to go into Haven."

"Do your people all have visions, too?"

"Almost none of us have them, no, and we don't call them visions. We call them extrapolations, connections, implications, likelihoods." She began to braid Genevieve's hair, humming once more, fingers moving swiftly. "There is nothing supernatural about them, vivid though they are, and

some of our visionaries have them to a greater or lesser degree. I take it you see things clearly?"

"Sometimes. I knew of my journey to Mahahm long before it took place. I saw this place, long before I came here. What is it, really?"

"Didn't the song of Tenopia tell you?"

"It was called a marae morehu. Awhero said that meant a house of refuge. Is it only that?"

"No thing, no person, no place is only one thing. For me, marae morehu is a home when I am away from Galul."

"There really is a Galul!"

"Oh, indeed there is a Galul. Our visionaries are there. Galul is where Tenopia first came from her island home. Our government, such as it is, has its seat in Galul."

"Aufors and I . . . we thought perhaps it was legendary, like Eden, a kind of Utopia. Aufors told me the original surveys show only ice at the southern end of the continent. And there's nothing in the archives more recent than that."

"There were glaciers over much of Galul when the survey was made, and also it was winter, with even the unglaciated areas covered in snow. Settlers are usually not very interested in areas covered with snow and ice, for which we were thankful. In the centuries between then and now the glaciers shrank and the winters became shorter. Indeed, Galul was warm and lovely long before these Mahahmbi came wandering in, unwelcome visitors to the north end of a landmass we had considered ours. Well, they settled in the desert, an area we had no use for, so we left them alone while we remained high in the southern mountains, drinking from pure streams that flow from ancient ice, our fields catching the rain that makes them green. Galul is our land. It was ours before the Havenites came."

"Before!"

"Weren't you told how Haven was discovered in the first place?" Melanie took a few long hairs from the comb, twisted them into a strand and fastened the finished braid with it, standing back to admire her work.

Genevieve fumbled to rearrange her thoughts. "I read Stephanie's book. A ship . . . an ark ship went down, and the book seems to say Stephanie's forebears were on it, though I was taught that all the crew were rescued."

"Oh, yes, the ship's *crew* was rescued. But the people who cared for the cargo were not. Nor was the cargo itself. The Captain of the ship simply abandoned the creatures he had sworn to carry away to safety, and us along with them."

"I was taught that many birds survived . . ."

"Actually, everything alive on that ship survived, including our ancestors, though we had our charges to thank for that! Once we got them free . . ."

"Your people were struggling in the water," cried Genevieve. "Trying to open a great door!"

"Exactly. You see? At some level, you knew about this. You were told something, likely by your mother, and you knew about this though your conscious mind had not made the connection. Our people got the seadoors open, and once we did, our charges came out and saved us in turn, carrying us to an island where we could live, bringing us food until we were able to find it or grow it for ourselves."

"How many?" Genevieve asked, her eyes wide with wonder. "How many of you?"

"Several dozens. Most of us young, luckily. So, we lived upon our island, and we begot children—huge numbers of them in that first generation, though we have become more sensible since. When our population grew too large for our island, our friends brought one group of us to Galul, the ones least suited to the sun and the sea, and took others of us to other islands. During those years, we and they have resurrected their ancient culture, the suitable parts of it at least, though now the language is used mostly for ritual."

"Awhero speaks it."

"Awhero, as I've said, plays her part to the hilt. She's an oral historian, and she lives the role."

"How did you keep the Mahahmbi out?"

"The seas around this island are full of our friends, the mountains are difficult to traverse. When the Mahahmbi first came, they tried to explore, but whenever they got close, we frustrated their expeditions in one way or another. More recently, since they've become devoted to the Shah's benefices, they've had no energy for exploration, no energy for anything but the lengthening of their own lives."

A hundred questions trembled on Genevieve's lips, but Melanie laid a finger upon them. "Come, now. We will be late for breakfast."

She waited while Genevieve stepped into her sandals and put on the soft robe, belting it around her. They went out into a long, cool hallway that led toward the murmur of voices, an occasional muffled clatter of crockery, the smell of food. At the end of the corridor a dozen or so people occupied a low, long room, lit only by wide, shallow arches that gave upon a shaded atrium. The trees there were wider than they were

tall, their branches filtering the sun through wine-red leaves to spread a rose-silver shade upon the paving stones. Those in the room glanced at Melanie and Genevieve, then returned to their food with studied uninterest. Two, however, a man and a woman, rose from their table and approached them.

"This is Joncaster," Melanie said. "And his sister, Enid. Enid and I were the two who . . . welcomed you last night. Go with them and eat a good breakfast. Do it quickly, for you have a long day ahead."

Joncaster, with light hair and skin freckled by the sun, went off to get her a plate. When he brought it, Genevieve was unsurprised to see more of the fruit she had been served the night before, along with a mug of tea, a wedge of soft cheese, and a small loaf of bread, still warm from the oven.

"Fuel?" Genevieve murmured. "For the oven?"

"Solar," said Joncaster in a crisp, not quite friendly voice. "We've been refining the ovens for generations. They are now very efficient."

"You will want news of your child," said Enid, returning to her own meal. "We have none except that he is safely away from the Shah and the Prince." She gave Genevieve a long looking-over, her face stern. "Is your father of their persuasion? Do we count him as one of them, or as a possible friend?"

Genevieve knotted her brow at this. "I don't know," she said honestly. "I don't know what persuasion you mean, or whether he is part of it. I've been at school since my mother died. I saw him seldom. Since leaving school, I seem to have irritated him most of the time . . ."

"How old is he?" demanded Joncaster.

"Sixty years," she said. "His birthday is not far off, when he will be sixty-one."

"He has no wife?"

"Not since my mother died."

"And she died of . . . ?" His eyebrows were raised, his lips curled in distaste.

Genevieve murmured, "Complications of childbirth, so the physicians said."

His face hardened. "You know that for a fact? You were there?"

Genevieve felt her face flame at this, half remembered grief, half anger at this continued questioning. "I was there. I was eleven. I saw her the day she died. I saw her in her coffin."

Joncaster frowned. "And your father has never been to Mahahm before . . . ?"

His sister interrupted. "It makes no never mind, Joncee. Many of the Prince's allies have never come to Mahahm, which doesn't prevent their receiving Mahahm's gift back on Haven. Her father could be one of them without ever having seen Mahahm!"

"Hush," said Melanie from behind them. "Whatever he is, Genevieve can't presume to speak for him. She can only speak for herself, and today we will give her a reason for doing so. For now, let her eat."

Irritated past endurance, Genevieve cried, "Do you know where my husband is? Does anyone know?"

A silence fell, almost as though those in the room had drawn breath together, and Melanie turned into that silence, saying, "Her husband is Aufors Leys. A Colonel in the Lord Paramount's armies, but a commoner."

"A commoner?" said her companions, both together.

Joncaster turned back to Genevieve with an almost friendly expression, "How did you manage that?"

"More important, why did you manage that?" demanded Enid, retaining her skeptical air.

Talking about Aufors was easier than answering their questions, so she talked . . . no, she spouted about Aufors, between sips of tea and bites of bread and cheese: how they met, why she ran away, why she returned, why she finally consented to marry him. She edited all of it, telling about her oath to her mother, but leaving out any reference to talking fish with or without human-seeming spokesmen; telling about Stephanie's book, but leaving out the exercises her mother had taught her. When she had finished, Joncaster seemed satisfied, and even Enid's expression had softened.

Enid said, "The airship was seen crossing the channel to the next island north. Whether the ship returned to Haven or stopped among the islands, we don't yet know, though it won't take long for our friends to find out."

Melanie had been talking with others in the room, but now she returned, asking them to hurry. "Will you go with us?" she asked Enid, who turned away from her with an expression of revulsion.

"I've seen enough of it," said Enid angrily. "She seems all right! Why don't you just tell her about it? Why put her through . . ."

"She has to see it," said Melanie firmly. "If she is to understand, she must see. I'll take her, and Joncaster can drive."

"Oh, yes, I'll drive," said Joncaster. "But Enid has the right of it."

Enid shrugged, took Genevieve's hand and squeezed it almost hurtfully, then abruptly left the table.

Melanie waited while Genevieve finished the last of the food before her. "Joncaster and Enid are intellectual heirs of the environmental engi-

neers on the ark ship, those responsible for maintenance of the machines that kept our cargo alive." This had a rehearsed sound to it, as though she had offered the explanation more than once.

"Oh, I like that," said Joncaster, with a wry twist of his lips. "Intellectual heirs. She says that just to cheer us. We're more like persistent fumblers. Trial-and-error tinkerers. Luckily, the machines we have today are practically foolproof, or we'd never make them work."

"Where do you get them?" asked Genevieve.

"Well, though we continually expect to be caught at it, we usually steal them from Haven. That's where we get sand-sleds, one of which we'll be using today. Come along. Melanie's right. We should leave before the wind rises. The sleds weren't designed to work in places as dusty as this, and they need constant fiddling with to keep them running."

Genevieve put on the hooded robe that Melanie handed her, the one with Aufors's smell to it, the one she had worn when she arrived, though the malghaste rags had been removed. They went out through the atrium to the rooms on the far side, a dormitory, a library, and down the hall between them into another wide, low room, this one reeking of oil and chemicals. The sleds rested before an overhead door, their tops only inches off the floor, and Joncaster showed Genevieve how to arrange herself by lying prone on the padded deck that slanted slightly upward to a pillowed chin rest. Her arms went on either side of the rest. Melanie lay on her right and Joncaster on her left, his hands on the controls, which were in a shallow well before him. He moved a lever and the overhead door rose slowly until it was just above their heads.

Genevieve wriggled uncomfortably, and he waited while she pulled her robe flat beneath her, saying, "For spying purposes, we've modified the sled to have a low profile. We removed the superstructure, took off the railings, turned the foot-operated controls into hand controls, padded the floor . . ."

His words were lost in a rush of air as they left the shed, skimming out beneath the door and darting away around a dune, immediately losing any sight of the refuge behind them.

"I hope you know where you're going," muttered Melanie.

"I have the desert well in mind, madam. I will not lose you in it."

Melanie continued unrepentently. "I trust someone found the flags?"

"Yes, Melanie. Of course, Melanie. I did. Early this morning. We'll pick them up at the farthest point south from Mahahm-qum. The procession won't reach it until afternoon."

"I walked for days," cried Genevieve. "And we can cover the distance in a morning?"

"You didn't really walk," soothed Melanie. "You stumbled, mostly, up and down dunes, through heavy sand. As the bird flies, we are not actually very far from Mahahm-qum."

Though Genevieve had a dozen questions she wanted to ask, the air was so full of grit that talking was impossible. Instead, she followed Melanie's example by lowering her hood over her eyes and turning her head to one side, resting it on the chin rest as on a pillow. Joncaster was the only one of them who had goggles, and even he soon wound a strip of fabric over his nose and mouth.

Close to the ground as they were, they seemed to go very fast, though not in any straight direction. Joncaster kept them low, zipping along the bases of the dunes rather than over their tops. The heat made Genevieve drowsy, and she let her body relax against the padding, aware of passing time but paying no attention to it, coming to alertness only when Joncaster murmured, "There," as he pointed toward the top of the nearest dune where a red scrap fluttered in the ceaseless wind. "I found a cave nearby that we can watch from."

"How far a cave?" asked Enid. "It's almost noon. We don't have much time."

"Patience, madam. Patience."

They veered widely around the base of the flag-topped dune, then went up another to encounter an outcropping of gray stone. Joncaster maneuvered the sled between two rough pillars and let it come to rest on an area of hard-packed sand beneath an overhang.

They rose, stiff from the motionless hours. When they stepped away, Joncaster pulled a pack of netting from under the padding and tossed it over the sled. Between the shadow of the rock and the effect of the netting, the sled disappeared.

"No one will see it unless they're looking for it, and so far as we know, no one's looking," said Melanie in a dispirited voice.

Joncaster had moved away around the outcropping, and he returned, beckoning. "Keep it quiet. I hear harptas grunting, so they're not far. They've covered more distance than I thought they would. They must have had fewer candidates than usual."

They found Joncaster's cave almost at the top of the outcropping, a shallow slit across the face of the rock, which Joncaster probed with a staff and a light, dislodging any of the desert's stingers and biters. They slithered into the crevice backward until the shadow covered their faces.

Melanie handed Genevieve a square of the same netting they had thrown over the sled, showing her how to drape it to hide her face.

"Now," said Joncaster, when each of them had wriggled a belly hollow in the sand carpeting the space. "You don't say a word, Genevieve. You don't cry out or scream or run out of this place in some crazy effort to stop anything that's happening, you understand? Nothing you can do will change what you see, and Madam Commander there says you have to see it, so stay quiet."

She was immediately rebellious, and the feeling must have shown on her face, for Melanie took her hands and squeezed them, tightly.

"What he says is true, Genevieve. Only your silence keeps us safe. If you are not concerned over your own safety, remember Dovidi, and your husband, and even Joncaster and me. You must watch quietly."

"Hush," hissed Joncaster. "They're here!"

Below them, within the scalloped rim of the lower dune, lay a broad blot of blood lichen, a few bristles of bonebush, a few taller sentinels of thorn. The flag marked one of the dips in the rim at the far side. Beside it rose the head of a man, then the head of a horse, then the bodies of both as the horse climbed over the rim. Once atop it, the horse was reined out of the line of march while four harpta lumbered past him, the first three accompanied by walking figures—half of them in black, half in white—and the fourth lizard burdened with basket panniers slung along its sides. From somewhere in the train, a baby cried, a single weak, querulous wail, and Genevieve's head came up, too swiftly.

"Shh," murmured Melanie. "Don't move. Don't attract attention. Just watch. The one on the horse is the Shah. The white-robed ones are the candidates. The black-robed ones are the aspirants or their proxies. They're called 'ritual masters.' "

The baby did not cry again. When all the persons and beasts were arrayed around the rim of the hollow, the Shah rode along their line, indicating this pair, that pair, this pair from among the black-and-white couples: six pair, all told, who knelt while the Shah raised his hands, mumbling something the observers could not hear.

"He's giving them his blessing," whispered Melanie.

The six black-robes moved to the pack-lizard, each taking a flat, woven basket from a pannier, each turning to guide one of the white-clad candidates down into the hollow. There each black-robe took a hooked blade from his belt and demonstrated to the candidate what was to be done: cut the lichen, so, near the ground; put the lichen, so, in the basket. The candidates knelt to the task, cutting the lichen close to the sand, placing

the cut pieces into the baskets, dark scallops, winy under the sun. If they missed a single frond, the ritual masters pointed it out. The patch of lichen was a large one. The cutting took some time, and the white-clad figures slowed as they worked, until they were barely creeping by the time all was cut. The black-clad ritual masters carried the filled baskets up the slope and emptied them into the panniers, stowing the baskets there as well. The knives were sheathed at each black-belted waist, and the six black-clad ones returned to the hollow where each waited beside a candidate, head bowed, while the rest of the procession left the hollow as it had come.

One harpta remained behind. It put back its head and bellowed to its departing kindred. An answer came from multiple throats. The interchange went on for some time, until the retreating calls faded into silent distance and the single beast was reduced to a gravelly muttering. Until that moment, not one human voice had spoken, not one word had been said.

Melanie took hold of Genevieve's hand and held it tightly.

One of the dark-clad figures uttered a command. The white-robed ones moved, uncertainly, and the command was repeated.

The white outer robes were dropped to reveal the forms of women, young women, standing uncertainly on the sand.

"Fold the robes," said the dark-clad leader. "Place them here."

Though the language was still strange to her, Genevieve understood the command. The robes were folded and piled neatly, leaving the women still voluminously clad, but with their heads and lower arms exposed. As one of the women turned, her veil pulled aside, showing her face. Genevieve started, only to be seized at once from both sides, Joncaster's hand over her mouth, Melanie's arm over her shoulders.

"You know her?" whispered Melanie.

Genevieve nodded. Joncaster took his hand away, slowly, watching her. "One of the Shah's wives," she whispered. The one who had spoken to her.

The women were led to the edges of the patch of lichen and evenly spaced about it.

"Kneel down," said the black-robed leader. "Here, facing the lichen bed."

"But," murmured one of the women in a drugged voice. "We are supposed to go . . . to go . . . to Galul."

Genevieve stirred again. She knew the voice. Not the Shah's wife, but . . . someone she knew. Who could it be that she knew?

"You will go," said the dark-robed one who had spoken. "This is your final task before going."

They knelt down. Another of the dark-robed ones went to each of them in turn, offering a drink from a flask, which they gulped thirstily. Another black-robe wrapped a strip of dark cloth around each one's eyes.

"We leave you now," cried their leader. "You must not make a sound. Those who will take you to Galul are on the way. You must wait patiently. Do you understand?"

"My child," said the familiar voice. "Please . . . my child."

"Will go with you, woman. Now silence!"

The four nodded, barely. The men marched in place, making crunching noises with their feet. One of the women swayed and fell forward, her face in the sand. The dark-robes waited silently as the other women swayed, then fell. One of the black-robes went to the woman who had fallen first, straddled her, pulled her head back, and with one, sudden motion, cut her throat with the curved, seabone knife he had taken from his belt. He dropped her head into the sand and stood away. Blood ran in a crimson stream, down across the sand, soaking in.

By the time Genevieve lifted her horrified eyes to the others, they, too, were bleeding their life's blood onto the sands. Somewhere among the slaughter, a baby cried.

"Shall I kill it?" asked one of the dark-robed ones, pushing his veils aside to wipe the sweat from his face on his sleeve. In that instant, Genevieve knew where she was. She was in Mrs. Blessingham's office, seeing a vision. There was the body she had seen, the blood, the knife in the hand of a man, and that man was Willum. What was he doing here, slitting the throats of Mahahmbi women? It had had nothing to do with Carlotta and Glorieta? Why had she thought it did! She shuddered and buried her face in the sand, trying desperately not to be sick.

"Leave it for the birds," said the leader, wiping his knife upon the woman's clothing then standing back to observe the flow of blood. "She made a good candidate for your father, Havenite."

Joncaster put his arms across Genevieve's back and held her firmly. The men climbed from the hollow, each picking up one of the abandoned robes before taking a position beneath the fins of the harpta and moving away, out of the hollow, back along the track they had made earlier.

Genevieve struggled against their arms, but they held her fast.

The men and the great lizard retreated, the lizard coughing in a dull, repeated complaint.

"Wait," whispered Joncaster. "Sound travels on the wind, and they are downwind of us."

Solemnly, slowly, the lizard moved away, grumbling, the silent men keeping pace beneath the shade of its fins until they vanished along the line of flags around a far dune.

"Now," said Melanie, with distaste. "Come!" She rose to her feet and started down the slope of the dune.

"I don't want to go down there," cried Genevieve in a child's voice. "I don't . . ."

"You will," said Melanie. "For your mother who could have died here; for all the women of Haven who have died here."

"Of Haven!" she cried. "Women of Haven? These are Mahahmbi women."

"You are of Haven," Joncaster said in an angry voice. "And you were supposed to be here, among these. You were warned, you escaped, otherwise you would have been here to drink their potion and kneel before their knives. And I am told there was to have been at least one other on your ship, one who did not come . . ."

"Lyndafal." She shuddered in disbelief. "The wife of the Earl of Ruckward."

Joncaster's iron hand pulled her erect and half carried her down the slope after him, she stumbling along in a mood of frantic denial. They went over the lip of the dune, into the cupped center, and stopped by the first body, white as a cloud, all its blood pumped away into the sand.

"Look," said Melanie, pointing. "This is what you have to see."

Where the blood had run, the sand had come alive! Questing scarlet tendrils writhed into the sunlight, tiny-toothed granules along their stems opening into flat, scalloped fronds that overlaid one another like feathers on a bird, rapidly covering the ground with winy scales. A high-pitched sound came from the sand, like the avid screaming of minuscule voices. Already, the patch of blood lichen that had been cut off at the ground had erupted into frantic regrowth wherever blood had flowed.

Joncaster knelt and turned the first body over. The face was peaceful, unafraid. "They give them a drug," he said. "At least the bastards don't terrorize them."

"Only because fear changes the blood chemistry," said Melanie. "If adrenaline helped the process, they'd terrorize them, believe me."

Joncaster pulled Genevieve after him as he went on to the second body, and the third, turning up their faces and feeling among the voluminous veils they wore. He came up with a bundle, which he unwrapped

carefully. A baby. "Dead," he called to Melanie, "from the heat and dehydration." He rewrapped the tiny bundle and replaced it by the mother's body. "A boy. They raise almost all the girl babies for their blood, but if the donor of the candidate already has an heir or two, they leave the boys for the carrion birds."

Genevieve cried, "I should think they'd grow them bigger, too. They'd have more blood, wouldn't they?"

"They say only women's blood makes the lichen grow like this," said Melanie. "Women of reproductive age, preferably nursing mothers. It has to do with the hormones."

"To make this stuff grow? What is it?"

"P'naki," said Joncaster, watching her narrowly.

She turned aside, retching, "They gave me P'naki, once. When I was a child. To protect me from the fever."

Melanie shook her head. "No, Genevieve. They gave you powdered bonebush, probably. It's evil-tasting stuff, and they told you it was P'naki, a protection against the fever. They told you that it came from Mahahm. You grew up thinking that only P'naki from Mahahm could protect you from the fever, and that explained why Mahahm was important, why the Lord Paramount traded with Mahahm instead of conquering it."

"I don't understand," she cried, as Joncaster dragged her to the fourth body. He rolled it over and removed the veil. Red hair tumbled across the sand, green eyes stared emptily at the sun, a soft mouth curved toward Genevieve, the lips slightly open, as though in a moment she would wake and laugh!

Genevieve wailed, the high, hopeless cry of a child, man or creature, lonely and lost. "Oh, oh, no . . . no."

Melanie grasped her by the shoulders and shook her, not gently. "Genevieve, stop it! Who is it!"

She sobbed, "Barbara. My schoolmate, Barbara. She married . . . she married Viscount Willum, of Halfmore. Oh, for the love of heaven, why? Why?"

"You haven't been listening to what we've been telling you!" snarled Melanie, shaking her. "Stop this!"

Genevieve shuddered herself silent while Joncaster felt along the body, coming away with a bundle that moved slightly. "Another boy child."

Melanie took it from him, a baby larger and older than the other had been. She took a nippled water bottle from the scrip at her side and thrust the teat into the little mouth.

"This is what you come for?" Genevieve said, wiping her face on her sleeve. "To save the babies?"

Melanie nodded. "The ones we can. There are other teams out covering the other locations. We have many among us now who were once children of the candidates."

Genevieve, kneeling to replace the veil over Barbara's white face, scarcely heard. "Will we bury her?" she cried, wiping her eyes as she stared about at the quiet bodies. "Bury them?"

"No," said Joncaster, rolling Barbara's body back onto her face, as he had already done the others. "We will do nothing except take this one living child back to the refuge. When he is strong enough to travel, he will go to Galul."

"Just leave her? Like this?" she cried.

Joncaster pulled her to her feet. "We will leave her with the others, so when the flagman's crew comes at the next holy season, they will see nothing except what the desert itself has done: perhaps a scattering of bones that the bonebushes have not eaten, which he will tidy away so the candidates won't be frightened by them. There are many carrion-eaters on the sands."

Melanie said, "Besides, if we buried them, the Mahahmbi might catch on to us."

"But surely the people from Mahahm-qum already know you're here," Genevieve said. "The refuge isn't hidden."

"Of course they know we're here," said Melanie. "But they don't know who 'we' are. Just as they hide P'naki in plain sight by defining it as something else, so we hide ourselves in plain sight by calling ourselves malghaste. So far as they're concerned, we're malghaste, therefore unimportant. They don't concern themselves with unimportance!"

"And the lichen isn't P'naki?"

"It isn't P'naki if you mean a preventive of a purely fictional fever," said Joncaster. "It is P'naki if you mean the stuff that Mahahm lives by, the stuff that is taken from here to a well-guarded storehouse just outside the south gates of Mahahm-qum, from which it is traded with the Lord Paramount for food and fabric and machines, that is then traded by the Lord Paramount with other worlds for all manner of things. It is P'naki if you mean that which the Lord Paramount uses to reward his faithful followers, just as the Shah uses it here in Mahahm. This stuff can extend men's lives indefinitely. Both the Lord Paramount and the Shah Effulgent have grown centuries old upon P'naki, and they grow craftier and greedier with age, while those of Haven who want to grow older grow more

numerous, and they, too, become more and more greedy. Those on far worlds, the powerful old men who trade off-world luxuries for P'naki, also grow greedy, always wanting more, and more and more."

Melanie said, "First the old men take it every twenty years. Then, when they are about one hundred, they need it every ten years, or five, and when they get to be a hundred fifty, they need it every year, every season, just to go on living. And for every dose, more or less, a woman dies."

Genevieve stared, her eyes glazed, lost in contemplation of the caverns beneath Havenor, piled high with useless treasures, paid for in blood. "How old can they get?" she cried. "Can they live forever?

Joncaster shook his head. "When it gets to the point they need it every day or so, usually something happens to them. They are said to die in hunting accidents, or they drown, or they fall down the stairs."

Melanie looked closely at Genevieve, noting her pallor, her trembling hands. "Come. Let's get out of this charnel house. Over the edge of the dune, at least."

"Go up to the flag," directed Joncaster. "No sense all of us climbing back to the sled in this heat. I'll get it."

Just over the edge of the dune, the two women sat on the sloping surface, Genevieve wiping her face with the hem of her robe while Melanie made a shade with her outer robe and laid the baby within it, still holding the bottle to his mouth. The baby sucked, then sighed, then sucked again.

"When Willum married Barbara," murmured Genevieve, forcing herself to consider what she had seen, "he knew she would end here, with his child?"

"As a candidate for his father, yes. Sons of the nobility know what is expected of them. No doubt Willum's father asked him to marry and provide a candidate. Under both Haven and Mahahmbi custom, a son owes filial respect to his father."

"And the Prince needed a candidate, so he would have married me, but I'm not his wife . . ." Genevieve murmured.

"There's a mystique about women of noble blood making the best candidates, but married to him or not, he'd have had to have someone else get you pregnant, Genevieve. This stuff makes men sterile and impotent. That's one reason they don't take it until they're older."

Thinking of the days and nights spent traveling back from Merdune, Genevieve shook her head sadly. "So the Prince really didn't care if I married Aufors. . . . And Father . . . well, Father couldn't have known."

Melanie moistened a cloth and wiped the baby's face. "If your father

didn't know prior to this trip, be sure he knew during, for he was brought along to serve as ritual master for the Prince."

"He was to have cut my throat?" murmured Genevieve, fighting the sickness she felt. "He did behave very strangely toward me. He must have known." She swallowed deeply and put her head on her knees. "What did Joncaster mean when he said a totally fictional fever?"

Melanie lifted the baby to her shoulder, sheltering it within her hood. "The commons are occasionally exposed to a carefully engineered off-world fever that wipes out a few of them, actually very few, for the nobles don't want a drop in population. The reports, however, always mention a fictional, large number of fatalities. Then some bitter-tasting but harmless stuff they call P'naki is dispensed, with maximum fanfare, and that reinforces the importance of P'naki in people's minds. That in turn explains both Haven's trade with Mahahm and why so many young women are said to have died."

"And when the Prince said he wanted the production of P'naki increased . . . ?"

"Well, of course he wants it increased. Our spies say the Lord Paramount promised him he might keep one-third of any increase in P'naki for himself. The Prince wants to hire mercenaries and buy war machines of his own. Most important, he wants to take over the throne of the Lord Paramount."

"And the Shah plays the same game?" murmured Genevieve.

"The Shah uses different words, but the game is the same, yes. At this stage of his life, the Shah no doubt needs a woman's life every few days to stay alive." She laid the baby down in the shadow of her body, offering the water bottle once more.

"Do all the babies end up out here as well?"

"We find quite a few boys. If a lord already has an heir or two, it isn't worth the money to rear a boy. Most of them are . . . well. There's Joncaster coming."

He stopped the sled at the bottom of the dune, where Melanie stowed the baby in an insulated compartment before lying flat beside the other two.

They had gone only a little way when Genevieve demanded, "Where did this lichen come from? Is it a native thing?"

"Our people on the ark ship were provided with a carefully engineered DNA antiagathic to slow down their aging after they landed on the new planet. Antiagathics had been outlawed on Old Earth, because of the crowding, but our people needed enough time to guarantee the survival

of the creatures from the ship. The antiagathic was kept alive in a cyano-bacteria inside an alga. When and if it was needed, the genetic code would have been extracted and inserted into a virus."

Joncaster offered, "The alga was used to perpetuate the stuff because algae was something we could grow on the ship very easily. It was never supposed to exist anywhere but in the ship's lab or the laboratory we would establish after landing. If the ship hadn't crashed, there'd have been no problem—"

Melanie interrupted, "But the ship did crash, and the bacteria was lost—so everyone thought—along with a lot of other things we really needed. Luckily, the people and creatures all survived, and they remained healthy long enough to carry on . . ."

"Carry on doing what?" Genevieve demanded.

"Our job was to help young creatures survive, to save seeds and cuttings, to hatch eggs, and to preserve adult members of long-lived species, the ones that needed to teach their young, to keep them safe from natural dangers until they got strong enough to hold their own among the species already on this world without destroying any of them. Every living species is a proper part of a world, and it would be tapu for us to destroy any of them."

Genevieve muttered, "I've seen the results of P'naki. Do you count it among all the living things that are proper parts?"

Melanie shook her head. "I've already said, the ship wasn't supposed to have crashed. We knew nothing about the survival of the bacteria until a few hundred years ago, when the Mahahmbi captured six of our women in the mountains and used them for sacrifice to the lichen. When we looked at the situation, we immediately remembered the antiagathic bacteria, and as soon as we could lay hands on some lab equipment, we took the P'naki apart and found out that's what it is—partly, at least. The bacteria survived, with its human genetic components, in the alga we'd transported it in. The human genetic components had mutated slightly, and the alga had teamed up with a terrestrial fungus—perhaps from spores carried by some of the birds on the ark—to create this foliose lichen."

Joncaster said, "The cyanobacteria produces nourishment from the sun while the fungus extracts minerals and water from the environment and offers protection. Together, so long as their environmental needs are met, lichens are very tough growths."

Melanie interrupted again, "Joncaster's right, and this one is tougher than most. Usually, when the fungus part of a lichen makes spores, the spores don't carry any alga, so when the spores hatch, they're just a fungus,

not a lichen. With this thing, however, the algal material is packed right in with the fungal spores. They spread on the wind, and when it comes alive, it doesn't do so as two separate, harmless organisms, it comes alive as P'naki."

"Presumably, you stopped them killing your women," Genevieve remarked.

Joncaster nodded emphatically. "We—that is, our people—made it very expensive for Mahahm to kill a malghaste. Wherever they had killed one of us, we destroyed the lichen patch where they did it . . ."

"I thought you couldn't destroy things," muttered Genevieve.

"Of course we can destroy members of a species. We're part of nature, and nature imposes a feeding chain, so some members of any species are killed by others all the time. What's forbidden is to destroy *species*. We were quite comfortable with wiping out individual patches of the stuff, though we might not have tried if we'd known how hard it would be!

"We had no herbicides or chemical killers of any kind. We couldn't have used them if we had, for all such things are forbidden. The only way we could remove a patch of lichen was to sterilize the sand it was growing in—and I do mean *in*. The rhizines are as thin as hair and they go down farther than you can imagine! We had no harpta to carry tools, and back then we didn't have sleds, either. It took an enormous amount of labor to dig out the sand in those areas and keep turning it over and over and burning it until the last of it was dead. And, of course, every time we disturbed the sand, the spore capsules were blown off in every direction."

"Do you have any idea how it works?"

Melanie said, "We hypothesize that lactating hormones stimulate some chemical process inside the genetic material, but we don't honestly know. Our ancestors on the ship had a great deal of technical knowledge, but their equipment and supplies and reference library went down with the ship. That's part of the reason we couldn't come up with a technical way to fight the stuff, or so we like to believe, though it could be we're just not smart enough. The best we could do was to create a myth about ourselves. We called ourselves the malghaste—that's a word the Mahahmbi already used for some of their own lowest caste people. We said we were divinely appointed to help them, and that our blood kills the lichen, and every time they killed one of us, a patch was killed. It didn't take them long to believe."

"That was a long time ago," Genevieve asserted. "Since then you've

learned how to lay hands on technology. You've had the opportunity to get herbicides and fungicides. Why haven't you wiped it out?"

Joncaster said angrily, "I've told you! We can't. We'd have to spray the entire continent of Mahahm! And we've all been reared on horror tales from Old Earth that make the idea repugnant."

Melanie patted her shoulder, "Genevieve, we honestly don't know how to kill it. Your muttering is pretty much the same as the muttering our own people do when confronted with the dilemma. We've considered wiping out the Mahahmbi, and we've considered wiping out the nobility of Haven. There's no way to do it without involving a lot of innocent people. We did the best we could when we created the story of the malghaste."

Genevieve snorted, "The Mahahmbi really believed that? I find that hard to accept!"

Joncaster cast her a quick glance, shaking his head. "The Mahahmbi scriptures are in writing. According to them, this makes writing so holy that it can't be used for anything but scriptures. As a result, they have no written history and their oral history is subject to a lot of revision. We had our people sing malghaste songs around the women and children, and when the boy children grew up, they remembered the songs. By now, the Mahahmbi think we've always been around. They already believed they were God's favorites when they came here, so it wasn't hard to persuade them God created slaves for them."

Melanie snarled, "And if you believe you're God's favorite, killing a few women and children doesn't bother you . . ."

"No more." Genevieve hugged herself to keep from shattering or screaming, as she felt about to do. "No more. I can't absorb half of what you've said. Don't tell me anything more."

She pillowed her head on her arms and tried to think of nothing, absolutely nothing. Blackness. No light, no sound, no nothing. Though it was only partially successful, the resultant mental fog was better than the assaults of the morning.

They went back the way they had come, winding among the dunes and arriving at the refuge as the evening bell tolled and the sun bled scarlet cloud rivers down the western sky.

Enid waited for them in the garage, where they brought the sled to a rest.

"She's seen?" she asked Joncaster, while peering into Genevieve's frozen face and staring eyes.

"More than she wanted to see," he said. "One of the victims was a friend of hers. . . ."

Enid shook her head, lips tightly clamped. She said to Genevieve. "I know you must be very sad . . ."

Genevieve erupted in laughter. "Sad? You know that I'm sad? I saw a girl I knew . . . a girl I loved! I saw her get her throat slit. Her last words were of concern for her child. And you think I'm sad? That's not quite it. Believe me, Enid, that's not quite the emotion I'm feeling!"

Their shocked faces brought her to herself. The violence in her own mind and voice frightened her. Anger was an emotion she had avoided all her life, but now she was drowning in it, unable to keep from screaming at them, "You asked if I'd seen. Well I've seen one thing quite clearly, and that is that while all this bloodletting and killing has gone on, you've stood by and let it happen. No matter what excuses you make, that's what you've done!"

Melanie began to stammer something, but Genevieve could not bear their shocked and angry faces or her own burning rage. She fled past them, pushing them aside, and went back to her own little cell, where she struggled with the sliding door in her attempt to slam it, finally jamming it half closed before she threw herself facedown onto her pillow and wept herself exhaustedly to sleep.

In the night, Genevieve woke to find Melanie sitting beside her bed, eyes closed, hands relaxed in her lap.

Her anger had not left her in the night. She murmured, half-resentfully, "Why are you here, Melanie?"

"I came to be with you. I thought you might be lonely."

She laughed, still angrily. "Oh, Melanie. Yes, I'm lonely, but you don't fill my empty niches. You're not husband or baby, so you won't do. Just go away."

"I thought we might talk."

"About what? Religion, Melanie?"

"Didn't your mother ever talk to you about religion?"

"She did, yes. She said it was important to be seen being pious. She quoted the covenants to me, about purity of soul. Women, she said, were required to be pure of soul."

"That's . . . rather what I wanted to talk about."

Genevieve sat up, not as annoyed as she pretended to be, surprised to find herself slightly curious. "It seems you won't be satisfied until you do! I'll listen, but that's all I'll guarantee."

Melanie refolded her hands, took a deep breath, and said, "The difference between our belief and the belief you were reared in is this: We don't believe people have individual souls. We believe living worlds have souls. We believe that all the species of life that have ever lived on a world are part of the soul of that world."

"Stephanie's book said something of that."

"In the old language we call it te wairua taiao—the world spirit. It starts out small and simple, and it grows and develops and learns as billions of years go by, becoming old and wise. It's of the world, our teachers say, an inevitable result of a living world, and it doesn't die when the world dies. It separates itself and goes elsewhere."

"Stephanie's book said that," Genevieve remarked, with something almost like amusement. "I discussed it with a strange little man named Jeorfy Bottoms, and we decided it was a concept one might accept, philosophically."

Stubbornly, Melanie went on: "The world-soul includes every living creature that has ever been on the planet, every microbe, every animal, every tree, not as individuals, but as races, and at any time upon any planet, some of those races are harbingers . . ."

"Harbingers?"

"Indicators. Signifiers. You know . . . if you dig in your garden, the soil is full of worms."

"If it's good soil."

"Exactly. If there are lots of worms, you know it's good soil. The worms are . . . harbingers of the health of the soil. So, on any given planet there are harbingers. If they are alive and healthy, then that planet is also alive and healthy. If the harbingers are dying or dead, then the planet will surely die."

"Then mankind couldn't have been a harbinger, for Earth died even though men were many."

Melanie's mouth twisted. "You're baiting me. You know Earthmen had no regard for other species. Even though it was the only soul they had, Earthmen evicted the soul of the Earth and moved out into space from a dead planet."

"So what are they now?"

Melanie sighed. "A friend of ours calls them irrelevant intellects."

"And all this time that I've worried over the state of my soul, I shouldn't have bothered," Genevieve said angrily.

Melanie sighed, moving restlessly in the chair. She said soothingly, "There's a little story my mother used to tell me about Haven. A scrutator

was sailing on Merdune Lagoon, and caught by a great fish who threatened to eat him, and the scrutator said it didn't matter, for his soul would go to heaven. And the fish asked him, 'When your soul gets to heaven, what will it say to enlighten the universe?' The scrutator said he wasn't that wise, and the fish said, 'You'd better learn wisdom while you're on the way down my gullet, because wisdom is the only thing that unlocks the gates of heaven.'"

"What else did your mother tell you?" Genevieve asked, suddenly intrigued.

"She told me that among the billions and billions of human beings, perhaps a few know some little thing of interest to the universe, and those few men are the leavening of mankind. Most men don't know anything except myths and manners. She told me only the wholeness of a world that has lived for billions of years can speak to the universe about anything meaningful. Men's lives are part of that, of course, and the wiser men become, the more they learn about the universe, the greater part they are, which is an incentive to study, so far as I'm concerned. If my life is a part of the world-soul, it is truly immortal."

"And what have harbingers to do with it?"

"They're just indicators. Like warning lights. Or alarm bells. They're born naturally, and they die naturally. They don't seek long life. Sometimes they're killed, but they don't look for unnatural ways to protect themselves. If a harbinger hunts, it hunts with what nature gave it. Sometimes it eats the prey. Sometimes the prey eats it. Harbingers don't play it safe, they adhere to the chain of life, and if the chain is healthy, so are they."

Genevieve closed her eyes, going inside herself to another place. Melanie's words resonated. Someone had said something like this to her before. Mother? Who else could it have been? "But if each living world has a spirit, didn't you simply invade another spirit's territory when you came here?"

"Spirits aren't territorial, they're inclusive. One joining another is like immigrants coming to a new land. They change the society, yes, but they broaden it and add to its wisdom. The spirit of Haven, the world, was not identical to the spirit of Earth that arrived with the creatures in the ark ship, but when the two united, the resultant spirit was not dichotomous."

Genevieve rubbed her forehead wearily. "Melanie, I know you want me to believe all this, but it seems little different from the religious stories we learned in school, esoteric and relatively pointless. I can believe your people came here to preserve Earthian species that were in danger of extinction. I believe that's why people on Old Earth built the ark fleet. I

believe you are sincerely religious, and I concede that your religious interpretation of what happened might be true, but I haven't even sorted out
the beliefs I was brought up to! I've no inclination toward adopting a new
credo just now unless I have to."

Melanie sighed. "Of course you don't have to believe anything. Mankind lived for a long time on Earth without believing in the spirit of the
world. Right up to the end people thought the Earth was the center of
the universe and the god of all creation was fixated on humans as a race.
Nonetheless, once the ark ships were gone, the world died."

Genevieve asked, "What does your world-spirit look like?"

Her jaw dropped. "I have no idea. None of us has ever seen it. I'm
not sure it's seeable."

"Well, your harbingers were sea creatures. They're great whales,
aren't they?"

"Yes. Very old, very big, very vocal. And dolphins, and some other
less bony things. And they can tell us things, sing us things we've learned
to understand."

"Do you go down, into the sea, to be with them?"

Melanie looked up, brows drawn together. "No, of course not. We lack
the equipment that would make that possible. This ocean on Haven . . . it's
huge! And deep. All Earth's oceans would plop into it without vastly raising
the water level."

"And you've never seen a great golden creature, lying like a floating
sun within the sea?"

"No," said Melanie, mystified.

"Ah." Genevieve laughed, a brittle little laugh, full of self-mockery.
"One more question. Who exactly was Tenopia?"

"Nobody knows, exactly! She's said to have been a confidante of the
spirits, a sacred woman. She was the first of her kind, a mystery. Her
mother was one of the island women, a tapu woman who claimed she had
been made pregnant by a wave from the ocean. The claim was heretical,
according to her people, so the claim was put to the proof. When the
child Tenopia was born, she was thrown into the sea, far from land. When
the sea returned her, alive, to the shore where her mother waited, everyone
knew her father was the sea.

"She grew up, she traveled all over Haven, and eventually, she came
to live in Galul. She told the people there that when she'd been in Mahahm, that she'd had to escape from the Shah, and she sang a song about
it. She bore many daughters in Galul. Some of us who live in Galul are
descended from her. She sent several of her descendents, some say most

of them, to Haven, and one of them was Stephanie, Tewhani, who became Queen."

Genevieve frowned wearily. "Stephanie also bore many daughters, who
bore many daughters. I can attest to that. I have paid attention. I have
heard of the world-spirit, the harbingers in the deep, and some . . .
considerable number of women descended from Tenopia. I pray that's all
of it? Please. For tonight?"

Melanie flushed. "I should have let you sleep."

"Oh, I have slept. I will sleep. Eventually. Go away, Melanie. Let me
lie here in the cool. There is a vast knot of confusion in my mind, and
something must untangle it."

Doubtfully, ruefully, Melanie went away.

ON THE ISLAND NEAREST MAHAHM, AUFORS LEY HAD REACHED A POINT OF no return with the Captain. Though Aufors was supposedly in command of the mission, evidently he could not command that the ship return to Mahahm to drop him off.

"We haven't enough fuel," the Captain reiterated, as he had been doing for two days. "We cannot return to Mahahm more than once and still make it back to Haven. Once we have returned to Mahahm-qum, the only movement open to us will be to return to Bliggen straight across the Southern Sea rather than along the arc of islands. If we go to Mahahm, we place ourselves at the mercy of the Mahahmbi. If they ask for you in return for the Prince, and if the Prince demands that you be turned over, I would have no choice but to order the men to deliver you."

The Captain regarded Aufors almost with desperation. "I've winked at evil too long, Colonel. If I'm to live with myself, I can't do it again. I won't see any of my men sacrificed by those bloodthirsty fanatics. If I take you back there, I'll have to leave the men and the provisions here. If I take only you, there'll be no one to pick off for slaughter but you."

"And no way to moor the ship."

"I could drop a message saying they must moor the ship from the ground if they want me to pick up the Prince. The Prince can't fly this ship, so he'll need me."

"And if you were free to choose what to do next?"

"Either go directly to Bliggen or, since we've plenty of food, wait here for a Frangian ship to come by, and negotiate a trip to Mahahm with them! Those are the only ways I can think of to stay here without danger to my men or myself."

"I can think of one additional precaution," said Aufors. "If you decide to approach Mahahm for any reason, alone or otherwise, I'd remove the cannon before you go. Mahahm might consider a life for the cannon

would be an appropriate trade-off. The life might be the Marshal's, or the Prince's."

The Captain paled. "I hadn't thought of that."

"As for the rest of it, I agree with your reasoning. It's probably best that I don't start my mission from outside the gates of Mahahm-qum. Have we any kind of small craft aboard? A skiff? Some kind of inflatable boat?"

The Captain nodded, relieved that Aufors had adopted a reasonable tone. Casting a quick look about to be sure they were not overheard, he said, "We do, yes. We have inflatable lifeboats in case of accident over the sea. They have electric motors with no very great range, but one of them has a solar regenerator. If you steal one, it would be only by accident that you might make off with that particular one. I, of course, would have no advance knowledge of your plans."

"I understand you completely, Captain."

"Get the steward to provision you, but try to keep me out of it. Be sure you have enough drinking water. You'll need that most. By the way, did you talk to the doctor?"

"I tried, on and off, between episodes of badgering you. He has some kind of professional oath standing betwixt him and telling me what I need to know, so he says. I think it's more fear than honor. He turned quite white when I opened the subject. Where is he from, anyhow?"

"The man is from Chamis. His homeworld is dying; its people are streaming off in all directions. He came here, with his wife and family, trading his expertise for permission to stay. You could probably frighten the information out of him if you threaten him. He has no stomach for violence, that one."

"Nor have I, Captain," murmured Aufors. "If I thought he could lead me to Genevieve, I'd do it, stomach or no, but the doctor knows no more about her whereabouts than I do, and cruelty for its own sake has no attractions for me. The very fact that there's something evil about the P'naki trade tells me where to begin looking. I've picked up hints of my own, and since you've indirectly affirmed most of them—though I'll never disclose that you did so—the rest will fill in."

"Where are you really going, Colonel?"

"After my wife and son." He raised his eyebrows. "Though, if anyone asks, it may be more expedient to say I have gone to rescue the Prince and the Marshal."

Aufors had already taken time to dye his hair and eyebrows. The dye was among the supplies he had fetched from Haven, for he had had a notion, even there, that the time might come when he would wish to pass

for a Mahahmbi, and there were absolutely no redheads among them. While the Captain kept his crew busy elsewhere, Aufors gathered his supplies together and set off across the sea toward Mahahm, getting the boat out of sight as quickly as possible. He did not wish to come ashore near the Frangian port or anywhere that could be seen from the Mahahmbi towers. His only real plan was to find the old woman who had been in his house, and though the house had been blown up, the subterranean ways to it still might be intact. If he could get into and through the city. If.

When Melanie left her, Genevieve fell into an exhausted and troubled sleep. At some later time she wakened to a sound that fell through that high window into the tall, narrow room, filling it, making it reverberate: the song of the sea. Surely, she thought, this would bring the whole refuge awake.

Seemingly, it did not. No one rose or scurried about. No one called in response to that song, not even Genevieve herself, who pinched her lips together and purposefully withheld response out of indecision whether it was wise or prudent to let her voice be heard.

Still, this was a stronger singing than she had ever heard, and even if she wouldn't reply, she felt a need to listen without walls in the way. Though the refuge was dark, with only a pale square of moonlight marking the window far above her head, she rose and went out into the corridor, feeling her way along the rough wall, scarcely aware of the chill of the stone on her bare feet. She made her way to the atrium, lighted from above by a dangling lantern. When she had come this way earlier in the day, she had seen stairs slanting upward along the base of the tower, rising upon themselves without a railing, with only a deep groove worn in the inner wall to show where people had trailed their hands as they went up and down. She climbed slowly, silently, moving from the upper step onto the flat roof of the lower story where a door was cut through to the inside of the tower.

Around a central pillar, thick and crusted as the boll of an ancient tree, stairs spiraled downward into darkness and upward toward the light, each step a thick slab of wood set fanwise upon the one below, one end buried in the central pillar, the other in the outer wall. Their cupped centers were smooth beneath her soles, worn glossy by generations of feet. The arched openings that pierced the tower on its inward side admitted slanting beams from the lantern to disclose venomous night hunters resting in the embrasures, creatures coiled or segmented or multilegged, all with huge many-lensed eyes.

Defiantly, she placed her right hand on the outer wall, the left hand on the pillar, stepping upward, feeling the roughness of mud brick and split wood, letting her hand trail needlessly near the stinging creatures. She was in a self-destructive mood, hating herself for not having known better what Barbara's fate would be, for not having pursued her own vision to find some means of warning her.

The stairs ended at the floor of the tower room. The trapdoor had been thrust up against the outer wall, which continued upward, enclosing a circular wood-floored, flat-roofed space, its radiating rafters supported at the center by a mud-brick pillar less massive than the one below. Open arches looked out in all directions, and on the courtyard side, a ladder led up to another trapdoor in the roof, this one closed.

She stepped up onto the floor, lowered the trapdoor to prevent her plunging down accidentally, and went toward the western arch, away from the courtyard, intending to lean there as she had leaned in her window at Mrs. Blessingham's. She could not. The stone trembled beneath her hands, her arms were shaken and thrust back by the song that she felt coming toward her across the desert like an arrow aimed at her heart. She staggered at the physical thrust of the sound, her lungs and throat conjoining without her consent to bellow defensively into the night, "I hear you, I hear you."

The words went from her like a shot from a great cannon. All tiny, subliminal sounds of the night stopped at once. The song stopped a moment later. A profound and waiting silence pervaded the desert. She leaned against the wall of the circular room, shivering, lips clamped tight shut to prevent any other sound from escaping her, her eyes fixed on the cleat across the room where the coils of the lantern rope were neatly hung.

The rope was a long one, long enough for the lantern to be lowered to the atrium floor for filling. Which meant it was long enough to bring here, to the outside, and lower over the outer wall. Though the gate was locked, she could climb down the rope and get away! If she didn't want to deal with that sound, she could run!

She shuddered, blinking angry tears away. Oh, yes, she could run, but she couldn't escape from today, not from Barbara's blind eyes, from the wail of the child, from Willum's sweaty face, his dull, matter-of-fact voice: "Shall I kill it?" His own son!

Or perhaps not. Knowing Barbara, if Willum had scorned her, she would have accepted passion elsewhere. Had Barbara ever, even for an instant, known what was going on? How long had she been drugged into acceptance? The marriage ritual between nobles required the noble bride

to drink from the so-called Cup of Acquiescence. Had Barbara been formally married in that way? Was the drug in that cup? Or did she receive her first dose later, at the wedding supper? Or later still, when she and Willum were alone together? Did all the nobles in Haven use it on their wives, their daughters? Was it routinely served at Mrs. Blessingham's? Did that explain Genevieve's own years of patience and resignation, her lack of rebellion?

"Oh, I have been so tender," she told herself with scathing self-loathing. "I have been so delicate, so pure. I've been well schooled not to look at ugliness, well trained not to experience life. I've cowered in corners and watched, refusing to take part. All my life I've had these visions and I've let them drift in and out of my mind like cloud pictures, spouting them out on command, all unquestioning. I've gathered information as a child collects shells on a beach, a mere pastime, knowing nothing about them, learning nothing! I loved Barbara, I might have saved her, but I did nothing to keep her from destruction!

"I've questioned nothing! For all I know, Aufors could have left me in that house in Mahahm just to give the men their chance at me. I could be lying out there on the sand, drugged and dead, blind to it all, deaf to it all! Dovidi could be a drying bundle against my belly for all the good sense I've shown! Now I see what should have been plain all along, and all I can think of doing is to run away!"

She bit her lip until it bled, tasted the blood, wiped it with her hand and stared stupidly at the dark stain of it as she turned back to the western arch. Here were no white curtains to suggest blown spray, no thrashing foliage to simulate waves. The ocean was present, nonetheless, in great billows of sand half lit by a sailing moon, half concealed by clouds whose scudding shadows lent the illusion of a heaving sea during storm. There was no storm. The clouds were only ragtag edges of a southern squall being swept out to sea. They were not heralds of the great tempest she craved, the cataclysmic event she longed for. She wanted something climactic to happen! Some form of resolution to take place, even a violent one! An end to this! A finality! Something to mark Barbara's passing.

Now that Willum had provided a candidate for his father, how soon would he remarry? And how much of the truth would he tell Glorieta? Glorieta, who might someday find herself paying someone to hide her daughter or granddaughter, just as the Duchess Alicia had hidden Lyndafal, pretending all the while that she did not know why, that she did not know from whom! But then, women were good at pretending. Women could survive a lifetime on lies, hope, and promises . . .

Genevieve had kept her promise. She had done as her mother required, she had gone with Delganor. She had seen what she was supposed to see. She had kept the faith, so now was surely the time to be done with subterfuge and mystery. Now there must be something more, something based on solidity and truth, though at the moment she could not define truth or foresee the results of it.

Neither the night wind nor the stars offered help. The wind had subsided to a whisper. Even the stars had seemed to still, as though the air that made them twinkle had turned to glass. Far to the west, a constellation swam along the horizon. No. Too low for stars. Very low in the east, on the sands, toward the coast, on that arrow-straight line song-cloven through the dark. On the airship's chart of Mahahm there had been a deep wedge cut into the western side of the land. Given that, and the fact that the western coastline ran diagonally toward the southeast, that cleft might not be far from this refuge. A few hours' steady walk from the sea, a walk made easier, quicker in the chill of night.

A decided thump on the roof made her flatten herself against the stone. Another thump, then one more, as though something heavy had been shifted. Out on the desert one light in the moving constellation blinked bright, like a nova, once, twice, three times. Another thump from above, then the upper trap door screeched open, and she pressed even more tightly against the wall as long, bare male legs came through the roof, as long arms closed the door above, and a single clad figure climbed down. When he saw the other trap door closed, he turned swiftly, like a man who fears a trap, seeing Genevieve's face clear in the moonlight.

"Ah," he murmured with a hint of laughter, miming fear as he wiped his forehead on his hand. "My Lady Marchioness. For whom I made such lovely clothing. Who thanked me by wearing very little of it!"

"Veswees?" she said, wonderingly. "Is that you, Veswees?"

He laughed, putting his arms about her and thumping her back kindly, as he might thump a friendly dog. "So, you have come to Mahahm and survived. I was worried about you."

"My friend, Barbara," she cried, "You knew about her. She . . ."

"I know," he murmured sadly. "They told me. As my own mother ended, so did she."

This gave her pause. You were one of the rescued babies," she asked wonderingly,

He nodded. "There are a good many of us, reared in Galul, but working either in Haven or among the malghaste in Mahahm-qum. Some of us were looking after you."

"Looking after me?"

"Um. A footman or two. A coachman. A dressmaker . . ."

She shook her head in wonder. "Enid has Barbara's child," she said. "And an old woman named Awhero has my child. And Aufors is gone, with the airship."

"I know, I know." He thumped her again, between the shoulder blades, making a drumlike sound. "Hear that? You are all hollow in there. You have been crying, and your heart is elsewhere, no? You are worried that Aufors is lost, or even worse? That he may be part of this evil? Yes, I know that feeling of doubt. Well, Aufors has no part of it. I know some of those who are involved. I wish I knew them all, for if I did, we would think of some way to destroy them. Aufors I do know, he is commoner through and through, and he has no wicked aspirations."

"My father?"

Veswees frowned, shaking his head. "I wish I could tell you he is not, Genevieve. It is true that in Havenor he was so naive that some men joked about it, but since he left Havenor . . . I don't know. There was a member of the Tribunal in your group, was there not?"

"Yes. He spent a good deal of time with Father."

He patted her again. "Then I'm afraid your father was enlightened—if one may call it that. Now. How are you getting along?"

"I don't know! I'm unsure of everything! While I had Dovidi, I felt quite complete, as though that was all I needed. That must be why some women have babies, over and over. One needn't worry about being anything else. Being a mother is a marvelous excuse for being nothing else. But with Dovidi gone, I feel like an arrow, shot a long time ago, flying all this time in thin air, carried by my own velocity until now I've come down with this great thump, throwing up the dirt, and I have no idea why! I've been up here yelling at myself for being so stupid."

"You yelled very quietly," he said, pulling her to the opening and pointing away across the desert where the light came closer, larger, breaking into disparate stars. "There is part of the answer. Here come the chieftains of the people of the islands. They come with their warriors and their singers and dancers. Their predecessors were the ones who talked with the depths generations ago. From among them Zenobia, Tenopia, was shot into the air as you were. Perhaps she, too, wondered where her duty lay and what was required of her. Now you may yell at them instead of at yourself. They are coming to hear what you will tell them."

"About what?" she cried.

"What we are to do," he replied. "When Zenobia was sent, when

Stephanie was sent, the depths told our people that in the fullness of time, Zenobia's daughters would return and tell us what to do. You are the first of those daughters."

She simply stared at him. "Veswees, since I was tiny, I have been taken to church and taught to be godly. My earliest lessons told me of my soul and of all I had to do for its sake, the meekness, the submission. I have believed . . . sometimes . . . that I could feel my soul. There were times in my tower when I heard the nightwind, saw the sky, felt the motion of the trees and felt a kind of joy that was . . . huge and marvelous. I told myself I was feeling my soul. Now, now they say that what I felt was no personal me-like thing, but something . . . what?"

"You already know," he said softly. "You felt something huge and marvelous of which you are part, and in the moments you describe, you forgot yourself for you were one with your world and with the sky above it, and even the stars looking down. There is nothing larger or more wonderful than that. Still, there are those who would prefer self. They will accept any belief, no matter how foolish, if it guarantees them personal immortality. I know people like that. But there are others who know themselves well enough to realize how limiting that is."

She drew a deep breath. "If I am to help, I would have to believe . . ."

He shook her gently, saying, "No, no, dear lady. No one ever has to believe! The universe *is,* it does not require belief. Do you think it will stop existing if you do not believe? Do you think far galaxies will harbor resentment against you if you do not believe? Do you resent the ant who does not look up and admire you? Never! Your disbelief can kill a world, but not the spirit of life within that world, and to that spirit, the sincere questioner is of more good than a thousand meticulous believers." He laughed.

She scowled at him, only for a moment. "Veswees, how quickly could you return to Haven?"

"Very quickly," he said in a dry voice. "More quickly than the Lord Paramount or the Prince might imagine!"

"You've been ordering equipment from off-world, haven't you? On the Lord Paramount's account."

"Now how did you know that!"

"Inference. You have some quick way to go, do you? An airship? Or some kind of powered boat?"

"I do, yes. I can get there very soon."

"Then go, my friend, for I am about to tell you something that will be useful to our world. Though I am confused about most things, there

is one thing I am sure of. The evil that besets Haven must be ended, and perhaps what I tell you will help to end it, when the time is right . . ."

"And how will I know when that is?"

"Oh, you will know, Veswees. Believe me, you will know." And she drew him close and murmured into his ear for a long time, while he nodded and nodded, murmuring, "Yes. I can do that. Yes, that can be done."

When she had finished, he stared at her, mouth open. "You're sure this is right?"

She laughed softly. "Sure? Oh, Veswees, who of us has time to be sure a thing is right? I am sure it is necessary. Will that do?"

He leaned forward, kissed her on the forehead, then lifted the trapdoor and went humming down the stair. She did not follow him, for he had given her the idea that she could act on her own, without having to believe anything. He had told her she could decide what needed to be done, and that warranted thinking out.

She had not really believed Aufors when he had told her she was an intelligent person, though his flattery had pleased her. She knew she was clever, yes, at scholarly things. Able to remember and compare. Able to feed back what had been taught. But intelligent? Or wise? Oh, if only she could believe that she was wise! If she could believe she had spent her life mastering something of value when so much of what she had learned was valueless, even evil! But, if she knew, if she claimed to know, she would have to make herself do all those things she had learned not to do. She would have to speak out, claim much, and spout like a geyser! She would have to assert! Demand! Rally!

"Genevieve?" Melanie's voice from below.

"I'm up here," she admitted, just loudly enough to be heard.

"I know. Veswees said. Will you come down now, or will you be busy thinking?"

The idea was startling! Busy. Thinking. Was it acceptable to be busy, thinking?

"Yes," she called, with only the slightest quaver. "I am busy thinking, Melanie. I will be thinking for some time."

"Later will be fine. There will be a lengthy welcoming ceremony, and the chieftains need to have something to eat and a bit of rest first. Take as much time as you need."

Genevieve did not ask "first" before what. No doubt Melanie thought that she already knew. She leaned in the embrasure once more, staring at the dawn and thinking of the lichen.

Mankind had always sought cures and reliefs in the local herbage, looking for omens in the shape of a leaf or the color of a pod. A leaf that was shaped and colored like a lung became lungwort, not because it actually cured sick lungs but because it should. A bandage-shaped leaf must be woundwort, a bladder-shaped pod, bladderwort. So the original observer of P'naki—the one who had first seen the lichen's rapid growth in response to blood—must have believed that anything burgeoning like that had to be a treatment for wasting diseases. Such as aging. So, he tried it, perhaps on himself, and the patient lived, and lived, and lived.

Now that discovery threatened thousands, maybe millions of lives, a fact that was known long ago by the powers that be, whatever they were. Stephanie-Tewhani and her sisters had been sent into Haven to breed up a crop of long-nosed cellar singers, female visionaries, presumably either to come up with or to expedite an answer. Genevieve was apparently one of them. So much effort on her behalf should culminate in an epiphany at least!

Take a deep breath and await the descending fire.

Nothing. Not a spark.

All that enormous effort had to have meant something! Had Mother known what it was for? Certainly Lyndafal had known nothing of what Genevieve had learned. Nor had Alicia. The song-line had failed in that line of descent. Perhaps in other lines as well. Despite all Zenobia's daughters, perhaps it had failed, over and over, leaving *only* Genevieve to hear the voice in the deep, only Genevieve to reply, only Genevieve who knew what she knew, though only heaven knew what it was good for?

Did it matter whether she was *one* or the *only one?* No. It really made no difference. A duty devolved upon *one* to the same degree as upon *only one*, if the *one* or the only could figure out what it was.

Now she could see the approaching company in some detail, a dark people, as dark as Stephanie had been, with tattoos on their faces and arms and legs. Their hair was knotted on top of their heads and decorated with sprays of green leaves. The group came toward the refuge in a choreographed movement, those at the center tall, facing forward, those on either side rowing their way across the sands with actual oars, carved and painted, flashing as the sun crept above the horizon. The assembled corps came in the guise of a fabulous ship, and she was reminded of canoes, marvelous canoes hewn from huge trees, with sails made of woven mats, moving across the stars. These were the descendants of the Kaikaukau Whetu, the star swimmers, the servants of those in the deep.

Of many such thoughts are understandings grown.

She went from window to window in the tall tower while light flooded the desert, while the nighttime cool leaked away, while the sun skipped into the sky like a released balloon. She saw a black-toothed wheel in the sky to the north, a gyre of carrion birds that plunged a few at a time while others assembled from the far hills and the shores of the sea, come to tidy up after the butchers. She put her face into her hands and shed tears once more for Barbara's son, somewhere in the fortress below her, and for her own son, somewhere unknown and unreachable.

Then she dried her eyes as the gates opened below her. Her mind heard the singing before her ears did, a woman's voice inside the tower singing an invitation: the kai karanga calling to the guests, *Haeremai, Haeremai, whakaeke mai*—welcome, welcome, come forward. She knew that song. Mother had taught her that song.

A woman from among the visitors sang an equally familiar reply, the karanga whakautu: We are the servants of the spirit, come from far islands to hear the words of the singer.

And again the call and the reply, the call in different words, but with the same sense. You of the spirit are welcome. With your ancestors, ascend into the house of our people. With your children, ascend into the house. Women's voices to call and women's voices to reply, for only women were free of warlike pride enough to know when it was safe to invite outsiders in, when it was safe to accept the invitation. Even as the women called *welcome*, the men postured *but beware*, threatening with their clubs. Welcome, but beware.

At last the women's voices won out and the people came into the courtyard, the servants of the deep into the refuge of marae morehu, place of survival.

There were further songs in the courtyard, ancient expressions of the culture of a sea and island people whose identity had been lost among the great press of other peoples on Earth; a people whose language had been preserved only in ritual; a people who had been chosen for a sacred duty, to fulfil a specific purpose. So said the words of Tewhani tapairu parauri. Stephanie, Dark Queen.

Unconscious of having made any decision, she found herself halfway down the stairs as the last of the songs dwindled to silence. She had been busy thinking. Now she had thought. It was time to talk to the chieftains of the people.

"We attack the malghaste to the south," said the Shah to his minister. His voice was high and petulant. His mouth was pursed. He looked,

thought the minister, like a fretful baby. "The malghaste have for too long existed on our border, affording refuge to those who escape from us."

Saelan knew that the escape of the Havenite woman annoyed the Shah past endurance. No woman could be allowed to escape. The Shah needed more women, not fewer of them!

"It is very early, and Your Effulgence has not had breakfast. Perhaps the decision . . ."

The Shah waved him silent, crying in a high, treble voice, "We will raze the nest of the rebels."

"Effulgent One, we do not know that the woman went to the place the malghaste call *mahrei*. Indeed, it is unlikely in the extreme. Her water bottle and a broken sandal were found far to the southeast, on the trail to Zimmi oasis . . ."

"It doesn't matter. If she had come to this *mahrei*, they would have taken her in."

"Effulgent One, is this . . . is this a proper time to wage war? You are holding Prince Delganor and the Marshal . . ."

"They are my guests," interrupted the Shah, with a curled lip and raised nostril. "As they must be, since their ship departed. I think, however, that I will make them my allies. The Marshal is a military genius, so he tells me. Perhaps I will put him in charge of the army. He can quell the malghaste in their *mahrei*. He can find his woman child and take her out in the desert, dedicating her to my use. Then I will consider elevating him."

Ybon Saelan swallowed deeply. "The ship departed, Effulgent One, because the Captain panicked, thinking the demonstration was directed at him or his men." As certainly it had been. Ybon had counseled the Shah against attacking the ship. Had the ship been destroyed, the Prince would have had no way to return home; the shipments of grain and fiber and other necessary material would not have arrived in Mahahm; the people of Mahahm-qum might well have arisen against the Shah. Driving the ship away was just as bad, since there was no way to reach it. The foolish people left in the house had destroyed the communications devices. All of which the Shah should have understood. Would have understood, in prior years.

He murmured, "We will hope that the Captain of the ship returns soon, Your Greatness."

"We will cut the Captain into pieces," said the Shah. "Before the eyes of the Prince. If the Marshal does not help us, we will cut the Marshal to pieces, as well."

Cursing silently, Ybon bowed. "Great One, the Marshal is of the nobil-

ity. And the Captain may be needed to return the Prince to his own land. From which our foodstuffs come. From which our bodies are clothed. From which our needs are met."

"Then we will take members of the crew. They cannot trifle with us in this way, Saelan! I am weary of it. The razing of this *mabrei* place will distract me while we wait for the ship to return."

The minister sighed and said the only thing he could. "Your Effulgence's word is our law. We will go south."

Inside himself, Ybon felt a tiny click, as though a switch had been thrown. As though a machine he had forgotten was there was now energized. As though a certain line of thought that had been unthinkable had been opened for leisurely contemplation.

In the marae, the people were ready to confer. The seven representatives of the many chieftains did not use their names while on such business, Melanie explained to Genevieve. Their names were local, tribal, familial. When they spoke for all the people, they used only their numbers, the order in which they had been appointed to this duty. First for the people, Tuatahi, had served longest. Seventh, Tuawhitu, had served least long. When a member died or resigned, the numbers below moved up a notch and a new seventh was appointed. Whoever was First at any given time was also chairman, and this one was tall and bulky, with long, strong brown arms and legs and a muscular torso half hidden by the length of fabric wrapped around his waist. Both men and women wore this garment, plus a loosely woven top to shield their shoulders, backs, and arms from the ardor of the sun.

The garments only partially hid the tatoos, which could not have escaped notice even though the contrast between the black patterns and the dark skins was not great. The patterns covered all faces, necks, and arms plus the backs of the women, the backs and chests and thighs of the men. Beginning at the sides of the faces, they swirled across cheeks and foreheads, symmetrically across chins and noses and lips, meeting in the center like the markings of some fabulous beasts. No two were marked alike, though all the designs were similar.

"It is polite to wait patiently while the chieftains speak," Melanie said, in an urgent tone. "Sometimes they speak rather lengthily, saying what everyone already knows, but it is still polite to wait."

Genevieve set herself to be patient, which was one thing she had learned that she could use. When she was seated before the committee,

all of them seated in a line, their symbols of authority arrayed around them, First gave her a long, weighing look, and then began to speak:

"Our ancient tongue is used now only for matters of honor and wisdom, mana and tapu. I speak in the language of your understanding, the language of this world:

"Long ago, when the canoes came to a new land, while most of our people worked to make us secure upon that land, a few of this family and that family were called aside and given great mana and heavy tapu, which we held secretly throughout the ages, for we were the star swimmers, the servants of the deep.

"From father to son and mother to daughter this knowledge was given, and those who learned it practiced it in hidden places. In the ages that followed it was known only to those who held it. Our foregoers called themselves the patient ones, nga whakamoumori, and we remained true, unmixed, learning in each generation the secret things of that generation, the mea huna, the mysteries.

"As the ages passed, men proliferated upon the earth and in time the earth was sickened unto death. Only man was left in any numbers, and the spirit of the world spoke to our people from the sea, saying that it must depart the earth, for the earth was dying. So, we went among the people of the world, and we cried a great shaming in the parliaments of mankind, speaking only of the creatures who should be saved, but not of the spirit, whom the powerful despised. Still, the spirit moved them to be ashamed, and the parliaments saw to the building of ships to carry the ancient creatures of the world away, to new worlds." He fell silent, to a murmuring among the listeners.

Second, a large, strong woman with a wild mane of dark hair took up the story. "And the creatures of the world entered into the ships, attended by the star swimmers and the servants of the deep, and the ships went out toward distant worlds. The captains of the ship were given destinations, but after they were launched, the spirit chose what worlds they would come to. The crews of the ships were confounded, and the ships were cast upon worlds chosen by the spirit rather than upon the worlds mankind had chosen."

Third, an elderly man, with white hair, went on: "We were on the last ship, the greatest ship. We remember the struggle to break free of the ship when it fell into the sea, as a bird must break free of its egg. With the help of the spirit, the star swimmers and the servants opened all the doors and all the gates, all those within were set free, and the spirit who had attended the ship from the old world flowed out into the new.

"We rejoiced, believing that all would be well with this new world and with us, and so it has been for many generations. But now the spirit cries out against this growth upon Mahahm, saying it carries the same destruction as that we left behind, the destruction of greed. The spirit says the evil will touch even the depths, and this world will die.

"We cannot understand why it says this, for the world seems healthy to us. We do not comprehend it, and we ask for enlightenment, but the spirit says we can do nothing but wait, that Tenopia was fathered from the depths, and her daughter Tewhani sent into the world that in time her daughters would return, bringing us understanding. You are the first to return. So it is said."

They fell silent, staring at Genevieve.

"The mana you were given, it was the singing of the harbingers' language, wasn't it? The voice of the sea?"

Wordlessly, they nodded.

She asked, "How many thousand islands have you settled?"

Two of them glanced at one another, then at Melanie, who sat nearby. She shrugged.

"She didn't tell me," murmured Genevieve. "But you dark-skinned people have obviously not interbred with the lighter-skinned ones. There are two types of you, and if one has settled Galul, the other must have settled elsewhere. There should be millions of you islanders, after forty generations."

"We have settlements on several thousand islands," First said. "Most of the populations are small, a few thousand. On Earth we were an island people, we have become so again."

"None of your villages would be evident from space, not even in Galul."

"You are correct," said Fourth. "Even there, we stay out of sight of the ships that come in." She was a slender woman with skin like brown satin.

"Galul was settled by your lighter-skinned people," Genevieve said. "Who were less well adapted to the sun and the sea."

"There was another reason," said Melanie. "Ten of the original keepers' staff were scientists, six of them so-called white, four so-called asian. The rest of the keepers were sea people, Maori they were called, who actually worked with the creatures."

First nodded. "There were different skills represented by the two groups, and all the skills were needed. Our ancestors lost much of their equipment and records, and they were not sure whether needed aptitudes would survive if we interbred. Retaining the original types became one of our customs, even after we learned that the skills existed in both groups.

Galul is still occupied mostly by those like Melanie whom we call shell-people, light skins. As you say, they are not as well adapted to the sun and the sea."

Genevieve nodded. "Which turned out to be a good thing, because when the settlers landed on Haven, they too were light-skinned. You'd have had a hard time penetrating that society if you hadn't had light-skinned agents. But Stephanie was dark, and though it's surprising, she managed to penetrate the society of Haven. How long have you been investigating the people of Haven?"

"Only since P'naki," said Third. "Only since the atrocities."

"You reacted to stop the Mahahmbi killing your women, but you did nothing about their killing other women. It's clear you could have done something. You are numerous enough that you could have killed the Mahahmbi who came out into the desert to perform those rituals!"

"But that wouldn't have stopped it," objected Second. "People on Haven knew all about the lichen, so we'd have had to kill most of the Mahahmbi and a great many of the Havenites, including many innocent persons. As for killing the lichen, even destroying a small patch of it was difficult, and we've found the spores on all the islands of the Stone Path and on the shore cliffs of Haven." She sighed deeply. "We thought we'd done everything possible, but the spirit doesn't agree! It agitates. It does not rest."

Melanie said, "Recently, when we figured out how to procure off-planet equipment, we set up computer models of various approaches we might take—"

"You managed to procure equipment," interrupted Genevieve, "by planting agents in Havenor and having them falsify purchase orders from the Lord Paramount. You intercepted the shipments when they arrived in Bliggen. You probably have quite a number of agents working in that so-called resort, as well."

"That's perfectly true," snapped First, "and how did you know?"

"My travels have been instructive," she replied. "I find that I can reliably infer all kinds of things I'd never thought of until this morning. In fact, I know a good deal more than you do about what happens to all the things the Lord Paramount buys with women's lives. I can also tell you why the spirit is so upset, the same reason your computer models will tell you, when you get around to running them."

"That's hard to believe," said Melanie.

Genevieve smiled grimly at her. "Then don't believe. Veswees tells me belief isn't necessary. Nonetheless, in a very short time there will be an

invasion from space. It will result in the subjugation of this world and an eventual depopulation of all landmasses . . ."

"Impossible!" cried First, turning on Melanie.

Melanie held out her hands, palms up, her face very pale.

"You can't know that," the dark man cried, his hand clenched on the table before him. "Melanie has just given the problem to the machines. They are just now working on it . . ."

"Machines or no machines, you will be invaded," said Genevieve calmly. "The first dose of P'naki that was sold off-planet made it inevitable. Once people out there learned that long life could be found on Haven, it became only a matter of time until they would attempt to take the planet. An invasion force may be already on the way."

"From where?" demanded Melanie.

"Among the planets most likely to attack I would guess either Chamis or Ares. They are closest. Of those two I would say most likely Ares, for the Lord Paramount's Aresian guards have had the freedom of the palace for several years and Aresia has a powerful motive. Their planet is dying."

"The spirit has departed their world?" asked Fifth.

Genevieve made a dismissive gesture. "Leave religion aside. I don't believe or disbelieve, but it doesn't affect what's going to happen. When the invading forces get here, they will do whatever is necessary to find out how the life stuff is produced. For a time they may be misled by the identification of P'naki as a fever medicine, for most of Haven, at least, believes that to be true. They may try to find out peaceably, but if that doesn't work, they will resort to torture, or drugs, or both. Once they find out, they will use every woman on this world to fertilize the lichen, including all your women, and they will enslave all the men."

She sighed, rubbing her forehead. "They will regret this deeply, but they will do it. It is likely all the children on Haven will be shipped to Ares, for their population is falling, and they desperately need more people.

"Then, having used up the women of Haven, they will buy or steal women from other worlds. This will inevitably lead to war among several worlds, and in the end this planet will be ruined for *all* forms of life." She paused, looking at each of them, significantly. "It is inevitable. It will not take long for it to happen. Unless the lichen is destroyed."

The room erupted in hubbub, people yelling at one another. Genevieve got up and left. She went to the kitchen and asked the cook if she might have something to eat. Inside she felt fiery, as though she had swallowed

a furnace. Two glasses of tea did nothing to put out the flame. Slowly she ate fruit and a circle of flat bread wrapped around a slice of fish in hot sauce,

"Brought by our visitors," the cook advised.

It didn't matter who brought it. She couldn't taste it. She was resolutely staring at her empty plate when Melanie came to fetch her.

"Have they stopped yelling?" Genevieve asked. "You know I won't talk to them anymore unless they've finished."

"There are still some raised voices."

"I will not be shouted at. I have told them what is necessary. I will not defend it against their doubts. If they have not wits to see it, then let them suffer the consequences."

"You are not the same girl who came here two nights ago, full of tears and sorrows," cried Melanie, with more than a little anger. "What got into you?

"I am doing my best to be someone else," Genevieve replied, her tight jaw belying the tears in her eyes. "For eleven years I was programmed by my mother to be two people, one public, one private. The public person was quiet and sedate and covenantly. The private person was something I can't even describe to you. I've been a conduit for Mother's forces and Father's furies, for intentions set into motion generations ago, for covenants decided millennia in the past. I'm through playing parts written by other people. This will have to be a role I will write myself. I may die of it, but it will be mine or no one's.

"And while I'm doing it, I won't accept rudeness, Melanie. Let them listen or not, as they choose, but I will not be shouted at."

"Don't hold it against them," cried Melanie. "This business has troubled us for generations! We were sent here as the protectors of the taiau wairua, but now the taiau wairua claims to be threatened, and you agree! So, if it is threatened, then we are threatened. We've made a vow, a sacred oath, the source of our mana, to protect the creatures, all of them, even bacteria! It is our vow, the source of our mana, to destroy no living species, to contaminate no world, but you say we must! If we do this, we will have betrayed our vow. If we do not, we will have failed our trust!"

Genevieve stared into the distance, her lips twisted into a bitter line. "You're no more troubled than I am, Melanie. If I don't act, I'll have failed my vow and my trust as well. The worst of it is that whatever we do may be wrong, and at the moment I haven't the least notion of anything we can do that will possibly set things right."

*   *   *

At the marae, talk went on throughout the afternoon, and as she learned additional facts, Genevieve filled in the outline of her understanding with implications and possibilities. All the theological-cum-ritual issues around which much of the talk circled lay outside her experience. That didn't matter, however. The covenants lay outside the experience of half the people in Haven, but everyone gave them lip service. It let people get on with life.

Believe or not believe, the longer she considered the problem, the more her understanding pushed up into the light, like a mushroom that thrust suddenly out of forest litter, a presence that was undeniable whether one knew anything about botany or not!

On the basis of one such understanding, she told them in midafternoon that it was necessary to evacuate the marae. "The Shah will soon attack the fortress. We should not be bottled up here."

Melanie said, "The committee says the destruction of the lichen must be discussed in Galul, with everyone taking part who wants to do so. Since we have no way to kill it, some strategy must be devised. Our scientist-persons are in Galul, so the committee and most of the rest of us will be leaving marae in a day or two."

Genevieve reached for Melanie's arm, shaking it. "Listen to me, Melanie. Not 'most of the rest.' Not 'in a day or two.' Everyone must leave here. Anyone left here will be as good as dead." She said it in an emotionless voice. She was seeing the bodies, lying on the sand. It was no longer enough merely to see and accept. Not if there were a chance at avoidance.

Melanie stared at her. "You're sure."

"I have said," Genevieve stated in a clear, direct voice that held more than a hint of anger. "What I have seen, I have said. I have seen the dead in Marae Morehu."

"Very well." Melanie frowned. "I suppose you mean soon. Tomorrow, perhaps?"

"Tonight," Genevieve replied.

Within the hour, Melanie came to her very flushed and teary to say that word had arrived from the malghaste in Mahahm-qum saying the Shah was mustering an attack against the marae.

"You were right," Melanie said, biting her lip. "I'm sorry I doubted you. Here we've been expecting you, or someone like you, for generations, and when you turn up, I doubt!"

"I don't care if you doubt me," Genevieve replied. "If I expected you to believe me, I probably should be carrying a flaming sword or something. I look in the mirror to see this witless girl and I doubt myself! So long

as you and I act upon what I know, it doesn't matter whether we doubt, but act we must. Otherwise, I'm no good to you, or to anyone. You'll all leave, won't you?"

"Most of the people here will go to Galul. We have seven sleds already loaded with supplies for the small refuges south of here, so seven of us—including Joncaster, Enid, and I—will drive them from here to the mountains. There's a range of stony hills along the shore where we'll leave the last load, then head south to Galul, after the rest. A few of us always remain in the small refuges. We never like to go too far from the Mahahmbi, for fear of what they may get up to."

Genevieve felt tears readying themselves, pooling. "I think I should go with you. Unless . . . is there any chance that Awhero could already be in Galul?"

Melanie frowned. "We don't know. We don't know where she is or what she's doing. We've had no word at all that she's been harmed, however, so you can be confident your child is safe."

Genevieve turned aside to hide the tears that spilled down her face. "I am trying not to think of Dovidi. If I think of Dovidi, I can do nothing. I would be easier in my mind if I could do something active and helpful."

"Help then. If we're to leave the marae, we need every hand we can muster."

The refuge was swarming like an ant hill. Furnishings, books, equipment, bedding, everything was being gathered up and taken through hidden doors into secret rooms and cellars. Some items were hidden between the walls of rooms, some of them were hidden under paving stones that rotated upward when a certain weight was applied. To Genevieve's astonishment, she found that almost every significant item had a label on it saying where its hiding place was to be: kitchen things near the kitchen, equipment near the garages or the laboratory. Solar panels on the flat roof slid into slots in the parapets and were covered with lines of mud brick. Books were on rotating shelves that turned a blind wall into the library. Bulkier things had wheels on them, and they were pushed down hidden ramps into empty caverns which, once the panels were closed, simply disappeared.

"You've done this before," she said to Joncaster.

"Every now and then our wells fail, and we have to leave the marae for a time. It would be impossible to equip it anew each time, and we daren't leave equipment where the Mahahmbi could lay hands on it, so everything gets hidden away. If some of our people need sanctuary, they can still find it, for they've been taught how to find emergency water or

food or a hiding place. When the marae was built, hiding places were built in."

Later, Melanie came to offer her tea, and Genevieve sank gratefully onto an earthen bench, built along a wall and not, therefore, storable.

"I've been thinking," Genevieve offered. "If this matter is to be discussed in the presence of your people, won't the so-called malghaste in Mahahm-qum want to take part?"

The question had barely left her lips when she shivered, eyes fixed on the space before her. Malghaste. A dozen of them crouched in an alley while men screamed by bearing strange weapons. A woman, clubbed from behind. "Ahhh," she murmured. "Get your people out of Mahahm-qum, Melanie. Get them out now!"

"But that will leave Mahahm-qum unobserved," said Melanie, puzzled.

"Listen to me!" she shouted. "You said you shouldn't have doubted me. Don't doubt me now! Get them out! Now! Or mourn their deaths."

"What are you seeing?"

She rubbed her head, her brow, fighting pain. "I see what will happen in Mahahm-qum! I see malghaste being killed in Mahahm-qum. Men, killing . . . perhaps out of frustration at not finding them here. Can the malghaste get out without attracting attention?"

"It's more difficult the more of them there are, but they can get out, whenever it's needful."

"It is needful now. Send word. Tell them to get to Galul."

In the warren beneath Mahahm-qum, Awhero sat beside an air duct which ascended along a narrow stair within the wall of a Mahahmbi house. Within the duct hung a thin strand of plaited leather bearing a tassel of broken glass bits. Awhero was feeding a fretful Dovidi, distracting him, passing the time until things settled down. There was too much tumult in the city, too much running hither and thither, too many chattering gatherings of the Mahahmbi, and great loadings of harpta panniers. War, people said. War against the malghaste. Word had gone today to the marae, warning the people there.

Dovidi pushed the bottle away and made a pained face. She put him across her shoulder and patted, waiting until he belched audibly. "Good child," she murmured. "Such quiet, good little boy." The good little boy cried fretfully, as though in pain. She put him in his cradle, a box lined with soft rags, and set it where he could see the light beam that came reflected from mirror to mirror down the airshaft. In the light hung a selection of objects—spoons and broken tiles and animals cut out of

paper—all turning in the least air, making an amusement for baby. Baby was not amused. He turned fretfully, and went on crying. She felt his forehead. Hot. Whatever this was, he'd had it since this morning. The change of food, perhaps. Some bug endemic to Mahahm that was not endemic to Haven. And, of course, loss of his mother's milk, with all the protection that afforded.

The plaited line in the airway trembled; the pieces of glass tinkled musically. And again.

Awhero went to the door and called deeper into the warren, "Bird is here, Kamakama."

A youthful form erupted into the room and launched itself up the narrow stairs, soft-footed, only a slight scratching betraying the climb to the pigeon cote above. The Mahahmbi used pigeons to train their hunting birds; the malghaste used them to carry messages. Within moments the boy was down again, passing the message capsule to Awhero and standing with cocked head while she took it apart.

"They go south," she said. "Everyone. They want us out of city. They say danger here, they want us on our way to Galul. Well, I can't go with this child sick, and nobody can go in direction Shah goes, before or behind, that's for certain. Best will be to wait until he and all his men march off toward marae, then we'll go another way. We can be gone by time he gets back."

The youth scratched his nose. "You want me to make rounds?"

"Better had," Awhero acknowledged. "Tell everyone to come here or send someone, so we can plan." Now what? She knew Genevieve had reached the refuge. She knew Aufors had been spotted by malghaste watchmen. He had been close in. Probably coming here, looking for her. Foolish man! If she could find him, he could accompany malghaste when they sneaked away. If she couldn't find him, likely he'd be taken by Shah's men and they'd end up killing him after all!

The malghaste would have to go far east or west to keep out of Shah's path. No point in their going by their usual desert routes, not with all Mahahm-qum watching them in moods of murder and mayhem. Some of those killed by airship's cannon had been old men, men about to receive His Effulgency's gift. Getting dead so close to immortality, why, that was shocking, no doubt. So said fathers and brothers, heatedly.

Well. If they asked her, she would recommend going by sea, as Aufors appeared to be going. Down the western shore, which route was, no doubt, also being chosen by some of those at the marae. They wouldn't

empty the small refuges. Some would stay nearby to keep an eye on the Mahahmbi. Perhaps to lead the Mahahmbi into mountainous country.

Awhero sucked her cheeks with pleasure, savoring thoughts of Mahahmbi among mountains. Then, as baby cried in real pain, she forgot pleasure. Pray heaven it was only colic.

THE MOUNTAIN RANGE THAT HAD BEEN PARTIALLY INUNDATED TO MAKE THE islands of the Stone Trail continued down the west coast of Mahahm, splitting just south of the desert into two ranges, one continuing south along the shore while the other veered eastward across the continent in the virtually impenetrable barrier of chasms and cliffs that protected the highlands of Galul. It was near a stony buttress slightly north of this split that Aufors found a mooring. He tugged the boat up behind the rocks where it could not be seen from the sea.

Getting this far had been simple enough, but now he had a fit of the niggling which-ways. Northeast to the city, or east along the foot of the mountains, looking for wherever Genevieve might have gone. The mountains enclosed a big territory, very steep, very dangerous, and if Genevieve had had some destination in mind, she had kept it to herself. If he went to the city, he would at least have a starting point from which he might trace her. Dislike it or not, he could only choose the city.

He put on the desert cloak he had brought, along with a tattered festoon of stained rags he had plundered from the machinist's store. Dirt on the face plus the few days' beard he had accumulated since fleeing Mahahm made the malghaste impersonation quite believable. He had purposefully arrived in midevening in order to make his trek in the dark. Though he carried a light, the stars would give him enough to travel by. A moment's reference to the locator gave him the heading he would need.

The wind had fallen to a whisper that moved only the smallest grains of sand. He covered a goodly distance in increasing darkness before becoming aware of others abroad in the night: a shadow against the stars at the top of a dune; a slither of falling sand to his right; a line of footprints along a sandy cleft, made very recently and heading southwest, toward the coast. At first these presences were widely separated, but as he penetrated farther, he saw more frequent signs, and he heard voices, too: a

pack animal being berated in murmured curses; vehement whispers telling a child to hush its crying; a muttered conversation between two men as to the landmarks of a trail that led southward among the mountains. Though he noted the landmarks in memory, he learned nothing as to who was going where, or why, except that there were a good many of them.

Since he did not known who the travelers were, or what had prompted their journey, he avoided them by going warily and stopping in this shadow or in that cleft while they passed him by, their numbers steadily diminishing. The sky had paled when he stumbled upon the first group of bodies strewn upon a cupped patch of blood lichen.

Warily, he backed off, scouted the area, then returned to the hollow with the tiny torch from his pack. He found six bodies, dried to sere leather, with their clothing torn to rags. Carrion creatures had been at them to the extent that it was hard to tell their sex. The first he uncovered was, he thought, a young woman because she had a dead baby bundled close to her. Though he would have preferred simply to walk on, the mystery of their presence here on the sands made him go on to each body in turn, all of them some days dead. Longer than that, there'd have been little left but bones. He saw no stains of blood, but necklaces of red lichen wound the mutilated throats and fronds emerged between leathern lips. The lichen had grown into them, or through them, which made him believe the site of the slaughter was no accident.

He thought they were all women. All women, at least one with a child. Almost as an echo, the Prince's words came back to him: "We always take new mothers along, for luck." And Genevieve's conversation with the Shah's wives. All young mothers. Going to Galul.

Was that a descriptive phrase that really meant something like "going to heaven?" Was it a religious ritual? Or just more of the Mahahmbi bloody-mindedness like cutting people into chunks to make a point?

Aufors hunkered down and considered. He had read of ancient societies that had revered certain trees or plants, societies that had made sacrifices when they cut a tree or used a plant. Did the Mahahmbi make some use of the bonebushes in the area? The Thorn trees? The blood lichen? Was this why it was called blood lichen? Was this ritual part of the quite impenetrable Mahahmbi religion? Or, since the Mahahmbi were known to be polygamous, had some one of them simply decided to rid himself of all wives at once?

Cursing under his breath, he used his dagger to cut a score of lichen fronds, fat ones, wrapping them in a square of the film that held his rations and storing the small bundle in his pack. If he ever got back to the airship,

he'd use the analyzer to find what if anything made them valuable to the Mahahmbi. If, indeed, this bloody ritual had anything to do with plant life.

Continuing his line of march, he came upon other groups of bodies in the dawn hours. More broken bodies, more swaddled infants. Once might be an aberration, but twice said this was indeed calculated, habitual. When the sun rose, he went on, sticking to the bases of the dunes, winding a sinuous trail farther eastward. He heard the screaming voices of the prayer-callers and risked climbing the nearest dune, where he saw first the lashing black banners of Mahahm-qum and then the walls of the city. He lay just below the crest with only his eyes above it, staring with amazement at the troop emerging from the southern gates!

Four men on horses. That would be . . . he focused the glasses more carefully. That would be Ybon Saelan, the minister to the Shah, the one who had escorted them around the town and bought them the daggers. He was flanked by the Prince and the Marshal! The fourth man, just behind, had to be the Shah himself, for the horse was caparisoned into virtual immobility. Behind the horses came a few dozen dark-clad men with fancy helmets, and behind them a motley assembly, shambling along in wavering ranks, twenty abreast, carrying a variety of weapons. Aufors lay quiet and counted a couple of hundred ranks, four or five thousand men. That would be almost the entire male population of the city, excluding very old men and boys.

At the rear of the procession came a line of baggage harpta, and he watched while this array made a wide, purposeful track around the base of the nearest dune to continue southward. The travelers he had seen during the night had moved singly and surreptitiously, but this bunch obviously didn't care who knew they were coming.

As the procession disappeared, a glitter of weapons brought his eye to a long, low building half buried in the dunes outside the gate. Though the Shah had taken virtually every man in the city with him, he had left a company of armed men to guard this unprepossessing building. He scanned it intently, intrigued by its odd shape, realizing finally that it was edged and topped by massive wooden shutters to hold back the sand that flowed above it and at either side.

Darkness would decrease his risk in entering the city, so he composed himself in the shade of the nearest convenient Thorn tree, one of several that stood outside a small patch of lichen. While removing food from the pack, he came across the packet of cut lichen. Seeing that it was already partly dried, he laid it in the sun to desiccate while he ate his bread and

dried meat and drank a long, slow ration of water. Finally he rolled in his robes and fell asleep immediately, as any soldier long in the trade learned to do.

When he woke, he was in the shade of the dune and the sun was just above the western horizon. The scraps of lichen he had cut earlier were thoroughly dry, and they crumbled to powder as he rewrapped them before stowing them in his pack. Then, as he pulled on his boots he noticed that the patch of lichen was now growing around the tree he had shaded under. Did he remember it wrongly? Or had the lichen moved nearer him while he slept?

Thoughtfully, he removed his dagger from its sheath, set the point against the vein at the base of his thumb, and nicked it. He held his hand above the lichen, dripping blood and counting slowly, one, two, three . . .

By the count of twelve the lichen came alive like a suddenly wakened tangle of tiny snakes, twisting and thrashing as they reached upward for the falling drops, the proximate disturbance gradually rippling outward to the far edges of the patch, the whole shrieking shrilly, like the high-frequency buzz of a swarm of tiny insects.

Considerably alarmed, Aufors moved away from the growth. The edge nearest him stretched as though to follow him, the frond tips questing like tiny snouts. Did it smell him? It sensed him somehow, that much was sure. With a slight shudder, Aufors wondered what would have happened to him if he had lain closer to the patch while he slept? Did it take spilled blood to get it going? Or could it dig through flesh all by itself?

And why, if making it grow was what the Mahahmbi were after, did they feed it only on women's blood—if he'd been correct about the bodies—when it had reacted very strongly to his own? He put on his gloves before cutting a good handful of the questing strands, wrapping them well and putting them into his breast pocket in order not to confuse them with the other sample in his pack.

When dusk fell he emerged onto the flat territory south of the city, plodding toward it in an unhurried and unbothered manner. The malghaste gate was to the left of the city gates, and he headed directly for it. When the prayer call screamed over the wall he stopped and bowed his head respectfully as he had seen the malghaste do. Malghaste could not sully the Mahahmbi religion by following it or adopting any of its rites, but neither could they show disrespect toward it. The quiet stance and the bowed head were sufficient to let them go unnoticed and unpunished.

When the call stopped, he slipped through the gate, seeing no one at all. No Mahahmbi. No malghaste. The house the Havenites had occupied

was at the south wall, so he needed to traverse the entire length of the city. The cellars there might provide a connection to whatever warren or system of tunnels the malghaste occupied, and if they had all departed, the cellars would at least serve as a temporary base of operations.

He walked slowly, head bowed, along the swerving alleyways. All the alleyways were alike, hard-packed earth; all the walls along them were alike, mud-brick, windowless, high and thick, with deeply inset doors made of heavy timbers. Aside from the occasional symbols painted on the brick, the small variation among hinges or lanterns, the sporadic use of tiles to outline entries or mark corners, one place looked like every other place.

When he judged himself to be halfway through the city, he heard the first footsteps. More than one person, and approaching. He stepped into an angled cul-de-sac, stopping just out of sight of the street to let them pass, which they did not do. Instead the two walkers stopped at the mouth of the narrow way, stepping just inside it to lean against the wall.

"So, he kills the ones out at the refuge," said one, in an angry whisper. "Then what happens to the ritual?"

The other said, "He's not thinking about the ritual."

"He'd damn well better. Without the ritual, Mahahm is going to starve to death in short order. When our people get hungry, they get mean, and when they get mean, the Shah's the first one they think of, Effulgence or no Effulgence."

"Keep shut," said the other. "Someone will hear you! Talking of it to anyone is forbidden, and people who do talk lose any chance of further elevation."

"You think there'll be any further elevations for either of us without the ritual? Without the Shah's blessing, the stuff won't work. I mean, we've seen what it does without the blessing! Old Gazar. He tried it without the blessing, and we know how he ended. A statue of himself, that's how!"

"I'm telling you, you offend the Shah and there'll be no blessing!"

"But it's such a damn silly idea! Taking thousands of men out into the desert to kill a few holed-up escapees. The refuge is malghaste. You can't get at escapees without hurting malghaste. And we hurt malghaste, what'll they do? They'll do what they did last time."

"That was most three hundred years ago."

"We haven't forgotten! What makes you think they have?"

The two fell silent, moving off down the street and leaving Aufors very puzzled behind them.

A little later he came to a place he recognized: a seven-sided polygon with alleyways radiating from the corners, a tiled doorway set into a blue-

painted wall with a prayer tower spearing the sky at one corner. He and the Prince and the Marshal had come this way on their tour of the marketplace. The Prince had remarked that the blue wall signified a house of worship. Aufors closed his eyes and visualized how he had first seen it—from across the plaza. He went there, and from the next corner he saw the city wall, and from the one after that, the gate. If there were guards at the gate, he could not see them.

He could see the house door, to the right of the gate, its splintered slabs lying across the entrance. Though debris littered the area, the entrance wasn't blocked. He stepped cautiously around the wreckage and went several paces inside and around a corner before using his light. The hallway was empty, the kitchen courtyard was full of broken mud-brick, blown out of the com-room along with tangles of wire and twisted chunks of metal. The kitchen was empty; everything had been taken. The hallway through to the large courtyard was empty, as was the courtyard itself. The well seal had been broken, and it seeped water onto the soil. The growing plants were gone, pots and all. Angrily, he hoped someone had tried to eat the greenery, for though colorful and sweet-scented, it was poisonous.

Upstairs, the rooms were bare of furniture, though a clutter of clothing and papers remained. Only Genevieve's things were untouched. It was likely the Mahahmbi religion forbade them looking at or touching women's things. He laid his hand on the gown she had worn the day he left. Soft as her skin was soft. He held it to his nose, taking in her musky-sweet aroma, ashamed to find himself shaking. He hadn't come for this. Or he had, but not in this way. He wanted the woman herself, not merely her scent, her gown, her memory! He shook furious tears from his eyes and went back down stairs, to the pantry behind the kitchen, where the downward route must be.

Even knowing it was there, he had to search for it: a door that didn't look like a door with steps going down into more darkness. He turned the torch up and lit his way down one flight to a series of comfortably furnished and neatly kept rooms. The malghaste might wear rags in public, but they did not seem to do so in private. A rack along the wall was hung with perfectly respectable garments; the rag garlands were thrown separately over a hook at the far end.

A tap set into a tiled section of wall above a floor drain explained where they got water. A tiny metal stove had a kettle atop it. Everything was neat, but no one was there, no one at all, and the tunnel led mysteriously into the dark.

After three hours, he had seen endless hallways, many of them with

rooms along the sides, some of them leading up into blind courtyards exposed to the sky, some of them leading up into occupied houses, where he could hear voices behind hidden doors. Women, mostly.

"We go Galul. Oh, happy, happy, we go Galul."

"You be good girl. You be good. Master not like bad girl."

"Oh, baby, baby, nice baby. Drink and get fat, baby."

When alone, the women evidently talked baby-talk Mahahmbi, for he could understand it perfectly well. Which meant they probably talked nonsense syllables when men could hear them. He was tired and hungry, so he decided to explore only a little farther and then, if he found nothing, go back to his house, the Prince's house, whosever it had been. He was getting nowhere down here, and his lack of success indicated that the people he had seen during the previous night had been the malghaste, leaving town.

It was after he turned back that he heard a voice, singing. Cautiously, he slipped toward the sound, stopping outside an ordinary door.

"Hush, hush," sang the voice inside. "Rock-a-byes. Shut his eyes. Oh, poor little one, Mama gone so far, Daddy gone so far, him all alone with old Awhero . . ."

He turned away, thinking it more of the same babble, but then stopped. The name. Awhero.

". . . alone with old Awhero, poor Dovidi . . ."

Aufors opened the door and walked in. His son was in a makeshift cradle-hammock hung a few inches from the floor; an old woman was swinging it to and fro. She leapt up when he entered and backed away toward the far wall, her hands covering her face.

Aufors gave her a predatory grin as he turned his light onto his own face. "Aufors Leys," he said. "Dovidi's father. Genevieve's husband."

"Ah," she murmured, dropping her hands from before her face. "Well . . . So beetle's dropped out of roofbeam, has it! I thought I'd have to go hunting you, and here you are. You've dyed your hair, too. Very sensible, though this is last place I'd have thought you'd come."

He gave her a weary smile, "My wife went down below, said the comman, and he was the last to see her. Where else should I go but down below after her?" He looked around at the room. A bed. Several small chairs. A skinny stove pipe running up the coiled stair and leading to a tiny stove, only large enough to hold the steaming kettle. From the smell of it, she was burning harpta dung.

"Well, you haven't come after Genevieve, lad, for love of creation. She's long gone. It's only baby that's here, and if he wasn't sick as wee

toad with belly-ache, he and I'd be gone as well. I think there's not twenty of us left in Mahahm."

Aufors went to the cradle and laid his hand on Dovidi's forehead, which was flushed and hot. He heard his voice quaver as he asked, "What's wrong with him?"

"He's not fond of sheep's milk, poor babe. So, I sent my helper to palace, for they've special food there for babies who have no mothers, you know. Sometimes mother dies, and baby is heir, and he's left behind, so palace buys food for such infants. My good Kamakama has gone thieving, and if he's done well, he should be back anytime."

"Dangerous, isn't it?" he asked, his voice still trembling a little. "Thieving from the Shah."

"Less so tonight than most nights . . . though it's almost day, come to that. Shah's gone hunting. He's off in southland with his army, and they're seeking runaways and escapees. I doubt there's two men awake in Mahahm-qum, and that wouldn't include supplies-man. No, my good boy'll make it back. He's quick, and he's quiet is my Kamakama."

"Your son."

"Not biological, no. Just one orphan boy I found and took."

Aufors considered this. "Did you find him, perhaps, out on the sands?"

She gave him a perspicacious look. "Oh, I'm so old it's hard to remember, but I might have. Then again, he could be water-baby."

"Water-baby?" He shivered.

"Half people, half fish, you know. They joke about such things, over in Merdune."

"And how would you know that?"

"Oh, they come here, salesmen from Merdune, looking to sell dried fish and loomed flax and what not. We listen, we malghaste. It's best amusement we have. You don't think funny?"

Aufors made a face. "I don't think funny, no."

Dovidi stirred with a brief, querulous cry, one echoed by a call that seemed to drop from above. In a moment they heard feet shushing on the stairs, and a lean, wiry youth exploded into the room, panting, with eyes wild. "They near had me," he whisper-shouted, conveying his disturbance by breadth of gesture rather than by volume. "Just behind me when I ducked into wall-way. Near as makes no difference!"

"Who?" asked Awhero. "Town is empty."

"Don't know who. Didn't stop to look or ask. They came around corner, yelling for me to stop, I went other way, kamakama."

Awhero rose and put her hands on her hips. "So you forgot milk?"

"Not me," he boasted. "Enough for six bratties and some left over for breakfast."

"This is Aufors Leys, Dovidi's daddy," the old woman said, coming to take the package from him.

The boy bobbed a half greeting, without looking Aufors in the eye, asking from the side of his mouth, "What's he doing down here?"

"Ask him," she said. "He can talk." She opened the pouch and took out a single packet.

"I came looking for Dovidi," Aufors offered.

The boy nodded, looked him over astutely from head to toe, then went to lean against the wall at the foot of the stairs.

"I came for Genevieve, too," said Aufors. "You haven't told me where she is."

"Nor can," said the old woman, peering at the writing on the back of a packet the boy had given her. "She's safe, so far. She got to marae, refuge, then marae up and departed, so she's wherever it went to. Galul, most likely. Unless she's decided to help out with Shah's army."

"Your people are going to fight the Shah's army?"

She giggled, sounding like a girl. "Oh, Aufors Leys, wouldn't that be spectacular. More blood and gore than all lichen could soak up, most of it malghaste blood. No. Fighting isn't malghaste way. We don't fight. We run. They run after us. Then they have accidents." She went to the stove, took the kettle from atop it, and poured hot water into a cup.

"Accidents?"

Kamakama laughed. "Avalanches bury them. Rocks fall on them. Chasms open up and swallow them. Serpents bite them. Large animals tear them to pieces."

Awhero said, "You go on up there, boy. Keep watch." As he departed, she busied herself with the kettle and the packet she had torn open, turning to remark, "Yes, it's dangerous world on way to Galul."

Aufors half whispered, "It must be dangerous. I saw bodies out there. Fairly fresh. All women."

The old woman frowned as she stirred the baby food into the cup. "We know. Some of them Mahahmbi women, some of them Haven women. New mothers, all."

He decided on a stab in the dark. "Why women? It grows perfectly well on men's blood."

She turned, amazed. "Oh, does it now? What did you do? Bleed on it? Oh, I've wondered on that many times."

"Wondered?" he exploded. "You mean you've never tried to find out? Never experimented with it?"

"Never," she said solemnly. "Lichen is tapu. Our people destroyed some, long and long ago, then they made it tapu. Untouchable."

Another stab, in not quite so deep a dark this time. "But evidently a man can live as long as he likes on women's blood, eh?"

She stared at him for a long time, wordless. "This is secret, you know?"

"Oh, I know. But it's an evil secret, Awhero. Answer me. A man can live as long as he likes on women's blood?"

"Oh, man can live long, yes. Not forever. No. I think not." She made a momentary clatter with cup and bottle and the hot water kettle, then added a dipper of cool water to the mix, tested it upon her tongue and filled a bottle.

"What makes you think not?" Aufors asked.

She put the nipple in the baby's mouth. He pushed it away fretfully before finally accepting it, though reluctantly. Holding baby and bottle, she sat down, cocking her head. "If I tell you, you promise not to say Awhero told you? This is maybe forbidden knowing, but I am nosy old thing."

He held up a hand, "I promise."

"Well, then," she said, "Well, then. We malghaste, we have ways to go in walls of houses, you know?"

"I know."

"One of ways I go is in walls of Shah's rooms, in palace. So, one day I am in walls, and guards bring in Old Friend, very Old Friend."

"An old friend of the Shah?"

"Oh, yes. Old Friend Gazar, from one hundred years, two hundred years. So, Old Friend comes in, na, na, na, talk talk, no sense. Shah says, 'How are you today, Old Friend.' Old Friend goes on, na, na, na, sky is blue, walls are gray, nice walk, time for good roast mutton. No sense. So, Shah goes to locked cupboard, unlocks it, takes out small box, unlocks that. I am looking down on this, and inside is powder, like lichen powder."

"You could see it?"

"Oh, yes. From inside walls, very clear. So, Shah puts powder in glass of wine, gives wine to Old Friend. Old Friend drinks."

"What happened?"

"Oh, ho, here is this old man who got silly in head, no more mind than harpta. Here is old man who can't follow orders. Here is old man two hundred tiresome years old. Here he is, needing woman's blood every day or so, but he is no use to anybody. What you think happened?"

"What should I think?"

"What happened was, after Old Friend drinks, Shah talked to him, na, na, na, na. Time went by, then Shah asked him, 'You all right, old friend?' Ha! Old Friend did not answer. Only blinked, very, very slowly. Then Shah tried to lift Old Friend's arm. Stiff. Like wood. Then Shah called guards and they picked him up, chair and all. They took him away."

"Where? How?"

"Listen, I am telling you. So, from inside walls I watched, I followed. They went out palace gate, across desert, to that building out there."

"The one with all the guards and the sand shutters?"

"That one, yes. I could not go to building, no cover for me, but I watched, and after time, they came back without Old Friend. So, Old Friend stayed in building. Then, I waited, listened while Shah talked to minister about other old men also tiresome, also due for 'accident.' Whatever powder is, is not P'naki."

"P'naki!"

"You think P'naki is to stop plague. No. Real P'naki is long-life stuff. What you call P'naki in Haven is just . . . nothing. Distraction."

Aufors thought this over. "What did they say killed him? More avalanches? More wild beasts?"

"No. Nothing so strange. Next day, in throne room, Shah makes sad announcement. Poor Old Friend took P'naki not blessed by Shah. Pity. Poor Old Friend is dead. Same happen to anyone taking P'naki not blessed by Shah." She put down the bottle and hefted Dovidi over her shoulder, patting him until he burped loudly. When she offered the bottle again, he seized it and sucked strongly. "Later I see Old Friend out in front of palace, in chair, people poking him, whispering about what happens when people take P'naki Shah did not bless."

"I see. Once the old guy is no longer in a position to help the Shah, he'd rather give the good stuff to some other old guy. And at the same time, he warns them off trying to get the good stuff by themselves."

"You say very accurately. Oh, very accurately."

They sat for a time in companionable silence, broken when Aufors reached out a hand to touch his child, still suckling.

"He seems to like that stuff."

"Good. I have nothing else to try, so it is good he likes this."

"So, what now?"

"What now? Well, night is over, so we cannot go now. So we wait until night comes again. Then if baby is all right, not crying, not fussing, we go through burrow to place near wall. Danger will come, so refuge

tells us, from Shah's men, but Shah cannot get back with all his men for another day or two, so this should be easy. Then we go out malghaste gate, and away. Like Tenopia."

"I heard about Tenopia. Seven days ago, Genevieve ran off, like Tenopia, right?"

"Good role model," said Awhero, with a gap-toothed grin. "We go south, where Genevieve is, most likely."

They waited. Awhero offered tea. Aufors got out his food pack and offered bread and dried meat. He went through his pockets, saw that the second lichen specimen was dry, crushed it to powder, wrapped it a bit more securely, and returned it to his breast pocket. The flat packet made no bulge. He could not even feel it through the fabric.

"You got that P'naki where women's bodies were, right?" asked Awhero, "You could sell that for fancy price on another world. What will you do with it?"

"Test it," he murmured, without explaining what it was. "See what it's made of, chemically."

When they had eaten, they napped, and when Aufors awoke, the little light that had seeped down the stair was gone. They prepared for their journey in moments. The boy carried a light pack. Awhero carried the baby inside her robe. Aufors carried his own pack, mostly food and water, plus his weapon, locator, and glasses. Awhero said he looked quite dirty enough to be true malghaste.

They went up the stairs to a slightly higher network of tunnels, one that led through the walls of contiguous houses, dropping here and there to go under an alleyway.

Awhero stopped, listening. "People out there," she said. "We'll go around."

"The place near palace," suggested Kamakama. "Where I lost them yesterday."

They went around, a longer way, farther down, coming up at last to a place where torchlight fell in from a high, barred window.

"Two turns right," whispered the boy. "It opens in alley near palace. Then we have to cross little way to get to malghaste gate."

They found the narrow notch behind a buttress at the end of a blind alley, the way blocked by a tumble of trash that, remarkably, hung all together and swung away on silent hinges when pushed from behind. They oozed through the hole, Aufors in the lead, then started for the alley entrance. Directly across from it was a malghaste gate, marked by

the dung-bucket that hung above it. They waited at the alley entrance. Nothing.

They went out into the open area where a sudden, blinding light fell upon them from all directions and a stentorian voice bellowed:

"Halt! Stand where you are! Be silent!"

"I thought you said the Shah couldn't get back so soon," cried Aufors to Awhero, under his breath. He had no chance to say more, for he was struck violently on the head with the butt of a weapon.

"We said, be silent," roared the voice. "You are the prisoners of the Ares Expeditionary Forces."

The Shah and his army arrived at the marae late in the afternoon, coming up over the rise beside the river to look across its empty bed.

"We shall attack," said the Shah, impatiently.

"Seemingly there's no need," drawled the Marshal. "The gates are open."

The Shah peered near-sightedly. The gates were indeed open. Almost reluctantly, he urged his horse forward, the others following across the dry river bed and up the hard packed surface beyond. The army shuffled after, gathering in a wide arc outside the gate where the bell loop hung almost in their faces. One of the officers grasped it and pulled, only to let out a howl and throw himself away, wildly waving his arm.

"Thorn!" he cried. "Black thorn."

"Fool," muttered the Marshal. "Look first. Think first. This could be a trap."

"Saelan," the Shah breathed. "Take some men and go in."

The minister paled, bowed, turned to select half a dozen companions, none of whom seemed eager. They slid through the open gate and disappeared inside while the others shifted uncomfortably from foot to foot. After a lengthy wait, the minister reappeared.

"No one here," he said in a voice that did not disguise his relief.

The Shah did not wait, spurring his horse almost over his minister and riding down the tall hallway into the atrium beyond. The doors from there were too low to admit a mounted man, and he dismounted, his annoyance plain at having to do so. On foot, the Shah was far less prepossessing. As his feet hit the ground, the others in the group crouched slightly, walking with knees bent beneath their robes. They were well aware of the Shah's mood, and no one wanted to incur his wrath by towering over him. Following his minister, with the Prince and the Marshal trailing behind, the Shah made a circuit of the refuge.

They found nothing, no water, no furnishings. The storage of all moveable items had been quite successful. The false panels that shut off the storage areas had been capably designed. They did not look or sound hollow. The water taps were in recesses that had been sealed off with a few hastily laid mud-bricks. Even the lantern that had lit the atrium was no longer there. The garages were empty of vehicles. Only a lingering smell of lubricants and cleansing agents betrayed the fact that work might have been done there within recent times.

The kitchens were cold, their pantries empty. The only signs of life in the place were the purple-leaved trees in the atrium, and they did not long withstand the Shah's fury. He had them chopped down and burned as fuel to warm his dinner. While the Shah ranted and roared, the Marshal went out onto the desert, selected a few dozen men to serve as sentries, and posted some well out upon the dunes and others upon the walls while the horde itself was directed to bivouac around the refuge.

"Thoughtful of you," said Ybon Saelan, from the doorway. "I was about to do that myself."

"It could still be a trap," rumbled the Marshal. "Is this the place the Shah thinks my daughter escaped to?"

"He claims to believe so, Marshal. Your daughters' belongings, however, were found on the trail to Zimmi oasis, far from here. I think it unlikely she escaped to anywhere or reached any place of safety."

"Someone alerted these people," the Marshal opined. "Someone told them we were coming."

"Well, we did not muffle our drums, did we. We marched out in full array in the light of day, and as we have rested in the heat of the day, it has taken us almost three days to get here. We know the malghaste use messenger birds. We think they also use drums to send messages. All in all, we chose to eschew surprise, so they've had time to flee to the ends of the earth . . ."

He was interrupted by a shout from one of the sentries. The man, who stood in the last of the light atop a dune, was pointing toward the southwest. The Marshal left the minister and ran to the dune, where his motion became more flounder than forward. Nonetheless, his struggles brought him to the top of the dune in time to see a dozen or so dark figures disappearing into a valley away to the southwest, toward the coast. When he returned, the minister had been joined by the Shah himself, and by the Prince.

"I'd say they were people from here," said the Marshal. "Heading southwestward, at some speed. They got warning of Your Effulgence's intent

and simply departed. From the looks of the place, I'd say it has never been more than a way-station. A camp. Unless there's a hidden well, they have to carry water in, which means they can't use it for protracted periods."

"They intend to hide in the mountains," grated His Effulgence. "I won't have it! We'll go after them."

"I wouldn't recommend it," said the Marshal, unthinkingly.

"Cut that man's tongue out," said the Shah, staring at the Marshal. "Who is he to recommend to the Effulgence of the World, the Divine Sun, the Glory of the Galaxy?"

"My apologies," cried the Marshal, suddenly aware of acute danger as he fell to his knees. "My desire is to protect Your Effulgence from harm, and there could be harm waiting in the mountains."

"There is truth in what he says," murmured Ybon Saelan. "We are only trying to protect you, Great Sun. The Marshal is well known in Haven as a superb tactician. We should not dismiss his words, no matter how insolently uttered."

"No harm waits," said the Shah. "What harm can befall a god? Am I not a god? Do I not warm the worlds with my rays?"

"Certainly. This is true," said Ybon, bowing deeply.

The others had sense enough to say nothing.

"If he is such a great tactician, he can no doubt foresee any danger," murmured the Shah, with a piercing look at the Prince. "You know him. Can't he foresee danger?"

The Prince turned his head slightly, painfully, as though something had rusted in his neck. He said unwillingly, "The Lord Paramount trusts the Marshal greatly, Effulgence."

"Well then, so will we. We will go into the mountains, in pursuit of our prey, and the Marshal will foresee any trouble in time to warn us of it. If he does not and we come into danger, we will kill him."

The Marshal bowed low in apparent acceptance while the Shah contented himself with sneering in his general direction.

Aufors, meantime, along with Kamakama, Awhero, and the baby, was sitting on the floor of the palace entryway, waiting to be questioned by the Aresian officer in charge, one Terceth Ygdaleson, youngest son, so the guards had said, of Ygdale Furnashson, the Chieftain of Aresia. Aufors, head bent forward between his knees, was still dizzy and bleeding from the wound at the back of his head. Still, he could hear Awhero clearly enough as she murmured to him:

"They will ask why you have weapons. You will say you have weapons to protect us from wild animals in southern mountains, where we are going. They will ask why we are going. You will say the Shah is angry with all malghaste, and we must flee before he returns. We did not go with others for baby was sick. Your name is Taipa, which means 'be silent.' You are my son and only child. Kamakama is an orphan I am fostering. The baby is not yours, or mine, just a baby I am caring for. Understand?"

Aufors nodded slightly, even the tiny motion enough to set up waves of nausea and pain. They had taken his pack and his weapon. Well, there was nothing in the pack to identify him. The weapons were ones the malghaste might have stolen from the Mahahmbi. The locator was an exotic item, but it and the glasses might have been traded for. The few items of clothing were anonymous. Other than that there were only food and water. Awhero carried food for the baby. The boy had nothing suspicious on him. He took a deep breath and concentrated on finding the pain. If he could find it, trace it to its source, he could cope with it, a trick an old warrior had taught him. "Concentrate on where it starts, and you have it trapped," he had said. So Aufors concentrated upon the back of his head, a certain spot, perhaps as wide and long as the first joint of his thumb. All the pain was in that one spot. He had it trapped. It could not spread from that one spot . . .

"You!" Someone jerked his head up by the hair. Pain exploded across his eyes. The nausea billowed up, uncontrollably, and he vomited across the man's boots.

"For the . . . What in hell!" The guard drew back a boot to kick Aufors, only to be stopped by Terceth himself, who jerked him roughly away.

"Men don't heave for the joy of it, Obrang! He's been hit on the head."

"Bassid didn' stop when I tol' im, Prince Terceth."

"Obrang, you can't get information from an unconscious man. I've told you that before!"

The man went away cursing, to clean his boots, while the other knelt before Aufors and offered water. Aufors shook his head. "It won't stay down," he murmured.

"Rinse out your mouth at least," said the other. "So you won't stink so when you answer me."

Aufors did so, turning slightly to spit in the place Awhero had just moved from.

"Now," said Terceth. "Who are you, the three of you?"

"My mother," said Aufors, gesturing weakly with an elbow, concentrating on the words he used, trying to sound like Awhero. "That's her foster

son, Kamakama. She's taking care of baby for one of her friends, I don't know who. My name's Taipa."

"You're what? A citizen of Mahahm?"

"No." Aufors tried shaking his head, quickly giving up the effort. "We're malghaste. Ah . . . servants. Ah . . . untouchables. We carry out shit."

Terceth thought about this. "The town's almost empty? Did you know that?"

"Yes. Shah went out. He took most all men. Our people went then. Only few of us left. Baby was . . . sick so we waited to go. We got left behind."

"Why is everyone leaving? Except the women, young children, and babies, that is. And a few old men."

"Shah, he's on rampage. He wants to kill all . . . malghaste. He says we are traitors. It's not true. We don't know why he's saying so."

"The women don't seem to understand the language we're speaking, but you do. We learned both Mahahmbi and Haven-tongue, but the women don't seem to understand either one."

"They do," Aufors said. "But they aren't allowed to speak it. Women evighaste. Dirty. Can't use men's words without making words dirty. If they talk Mahahmbi, they have tongues cut out. They're afraid."

"Umm," hummed Terceth. "I don't suppose you'd care to tell me where you got the weapon, and what it was for."

Aufors raised his head, fixed the officer with an innocent stare. "Stole it from Mahahmbi palace. Stole food for baby, too."

"That's right, sir," said one of the men standing by. "We almost caught somebody coming out of a storeroom there yesterday. There was baby food all over the place."

Aufors sulked, "Need food for baby, need weapon. We travel all alone. Animals are fierce in mountains. Must have protection."

"Did the others all have protection?" Terceth asked in a suspiciously neutral tone.

Aufors risked shaking his head, very gently. "Not many had weapons. But there are very many many of them. They can make loud noise, wave torches, frighten animals away. Old woman doesn't count, so only two of us, boy and me. Not enough to frighten."

"So, if the Shah wants to kill you all, where is he?"

"Malghaste camp place south of here. He went there. To kill many malghaste. We need to go before he comes back."

"Oh. He's coming back?"

Aufors did his best to look honestly amazed. "Where else he go?"

Terceth stared at him a long time, a stare which Aufors returned with a wounded, reproachful look of his own. Finally the man reached into his pocket and took out the packet of lichen powder that had been in Aufors's pack. "Can you tell me what this is? And where you got it?"

"Stole it," said Aufors, who had anticipated the question. "From palace. It was in locked box, so I thought it was important. Medicine. Valuable, maybe?"

"Ahh," said the officer. "Well, well. Can you show us where you got it?"

Aufors scratched his head, reached back, tenderly touched his wounded head. "No."

"Why no?"

"Can't remember where. Remember going to palace. Remember weapon. Remember box. Can't remember palace. Head hurts when I try. What'd he hit me for?" Aufors, listening to himself, thought he sounded an absolute fool which was, probably, what was wanted. He glanced up to see Awhero beaming at him approvingly.

"You don't mind if we keep this, then?" asked Terceth.

"Keep it. Don't need it. Do need weapon and food and water. You give them back, we go away, not bother you."

"We'll see. You just wait patiently. You shouldn't move too much right now anyhow. Let your head settle."

Terceth moved to Awhero, drew her away, out of earshot, and questioned her, the old woman answering volubly, waving her arms. The baby began to cry, and the old woman took out a pack of baby food and waved it about, making demanding noises. Someone was sent to bring hot water.

Well, except for some of them like Obrang, they weren't barbarians by nature. They weren't trying to be cruel. They were just set on taking over Mahahm. Or . . .

Aufors looked up at the nearest guard and said plaintively, "You should go to Haven. Haven has good land. Haven has wine, and lots of food. Good things. There's nothing good here."

"Don't you worry, desert-rat. By this time we've got Haven, too." The guard grinned. "Some of us landed in Havenor soon after we landed here. We're taking over the whole place. And we're all going to live forever!" He laughed, a quiet and very satisfied chuckle.

Aufors subsided against the wall. Well, and well. He could fill in the blanks. The Lord Paramount had been selling long lives in return for frippery and security forces. Some of his customers on Ares figured the price was too high—or they couldn't buy enough—so the customers decided to take over the store. But they didn't know where the store got

the stuff, not yet. They were looking for something, but they didn't know what they were looking for. If they went out onto the dunes and found those bodies, they might figure it out soon enough.

Awhero said something to Terceth, who threw up his hands and let her go. Cradling the hungry baby in her arms, bottle at the ready, she came to sit next to Aufors once more.

"I'm going to try to get them to let you go," said Aufors. "These people are looking for you-know-what, and if they find those bodies out in the dunes, they'll soon figure out why they're there. Somehow, you've got to get your people to dispose of them."

She rocked to and fro. "I can't reach my people. All messenger birds went south. Malghaste left marae, now they hide. Some go to Galul."

"How far? Too far? Damn. Who's left in the city?"

"Women," she said. "Babies."

"Women." He thought about it. "Could they . . . ?"

She whispered, "If they were not drugged, perhaps they could understand, but they are drugged."

"But with most of the men gone, who's doing the drugging?"

"Old men. Keepers. Maybe it's in their water. I don't know."

"So they probably can't bury the bodies?"

"Why bury them? Just dragging them away from where they are would be enough. I don't think Mahahmbi women could do even that."

"I can't figure out how the Shah keeps the secret? I can't be the first traveler to have stumbled over bunches of bodies. Even having seen the Old Friend, you'd think some Mahahmbi men would have gone out there and tried themselves."

She shrugged. "Perhaps risk seems too great. If they do not want to become statue, Shah's blessing is essential."

Remembered the conversation he had overheard in the city, he fell silent. It was true the two old men had spoken of the blessing. And of the vow of silence. Pray heaven they kept silent. It would be a very bad thing if the Aresians found out where the life-powder came from.

OF LATE THE LORD PARAMOUNT HAD FOUND HIS NIGHTTIMES INCREAS-
ingly wakeful. He was often aroused by small disturbances or sounds which
would not have bothered him a few years before. It was true that the
longer he reigned, the more anxious about his reign he became, for he
was fully aware of the machinations of Prince Delganor. He knew the
Prince had killed others in the line of succession. He knew the Prince
conspired against himself, Marwell. He also knew, however, that allowing
the Prince to operate with apparent freedom limited the field of possible
aspirants, rather as turning goats into a pasture keeps down the weeds,
not wiping them out, necessarily, but preventing their seeding or spreading. Better an evil one knew intimately than an evil one only guessed at.
Thus far, the Prince had served admirably in the capacity the Lord Paramount had assigned him. Mower of aspirants. Cutter down of
presumptives.

Marwell had always known the Prince would eventually become so
powerful and so intricately enmeshed in Havenor's affairs that it would be
necessary to kill him. The Lord Paramount knew that this point had now
been reached, which required that he, himself, watch matters very, very
closely and make his moves very, very cautiously. These concerns made
the Lord Paramount sleep even more lightly than usual.

On the night of the invasion, therefore, when he was wakened by a
scuffle in the courtyard, he made no attempt whatsoever to investigate the
cause, but did instead what he had many times practiced doing: he stepped
directly from his bed to the control panel of his secret elevator, opened
the concealed door, closed the double layer of sturdy, metal-backed panel-
ing behind him, and dropped the cage halfway down its shaft before he
was even fully awake.

The elevator was well supplied with sensors covering most of the
palace, inside and out, and from the safety of his cell-like enclosure, he

observed the palace being occupied by his own Aresian guards, their forces supplemented by a great many other Aresians who seemed to have materialized out of thin air.

The Lord Paramount was shocked and surprised. He felt the shock quite palpably. He had imagined an attack from every quarter but this! He was at first a bit dazed, though when it became clear there was no level aboveground free of Aresian troops, he managed to calm himself sufficiently to dress and arm himself. Then, for the first time in almost a century, he went on down to the "upper cellars" beneath Havenor. Though the Aresians knew there were belowground warehouses—they had seen freight shipments being lowered—it would be some time before they found the access routes and began a search. By that time the Lord Paramount had gathered additional weapons and some other odds and ends of supplies before dropping even further down, into the gigantic lower caverns that constituted his subterranean storehouse. This area was known only to him, to the criminals he had sentenced to work there, and to the computer that ran the inventory. The last act of the Lord Paramount before leaving the elevator was to press a button which sealed off all the access shafts to these lower caverns as well as closing access to the inventory computers. If all went well, he could cancel this order at some later time, but he would have to do it from the elevator itself.

When, very shortly thereafter, the Aresians searched the upper caverns, they found a great quantity of light weapons and an enormous quantity of junk, all of it ill stored and in general disarray. There was no sign of the Lord Paramount. The occupying force considered this disappointing but not critical, as it was assumed many noble Havenites would possess the knowledge the men of Aresia wanted.

In this they proved to be mistaken. No one they spoke to knew anything at all specific about long-life stuff. There were no very old men to be found, though there were a surprising number who looked and claimed to be between the ages of sixty and eighty. There were no very old women, either. In fact, there was a definite shortage of women of any age!

When questioned, Count Daviger of Farmoor said yes, the Lord Paramount did give an expensive health drug to certain favorite courtiers, but he got it from off-planet somewhere in exchange for women. This was confirmed by Gardagger, Duke of Merdune, and by Lord Listley, Earl Northmarch, and by Prince Thumsort of Tansay in Sealands, plus all the other earls or counts or barons residing in Havenor, most of them in that highly suspect sixty to eighty year range.

When the invaders in Mahahm had time to question the few old men

in Mahahm-qum, they learned that the Shah did dispense a health drug
to a few favorites, and that he obtained the stuff from Haven in return
for women.

Would the drug let them live forever? the informants were asked.

No, of course not, said the prisoners. What a silly idea.

So stymied for the moment, brothers Ogberd and Lokdren Ygdaleson
summoned brother Terceth to Havenor for a strategy conference with
their father, Ygdale Furnashson. Terceth arrived in his own battle cruiser,
settling it outside the city next to those of his father and brothers and
the several smaller vessels owned by minor Aresian warlords, the four large
and several small vessels constituting the entire Aresian fleet. The Chieftain
and his sons, after a nightlong discussion, settled down to a more lengthy
occupation than had been planned. They did not believe the long-life stuff
came from off-planet. They did not believe it was only a health drug.
While they were not barbarians, while their sportsman's code made them
dislike inflicting pain and suffering, it was obvious that they were not
going to get the information they needed without some very cruel methods
of extraction.

The men of Ares were so very body-oriented, so very out-of-doorsy,
so very much into tramping and swimming and climbing, and overall
heartiness, so very much unaccustomed to sedentary pursuits that they did
not consider the possibility of archival technology. No one among them
considered examining the archives to determine the real ages of the men
they questioned. Inasmuch as the lower levels of the archives had been
blocked as tightly as the lower levels of the caverns, even if the Aresians
had thought of it, they would probably have found nothing.

Deep below Havenor, the Lord Paramount, dressed in mufti with his
second-best crown a-cock, wandered in darkness of air, darkness of stone,
and darkness of dust lying deep. Oh, the caverns were darker than remembered, or than he remembered remembering. Had he actually come here,
ever? Or had he only told people to create these spaces, drain them, warm
them, make them fit for storing all the treasures, all the pleasures of the
king. The king. Himself, who had always been a king though he was not
called a king. The cosettlers had not wanted a king, but they had accepted
a Lord Paramount, a chief Lord, a more lordly lord than lesser lords.
Marwell would have preferred to be king. He had always preferred to
be king.

When he had seen his own guards taking over the palace, caverns,
something strange had happened to him. He had been furious, of course.

He remembered his anger. And he remembered it building into a fury which had grown tighter and tighter, humming like a taut violin string which had then, oddly, snapped as he stepped out into this dark world. He had felt the tightness break, a quite tangible and organic feeling, a cord somewhere inside himself giving way, as though something springy but nonessential had been stretched too far. The sensation had been disquieting, and for the moment he had forgotten his anger, and when he returned to it a moment or so later he could not find it. Anger was more or less gone. Or perhaps it had merely lost its focus. What had been red fury was now only . . . a sallow swirling, an ashen agitation, a pale pique. He giggled at this. His fury was still there, oh, yes, but it was no longer such an irritating ire. Not anymore.

Without it he felt more comfortable, less driven to do or accomplish at once. There was time. Plenty of time. So, he wandered, lantern in hand, along a roadway deep in dust that rose before his feet in little clouds. He had dressed in his disappearance clothes and shoes, but no matter how he tried, he could not step high enough in those shoes to avoid kicking up the dust. Sometimes he kicked it up just for fun. Some places it rose high, making him sneeze. Other times it merely fountained and fell in opaque puffs, a recurring geyser at his feet.

He spent some time exploring a mountain of crockery. Much of it he remembered seeing before; the patterns were strangely evocative; the extravagant ornamentation of gold and platinum carried hints of old longings and desires. Oh, with a dinner service like that, everyone would know he was more than merely Lord Paramount. So, why had he sent it down here to be stored so clumsily? Who had let it fall so far, who had let it break into such tiny pieces? It was kingly china, he was sure of it, sure as he had been at the time, most kingly, as were the porcelain ornaments in the next box and the crystal goblets in the next heap—one of which he found unbroken and carried with him as he examined scraps of linen and lamé in the next pile over but one. When he struck the goblet with his thumbnail it rang, like a tiny bell, and so he went, *ting-a-ling, ting-a-ling,* betimes straightening his crown, which did not accord with his clothing, but which, nonetheless, he refused to forsake.

He found carpets. He remembered those carpets. He had contemplated them for a year before ordering them, deep, and rich in color, and made by the innocent hands of children in the far mountains of some other world. Chamis, perhaps. Or Alfrenia. Or Verchop's World. Oh, there had been many carpets, so many, enough for the whole palace, but they had

been improperly stored, fallen into ruin and decayed, soaked with lizard filth and burrowed through by creatures.

Oh, he told himself calmly, he would hold someone responsible, yes, he would. But first, first he had to find the war machines, somewhere down here, and put them into action, to drive away the invaders, the Aresians, the faithless, the false, the traitorous, the terrible . . . The adjectives were enough. He did not need to feel anything. So long as he knew they were dreadful people, that was enough.

He hummed a little as he went, licking a finger now and then before thrusting it into the small jar he carried, bringing it out laden with P'naki to be sucked off, like a child with a lolly as he went singing-tinging, crown-acock, down the lanes of his fortune, his treasury, his wonderful, wonderful things. So, they were a bit tattered, but they could be mended. They were quite all right, really, quite fixable, once he had found the machines, he would set about putting things to rights . . .

But, obviously, someone had erred. People down here had not Done Their Jobs Correctly. Things were Not in Good Order. Why, here, here, see! His pets! How long had they been here? When had they arrived? And why had no one told him they had come? Pretty things. Oh, pretty things. Well, now, he would put that to rights himself! It was only a matter of pulling the little tabs and setting the little valves into motion. He would let them out into the world, he would, of course, where they belonged. There, one. And there, another. And here a whole bunch of them in a row, eyes staring out through glassine and vitreon, eyes staring deep into his own. And here others, and there, down a twisting aisle barely wide enough to wriggle through, more, and more yet.

So the tabs were pulled and deep within lights began to glow and wheels began to turn and fluids began to pulse in tubing as creatures long, long asleep began to waken. And he, Lord Paramount of Haven, burrowed into the stack, finding them all, setting them all in motion before he came out, humming, to continue down the dusty way, seeking the person responsible for this inadequacy, this disorder, this mismanagement of the dream, this corruption of his Eden.

WHEN YBON SAELAN WOKE AFTER AN UNCOMFORTABLE NIGHT IN THE BARE and waterless refuge, the others were still sleeping, except for the sentry officer who stood bolt upright in the outer gateway, pivoting to keep each of his dune-top sentries in view.

"Report," grated the minister.

"Nothing to report, sir. The night was quiet. We didn't see anyone or hear anyone. Marshal came to take a look at the sentry posts early this morning, before dawn. That's the sum total of it."

Ybon seated himself on a convenient rock. "Was the Marshal satisfied with your sentries?"

"Don't know, sir. Haven't seen him since he went out there. He's quite the soldier, sir. Came out in full pack."

"Ah," said Ybon again, puzzled.

"Sir?"

"Yes, Guardsman."

"I . . . maybe I shouldn't mention it, sir, but the men are muttering and turning quarrelsome. It's worrisome. They're not regular guards. They don't have the discipline to go along without knowing all the details . . . well sir, it's the Shah's manner that's got them uneasy. He's headed us off nobody knows where, and he's ready to cut out the tongues or chop off the heads of most anybody, maybe the whole lot of us . . ."

"Ah," mused Ybon. "I'm sorry to hear that. Well, I'll see if I can't calm him down."

He went back into the refuge, to the room where the Shah's bedding and furniture had been set up, where the Shah himself was still noisily asleep, the rasp of his breath clearly audible. On the small table by the door stood a carved box, an ornamental water cooler of porous clay, a folded napkin, a cup, and a small spoon carved of seabone. The box contained P'naki. The Shah had a spoonful of it on his morning cup, every

day. The Shah, as a matter of fact, was by now using almost as much of the lichen as the rest of Mahahm put together.

Ybon stared at the P'naki box for a long time, finally stepping forward to take both spoon and box with him into the anteroom where he shut himself into a privy closet. There, he took a key from a secret pocket and opened the box. It was full of P'naki, the dark red powder fine as talc. He took a small pouch from beneath his clothing and opened it also, displaying contents that looked as finely powdered, as darkly red. With the seabone spoon he made a careful hollow in the P'naki in the box. Then he dipped the spoon into the pouch, brought it out heaped full, carefully wiped clean its convex side, then lowered it into the already created hollow in the box and left it there. The spoon now held a measured dose which looked in all respects like P'naki, and the lid, as he had already established, would shut and lock even with the spoon in place.

The key went back in the secret pocket and the pouch returned to its hiding place. Just before this expedition Ybon had stolen the substance in the pouch from a little box in a locked cupboard in the Shah's private rooms. Not that Ybon had decided to use it, but he'd always thought something of the kind might be needed when the Great Effulgence, to everyone's dismay and infinite regret, was no longer . . . radiant.

Moving softly, carrying the box with exquisite care, he returned it to the table in His Effulgence's room. From his pocket he took a seabone spoon to lay where the other spoon had been. It wasn't identical, but it was close in shape and size, and if he was lucky, no one would see it close up. Then he returned to the uncomfortable pallet on which he had spent the night, where he was wakened some time later by Prince Delganor, who wanted to know where the Marshal was. Shortly thereafter, the Shah was wakened by a lively discussion between the minister, the Prince, and two of the officers in the antechamber.

"What's going on?" demanded His Effulgence, pulling himself higher on his pillows.

Ybon Saelan prostrated himself in the doorway.

"It's the Marshal, Your Effulgence. He seems to have wandered off. He may be lost. It's difficult to keep one's way in the dunes when one is unaccustomed to the desert."

"Went out in the dark did he?"

"Would you like the officer to tell you? He's just outside."

The Shah frowned but did not object. The officer came to the door, prostrated himself, then, nose almost on the floor, explained about the Marshal. Prince Delganor, meantime, stood just outside the doorway, his

brow furrowed, listening to the story. He didn't believe for a moment the Marshal was lost; he very much wished to know what the Marshal was up to.

The Shah grunted, waving the officer out. "My cup, Saelan!" he demanded.

The minister crept forward to the Shah's right hand. The Shah fumbled in a pocket of his nightdress and came up with a key. Saelan crept away to the table, then rose. From their positions just outside, the Prince and the officer saw him use the key to unlock a box on the table; saw him pour a cup of water; saw him pick up the spoon from the table; saw him move the spoon to the box, which was now hidden by his body, then bring forth the spoon laden with powder, which he sprinkled upon the water in the Shah's cup. They saw him pick up the waiting napkin, wipe the spoon with it, and replace the spoon upon the table before relocking the box, and carrying both key and cup to his master.

The Shah accepted the key with one hand and the drink with the other, absently draining the glass.

"What did the Marshal say, again?" he called impatiently.

"He said he was going to check the sentries," murmured the officer from outside the door. "And he went up onto the dunes. That's the last anyone's seen of him."

The Shah did not speak. The minister remained bowed at his side as he gently dropped the extra spoon from his sleeve into the side pocket of his robe.

"What time was . . . that?" asked the Shah in a peculiar voice.

The Prince looked up, alertly. The minister raised his head, an expression of concern on his face.

"Well after midnight, Great One," said the officer from the doorway.

"And he . . . went . . . went . . ." said the Shah.

"Out onto the dunes, Great One," said the puzzled officer.

"Your Effulgence," cried the minister. "Are you all right?"

"All right . . . all . . . all . . ." murmured the Shah, stopping with his mouth half open.

"Great One, answer me! Are you in pain? What's the matter?"

"He seems to have stopped," said the Prince, in an interested voice as he stepped forward into the doorway. "Like a clock! What was that you gave him?"

"His morning medicine. He has taken it every morning, for years."

"P'naki?"

The minister shook his head, put his finger to his lips and said to the kneeling officer, "You're excused. The Shah is obviously unwell."

The officer scurried away as quickly as he could on all fours.

"Then it was P'naki," said the Prince, when the officer had gone. He stepped into the room.

"Oh, yes, Prince Delganor. Of course."

"Every day, hmm?"

"The merest sprinkling."

"Maybe it went bad," suggested the Prince.

The minister heard this with open-mouthed amazement. "I've never heard of it doing that, Prince Delganor."

"You also take P'naki."

"Yes, sir. But only once every . . . oh, ten years or so."

"You wouldn't mind taking some from the Shah's supply?"

"Sir! Are you suggesting . . ."

"Just the merest sprinkling, as you say. It can't hurt you."

"No, it certainly cannot," said the minister, wrathfully, as he laid his master back upon his bed and took the key from between stiffened fingers. He unlocked the box, poured a cup of water, sprinkled a spoonful of dust on the surface, and downed the drink, the whole while maintaining his expression of dignified outrage.

"Tell me about P'naki," purred the Prince.

"I can tell Your Highness nothing Your Highness does not already know," snapped the minister. "We know you want the supply increased. It cannot be increased. We have explained that. The desert grows only so much, no more." Actually, the desert would grow all the Shah could bless, but the Shah would bless only as much as he needed and was convenient. And lately they'd had trouble getting enough candidates even for that!

"But if we plant it in Bliggen?" The Prince watched him narrowly, looking for signs of incipient stalling.

The minister moved back to his Shah, smoothing back the hair, covering the supine body with a coverlet. "It would not grow in Bliggen. It grows only in the desert of Mahahm, and even there it grows to its proper purpose only with the blessing of the Shah."

"Whom, it seems, you no longer have around to do the blessing," said the Prince, joining him near the bed. He poked the body lying there and received, in response, a flicker of eyelid. "Is he still alive?"

"That is a question for the doctors, Your Highness, and we should

certainly return to the palace at once. We have no doctors here, but there are doctors in Mahahm-qum."

"Oh, by all means," murmured the Prince. "And what do we do about the Marshal?"

"He will either find his way back here, or to Mahahm-qum, or he won't. We cannot afford to spend time and effort hunting for him with the Shah in this condition."

"I agree." The Prince smiled. "We certainly can't."

"If Your Highness will permit," said the minister, bowing toward the door.

"Since it seems you did not poison the Shah, we will permit, yes," said the Prince in an uneasy voice. For the first time, he considered that there might be an end to life even with P'naki. Was P'naki then, only a long delay and not a reprieve from mortality? "If it wasn't poison, what was it? Was he very old?"

"He was, is, very old, Your Highness. Very, very old."

So was the Prince, very old, and he did not like the thoughts those words brought to his mind. He himself was about due for his next dose of P'naki. Since his own supply was probably no longer available, it would be necessary to borrow some from Ybon.

Within a short time, the expedition set out, thousands of weary men who muttered amongst themselves while throwing curious glances at the litter bearing, all too clearly, the person of the Shah. They had come a very long way for no better purpose than the chopping of a few ornamental trees, and there was muttering in the ranks as they straggled rather than marched, following the wind-blown tracks they had made coming out, paying little if any attention to the world around them.

The strange ship that hovered silently above the procession had to fire a glittering burst into the sand ahead of them to get their attention. The horses reared, the harpta bellowed, the army milled about, and the twenty-member crew of the ship took them all captive in a matter of moments by virtue of superior weapons. The announcement that the world of Haven had been conquered by an off-world power came to the Mahahmbi, and to Prince Delganor, as a total and most unwelcome surprise.

A worse surprise came when he and Ybon were searched and the box that had contained the Shah's P'naki was found to be empty.

"It contained foot powder," said Ybon, when their captors questioned the empty box. "My horse reared and it was spilled when we were taken prisoner."

*　　*　　*

Aufors was kept waiting by the Aresians all the following day. In late afternoon, he was taken by a Captain Dunnel of the Tracker's Team, to meet again with Terceth Ygdaleson.

Terceth smiled grimly at him. "There's a so-called Prince Delganor with the Mahahmbi army."

Aufors looked up, questioningly.

"We've captured the army, all of it. And the Prince is looking for someone about your size."

Aufors shrugged. "Many men my size."

"True. Tell me, if we wanted to know something about Mahahm, would it do any good to ask Mahahmbi women?"

Aufors shook his head. "Mahahmbi women don't know anything. Mahahmbi don't even talk to women."

Terceth exchanged an exasperated look with his officer.

Dunnel offered, "This man isn't likely to be the man the Prince mentioned, Sir. He's the right size and general description, all right, but the one the Prince mentioned was upper-mid-caste from Havenor, wasn't he? This one is just like all the other malghaste we've picked up."

Terceth smiled, eyes fixed on Aufors. "By which you mean dirty and stupid, Dunnel? Dirtiness is a condition, not an attribute, and stupidity can be a strategy. You're probably right, but we'll hang on to him, nonetheless. You can let the woman, the boy, and the infant go. Let this one have his belongings, except for his weapon, but keep him until I can have the Prince take a look at him."

The officer took Aufors to the room where Awhero was, and as he packed his few belongings he whispered a few quick words.

"They're not letting me go, but they are freeing you and the boy. I'll have to think of some other way to get loose." Putting his hand to the back of his head, he winced, closing his eyes. The wound there was puffed and angry, probably infected. "Awhero, take my son to Galul. Promise."

"Of course," she said, giving him an anxious look. "I will do it, Aufors Leys. That wound needs attention."

"I'll attend to it when I figure out how to get away."

Since the few captive Mahahmbi refused to have a malghaste imprisoned among them, Aufors was taken out onto the sands and chained to a metal ring set in the side of a hastily erected sentry hut. Something about the site bothered him. He was not far outside the malghaste gate through which he had entered the city. He stared at the gate and at the desert for some time before realizing that the much-guarded building he

had seen through his glasses was gone. No, certainly not gone, though as certainly invisible. A great flow of sand had covered it.

Until this moment, he had assumed that the building would have been discovered by the Aresians, who would therefore also have discovered at least a few hardened Old Friends. Some of them must have accumulated over the years. Since they had not found P'naki in the palace, it stood to reason the Shah must have kept the stuff in the guarded building. If the building had been covered at the first alarm, however, then the Aresians had neither found the store of P'naki, nor had they seen what happened to Old Friends.

Aufors was not positive what had been given to the Old Friends, but he had a hunch he had some of it in his breast pocket: the lichen he had allowed to eat his own, male blood during his hike across the desert to Mahahm-qum. Though the guards had patted him down, the packet of lichen powder was so thin they had not felt it.

The sentries changed their post in early evening. Obrang, the same soldier who had beaten Aufors over the head previously was the one assigned to the post where he was chained. Aufors showed no recognition. In the evening, both he and the guard were provided with a meal. The guard gave Aufors a sneering look while taking half of Aufors's ration to add to his own. He ate greedily, with much lip smacking aimed in Aufors's direction, then began gaping almost as soon as the meal was over, his normally torpid wits damped further by too hearty a meal.

Interrupting Obrang's yawn, Aufors said softly, as though talking to himself, "My woman is in south. I would give much to rejoin my woman, my children."

The guard stopped gaping and grinned. "Yeah. And what *much* might you have to give, shit-toter?"

"Everyone here is looking for long-life stuff, very rare, very valuable. I have some. I would give that."

The guard's grin vanished. He came nearer Aufors and knelt down. "Yeah? And where would that be?"

"Not here. I will show where, if you let me go."

The guard stared at him for a moment, his dull wits struggling with the dimly recognized possibilities.

"I can search you," blustered the guard.

"I don't have it here. But close."

"Tell you what," the guard said after some time had passed. "I put a shackle on you. I lock the other end to me. You take me to the place, if the stuff is there, I let you go."

"You have to use it right away," murmured Aufors. "It's already more'n two days old, and it's only good for three days. I had more, but your commander took it."

Obrang's eyes swiveled. "The Prince? Terceth? Him?"

Aufors nodded.

The guard dithered. Terceth was known to be a good deal smarter than the average Aresian. Besides, he was the Chieftain's son. Keeping his voice affable with some difficulty, Obrang said, "All right. You show me where."

"Bring water," murmured Aufors. "You have to use it right away."

The guard fetched his water bottle, giving Aufors a chance to take the packet from his pocket and hide it up his sleeve. The guard shackled Aufors to him, pocketing the key, and they moved away from the guard post to the nearest dune that hid them from the city. There Aufors pretended to look for landmarks, finally settling on a dead bonebush, where he fell on his knees and dug into the sand at its root to come up with the packet.

The guard tried to snatch it, but Aufors turned away.

"I'm not fightin' over it," said the guard, with an evil grin. "We go back and I lock you to your post again. Then I'll just take it."

"You try, I yell," said Aufors. "Guards come running. They'll take that away from you. This is too valuable for me to give for nothing. You let me go first."

The guard took a moment to arrive at a conclusion in which Dunnel and General Terceth both figured prominently. "All right," he said with false geniality. "But I'll use it first, then I'll unlock you."

"Pour water into cup," said Aufors, waiting until the guard had complied to lean forward and sprinkle half the powder.

Obrang sniffed it, then gulped it down, grinned his evil grin, and started to move away.

"Be still," said Aufors. "You have to be still for minute, let it work. Otherwise no good."

The guard sat, staring ominously at Aufors and jingling the chain between them like a threat. Aufors hummed in time to the jingling. First an impatient quick time march. *Chink chink chink chink.* Then an adagio: *chinkle . . . chinkle . . .* Then a dirge: *clunk . . .* silence *. . . clunk . . .* silence *. . .*

Aufors leaned forward and took the key from the guard's pocket. The guard's eyes followed him, though slowly. Aufors unlocked and removed the shackles and replaced the key. He took the guard's weapon, then took

both cup and bottle back to the guard post where he rinsed the cup, then emptied Obrang's water into his own water bottle before replacing the guard's cup and locking one end of the shackle to the hut.

Darkness was falling as he walked away from the city, feeling, so he told himself, perfectly all right, though he staggered as he walked. The night winds wiped out his wavering footprints as he went, a single intention in his addled mind: somehow to get back to his boat, and then . . . then . . . find Genevieve.

Deep in the caverns beneath Havenor, beings had awakened. Some were small and some large. All were what the malghaste might once have defined as harbingers of their respective worlds; all were from worlds no longer living. It was not chance that had brought them to Haven, any more than it had been chance that brought them to these protecting caverns. Vast and wondrous spirits had chosen that the harbingers come here, to await their future in a place better suited to their needs. They had come to a refuge in chrysalises of fiber and metal made by men, the chrysalises had been broken, and now was time to leave this dark place and move on.

The beings left their cartons and moved into the dusty aisles, noses smelling, eyes seeing, tongues tasting the air. Their senses led them to the food nearby, purchased long ago and stored for their eventual benefit. Latigern and betivor, chamaris and thalliar, bruk and bralt, they among a hundred others wakened and fed and turned unfalteringly toward a desired exit, one southward under the mountains, one that led far from this place but much nearer the place they would go.

Swift as the sailing moon they went, hoofed and taloned, many-legged and legless, winged and finned, armored or furred or feathered, the larger carrying the smaller, away down dusty aisles, past towers of treasured artifacts and precipices of coveted devices, all, all fallen into ruin.

In a far nook, curled like a worm in a nut, lay the Lord Paramount. He had sucked up all but a tiny bit of the P'naki he had brought with him from the elevator, more than he had ever had all at once before, and he had been thinking about finding his way back to his elevator to fetch some more. As the creatures went by, their wild flight made him lose track of these thoughts, and he sat up to watch. There were his pets, his lovely zoo, his curiosities, his specimens, his amusements, his possessions. There they were, moving, running, going past. He lifted one little hand to wave. Byedy-bye to all that marvel, byedy-bye to all that wonder, byedy-bye, see them go, all gone. He began to hum to himself, a buzzing

little hum, like a sleepy bee, musing over all those lovely creatures. Though he could not remember ordering some of them, surely he had. And quite right. They belonged here. He was quite certain they belonged here.

The creatures saw him as they passed, though they disregarded him as a function now obsolete, an actor whose sole act was done. They went from his view into tunnels no man had ever traveled, where they fled past underground rivers, slaking their thirst on dark waters that had never seen the sun. In time, sooner than anyone on the planet would have considered possible, they emerged from the seacliffs south of Bliggen, west of Frangia, near the Stone Trail. The separating seas meant nothing to them. Those who could not swim would be carried by those who could, and creatures of this world were already coming from the sea to offer assistance.

However they chose to go, they would end on Mahahm, Mahahm, which had been meant for them, from the time the first one of them was stricken down by the weapons of mankind.

The seven supply sleds were driven by Joncaster, Enid, and Melanie, plus three men from the marae: Jorub, Etain and Gilber; and one woman, Ithil. Genevieve was the only passenger as they worked their way slowly southwest, stopping each night at one of the refuges and moving on each morning. When the refuges had been resupplied, the sleds would go on to Galul for safekeeping. They were too hard come by to leave behind.

They left the marae in the early morning of the sixth day after Genevieve had fled from Mahahm-qum, spending all that day and the two following along tortuous trails. Each morning they started well before sunrise and stopped at some shaded place midmorning for food and rest while the sun was at its zenith. During these stops, Genevieve usually fell asleep, for though she felt exhausted by the end of each day, she lay half awake in the night silences, haunted by sounds and visions that seemed always to stay just beyond her understanding.

So, this morning, when she fell into a doze, the others moved around her quietly, letting her sleep, only to be startled half out of their wits as she sat up suddenly and screamed. It was an enormous cry, one that went out of her like a visible thing, like a great wing of sound, reverberating among the rocky cliffs, propagating as it soared over the desert, going away among its own echoes still sounding, plangent as an enormous bell.

This was followed by a profound hush, during which her companions scarcely breathed. Thus, silenced within silence, they heard from afar an answering sound, lower, and yet alike, a sound that did not diminish but went on and on, like the endless vibrations of a tuning fork.

Genevieve staggered to her feet in one panicky motion, and the others shook off their immobility and surrounded her, as she glared with wide eyes into the cliff face that sheltered them as though it were a door into some other world.

"I see," she cried. "Oh, I see."

"What," urged Joncaster, coming to place his hand on her shoulder. "What do you see?"

"They said call upon them on the sea," she whispered, eyes focused on something they could not see. "We must get to the sea. There is a place by the shore where a pillar of stone rests on a black pedestal. I see a great stone serpent, a horned serpent . . ."

"We know the place," said Gilber. "It marks on offshore deep . . ."

"A ship is coming there."

"What . . . Who . . . told you?" asked Melanie.

Genevieve laughed, almost hysterically. "Your spirit, I suppose. The one you're so determined to convince me of!"

"Te wairua taiao?"

"The one you say you've never seen." She put her head in her hands, shuddering. "Oh, Aufors, Aufors . . . Please, someone, help him! He's . . . he's wounded. He's sick. He needs help."

"Where?" cried Joncaster. "How?"

"I see a red cliff with a black layer in it, like a wide stripe. I see him moving . . . moving bodies. Moving women's bodies away from the lichen, so they won't be found there. He is wounded, the wound is infected. He's delirious. I don't know if he lives . . . ah, Aufors . . . I see a red cliff and I see rocks covered with birds, along the shore . . ."

"You've seen three separate places," muttered Joncaster.

"Aufors at the red cliff or the bird rocks," Genevieve cried. "The serpent rock is something else . . ."

"We'll empty two sleds at the refuge tonight," offered Enid, "and send one to the bird rocks and one to red cliff . . ."

"No," said Joncaster. "We've seen proof of her visions already, Enid. We've seen that delay is a mistake. We've already reduced the loads by half, so we'll unload two of them onto the other five. If her man is there and wounded, best we find him while he's still alive."

"Wait, wait, wait," Genevieve muttered. "Take care. Oh, Joncaster, *that's* why Aufors was moving bodies! I said they would come! They *have* come! The Aresians! Mahahm-qum is taken. Havenor is taken. The Lord Paramount, oh, see him go down, down. Oh, now he lies deep, deep in the tunnels below Havenor. The Shah is no more. Oh . . ." She put her hands

to her head, her eyes wide, unseeing. "More. Animals? From below Havenor? I told Veswees . . . it wasn't supposed to be animals . . ."

"What do you mean, wasn't supposed?"

"I'd seen something else moving from Havenor. No matter, no matter, it will have to wait. My father. He's up there behind us, following us. He has murder in his eyes. There is danger . . ."

"What else?" murmured Melanie, with a shocked look at the others.

She started to speak, started to scream, then held it in, clamped down upon it. "Nothing," she murmured. "Nothing. Only the sea, the waves of the sea, the surf breaking on the serpent rock. You must bring Aufors there . . ."

Joncaster shared a look with Melanie, half awe, half skepticism. "You've seen enough to keep us all busy, Genevieve," he said at last. "The rest of you head for the standing stone. Jorub and I know where both the other places are."

They began to bustle, unloading and reloading the sleds, while Genevieve sat with her head down, concentrating. The last of the dream. After she had seen the serpent rock. She was there with Aufors and the baby. Someone . . . someone was threatening her. Someone said, "Genevieve knows, she's such a clever, clever girl . . ." and then someone else pursued her, and she climbed onto that horned rock, with Dovidi. Oh, Dovidi. She climbed that rock, carrying the baby and then . . . then . . .

She looked up, shuddering.

Joncaster put his hand upon her shoulder. "What is it, Genevieve? Something else we should know?"

Her eyes focused and she took control of herself. She would not speak of the stone. Not yet. "My father wants to kill you, and then he will give me to the Prince."

"Gilber can circle behind your father to keep him off you. Jorub will go to the bird rocks, and I'm taking Etain with me," said Joncaster, nodding toward the men from the marae. "If your husband is at red cliff, he's still near where the bodies are, and if he hasn't moved them all, perhaps we can finish the job. The Aresians mustn't find out what they're there for . . ."

"I'll circle out behind your father," said Gilber. "You're sure he's out there alone."

"Yes," said Genevieve, positively, almost pityingly. "He's always been alone."

From a rocky height some distance to the west, the Marshal peered down at a straggling and almost invisible track leading toward the rocky

wilderness along the coast. He had followed the track all day, even catching recurrent glimpses of the travelers. Once he had seen a line of sleds sliding over the top of a dune and had counted the people on them: seven drivers, plus one.

The one was surely Genevieve. He had not believed she had gone elsewhere, no matter what Y'bon Saelan had said. Genevieve had inherited her mother's unwarranted cleverness, her mother's ability to gather information she should not have any inkling of and put it together to draw a conclusion that was always and infuriatingly correct. Women were quite bad enough when they were as stupid as they were expected to be. When they were intelligent, perceptive, when they saw through each courteous evasion to the facts one would prefer not to discuss . . .

Why should a man be labeled a monster by laying his motives out in that way when a few harmless evasions would allow his reputation to be unstained and his family to be comfortable? Genevieve's mother could not have been comfortable in paradise! The questions she used to ask! The way she worried at things! The answers she came up with! She had probably known all about P'naki years before he did. He was certain of it. He remembered her looking at him almost pityingly, with those strange, all seeing eyes. . . .

The previous afternoon, when he had sneaked close to the ones he was following, downwind of them, he had heard his wife's voice, coming over the sands. He had actually looked up, expecting to see her, before realizing it was not wife but daughter he heard. Genevieve was like her, so like her, with that same voice, that same cleverness. Oh, depend upon it. She knew! She knew all about it.

Women were not supposed to know the truth! They had their youth, their comforts, their purity of soul to guarantee them an eternity fluttering like butterflies among the flowers of paradise. So the Invigilator had said. Being butterflies wasn't an immortality a man would want, but no doubt it served for women. Thank heaven Genevieve's mother had died. Knowing what he knew now . . . he was glad she had died.

And what a fool he had been not to have known sooner! Of course, his own father had died young, in battle, while he, the Marshal, was only a boy. There were no other male relatives. So, it had been left to Rongor, though the fool had given him as much misinformation as fact! Rongor had intimated the Prince was in charge of the P'naki matter. Perhaps Rongor had merely inferred this from the Prince's lordly manner, but in any case, he had been mistaken. It was the Shah who controlled P'naki, and the Shah had no high regard for the Prince. Idiot Rongor, who had

worshipped the Prince and who had not known the truth until it was too late. . . .

And he, himself! He had tried to expedite the delivery of his daughter into the hands of the Mahahmbi! He had left the doors open, so they could come in and get her, and he had gone to the palace to announce that fact. Instead of being congratulated for solicitous behavior, he had been taken prisoner and his guards had been slain before his eyes. Even then, perhaps, things could have been differently managed if he had known the Shah's true feelings.

"What does this mean?" he had asked, when the Prince and Rongor had involuntarily joined him in the palace guest suite.

"A momentary hitch," the Prince had said, loftily. "The Shah is merely making a point. When he is finished making it, all will be well."

"Then there is no danger?"

"I am in no danger, Marshal. Don't concern yourself. I have seen these little fits before."

Well, the Prince had been in no danger, that much was true, though the Marshal had foolishly allowed himself to be misled by that fact and by the Shah's soft words. The Shah had referred to them as his "guests." The Shah had spoken regretfully about the "misunderstanding" with those on the ship. The Marshal had been lulled.

His comfort had ended that night when the three of them were summoned onto the desert by the Shah's minister—to admire a comet, so the minister said. There had been no comet, though they had stood awhile in a patch of blood lichen, looking upward at starry heavens. While they were thus distracted, the Shah's men had surrounded Rongor and cut him down. He, the Marshal, would have moved to defend the Invigilator had not the Prince held fast to his arm. The Prince's face had remained impassive. He had not even looked at the Marshal as he held him fast.

So were the Shah's true feelings and power made clear. So was the Prince's subordinate position illustrated. So was the Marshal's danger made manifest. While they watched, the Invigilator's dry-sucked head had been put on a stake in the center of the lichen. A warning, said Ybon Saelan, in a loud clear voice, a warning that this place was unblessed by the Shah, *and there could be no P'naki without the blessing of the Shah.*

Meantime, the Shah himself had smiled and smiled, at the Prince, at the Marshal, at the others there, letting them all know that P'naki belonged to the Shah, only the Shah, and they had best not try to interfere again.

After that, they had stayed penned in the palace during the so called holy days and while the people of Mahahm-qum prepared for war. Day

on day they had sat in the Shah's throne room, eaten at the Shah's table, and observed the Shah's growing irrationality, his putrefying resentment, his erratic malevolence. It was obvious the Shah was teetering on the edge of sanity and standing too near him was to woo death.

While matters were in such flux in Mahahm, the Marshal felt it made good sense for him to be out of reach. It was not quite honorable of him to have left the Prince, true, but since he had learned how much additional life Genevieve's blood would buy him, honor had seemed less important. He wanted those extra years. He had earned them. He deserved them. And he would return Genevieve to Mahahm-qum to be a candidate for the Prince!

On the eastern side of the Stone Trail, the Frangian ships were plowing steadily southward, toward their enclave on the continent of Mahahm. The Lord Paramount's airship had been spotted earlier that day, the Lord Paramount's message had been delivered, and the airship had reinflated itself and flown away northward. Now they had the next duty to perform, which did not trouble them. Being Frangian, nothing troubled them much.

Therefore, there was some wonder at the tone of the lookout's voice when he shouted in panicky fashion, "Yo. Sir. Something out there. Something . . ."

Those on deck followed the direction of the lookout's flailing arm, seeking along the line of islands for whatever it was that had caused such consternation. At first they saw nothing, but then . . . well, they saw a something. A very large something protruding from behind one of the rocky islets, something vaguely goldish in color and enormous in size and roundish in shape, though no one could give a name to it. On the back of Whatever-it-was were other whatevers they could not identify, and above and around were other whatevers yet in the sky and in the sea. All of these things or creatures were moving south along the outer or western side of the islands, all of them silent, all of them taking no notice whatsoever of the Frangian ship.

The men turned, as was their habit, to the Captain for reassurance in their faith.

"Whatever happens," said that worthy. "Whatever is inevitable. Whatever always differs from what was. Be at peace in the Whatever. Let us offer our adoration."

When they turned to adore, however, Whatever was gone. Still, they had marked its direction. They would follow it, for it was the Frangian way always to discover whatever. The ship heeled in the brisk wind and

began a westward tack that would take them between two rocky isles and down the west coast of Mahahm.

Outside Mahahm-Qum, Terceth Ygdaleson sat in his tent with Captain Dunnel, watching a straggling caravan approach across the sands. In the lead, ahorse, were two men, a prince of Haven and a minister of Mahahm, and in a horse-drawn travois between them was the body of the Shah, a statue of his former self.

"Sir," said Dunnel. "That sounds exactly like what happened to Obrang!"

"One of their men disappeared, also, a high-ranking Havenite, the Marshal," said Terceth. "The man who disappeared here was a malghaste. So you said."

"I may have been wrong sir. The man the Prince wanted was the Marshal's son-in-law. The man we had might have been him."

"Wrong coloring, you said."

"He could have dyed his hair, sir. I should have checked at the time . . ."

"Nonsense, Dunnel. It wasn't as though you turned him loose! I said hold him, you held him, it wasn't your fault he vanished like piss in the sand. That blockhead, Obrang, was responsible if anyone, and his fate fit him like a glove. Once a blockhead, why not a blockbody as well, ah? Assume the prisoner was the one the Prince wanted. You think this is some kind of family poison? Something they all carry?"

"I don't know, sir."

"Well, it's one of many questions I'd like answered. My brothers seem to think we're going to be here a while. They've taken the capital of Haven without a fight and we've captured the entire Mahahmbi army, such as it is. Haven isn't up to much, resistance-wise, but it seems to be impenetrable where information is concerned! My brothers are now asking the common people what they know, to no avail. Eventually, Father will tire of it, and then . . . well, I'd rather not think of then.

"In the interim, I'm leaving the camp in Colonel Morfat's hands and taking you and your Trackers to see if we can find this man who vanished. Since this Prince of Haven can identify his missing man, we'll take him as well. If anyone can find him, your Trackers can."

At the foot of a high, red cliff, half-hidden behind a pillar broken from the face, Aufors lay unconscious, afire with fever and entranced in dream. He was searching the desert for women's bodies, finding them everywhere. Each one had to be pulled a long way away from the bed of squirming snakes it lay upon. He struggled up the dunes, tugging the mummified corpses after him, the wind drying his eyes, the sun crisping his skin, himself burning, burning with the job not yet done. Worst of all, the bodies spoke to him.

"Galul," they whispered. "We were promised Galul. Be resigned, they said, until you are grown. Then you will go to Galul. Be resigned, they said, until you are married. Then, then you will go to Galul. Oh, be resigned, for when you have children, then, oh, then you will go to Galul."

"Galul," they whispered, "where we may lie bare-skinned in the soft surf and make castles in the sand. Galul, where we may speak aloud. Galul, where we may dance among the flowers . . ."

He told them that Galul was only over the next dune, but still they would not let him rest. No matter what direction he took, there they lay, speaking to him.

"I wanted to leave the old man and go to heaven."

"They gave me to him when I was only ten, when I was only a child."

"I was the fourth wife of the Duke of Highland. He was an old, old man, long past the ways of love. He left me alone with a young guardsman, who said he loved me. When I was with child, the guardsman went away, and my husband sent me here . . ."

"My child, my child! Here by my side. Is he alive? Take him, save him! Oh, please, take my child . . ."

They spoke in his mind, they disputed with one another, they were angry at themselves, they boiled with disappointment, their heat charred him, turned him into ashes . . .

"He's burning up," said a voice.

"Look at that wound on his head. It's puffed up like a melon. I've brought the all-heal. Here, hold his arm . . ."

He didn't even feel the pinprick though he gulped thirstily at the water they gave him. He couldn't hear their voices over the voices in his head.

"You don't understand," he told the shadow women. "They planned to kill you all along. It's your blood that makes the lichen work. The blood of nursing mothers. If men bleed on it, it becomes something else. It turns people to wood."

Etain said, "Listen to him. He says if a man bleeds on the lichen, it becomes something else. Could that be true?"

Joncaster felt Aufors's head, playing the words over in his head. "Look at his hands. They're covered with cuts. He's been cutting himself, so it looks like he believes it's true."

"Wouldn't we have heard of that if it were true?"

"The lichen's been tapu for us for a long time, Etain. We haven't even gone near it. But for him . . ."

"Would bleeding on it be tapu for us?"

"I don't see how. Scout around. See if you can find a patch of lichen close by."

Etain departed. Joncaster settled Aufors more comfortably in the shade. He had heated water, applied an herbal compress to the wound on Aufors's head, and was readying a replacement before Etain returned, sliding down a dune in an avalanche of sand.

"There's a patch just over there. He'd moved two bodies. There were still four of them there. I moved them. Then I bled a little on the lichen, just to see. It went crazy. More than when the women are killed on it."

"How much blood?"

"Only a little, Joncaster. Really. I've bled more shaving!"

"How many patches are there, close around here?"

"The Mahahmbi did fifteen, last holy days."

"He couldn't have happened upon more than three or four of them if he aimed for the sea. If this . . . if this works, we ought to do it everywhere, now! Before the Aresians find the women's bodies and put two and two together."

"Aresians," cried Aufors, becoming agitated. "They want to know about P'naki. Don't let them find out about P'naki."

Joncaster muttered soothingly to him, then turned to Jorub. "You brought a couple of birds didn't you? What's home for them."

"Refuges Four and Six."

"Melanie should get to Six by tonight. Give the birds enough water to get them through a day's flight." Joncaster busied himself with paper and marker: *Aufors found, important to move bodies, put drops of male blood on lichen.* He rolled the messages into the slender quills the birds were trained to carry. Meantime the birds drank, cooing softly between themselves. Then they were aloft, headed southward.

Joncaster muttered, "If Melanie gets the message and they work through the night, they can get most of the bodies moved."

"We could do some of them ourselves, the nearest ones."

"This man should rest, but I hate to leave him alone. She said he had to go to the standing stone."

"You believe her?"

Joncaster stared at the sky. "She doesn't . . . she doesn't share our beliefs, but that doesn't mean she's wrong. You heard that sound she made."

"Like *it*."

"Right. We have lots of singers in Galul, but I never heard one of them make a sound like that. And it was answered."

"It could have been an echo."

"It wasn't an echo. That was real. That was *it* speaking."

"Have you ever seen it?"

"Never. But . . . I wouldn't be surprised to learn she has."

"I'll go for a while, do what I can, then come back," offered Etain.

Joncaster nodded. "Go. But take care. We don't know what kinds of equipment the Aresians have. They may have detectors, so be cautious."

Etain saluted, took up his water bottle and a packet of food, threw himself upon the sled and slithered it around the base of a dune, heading inland. Joncaster replaced the compress, then applied another when it cooled. Gradually the crustiness of the wound was softening, and when he changed the compress for the fourth time, the evil matter inside the wound began to flow out. Joncaster cleaned it away, looked at his time-piece, and readied a second injection.

The sun slipped behind the dune to the west, leaving them in deep shade. Though the temperature did not drop significantly, and would not until night came, the absence of the sun's glare made matters more bearable. Aufors stirred. "Who?" he asked.

"A friend," said Joncaster. "A friend of Genevieve's, as well."

"Is she . . . is she . . ."

"She's well. Tired, but well. As soon as we can get your fever down, we'll take you to her."

"Aresian guard hit me," Aufors said clearly. "No reason for it, just stupidity. His officer read him off. I should have asked for something to treat it with. It didn't seem that bad."

"Can you tell me about the lichen?" murmured Joncaster.

Aufors eyes flew open, full of awareness. "Who are you?"

"I said, a friend of Genevieve's."

Aufors's eyes closed. He was silent.

Right, Joncaster thought. And how does one prove one is a friend of Genevieve's?

"Do you know about Awhero?" Joncaster murmured. "I also know Awhero. And your son's name is Dovidi."

Aufors's eyes opened halfway, a mere slit. "You could have found out names in many ways. You could be Aresian."

"All right," Joncaster said, shaking his head. "Go back to sleep. I've sent Etain to bleed on as many patches of lichen as he can find. I hope that's what you think is best."

Stubbornly, Aufors did not reply.

South along the shore from the red cliff, a stony stretch of coast was known to the malghaste as "the bird rocks." A submarine trench that reached deeply into the planet's crust lay just off shore, and the rising water was alive with food for the nesting birds. No matter the season, the wave-splashed stones were white with waterfowl or their droppings, and their cries could be heard for miles inland.

Awhero and the boy had come to the rocks along a narrow strip of beach that wound among the stones. They had arrived at a cavern on the sea where a freshwater spring dripped into a deep crevasse far back, out of sight of the shore. This cool, moist retreat was well known to the malghaste.

"Thank wairua taiao for bit of rest," said Awhero. She untied her shawl and unwrapped a fretful Dovidi who began to wail. She spread her blanket beside the pool outlet and settled herself and the child upon it. Poor thing, he was prickly from the heat and fretful as well. She lowered his naked, reddened body onto the sand at the edge of the deep pool and ladled water over it while the fretful whimpering turned into chuckled sounds of enjoyment. Good enough.

Kamakama was lying full length upon the sand, his face submerged in the water. Now he pulled up his head with a great spuming and blowing. He cried, "Oh, kuia, that's good."

"Soon you'll be in Galul, boy. You can put your whole body into water there. There's lakes to swim in."

"I'd like that. Is swimming hard?"

"Is walking hard? Everything is when you start out, getting easier as you go."

"Except life," said the boy in a grim voice. "It starts out hard then just gets harder the more we go on."

"There is that," she agreed. "We didn't count on these Aresians. I hope we got enough bodies moved . . ."

"We got the ones south of Qum. They were the closest ones."

"All we could do with this child along." She lifted the baby from the water, patted him dry, and laid him on the blanket, where he promptly put his thumb in his mouth and closed his eyes.

"Well, he's gone quick enough," the boy said.

"He's slept hardly at all on way," she answered. "He's tired out. And so are we, but watch should be kept. You rest, boy. I'm too jumpy to sleep yet."

Kamakama stretched out on the blanket next to the sleeping baby and let himself relax, wriggling his hips and shoulders into the sand while Awhero took her pack to the cave entrance and arranged it to make a backrest. From this vantage point she could see north and south along the coast, though her view inland was blocked by the ridges stair-stepping upward above the cavern. From this point south, the seacliffs blocked all passages from the sea, at least any that were visible from the shore.

The entrance to the cave was well hidden. The state of constant vigilance they'd been in for the last four days meant she and the boy had slept little better than Dovidi. She leaned back her head and shut her eyes. Just for moment, she told herself. Not long. Just . . . moment.

And she woke to an erratic sound, like a disturbed bee or hornet, caught in some cul-de-sac. A whiny noise. Like a malfunctioning sandsled . . .

She moved slowly, carefully to the entrance, standing in the shadow. There it was, down on the shore path, with the tide moving in. And there was . . . well, Jorub! Now what the devil was he doing out here? She stepped into the clear, put her hands to her mouth and called through them, "Hai-eee."

He couldn't hear her over the sound his engine was making. It went on whining, then suddenly stopped. She put her hands up and called again. This time he looked up. She waved. He got off the sled and kicked it petulantly.

Shaking her head, Awhero went down among the rocks. "You got water in intake, didn't you?"

"I don't usually come this way, to or from," he said. "I was looking for Aufors Leys. Is he with you?"

"Looking here?"

"The woman, Genevieve, she saw the bird rocks and the red cliffs and her man was supposed to be at one or the other."

"Well, then he's at other. She saw this place because her child is here."

He shrugged. "So, I've wasted a little fuel."

"Not a drop was wasted, and I'm mightily glad you came. We could use little faster travel, which we won't have if we don't get this sled up out of wet."

Together they dragged it along a sloping shingle, halfway up the shore path, out of the reach of the tide, while Jorub shared his news of Genevieve and the Marshal and Joncaster, gone to find Aufors Leys. "We'll meet at the standing stone," he concluded.

"Te marae's empty, is it?" Awhero asked.

"We shut it down before the Shah got there. We've been making a supply run since, and we were at the canyon house when Genevieve got the galloping visions . . ."

"I heard someone . . . something call," Awhero offered, tentatively.

"You and the rest of the world," muttered Jorub. "I thought those shouters in Mahahm Qum were loud. She let out a bellow like I've never heard."

"I also heard . . . answer."

He mumbled, looking over his shoulder, "So did Melanie. She says. Well, so did I. It could have been an echo."

"Ah. I can see why you'd rather think so. You can take us to meeting place?"

"If the sled'll run, sure. I came out here to rescue whoever, and I guess you're as whoever as the next one."

"We may as well have little rest, while sled dries out."

They climbed the slope to the cave entrance, slipping into the entrance hidden in the shadow between two stones.

"Who's that?" demanded Jorub.

"Kamakama. Boy I rescued years ago. He's been in city with our contingent." She took off her hastily snatched up shawl and resumed her seat at the entrance.

"I thought you said you had a baby with you?"

"There, lying next to . . ." She rose, eyes wide. There was no Dovidi

next to Kamakama. She ran to the blanket, knelt down upon it, searched the cavern with her eyes. Jorub came up behind her with his light, shining it into crevices. A slight disturbance of the water caught their eyes. There the baby was, deep in the pool, floating facedown, motionless.

"Oh, by heaven," cried Awhero.

"I'll get him," said Jorub, throwing off his robes and diving into the water. As he thrashed toward the child, some errant eddy took the small body and turned it, moved it away. The little feet flipped, the little arms paddled, up he came while his would-be rescuer plunged about below, searching for him.

Jorub rose, spewing water, to see Awhero holding the child and shaking as though she had just taken death by the hand.

Jorub climbed out, panting. "How did you get hold of him?"

"He . . . he washed up toward me," she said, holding the baby tightly. "When you jumped in, it must have made current."

Dovidi made a little crowing sound, half question, half joy.

"He's none the worse for it," said Jorub.

"No," she murmured, drying the baby's neck and shoulders. "No. I guess he . . . held his breath. Instinctive, you know."

"He was asleep next to me when I lay down," said Kamakama. "I never felt him move."

"In future, we'll keep him away from water," said Awhero, with a tremulous smile. "Unless we're with him. And awake."

Jorub settled onto the blanket. "Genevieve said the Aresians had come. Is that true?"

"It is true, my boy; they came with vengeance. Kamakama and I were afraid they'd find bodies out on sands, so we moved all we came upon."

"There were sixty-eight, last holy days."

"We moved twelve. Maybe Joncaster did, too."

"It wouldn't be good if Aresians found out, would it?"

She said, "Hand me that pack, boy. The baby's milk is in it." Then, after a few moments she answered him. "No. It wouldn't be good if Aresians found out."

The messenger bird arrived at Refuge Six shortly after Melanie and her group arrived there. They immediately unloaded four of the five sleds and sent them away, Enid and Ithil driving two of them, and two men from the shelter the other two, leaving Melanie to escort Genevieve on to the standing stone.

"We've been days on this trip," said Genevieve. "How can they get back there tonight?"

"We've been days," Melanie replied, "because we've gone slowly, the long way, not wanting to waste fuel. This matter is worth the waste of fuel. Come morning, you and I will head for the standing stone while Enid and Ithil go past Refuge Five and the other two sleds take the high route to Four. Each sled will pick up a man to help with the work."

"Heavy, horrible work," cried Genevieve.

"Horrible perhaps, but not heavy. The bodies will be mere husks, dried leaves. The business about bleeding on the lichen is probably unpleasant, but Joncaster says to give it only a taste. That's why we'll have men on every sled."

"You've decided it isn't tapu to bleed on it?"

"We're not killing it or using it. Those would be tapu. Is this tapu? I don't see why it would be."

Genevieve stared at her hands, clenched to prevent the spasmodic, purposeless movement they seemed determined to make. "It seems impossible that the lichen would have such a different effect just from the hormonal content of the blood! If that's what it is."

"It could equally well be something in the DNA," said Melanie, taking Genevieve's hands and uncurling them, stroking them quiet. "It could be that any women's blood does the trick, and the nursing-mother bit is pure superstition."

"Or, perhaps, the two states of being are different only in degree," said Genevieve. "And the ones who turn to wood are still alive. Certainly Prince Delganor seemed wooden enough to me! I wonder how Aufors found out?"

"It may have been an accident. After all, he was wounded." Melanie dug her hands into Genevieve's neck and shoulders, kneading the flesh. "Joncaster is extremely good in emergencies. He will see that Aufors is properly cared for, believe me."

"It is important to take time to move the bodies," Genevieve agreed, gritting her teeth at the idea of any delay. "Isn't it?"

"Very, very important."

Two sleds, one bearing Genevieve and Melanie, one bearing Jorub with Awhero, Kamakama and the baby, arrived at the standing stone within an hour of one another. The pillar, split from the face of a black cliff, was a well-known landmark, as was the black stone serpent at its base, a tapering tail that plunged into the sea then rose and fell in a rounded hump and

rose still again in a long neck and horned head that jutted out over the deep off-shore crevasse. From a distance, it did resemble a serpent swimming out from the land, particularly when glistening with spray. Above the tumbled stone, at the base of the cliff, was a hidden cavern with a freshwater seep hole above a stone well.

When Awhero came to the cave carrying the baby, Genevieve wept with joy, clutching him to her so tightly he struggled and complained, then began nuzzling at her. This refreshed her tears.

"They gave me medicine," she said to Awhero. "To dry my milk. Oh, poor baby, I can't feed him!"

"We have food, lady," Awhero answered. "We have food, and drink here at this spring, and shelter above us."

Melanie said, "You'll feel better if you take a few moments to rest and eat something and play with your son before he forgets who his mother is!"

"Ah, Dovidi, Dovidi, would you forget your mother?" she asked the child.

"Very unlikely," muttered Awhero. "Seeing who . . . and what . . . his mother is."

Genevieve flushed and began to babble to the baby as the others set up their camp within the cavern, distributing food supplies and sleeping mats and repeatedly sprinkling the sandy floor with water to make it cooler.

Not far to the north, Joncaster eased a sled across a stretch of rocky ground. "You think we got all of them?"

"I think so," said Etain, not for the first time. "We divided up the territory pretty well."

Joncaster murmured, "Is the Colonel still unconscious?"

"He moaned a little, a way back. He's still way too hot."

They drove on, unaware of the float-craft that slipped silently along the dunes behind them, one that followed Dunnel's loping form as he unerringly spied a fan of sand expelled by an ejection valve or a carved line that curved against the wind, both evidence of a rigid skirting that had dug into the dune. Other trackers found footprints and drag marks and mummified bodies so broken and shattered it was impossible to know whether they were male or female, not that the Trackers particularly cared.

"It's probably how they bury their dead," opined Dunnel, who had allowed the hover to catch up to him while he rested a moment on the sands.

"Where's that Havenite prince? Dunganor?" asked Terceth.

"Dalgabor, sir. I have him shackled to the aft rail."

Terceth went to the aft rail where Delganor sweated in the sun. The man looked seriously unwell.

"Hot," murmured Terceth. "Would you like some water?"

"Of course I'd like some water," said the Prince, through his teeth.

Terceth poured a cup of water from a nearby canister and offered it to the Prince, who drank greedily then remained with his head down for a long moment, panting.

"You seem stressed," said Terceth.

"I am accustomed to a certain medicine which I have not had for some time. Normally, I take it every few days . . ."

"Pity," said Terceth, taking the emptied cup. "When we find your man, if we find him, we'll return to the city. Surely you have a supply there?"

The Prince grimaced. "I had a supply when we were captured. The Shah's minister was . . . carrying it for me, for safekeeping."

"Ah," said Terceth, making a mental note. "Indeed. Well, when we return, I'll inquire."

He returned to the cabin and turned the floater to follow the Tracker toward the sea and then south. A little later, they came upon him, staring out to sea.

Following his gaze they saw a ship moving southward quite close to shore, and through the glasses they could see its men were all at the far railing, peering into the distance.

"Can we get out there, Captain?" Terceth called to his pilot.

"Of course, Prince Terceth. Do you want all our men?"

"Best, yes. The crew of the vessel may not surrender peaceably."

"I'll round them up," said Dunnel, speaking rapidly into the device pinned to the shoulder of his robes.

The Frangians on the ship had been following a vision of whatever for some time. Their search images did not include a hover vehicle coming at them from behind, low over the water, and their first awareness of the Aresians came with the men who vaulted over the rail. There was only momentary confusion, and the Frangians' immediate surrender did nothing to contradict the Aresian's impression of Havenite spinelessness.

"Now where were you going?" Terceth inquired of the man identified as the Captain.

"Well," said he, trying to focus on this new whatever when the former whatever was still very much on his mind, "we were going to Mahahm, to pick up P'naki for the Lord Paramount of Haven. But then we saw a wonderful whatever, so we set off to pursue that . . ."

"P'naki?" asked Terceth. "And what's that?"

"It's a medicine, to prevent batfly fever."

"And where does Mahahm get it?"

"Why as to that, sir, I don't know."

"So you're following this creature, eh? You wouldn't object if we came with you?" said Terceth.

"But, sir . . ." said the head Tracker.

"Peace, Dunnel. I've nothing else to do at the moment. The ship is headed the same way we are. Why not enjoy a sea voyage while they search for this wonder. Perhaps we will come upon the man we are seeking. . . ."

In the cave at the standing stone, Genevieve lay asleep by the pool, Dovidi beside her. Awhero, Melanie, Kamakama, and Jorub had disassembled the drive mechanism of Jorub's sled and were painstakingly cleaning out the sand it had gulped at the previous halt.

"I suppose we should wait for Joncaster and them," said Jorub. "Though we could just leave a message."

"She won't go," said Awhero, in a low voice. "Look at her. Smiling in her sleep. First time since she left Mahahm-qum, probably."

"She knows he's safe," argued Melanie.

"Knowing isn't having," said Kamakama. "He'll be needing her, too, when he comes."

"Wise head on young shoulders," remarked Awhero, with approval.

"Soon to be lopped off," said a cold voice.

They were aware too late, for the Marshal was already in the entrance to the cave, pointing a complicated weapon at them and obviously ready to use it at the first movement. "Wake her," he snarled at Awhero. "Bring her and the child over here. The rest of you, sit against the wall."

Reluctantly, Awhero rose to her feet and stepped to the blanket where Genevieve and the baby slept. As Awhero knelt down, she saw that Genevieve's eyes were already open, peering deeply into Awhero's with complete awareness.

"I'm coming," she murmured, rolling over to gather Dovidi to her in one smooth movement that brought her to her feet. "Good day, Father," she said in a casual voice. "I am relieved to see you well. We had heard the Shah was creating much havoc, and we feared you might be caught up in it."

"And your fear for me set you running as far away as possible," he sneered.

"No," she said. "My fear for Dovidi did that. Particularly as you were already with the Shah by the time we knew anything about the furor."

"A dutiful daughter would have inquired from the Shah as to my safety."

"You ordered me not to concern myself with your safety, Father. Don't you recall? Besides, even a dutiful daughter would have had difficulty doing anything else, since the house and the ship were under attack by a mob."

"How did you get out?" he demanded, waving his weapon at her and at Awhero, who went to join Jorub and Kamakama against the wall.

Genevieve leaned down to pick up the baby's blanket. "I had watched the malghaste leaving the house, and I went out by their route."

"Well, it is time to return. The Prince has need of you."

Genevieve joined the others against the wall and sank down next to Melanie, resting her back against the stone as she cradled the child. "The Prince has a need to slaughter nursing mothers," she said. "Have you seen them do it, Father? Have you seen the great, strong, proud men cut women's throats on the desert? How unfortunate that my separation from Dovidi has dried my milk. I can no longer provide years of extra life for the Prince."

The Marshal turned pale, then furiously red, as though he had been drained then refilled to overflowing, eyes swollen with fury. "You are what?"

She merely looked at him, unspeaking. He had heard her. He might kill her now, she supposed, which she would prefer to having her throat slit on the desert. If he was as furious as his face, he would probably kill them all.

"We gave her medicine to dry her milk," said Melanie. "It was the only sensible thing to do."

The Marshal growled, and Awhero made a tiny motion, pressing her hand against Genevieve's thigh. She rolled her eyes toward the entrance, just enough for Genevieve to see. Gilber was just outside. As the Marshal turned to look around him, Gilber slipped out of sight. The Marshal focused on his captives once more.

"I am to be elevated," he muttered in Genevieve's direction, chewing his cheek as though it were a cud. "You are my candidate, dedicated to the Prince's use, whatever use that is. You have had your youth. You have had your years of joy. Now, you will serve me. Put the child to your useless breasts and pray he can suck the juice back into them, or he will die before you!"

"The baby just ate," said Awhero in a whining voice. "He won't be

hungry for some time. It's possible his suckling will make her milk flow, I've known it to happen." She nodded, rolling her tongue in her mouth and swiveling her eyes like a witless witch. Genevieve relaxed against the stone. Awhero was playing for time.

"You," snarled the Marshal, pointing at Kamakama. "Get me food. My rations ran out two days ago. You," he indicated Jorub, "reassemble that sled. It'll make my trip back to Mahahm-qum an easier one."

"You're going back to Mahahm-qum?" squeaked Kamakama, his voice splitting and sliding. "Back to the Aresians?"

"What Aresians?" the Marshal demanded.

"Men from Ares have taken the city, Father," said Genevieve. "They've also taken Havenor. They are here to find the source of your promised elevation, for they, too, have many men wanting to ascend onto that height."

"Ares? But they furnished the Lord Paramount's guards!"

"No longer. The Lord Paramount is gone, Father. The Prince is in the hands of the Aresians. The Shah . . . the Shah is no more."

He laughed shortly. "No doubt the several of you could have come up with a better lie than that, daughter, if you'd had more time. The Aresians, eh? There aren't enough of them on Haven to conquer a provincial market town."

"They came in ships," said Genevieve, looking through him at the wall. "The three sons of the Chieftain came, with all their men, and their warlords. And they have taken Havenor without a fight. Your armies did nothing to oppose them."

He laughed again, mockingly. "I'll credit that when I see it."

"Food," said Kamakama, bringing it to him. "And drink."

"Go help your friend get the sled back together," said the Marshal in high good humor. "While I am amused at stories about invasions from space." He sat upon a convenient stone, arranging the food in easy reach and keeping one hand always upon the weapon.

Jorub and Kamakama set about reassembling the sled, carefully reinserting sand into those parts that would almost certainly guarantee a breakdown if they tried to go anywhere. When they had the mechanism in one piece, the Marshal told them to go out in single file, then Awhero, Melanie, and Genevieve. He wanted the motor reinstalled, he said, so he and Genevieve could get out of there and if the others behaved themselves, he would leave them unharmed. He came behind, weapon at the ready, only to be grabbed from behind the moment he emerged fully from the concealing stones.

"Drop it," said Joncaster in an angry voice. "Sit on him, Etain, while I find something to tie him up. Gilber, you and Jorub get Aufors Leys into the cave where it's cooler."

There was a momentary confusion, threats from the Marshal, imprecations from Joncaster, moaning from Aufors, which caused a freshet of tears from Genevieve, after which they all returned to the cool of the cave, this time with the Marshal trussed up like a pig on its way to market. Genevieve immediately huddled over Aufors, willing him to open his eyes while Awhero bathed his face, arms, and chest with cool water from the spring.

"I heard Joncaster's sled," said Gilber to Melanie, in answer to a question. "So I ran down the shore to catch him before the Marshal heard him. We'd no sooner come up outside than you all came out!"

Aufors groaned and opened his eyes. He blinked several times and murmured, "Jenny?"

"Oh, yes, love. I'm here."

"Dovidi . . ."

"He's here, too."

"Ah," he said, licking his lips. "Dry . . ."

"Here's water, love."

"Tea," he whispered. "I want lemon tea . . ." He tried to smile, failed, managed to get his hand onto hers, squeezed it, then lapsed into sleep once more.

She rose at once and went to the supplies, to search for tea. Meantime, Jorub and Etain dragged the Marshal back through the open area into the lengthy branch of the cavern that led to the crevasse used as a privy. They returned as Joncaster was saying:

"Among us and the other sleds, I'd guess we've moved all the bodies. What we don't have is any information about where the stock of the stuff was kept . . ."

"Oh, yes," murmured Awhero. "I know where P'naki was kept! So do Genevieve, and Aufors."

Aufors, hearing his name, opened his eyes. "What?" he cried. "Jenny? What did she say?"

Genevieve was still across the cavern, and unthinkingly she called, "She said I know where the stuff is kept." She put her hand over her mouth, guiltily, looking toward the back of the cavern.

Joncaster laid a finger over his lips, whispering, "What do you see happening in Haven?"

She replied softly. "I see nothing about P'naki. For some time I caught

glimpses of the Lord Paramount. He was down in the caverns, singing to himself and eating something out of a jar. Licking it off his fingers. Now I see him curled in a dark corner somewhere, sleeping. I've seen him in that same position for a long time. As though he were carved. He doesn't move."

"Carved, eh?" said Awhero. "Now that's odd and interestin' . . ."

"Could it have been P'naki? A whole jar full?" wondered Joncaster in almost a whisper. "I've been wondering if too much of the stuff at once would do the same thing Aufors told us about."

Genevieve rose, bringing the cup of tea she had brewed to Aufors's side. "Awhero told Aufors about it, but she didn't know it was men's blood that did it."

"How did you know?" Melanie asked Awhero. "And why didn't you tell us?"

"Never had a chance until now," said Awhero, going on to tell her story about the Old Friend, while Joncaster and Melanie listened with their mouths open, and Genevieve knelt above Aufors, feeding him sips of tea and pondering the existence of Old Friends with great concentration. She was about to ask Awhero an important question when a call from the entrance interrupted her. Jorub.

"Joncaster," he cried, "Melanie! Come look! It's a Frangian ship sailing down the coast. They don't do that! They stay east of the Stone Trail, always . . ."

Joncaster went to the entrance, and except for Genevieve, who was holding the cup to Aufors's lips, he was joined there by the rest of the group. Intrigued by the appearance of the ship, they moved down to the shore where they stood with the waves washing their toes, shading their eyes from the setting sun and murmuring among themselves. Since the hovercraft behind the ship was low on the water, lost in the dazzle of the sun-splashed waves, they did not notice when the craft left the cover of the ship, slipped across the narrow strip of water to the land, hidden from them by protruding stones.

They were still standing, still watching, when Terceth, Dunnel and the other Trackers arrived, dragging behind them an unwilling Prince Delganor. It was the Prince's curses that spun them around.

"Well," said Terceth, upon seeing Awhero and the boy. "We've met before, madam."

"We have," she assented with some discomfort. "And no reason to meet again, so far as I can see."

"Happens we're looking for your son, madam. Or the man you claimed

was your son. He left a mystery behind him. One we'd mightily like to solve."

"Taipa? What mystery to him? Oh, he's done bit of thievery, but that was just to save baby's life . . ."

"Where is the child?" asked Dunnel. "I don't see a child."

Awhero's response was aborted by a wail from the cave. She shook her head in irritation. "Up there. I'll get him. . . ."

But Dunnel was already halfway to the cavern, where he immediately discovered Genevieve and Aufors. His shout brought the others, who arrived to find Genevieve speaking indignantly to him.

". . . we're Havenites come to Mahahm to trade for P'naki, which is a medicine against the fevers. This is my husband, Aufors Leys, and he was wounded when he went back into the city to rescue our child."

"What's your name?" demanded Terceth from the cave entrance.

"Genevieve, Marchioness of Wantresse," she said, drawing herself up and glaring at him, the red light of sunset glittering in her eyes. Between him and herself was a roiling of shadows, a vortex of images. Events were spinning out of control. She took a deep breath. There was danger coming. She could only see shadows, but they were full of danger.

"Well, Marchioness. What do you know about long-life stuff?"

She swallowed, saying slowly, "Long-life stuff? I know it is something the Lord Paramount gets from off-planet."

"The Lord Paramount," he mused. "And the Shah?"

"I suppose the Shah could too," she answered. "They use it to keep their subjects in line. If men don't behave, they don't live long."

Terceth seated himself on a stone and crossed his legs, leaning forward intently. "And what do they give for this drug?"

Genevieve shrugged, watching the shadows move and gather. She could say this, which was dark, or that, which was lighter. "Women, it's said. I thought everyone knew that."

"And the stuff is called P'naki," said Terceth, as though thinking aloud, though he watched her closely.

"No, no," corrected Genevieve. "I've taken P'naki myself as a preventive against batfly fever, but only men take the long-life drug."

This accorded completely with what the Frangians on the ship had said, but it was not what Terceth wanted to hear. He snarled in irritation. "What does it look like, this P'naki?"

Genevieve shrugged. "I don't think I ever saw it except stirred into fruit juice."

"Well then, what world does the long-life drug come from?"

She shook her head. "I don't know. Do you know, Melanie?"

"I imagine the Lord Paramount and the Shah keep it a secret," said Melanie demurely, her eyes on her feet.

Aufors moaned, opened his eyes, blinked, and tried to sit up. Genevieve was beside him at once, but so was Dunnel, turning out his pockets and feeling for weapons.

"Prince Terceth," said Dunnel, drawing the packet from Aufors's breast pocket, "Here's more of the stuff he gave you."

"Which he said he stole from the palace," mused Terceth.

"Well, and he did," asserted Awhero. "We needed food for baby, and I told him that was only place I knew of we could get it. He told me all about it."

Terceth demanded, "What did he tell you?"

"He said he found food, and then he found weapon, and then he went into big room, like bedroom, and there were boxes with packets in, and he took two packets, just curious. And you took one packet from him in Mahahm-qum."

"Indeed I did. I still have it." He took it from his pocket and held it with the other, musing. "We searched the palace for more of it, but we found none. What is the stuff for?"

"Who knows! Locked up stuff in fancy boxes, usually that kind of thing is worth something, isn't it? I told him to try to take something light, something we could trade on our way south."

Dunnel murmured, "He could have given some of it to Obrang, sir. In return for being set loose."

"What's an Obrang?" asked Awhero, looking up suspiciously.

"One of my men. Seemingly turned to stone."

Awhero licked dry lips and swallowed. "Well, likely he got into some bonebush."

"Why would he have done that?" asked Dunnel, curiously.

"Well," she said, wildly concocting, "here you are, hunting high, hunting low, looking for long-life stuff, and here's this funny-looking bush, so some idiot in your army tells some other idiot in your army to taste it and see if that's it."

"And you don't know what this stuff is?" murmured Terceth. "Well, we can test it on the Prince. Bring him."

Dunnel departed. Aufors struggled to sit up, and Awhero and Genevieve propped him against the wall, where he blinked owlishly, feeling the top of his head, where the excruciating pain of the last few days had been succeeded by a dull ache. Outside, night had fallen. Dunnel returned

carrying a lantern and leading Delganor by his shackles. On seeing Gene-vieve and Aufors, Delganor's lips thinned.

"At last," he quavered. "My runaway bride. And her faithless husband. I am gratified to see you looking unwell, sir!"

In her shock at his appearance, Genevieve ignored what the man said. Delganor stooped; his face was deeply wrinkled and darkly spotted with age.

"We've brought you here for a purpose," said Terceth. "This man was carrying something we're eager to know about." He held out the two packets of powder, dangling them before the Prince's eyes. "This man stole these from the Shah's palace."

Genevieve, who was at one side, saw the tightened jaw, the very slight motion the Prince made toward the packet. Awhero, who had been alerted by the story of Obrang to the realization the packets might not be identi-cal, virtually stopped breathing.

With great effort, Delganor managed to keep his voice uninterested as he said, "What is it?"

"You don't know?"

"How would I know?"

"It isn't P'naki?"

"No," he said craftily. "I buy P'naki from the Mahahmbi all the time. P'naki is gray. And more granular."

"Could it be the health drug your Lord Paramount gives to his faith-ful supporters?"

Delganor frowned. "That drug is a similar color, though it is usually a much finer powder."

"You wouldn't mind trying this, then?"

"For what reason?"

Again, Genevieve saw the tightness at the jaw, the eager flicker of the eyes toward the packet as he struggled for self-control. The whirling shad-ows still hung between her and the others in the cave, a vision of the near future where events spun madly, sucking her in, sucking her down . . .

Awhero had been holding her breath. She gasped, covering it up with a coughing fit.

"Take the stuff because I say so," Terceth said to the Prince.

Dunnel poured a cup of water and brought it to Delganor. Terceth handed over the packets, and the Prince sprinkled the contents of one packet on the water and drank it. The others watched him closely. He did not move but merely glared at them.

"How do you feel?" asked Terceth.

"It's not . . . not . . . not . . ." Delganor murmured. "Not . . . P'naki."

"So you said," Terceth agreed, cocking his head in wonder.

The Prince took a deep breath. He stood straighter. The weariness in his face smoothed away. His eyes cleared.

"Now, that must be your 'health drug,'" Terceth crowed, his eyes alight.

"Yes," said the Prince. "That's what it feels like." He spoke as though he were drugged or drunk, but his fingers curled around the unused packet.

A sound came from the darkness at the back of the cavern, a rock falling, a scraping. They all started.

"Dunnel," murmured Terceth, jerking his head in that direction.

Dunnel took a torch from his belt and followed its beam into darkness. Genevieve glanced meaningfully at Awhero. Awhero pinched Dovidi, making him wail in pain and surprise. Genevieve exclaimed and took the baby from her, put him on her shoulder, and began walking to and fro, patting him into quiet. Each time she turned, she came closer to the cave entrance.

Dunnel called, "There's a man back here, sir. Bound and gagged."

"Bring him here!"

Genevieve said in a casual tone, "The captive is my father. He planned to take me from my husband and child, and give me to Prince Delganor. Prince Delganor planned to sell me in return for the drug. My father was dragging me away by force when my friends stopped him. That's why he's tied up!"

"So you're one of the women who was going to be sold, are you?" asked Terceth in an interested voice.

"I am not the Prince's property to dispose of," she said. "Neither my husband nor I belong to Prince Delganor!"

"All the Prince's subjects belong to the Prince!" the Marshal shouted, staggering into the lamplight, his face contorted with rage.

"I am not the Prince's subject," retorted Genevieve. "Nor are you. We are both subjects of the Lord Paramount. You seem inclined to forget that, Father."

"You know the Lord Paramount?" Terceth asked her, in a deceptively casual manner.

"I have met him, yes," she said, looking over the Marshal's shoulder at Aufors. Joncaster had helped him rise, and he stood in the shadows.

"And what else might you know about long-life stuff?" Terceth asked.

"Just what I've told you," she said. "It's given only to men, and it's expensive, and they get it from off-planet."

"Hah!" shouted the Marshal, his rage outrunning his good sense. "The

presumptuous chit knows more than that. I heard them talking out here!
She knows where a supply of the stuff is, a great supply!"

Genevieve's spinning shadows collapsed upon themselves, and she
waited for nothing more. Even as Terceth turned toward her with a triumphant shout, she darted out the entrance and down the slope, Dovidi on
her shoulder. On the pebbled beach she evaded the astonished group of
Trackers and raced out along the serpents tail. The tide was low. She
splashed through the shallow water that led to the hump, then over the
hump through deeper water to climb up the neck of the serpent and onto
its head, where she grasped the horn and stood silhouetted against the
last of the light.

Terceth stalked angrily down the slope, gathered the Trackers, and
went out onto the tail stone.

"She'll jump if you threaten her," Awhero screamed from up the hill.
"She will!"

"She won't jump with the child," growled Terceth to his men, staring
up at Genevieve. The neck stone was the height of five or six tall men,
and it was slick with spray. Genevieve stood with one arm clutching
Dovidi, the other grasping the stone horn, her face turned outward to the
sea and her body leaning dangerously above the deep.

Terceth snarled at two of his men, "Go up there and get her."

They began to splash toward the neck stone.

At the first splash, Genevieve opened her mouth and called. The great
sound went out of her visibly, plangent and sonorous, the air wavering as
though from rising heat, the cry undiminished by distance. Even when
she closed her lips, the air throbbed vibrantly for an endless time. Before
the sound faded, a wave leapt up from the deep and came swiftly toward
the shore to wash the Trackers from the stone and tumble them in the
surf. Another, larger wave threatened all those on the shore, and they fled
before it.

Terceth turned as the water slithered away in runnels of foam and saw
a sun rerisen in the west, monstrous and golden, with huge dark shapes
arcing before it. The dark shapes leapt and soared from fountains of foam,
jumping again and again, higher and higher. A wail arose from the Frangians on the ship. "Whatever! Oh, Whatever!"

Terceth snarled, strode back down the slope, thrust himself through
the waves to the bottom of the neckstone and began to climb.

Above, Genevieve turned and sought Aufors, where he stood in the
cave entrance, supported by Joncaster, his eyes fixed on hers. She lifted
her hand.

"Aufors," she cried in that great voice. "Aufors wait for me . . ."

And she threw herself out into space; folding the child between her arms, bending her head to cover his, she arrowed down, slipping into the water as into a silken gown, and was gone.

"What was that?" cried Terceth, staring at the horizon where the rerisen sun had just disappeared into the sea. "What in the universe was it!"

The Frangian ship was close enough that its captain heard him. "Whatever," he shouted exultantly. "Oh, whatever."

"Te wairua taiao," sang the malghaste, as they poured down from the cavern above. "Oh, wairua taiao!"

"What are they going on about," Terceth angrily demanded from Dunnel.

"I don't know, sir," Dunnel whispered, his eyes still moving between the horizon and the spot where Genevieve had fallen.

All those from the cave came down the hill, including Aufors, supported by Joncaster and Jorub. Lagging behind were the Prince and the Marshal, keeping a considerable distance from the others.

"What was it?" Terceth demanded of the malghaste.

"The spirit of this world," Melanie rejoiced. "Together with a company of great whales and many other creatures."

"What do you mean, the spirit of the world?" he grated, reaching out to grasp her by the shoulder.

Joncaster lowered Aufors on a convenient sitting stone and came to remove Terceth's hand from Melanie's shoulder, putting himself purposefully between them. "You saw the spirit of Haven. Your world once had such a spirit also."

Terceth snarled wordlessly. This was nonsense!

Melanie saw his furious expression over Joncaster's shoulder. "But it's true! Your world did have a spirit! You saw it depart."

"What are you talking about?"

"Our people in Havenor have heard you speak of the night the fires departed from Ares. Surely you remember it."

"I remember," said Dunnel, white-faced. "My parents got me up, and we watched it go . . ."

"This is nonsense," blustered Terceth. "Arrant nonsense."

Melanie shrugged. "Well, it is easy to know whether I speak truth. If life is dying on your planet, then your world's spirit has departed."

"We have a disease," said Dunnel. "People just . . . stop. They keep trying to remember something . . ."

"Of course," said Joncaster. "They wake one morning no longer feeling alive. They try to remember the feeling of life. They wander, searching for it. They rove among their human kin, but they cannot find what they are seeking. They take a pet cat into their laps, or lean to pat a dog, and for a moment they feel peace, but only for a moment. At the end, they realize what has been lost and they cry out, most piteously, and soon after they die. Is this not the way of it?"

"How did you know that?" cried Terceth, clenching his fists, ready to assault them all.

"It's not a secret," said Melanie, impatiently. "Yours isn't the only world it's happened to."

He jeered, "And I suppose the Marchioness of Wantresse summoned up the spirit of Haven and then went to join it, did she?"

For a moment, Melanie was stunned, then eager surprise lit her face and she gripped Joncaster by the arm, crying, "She did call the spirit, Joncaster! We heard her! But she wasn't a believer! Could she have . . ."

Joncaster nodded slowly. "It might not matter. Perhaps the spirit doesn't care why we do the right thing so long as we do it."

Terceth cried, "The right thing! To drown yourself and your child in the ocean!"

"Better than die at the hands of Aresian torturers!" said Aufors, tears streaming down his face.

"We are not torturers," Terceth blustered, flushing as he confronted Aufors's pain-racked face and the accusing stares of those around him.

"I was quite well until I met the Aresians," Aufors murmured. "Call your treatment what you will."

Terceth glared in frustration, grinding his teeth as though to gnaw the situation into something more malleable.

"If our world is dead, what do we do to resurrect it?" Dunnel pled.

"You can't," said Melanie.

Dunnel cried, "But we must. We've already brought in animals! We've imported trees!"

Joncaster shook his head. "There are too many vital pieces left out,

hundreds of thousands of tiny living things you never knew were there. How can you restore what you never saw in the first place?"

Aufors bent forward with a moan, trembling, his hands clenched, his forehead beaded. "Jenny," he whispered, as though to himself. "Oh, Jenny . . ."

Awhero put her arms around him, murmuring, "You heard your Jenny, Aufors. She said to wait. Believe in her. She didn't drown herself. And she didn't drown Dovidi."

Terceth was too frustrated to let this go unchallenged. "Oh, she most certainly did, old woman. She's committed suicide!"

"No," cried Aufors, his eyes wild and unfocused as he tried to stand on legs that would not hold him.

"She'll be back," whispered Awhero, dragging Aufors back onto the stone, holding him there.

Terceth ranted, "She won't be back unless she's part fish! And the child won't be back unless he's a fish's whelp!" He spun around, gesturing. "Dunnel, go back to the ship and get it out into the sea. If that woman or creature or whatever she is comes up with or without the brat, I want her."

"Fish's child," said Aufors, his face becoming even more pallid and clammy. Part fish, his mind blathered, running back into his childhood, full of jeering brother-noises and night terrors. Part fish. He was unable to escape the idea. Maybe it was true. Genevieve had encountered something in Merdune Lagoon. Something shapeless, she'd said, but what did shape matter? Had something happened to her she hadn't wanted to tell him . . . ?

This led him into a thicket full of clammy monsters, bogeymen of grief and jealousy that he was not strong enough to recognize, much less analyze. He slumped, unable to hold up his head. Joncaster picked him up and strode up the hill with Awhero and the other malghaste following. Delganor and the Marshal followed Terceth and Dunnel, who went on down to the shore, Dunnel very pale and quiet while Terceth, who had been raging at the world of Haven and everyone on it, grew gradually quieter and more thoughtful and more anxious. In an impotent fury he admitted to himself that there might well be things going on he did not understand. It might well be that this expedition had not been a good idea. Perhaps, oh, perhaps all the Aresian forces now on Haven would be better off somewhere else.

On a hillside not far from Havenor, among an untidy litter of furnishings and materiel, two watchers sat comfortably in dusty chairs observing

a procession of exotic and complicated robots emerging from a vertical cleft in the rock. Variously, the machines rolled or strode or bounced westward in eerie procession on a shadow carpet cast before them by a rising moon. They might almost have been spectral, they moved so silently. Even after centuries of storage, not one of them squeaked.

The watchers, Veswees and Jeorfy Bliggard nee Bottoms, had only recently discovered this deep fissure leading into the Lord Paramount's caverns, one better suited to the emergence of bulky machinery than any of the eel-burrows or squirmy mazes they had explored theretofore. The departing procession was the final one for this evening, though on previous nights many waves of flying or fast-running machines had come out like monstrous hatchlings from a dragon's nest. The earlier departures had allowed more travel time, but this group was destined for duty in the villages around Havenor itself.

"You know," said Jeorfy in a disappointed voice, "I expected them to clank. When we unpacked and programmed them, down below, they looked like they'd clank. And make sparks."

"And utter threats in loud voices, no doubt," said Veswees. "If you're trying to sneak up on people, you don't want things that clank or spark or shout."

"We're not really trying to sneak . . ."

"What would you call it?"

Jeorfy gave this his complete attention. "I'd call it getting people's attention modestly, politely, occasioning no alarm."

Veswees smiled only slightly. "Clank or no clank, I can't imagine any of these creatures entering a village without occasioning alarm. The less alarm the better, however, so the villagers can give the messengers a fair hearing."

"It's good there were so many machines that can talk," agreed Jeorfy. "But I wish you'd allowed me a little more variety in their modes of speech."

"Clarity was most important," Veswees said firmly. "Declamations in foreign accents or complicated verse forms would not have helped!" Veswees stared after the retreating forms, now vanishing in the dark. "I hope to heaven we've programmed them correctly. I shudder to think what may happen otherwise."

"Certainly I programmed them correctly," said Jeorfy, indignantly. "Even though I'd never tried it before it came quite naturally to me. I did it correctly. I think."

Veswees sighed deeply. "You think?"

"I'm quite sure," Jeorfy tittered, hugging himself. "Oh, Veswees, if you could see your face!"

"I'm tired, Jeorfy. When you tease me it makes me wonder how it could have sounded like such a good idea when Genevieve told me about the robots down there . . . and about you."

Jeorfy's face lit up. "Genevieve! Now, that should relieve your mind completely."

"How so?"

He stood, adopting a declamatory posture: "Genevieve sees the future, dark or bright? So she's already seen my programming, right? And she wouldn't have told you to come find me, unless I'd done or would do it successfully!"

Veswees laughed, though briefly, all he had strength for. The past days had been overfull of travel, exploration and mental strain. Finding Jeorfy. Finding the machines. Using the huge cargo machines to widen the way out. Making lists. Determining which would go where, when! Composing and re-composing the message! Jeorfy's talking in verse only complicated things. "Genevieve also told me you'd given up rhyming."

"I have. Mostly." Jeorfy pulled at the closest pile of materials the cargo machines had carried outside over the last few days, tugging out a gold-framed mirror that he propped against a topless packing case. The case held the desiccated body of an old, old man with his arms tightly curled around an empty jar. When they had found him in the caverns he had had a very complicated little code book in the pocket of his dusty trousers and he had also been wearing the dented crown that Jeorfy now wore tilted over his left eye.

"What shall we do with him?" Jeorfy asked, indicating the dried-up body.

"Fasten the top on that box and bury him," said Veswees. "I still say he's the Lord Paramount. No one else would have had that crown. Or that code book."

"What would the Lord Paramount have been doing in the darkest corner of the bottommost cavern? And how did he get there?"

"Maybe your friend Zebulon Coffin put him there."

"We found Zeb where the pile of stuff fell on him—poetic justice, since he's the one who stacked it off balance in the first place! There was nothing left of him but lizard-gnawed bones, so he died long before this one. And all the access routes were locked, so no one could have gotten in. . . ."

"Probably the Lord Paramount got in before the computers locked. Probably he's the one who locked them," Veswees mused.

"That would explain the code book," Jeorfy agreed, "though I didn't know the Lord Paramount had anything to do with the files personally . . ."

The tiny notebook, though it was full of codes for this and that and the other thing, had not included any reference to the secret elevator. The Lord Paramount had never, ever written down anything about the elevator, and only one person now living knew anything about it.

". . . but whoever he was, the book gives us total access to the files," crowed Jeorfy, as he'd been doing since discovering it. He straightened the crown and posed before the mirror. "Oh, what we'll find out."

"I think what we've already found out will be more than adequate." Veswees yawned hugely. "We've already found out all we needed for the machines to do their job. And we've kept the cargo machines to bring stuff out of the caverns."

Jeorfy stopped posing and sat down, his face serious. "Right until the last, I doubted we'd find enough citations to cover the whole Tribunal. I can't understand how they could have let things like that become a matter of record."

Veswees grinned, showing his teeth. "They had to record it. Their continued lives depended on bookkeeping. So much blood credited to this one, so much blood for that one. The names and dates of each and every woman who had been furnished by this or that member of the Tribunal, every daughter, every wife, every abducted housemaid they sent off to be slaughtered . . ."

"Sickening," Jeorfy said, making a face.

"It'll be behind us soon. Then we can go on to something else."

"Like what?"

Veswees glanced at Jeorfy from the corner of his eye. "The first thing I want to look into is seafaring technology."

"Seafaring? Why do that?"

"Haven't you noticed we're losing a lot of dry land? The seas are rising."

"Not all that much," said Jeorfy, tilting the crown over his other eye and rising to take another look at himself.

Veswees shook his head reprovingly. "I do hope you're not considering starting a new monarchy?"

"I'm amusing myself," said Jeorfy. "And why not!" He bent and turned, trying to get a good view of the rest of himself in the mirror. King Jeorfy, he muttered to himself, enjoying the idea. King Jeorfy the First! "But if

you don't want amusement, then you do whatever you like, partner. Whatever you like."

"I've already done most of that," Veswees murmured. "These last few
days, I've had fun enough for anyone."

In a hamlet near Havenor, the populace—only recently retired for the
night—was awakened by a brazen voice calling, "Oyez, oyez, oyez, draw
near and hear what it is right you should know, draw near and hear, draw
near and hear . . ."

Men rolled out of bed cursing or frightened, as their characters dictated, drawing on their trousers and boots while they urged their women
and children into hiding. The more belligerent among them picked up
pitchforks or scythes or whatever other sharp or heavy implements were
at hand and plunged out of their houses toward the village square. When
they arrived, however, they found a device, one more exotic than threatening, occupying the steps of the town hall as it trumpeted its invitation. A
few of the men shook their heads and turned back, only to be stopped
by a voice like a trumpet.

"Fetch your wives, your children, your aged parents," the machine blat-
ted. "Hurry up, for I must take this message to twenty other towns by
dawn. . . ." Seeing several who shook their heads and seemed determined
to return to bed, the machine allowed bolts of lightning to spit from its
eyes as it stamped its foot, crushing the stone of the steps.

So encouraged, the populace was hastily assembled, though at first it
made little sense of the machine's message. Only when the words "disappearing women" focused their attention did they begin to understand what
was being said. On the third reiteration, as the brazen voice repeated the
names of specific women and the names of the men who had taken the
women and the reason the women had been taken, even the machine had
difficulty outshouting the uproar. During every lull in the tumult, however,
it went on repeating the message until every person present understood
each and every fact that Jeorfy and Veswees, by use of the Lord Paramount's code book, had extracted from the files: Such and such a noble
had abducted such and such a woman and had provided her to the Mahahmbi for such and such a purpose. Such other noble had taken such
other woman, and this daughter had been sent for that father, and this
young mother for that grandfather, and these several ones for the Lord
Paramount, and that one for the Shah of Mahahm, and so on and so on.

The catalog was in mid-repetition when one very large, red-faced
farmer (a sometime-malghaste on duty in Haven) lifted his scythe and

cried loudly, "Enough. We know enough! To the home of the Duke of Merdune! Follow me!"

There was sufficient outrage that virtually the entire village did follow him. The machine, left behind, noted that its first mission had been a success and trundled itself off to the next village on the list.

In Havenor, Gardagger and Alicia, Duke and Duchess of Merdune, were at late supper with a number of guests—among them Prince Thumsort and the Prince's son, Edoard—when they heard a great clamor outside. It was not the orderly sound of an Aresian clamor, which regardless of purpose always included a thunderous tramp, tramp, tramp plus an uproar of drums, a bray of trumpets, or at the very least a loudly shouted marching song. The current clamor sounded, Gardagger thought, like a bunch of peasants in a fury, and he stalked wrathfully out onto the terrace to put an immediate end to the insolence.

Curious as to the cause of the event, Prince Thumsort and Edoard followed, though other guests remained at the table. Among them, the Duchess Alicia sat quite still for a long moment, her eyes wide as she experienced what was almost a vision for the first time in her life.

The peasantry had climbed the fence and assembled at the foot of the terrace, well armed with implements and torches, but the Duke Merdune felt no terror as he raised his hands and demanded silence, which he received. The quiet was immediately broken by the voice of the very large red-faced man who came to the front of the mob and shouted:

"Gardagger, Duke Merdune, we require you to answer for the deaths of our wives and daughters and your own! You, Gardagger, gave women to the Shah of Mahahm to be sacrificed on the sands of Mahahm, and in return you were granted extension of life by the Lord Paramount. You, Gardagger, are now one hundred thirty years old. Deny or affirm."

Gardagger, very red in the face, shouted, "I deny . . ."

The large man scarcely paused: "Morion, the daughter of Hesbet, the baker, had her throat slit on your behalf."

Hesbet and his colleagues screamed for Gardagger's blood.

"I am the son of Morion. When she was killed, your name was spoken aloud as the man who would profit from her blood, and this was overheard by those who rescued me as a baby from death on the sands of Mahahm.

"Forty years ago, she died, and you have had five other women killed since then, including Sybil, daughter of your wife, Alicia Bellser-Bar . . ."

Gardagger, ashen-faced, raised his hands, patting them outward as though to push away the crowd assembled below him, but the threat came

from behind him as Alicia lunged wild-eyed onto the terrace, a carving knife from the table glittering in her hand.

"Gardagger," she screamed, "you said no. You said not. You said she died in childbirth . . ." And she flung herself at him while Prince Thumsort vainly tried to stop her.

The Prince would have been better advised to look to his own safety, for the horde waited no longer. It poured up onto the terrace to make a short and bloody work of Duke Merdune and then flowed away again, leaving Thumsort and Edoard bruised and battered behind them.

The trumpet-voiced man turned as he departed. "Prince Thumsort, Duke Edoard, the people from Sealands will be seeking you. They know which of the women of Sealands you have used. We leave the exacting of justice to those to whom justice is due. . . ."

The crowd went cheering into the night, waving their torches and leaving behind Gardagger's body, bleeding onto the marble as Alicia kicked at it, over and over, first with one foot then the other. Only when her shoes were sodden with his blood did she turn screaming toward the house.

Behind her, Prince Thumsort and the Duke Edoard, much bruised, crawled toward one another in terror.

"Father . . ." Edoard cried.

"They can't prove it. There's no proof . . ." Thumsort looked around for someone to confirm this fact, one he had always been assured of, one he had always believed.

"They'll find proof," cried his son. "They do say who, out on the sands, when the throats are slit. They do say who the blood is for. When I was a ritual master, I heard them! If someone was listening, if they found out about Gardagger, they'll find out about you. You've had dozens. You had my first and second wives, and both their daughters, and some of those you used had sons, and if the sons lived . . . why, I didn't know they ever lived. No one told us any of them lived! And the maids from our place in Tansay that you took . . . And the women I got you from those raids into Dania, and . . ."

"You, too," his father snarled. "You've had your own candidates!"

"You told me it was safe. You said they'd never find out!"

"Leave it! It doesn't matter. We have to decide what to do now. Where we can go. To be safe . . ."

Alicia stood in the doorway, cackling like a witch. "There is no place to be safe, Prince Thumsort. They'll find you, and they'll find Duke Edoard. I know who set this in motion and believe me, she'll find you all." Then

she fell to keening as though she could not stop, a hideous noise that drove the rest of the guests out of the house, into the dangerous night.

When Genevieve leapt from the serpent rock, she and Dovidi fell as one, as one entering the waves, arrowing downward as the light faded behind them. She drove them deeper with thrusting legs. The child struggled, freed his limbs and swam with her, kicking with his tiny feet even within the circle of her arms. The pudgy folds at the sides of his little neck swelled, then opened. Seeing this, Genevieve gave a great gulp of relief, and the almost invisible lines that circled her own neck opened to let the fringed tissues inside extrude like a great, frilly collar that drew the oxygen from the water flowing through it. She blinked and transparent lids lowered to protect her eyes. Oh, it had been so long since she had done this. Only that once since mother died, before she went to Havenor. So long since those endless exercises in the pool beneath Langmarsh House. So long since Mother went away.

Dovidi moved his jaw with a clicking noise, like a question, and she turned her head in the direction he was staring. Almost touching them were scores of skeining dolphins, weaving patterns in the water, talking among themselves in a series of snaps and pops, their cheerful faces and bobbing bodies encouraging their descent. As they went deeper, the dolphins were replaced by black-and-white orcas with great teeth in their smiling jaws, and then by bigger creatures yet, huge whales, some with pointed heads and others with great, broad faces above enormous mouths. Beyond these familiar shapes were others she could not recognize, deep dwellers of races she knew nothing of, huge and writhing, with multiple eyes, the leviathans of Haven.

The sparkling blue changed to bright sapphire and that darkened to lapis and that to purple and that, soon, gave way to an ebon realm of endless space glittering with living galaxies, with luminescent constellations moving and spinning in the dark as they hummed and clicked and sang. As they went deeper yet, the water began to glow, and they looked down upon a golden continent, the largest of all the sea shapes, one that shone with its own light, the great golden creature Genevieve had seen in Merdune Lagoon, now rising toward them, turning beneath them, to bring the tip of its huge dorsal fin within reach of her hand.

She grasped the apex, like grasping the tip of an ornamental spire at the top of a great tower above a vast city. Her eyes swooped down across the creature-scape of the being, a distance so great that she could not see its end. Behind her, the mighty tail waved in powerful thrusts that drove

them deeper yet. She should have been swept off, but she was held to the surface of the fin as though glued to it, surrounded by an intention that would neither let her go nor harm her while she stayed.

Inside her a half familiar discomfort built as something shifted, as an inner pressure built to match outer pressure, as air bled from certain cavities, releasing inert gases. The pools at Langmarsh had not been deep enough for this, but she had been told to expect it. She looked intently at Dovidi to see if he felt any distress, but his tiny hand rested easily beneath hers on the great fin and he chortled at their going.

The sound of his joy released her. All her anxieties fell away like weights dropped from a diver's belt, leaving her free in the great ocean. Here was where she belonged and where she had been meant to come.

"So, daughter," the voice spoke all around her in the sea. "You have come."

"I've come," she replied with her mind, her lips still sipping the sea, her gills still breathing for her. "Oh, yes. I didn't believe in you, but still, I've come."

"You have refused to believe in me," said the voice, with a hint of laughter. "You have been a doubter?"

Genevieve floated, spirit and mind, untroubled. "You seemed unlikely," she said. "You seemed . . . invented."

"Ah, well, yes. Invented by time, made likely by space. We living things work so hard to acquire knowledge. Surely you wouldn't suppose it wasted?"

"No," she confessed. "It's better not wasted."

"Which is why you were sent," the spirit said. "Your lineage was sent to see the world and the creatures in it, those like you and those unlike you. Your lineage was meant to learn their beliefs and their doings, to judge them and return with that judgment."

"I have judged," she said, utterly unworried at this verdict. She need not concern herself with ifs or buts. What she knew was simply correct. "There are many good folk on Haven, but the use of the lichen is wrong. Those who have used it should perish."

"And those from outside, who seek to use it?"

"Should also perish if they will not repent of it."

"And the innocent?"

"You have already prepared for the innocent," she said. "How long ago did Tenopia go into Mahahm? How long ago did your own people make for them a refuge in Galul?"

"Those are called rhetorical questions," said the spirit with something very like laughter in its voice.

"Indeed," said Genevieve with matching laughter.

"Hundreds of daughters in the first few generations of Tenopia's line. Hundreds of daughters more from Tewhani's line, then both daughters and sons. But you are the first child with Tenopia's blood from both parents. You are the first, and Dovidi is the second."

"My father is of that lineage?" She could not imagine the Marshal of that lineage.

"Not the man you are thinking of."

"My father was someone . . . else?"

"It is self-evident. No such brutal warrior could have come from our lineage. Would one of our lineage act as he has done?"

She thought not. No.

"Your husband's mother, she also was of Tewhani's blood. There will soon be many others like you and Dovidi, returners to the sea, but they will come in their own time. Before that, you have a duty to perform. Do you know what it is?"

"I have the duty to explain. People will need an explanation when the lichen is gone and all its works and customs are abandoned."

"That will be soon. We are singing the furnaces of the world to raise the floors of the sea. If the sea floors are raised beneath the deeps, then the water in the shallows also is raised."

"There are good creatures of this world who need dry land. Does their Haven remain?"

"Haven always remains."

She smiled, feeling the pulse of the sea around her. "I was afraid, for a time, that whatever was done would be too late . . ."

"Very late, certainly, and perhaps too late except for the father of your child. He saw what needed to be done and by doing it, he has bought this world the necessary time. We approve of him. He is of our lineage. He is among our people."

The words filled her with delight and wonder, an inner warmth she had felt only once before, in Weirmills, when she had lain within Aufors's arms. Dovidi squirmed in her grasp, waving his hands at the creatures all around them, his expression echoing her own.

It seemed to Genevieve that they talked for some time after that, the creatures of the deep glittering like sequins and the songs of the sea moving among them like the surge and collect of the waves. At last,

however, the voices stilled and the one voice said regretfully, "Now is time to go up."

Slowly the marvelous cortege sang its way upward, a long, slanting line that ascended into the pale greeny glimmer of surface light.

She said, "The malghaste said . . . they had a tapu against killing anything, any form of life. I thought the lichen couldn't be destroyed . . ."

"But the lichen is not a species! It is only an evil alliance. It is an alga that lives in the sea, a fungus that grows in the mountains, it is only on the desert of Mahahm that they grow together. Only there."

"Awhero said there's a great store of the stuff in a buried house outside Mahahm-qum," she murmured, feeling a momentary panic.

"Where you will go now, for we have brought you to that place." She turned in the water, staring upward to the shattered glimmer of the surface, seeing it darken in a long, heavy line which moved slowly across the light.

"Observe," said the voice in her mind. "The power of the sea. That power will come when you call it. It will go where you will it. You have seen the evil. You will summon the remedy. You will explain the result."

At Terceth's order, the Frangian vessel had sailed back and forth along the western shore near the standing stone, looking for Genevieve. After two days, Terceth had lost patience and had had everyone, including the Frangians and their ship, moved north from the standing stone to the vicinity of Mahahm-qum, where the Aresians had their camp. The camp had grown larger, for all the Aresians on Haven had assembled there within the past few days. The great battleships had landed on the sand and stood there now, those of the warlords, those of the brothers Ygdaleson, and that of the Chieftain as well. Some of the officers had billeted themselves in houses inside the wall, from which the Mahahmbi had been evicted, and the rest were bivouacked in tents outside the city walls.

Dunnel and two of his Trackers had remained on the Frangian ship, which was anchored just offshore, and it was they who first saw Genevieve as she leapt straight up from the water, an arrow silvered with the sea, carrying the child in the curl of her arm. She landed lightly on the deck, on her feet, to the open-mouthed amazement of the crew.

When the two Trackers shook off their stupefication and started for her, a tentacle came across the railing, dragged them overboard and left them thrashing in the water alongside.

"Pull them out," Genevieve said cheerfully to Dunnel. "And don't let any others of your men make the same mistake. I have come with a

message for the warriors from Ares. If you interfere, the sea creatures will make a breakfast of you."

"We bow before the Whatever," cried the Captain, falling to his knees. "Nothing shall interfere with the Whatever."

Dunnel pulled his thoroughly frightened men aboard and made no further attempt on Genevieve. Since the episode at the standing stone, he and Terceth had discovered they shared the same doubts. Both of them were now convinced it was a mistake for Ares to have invaded Haven. Genevieve seemingly read his mind.

"Dunnel. That's your name, isn't it?"

He nodded.

Where is Terceth Ygdaleson? And the others of his family?"

He pointed to the cluster of tents around the ships. "The tallest ones," he said uncomfortably. "With the most banners."

"And the Prince and the Marshal?"

"There. With them."

She smiled at him and at the ship's captain. "Dunnel, if you are fond of these men of yours, and you, Captain, if your crew is fond of life, stay here."

"Where, lady?" murmured Dunnel.

Here, on this ship. How long would it take you to sail to the east side of that nearest island?" She pointed north to the first island of the Stone Trail. She had seen it from the air, a rocky peak with a curved deepwater bay on its eastern side.

"Not long, lady. An hour or so."

"Remember that, and wait here for word from me."

They put out a little boat to take her to shore, and as they neared the pebbly beach, old Awhero came wading hip-deep into the sea. She reached for the child with a cooing noise and an armful of dry clothing.

"So you've been below with your destiny, have you?" she asked, with a sidelong glance at Genevieve "You look like drowned cat. I've been waiting for you to come back from following your road."

"It was a deep, dark sea-road, Awhero, and I don't know how long it took."

"Last we saw of you was four days ago."

She gasped. It hadn't seemed . . . "Is Aufors all right?"

"He's over there in camp, and no, I wouldn't say all right, exactly. His body's most recovered. I told him you'd be back, but he's turned odd. All of sudden he's got strangeness in him about you and Dovidi."

"What do you mean?"

"If I knew what it meant, it wouldn't be strangeness, girl." She puckered her lips, thinking better of what she had been going to say. "He was rambling on and on about fish!"

Genevieve wrinkled her forehead in thought. "Are you and the other malghaste free to move about, Awhero?"

"Only three of us still here: all of us but Melanie, Joncaster, and me slipped away to Galul soon after we got here. The three of us left can move around, yes, and those Aresians are letting us alone. We all said Marshal misunderstood what he heard, that all you knew about was where P'naki was to cure fever, that's all."

"What about the Marshal? Has he been volunteering any more information?"

"Delganor got at him, and they're keeping their mouths shut now, still trying to wriggle out of trap they're in."

"Still trying to bluff the Aresians? I thought by now the Chieftain would've started torturing people."

"They have done that. Ogberd, he started with old Ybon, Shah's minister. I'm told they set hot iron to him, and minute it touched him, he died, just like that. These real old ones, they're kind of like dried flowers. Touch them and they fall apart."

Genevieve made a face. "Well, then, there's no time to waste. Those of you who were at the standing stone, take Aufors and go out to that Frangian ship . . ."

"We can't get at Aufors now. Ogberd, he has Aufors under guard, just in case you come back."

Genevieve sighed. "Never mind, then. The rest of you go. And you tell the Captain to sail around to the east side of that first, rocky island and make the ship fast close inshore."

"Then what?"

"Just wait. You'll know."

The old woman nodded. "I'll take baby . . ."

"No," Genevieve said in a very quiet voice. "Dovidi will be quite all right with me."

The guard outside the Chieftain's tent was the first to see Genevieve walking across the sands toward the encampment. Within moments, the Chieftain and all three sons were outside under the shade of the tent flap, watching her approach.

"Shall I send some men out?" muttered Ogberd.

"She's already headed in this direction," said Terceth in a voice that

sounded worried, even to him. "Just let her come. Get a chair for her. Let's start with courtesy, at least."

The Chieftain sneered at this but let it pass.

When she came near enough, Terceth went out to walk with her. "Marchioness."

"You may call me Genevieve," she said. "I've come with a message for you."

"You are in great danger," he whispered.

"We all are," she murmured as they came to the tent where the others waited. Terceth offered her a chair in the shade of the tent flap, which she accepted gratefully. The sand was hot, and her sandals were full of sharp grains. The men watched, bemused, while she took off the sandals and emptied them out. She took notice of the arrangements, betimes. The Marshal and the Prince were at the rear of the tent, guarded but unfettered, both of them glaring at her with hot eyes. Though she saw that the Marshal held the Prince's clenched fist with both his hands, and though she guessed what was in that fist, she ignored them for the present.

"I've come with a message," she repeated.

"What message?" asked the Chieftain.

"Before I can deliver it," she said, "I must be sure we speak the same language."

"We are speaking the same language."

"Perhaps we are, but when I return to my . . . my mentor, I must be sure. Let us see. I understand you tortured the minister of the Shah to extract information from him."

Terseth flushed and turned his face away.

"We attempted to persuade him," grated Ogberd.

"That's what I meant by difference in language," Genevieve said, shaking her head. "You say persuade, I say torture. So, when I go back to my mentor, I will say to . . . him, the Aresians are torturing the Mahahmbi.

"Now, it is my understanding that you wish to gain access to the long-life stuff the Shah of Mahahm has made available to Haven and to certain outside worlds, is that correct?"

Lokdren snarled, "Quite correct."

"And you will use any *persuasion* to gain this access. Will you murder for it?"

"Why should it be necessary to murder or persuade for it," grated the Chieftain, "once we are told what we need to know?"

"The substance is potentiated by being mixed with the blood of young

mothers," said Genevieve. "Each dose requires that a young woman be slain."

"Uncovenantly bitch," bellowed the Marshal from the rear of the tent.

"Traitoress," cried the Prince, more feebly.

"Nonsense!" said the Chieftain between his teeth.

"Not nonsense, no. The reactions of your prisoners should tell you I speak the truth. Whether you believe me or not, I will tell you nothing but the truth."

"Father," said Terceth, reaching out his hand. "I don't think . . ."

"No," snarled Ygdale. "You don't think, but I do! None of us like the steps to which we are driven, but I have a world to consider." He strode to the back of the tent where he stared at the two men there for a long time, twisting his mustache the while and lifting one nostril as though to sniff something out that eluded him. At length he returned, saying, "Tell your . . . mentor, that we regret finding it necessary to make some sacrifices . . ."

"Ah," she said. "That is very much what the noblemen of Haven and the men of Mahahm have always done. Even your vocabulary is similar to theirs. On Haven we women were taught resignation. On Mahahm they were drugged into acceptance. Even so, eventually one runs out of young women. Are you prepared to abduct women from other worlds to make this medicine?"

"Father," cried Terceth. "Think what she's saying!"

His father snarled to his guards, "Take my youngest son to his tent." Then, when they had escorted him away, to Genevieve, "We consider that our first responsibility is to our own families. Our children. Our wives."

"No," Genevieve interrupted him. "The medicine does not work on women. You will have to sacrifice your own wives and daughters."

Silence for a long moment, then, reluctantly he said, "If doing so will restore life to our world . . ."

"Only the lives of old men. No others."

"But men are the real Aresians," blustered Lokdren. "Ours is a very masculine world. We revel in masculine things . . ."

"Men who take this medicine do not revel," she said. "They do not sport, or dare. They are impotent, but greedy for life. They do not ride or hunt or take any risks at all, but every few days they drink the blood of slaughtered women."

"Still . . ." murmured Lokdren.

"Wisdom comes with age," said the Chieftain ponderously. "Perhaps through wisdom we will learn some way to avoid the necessity . . ."

"An interesting interpretation of wisdom," she said. "So when I return to my mentor, I am to say you are willing to sacrifice and persuade in order to become wise?"

"What makes you think you will be allowed to return with your telling?" grated the Chieftain. "I allowed you to speak merely to see what you had to say of interest. Now you have said it, and it is not of interest! Do you think you, yourself will not be affected by the *persuasion* of your husband, by the *sacrifice* of your child!"

"Oh, I would be affected," she said. "I would tell you anything you want to know."

"The location of the drug!"

"I know where a great store of it lies, and you need not persuade either my husband or my child. I will tell you without that. I ask only that you let me see him, alone, for a little time."

The Chieftain met her limpid gaze with a hard, brittle glare of his own. "A very little time. Ogberd, take her."

They went out into the glare of the sun and down a line of tents to a small one where Aufors slumped in a disconsolate huddle against a roll of blankets. Genevieve went in and laid the baby beside him. He looked up, saw her face, and turned a furious red, a shamed red, then turned his face away from her, shuddering.

"I'll wait," said Ogberd, sneering. "Don't look like I'll be long."

Genevieve turned toward him, saying, "Out of earshot. Please, let us have some privacy."

He shrugged and walked to a nearby tent where Terceth sat cross-legged in the opening, and they two were soon joined by Lokdren, who gestured toward Aufors's tent and said, "What do you think, her wandering in like that?"

"I think Father'll kill her if she crosses him," Ogberd offered.

Lokdren shook his head. "I think she's going to tell him where the stuff is."

"Why would she?" Ogberd asked.

"Because she knows something we don't," Terceth spoke from his place in the shade of the tent flap. "I've been thinking about what happened south of here. I think we're making a mistake. I have a bad feeling about this."

Ogberd snorted. "Oh, for the love of Hotipah, you don't believe that stuff about sacrificing women, do you? She made all that up, just to put us off!"

Terceth replied, "Oh, yes, I believe it. The two Havenites in there,

they knew she spoke truth, and so did Father. That's why he's so angry. He has his mind set on doing anything he needs to do to get the stuff, and she knows that if we've decided to do that, then we've changed the kind of people we are—or thought we were."

"Life is change," sneered Ogberd. "We'll be whatever kind of people we need to be."

Terceth murmured, "I'd like to know who's this *mentor* she talks about?"

"It doesn't exist," said Ogberd. "She's trying a bluff. By Hotipah, Terceth, sharpen up! Don't you care if Ares dies? If our family dies?"

"Ares died a long time ago, and when Father commanded that iron to be heated and you put it against that old man's chest, so did we," said Terceth.

Ogberd stalked away at that, Lokdren following him, leaving Terceth to sit alone, brooding over the two across the way.

Inside the tent, Aufors had gone on staring, either unable or unwilling to speak.

"I told you I'd come back," she whispered. "Aufors, talk to me!"

He drew a deep breath, put his hand on her hair, still sodden from the sea, hanging in long strands around her face. There was seaweed in it, and the smell of the ocean was on her.

He said, "Awhero told me . . ."

"Told you what, dear one?"

"She *told* me . . . so you needn't pretend anymore."

Puzzled, beginning to feel angry, she said, "Told what? Pretend what?"

"I've found out about Dovidi. Do you know who his father is? Does anyone know who his father is?"

She staggered back from him, as though he had slapped her. "Aufors, this child is your son."

"He couldn't be my son. No. Half fish. That's what Awhero said. He's half fish. It's all been . . . it's all been some kind of mystery . . ."

She took a deep breath, clenching her fists. "Do you remember your mother?"

"Not well," he gulped, astonished.

"Do you remember what she looked like?"

"Only from her picture. In the hallway at home."

"You had a copy of that portrait with you on the ship, when we came here."

"In my wallet. It's . . . still there."

"Where is it? In this pack. Good." She rummaged among his belongings, coming up with the familiar folder. "Look at it, Aufors."

He opened it with fumbling fingers, finding the picture with some difficulty. He took it out and stared at it, looking from it to Genevieve with puzzled eyes.

"Notice the nose, the eyes," she said. "She resembles me, does she not?"

He started to speak, cleared his throat, managed to say, "Somewhat, yes. But . . ."

"That's because we were related, Aufors. Distant cousins to be sure, but both she and I were of Stephanie's line." Almost she started to tell him what lineage that was, but swallowed the words. He'd never believe that!

He stared, licked his lips, swallowed deeply and painfully. "How do you know about my mother?"

"I know because I was told. More important, I know because Dovidi could only have been born to two parents who were each of Stephanie's line. Just as I could have been born only to two such parents."

He barked laughter, without humor. "The Marshal? Tell me another tall tale."

"The Marshal is not my father. He fathered a number of children on my mother and all of them died. I lived. I should have realized what that meant a long time ago. My mother must have had a lover."

"Awhero said he . . . Dovidi would be able to breathe, down there," he said.

"That's true," Genevieve agreed. "Though I don't know how she knew."

"During their trip, he fell in the pool, or wriggled in, and she saw him swim. She says he has gills . . ."

"Like gills, yes. But not just that. Other things, inside, that let us go down, very deeply, as the harbingers do."

He gave her a quick, frankly curious glance, started to say something, then stopped, shaking his head.

"You want to see," said Genevieve. "But I can't show you. The skin doesn't open unless I'm under water."

"And . . . Dovidi is . . ."

"Dovidi is your son. As we both know. As you should never have doubted." Try as she would, she could not keep the outrage from her voice.

He struggled to his feet in sudden agitation, her anger stirring his own. "It's late to tell me that. You said . . . when we met in Barfezi you said you'd been taken prisoner in the caverns. And you said there'd been someone . . . someone on the boat with you. A presence. You said, you couldn't really remember. When Awhero said he, Dovidi, was part fish I thought . . . oh, I thought . . . you should have told me before we were married . . . shouldn't have let me find out . . ."

She shouted, "Told you *what?* Let you find out *what?*"

"About . . . you know. Your . . . difference. Your . . . abilities."

She took a deep breath and counted slowly to ten. "My mother made me swear never to tell anyone until the ability was needed, and the first time I ever needed it was when I dived off that stone into the sea with Dovidi in my arms. I suspected about Dovidi only after he was born, and I didn't really know until we were underwater. And you will recall that I suggested we wait to get married, but you insisted, and you will also recall that during the entire time since I have had something I *could* tell you, we have been separated by a war, an ocean, a desert, an army, or this . . . this stupidity!"

He sat down, glaring at his feet. "You should have told me. I mean, how long have you known you could do this?"

"How long have I really known? About four days. Covenantly daughters don't swim. They don't go in the sea or in rivers or pools. Except for the pools under Langmarsh House, I've never been in water deeper than a bathing tub. So, when I took that leap away from those men, I only hoped. I didn't know."

He shook his head wearily, too far sunk in doubt to be able to swim out of it.

She aped his head shake, speaking between her teeth in irritation. "Aufors, we don't have time for this. Tell me, do you value your life?"

"Of course," he snapped, angry again. "Though perhaps . . ."

"Perhaps nothing! You are going to have to believe in me. In a moment, I'm going to walk out of here to tell the Chieftain and the Prince and my un-Father where they can find the great store of life-stuff they're looking for."

"You wouldn't!"

"I will. I will for good reason. And if you trust me and come with me and stand beside me, you'll be safe and all our people will be safe, no matter what happens."

"And Dovidi?"

"Including Dovidi, of course. I would never threaten Dovidi's life, or yours. Whatever's chewing on you, can you set it aside? For the love you claimed you bore me . . ."

"Claim! I did . . . do love you!"

"Then prove it. Stop sulking and follow me!"

He rose, breathing heavily, his face reddening as he bent to take up his cloak and pack.

"Leave them," she whispered. "We can save only ourselves."

Reluctantly, he followed her out of the tent. Terceth still watched, and as they passed, Genevieve said to him, "Terceth, do you see that great rock outcropping a little south and west of your ship? If you would live, get yourself to the top of it, together with any whose lives you treasure."

He started to speak, but her glance quelled him, and as they departed, Aufors turned back to see him leave the tent and run toward the outcropping she had mentioned. He ran alone.

The Chieftain and his two elder sons awaited them in the high tent, where Genevieve went with Aufors close behind.

"I would speak a word to the Prince, to the Marshal."

"Speak," the Chieftain said, "but don't take long."

She went back to where they sat on a carpet at the rear of the tent. The Prince looked as he had at the Standing Stone, mummylike, aged beyond belief. The Marshal was unchanged. He still gripped the Prince's hand, and Genevieve could see a bit of food wrapper protruding between the fingers. So. They were disputing over who should have the dose.

"I have only a little question," she murmured. "If either of you had it to do over again, would you do anything differently?"

The Prince wheezed. "I'd have killed that old fox Marwell long ago. And I'd have rejected you as a candidate, girl. You've brought our world down around us."

She turned to the Marshal, questioning only with her eyes.

"I'd have had your mother done away with after you were born," he snarled. "And you with her!"

She smiled, radiantly, so brightly that they were caught in the light of it, unable to turn away.

"No last-minute conversions. No remorse. Consistent to the end."

"What end?" breathed the Prince. "Tides turn, girly. Tides turn . . ." His fingers worked, and he nodded at the Marshal, as though in agreement.

So. They would share it. She turned to walk back through the tent and out onto the sand, summoning the Aresians to follow her. There she pointed at a slope of sand near the city walls and said, "Under that sand is the store of life stuff buried. Dig down, and you will find the building. I ask only to take my son and my husband and depart."

"Oh, no, no," laughed the Chieftain. "Not until we've proven you right, lady. Then you can take whom you will. Take your papa as well, and that old mummy back there who's fading by the minute."

"Very well," she said. "I will stand here, where I can see your men digging. You have decided to dig it up, no matter what I've said?"

Lokdren made an abortive gesture, but Ogberd caught his arm and held it.

"No matter what you or anyone might say," the Chieftain agreed. And with that, he turned to his men and trumpeted an order. Within moments, a horde of diggers were converging on the slope.

"There is a song to be sung on these occasions," Genevieve said. "You will not mind if I sing it?"

"Sing to your heart's content," sneered the Chieftain. "I'm going to join the treasure hunt."

When he approached the diggers, Genevieve stepped away from the tent, tugging Aufors along by one lax hand. When the first shovel entered into the sand she began to sing, and for the first time in all her singing, she did not bother to soften her voice.

In Mahahm, every prayer-caller woke to sudden attention. In the oases across the deserts, Mahahmbi stopped what they were doing to hearken. Among the armies of Aresia, no man moved. The shovelers stopped, stooped. The officers froze, mouths open. The Chieftain stood as one turned to stone. Out on the sands, near the stone outcropping, Terceth staggered, then picked himself up and ran on. On the Frangian ship, the sailors heard, and hastened to bring their ship into the bay.

In far Galul, people heard the song and stood amazed while the beasts of the fields stopped grazing and put their heads high, swiveling their ears. Her voice did not blare, it was not loud, it simply filled all space with total sound, emerging as smoothly as the reverberation of a great temple gong, setting forth melody note by note, each note unfading as the next joined with it in harmony, slow, measured, a call that went forth across the sea to its farthest edges.

And was answered.

They heard the answer first, then the shock, as though the world shook.

"Stand by me," whispered Genevieve to Aufors. "Stand close. Hold on to me."

Another shock, this one larger, and this time the world quivered, like the hide of a horse, shaking off a fly.

"What's happening?" bellowed the Chieftain.

"I have sung to my mentor," cried Genevieve in her huge voice. "I have told the spirit of the world of your decision."

A third great shock, and this time the desert shook, sands dancing above its surface like rain upon a pavement, the city of Mahahm-qum

wavering against the sun-cooked sky, its towers cracking, great billows of dust rising.

They heard it coming. Heads turned, everywhere.

"Storm?" breathed Aufors, clinging to Genevieve's arm. "Wind?"

"A quake," she murmured to him, drawing him closer. "And behind the quake, the wave . . ."

They saw it coming then, beyond the walls of the city, a long black line across the horizon, one that grew in height as it approached, a wave that loomed above the tallest tower of Mahahm-qum, one that reached almost to the top of the rocky outcropping Genevieve had pointed out to Terceth, a tidal wave that met the shore of Mahahm and just kept coming. Beyond it, Aufors saw another, higher!

"Take a deep breath," said Genevieve, drawing Aufors into the circle of her arms, Dovidi close between them. "And hold on."

THE CREST OF THE WATER CURLED ABOVE THEM IN A GLASSY MOUNTAIN, FOAM edged, growing higher and more curled, then higher yet, breaking at last as the wave lipped over the walls, gulping the city into the maw of the sea. The assembled diggers broke and ran as the surge deepened and swirled, dissolving the walls, the roofs, the alleys, clear water turning dark in a muddy maelstrom that foamed through doors and windows, eating the houses from the inside and outside at once, drowning both the inhabitants and their cries, carrying all before it in a furious flood that raced toward the encampment on the heels of the runners, sucking them up and racing on.

When the water reached Genevieve and Aufors, it was full of struggling bodies, but among them were creatures with flippers and tails who darted invisibly through the groaning torrent. Genevieve held tight to Aufors while the finned creatures of the sea lifted them both up, keeping all their heads above water as thick as soup, while the great wave ebbed and the second, greater one rushed in.

Aufors's eyes were full of mud. His hands were gripped tight in Genevieve's hair. He was lost in tumult, swallowing muck, gasping for air, always losing it, always finding it again, plunging deeply only to rise like a buoy as the flood rolled around him, catching panicky breaths while it lifted, while it ebbed, and while other clear waves followed, time after time after time. At the end the water was like crystal; he could see the creatures who helped them though he could not imagine how many of them there had been. He did remember that Genevieve never let go of him nor he of her, and he also had graven into his mind the sight of Dovidi surfacing beside him in the midst of chaos, in company with a great, black-and-white whale who caught Aufors's shirt in his teeth and held him steady while the water ebbed once more. The sleek body left them only at the last to thrash its way outward with the ebb, into the calmer sea.

When the last wave ebbed, leaving only its foamy followers shushing across the shore, Aufors lay supine beside Genevieve on the sodden, silt-coated sands with Dovidi sprawled across her belly, the baby crowing as though he were being tickled.

When they had the strength to sit up and look, the city was gone.

They stood then, staggering, heads spinning, trying to find any land-mark to which they could hold. The city had vanished totally. Nothing of it remained. No house, no tower, no remnant of wall. West sparkled the sea. East lay the wrack of the wave, and as though by mutual consent they walked the considerable distance to the first line of bodies, the soaked and leveled sands like an endless beach, a harder and easier road than the desert dunes had been.

The Aresian ships lay on their sides, battered and broken. Bodies were tumbled like storm-wrack, here piled high, there spread apart, men from Mahahm and Ares together, a sprinkling of the women and children of the town, not many. There had never been many Mahahmbi women, and recently there had been all too few. Even the few were too many, Gene-vieve thought, as she wept over them.

Aufors turned, seeking the swell of sand that had covered the Shah's treasure house. "Gone," he said, gesturing widely. "I thought you were giving them the P'naki, but it's all gone."

"Not only what was stored, but what was growing," she agreed. "It will not grow again where the seas sow salt."

"The wave went all the way across the desert?" he cried, incredulously.

"Not this time," she said. "Not while we were here, but when we have gone, next time, yes."

"Next time!" He gave her a look of disbelief, then walked farther among the bodies, here and there saying a name as he recognized some from among his captors, calling out loudly as he came upon a particular group of bodies: the Marshal and the Prince, turned to wooden statues, their hands locked around one another's throats in a final conflict. Nearby were Ogberd and Lokdren and their father, clinging to one another, eyes wide and empty.

Aufors's face was ashen as he said, "You did this. You called this down on them."

She thought about it. "No, and yes. It was the only way to destroy the lichen. Also, it was the only way to destroy both those who knew about the lichen and those who coveted it."

"You have . . . that power? Oh, Jenny, what am I to do?"

"About what?" she asked wearily, turning to lead them away from the

piled corpses, for already the carrion birds had come to spin their toothed wheels in the sky, while across the sands they saw the tiny figure of Terceth as he came slogging toward them from the rocky pinnacle he had achieved just in time.

"I considered myself worthy of you," Aufors said in a hopeless voice as he trailed five paces behind her. "Though you were noble and I was common, I was proud of my accomplishments and I knew you valued me. And you were worthy of me, also, for you were honest and kind and intelligent, unlike many of the nobility, and I loved you to distraction. When your father . . . when the Marshal told you to take no concern for your safety, I hated him and valued myself, for I thought I could protect you if he would not. I wanted to protect you, treasure you, care for you. And when you leapt into the sea, I thought . . . well, you know what I thought, or felt, that I could not protect you as I had hoped to do . . .

"And now, now I feel like a fool. How could any common man have any role at all with . . . what you have become?"

She laughed, then cried, then did both together. After a moment, she stopped walking, laid Dovidi on the sand and collapsed cross-legged, bent into her lap still laughing, sobbing, able at last to lay down all pretense of being in control of events. "And what have I become, Aufors Leys?"

"You are, you can . . . summon the sea!"

"Did you never post a signalman to summon the army when the enemy appeared? Did the signalman create the army, or command it? He signals because that is his assignment, and good soldiers carry out their assignments. So I called the sea because that was my assignment, and among creatures of honor, I will do what I can." She tried to wipe her eyes on her soaked sleeve, then wrung it out instead, laughing almost hysterically at herself. "If I tried to summon the sea now, I could sing until sundown and nothing would happen. I can't even hurry the tide! Oh, Aufors. I am no more nor less than I was when you met me. It may be I have already done most of what I have to do in my entire life. It may be I will never again dive that deep or do that much to such purpose . . ."

"What good has it done?" he cried. "There are men on Haven who know everything these men knew!"

"No," she said, shaking her head at him. "If Veswees has been as capable as I judge him to be, if he has used what I told him, and if everything is happening as I have seen it happening, the old men of the Tribunal are already dead or under sentence of death, and Haven's store of P'naki is lost forever, buried so deep no one will ever find it. It doesn't matter who knows about it if none of the stuff exists. I am just me, Aufors.

The only difference between this dripping wet Jenny and the Jenny you knew before is that I know what my task is."

"After all this?" he cried. "Still more?"

"Only a little more. I have yet to explain," she said, wiping her eyes with her fingers, rocking to and fro, picking up her child to rock him with her in an endless, swaying comforting motion, the motion of a cradle or a rocking chair in some homely quiet place. "Someone has to explain."

After a time she swallowed her tears and rose again to move off toward Terceth, who had stopped when he first caught sight of all the bodies piled in the distance before him. They joined him silently and walked with him to the sea, where they made a rough camp and waited.

That night, deep in the dark hours, when Aufors was securely locked in sleep, Genevieve swam out into the sea with Dovidi. He was hungry, and she had nothing to feed him. There among the little wavelets she called a tiny call, a wee meeping call, and a warm sea creature came to share its milk between its calf and Dovidi, who drank it underwater and was satisfied.

It was an innocent, necessary thing to do, but Genevieve did not tell Aufors about it on the morning. Given his temperament and present mood, there might be some things it would be better for him not to know.

A day later, the Frangian ship returned to take them home.

It was not long thereafter that Genevieve woke one dawn to the sound of the siren-lizards in the vines. She knew the room well, her own tower room at Mrs. Blessingham's, and she was alone in the room as she had used to be, for Aufors was at Langmarsh House, with Dovidi. It was time, she felt, they should get to know one another and feel their kinship. Though Aufors still gave her very strange looks from time to time, she continued day by day being as dull as possible, as merely motherly as she could manage, and his doubts became less frequent. When she felt like singing, she repressed the urge. Repression was no more than she had practiced for many years, and doing so now might help him accept the situation. Aufors himself felt he was accepting it, though it required all his forbearance and powers of pragmatic analysis to do so.

Genevieve slipped out of bed and went to the window. Sun sparkled on leaves, siren-lizards sang, the world seemed unchanged. A pity it seemed so, considering how it was changed. Nothing was as it had been before.

They had returned from Mahahm aboard the Frangian vessel, bringing the Marshal's body, though not the Prince's, whose hands Aufors had taken

some pleasure in severing from the Marshal's neck. Genevieve had felt the sands of Mahahm a proper tomb for the Marshal, but Haven's propriety required that he be buried in the tomb of his ancestors. By all means, she had told herself. Bury him in Langmarsh. Do nothing that might reduce her respect among the women of Haven, for they would find her announcements hard enough to accept from a Duchess, much less a disreputable commoner.

Now a siren-lizard dropped from a tree branch onto the windowsill and stared at her, as though about to speak.

"It's a strange feeling, being here again," she murmured to it, leaning into the breeze. "I'd honestly rather be elsewhere, in Galul, perhaps, but someone has to explain to the women of Haven, and since most of them respect the schools in which they were reared, the schools are the best place to start."

The lizard opened its frills and sang to her, and she sang a tiny whispered song in return as it flew out into the tree once more. There were no longer any scrutators to penalize noble women for singing, though it would probably take some time before noble women were comfortable doing so. Or comfortable not being noble, which might come harder.

Mrs. Blessingham herself had not been easy to convince. Explain though Genevieve would, the schoolmistress had found it difficult to understand all that had happened and even more difficult to determine what should be done about it now. First, of course, people had to be informed. After much discussion, it had been decided to hold a conference for all the schoolmistresses on Haven, so that each schoolmistress might then go back to her own students and to those who had been her students, and to their mothers.

"Though it will take far too long for all of them to get here," Mrs. Blessingham had fretted.

Genevieve had already planned for it. "Aufors has offered to help in all possible ways, and I've sent word to Langmarsh, asking him to commandeer the Lord Paramount's airships. He can forge a letter from the Marshal. No one knows yet that the Marshal's dead. If they come by air, the schoolmistresses can all be here in a few days."

"I suppose no one is in any condition to gainsay the Marshal," Mrs. Blessingham had said, a little bitterly. "Not the Lord Paramount, who has simply disappeared. Not the Tribunal, for better than half the members have been slaughtered by mobs of commoners, and all the rest are dying for lack of . . . what you told me of. Even younger men have been killed, men who've lost . . . well, *sacrificed* a first or second wife. The commons

are being quite ruthless in rooting them out, and the ones the commons haven't slaughtered, the machines have!"

"You sound disapproving."

"Oh, Genevieve, no, no. How could I disapprove? It's just, my world is upside down, too. Without a nobility, what need for places like this school? What need for women like me? Ah?"

"There will always be a need for women like you," Genevieve had told her, honestly. "No matter what happens."

The first of the schoolmistresses had arrived last evening. By tomorrow or the next day, they would all be here. Though it was still very early in the morning, Genevieve dressed herself and went down to Mrs. Blessingham's office.

"I've come to ask a favor," she said.

"Of course, my dear."

"Who was my real father?"

"Oh, Genevieve, why do you imagine I would know . . ."

"Don't put me off. You were Mother's friend, and if anyone knows, you do."

Mrs. Blessingham fretted. "I swore never to tell, but well, it doesn't matter now, does it? He was a commoner. A lovely man. A bit of a poet, a bit of singer, an artist in fabrics. He had a weaving shop here in Avanto. When the Marshal married your mother and took her to Langmarsh House, he sold his shop and moved into Vena, to be near her."

She sighed, remembering. "After you were born, she gave him up, for duty's sake. For the sake of her soul. He stayed in Vena, just in case she should ever need him."

"Is he still alive?"

"I have no idea," she replied, honestly. "After your mother died, he moved away."

"If he is alive, I will find him," she said, tears in her eyes.

Mrs. Blessingham said, "It's odd you should bring this up this morning, for last night I had the thought that many of the women of Zenobia's line must have had lovers. If they had to be married to nobility, as your mother was, how else could they have stayed sane?"

"So I am a commoner, really."

"If it matters now."

"It does matter to me. I have always hated the idea of being a Marchioness or Duchess by accident of birth. Now that I know my birth was no accident . . . Well, say that I am happier knowing it."

Her happiness was short-lived. That evening, as she was readying herself for bed, her door was thrust open, and Glorieta came storming in.

"What's this terrible lie you're telling about Willum?" she shrieked. "How could you, Genevieve!"

Breathlessly, Mrs. Blessingham came in behind her. "I'm so sorry, Genevieve. Glorieta, my dear . . ."

Glorieta spun around, thrusting out her jaw. "Don't my dear me! I was in Poolwich when I heard what's being said! As if it wasn't bad enough, Father's death, Willum's father's death, everything that's happened . . ." She started for Genevieve, then stopped, her eyes filling with tears. "It isn't true! It can't be true!"

Genevieve had expected this to happen, someday, somewhere. She had decided that when it did, only the truth would do. "I saw him slit Barbara's throat. I was there. I saw him leave her and her son, perhaps his son, on the desert to die. He did not slit your throat. He did not kill a child you and he had together. He chose to kill someone else instead because of his love for you."

Seeing Mrs. Blessingham's astonished face, Genevieve realized she had sung the words, as the spirit or the harbingers might have sung them, in a very large voice. Glorieta was staring, her mouth open, her face very white. Well, come to think of it, it had sounded impressive. Perhaps awkward truths needed to impress in order to be taken seriously.

"I can't believe it," sobbed Glorieta. "That he would do such a thing . . ."

"He will never do it again," said Genevieve in her own, quiet young woman's voice, not adding that there would be no advantage for him to do so. Glorieta would figure that out for herself.

Glorieta, sobbing uncontrollably, turned to leave, supported by Mrs. Blessingham, who threw a tragic glance over her shoulder at Genevieve. Genevieve did not see it. Instead she saw between herself and the retreating figures a cliff, high above the sea and the jagged rocks upon which the waves broke, and on the rim, Willum, leaping out . . . out . . . far out . . . This thing was happening now, not later, not in the past, but now. Well, then. Glorieta would not need to choose. Either Willum knew that Glorieta could not love him, knowing what he had done, or he had chosen not to wait for the mobs or the machines to find him.

After one more day during which nothing at all seemed changed, not even, Genevieve thought wryly, the dull menu offered by the school kitchens, all the schoolmistresses had gathered, and Mrs. Blessingham told them

about P'naki in a session marked by equal parts of horror, grief, and disbelief. There was no hurrying the enlightenment. Everyone present had to express every doubt she was capable of feeling, not once but several times, in different words, antiphonally, like a chorus gone mad.

When they were all, more or less, worn out, Genevieve told them the rest of it. By the time she had finished, Genevieve was thoroughly sick of submerging herself in the school fishpond to illustrate what was meant by the coming change.

Several days' constant chatter, like the wear of wind or water, smoothed them into acceptance. They knew the waters were rising, but slowly. They knew the descendants of Tenopia and Stephanie were to inherit a sea-world. Genevieve had decided not to explain why it was philosophically preferable and had talked instead about prestige. The sea-lineage would be more prestigious. On a planet used to nobility, prestige did well enough. More troublesome were the discussions of how the schoolmistresses could find sensible and useful employment educating the future generations and, most important, arranging appropriate marriages for women who were no longer of the nobility.

Mrs. Blessingham had frowned at this, saying musingly, "Not necessarily marriages. Some marriages may still be made for reasons of pride, so we must concern ourselves with matings. The young women of Haven may marry who they will, but they should pick their children's fathers very carefully. And vice versa. We'll need to establish a . . . well, a stud book."

As she had before, Genevieve blinked at Mrs. Blessingham's pragmatic decisiveness in the face of utter confusion. The schoolmistresses, by now imperturbable, nodded to one another. A stud book, they agreed. And perhaps even some imported reproductive technology. Genevieve was able to assure them that the spirit of Haven did not desire to cause them pain. "There'll be lots of time for our descendants to change."

"And there will be some dry land left?" queried a schoolmistress from Dania. "We would miss our forests."

Genevieve assured her, "Anything at the altitude of Galul or above. That will include the uplands of Langmarsh, the mountains of Sealands, most of Dania, all of Havenor and Upland, though Barfezi will become marshlands, and virtually all of Merdune and Frangia will be submerged. Havenpool will be nothing but a shallow lagoon of the sea. Since there is considerable vulcanism involved, however, there will also be new islands, some of them of considerable size. Though we will not live to see all these changes, our children's children will."

"We will not see the depths of the sea, either," said Mrs. Blessingham firmly, though sadly. "But our children's children will."

Genevieve went home to Langmarsh House, where, as they had agreed on their way home, Aufors Leys had been busy reorganizing the Duke's estates and parceling various farms and businesses out to the men and women who had always worked them. Genevieve, watching him before he knew she was there, saw the satisfaction in his face. He actually looked happy! His welcome, when he saw her, was almost as ardent as she remembered.

"All finished?" he asked.

She heaved a great breath. "I think so."

"And what now?"

She surprised herself by weeping, tears spilling down her cheeks as though his words had released a dam. "Oh, Aufors, I feel finished, too. Done with my purpose in life! I think it's a great pity to come to the end of one's purpose in life when one is not yet twenty-two."

He actually laughed. "You think you've come to the end, do you?"

He said it teasingly, but it rankled nonetheless, and she frowned, aware she was behaving childishly, unable to behave in any other way. Too much had happened to her. Too much all at once.

"Come," said Aufors, reaching for her hand. "I want to see."

"See what?"

"See the cellars where your mother took you." He caressed her hand, and though she could not fathom his reason, his tone said it was important to him. They went down the stairs, she leading him by one hand, a candle in the other, as she herself had been led all those years of her childhood. They traversed the extensive cellars, far under the foundations of Langmarsh House, to those deep pools where she had learned to be what she was.

He looked at her, and at the pool, and at her again. The candlelight reflected on the pool in little shattered ripples of fire. Far off, the water dripped ceaselessly with a musical phrase that repeated, with variations, over and over. He ran his hands down her neck, where he felt nothing at all but sweet flesh and soft skin, though his eyes told him there were little lines there that other women might not have. Some other women.

"It's only a deep pool of water," he said, gesturing. "I thought it would be more mysterious."

"It's pretty mysterious at two in the morning, especially in winter. It's cold in there, and it's dark," she murmured, half hypnotized by the ripples

on the water. "I was always afraid there were eely things in there. Still, it's not unnatural, and I'm not unnatural either, anymore than whales are unnatural. We are both creatures born to the land who are going back to the sea."

"That's the part you haven't explained," he said. "It's why I wanted to come down here. I want everything. Everything the spirit said to you. All that you've told me so far, I've managed to accept, but you haven't really said why. Why are we to go back to the sea?"

"Fingers," she murmured, remembering the words of the spirit. "We got fingers before we got good sense. You know, one of our early ancestors was called Homo habilis, the toolmaker. We learned to manipulate and change things before we learned to look at what we were changing. So did the whales, and the dolphins, long before us, but they have bigger brains than we do, and after they made a few mistakes, they decided— philosophically, you understand—that it would be better to go back to the sea and practice humility first by thinking things out thoroughly. Then, when they'd done that, they could crawl back up on the land in a few million years or so. Only they never got the chance because of us! We . . . we made mistakes, too, but we didn't have any humility. We never both- ered to think things out. We just . . . went on. Wreck this, destroy that, gamble our souls on the odds of whether we'd ever do it right . . ."

"So," he said.

"So, the spirit of this world made one tiny change in one woman— Tenopia's mother really was impregnated by a wave—and that woman passed on that one tiny change to all her lineage, and that lineage will turn us around and let us go back."

The water dripped and rippled. The light on the ripples came and went.

"What will happen to Ares?" he asked at last.

"Terceth asked me that, before he left for home. The Aresians that are left will have to emigrate to other worlds. The planet will lie barren for an age, or an eon, until a spirit of life visits it again. Perhaps in time its own harbingers will return to it from their haven here. Life always goes back. It always tries again. Meantime, the spirits of several dead worlds have found a haven here, and their harbingers with them. The spirit said, 'The latigern and betivor graze the hills of Galul. The chamaris and thalliar roam the mountain ranges. Bruk and bralt lie in deep grass along the rivers, where the Thal-flower grows amid the reeds.' So the spirit said, that they have come to their Haven, as we will come to ours."

"And that's the end?"

"There's never any end," she said. "The world souls sunder and they join. Sometimes they win, sometimes they lose, but eventually, wisdom spreads and there will be more of those whose covenant is life, not mere living for one species at the expense of all, but life in such variety that there will be no place in the universe it does not exist, and all that exists will think as with one mind . . ." Her voice trailed into silence.

"And that's all you know?"

"Every jot. I'm sure there were things being said that I was too stupid to understand, but you've heard everything I can remember."

"Then your being half fish shouldn't bother me," he said, as though trying to convince himself.

She watched him narrowly, then pressed herself against him, unbuttoning his shirt and her own, to let their skins lie next to one another.

"Fish aren't warm," she whispered. "I'm warm, aren't I?"

He gulped. "Oh, yes."

She slid her hands lower and caressed him.

"If I am only *part* fish, it's no part that's important to *us*, is it?"

After a long moment, he laughed tremulously, putting his arms around her to hold her as he had not truly held her since she had sung to the sea.

In the pool, something small and golden surfaced only long enough to see the two of them locked together in the light of the candle. It flipped away as quickly as it had come. Nothing had ever happened on Earth that the Earth-soul had not seen and remembered. Nothing had ever happened on Ares, or Chapin, or Dowes world that their world-souls had not seen and remembered. Nothing happened anywhere on Haven that was not added to those memories.